Turning up the heat

Turning up the heat

Urban political ecology for a climate emergency

Edited by

Maria Kaika, Roger Keil, Tait Mandler, and Yannis Tzaninis

MANCHESTER UNIVERSITY PRESS

Copyright © Manchester University Press 2023

While copyright in the volume as a whole is vested in Manchester University Press, copyright in individual chapters belongs to their respective authors, and no chapter may be reproduced wholly or in part without the express permission in writing of both author and publisher.

Chapter 15 is adapted from 'Green and Gray: New Ideologies of Nature in Urban Sustainability Policy' by David Wachsmuth & Hillary Angelo, *Annals of the American Association of Geographers*, copyright © American Association of Geographers, by permission of Taylor & Francis Ltd, http://www.tandfonline.com on behalf of American Association of Geographers.

Published by Manchester University Press
Oxford Road, Manchester M13 9PL

www.manchesteruniversitypress.co.uk

British Library Cataloguing-in-Publication Data
A catalogue record for this book is available from the British Library

ISBN 978 1 5261 7004 0 hardback

ISBN 978 1 5261 6799 6 paperback

First published 2023

The publisher has no responsibility for the persistence or accuracy of URLs for any external or third-party internet websites referred to in this book, and does not guarantee that any content on such websites is, or will remain, accurate or appropriate.

Typeset by Newgen Publishing UK

Contents

List of figures	vii
List of contributors	ix
Acknowledgements	xvi
Prologue: Losing California – The political ecology of the megafires – Mike Davis	xix
Introduction: Urban political ecology for a climate emergency – Yannis Tzaninis, Tait Mandler, Maria Kaika, and Roger Keil	1

Part I: Extended urbanisation: Moving UPE beyond the 'urbanisation of nature' thesis

1 Capital's natures: A critique of (urban) political ecology – Erik Swyngedouw	37
2 Urban political ecology versus ecological urbanism – Matthew Gandy	56
3 Towards the urban-natural: Notes on urban utopias from the decolonial turn – Roberto Luís Monte-Mór and Ester Limonad	67
4 Circuits of extraction and the metabolism of urbanisation – Martín Arboleda	91
5 Hinterlands of the Capitalocene – Neil Brenner and Nikos Katsikis	105

Part II: Situated urban political ecologies

6 The case for reparations, urban political ecology, and the Black right to urban life – Nik Heynen and Nikki Luke	129
7 Urban climate change and feminist political ecology – Andrea J. Nightingale	143
8 Nairobi's bad natures – Wangui Kimari	159

9 Situating suburban ecologies in the Global South: Notes from India's urban periphery – Shubhra Gururani 169
10 Infrastructure beyond the modern ideal: Thinking through heterogeneity, serendipity, and autonomy in African cities – Mary Lawhon, Anesu Makina, and Gloria Nsangi Nakyagaba 186

Part III: More-than-human urban political ecologies and relational geographies

11 Extending the boundaries of 'urban society': The urban political ecologies and pathologies of Ebola virus disease in West Africa – Roger Keil, S. Harris Ali, and Stefan Treffers 207
12 In formation: Urban political ecology for a world of flows – Kian Goh 222
13 Insurgent earth: Territorialist political ecology in/for the new climate regime – Camilla Perrone 244

Part IV: Addressing disjunctions between policy, politics, and academic debate

14 Populist political ecologies? Urban political ecology, authoritarian populism, and the suburbs – Alex Loftus and Joris Gort 265
15 Greenwashing and greywashing: New ideologies of nature in urban sustainability policy – David Wachsmuth and Hillary Angelo 284
16 The peasant way or the urban way? Why disidentification matters for emancipatory politics – Irina Velicu 302
17 Urbanising islands: A critical history of Singapore's offshore islands – Creighton Connolly and Hamzah Muzaini 319
18 The circular economy of cities: The good, the bad, and the ugly – Federico Savini 333

Epilogue: Is an integrated UPE research and policy agenda possible? – Tait Mandler, Roger Keil, Yannis Tzaninis, and Maria Kaika 347

Index 358

Figures

5.1 Night-time lights of the world. Visualisation by the authors based on the publicly available dataset: VIIRS, DNB, Nighttime Lights Composites, NOAA, National Center for Environmental Information (NCEI). 109
5.2 Spiky world: Geographical distribution of global GDP in a three-dimensional perspective. Visualisation by the authors based on the original idea of the spiky world by Florida (2005). This image is derived from the publicly available dataset: UNEP (United Nations Environment Program), 2012. Gross Domestic Product 2010. 109
5.3 The hinterland of the 'isolated state': Von Thünen's visualisation (1826). 112
5.4 Agglomerations and the 'used area' of the planet in the early twenty-first century. Visualisation by the authors based on the following sources and publicly available datasets: European Commission Joint Research Center, 2016, Global Human Settlement Layer; Erb et al. (2007); Vector Map Level 0 (VMap0) dataset released by the National Imagery and Mapping Agency (NIMA), 1997. 114
5.5 Growth in global trade of basic materials, 1960–2010. Over the past decade, the global trade in primary commodities increased more than threefold. This reflects the increasing globalisation of hinterland economies. Visualisation by the authors based on data from Krausmann et al. (2009). 116
5.6 Worlds of specialised agricultural production, 2000. This map series depicts the geographical distribution of production sites for the five most globally traded agricultural commodities as of 2000. Visualisation by the authors based on data presented in Monfreda et al. (2009). 117

5.7 Hinterlands of hinterlands, 2000. This map series depicts the geographical distribution of cropland areas dedicated to food, feed, or non-food uses. Visualisation by the authors based on the publicly available datasets in Cassidy et al. (2013). 119

5.8 Mechanised, monoculture landscapes of corn and soybean production in the US Midwest, 2018. Visualisation by the authors based on the following publicly available dataset: USDA National Agricultural Statistics Service Cropland Data Layer (2018), published crop-specific data layer, available at https://nassgeodata.gmu.edu/CropScape/, accessed 12 August 2022. 120

5.9 Intensity of synthetic fertiliser application (nitrogen) over the global croplands, 2000. This map depicts annual levels and locations of nitrogen fertiliser use through a black-dotted gradient pattern. Visualisation by the authors based on the following publicly available datasets: Ramankutty et al. (2010); Potter et al. (2012). 121

9.1 Number of water bodies lost in the Gugugram region of India over 60 years. Source: GMDA, 2019. 175

9.2 Ghata lakebed used as a dumpsite and as settlement area for migrant workers. Source: Author, December 2018. 179

12.1 Diagram of global-urban networks. Source: Author. 231

12.2 Diagram of conceptual interfaces, relationships, and formations. Source: Author. 235

17.1 Map showing the location of Singapore's Southern and Western Islands, with the Southern Islands of St John's, Lazarus, and Kusu circled as the focus of our field research. 324

17.2 Signboard showing map of Semakau Landfill. Source: Author. 327

Contributors

S. Harris Ali is Professor of Sociology at York University in Toronto, Canada. His areas of research interest include: disaster research, environmental sociology, environmental health, and the social and political dimensions of infectious disease outbreaks. He is currently conducting research on Ebola in sub-Saharan Africa.

Hillary Angelo is an Assistant Professor of Sociology at the University of California, Santa Cruz, whose work explores the relationship between nature and urbanisation from historical, theoretical, and ethnographic perspectives. She has been published in leading social science and geography journals, including the *Annals of the Association of American Geographers*, *Theory and Society*, and the *International Journal of Urban and Regional Research*. Her new book is *How green became good: urbanized nature and the making of cities and citizens* (University of Chicago Press, 2021).

Martín Arboleda is Assistant Professor of Sociology at the Universidad Diego Portales, Santiago de Chile. His research interests include the fields of global political economy, critical social theory, and development studies. He is the author of the books *Planetary mine: territories of extraction under late capitalism* (Verso, 2020) and *Gobernar la utopía: sobre la planificación y el poder popular* (Caja Negra Editora, 2021). His research on the political economy of resource extraction in Chile and Latin America has been published in several scholarly journals. He is currently working on a long-term research project on the political economy of the globalised agro-food system, as well as on the intellectual history of economic planning during the 1960s and 1970s in Latin America.

Neil Brenner is the Lucy Flower Professor of Urban Sociology, the Director of the Urban Theory Lab, and the Chair of the Committee on Environment, Geography and Urbanization (CEGU) at the University of Chicago. His books include *New urban spaces: urban theory and the scale question*

(Oxford, 2019) and *New state spaces: urban governance and the rescaling of statehood* (Oxford, 2004).

Creighton Connolly is an Assistant Professor in the Department of Urban Planning and Design at the University of Hong Kong. His research focuses on cultural politics, urban political ecology, and contestations over urban development in Malaysian cities. He uses a collaborative, action- oriented approach for his research, which involves working closely with civil society actors in research sites to identify challenges in the areas of transportation planning, environmental sustainability, public health, and heritage conservation and how they may be overcome.

Mike Davis (1946–2022) was Professor Emeritus at the University of California at Riverside. Davis, the author of *City of quartz, Late Victorian holocausts, Planet of slums,* and *Ecology of fear,* is considered one of the founding thinkers of UPE. He was the recipient of a MacArthur Fellowship and the Lannan Literary Award. Davis was most recently the co-author with Jon Wiener of *Set the night on fire: L. A. in the sixties* (Verso, 2021).

Matthew Gandy is Professor of Geography at the University of Cambridge and an award- winning documentary filmmaker. His books include *Concrete and clay: reworking nature in New York City* (MIT Press, 2002), *The fabric of space: water, modernity, and the urban imagination* (MIT Press, 2014), *Moth* (Reaktion, 2016), and *Natura urbana: ecological constellations in urban space* (MIT Press, 2022).

Kian Goh is Associate Professor of Urban Planning at University of California, Los Angeles (UCLA) and Associate Faculty Director of the UCLA Luskin Institute on Inequality and Democracy. She researches urban ecological design, spatial politics, and social mobilisation in the context of climate change and global urbanisation. She is the author *of Form and flow: the spatial politics of urban resilience and climate justice* (2021, MIT Press).

Joris Gort is a PhD Candidate in the Department of Geography at King's College London. His research focuses on the political ecology of Dutch water management throughout the nineteenth and twentieth centuries and the way rational water management has asserted liberal hegemony. He also researches authoritarian populism and hegemony through the lens of relational comparison more broadly.

Shubhra Gururani is Associate Professor in the Department of Anthropology at York University. She also serves as the Director of York Centre for Asian Research (YCAR). Gururani's research draws on extensive ethnographic fieldwork in the city of Gurgaon in India and focuses on the politics of land, property, urban nature/ecologies, planning, villages in the cities, agrarian-urbanism, waste, sewage, and infrastructure. Her recent publications have appeared in *Urban Geography, Urbanisation*, and *SAMAJ*.

Nik Heynen is a Distinguished Research Professor of Geography at the University of Georgia and visiting scholar at Spelman College. He studies abolitionist politics, political ecology, and cities. His main research foci relate to the analysis of how uneven social power relations – including race, gender, and class – are inscribed in the transformation of nature and space and how in turn these processes contribute to uneven development.

Maria Kaika is an urban political ecologist. She works on cities and crisis, urban radical imaginaries, and land financialisation. She is Director of the Centre for Urban Studies and Professor in Urban Regional and Environmental Planning at the University of Amsterdam. Her most recent book is *The political ecology of austerity: crisis, social movements, and the environment* (edited with R. Calvário and G. Velegrakis; Routledge, London, 2022).

Nikos Katsikis is Assistant Professor of Urbanism at TU Delft and affiliated researcher at Urban Theory Lab – Chicago. He works on the intersection of urbanisation theory, design, and geospatial analysis. He holds a Doctor of Design from the Harvard Graduate School of Design.

Roger Keil is Professor in the Faculty of Environmental and Urban Change, York University. The inaugural Director of the university's City Institute and a former York University Research Chair, Keil has authored *Suburban planet* (Polity), co-authored *Pandemic Urbanism* (with S. Harris Ali and Creighton Connolly, Polity) and edited several books including *The globalizing cities reader* (with Xuefei Ren; Routledge), *After suburbia* (with Fulong Wu; University of Toronto Press) and *Public Los Angeles* (with Judy Branfman; University of Georgia Press).

Wangui Kimari is an anthropologist based at the Institute for Humanities in Africa (HUMA). Her work draws on many local histories and theoretical approaches – including oral narratives, assemblage theory, urban political ecology, and the black radical tradition – in order to think through urban spatial management in Nairobi from the vantage point of its most marginalised residents. Wangui is also the participatory action research coordinator for the Mathare Social Justice Centre (MSJC), a community-based organisation in Nairobi, and an editorial board member of the online publication *Africa Is a Country*.

List of contributors

Mary Lawhon is Senior Lecturer in Human Geography at the University of Edinburgh. She is a political ecologist whose work focuses on the ways in which politics shapes and are shaped by urban infrastructural flows including waste and sanitation. Her work draws on and contributes to postcolonial theory, the politics of socio-technical sustainability transitions, and urban political ecology.

Ester Limonad is Full Professor in the Department and Graduate Programme of Geography at the Fluminense Federal University (Niteroi, Brazil), where she directs a human geography and critical territorial planning research group. Her main teaching and research interests include emerging problems and conflicts related to extended urbanisation, the production of space and everyday life concerning uneven social power relations, and the appropriation of nature, with an emphasis on Brazilian urbanisation trends.

Alex Loftus is Reader in Political Ecology at King's College London. His research addresses questions in political ecology, ranging from debates over water privatisation, to struggles over water in post-apartheid South Africa, around the right to water and, more recently, debates over the financialisation of water infrastructure. More broadly, Alex has sought to reframe political ecological questions through a philosophy of praxis as articulated through the work of Antonio Gramsci.

Nikki Luke is Assistant Professor of Geography at the University of Tennessee. She studies energy, labour, race, social reproduction, and urban political ecology in the US South. Her work has been published in *Antipode*, the *Annals of the American Association of Geographers*, *American Quarterly*, and *Social and Cultural Geography*.

Anesu Makina holds a PhD from the Department of Geography and Environmental Sustainability at the University of Oklahoma. Her work focuses on urban environmental issues.

Tait Mandler completed a PhD in Anthropology and Urban Planning at the University of Amsterdam. Their research interests include urban political ecology, agro-food economies, human-chemical entanglements, and anthropology of the senses.

Roberto Luís Monte-Mór is Full Professor at Centro de Desenvolvimento e Planejamento Regional at the Federal University of Minas Gerais. He teaches and researches in the areas of economics and urbanism, with an emphasis on theories of urbanisation, urban and regional planning, metropolitan planning, regional and urban economy, popular and solidarity economy, organisation of space and environment, production of space among traditional populations, and urbanisation and development alternatives in the Amazon.

Hamzah Muzaini is Assistant Professor with the Department of Southeast Asian Studies at the National University of Singapore with research interests on topics related to war heritage and memoryscapes, geographies and politics of theme parks, migration heritage making, and island geographies and heritage. He is author of *Contested memoryscapes: the politics of second world war commemoration in Singapore* (with Yeoh; Routledge, 2016) and editor of *After heritage: critical perspectives of heritage from below* (with Minca; Edward Elgar, 2018).

Gloria Nsangi Nakyagaba, alias Gloria Nsangi, is a PhD student and Teaching Assistant (Human Geography/GIS) at the University of Oklahoma. She is an enthusiastic urban researcher in urban infrastructure including sanitation, energy, food systems, and climate change. Her current research is examining the links between nature, environment, and modes of sanitation in Kampala which is funded by RJ Nature Project (KTH Royal Institute of Technology). She holds a Master of Arts degree in Geography from Makerere University, Kampala Uganda. Recent publications include 'Towards a modest Imaginary? Sanitation in Kampala beyond the modern infrastructure ideal' (*Urban Studies*, 2022) and 'Power, politics and a poo pump: Contestation over legitimacy, access and benefits of sanitation technologies in Kampala' (*Singapore Journal of Tropical Geography*, 2021).

Andrea J. Nightingale is Professor of Human Geography, University of Oslo, and Research Fellow, Swedish University of Agricultural Sciences. Her current research passions seek to account for power and politics within dynamic and unpredictable environmental change in Nepal, Kenya, and Nicaragua. Her interests cross between climate change adaptation and transformation debates, collective action and state formation, the nature-society nexus, political violence in natural resource governance, and feminist work on emotion and subjectivity in relation to development, transformation, collective action, and cooperation. Her recent book is *Environment and sustainability in a globalizing world* (Routledge, 2019).

Camilla Perrone is Associate Professor on Urban and Regional Planning at the University of Florence and Founding Director of the Research Laboratory of Critical Planning and Design. Her fields of interest cover critical planning and design, DiverCity and interactive design, social, spatial and environmental justice, new sustainable forms of city and regional planning beyond traditional city design and town planning, contemporary regional urbanisation processes, interdisciplinary urban and environmental studies, and research methodology. She has published articles and books on spatial planning, participatory design, and urban policies for managing diversity.

Federico Savini is Assistant Professor in Environmental Planning, Institutions and Politics at the University of Amsterdam. In his works he studies the politics that drive institutional change, focusing on the different sets of regulations that shape city-regions and influence their ecological impact on the planet. His work envisions a degrowth path for city-regions. His most recent publication is the edited book *Post growth planning: cities beyond the market economy* (Routledge).

Erik Swyngedouw is Professor of Geography at the University of Manchester, UK. He holds degrees in environmental engineering, urban and regional planning, and geography. His was previously Professor of Geography at Oxford University and held the Vincent Wright Visiting Professorship at Science Po, Paris, 2014. He also holds Honorary Doctorates from Roskilde University (Denmark) and the University of Malmö (Sweden). His research focuses on political ecology, critical theory, environmental politics, democratisation, urbanisation, urban governance, politicisation, and socio-ecological movements.

Stefan Treffers is a PhD Candidate in Sociology at York University, Toronto, Canada with broad interests in urban sociology and critical criminology. His doctoral work explores the politics of urban revitalisation in post-bankruptcy Detroit. He has recently co-authored several refereed journal articles on various topics in *Environment and Planning E: Nature and Space*, *Journal of Urban Affairs*, and *Housing Studies*.

Yannis Tzaninis is an urban and social geographer at the University of Amsterdam. His current research focuses on urban political ecology, European suburbanisation, and discourses of space. He has published on cosmopolitanism, the urban–suburban dichotomy, utopias, place-making, and educational inequalities.

Irina Velicu is a political scientist working on environmental conflicts in post-communist countries. Her research interests revolve around political theory and aesthetics, social transformation, and equality. She is currently a co-coordinator of the PHOENIX Horizon2020 project related to green citizenship. She holds a PhD in Political Science from the University of Hawaii (USA) and an MA in International Studies from the University of Warwick (UK). Her recent publications can be found in the *Journal of Rural Studies, Sociologia Ruralis, Antipode, Environmental Politics, Theory, Culture and Society, Ecological Economics, Geoforum,* and *Globalizations.* Dr Velicu has recently edited HRANA, a collection of peasant storytelling, and is frequently a contributor to Undisciplined Environments and the Berliner Gazette.

David Wachsmuth is the Canada Research Chair in Urban Governance at McGill University, where he is also an Associate Professor in the School of Urban Planning. He directs UPGo, the Urban Politics and Governance research group at McGill, where he leads a team of researchers investigating pressing urban governance problems related to economic development, environmental sustainability, and housing markets. Dr Wachsmuth has published widely in top journals in urban studies, planning, and geography, and his work has been covered extensively in the international media, including the *New York Times,* the *Wall Street Journal,* the Associated Press, and the *Washington Post.* He is the Early Career Editor of the journal *Territory, Politics, Governance* and serves on the editorial boards of the journals *Urban Geography* and *Urban Planning.*

Acknowledgements

This book has long- and medium-term histories that have accumulated multiple layers of intellectual, institutional, and personal indebtedness that we can only acknowledge here briefly. Among the long histories is certainly the collaboration of Kaika and Keil on matters urban and nature that goes back to the 1990s. Most of our close co-conspirators and comrades from the early period of UPE are in this book and we are grateful to them for allowing us to share a path in critical solidarity over those years and decades in creating one of the most rewarding, inspiring, and productive projects of our careers. It is the now time-honoured *collective* project of attempting to understand the urbanisation of nature that we acknowledge here as the seedbed for this particular contribution we have put between these covers.

Among the more short-term histories that need mentioning here is the opportunity that arose at the end of the Major Collaborative Research Initiative on Global Suburbanisms, sponsored by Canada's SSHRC, and housed at York University, to look specifically at the intersection of global suburbanisation – or as we would also call it, extended urbanisation – and urban political ecologies. Global Suburbanisms funded the research for a paper, with the lead authors Yannis Tzaninis and Tait Mandler: Tzaninis, Y., Mandler, T., Kaika, M., and Keil, R. (2021). Moving urban political ecology beyond the 'urbanization of nature', *Progress in Human Geography*, 45(2): 229–52. This paper also provided the basis for the Introduction, and eventually also the Epilogue of this current book.

The paper initially provided the impetus for the Sub/urban Political Ecology Workshop, also funded and co-organised to great extent by Global Suburbanisms, and co-organised and hosted by the University of Amsterdam in February 2019. We would like to specifically thank Cara Chellew and Lucy Lynch at York and Yannis Tzaninis in Amsterdam for their tireless efforts to make the event a huge success. In addition to most authors in this book, Jochen Monstadt, Sara Macdonald, Samir Harb, Marco Armiero, Cara Chellew, Lucy Lynch, Justus Uitermark, Joris Tieleman, Debra Solomon, and Mendel Giezen provided valuable input during the workshop.

It deserves mentioning that the editors met again a year later in Amsterdam, in February 2020, to forge the detailed conceptual framework for this book. It was the last collegial in-person meeting any of us attended before the world shut down due to the pandemic. We are grateful to our authors to have stuck with us during quarantine and lockdowns, grinding uncertainties as our attention shifted to an economy of care, that has preoccupied our urban world since, and to have provided us with the exceptional papers that we have assembled here. The pandemic is written into the pages of this book explicitly and implicitly. The project's original framing around the climate emergency – fuelled by the editors' recent first-hand experiences of the devastating fires in Australia and Greece – had provided the backdrop. In this context, we are particularly grateful to Mike Davis for setting the tone for this volume with his prefatory essay on the political ecology of California's megafires.

In keeping with this theme, on 5 May 2022 Leto Bengtsson, the son of one of the editors, produced a captivating hand drawing. When asked what it depicted, Leto said it was Australia: its sun, its sky, and the smoke under the sky. Then when asked what the yellow-red colours and stick figures depicted he said it is Australian people dying in the wildfires. Leto called this grim, sobering picture 'The Fire Land'.

Leto Cornelis Bengtsson gave permission to use his beautiful artwork for the book cover. Thomas Dark, Laura Swift, and Victoria Chow worked hard to deliver a well edited manuscript. Judy Dunlop produced the meticulous index.

As we were finalising this volume, the sad news of Mike Davis's death reached us. Mike had been ill for a while and we had been in touch with him with encouragement as he was ultimately going into palliative care. We kept him abreast of the progress of the manuscript and sent him an early sketch for the cover that used Leto Tzaninis's painting. A children's book author late in life himself, he noted 'Love it!' and his wife Alessandra Moctezuma said it was 'a beautiful cover'.

With Mike, we are losing an early proponent and profound defender of the urbanisation of nature debate that drives the discussion in this book. Nobody amongst us who has participated in that debate took it as far as Mike did over thirty years of critical interventions on the topic. He wrote about the water of the LA River, the political ecology of slums, the fragility of the desert environments, even the glacial pace that underlies our existence, and importantly the political pathology of infectious disease. And much more.

We were honoured and delighted that Mike gave us access to the text that now stands as the Prologue of this book. It is a tremendous statement of both the challenges and political opportunities that await. In the end, he wrote about fire, and he left us with this Prologue as a strong signal at the outset of the volume before us. We will honour his demand and cry to continue the struggle even in the darkest times. In the end, the collective project towards a better socio-natural future will have the upper hand. We will miss him.

Amsterdam and Toronto, October 2022

Prologue: Losing California – The political ecology of the megafires

Mike Davis

In the 1947 novel *Greener than you think* by the left-wing sci-fi writer Ward Moore, a mad scientist in LA, Josephine Francis, recruits a down-and-out salesman named Albert Weener, described as having 'all the instincts of a roach', to help promote her discovery: a compound called 'the Metamorphizer' that enhances the growth of grasses and allows them to thrive on barren and rocky soils. She dreams of permanently ending world hunger through a massive expansion of the range of wheat and other grains. Weener, a scientific ignoramus, thinks only of making a quick buck, peddling the stuff door to door as a lawn treatment. Desperately needing cash to continue her research, Francis reluctantly agrees and Weener heads out to the yellowed lawns of tired bungalow neighbourhoods.

To his surprise the treatment, which alters grass genes, works – only too well. In the yard of the Dinkman family, crabgrass is converted into a nightmare 'Devil Grass', resistant to mowing and weedkillers, that begins to spread across the city. 'It writhed and twisted in nightmarish unease ... inexorably enveloping everything in its path. A crack in the roadway disappeared under it, a shrub was swallowed up, a patch of wall vanished' (Moore, 1947: 59). It continues to eat pavements and houses and finally consumes the city: a monstrous new nature creeping toward Bethlehem.

Greener than you think is both hilarious and slightly unnerving. But in the strangest of turns, its absurd premises are being turned into reality by climate change. Devil Grass is actually Bromus, a tribe of invasive and almost ineradicable weeds bearing appropriately unsavoury names such as ripgut brome, red brome, and cheat grass. (Their sinister allies from other tribes include scourges of medusahead, tall fescue, false brome, and barbed goat grass.) Invasion is an old California story. In the first wave, black mustard and oatgrass arrived from Europe in the Spanish period and thanks to overgrazing by wild cattle soon replaced native perennial grasses. The bromes, originating in the Mediterranean and the Middle East, came as a second wave in the late 1880s. They were described as a 'contagion' that ate away at the endless carpet of wildflowers whose spring displays in the foothills and valleys had stunned early visitors and put 'golden' in the state's nickname (Minnich, 2008). But now increased fire frequency and exurban sprawl have become the bromes' Metamorphizers, allowing them to rapidly conquer and degrade ecosystems throughout the state.[1]

The Eastern Mojave Desert is a tragic example. En route from LA to Vegas and 20 minutes away from the state line, there is an exit from I-15 to a two-lane blacktop called Cima Road. It is the unassuming portal to one of North America's most magical forests: countless miles of old-growth Joshua trees mantling a field of small Pleistocene volcanoes known as Cima Dome. The monarchs of the forest are 45ft high and centuries old. In mid-August 2020 an estimated 1.3 million of these astonishing giant yuccas perished in the lightning-ignited Dome Fire (Boxall, 2020). This is not the first time that the Eastern Mojave has burned, a megafire in 2005 scorched a million acres of desert but it spared the Dome, the heart of the ecosystem. Over the last generation, increasing invasions of red brome have created a flammable understory to the Joshuas and transformed the Mojave into a fire ecology (Underwood et al., 2019).[2] (Invasive cheatgrass and wiregrass have played similar roles in the Great Basin and eastern Washington's prairies for decades.) Most desert plants, unlike California oaks and chapparal, are not fire-adapted, so their recovery may be impossible. Debra Hughson, the chief scientist at the Mojave National Preserve, indeed described the fire as an extinction event: 'The Joshua trees are very flammable. They'll die, and they won't come back' (Olalde, 2020).

The invasive grass–fire cycle

Our burning deserts are regional expressions of a global trend: the fire-driven transformation and replacement of native land-cover from Greenland (where wildfires are now an annual event) to Hawai'i. Even the Antarctic Peninsula now has an invasive weed problem (Hughes et al., 2020). In most cases, exotic plants – especially annual grasses and forbs – are the culprits. In southeastern US forests the devil is cogongrass from East Asia; in Australia, serrated tussock from South America; in Hawai'i, guinea grass from Africa; and in Spain, pampas grass from the Rio Plata. But bromes, superbly adapted to the Anthropocene, rule the West Coast. As Travis Bean, a weed scientist at UC Riverside, warned in 2019: 'We have all of the nasty non-native Bromus species here in California, and the ubiquitous weeds are key drivers of increasing fire frequency' (Kan-Rice, 2019). Increased fire frequency, in turn, opens new spaces for the propagation of these fast-growing and easily dispersed species. Where mountain chapparal, for instance, requires 20 years after fire to restore biomass, bromes need only one or two winters' rain to sustain a large fire. Once established, the ensuing 'invasive-grass–fire cycle' is almost irreversible.

This is happening in all Mediterranean biomes, despite the fact that their vegetation has similarly coevolved with fire and requires episodic burns to reproduce. The current wave of annual extreme fire in the Iberian Peninsula, Greece, Australia, and California is overriding Holocene adaptations and pushing native ecosystems, many of them already degraded, past their survival tipping points. Southern California's coastal sage scrub, for instance, is estimated to have lost 68 per cent of its area to bromes and other invading weeds (Martinson et al., 2008: 264). Although Australia is a close contender, it is California that best illustrates the vicious circle where extreme heat leads to frequent extreme fires that prevent natural regeneration and, with the help of tree diseases, accelerate the conversion of historic landscapes into parched grasslands and treeless mountain slopes. And with the loss of native plants goes much of the native fauna, from salamanders to owls.

Climate change drives landscape conversion in several different ways. From an earth-system perspective, the warming of the equator is expanding the Hadley cell, the vast system of overturning circulation that pumps hot, moist air upwards, producing tropical rainfall, then the same air masses descend in the semi-tropics as high-pressure ridges, blocking rainfall and creating most of the world's deserts and arid lands. According to cutting-edge climate modelling from Columbia's Lamont-Doherty earth science campus, the impact on lower-latitude temperate landscapes such as California will be profound.

> The ongoing climate change and future change, if it follows the model projections, will transform and move Mediterranean-type climate regions. At the core latitudes of the regions, aridity will increase as winters become drier and temperatures increase through the year. On the equatorward flank some locations that are currently Mediterranean-type climates are likely to transition into subtropical desert or subtropical steppe.
>
> (Seager et al., 2019: 2911)

This is likely the future of Southern California. On the other hand, the Mediterranean climate will probably move poleward into Oregon and even Washington, threatening many forests. LeRoy Westerling at UC Merced believes this transition is fully in progress and that it explains the recent epidemic of extreme fire north of San Francisco: 'Climate change is giving [Northern California] a climate like Southern California, in terms of the degree of drying that the fuels undergo' (Serna and St John, 2020).

Indeed, state water planners and fire authorities since the turn of the century have been intensely focused on the threat of multi-year droughts caused by intensified La Niña episodes and stubbornly persistent high-pressure domes. They also anticipated that the drying of forests would increase vulnerability to insect infestations and tree diseases. Their worst fears were realised in the great drought of the last decade, the biggest since the sixteenth century, which contributed to the death of more than 100 million bark-beetle-infested trees, which subsequently provided fuel mass for the firestorms of 2017 and 2018. At the same time an exponentially spreading fungal pandemic called 'sudden oak death' – which is also facilitated by drought – has killed millions of live oaks and tanoaks in the coast ranges from Big Sur to the Oregon border (Wheeling, 2020). Since the tanoaks, especially, grow in mixed forests with Douglas-firs, redwoods, and ponderosa pines, their dead hulks should probably be accounted as million-barrel fuel-oil equivalents in the current firestorms raging in coastal mountains and Sierra foothills (Frankel, 2007; Valachovic et al., 2011).

In addition to ordinary 'dry' droughts, however, scientists now talk about a new phenomenon in California, the 'hot drought'. Even in years with average twentieth-century rainfall, extreme summer heat, our new normal, is beginning to produce massive water deficits through evaporation in reservoirs, streams, and rivers. In the case of Southern California's lifeline, the lower Colorado River, a staggering 20 per cent decrease in the current flow has been predicted within a few decades, independent of whether or not watershed precipitation declines (Udall and Overpeck, 2016). But the most devastating impact of Death-Valley-like temperatures (it was 121°F (49.4°C) in the San Fernando Valley recently) is the loss of plant and soil moisture. A wet winter and early spring may mesmerise us with extravagant displays of wildflowers but they also produce bumper crops of grasses and herblike plants (forbs) that are then baked in our furnace summers to become fire starters when the devil winds return.

The invaders' Darwinian edge

The bromes and other pyromaniacal weeds like black mustard, pampas grass, and French broom are the chief by-products and facilitators of this new fire regime. Years of research at experimental plots, where the scientists burn different types of vegetation and study their fire behaviour, has confirmed their Darwinian edge. They burn at twice the temperature of herbaceous ground cover, volatilising soil nutrients essential to the regeneration of native species. Whereas the historical fire season for the state's major savanna and chapparal species – oak, chamise, manzanita, sage, and buckwheat – is six months long; the invasive bromes can burn anytime during the year. A study published in 2019 by the National Academy of Sciences estimated that invasive grasses 'are already increasing fire occurrence by up to 230% and fire frequency by up to 150%' (Fusco et al., 2019). They also have a formidable capacity to alter soil conditions in their favour. According to UC Riverside researchers, the invaders 'accelerate the onset of the summer drought and decrease deep soil water recharge ... inhibit[ing] the re-establishment of native shrubs and further increase vulnerability to invasion' (Phillips et al., 2019: 1216). In addition, they sponsor the growth of microbial communities inimical to endemic plants, especially those that constitute Southern California's coastal sage scrub ecosystem (Pickett et al., 2018).

As a result, weeds replace, often permanently, the woody native shrubs that provide net carbon storage. 'This ecosystem conversion,' warned scientists back in 2006, 'has changed portions of the western US from a carbon sink to a source, making previous estimates of a western carbon sink almost certainly spurious' (Bradley et al., 2006: 1815). Now annual firestorms kindled by weed growth are overwhelming the state's highly advertised efforts at curbing greenhouse emissions. In seven weeks from the beginning of August 2020, megafires in California had released significantly more carbon dioxide (91 million metric tons) than produced by all the cars, cities and industries in the state in 2019 (Alberts, 2020).[3]

And weeds can pop up literally everywhere. It was once believed that mountain chapparal was invulnerable to the brome threat but today the wild grasses have taken over one-third of the surface area (Park and Jenerette, 2019: 460). Chapparal is adapted to intense burns within a range of 20 to 50 years, but high fire frequency – one to 15 years – ensures the dominance of invasive species and a type conversion to grasslands (Klinger et al., 2008: 185–6). Likewise closed-canopy West Coast forests have never seemed threatened because they are too cool and shaded. But a research group at Oregon State's College of Forestry that is studying the question now warns forest managers that the species called false brome actually adapts well to forest gloom while cheatgrass immediately colonises forest burn sites. Once a durable feedback loop with fire is established, a forest grass invasion becomes, in their words, a 'perfect storm'.

Like Weener's Devil Grass, the invaders repel extermination campaigns. 'Management actions,' write the Oregonians, 'such as thinning and prescribed fire, often designed to alleviate threats to wildfires, may also exacerbate grass invasion and increase fine fuels, with potential landscape-scale consequences that are largely under-recognized' (Kerns et al., 2020: 2). UCLA's Jon Keeley, a world-renown expert on fire in California ecosystems, had made the same point earlier: 'Complete clearance can actually enhance fire spread by both increasing alien weeds that comprise flashy fuels, and by eliminating important "ember catchers" such as oak trees that can dampen the fire threat around homes' (Keeley et al., 2010: 5). In any event, clearance by itself affords little or no protection. In 2019, Keeley and his colleague

Alexandra Syphard published the first major survey of homes destroyed in the last decade, arriving at the 'surprising finding' that 'of the structures that did have more than 30m of defensible space the vast majority were destroyed in these fires' (Syphard and Keeley, 2019: 14; Keeley and Syphard, 2019).

In other words, the textbook prescriptions for reducing fire hazards may only reproduce them in a new form – something that is poorly understood, if at all, by public officials. This is the Achilles heel of the emergency legislation that Dianne Feinstein, with the support of Governor Newsom, is trying to push through Congress that would override federal environmental regulations to accelerate the thinning of forests and the clearance of chapparal and brush. The bulldozers and torches would invite bromes into cleared landscapes without factoring in their ability to annually generate large fuel loads. Only a sustained annual effort to reseed native plants and remove, to the extent possible, the bromes and their friends – something that would require a large army of full-time forest workers and the cooperation of landowners – could theoretically postpone the weed apocalypse. It would also require a moratorium on new construction as well as on post-fire rebuilding in the most extreme fire hazard areas, but this is hardly palatable in Sacramento even in the era of a Democratic supermajority.

Wildland gentrification

Governor Newsom and other liberal leaders address every fire emergency as the result of climate change and call for urgent action to reduce emissions. In doing so, they deliberately elide the question of what needs to be done on the ground, here and now. Such an agenda would have to directly confront the continuing dictatorship of land-extensive real-estate development, especially the sprawl along what fire experts label as the 'wildland-urban interface' (WUI). The Forest Service definition of WUI distinguishes between two conditions. 'Interface' is when suburban housing is near wildland vegetation, as in the Coffey Park subdivision of Santa Rosa destroyed by the 2017 Tubbs Fire. 'Intermixed', on the other hand, describes the intermingling of housing with brush and trees, the case with many homes in the doomed town of Paradise, incinerated in the 2018 Camp Fire.

A majority of new housing in California over the past 20 years has been built, profitably but insanely, in such fire ecologies and by one estimate over a quarter of the state's population (11 million people) now lives in the WUI (Lowrey, 2020). Despite the fire storms, moreover, the juggernaut seems unstoppable. According to 2018 research by *Bloomberg Business Week*, 'an estimated one million new homes will be built in California's high-risk wildfire zones by 2050' (Flavelle, 2018). In San Diego County alone, supervisors recently approved 10,000 new homes in 'extreme fire-hazard locations' in the backcountry (Smith, 2019). The exponential increase in exposure to the fire hazard can be illustrated by a recent Northern California example. 'In 1964 the Hanly Fire in Sonoma County destroyed fewer than 100 homes. Last fall the Tubbs Fire [2017], which covered almost the same ground, destroyed more than 5,000 homes and killed 22 people' (Flavelle, 2018). Since 40 per cent of the state's 33 million acres of forest are privately owned (57 per cent is federal land and only 3 per cent is under state or local control), there are few restraints on future development without forceful legislative action (University of California Agriculture and Natural Resources, n.d.).

Yet such legislation, even that with the weakest wording, has always been headed off at the pass by successive Democratic and Republican governors under the sway of campaign contributors and elite voters. Thus, Newsom recently vetoed a bill that would have required local government to restrict building permits in 'very high fire risk areas' to only those homes that met the new fire prevention standards detailed in the bill (Weil and Simon, 2020). County ballot propositions to slow growth and protect wildlands have met the same fate up and down the coast, even in the immediate wake of local fire catastrophes. The only real restraint is the increasing reluctance of insurers to issue fire coverage, but this mainly affects ordinary homeowners not wealthy rural gentrifiers, who can easily afford higher premiums and can pay for the private fire crews recommended by the large insurers.

The uncontrolled expansion of the residential frontier into disaster-prone landscapes of course is not just a California trend: think about the building boom on Atlantic and Gulf coast barrier islands episodically submerged in hurricane storm surges. According to geographers Laura Taylor and Patrick Hurley,

> Despite the common perception that the United States has become a 'suburban nation' …, exurbia has emerged as the dominant settlement pattern across the country …, characterized by different patterns of development and different lifestyle expectations from cities, towns, and suburbs, with houses in scenic, natural areas on relatively large acreages (often with one house per 10, 20, or 40 acres or more).
>
> (Taylor and Hurley, 2016: 1)

Instead of densifying housing on the footprints of older suburbs, especially near rapid transit, which is the rational approach to the national housing affordability crisis, market forces are poaching the wildlands and increasing car dependency while shifting the cost of wildfire protection onto county, state, and federal governments.

But there are two very different migration streams to the backcountry. Some, like the inhabitants of Paradise, the Sierra foothill city incinerated in 2018, are rent refugees from the state's housing crisis or ordinary folks, especially retirees, who want to own a tiny piece of the state's beauty. Many live in trailers or manufactured homes, blending in with traditional low-income rural populations in the shadow of declining extractive industries. But they are minor players compared to the influx of wealth from the coast. Rural areas that were once ruggedly blue-collar and derided as 'Appalachia' (the insult long attached to eastern San Diego County where I grew up) now boast 'starter castles', high-end subdivisions and spa retreats. From Mendocino on the north coast to the Sierra foothills in the east and the San Diego mountains in the south, upper 5 per cent migration has been gentrifying the urban hinterlands, especially those areas with high amenity values such as ocean views, wineries, forest lakes, and colourful local histories. Increasing numbers are second or weekend homes, affordable by those who have a solid anchor in soaring coastal home equity.

An equally prized if unspoken amenity is their racial homogeneity. 'Exurbanisation' is often a euphemism for white flight from metropolitan diversity. California's high-income exurbs, regardless of their politics, are almost entirely monochromatic. Nevada County, one of the fastest growing Sierra exurbs, is just 0.4 per cent Black, while more liberal Mendocino County is 0.7 per cent. As California's suburbs turn to technicolour and become more Democratic, the population in the WUI – especially inland from the coast – trends hardcore conservative and fiercely anti-government except in fire season. One of their leading voices was Duncan Hunter, now on his way from Congress to prison, who represented the exurban corridor along I-15 from San Diego to Temecula. For years he fought endangered species legislation and restrictions on backcountry development with the same zeal that he opposed Latino immigrants and affirmative action.

This is a mindset, blind to the consequences, that allies itself to the botanical counterrevolution. Relentless land clearance and home construction fragment habitats, introduce myriad new ignition sources and promote weed invasion. Yet the newcomers in their majority are unwilling to accept state enforcement of building material codes or proposed fire zoning regulations and raise hell when foresters attempt prescribed burns (Edgeley et al., 2020). A recent report from the National Bureau of Economic Research, summarised by two journalists from ProPublica, targeted the perversity of using general tax funds to provide fire protection to wealthy exurbanites who take so little responsibility for their own safety.

> The very fact that firefighting is publicly funded decreases the incentive for WUI residents to fireproof their properties [thereby] distorting the housing market further and creating moral hazard: Because much of firefighting budgets comes out federal disaster funds, publicly funded fire response decreases

the incentive for a city or state – hello, California – to create and enforce wildland building codes.

(Weil and Simon, 2020)

Meanwhile undermanned fire crews are under tremendous pressure to defend individual home sites, making it almost impossible to adhere to the Forest Service's doctrine of 'disengag[ing] suppression activities immediately if strategies and tactics cannot be implemented safety'.[4] The result has been an epidemic of deaths and injuries among firefighters. After fires, moreover, most exurbanites seem incapable of drawing the obvious lessons. In 2003 a firestorm destroyed over 1,000 homes in the unincorporated towns of Alpine and Crest in the mountains east of San Diego. When I took a documentary film crew there in 2019, the lost homes had been replaced by even larger houses and residents assured us that thanks to brush clearance the fire hazard had been mitigated. Despite their own experiences they had bought into the idea of 'defensible space' and the illusion that evacuation would no longer be necessary.

'This "stay-and-defend" approach has effectively privatized disaster prevention and management by shifting fire safety responsibility to homeowners and private contractors', making it popular amongst developers and insurance companies seeking to defend property (Galbo et al., 2020: 2).[5] But as we have seen from the Keeley and Syphard research, firestorms that create their own tornadic weather systems and can hurl fiery debris a mile ahead of the flame front are not deterred by a 300ft circumference of brush clearance or some carefully watered beds of ice plant. Nor can 'fireproof' homes resist combustion when extreme heat blows out their windows and ignites their garage doors.

The victory of the weeds

How should we understand the large-scale ecological consequences of the invasive grass/wildfire cycle? One, perhaps surprising, analogue is the aftermath of the fire-bombing of Germany during the Second World War. In the late 1940s the ruins of Berlin became a laboratory where naturalists studied plant succession in the rubble. The expectation was that the original vegetation of the region – oak woodlands and their shrubs – would soon gradually re-establish itself. To their surprise this was not the case. Instead escaped exotics, some of them rare garden ornamentals, established themselves as the dominants within a new 'ruderal' ecosystem. As one startled but fascinated researcher emphasised: 'The unexpected spread of foreign species made possible by the destruction of broad areas of Berlin was such a radical event that it had rendered previous work on the flora of the city completely insufficient' (Lachmund, 2003: 235). The botanists, who until 1961 included those from the east, continued their studies until the last major rubble site, the Dörnberg-Dreieck, which had become 'the most intensively studied ecosystem within a city that had ever existed', was cleared, despite loud protests, for hotel construction in 1986 (Lachmund, 2003: 244).

'The repopulation of rubble,' wrote another naturalist, 'created in many cities due to the activity of bombers in the last war, has unintentionally become a tremendous natural experiment, which with respect to its size, must be compared to the populating of new habitats created by volcanic activity' (Lachmund, 2003: 239). The persistence of this dead-zone vegetation for a generation after the war and the failure of the plants of the Pomeranian woodlands to re-establish themselves prompted a debate about 'Nature II'. The emergent consensus was that the extreme heat of incendiaries and the pulverisation of brick structures had created a new soil type that invited colonisation by rugged plants that had evolved in on the moraines of Pleistocene ice sheets, if not at the edges of lava flows (Sukopp and Hejny, 1990: 57). The faunal velociraptor in the Berlin rubble was the evil-smelling Chinese 'tree of heaven' (Ailanthus), one of the most aggressive and ineradicable tree-weed species on earth, superbly adapted to every sort of human landscape disturbance from 1,000lb bombs to freeways. (In contemporary California it can be found almost everywhere, sprouting from cracked asphalt in LA parking lots, colonising foothill streambeds and so on.)

An all-out nuclear war, of course, would reproduce Berlin-Year-Zero conditions and replacement ecology on a vast scale.[6] According to a 1960 US study, 'under certain conditions ultimate spread [of fires] from one nuclear weapon has been estimated to be as great as 10,000 square miles'. To model such firestorms, Army and Forest Service researchers in the early 1960s used recent fires in the Santa Monica Mountains, among others in California, as analogues. They were particularly interested in the energy and intensity of wildfires in various environments, establishing a precedent for calculating fire energy in terms of tonnage of TNT (Countryman, 1964: 1). In the aftermath of Victoria's Black Saturday fires in early 2009 that killed 173 people, Australian scientists calculated that their released energy equalled the explosion of 1,500 Hiroshima-sized bombs. Even greater energy has produced the pyrocumulus plumes that for weeks towered over Northern California and Oregon. In fact, the toxic orange smog that shrouded the Bay Area might be considered a miniature nuclear winter.

Megafires in the Anthropocene, in other words, can easily be seen as the physical equivalents of nuclear war without fallout. As a result, a new, profoundly sinister second nature is rapidly emerging from our fire rubble at the expense of landscapes we once considered sacred. Weeds and weedy species of all kinds will continue to win victories within the new evolutionary spaces opened by climate change. And the worst is yet to come. According to a research team from Lamont-Doherty, Scripps, and UCLA, 'the effects of anthropogenic warming on California wildfire thus far have arisen from what may someday be viewed as a relatively small amount of warming' (Williams et al., 2019: 905). Over the next generation fuel dryness, as measured by the atmospheric vapor-pressure deficit, is expected to double. 'Given the exponential response of California burned area to aridity', even greater holocausts are probably inevitable, their scope limited only by available fuel mass (Williams et al., 2019: 905). Our imaginations can barely encompass the speed or scale of this catastrophe. Gone California, gone.

Notes

1. The process of invasion continues in the twenty-first century: in 2008 a new Mediterranean alien, Wards weed, arrived in the beach town of Carlsbad, north of San Diego, and, thanks to its extraordinary seed production (30,000 per square metre), rapidly spread inland. It is a notorious fire plant that invaded Australia in the 1920s and helped increase fire frequency along that continent's arid south coast. Chances for stopping its proliferation look slim (see Diehl, 2019).
2. Three-quarters of the Mojave is deemed 'highly' or 'very highly' susceptible to grass invasion and 'type conversion'.
3. The 257,000-acre California Rim Fire alone released as much CO_2 as the annual emissions of 2.57 million automobiles (Garcia et al., 2017: 340).
4. After the death of four firefighters during Washington's Thirtymile Fire in 2001, the agency published the Thirtymile Fire Investigation report (www.fs.fed.us/t-d/lessons/documents/Thirtymile_Reports/30mile_actionplan%5B1%5D.pdf).
5. Half a million people were forced to evacuate during San Diego County's Witch Fire in 2007.
6. See 'Dead cities: A natural history', Chapter 17 in my book *Dead cities and other tales* (Davis, 2002).

References

Alberts, E. 2020. 'Off the chart': CO_2 from California fires dwarf state's fossil fuel emissions. *Mongabay*, 18 September. https://news.mongabay.com/2020/09/off-the-chart-co2-from-california-fires-dwarf-states-fossil-fuel-emissions/, accessed 12 August 2022.

Boxall, B. 2020. Mojave Desert fire in August destroyed the heart of a beloved Joshua tree forest. *LA Times*, 6 September. www.latimes.com/environment/story/2020-09-06/mojave-desert-fire-destroys-the-heart-of-a-beloved-joshua-tree-forest, accessed 12 August 2022.

Bradley, B.A., R.A. Houghton, J.F. Mustard, and S.P. Hamburg. 2006. Invasive grass reduces aboveground carbon stocks in shrublands of the Western US. *Global Change Biology* 12(10): 1815–22.

Countryman, C. 1964. Mass fire and fire behavior. Res. Paper RS-RP-19. Berkeley, CA: Pacific Southwest Forest and Range Experiment Station, Forest Service, US Department of Agriculture.

Davis, M. 2002. *Dead cities and other tales.* New York: New Press.

Diehl, P. 2019. Invasive plant found in California threatens to spread across southwest. *Phys.Org*, 17 April. https://phys.org/news/2019-04-invasive-california-threatens-southwest.html, accessed 12 August 2022.

Edgeley, C.M., T.B. Paveglio, and D.R. Williams. 2020. Support for regulatory and voluntary approaches to wildfire adaptation among unincorporated wildland-urban interface communities. *Land Use Policy* 91. www.sciencedirect.com/science/article/abs/pii/S0264837719306374, accessed 12 August 2022.

Flavelle, C. 2018. Why is California rebuilding in fire country? Because you're paying for it. Bloomberg, 1 March. www.bloomberg.com/news/features/2018-03-01/why-is-california-rebuilding-in-fire-country-because-you-re-paying-for-it, accessed 12 August 2022.

Frankel, S. 2007. Climate change's influence on sudden oak death. Forest Service, US Department of Agriculture. www.fs.fed.us/psw/cirmount/meetings/paclim/pdf/frankel_talk_PACLIM2007.pdf, accessed 12 August 2022.

Fusco, E.J., J.T. Finn, J.K. Balch, and B.A. Bradley. 2019. Invasive grasses increase fire occurrence and frequency across ecoregions. *PNAS*, 19 November. www.pnas.org/content/116/47/23594.short, accessed 12 August 2022.

Galbo, K., R. Le, and R. Zaman. 2020. *A 'wicked problem': post-wildfire restructuring in exurban San Diego.* Columbia University. https://cdn.filepicker.io/api/file/laPBO1s6RBS5giHvZldb?&fit=max, accessed 12 August 2022.

Garcia, M., S. Saatchi, A. Casas, A. Koltunov, S. Ustin, C. Ramirez, J. Garcia-Gutierrez, and H. Balzter. 2017. Quantifying biomass consumption and carbon release from the California Rim fire by integrating airborne LiDAR and Landsat OLI data. *Journal of Geophysical Research* 122(2): 340–53.

Hughes, K.A. et al. 2020. Invasive non-native species likely to threaten biodiversity and ecosystems in the Antarctic Peninsula region. *Global Change Biology* 26(4): 2702–16.

Kan-Rice, P. 2019. California's bad romance with Bromus fuels wildfire. *UC Agriculture and Natural Resources*, 23 July. https://ucanr.edu/blogs/blogcore/postdetail.cfm?postnum=30883, accessed 12 August 2022.

Keeley, J.E. and A.D. Syphard. 2019. Twenty-first century California wildfires: Fuel-dominated vs wind-dominated. *Fire Ecology* 15(2).

Keeley, J.E., J. Franklin, and C.M. D'Antonio. 2010. Fire on California landscapes. *Fremontia* 38(2–3): 2–6. https://citeseerx.ist.psu.edu/viewdoc/download?doi=10.1.1.732.8673&rep=rep1&type=pdf, accessed 12 August 2022.

Kerns, B.K., C. Tortorelli, M.A. Day, T. Nietupski, A.M.G. Barros, J.B. Kim, and M.A. Krawchuk. 2020. Invasive grasses: A new perfect storm for forested ecosystems? *Forest Ecology and Management* 463.

Klinger, R., R. Wills, and M.L. Brooks. 2008. Fire and nonnative invasive plants in the Southwest coastal bioregion. In K. Zouhar, J.K. Smith, S. Sutherland, and M.L. Brooks (eds.), *Wildland fire in ecosystems: Fire and nonnative invasive plants.* Ogden, UT: US Department of Agriculture, pp. 175–92.

Lachmund, J. 2003. Exploring the city of rubble: Botanical fieldwork in bombed cities in Germany after World War II. *Osiris* 18(1): 234–54.

Lowrey, A. 2019. California is becoming unliveable. *Atlantic*, 30 October. www.theatlantic.com/ideas/archive/2019/10/can-california-save-itself/601135/, accessed 12 August 2022.

Martinson, E.J., M.E. Hunter, J.P. Freeman, and P.N. Omi. 2008. Effects of fuel and vegetation management activities on nonnative invasive plants. In K. Zouhar, J.K. Smith, S. Sutherland, and M.L. Brooks (eds.), *Wildland fire in ecosystems: Fire and nonnative invasive plants*. Ogden, UT: US Department of Agriculture, pp. 261–6.

Minnich, R.A. 2008. *California's fading wildflowers: Lost legacy and biological invasions*. Berkeley: University of California Press.

Moore, W. 1947. *Greener than you think*. New York: Sloan Associates.

Olalde, M. 2020. Dome fire torches 43,000 acres in Mojave National Preserve, many Joshua trees burned. *Desert Sun*, 17 August. www.desertsun.com/story/news/2020/08/17/dome-fire-burns-in-mojave-national-park-as-temps-soar/3383180001/, accessed 12 August 2022.

Park, I.W. and G.D. Jenerette. 2019. Causes and feedbacks to widespread grass invasion into chaparral shrub dominated landscapes. *Landscape Ecology* 34: 459–71.

Pickett, B., I.C. Irvine, E. Bullock, K. Arogyaswamy, and E. Aronson. 2018. Legacy effects of invasive grass impact soil microbes and native shrub growth. *Invasive Plant Science Management* 12(1): 22–35.

Phillips, M.L., B.E. McNellis, M.F. Allen, and E.B. Allen. 2019. Differences in root phenology and water depletion by an invasive grass explains persistence in a Mediterranean ecosystem. *American Journal of Botany* 106(9): 1210–18.

Seager, Richard, T.J. Osborn, Y. Kushnir, I.R. Simpson, J. Nakamura, and H. Liu. 2019. Climate variability and change of Mediterranean-type climates. *Journal of Climate* 32(10): 2887–915.

Serna, J. and P. St John. 2020. How wine country became the epicenter for fires in California. *LA Times*, 29 September. www.latimes.com/california/story/2020-09-29/how-wine-country-became-the-epicenter-for-fires-in-california, accessed 12 August 2022.

Smith, J.E. 2019. San Diego's latest backcountry development to be built where California suffered one of its most historic wildfires. *The San Diego Union Tribune*, 27 May. www.sandiegouniontribune.com/news/environment/story/2019-05-25/san-diegos-latest-backcountry-development-to-be-built-where-california-suffered-one-of-its-most-historic-wildfires, accessed 12 August 2022.

Sukopp, H. and S. Hejny (eds.). 1990. *Urban ecology: Plants and plant communities in urban environments*. The Hague: SPB Academic Publishing.

Syphard, A.D. and J.E. Keeley. 2019. Factors associated with structure loss in the 2013–2018 California wildfires. *Fire* 3(3): 1–15.

Taylor, L.E. and P.T. Hurley. 2016. Introduction: The broad contours of exurban landscape change. In L.E. Taylor and P.T. Hurley (eds.), *A comparative ecology of exurbia: Planning, environmental management and landscape change*. Cham: Springer, pp. 1–29.

Udall, B. and J. Overpeck. 2016. The twenty-first century Colorado River hot drought and implications for the future. *Water Resources Research* 53(3): 2404–18. https://agupubs.onlinelibrary.wiley.com/doi/full/10.1002/2016WR019638, accessed 12 August 2022.

University of California Agriculture and Natural Resources. n.d. Forest research and outreach: California forests. https://ucanr.edu/sites/forestry/California_forests/, accessed 12 August 2022.

Underwood, E.C., R.C. Klinger and M.L. Brooks. 2019. Effects of invasive plants on fire regimes and postfire vegetation diversity in an arid ecosystem. *Ecology and Evolution*. https://onlinelibrary.wiley.com/doi/pdf/10.1002/ece3.5650, accessed 12 August 2022.

Valachovic, E.C., C.A. Lee, H. Scanlon, J.M. Varner, R. Glebocki, B.D. Graham, and D.M. Rizzo. 2011. Sudden oak death-caused changes to surface fuel loading and potential fire behavior in Douglas-fir-tanoak forests. *Forest Ecology and Management* 261(11): 1973–86.

Weil, E. and M. Simon. 2020. California will keep burning, but housing policy is making it worse. *ProPublica*, 2 October. www.propublica.org/article/california-will-keep-burning-but-housing-policy-is-making-it-worse, accessed 12 August 2022.

Wheeling, K. 2020. Sudden oak death taking a toll on US West Coast. *EOS*, 29 July. https://eos.org/research-spotlights/sudden-oak-death-taking-a-toll-on-u-s-west-coast, accessed 12 August 2022.

Williams, A.P., J.T. Abatzoglou, A. Gershunov, J. Guzman-Morales, D.A. Bishop, J.K. Balch, and D.P. Lettenmaier. 2019. Observed impacts of Anthropogenic climate change on wildfire in California. *Earth's Future* 7. https://agupubs.onlinelibrary.wiley.com/doi/pdf/10.1029/2019EF001210, accessed 12 August 2022.

Introduction: Urban political ecology for a climate emergency

Yannis Tzaninis, Tait Mandler, Maria Kaika, and Roger Keil

Urban political ecology as intervention to the current socio-environmental emergency

In the opening scene of *Blade Runner*, Ridley Scott's iconic 1982 movie, the cinematic gaze is drawn on downtown LA; a dense 'centre' made up of messy, smoggy, dirty, rainy streets, where a seething mass of people, cars, and flying objects move in chaotic trajectories. Soon after its release, the film became the exemplary depiction of dystopian urban futures. However, 35 years later, the film's sequel presents a different type of dystopia. Moving the gaze away from the city centre, the opening scene of *Blade Runner 2049* (directed by Denis Villeneuve, 2017) focuses on the horizontal planes of everywhere. It is a dystopian future of extensive sprawl, of homogenised landscapes of an never-ending 'outside', dominated by synthetic farms and solar panels. The future of Los Angeles's extended periphery seems to have no end; it is a horror-scenario of the 'continuous city' sprawling over an ever-warming planet (Berger et al., 2017; Hern and Johal, 2018; Lerup, 2017); the ultimate state of capitalism's environmental ills, ironically combining ecological collapse with renewable energy, free/slave labour, and mass-produced synthetic food (Astley, 2018). There is no possible escape to an alternative 'outside'; the outside and inside are blurred; the only possible outside left is ex-planetary uninhabitable landscapes of waste and labour, those elements that Marx once thought of as the indispensable conditions of capitalist accumulation.

The juxtaposition of the original to the new cinematic *Blade Runner* landscapes is an analogy for the shifts that real landscapes of urbanisation underwent in less than one generation. While humans have become more urban both in location and lifestyle, they have done so on an exceedingly expansive terrain. Today, the dynamics of relentless and uneven capitalist growth create extended urban landscapes that blur the boundaries of the inside and the outside, and transcend the classical city/countryside, city/

periphery, city/nature boundaries that had been constitutive of urban studies. This shift, that occurs under the threat of climate change, is what generated the need to put together this edited volume as a call to expand the empirical and theoretical scope of UPE's early call to overcome the distinction between core and periphery, inside and outside, city and nature.

The aim of this edited volume is to showcase urban political ecology (henceforth UPE) as an intervention – in theory, methodology, and practice – to the socio-environmental emergencies of the twenty-first century. Understanding extended urbanisation to be both a political and an ecological matter of concern, we argue that climate change is a socio-environmental condition that adds urgency to the way debates and methodologies advance within UPE scholarship. The volume brings together theoretical discussions and empirical analysis by key scholars spanning three intellectual generations focusing on the link between theory and policy/politics, and on the need to advance UPE's theories, methods, and empirical analysis around situated and southern urbanism, abolitionist urbanism, more-than-human entanglements, and extended urbanisation.

As extended urbanisation and violent 'feral' suburban development (Shields, 2012) lead to new waves of destruction, the role of cities and urbanisation has become central in recent years in local and international policymaking and discussions on how to cope with the climate emergency. The fires that burned in Alberta's tar sands in 2016, across Australia in 2019, and California in 2018–19 and 2020, and the floods that devastated many European cities in 2021 bring into sharp relief the consequences of urban development where there should not be any or development that has burned in the past only to be rebuilt with public blessings and even subsidies (Arellano, 2018; Davis, Prologue in this volume; Goh, 2019a; Maginn and Keil, 2019; Serna, 2019).

However, as international policymaking organisations – from the UN Habitat's New Urban Agenda to EU's Green Deal – discover cities as key points of intervention for climate change mitigation and adaptation, the strategies around urbanisation and environmental protection become increasingly dominated by market-led solutions or populist and racist discourses. It is therefore crucial for UPE scholarship to turn its critical energies towards a politically engaging debate over what role extended urbanisation processes can and should play in addressing socio-environmental equality in the context of climate change and related anthropocentric and metabolic rifts – both real and discursive (Ernstson and Swyngedouw, 2018).

This interdependence between the 'ecological' and the 'urban' has been the central focus of urban political ecology (UPE) for almost two decades (Connolly, 2018). As noted by Swyngedouw and Kaika (2014), a key characteristic of UPE scholarship is the development of an understanding of the 'urban' not as a bounded space within which political-ecological contestations are played out, but as a process of continuous socio-ecological flows and transformations. UPE's radical reading of cities not as bound spaces was a critical response to the canon in urban studies that viewed 'cities as purely social spaces ... entirely separate from the countless non-human entities and organisms that are enrolled in, and help shape, urban life' (Braun, 2005: 635).

Today, however, the dystopian present and future we face emphasise that the matter of concern is not cities per se, or environments per se, but rather 'the urbanization of nature', i.e., the process through which 'all types of nature are socially mobilized, economically incorporated (commodified), and physically metabolized/transformed in order to support the [continuous] urbanization process' (Swyngedouw and Kaika, 2014: 462). Although politics commonly precede academic enquiry and policymaking lags behind scientific research, the unfolding of the climate emergency within a context of extended urbanisation means that this disjunction between academic debate and the policy and politics of climate change has urgent socio-ecological implications that UPE scholarship cannot afford to ignore.

In this volume, we put forth an integrated UPE agenda enriched by the expansion of the scope of its inquiry, and therefore better-suited to address contemporary environmental issues in theory and practice. We make a case here for an UPE focused on extended urbanisation; a UPE better informed by situated knowledges; an embodied UPE that puts equal attention to the role of postcolonial processes and more-than-human ontologies of capital accumulation within the context of the climate emergency and abolitionist thinking, anti-Black and anti-Indigenous racism. Within this context, we identify four key debates in the contemporary UPE agenda which we bring into generative dialogue in order to address the climate emergency.

The first debate (Part I of the edited volume) discusses how UPE can be strengthened through new ontologies of 'the urban' and debates over 'extended urbanisation', 'suburbanisation', and a critical take on 'planetary urbanisation' that can contribute to an 'ecological, political understanding of contemporary urbanization' (Angelo and Wachsmuth, 2014). The second debate (Part II) is the call for a 'situated' UPE coming from scholars working on and in the Global South and from feminist and intersectional UPE scholars who aim to create 'the possibility for a broader range of urban experiences to inform theory on how urban environments are shaped, politicized and contested' (Lawhon et al., 2014: 498). This work overlaps with theoretical and practical interventions ascribed to Southern urbanism, postcolonialism, feminism, and racial capitalism (Bhan, 2019; Dorries et al., 2019; McFarlane and Silver, 2017; Silver, 2014; Simone, 2004; Wu and Keil, 2020; Yiftachel, 2020). The third debate (Part III) examines the conceptual and methodological challenges and policy implications of bringing more-than-human actors and entanglements into UPE and into the climate change agenda, by showing not only how 'cities are produced through socio-natural metabolic flows originating "elsewhere"; but also, how cities and their specific sociopolitical contexts and spatial configurations have strong implications for how … non-human natures are urbanized' (Connolly, 2018: 2). The fourth debate (Part IV) addresses the disjunction between policy, politics, and academic debates, and explores what UPE can contribute to contemporary environmental policy and politics – and vice versa.

As present-day capitalism shows its ugliest face, the analysis of the link between racial capitalism, class struggle, and the politics of climate change, that has been on UPE agendas for over a decade, needs to be emphasised and better integrated into present-day politics and social debate. The additional challenges revealed by the urban political pathology of COVID-19 make this UPE debate ever-more urgent today (Bressan, 2021; Connolly et al., 2021; Keil et al., Chapter 11 in this volume).

One of the strengths of this volume is the diversity in the linguistic, conceptual, and cultural background of the authors. The authors and editors tried to transpose this diversity and multiplicity into a coherent English language text while being cautious not to try to mould diverse manners of speech into a stylistic norm that may be acceptable only to middle-of-the-road Anglo-American standards.

Urban political ecology's past and present: Why UPE's heterodoxy is an asset when it comes to addressing climate change

Over the past two decades, UPE has advanced and diversified theoretically, empirically, and methodologically. Using a chronological stage model, Heynen (2014, 2016, 2017) identifies two 'waves' of UPE scholarship. The first includes foundational texts: *Concrete and clay* (Gandy, 2002), *Social power and the urbanization of water* (Swyngedouw, 2004), *Nature and the city* (Desfor and Keil, 2004), *City of flows* (Kaika, 2005), and *Lawn people* (Robbins, 2007). The first 'wave' culminates with the 2006 volume *In the nature of cities*, edited by Heynen, Kaika, and Swyngedouw (see also Collard et al., 2018). While a variety of approaches to, and applications of, UPE are present in that volume, most draw theoretical inspiration from Swyngedouw's framing of metabolic circulation (Swyngedouw, 2006). The second 'wave' of UPE, according to Heynen (2014, 2016, 2017), comprises an emerging body of literature that is critical of UPE's early framing. It includes research more attentive to race, gender, and sexuality, and incorporates postcolonial, Indigenous, feminist, and queer theory. While some authors maintain a commitment to a metabolic circulation framing, others move in new directions, often more concerned with everyday life, and micro-politics. Heynen's chronological framing of UPE in two distinct waves is didactic and advances our understanding of the genealogy of the field (see also Connolly, 2018).

The current edited volume depicts the heterodoxy in UPE's past and recent scholarship not only as a fruitful engagement among scholars, but also as central to UPE's unique position to address the urgent political questions around climate change. Without editing out the rich ontological and epistemological debates and complexities in the field's intellectual history (Connolly, 2018), we attempt to amalgamate the contribution that UPE scholarship can make in twenty-first-century debates and praxis over urbanisation and the environment. Our position is that critique is significant not only for moving the field forward but also for moving into new forms of action. Therefore, the editors do not attempt to force diverse pathways to congeal; what drives this endeavour instead is the urgent scholarly and political need to assess which epistemologies, ontologies, and methodologies within UPE's pathways might be best suited to deal with the integrated, compound, and systemic disaster we call climate change.

To do this, we focus on the unity within UPE's diverse debates; on the fact that, while hybridising, UPE's intellectual debates share a common goal: to move the intellectual and political debate about 'green and grey cities' (to use Angelo and Wachsmuth's term) into new productive territory. So, without glossing over the critical edges UPE literature has generatively developed over the past two decades, and recognising that UPE is further branching out and hybridising, the book identifies four distinct 'pathways'/directions within contemporary UPE agendas. Each part of this book engages with one of these debates.

Part I: Extended urbanisation: Moving UPE beyond the 'urbanisation of nature' thesis
Part II: Situated urban political ecologies
Part III: More-than-human urban political ecologies and relational geographies
Part IV: Addressing disjunctions between policy, politics, and academic debate

This 'typology' exercise serves two purposes. First, it allows us to compare and contrast the ways in which each distinct pathway/debate addresses (epistemologically, ontologically, and methodologically) current socio-environmental challenges. Second, and most important, it opens a dialogue among these pathways/directions over what UPE scholarship can offer to the politics of climate change, and over how UPE scholarship can move squarely into current debates about urbanisation and climate change, taken to be a political as much as an 'ecological' problem. All of the book's collected chapters embrace this dialectic between critique and call to action in different ways. Although the edited collection does not come up with a unified and singular answer, it does identify different possibilities of action at different scales and geographical locations.

Part I: Extended urbanisation: Moving UPE beyond the 'urbanisation of nature' thesis

Until the 1990s critical urban geographical research and progressive urban practice remained stubbornly focused on the urban centre. When Henri Lefebvre (1996: 208) visited Los Angeles in the 1980s he was both stupefied and fascinated by the fact that Los Angeles was a clear material digression from the concept of a 'city' which has a clear centre and a clear periphery; 'you don't know exactly when you are entering … or leaving [the city]' as it stretches for 150km. The Los Angeles School of urban scholarship emphasised this point further and it took another 30 years for urban scholarship to finally acknowledge that not all future cities will look like Los Angeles; and not all future cities will follow the centralised Euro-US trajectories that Lefebvre and twentieth-century urban sociology and geography took as the model from which they considered Los Angeles (or Houston, Johannesburg, Shenzhen, São Paulo, or Djakarta) to be an aberration. But in the meanwhile, the focus on a core central city had entered prescriptive and normative assumptions underlying urban sustainability policies (see for a critique Wachsmuth et al., 2016; Wachsmuth and Angelo, 2018).

Transcending the dichotomies that have been constitutive of urban studies and urban environmental policies has been a key concern of UPE scholarship since its inception in the 1990s. UPE focused from the onset on blurring traditional understanding of 'cities' as distinct ontological entities, separate from the outside, from 'nature' and peri-urban landscapes and developed methods for examining how the production of human settlements is metabolically linked with networked flows of resources, technology, labour, capital, and more-than-human actors and ecological processes. However, UPE's early call *not* to examine 'cities' or 'natures' per se, but the 'urbanization of nature' (Kaika, 2005) as a set of metabolic flows and socio-environmental processes, also often privileged a perceived 'centre' as the *point-de-capiton* around which these flows and processes fester. While there is nothing inherently wrong with research on cities, Angelo and Wachsmuth (2014: 23) suggest that there is a danger to this being the overwhelming norm in UPE research (see also Connolly, 2018, for a response).

But today, despite advanced theoretical debate and increased empirical attention on extended urbanisation, an integrated research agenda for a UPE beyond the city has yet to be concretely developed. In response to this need, this edited volume pushes the UPE debate beyond this 'centre' in order to shed light on spaces and lives outside urban centres that have been largely overlooked (McKinnon et al., 2017) and on the socio-ecological and spatial processes and practices beyond privileged scales. This volume responds to the call to resist the reduction of what goes on outside of cities to the dynamics and processes that emanate unidirectionally from cities. And to do this, we urge to realign the focus of UPE with the new urban forms and processes of urbanisation that we witness since the last quarter of the twentieth century, which we articulated around the notion of 'extended urbanisation'. Extended urbanisation is understood here as a global process that exceeds the conventional conceptualisations of 'the urban' to include a vast variety of expansions of form and process, forms of densely layered dynamics of growth and decline, densification and de-densification, demographic and economic growth and diversity (Tzaninis, 2020) and contradictory socio-economic dynamics (Johnson et al., 2018; Lawton, 2019). Our concern with extended urbanisation includes the combination of non-central forms of population and economic growth with spatial expansion of various forms, from 'suburban', 'peri-urban', 'post suburban', corridor urbanisation, informal settlements, gated communities, tower estates, massive production sites, logistics 'cities', brutalscapes, deforestation, and vast agricultural landscapes, but also suburban residential sites, be it concrete high-rises or picket-fenced homes, kampungs, desakota, peri-urban villages, extensive employment zones, office cities and aerotropolises, as well as extended recreational and infrastructural spaces (for elaboration see Brenner and Katsikis, Chapter 5 in this volume; Ekers et al., 2012: 407; Keil, 2018d, 2018e; McGee, 2011; Monte-Mór, 2014a, 2014b; Simone, 2019).

The arguments centred around the notion of 'extended urbanisation' in this volume build on significant work that has already began. In a series of articles Ekers and Prudham (2015, 2017, 2018) theorise the 'socio-ecological fix' which may help us understand landscape transformations without relying on bounded notions of 'urban' and 'rural' (see also Andreucci et al., 2017). Coplen's (2018) work on food systems also follows complex supply chains as a method for researching across urban–rural divides (see also Agyeman and McEntee, 2014; Alkon, 2012; Hovorka, 2006). Saguin (2017) explores the production of non-urban 'hazardscapes' through urban-rural metabolisms, while Rice and Tyner (2017) offer a compelling UPE of rural mass violence in Cambodia. Gururani (2002) demonstrates how rural women in the Indian Himalayas constitute their identities through everyday practices, and calls for a culturally embedded analysis of nature–society relations. Harrison and Popke (2017) focus on the Caribbean to conceptualise 'island energy metabolism' through the relations between the particular materialities of energy sources, island geographies, and particular territorial, infrastructural, and geopolitical characteristics. A cross-fertilisation between UPE and agrarian political economy has also produced significant methodological insight for moving UPE beyond the city. As Karpouzoglou et al. (2018: 491) note:

> social inequalities arising from land-use change, inequalities in terms of access to safe and clean water, and the management of industrial waste are only some of the pressing issues that ... will require a joint endeavour of thinking across UPE and peri-urban scholarship.

Another significant body of recent UPE scholarship focused on suburbanisation processes (Angelo, 2017; Keil and Macdonald, 2016; Taylor, 2011). The suburban was traditionally depicted as the dumping ground for the by-products of core functions and for undesirable people: from factories, nuclear plants, and garbage dumps, to retirement homes and revalidation centres. The bias of urban studies towards the core led to a certain blindness 'to the views and perspectives of those marginalised in everyday ecologies, and the differences within and among these groups' (Shillington and Murnaghan, 2016: 1022). We must focus on the quotidian revolutions in the sub/urban political ecologies of everyday life through which we can reconcile seemingly opposing claims between situated UPE and the call for a post-cityist UPE. This begins with acts of 'dissensus' as living indicators for tackling socio-environmental inequality (Kaika, 2017; see also Velicu and Kaika, 2017). Nowadays some of the most dynamic socio-political changes happen in the periphery and indeed, recent political ecology research on the spatial periphery intersects with inquiries on social marginalisation. Gustafson's (2015) work in southern Appalachia and Schmidt's (2017) work on the re-production of wilderness in Houston's suburbs are cases in point; they both explore how the exurban is produced through local contestations over knowledge and power. Also focusing on practices of marginalisation, Batubara et al. (2018) recently explored the politics of flood infrastructure in Jakarta to demonstrate how inequality is reproduced through the extraction of cement from the periphery that is utilised to transform the city. Parés et al. (2013: 342) show how the suburbs of Barcelona emerge through a dialectic of capital flows and the materialisation of desires for consumption (homes in this case), a kind of intertwined process of morphological suburbanisation and new suburban ways of life. Finally, Bruggeman and Dehaene (2017) propose a distributed model of urbanisation through a study on the expansion of electricity infrastructures in Belgium across urban and rural spaces. Valdivia's (2018) recent work is one such example that intersects periphery, everyday life and fossil capitalism with the embodied ecologies of an oil refinery city in which conditions of social and chemical toxicity characterise everyday life, but also where desires for social justice manifest through optimism and dignity. The very concept of suburbanisation is expanded in these studies to be understood as a 'global process' that exceeds conventional conceptualisations. Tzaninis and Boterman (2018: 58) argue that the transformations of cities and suburbs are not even 'two sides of the same coin' but rather resemble a 'cyclical, non-dichotomous spatio-temporal process'. As Keil (2018e: 496) notes, 'the notion of suburbanization as dependent on one centre has to be discarded as the form and life of the global suburb take shape through multiple centralizations and decentralizations'.

We distinguish the notion of 'extended urbanisation' from recent contributions to 'suburbanisation', but also from the 'planetary urbanisation' (PU) thesis. At the same time, we acknowledge the important contribution these bodies of thought have brought to the field. PU has recently received strident critiques from feminist, queer, and intersectional scholarship on the basis that the concept can be too comprehensive and violent to enable 'other' critical urban approaches to flourish (Buckley and Strauss, 2016; Butcher and Maclean, 2018; McLean, 2018; Oswin, 2016; Peake et al., 2018), or too close to what Haraway (1988) calls a 'god trick' that reproduces a 'conquering gaze from nowhere' (Derickson, 2017; see also Monte-Mór 2014a, 2014b). Notwithstanding the validity of these critiques, it is important not to throw away the baby with the bathwater. The planetary urbanisation (PU) debate has a significant intellectual history linked to over half a century of urban social movements and struggles. While acknowledging the importance of contemporary feminist postcolonial and intersectional concerns about the totalising and universalising effects of PU, we advocate that it is worth to politicise again some of PU's key insights (Keil, 2018a) including: the 'concern with the relational and hybrid nature of social relations; … the concomitant rejection of … dualisms like urban/non-urban' (Derickson, 2017: 558); the focus on 'simultaneity of process … temporal flows … and relentless, multi-directional spillages, leakages, causal criss-crosses, and trans-boundary processural connections' (Wilson and Jonas, 2018: 2); the traversing of 'spatial scales and analytical levels' (Angelo and Goh, 2020: 742). Through these heated debates, we find Alex Loftus's intervention particularly constructive, as he calls for 'a philosophy of praxis that begins from lived practices' and suggests that the 'grounded' and the 'planetary' do not comprise a dichotomy; instead, the two are mutually constitutive (Loftus, 2018a: 94). We also build on the work of scholars who advocate 'epistemic plurality' (Buckley and Strauss, 2016), 'chaotic research pathways' (McLean, 2018), and 'other fields of vision' (Peake et al., 2018), a plurality that the concept of extended urbanisation can better accommodate.

Acknowledging the fruitful yet contentious debate around naming urban peripheries worldwide (Harris and Vorms, 2017), in this volume we highlight the potential of the concept of 'extended urbanisation' to become generative of a situated UPE theory within the context of a climate emergency; a situated UPE of extended urbanisation that takes to heart the empirical, theoretical, and methodological insights of feminist, intersectional, and postcolonial debates. This contributes towards building an integrated political ecology that can advance the field in two distinct ways. First, it expands our understanding of marginality beyond 'traditional' notions, actors, and spaces. Second, it challenges the related 'traditional' policy discourses on urban sustainability that focus mainly on centres.

Yet, at the same time, we remain cautious to avoid 'extended urbanisation' becoming yet another 'vacuous shell for academic debate' (Keil 2018a: 1591). The situated urban political ecologies of extended urbanisation that this volume puts forward focus on 'the networked matrix ... on which urban-nature relations are made and unmade' (Keil, 2011: 716). A 'sociology of nature' for a planet of extended urbanisation needs to take into account that new forms of socio-nature take shape in sprawling regions of multiple densities. These spaces encompass past and present landscape and socio-ecological formations and contestations: from disputes over ancient land rights, rural remnants, agricultural residues, to sedimented leftovers of industrial society, mines, old factories that are now being reclaimed by open landscape or incorporated into new urban spaces (Keil, 2018c). For example, while the suburban fringe appears to Berger as 'a no-man's land of random, disaggregated and often uncomplimentary, informal and uncontrolled land uses' (2017: 525), we know that both the suburban and the landscape beyond have been structured by generations or millennia of preceding human-nature interactions. To phrase it in these terms – 'no-man's land' – might risk steamrolling over generations of human–non-human societal relationships with nature as well as the Indigenous relationships to land that have existed there for a long time.

In engaging with the notion of extended urbanisation, the editors and authors of this volume were inevitably faced with what AbdouMaliq Simone (2019: 991) calls a 'conceptual conundrum ... to identify how such processes [of extended urbanisation] entail a coherent series of maneuvers and logics without reifying the intensely malleable, shape-shifting ways in which urbanization articulates divergent trajectories of spatial production'.

All authors in this volume address this conundrum by exposing the socio-ecological metabolisms inherent in this process: Mike Davis's prologue on exurban fires, Savini's chapter on circular economies, Connolly and Muzaini's contribution on islands as urban extensions.

The authors in Part I of in this volume address this conundrum more explicitly. In Chapter 1, Erik Swyngedouw identifies the methodological, theoretical, and political challenges we face when trying to propel the (urban) ecological condition to a matter of global political concern within the context of extended urbanisation. He focuses particularly on the articulation between critical theorisations and political possibilities and on the need to better articulate critical policy and governance analysis with an understanding of 'the political'.

In Chapter 2, Matthew Gandy argues that current tensions around the definition of 'the city' as an object of analysis are further complicated by the increasing deployment of ecological metaphors in urban design and related fields. He argues that the limitations of urban ecology, as a coherent approach for urban analysis or intervention, stem from the dynamic, interdependent, and historically contested characteristics of urban nature and the ambiguous dimensions to ecology as a leitmotif for urban politics.

In Chapter 3, Roberto Luís Monte-Mór and Ester Limonad use the case of Brazil to exemplify how, while industrialisation divided 'cities' from 'natures' and treated nature as an obstacle to be removed, the alternative 'other' economies that either survived or emerged outside capitalist industrialisation reunited the urban and the environmental perspectives. The authors see the possibility of alternative socio-environmental futures in the increasing focus on collective reproduction of these 'other' economies (as opposed to the capitalist economy's focus production and accumulation).

In Chapter 4, Martín Arboleda puts forward the notion of extensive extractivism to analyse how transnational circuits of extraction contribute to extensive urbanisation. Extensive extractivism, he argues, signalled the integration of hitherto dispersed elements of social production and brought together natural resources and built environments, as well as city and non-city spaces, in novel and intricate ways.

In Chapter 5, Neil Brenner and Nikos Katsikis advocate a heterodox synthesis of UPE's theoretical orientations, epistemological framework, and normative foundations with conventional approaches to socio-ecological metabolism as a basis on which to explore the dialectics of concentrated and extended urbanisation. The chapter explores how the use of urban ecological footprints, anthropogenic biomes, material flows and urban land teleconnections can illuminate the role of non-city landscapes, or 'hinterlands' as essential arenas and products of the urbanisation process.

Part II: Situated urban political ecologies

This volume responds to the call for a situated UPE scholarship that mobilises a Global South perspective as a tool for conceptual and empirical reorientation, rather than simply as an afterthought. Moving UPE beyond the usual North–South divide gains increasing importance as extended urban systems are being prepared for climate adaptation and mitigation through global systems of financing, as well as engineering management knowledge and policy transfer (Goh, 2019b; Keil, 2020; Ranganathan, 2014; Ranganathan and Balazs, 2015). This extension significantly enriches the field with new research methods, theoretical framings, and practices from the Global South, thus provincialising North-centred UPE debates (Goldfischer et al., 2020; Lawhon et al., 2014, 2016, Chapter 10 in this volume; Loftus 2019a). It pays more attention to everyday practices (Loftus, 2012), mobilises a more nuanced examination of power as diffused and relational (Lawhon, 2012; Lawhon et al., 2014), and emphasises race, gender, and location (Loftus, 2019b; Njeru, 2006; Truelove, 2011).

It is important to note that the theorisation and conceptualisation of 'Southern urbanism' in this volume refers not only to the different forms, modes, and processes related to the urbanisation of nature in different geographical settings and to the politics and power relations involved in these. It also refers to the politics of research and theorisation of 'Southern urbanism', the call to de-centre the position from which theory itself is developed.[1]

Our call for a situated UPE is also in dialogue with the recent 'infrastructural turn' in urban studies; a critical response to the depiction of infrastructures as universal or uniform by urban theory produced in the Global North (Addie et al., 2020; Graham, 2010; Monstadt and Coutard, 2019). This turn proposes 'heterogenous infrastructure configurations' as an analytical lens that troubles the formal/informal binary and directs research questions towards 'the conditions under which ... socio-technical artefacts work, for whom they work, and what it means for infrastructures to work' (Lawhon et al., 2018: 730). This intervention is brilliantly elaborated in Chapter 10 by Mary Lawhon, Anesu Makina, and Gloria Nsangi Nakyagaba in this volume. Within the call for an 'infrastructural turn', Doshi (2017: 125) also advocates paying more attention to material embodiments, which currently remain 'under-studied and disparately theorized'. Drawing on research in the Global South, she offers five propositions: 'attention to [embodied] metabolism, social reproduction, intersectionality and articulation, emotion and affect, and political subjectivity'. Holifield and Schuelke (2015) also call for incorporating the aesthetic mobilisation of desires into UPE analyses of process and disruption.

Along with the infrastructural turn perspectives from the Global South, the call for a situated UPE also puts on centre stage Indigenous political ecologies, theories and practices of decolonisation, as well as abolitionist political ecologies (Heynen, 2016, 2018). The political urgency of a situated UPE was violently highlighted in 2020 with the brutal police murder of George Floyd and the global activism that followed, which questioned the legitimacy of the state, its institutions, and its infrastructures, but also raised again broader questions around the distribution of wealth and land and the clash between Indigenous and capitalist political ecologies (Taylor, 2019; Wilderson, 2021).

In recent years, situated UPE focused equally on highlighting the different forms that environmental racism takes across the world (Ahmed, 2021), particularly in settler colonial societies – such as Australia, Canada, and the United States – where the clash between suburbanisation as a Western lifestyle and traditional ways of living on the land is most pronounced (Maginn and Keil, 2019; Middleton, 2015; Veracini, 2012). This clash extends to all sites and products of extended urbanisation and relational connectivities. As Kipfer (2018: 474) illustrates in the case of Canadian pipeline politics, ecological thinking around extended urbanisation cannot do 'without resorting to … approaches that help us understand the settler-colonial aspects of Canadian urban history and grasp the inter-national dimensions of Indigenous politics' (see also Hern and Johal, 2018; Pickerill, 2018). But this literature also highlights potential alternative pathways of resistance. Simpson and Bagelman (2018) show how in occupied Colombia the production of nature continues to proceed through an ongoing interplay of colonisation and resistance; where the 'colonial socionatural order' has been imposed on millennia-old (Indigenous) Lekwungen socio-ecologies, the latter have in fact never been fully erased. Similar emphasis on 'counter-hegemonic' processes comes from Gururani and Vandergeest (2014), who suggest a shift of focus towards ecological knowledge produced by local actors. As Schulz (2017: 139) shows, colonisation is not only about recognising material processes of appropriation and subjugation but also hierarchies of knowing and being that structure research practices:

> The careful building of a pluriversal dialogue that is neither embedded in culturalism nor absolute particularism, but in the realisation that multiple loci of enunciation coexist and are entangled through the coloniality of knowledge, being and power, will thus be the major task that lies ahead for a decolonial-ecological critique in and of the Anthropocene.

We, the editors, remain conscious of our position as scholars embedded in Western/Northern academic institutions. For this reason, we were deliberately non-prescriptive/normative with our chapter authors in terms of how they should address this crucial question. Indeed, many of our authors address this problematic implicitly and others explicitly, especially those who speak from the Global South (Monte-Mór and Limonad, Lawhon, Makina, and Nakyagaba, Gururani, Kimari, etc.). Mary Lawhon's recent book *Making urban theory: Learning and unlearning through southern cities* speaks directly to that point (Lawhon et al., 2020).

In Chapter 6, Nik Heynen and Nikki Luke argue that white supremacist urbanism and colour-blind urban theory miss opportunities to produce more just cities. Mobilising insights from the Black radical tradition they discuss an abolitionist framing of Atlanta's land bank and the emancipatory potential of energy reparations connected to decarbonisation of the electrical grid in New Orleans.

In Chapter 7, Andrea Nightingale draws upon feminist political ecology and critical socio-natures scholarship to develop an analysis for thinking through urban climate change adaptation struggles that place an understanding of intersectional social inequalities and knowledge politics at the centre of policy debates. The author emphasises how intersectional social relations and knowledge politics can shape adaptation programmes and suggests that current approaches to planning are too static to allow the kinds of renegotiations that are required to address social inequalities within adaptation programmes. There is a need for deliberative, democratic practices that hold the politics of exclusion and multiple ways of knowing in the centre of adaptation processes in order to better respond to uncertainty and change.

Wangui Kimari discusses in Chapter 8 how Nairobi's colonial past has shaped and continues to shape urbanisation and subjecthood. The choice of the elevated, mosquito-free areas for European habitation left the low-lying flood plains to the 'native city'. Consequently, these racialised geographies of the past became the map on which racialised ideas about subjecthood were transcribed. These conjoint ecological and subject spatial configurations remain to date at the service of metabolisms engineered by racial capitalism.

In Chapter 9 Shubhra Gururani focuses on flooding as a 'critical event' that allows us to explore the imbrication of human and more-than-human ecologies and infrastructures in the ways modernist planning disrupts the seasonal rhythms of land and water and destroys local ecological knowledges and practices. Using the case of the 2016 floods at Gurgaon, at the outskirts of New Delhi, the author focuses on the deeply sedimented ecologies of lakes, ponds, aquifers, and water bodies that had been virtually erased, as well as on the long-established infrastructures of canals, channels, and drains that were ruthlessly undone by planning in the 1960s to make space for building Gurgaon. While 'old' ecologies are erased, the new discourses of sustainability and climate change pave the way for 'new' natures that are aesthetically pleasing, durable, and benign.

In Chapter 10 Mary Lawhon, Anesu Makina, and Gloria Nsangi Nakyagaba critique from a Global South perspective the majority of scholarship that seeks socially just cities focusing on increasing access to modern services. Highlighting the limitations of modernist urbanism whose basic logic of efficiency and order works against the 'make a plan' resilience practices embodied by many residents of the urban Global South, they mobilise Southern perspectives about uncertainty and resilience, to rework Western ideas about the relationship between people, planners, cities, and natures. Drawing upon two examples – waste picking in Tshwane, South Africa and 'alternative' sanitation technology in Kampala, Uganda – they point to the limitations of the idea of uniform services in contexts where houses and residents are heterogeneous, and jobs for everyone in contexts where unemployment is high, and life is unpredictable.

Part III: More-than-human urban political ecologies and relational geographies

The discussion about inside and outside, core and periphery, the urban and the exurban that this volume promotes cannot ignore the more-than-human elements involved in the production of space. Over the past decade, UPE scholarship significantly expanded its concerns on commodification, circulation, and metabolism to encompass the more-than-human lifeworld. Barua (2016, 2017, 2019) has shown how lively commodities and non-human work are part of the urbanisation processes. Barua's and Sinha's (2019: 1164) work explores 'how commodification or metabolization affects and alters the sentient experience of animals' (see also Barua, 2014). Gandy (2019) explored the intersections of urbanisation and non-human species as well as biodiversity more broadly (Gandy, 2016). The more-than-human lifeworld becomes of particular relevance as geographical concepts of ecologies are taking on board explicitly 'volumetric' perspectives (Graham, 2016). Still, an interest in more-than-human UPE is yet to benefit from in-depth cross-fertilisation and engagement with science and technology studies, ecology science, landscape ecology, the work of Tsing (1993), De La Bellacasa (2017), and the latest work of Haraway (2016), all of which cross disciplinary boundaries and disrupt the categories of centre/periphery but also of human/more-than-human.

Earlier work by Wu and Hobbs (2002: 358) on the spread of 'invading species' becomes particularly pertinent to debates around extended urbanisation. Wu and Hobbs refer to invading species as an 'increasingly important ecological and economic problem' – a statement that could just as easily refer to invasions of various spaces and habitats by our own species. Since Wu and Hobbs's (2002: 364) call to incorporate 'humans' and their 'perceptions, value systems, cultural traditions, and socioeconomic activities' into landscape ecology, there have been several attempts to integrate the analysis of the physical landscape with human activity (see Cumming, 2011). However, these focus mainly on issues of sustainability or 'resilience', and the analysis often misses the mark by taking a de-politicised perspective (Ahern, 2013; Lovell and Taylor, 2013). Landscape ecology literature for its part, largely reproduces the dichotomy of 'urban' and 'nature' (Jennings et al., 2017; Wu, 2013) and some authors even suggest that 'a small set of landscape metrics is able to capture the main spatiotemporal signatures of urbanization' (Wu et al., 2011: 7).

But the non-human lifeworld is not the only more-than-human matter of concern. Some of the foundational UPE texts focused on how water provision – or disruption – in cities illustrates the messy continuity of 'city' and 'nature' (Swyngedouw et al., 2022; Kaika, 2005). While water remains a key concern, many UPE scholars have focused in recent years on the dependency of extended urbanisation on the increased production of air, food, waste, concrete, electronics, etc. Extensive soil, water and air contamination and often irreversible transformations of terrestrial and marine ecologies in the service of perpetually extended growth and urbanisation, continuously increase 'the entropy spread to periphery environments' (Marull et al., 2010: 498).

The production and consumption of concrete and plastic has received particular attention in UPE literature. Capitalism's addiction to concrete is particularly pertinent to UPE debates as increased concrete production is directly linked to the extended urbanisation currently led by China, India, the US, and Turkey (Keil, 2018d; see also Harvey, 2018: 177). Today, concrete is 'second only to water [as] the most consumed material' in the world (Gagg, 2014). Concretisation is a violent, fetishised process of unabated, seemingly endless expansion; the production of one ton of cement releases almost as much CO_2 while soil contamination, water runoff problems, and lung disease from dust are only some of the serious (socio-environmental) effects of the widespread use of cement across the world (Chang et al., 2016; DeJong et al., 2010; Naik, 2008). Although policymaking focuses on finding innovative techno-managerial solutions, 'wonder materials' (Gabbatiss, 2018)[2] that can 'repair' the ecological damage caused by extensive concrete and plastic use, the politics of ecology remain especially discerning.

However, even the politics of something as fundamental as air and oxygen become increasingly instrumental in oppressive policing of the body, making air an 'integral part of sovereign power', as Nieuwenhuis (2016,

2018: 90) illustrates through the case of gassing events during global protests, reminiscent of the genocidal weaponisation of air in the First and Second World Wars. Gandy (2017) situates urban air through an ontological discussion on 'urban atmospheres' and 'affect': the (uneven and unequal) geography of air reminds us how 'air spaces have been constituted in part by the racialized and classed bodies that live, work, and play in them' (Choy, 2011, cited in Gandy, 2017: 364). While urban areas are generally positioned as sources of heat and pollution that harmfully diffuse to less urbanised areas (Graham, 2015: 196), the movement of air has little concern for such categories as it crosses bodily and territorial boundaries with troubling nonchalance. Nieuwenhuis (2018: 91) proposes an alternative decolonial reconnection of nature and society by 'seeing the "right to life" not as a hierarchical relationship that originates from a metaphysical authority of human law over "nature" but as recognition for our always already atmospheric being-together-with humans and more-than humans'.

These significant debates in UPE regarding more-than-human actors and lifeworlds are central in Part III of this book. In Chapter 11 Roger Keil, S. Harris Ali, and Stefan Treffers add disease spread and zoonosis to UPE's arsenal of metabolic explanations that include the more-than-human world. Examining the intertwined histories and geographies of infectious disease and the mobility of bodies through an increasingly urbanised space, the authors exemplify their theoretical arguments through the case of the 2003 SARS outbreak, the 2014/15 West African Ebola pandemic, and the recent COVID-19 outbreak, all of which exposed the connectivities of economies and populations in an extensively urbanised world. The authors argue that a 'spatialized political ecology of infectious disease' can help better understand the challenges and mitigate the impact of disease outbreaks in a continuously urbanising world.

In Chapter 12, Kian Goh illustrates the formation of global-urban networks and multiscalar, multilevel connections through which capital, knowledge, and influence flow into climate change mitigation policies and practices. Focusing on how Dutch water expertise internationalises out and forms relationships within and between Rotterdam, New York, and Jakarta, the author probes the ways in which these networks emerge to mobilise ideas and influence across geographical scales and political boundaries, driven and defined by interrelated factors including economic relationships, historically defined situational relationships, and interface conditions including narratives of culture and environmental urgency.

In Chapter 13, Camilla Perrone advocates a shift of the geographical focus of UPE from cities to overlooked peripheries and hinterlands as a theoretical domain in which to explore new possibilities for encounters between human and more-than-human actors. This call is addressed with reference to the theoretical debate that questions the centrality of the earth itself, and of its ability to act autonomously (insurgency). The chapter supports the idea that the terrestrial/earthling is an agent/actor of a new political interplay between geo-sphere, socio-sphere and bio-sphere. Accordingly, the planetary urban future is tackled with a questioning on 'who' owns/governs/acts the earth in the processes of capital accumulation.

Part IV: Addressing disjunctions between policy, politics, and academic debate

While academic debate moves beyond privileging cities as objects of inquiry, cities increasingly become the preferred sites for policy and governance experiments to address climate change. A proliferating number of 'urban laboratories' across the world (Turner and Kaplan, 2018: 7) are advocated and supported by international policymaking organisations (e.g., UN Habitat's New Urban Agenda, the EU's New Green Deal) focusing on how cities are now expected (in policy rhetoric) 'to save the planet' (Kaika, 2017; see also Angelo and Wachsmuth, 2020) through technomanagerial innovation: circular economies, smart cities, 'translocal' responses (Bulkeley et al., 2014), 'climate change experiments' (Broto and Bulkeley, 2013), 'municipal voluntarism' (Bulkeley and Betsill, 2013), and urban resilience planning (Camponeschi, 2021).

Documenting these new urban governance practices has become central in contemporary UPE literature and strengthens the original UPE focus on governance issues, particularly in the context of neoliberal reorganisations and shifting discourses and practices of urban sustainability, circularity, and resilience (Gabriel, 2014; Leitner et al., 2018; Lynn, 2017). For this growing literature, key matters of concern are: the changing role of the state (Loftus, 2018b); the rescaling of environmental governance, the articulation of new forms of governance with environmental justice (Amuzu, 2018); the administrative friction in planning and policy for urban resilience and security (Monstadt and Schmidt, 2019); carbon governance (Rice, 2014); and the financialisation of infrastructures especially in the urban periphery (Christophers, 2018; see also Bryant, 2018; Loftus et al., 2019; Macdonald and Lynch, 2019; Ouma et al., 2018; see also Harker, 2017, on debt). The articulation of housing with provision of key resources and infrastructure is also an important advancement in recent UPE literature. Mee et al. (2014) construct a UPE of housing through the lens of water while Edwards and Bulkeley (2017, 2018) research 'climate changed housing as infrastructure', arguing:

climate change reconfigures the circulations of the city in ways that allow both the state and capital to reach further into the home. It does so by transforming who is governing housing, how housing is being governed, and whose housing stands to benefit.

(2017: 1128)

In other words, 'there is no such thing as an unsustainable city in general, but rather there are a series of urban and environmental processes that negatively affect some social groups while benefiting others' (Heynen et al., 2006: 10).

There is extraordinary richness of empirical and conceptual analysis around documenting these key shifts in neoliberal reorganisations of urban governance discourses and practices in the context of climate change emergency, resilience adaptation and mitigation (Gabriel, 2014; Leitner et al., 2018; Lynn, 2017). In a way, the field has been playing catch-up with the fast and snowballing local and global policy changes within this context.

However, UPE literature that is more concerned with questions of new *policy* and governance arrangements is less (or not) concerned with theorising the new *politics* of urbanisation under climate change governance. But engaging with the ways in which policy articulates with politics is important if we are to start imagining alternative futures. Important as it is to document and analyse the fast and sweeping changes in urban governance, there is also an urgent need to understand and theorise the more profound effects these changes have in the way policymaking articulates with politics. As Swyngedouw and Erntson (2018) argue, shifts in policy rhetoric and practice linked to the climate change emergency and the focus on technocratic risk management have led to a 'depoliticisation' of key socio-environmental issues. Cohen and Bakker (2014: 123) agree; the rescaling of environmental governance through ecological concepts like bioregions, they argue, becomes a depoliticising move, an eco-scalar fix, 'a strategy of either internalizing or externalizing socio-environmental externalities, or both, thereby displacing conflicts and crises, often through the construction of (purportedly "natural") ecological scales, which simultaneously depoliticize and repoliticize governance'. Similarly, Macdonald and Keil (2012) interpret the Ontario greenbelt as a scalar fix that benefits the protected greenspace on the suburban and rural fringe while intensifying growth off the greenbelt. Kaika (2017: 91) demonstrates the problem of using resilience uncritically in the current literature and policy by criticising the idea that nature can be 'injected' into cities through parks or green roofs. Consequently, she proposes focusing instead: 'on identifying the actors and processes that produce the need to build resilience in the first place. And try to change these factors instead' (2017: 95). Performing a comprehensive analysis of municipal climate action plans in New York and Copenhagen, Camponeschi (2021: 78) also points to the predominance of technocratic and apolitical associations with narratives that narrow down 'complex social-ecological analyses of vulnerability into a more manageable – thus easier to manipulate – idea of resilience'.

Still, although the new forms of urban policies and governance for resilience and climate change adaptation and mitigation lead to technomanagerial solutions, they are also generative of new forms of politics. Part IV of this edited volume focuses on these emerging *politics* that try to operationalise and spatialise alternative forms of socio-environmental responses to climate change (for an analysis of the spatialisation of the political see Kaika and Karaliotas, 2016). For coherence, the book adopts Nancy's (1991: xxxvii) definition of *politics* as the act that not simply questions instituted ensembles and practices, but also moves beyond 'the locus of [existing] power relations'. In this sense, *politics* is neither what is being enacted by the institutions of a constituted political order (parties, legislative bodies, etc.), nor is it simply the act of protesting and staging dissent against those institutions. Rancière reserves the term *politics* only for those practices that go beyond simply staging dissent and go into creating methods and practices that can modify 'the map of what can be thought, what can be named and what can be perceived' (Rancière in Lévy et al., 2007: 4; for an overview of the argument, see May, 2008). These are practices that can potentially lead to *the political event*; the particular moment or action that not only calls into question the principles of the established order, but also produces new social imaginaries and suggests new institutions. The inherently antagonistic dimension of socio-environmental relations that produce climate change is central in generating *the political* event; the moment that can potentially change everything (Marchart, 2007; Mouffe, 2005; Stavrakakis, 1999, 2007). The chapters throughout this book but in Part IV in particular attempt to articulate the dialectic between socio-environmental *policy* or governance and socio-environmental *politics* and point to emerging methods and practices that can lead to the political event, coming from contexts in both the Global South and the Global North. In Chapter 14 Alex Loftus and Joris Gort suggest that the situated, process-oriented approach developed within UPE fits well with recent efforts to develop conjunctural and relational interpretations of a range of authoritarian populist political projects. The authors make the case for an urban political ecology that is understood as a philosophy of praxis attendant to the situated practices and knowledge forms emerging around distinct socio-ecologies. In such ways, UPE might provide not only better understandings of the current political conjuncture but also, perhaps, point to cracks within which a popular political ecology struggling for social and ecological justice might be fostered.

In Chapter 15 David Wachsmuth and Hillary Angelo draw upon Lefebvre's ideas of 'realistic' and 'transparent' illusions as the constitutive ideologies of the social production of space, to explain the preponderance of greenwashing and the focus on green urban nature as a key strategy in contemporary responses to climate change.

In Chapter 16 Irina Velicu explains how policy rhetoric about a singular future of Romania as an 'urban-industrial state' results in invisibilising and marginalising the country's large population of peasants as an 'unproductive' and 'irrelevant' social category. This rhetoric also enables land grabbing and practices of dispossession. At the same time, however, this policy has given rise to a new politics; a new consciousness for a growing number of people who proclaim themselves to be politically active under the broad umbrella of *Via Campesina*, a movement that challenges land grabbing and industrial agro-food production. The author focuses on the new politics and vision for land/food/socio/environmental justice that these new forms of subjectification bring as the movement establishes processes for feeding the nation its own (traditional) products.

In Chapter 17 Creighton Connolly and Hamzah Muzaini focus on the socio-ecological transformation that Singapore's offshore islands underwent after Singapore was expelled from the Malaysian Federation in 1965. While most islands had thriving traditional Indigenous communities and economies (*orang asli*), these were displaced as the islands were developed to service the needs of Singapore when it became a city-state without a periphery to service the core. The islands were repurposed to serve landfilling (Pulau Semakau), oil refinery (Pulau Brani), shipping (Keppel Island), and leisure/tourism (Pulau Ubin, Serangoon Island, Sentosa). In doing so, the chapter contributes to the volume's objective of examining how spaces on the urban periphery are deeply bound up with processes of urbanisation, given their important role in processes of urban metabolism.

In Chapter 18 Federico Savini focuses on circular economy, one of the most popular practices adopted for socio-technical transitions in contemporary policymaking – from water to energy, waste to logistics. Focusing on the region of Amsterdam, the Netherlands, Savini argues that these policies lead to an unfolding regime of ecological accumulation in city-regions that thrive out of the valorisation of urban waste. The author shows how, despite its green credentials, circular economy is a development paradigm which unfolds through a 'wicked' partnership between three parties: a local consumers economy who engages in recycling and repairing; a regional economy of biomass and incineration that produces energy at the city region level; and a global economy of multinational recycling corporations which invest in secondary materials.

Moving UPE beyond apocalyptic scenarios: Situated ecologies and politics of extended urbanisation against climate change

One of this book's key aims is to resist the reduction of what goes on outside cities to the dynamics and processes that emanate unidirectionally from cities (Keil, 2018a). For this reason, we advocate a shift in UPE's vantage point away from a privileged urban 'core' or 'inside' and sketch an integrated research agenda for a UPE beyond the city, by exploring if – and to what extent – it is also (or even mainly) the 'margin', the 'outside', and the 'periphery' that dictates the logic of the 'core', the 'inside'.

In addition, the book is also a call to move UPE beyond the (inevitable) apocalyptic scenarios of extended urbanisation and climate change. Sieverts (2003) gives an interesting perspective on the future of the new lands of extended urbanisation and the spaces in between dense urban formations that goes beyond doom and gloom. To him, the *Zwischenstadt*, the in-between city, may become the historico-geographic terrain on which new forms of 'rurbanity' can help sustain life on a planet of 10 billion. This would mean the 'merging of urban and rural, of cultural and natural characteristics in this urbanization process' (Sieverts, 2017: 3), an increase in food production, heightened conflict between industrial agriculture and more diverse forms of cultures in and around cities, and the spread of 'horizontal metropolises' that will have to develop 'their wildnesses, their areas of adventure and recreation, in themselves, as fractal urban landscapes' (2017: 4). Sieverts contends that these new socio-ecological metabolic relations can 'lead to fascinating forms of an urban-rural continuum, fascinating new urban landscapes' (2017: 4). This volume's call to heighten our attention to extended urbanisation can give us a better empirical and conceptual understanding of the production of new spaces of marginality and of new processes leading to environmental hazard; but also of emerging grassroot practices and imaginaries for alternative socio-environmental arrangements.

But this volume also aims to encourage a better focus on southern urbanisms, the diversity of urban environments, and a situated UPE that focuses more on thus far neglected actors, relations between institutions and political and economic forces, and everyday practices involved in the urbanisation of nature (Birkenholtz, 2010; Lawhon, et al., 2014; Loftus, 2012; Roy, 2009; Silver, 2017; Simpson and Bagelman, 2018; Truelove, 2011, 2016; Velzeboer et al., 2018; Zimmer, 2010). As Kipfer (2009: 68) suggests:

> The urban functions as a level of analysis mediating between macro- and micro-levels of reality and possibility. In other words, the urban leads not only to analysis of the macro-realities of the state, capital and empire but also to a differential and dialectical critique of everyday life.

Our call to also expand UPE's focus and analysis beyond the human lifeworld (Part III) adds to the opening of possibilities for developing an integrated urban political ecology that examines processes management practices beyond privileged scales places and actors.

However, at the end of the day, the question of the urban condition is a political question that we cannot afford to ignore (Part IV). The world is in a state of continuing cascading crises that are universal and truly planetary. 'Turning up the heat' is a metaphor for the most severe dimension of these crises, the climate catastrophe which has myriad impacts around the world and is part of everyone's horizon of experience. The recent COVID-19 pandemic demonstrated that the universal nature of emergencies can take different forms and that crises and their impacts can be intersecting and can have ripple effects and unforeseeable consequences. This is the first time in history that global events like climate change and the pandemic presented themselves in a world of extended forms and processes of urbanisation.

Pointing at global capitalism as the source of all aspects of these cascading crises does not suffice; and the truth is we do not have strong or coherent alternatives to move beyond technomanagerial solutions. But we can say for sure that capitalism in its present incarnation has produced an 'imperial mode of living' which, in a nutshell, means that 'everyday life in the centres is essentially made possible by shaping social relations and society-nature relations *elsewhere*, i.e. by means of (in principle) unlimited access to labour power, natural resources and sinks ... on a global scale' (Brand and Wissen, 2021: 39–40, emphasis in original).

As for finding a way out of this predicament, many progressive political ecologists have been debating whether we need to pull the brakes on (capitalist) growth altogether or whether some form of growth and redistribution may still need to be part of the way forward. However, as Paul Robbins (2020: 5) discusses, there is an 'impasse' between the movement for degrowth and those he calls socialist modernisers: 'this impasse, it seems, is less about what is desirable, or even possible, than it is about the problems with both dystopia and utopia, which haunt all ecological futures'. Robbins does not attempt to resolve the stalemate but suggests that 'there must be good forms of hope and despair, which acknowledge terrible realities, uneven injustices, and structural barriers, while moving towards revolutionary change'. He tasks political ecology with some bridging work to escape 'the shadows of bad utopias and bad dystopias they both abjure. The role of political ecology must be to catalogue experiments in these kinds of visions of the future, and to chase away these shadows' (Robbins, 2020: 5).

The conversations evoked by Brand and Wissen in their work on the imperial mode of living and the debates that Robbins wants to reconcile do not have an explicit urban focus. But if we accept that the new forms of extended urbanisation are indeed the 'chief artefact of the Anthropocene and terrain of new political performativities', as Keil (2018b) argues, the imperial mode of living has a home and climate change has an address: it is the extended urban world in which we live. Hermann's (2021) suggestion for a solidarity mode of living could be a way forward. A mode of living that

> could start with a massive redistribution of wealth and the expansion and improvement of public goods and services, including efficient public transport and sustainable public housing, in advanced capitalist countries. The solidarity mode of living would be attractive not only to people in the Global South but also to the majority in the Global North whose lives are far from luxurious.

This book was put together as a response to the urgent need to both expand and integrate UPE's theoretical empirical and political scope in the face of extended urbanisation under climate change. The book emphasises that staying with urbanisation as a matter of concern does not have to mean succumbing to reformist, technocratic, and mechanical suggestions for 'cities to save the world' (Wachsmuth and Angelo, Chapter 15 in this volume). We argue that this is UPE's political and intellectual challenge if the field wants to remain relevant to the politics of a heating planet.

Notes

1 Many thanks to an anonymous referee of the book manuscript for emphasising this point.
2 Chang, Im, and Cho (2016) propose to look for solutions in biopolymers when addressing carbon emissions due to the extended use of cement. Bacteria are also seen as the new method for concrete to 'self-heal' through a process called bacteria-based calcium carbonate precipitation (Wang et al., 2014). Bacteria-induced enzymes are also regarded as saviours against plastic pollution.

References

Addie, J.-P.D., M.R. Glass, and J. Nelles. 2020. Regionalizing the infrastructure turn: A research agenda. *Regional Studies, Regional Science* 7(1): 10–26. DOI: 10.1080/21681376.2019.1701543.

Agyeman, J. and J. McEntee. 2014. Moving the field of food justice forward through the lens of urban political ecology. *Geography Compass* 8(3): 211–20.

Ahern, J. 2013. Urban landscape sustainability and resilience: The promise and challenges of integrating ecology with urban planning and design. *Landscape Ecology* 28(6): 1203–12.

Ahmed, A. 2021. The father of environmental justice isn't done yet. *The Nation*, 3 May.

Alkon, A.H. 2012. The socio-nature of local organic food. *Antipode* 45(3): 663–80.
Amuzu, D. 2018. Environmental injustice of informal e-waste recycling in Agbogbloshie-Accra: Urban political ecology perspective. *Local Environment* 23(6): 603–18.
Andreucci, D., M. García-Lamarca, J. Wedekind, and E. Swyngedouw. 2017. Value grabbing: A political ecology of rent. *Capitalism Nature Socialism* 28(3): 28–47.
Angelo, H. 2017. From the city lens toward urbanisation as a way of seeing: Country/city binaries on an urbanising planet. *Urban Studies* 54(1): 158–78.
Angelo, H. and K. Goh. 2020. Out in space: Difference and abstraction in planetary urbanization. *International Journal of Urban and Regional Research* 45(4): 732–44.
Angelo, H. and D. Wachsmuth. 2014. Urbanizing urban political ecology: A critique of methodological cityism. *International Journal of Urban and Regional Research* 39(1): 16–27.
Angelo, H. and D. Wachsmuth. 2020. Why does everyone think cities can save the planet? *Urban Studies* 57(11): 2201–21. DOI: 10.1177/0042098020919081.
Arellano, G. 2018. Revisiting Mike Davis' case for letting Malibu burn. *LA Times*, 14 November.
Astley, D.L. 2018. An eco-Marxist blockbuster – on *Blade Runner 2049*. Political Economy Research Centre. www.perc.org.uk/project_posts/eco-marxist-blockbuster-blade-runner-2049/, accessed 12 August 2022.
Barua, M. 2014. Bio-geo-graphy: Landscape, dwelling, and the political ecology of human–elephant relations. *Environment and Planning D: Society and Space* 32(5): 915–34.
Barua, M. 2016. Lively commodities and encounter value. *Environment and Planning D: Society and Space* 34(4): 725–44.
Barua, M. 2017. Nonhuman labour, encounter value, spectacular accumulation: The geographies of a lively commodity. *Transactions of the Institute of British Geographers* 42(2): 274–88.
Barua, M. 2019. Animating capital: Work, commodities, circulation. *Progress in Human Geography* 43(4): 650–69.
Barua, M. and A. Sinha. 2019. Animating the urban: an ethological and geographical conversation. *Social & Cultural Geography* 20(8): 1160–80.
Batubara, B., M. Kooy, and M. Zwarteveen. 2018. Uneven urbanisation: Connecting flows of water to flows of labour and capital through Jakarta's flood infrastructure. *Antipode* 50(5): 1186–205.
Berger, A.M. 2017. Belting future suburbia. In A.M. Berger, J. Kotkin, and C.B. Guzman (eds.), *Infinite suburbia*. New York: Princeton Architectural Press, pp. 522–51.
Berger, A.M., J. Kotkin, and C.B. Guzman (eds.). 2017. *Infinite suburbia*. New York: Princeton Architectural Press.
Bhan, G. 2019. Notes on a Southern urban practice. *Environment & Urbanization*, 1–16. DOI: 10.1177/0956247818815792
Birkenholtz, T. 2010. 'Full-cost recovery': Producing differentiated water collection practices and responses to centralized water networks in Jaipur, India. *Environment and Planning A: Economy and Space* 42(9): 2238–53.
Brand, U. and M. Wissen. 2021. *The imperial mode of living: Everyday life and the ecological crisis of capitalism*. London: Verso.
Braun, B. 2005. Environmental issues: Writing a more-than-human urban geography. *Progress in Human Geography* 29(5): 635–50.

Bressan, D. 2021. Climate change could have played a role in the COVID-19 outbreak. *Forbes*, February 8; www.forbes.com/sites/davidbressan/2021/02/08/climate-change-could-have-played-a-role-in-the-covid-19-outbreak/?sh=4deacbf911ef, accessed 12 August 2022.

Broto, V.C. and H. Bulkeley. 2013. Maintaining climate change experiments: Urban political ecology and the everyday reconfiguration of urban infrastructure. *International Journal of Urban and Regional Research* 37(6): 1934–48.

Bruggeman, D. and M. Dehaene. 2017. Urban questions in the countryside? Urbanization and the collective consumption of electricity in early twentieth-century Belgium. *Planning Perspectives* 32(3): 309–32.

Bryant, G. 2018. Nature as accumulation strategy? Finance, nature, and value in carbon markets. *Annals of the American Association of Geographers* 108(3): 605–19.

Buckley, M. and K. Strauss. 2016. With, against and beyond Lefebvre: Planetary urbanization and epistemic plurality. *Environment and Planning D: Society and Space* 34(4): 617–36.

Bulkeley, H. and M.M. Betsill. 2013. Revisiting the urban politics of climate change. *Environmental politics* 22(1): 136–154.

Bulkeley, H.A., V.C. Broto, and G.A. Edwards. 2014. *An urban politics of climate change: Experimentation and the governing of socio-technical transitions.* Routledge: New York.

Butcher, M. and K. Maclean. 2018. Gendering the city: The lived experience of transforming cities, urban cultures and spaces of belonging. *Gender, Place & Culture* 25(5): 686–94.

Camponeschi, C. 2021. Narratives of vulnerability and resilience: An investigation of the climate action plans of New York City and Copenhagen, *Geoforum* 123: 78–88. https://doi.org/10.1016/j.geoforum.2021.05.001

Chang, I., J. Im, and G.-C. Cho. 2016. Introduction of microbial biopolymers in soil treatment for future environmentally-friendly and sustainable geotechnical engineering. *Sustainability* 8(3).

Choy, T. 2011. *Ecologies of comparison.* Durham: Duke University Press.

Christophers, B. 2018. Risk capital: Urban political ecology and entanglements of financial and environmental risk in Washington, DC. *Environment and Planning E: Nature and Space*, April.

Cohen, A. and K. Bakker. 2014. The eco-scalar fix: Rescaling environmental governance and the politics of ecological boundaries in Alberta, Canada. *Environment and Planning D: Society and Space* 32(1): 128–46.

Collard, R.C., L.M. Harris, N. Heynen, and L. Mehta. 2018. The antinomies of nature and space. *Environment and Planning E: Nature and Space* 1(1–2): 3–24.

Connolly, C. 2018. Urban political ecology beyond methodological cityism. *International Journal of Urban and Regional Research*. DOI: 10.1111/1468-2427.12710.

Connolly, C., R. Keil, and S.H. Ali. 2021. Extended urbanisation and the spatialities of infectious disease: Demographic change, infrastructure and governance. *Urban Studies* 58(2): 245–63. https://doi.org/10.1177/0042098020910873

Coplen, A.K. 2018. The labor between farm and table: Cultivating an urban political ecology of agrifood for the 21st century. *Geography Compass* 12(5): e12370.

Cumming, G.S. 2011. Spatial resilience: Integrating landscape ecology, resilience, and sustainability. *Landscape Ecology* 26(7): 899–909.

DeJong, J.T., B.M. Mortensen, B.C. Martinez, and D.C. Nelson. 2010. Bio-mediated soil improvement. *Ecological Engineering* 36(2): 197–210.

De La Bellacasa, M.P. (2017) *Matters of care: Speculative ethics in more than human worlds.* Minneapolis, MN: University of Minnesota Press.

Derickson, K. 2017. Masters of the universe. *Environment and Planning D: Society and Space* 36(3): 556–62.

Desfor, G. and R. Keil. 2004. *Nature and the city: Making environmental policy in Toronto and Los Angeles.* Tucson: University of Arizona Press.

Dorries, H., D. Hugill, and J. Tomiak. 2019. Racial capitalism and the production of settler colonial cities, *Geoforum* 132: 263–70. https://doi.org/10.1016/j.geoforum.2019.07.016

Doshi, S. 2017. Embodied urban political ecology: Five propositions. *Area* 49(1): 125–8.

Edwards, G.A. and H. Bulkeley. 2017. Urban Political Ecologies of housing and climate change: The 'Coolest Block' contest in Philadelphia. *Urban Studies* 54(5): 1126–41.

Edwards, G.A. and H. Bulkeley. 2018. Heterotopia and the urban politics of climate change experimentation. *Environment and Planning D: Society and Space* 36(2): 350–69.

Ekers, M. and S. Prudham. 2015. Towards the socio-ecological fix. *Environment and Planning A: Economy and Space* 47(12): 2438–45.

Ekers, M. and S. Prudham. 2017. The metabolism of socioecological fixes: Capital switching, spatial fixes, and the production of nature. *Annals of the American Association of Geographers* 107(6): 1370–88.

Ekers, M. and S. Prudham. 2018. The socioecological fix: Fixed capital, metabolism, and hegemony. *Annals of the American Association of Geographers* 108(1): 17–34.

Ekers, M., P. Hamel, and R. Keil. 2012. Governing suburbia: Modalities and mechanisms of suburban governance. *Regional Studies* 46(3): 405–22.

Ernstson, H. and E. Swyngedeouw (eds.). 2018. *Urban political ecology in the Anthropo-obscene: Interruptions and possibilities.* London: Routledge.

Gabbatiss, J. 2018. Plastic-eating enzyme accidentally created by scientists could help solve pollution crisis. *The Independent*, 16 April. www.independent.co.uk/news/science/plastic-eating-enzyme-pollution-solution-waste-bottles-bacteria-portsmouth-a8307371.html, accessed 12 August 2022.

Gabriel, N. 2014. Urban political ecology: Environmental imaginary, governance, and the non-human: UPE: Imaginary, governance, and the non-human. *Geography Compass* 8(1): 38–48.

Gagg, C.R. 2014. Cement and concrete as an engineering material: an historic appraisal and case study analysis. *Engineering Failure Analysis* 40: 114–40.

Gandy, M. 2002. *Concrete and clay: Reworking Nature in New York City.* Cambridge, MA: MIT Press.

Gandy, M. 2016. Unintentional landscapes. *Landscape Research* 41: 433–40. DOI: 10.1080/01426397.2016.1156069.

Gandy, M. 2017. Urban atmospheres. *Cultural Geographies* 24(3): 353–74.

Gandy, M. 2019. The fly that tried to save the world: Saproxylic geographies and other-than-human ecologies. *Transactions of the Institute of British Geographers* 44: 392–406. DOI: 10.1111/tran.12281.

Goh, K. 2019a. California's fires prove the American Dream is flammable. *The Nation*, 23 December. www.thenation.com/article/archive/california-fires-urban-planning/, accessed 12 August 2022.

Goh, K. 2019b. Flows in formation: The global-urban networks of climate change adaptation. *Urban Studies* 57(11): 2222–40. https://doi.org/10.1177/0042098018807306.

Goldfischer, E., J.L. Rice and S.T. Black. 2020. Obstinate curiosity and situated solidarity in urban political ecology. *Geography Compass*. DOI: 10.1111/gec3.12479.

Graham, S. 2010. *Disrupted cities: When infrastructure fails*. New York: Routledge.

Graham, S. 2015. Life support: The political ecology of urban air. *City* 19(2–3): 192–215.

Graham, S. 2016. *Vertical: The city from satellites to bunkers*. London: Verso.

Gururani, S. 2002. Forests of pleasure and pain: Gendered practices of labor and livelihood in the forests of the Kumaon Himalayas, India. *Gender, Place and Culture: A Journal of Feminist Geography* 9(3): 229–43.

Gururani, S. and P. Vandergeest. 2014. Introduction: New frontiers of ecological knowledge: Co-producing knowledge and governance in Asia. *Conservation and Society* 12(4): 343–51.

Gustafson, S. 2015. Maps and contradictions: Urban political ecology and cartographic expertise in Southern Appalachia. *Geoforum* 60: 143–52.

Haraway, D. 1988. Situated knowledges: The science question in feminism and the privilege of partial perspective. *Feminist Studies* 14(3): 575–99.

Haraway, D.J. 2016. *Staying with the trouble: Making kin in the Chthulucene*. Durham: Duke University Press.

Harker, C. 2017. Debt space: Topologies, ecologies and Ramallah, Palestine. *Environment and Planning D: Society and Space* 35(4): 600–19.

Harris, R. and C. Vorms (eds.). 2017. *What's in a name? Talking about urban peripheries*. Toronto: University of Toronto Press.

Harrison, C. and J. Popke. 2017. Geographies of renewable energy transition in the Caribbean: Reshaping the island energy metabolism. *Energy Research & Social Science* 36: 165–74.

Harvey, D. 2018. *Marx, capital, and the madness of economic reason*. New York, NY: Oxford University Press.

Hermann, C. 2021. Everyday life and the ecological crisis of capitalism. *The Bullet*, 3 June. https://socialistproject.ca/2021/06/everyday-life-and-ecological-crisis-of-capitalism/#more, accessed 12 August 2022.

Hern, M. and A. Johal. 2018. *Global warming and the sweetness of life: A tarsands tale*. Cambridge, MA: MIT Press.

Heynen, N. 2014. Urban political ecology I: The urban century. *Progress in Human Geography* 38(4): 598–604.

Heynen, N. 2016. Urban political ecology II: The abolitionist century. *Progress in Human Geography* 40(6): 839–45.

Heynen, N. 2017. Urban political ecology III: The feminist and queer century. *Progress in Human Geography* 42(6): 839–45.

Heynen, N. 2018. Toward an abolition ecology. *Abolition: A Journal of Insurgent Politics* 1: 240–7.

Heynen, N., M. Kaika, and E. Swyngedouw (eds.). 2006. *In the nature of cities: Urban political ecology and the politics of urban metabolism*. New York: Routledge.

Holifield, R. and N. Schuelke. 2015. The place and time of the political in Urban political ecology: Contested imaginations of a river's future. *Annals of the Association of American Geographers* 105(2): 294–303.

Hovorka, A.J. 2006. The No. 1 Ladies' Poultry Farm: A feminist political ecology of urban agriculture in Botswana. *Gender, Place & Culture* 13(3): 207–25.

Jennings, V., M.F. Floyd, D. Shanahan, C. Coutts, and A. Sinykin. 2017. Emerging issues in urban ecology: Implications for research, social justice, human health, and well-being. *Population and Environment* 39(1): 69–86.

Johnson, C., T. Baker, and F.L. Collins. 2018. Imaginations of post-suburbia: Suburban change and imaginative practices in Auckland, New Zealand. *Urban Studies*. DOI: 10.1177/0042098018787157

Kaika, M. 2005. *City of flows: Modernity, nature, and the city*. New York: Routledge.

Kaika, M. 2014. The uncanny materialities of the everyday: domesticated nature as the invisible 'other'. In S. Graham and C. McFarlane (eds.), *Infrastructural lives: Urban infrastructure in context*. New York: Routledge, pp. 153–66.

Kaika, M. 2017. Don't call me resilient again! The new urban agenda as immunology … or what happens when communities refuse to be vaccinated with 'smart cities' and indicators. *Environment and Urbanization* 29(1): 89–102.

Kaika, M. and L. Karaliotas. 2016. The spatialization of democratic politics: Insights from Indignant Squares. *European Urban and Regional Studies* 23(4): 556–70. https://doi.org/10.1177/0969776414528928

Karpouzoglou, T., F. Marshall, and L. Mehta. 2018. Towards a peri-urban political ecology of water quality decline. *Land Use Policy* 70: 485–93.

Keil, R. 2011. Transnational urban political ecology: Health and infrastructure in the unbounded city. In G. Bridge and S. Watson (eds.), *The new Blackwell companion to the city*. Oxford: Blackwell, pp. 713–25.

Keil, R. 2013. Welcome to the suburban revolution. In R. Keil (ed.), *Suburban constellations*. Berlin: Jovis, pp. 8–15.

Keil, R. 2018a. The empty shell of the planetary: Re-rooting the urban in the experience of the urbanites. *Urban Geography* 39(10): 1589–602.

Keil, R. 2018b. Paved paradise: The suburb as chief artefact of the Anthropocene and terrain of new political performativities. In H. Ernstson and E. Swyngedeouw (eds.), *Urban political ecology in the Anthropo-obscene: Interruptions and possibilities*. London: Routledge, pp. 165–83.

Keil, R. 2018c. Political ecology beyond the city: Situated peripheries and capitalocenic limits. In *RC21/ISA Annual Meeting, IJJUR Lecture*, Toronto, Canada, 19 July 2018.

Keil, R. 2018d. *Suburban planet: Making the world urban from the outside in*. Cambridge: Polity.

Keil, R. 2018e. Extended urbanization, 'disjunct fragments' and global suburbanisms. *Environment and Planning D: Society and Space*. https://doi.org/10.1177/0263775817749594

Keil, R. 2020. An urban political ecology for a world of cities. *Urban Studies* 57(11), 2357–70. https://doi.org/10.1177/0042098020919086

Keil, R. and S. Macdonald. 2016. Rethinking urban political ecology from the outside in: Greenbelts and boundaries in the post-suburban city. *Local Environment* 21(12): 1516–33.

Kipfer, S. 2009. Why the urban question still matters: Reflections on rescaling and the promise of the urban. In R. Keil and R. Mahon (eds.), *Leviathan undone? Towards a political economy of scale*. Vancouver: UBC Press, pp. 67–83.

Kipfer, S. 2018. Pushing the limits of urban research: Urbanization, pipelines and counter-colonial politics. *Environment and Planning D: Society and Space* 36(3): 474–93. https://doi.org/10.1177/0263775818758328

Lawhon, M. 2012. Relational power in the governance of a South African e-waste transition. *Environment and Planning A* 44(4): 954–71.

Lawhon, M., H. Ernstson, and J. Silver. 2014. Provincializing urban political ecology: Towards a situated UPE through African urbanism. *Antipode* 46(2): 497–516.

Lawhon, M., J. Silver, H. Ernstson and J. Pierce. 2016. Unlearning (un)located ideas in the provincialization of urban theory. *Regional Studies* 50(9): 1611–22.

Lawhon, M., D. Nilsson, J. Silver, H. Ernstson, and S. Lwasa. 2018. Thinking through heterogeneous infrastructure configurations. *Urban Studies* 55(4): 720–32.

Lawhon, M. with L. Le Roux, A. Makina, and Y. Truelove. 2020. *Making urban theory: Learning and unlearning through southern cities*. London: Routledge.

Lawton, P. 2019. Unbounding gentrification theory: Multidimensional space, networks and relational approaches. *Regional Studies* 54(2): 268–79. https://doi.org/10.1080/00343404.2019.1646902

Lefebvre, H. 1996. *Writings on cities*. Selected, translated and introduced by E. Kofman and E. Lebas. Oxford: Blackwell.

Leitner, H., E. Sheppard, S. Webber, and E. Colven. 2018. Globalizing urban resilience. *Urban Geography* 39(8): 1276–84.

Lerup, L. 2017. *The continuous city: Fourteen essays on architecture and urbanization*. Houston: Rice Architecture.

Lévy, J., J. Rennes, and D. Zerbib. 2007. Les territoires de la pensée partagée. *Entretien*. www.espacestemps.net/articles/jacques-ranciere-les-territoires-de-la-pensee-partagee/, accessed 12 August 2022.

Loftus, A. 2012. *Everyday environmentalism: Creating an urban political ecology*. Minneapolis, MN: University of Minnesota Press.

Loftus, A. 2018a. Planetary concerns. *City* 22(1): 88–95.

Loftus, A. 2018b. Political ecology II: Whither the state? *Progress in Human Geography*. https://doi.org/10.1177/0309132518803421

Loftus, A. 2019a. Political ecology I: Where is political ecology? *Progress in Human Geography* 43(1): 172–82. https://doi.org/10.1177/0309132517734338

Loftus, A. 2019b. Political ecology III: Who are 'the people'? *Progress in Human Geography* 44(5): 981–90. https://doi.org/10.1177/0309132519884632

Loftus, A., H. March, and T. Purcell. 2019. The political economy of water infrastructure: An introduction to financialization. *WIREs Water*. https://doi.org/10.1002/wat2.1326.

Lovell, S.T. and J.R. Taylor. 2013. Supplying urban ecosystem services through multifunctional green infrastructure in the United States. *Landscape Ecology* 28(8): 1447–63.

Lynn, K.A. 2017. Who defines 'whole': An urban political ecology of flood control and community relocation in Houston, Texas. *Journal of Political Ecology* 24(1): 951–67.

Macdonald, S. and R Keil. 2012. The Ontario greenbelt: Shifting the scales of the sustainability fix? *The Professional Geographer* 64(2): 125–45.

Macdonald, S. and L. Lynch. 2019. 'Greenfrastructure': The Ontario greenbelt as urban boundary? In P. Filion and N. Pulver (eds.), *Critical perspectives on suburban infrastructures: Contemporary international cases*. Toronto: University of Toronto Press.

Maginn, P. and R. Keil. 2019. Why we need suburbia if we want to save the city in the climate emergency. *The Conversation*, November.
Marchant, O. 2007. *Post-foundational political thought: Political difference in Nancy, Lefort, Badiou and Laclau*. Edinburgh: Edinburgh University Press.
Marull, J., J. Pino, E. Tello, and M.J. Cordobilla. 2010. Social metabolism, landscape change and land-use planning in the Barcelona Metropolitan Region. *Land Use Policy* 27(2): 497–510.
May, T. 2008. *The political thought of Jacques Rancière: Creating equality*. Edinburgh: Edinburgh University Press.
McFarlane, C. and J. Silver. 2017. Navigating the city: Dialectics of everyday urbanism. *Transactions of the Institute of British Geographers* 42: 458–71 DOI: 10.1111/tran.12175.
McGee, T. 2011. Rethinking the urban fringe in Southeast Asia, Policy and Research Agendas. Paper presented at the workshop on Issues in the Peri-Urban Regions and Ways towards Sustainable Peri-Urban Futures.
McKinnon, I., P.T. Hurley, C.C. Myles, M. Maccaroni, and T. Filan. 2017. Uneven urban metabolisms: Toward an integrative (ex)urban political ecology of sustainability in and around the city. *Urban Geography* 40(3): 352–77.
McLean, H. 2018. In praise of chaotic research pathways: A feminist response to planetary urbanization. *Environment and Planning D: Society and Space* 36(3): 547–55.
Mee, K.J., L. Instone, M. Williams, J. Palmer, and N. Vaughan. 2014. Renting over troubled waters: An urban political ecology of rental housing. *Geographical Research* 52(4): 365–76.
Middleton, B.R. 2015. *Jahát Jat'totòdom*: Toward an Indigenous political ecology. In R.L. Bryant (ed.), *The international handbook of political ecology*. Cheltenham and Northampton, MA: Edward Elgar, pp. 561–76.
Monstadt, J. and O. Coutard. 2019. Cities in an era of interfacing infrastructures: Politics and spatialities of the urban nexus. *Urban Studies* 56(11): 2191–206. DOI: 10.1177/0042098019833907.
Monstadt, J. and M. Schmidt. 2019. Urban resilience in the making? The governance of critical infrastructures in German cities. *Urban Studies* 56(11): 2353–71. DOI: 10.1177/0042098018808483.
Monte-Mór, R.L. 2014a. Extended urbanization and settlement patterns in Brazil: An environmental approach. In N. Brenner (ed.), *Implosions/explosions*. Berlin: Jovis, pp. 109–20.
Monte-Mór, R.L. 2014b. What is the urban in the contemporary world? In N. Brenner (ed.), *Implosions/explosions*. Berlin: Jovis, pp. 260–7.
Mouffe, C. 2005. *On the political: Thinking in action*. London: Routledge.
Naik, T.R. 2008. Sustainability of concrete construction. *Practice Periodical on Structural Design and Construction* 13(2): 98–103.
Nancy, J.-L. 1991. *The inoperative community*. Minneapolis, MN: University of Minnesota Press.
Nieuwenhuis, M. 2016. Breathing materiality: Aerial violence at a time of atmospheric politics. *Critical Studies on Terrorism* 9(3): 499–521.
Nieuwenhuis, M. 2018. Atmospheric governance: Gassing as law for the protection and killing of life. *Environment and Planning D: Society and Space* 36(1): 78–95.
Njeru, J. 2006. The urban political ecology of plastic bag waste production in Nairobi, Kenya. *Geoforum* 37(6): 1046–58.

Oswin, N. 2016. Planetary urbanization: A view from outside. *Environment and Planning D: Society and Space* 36(3): 374–86.
Ouma, S., L. Johnson, and P. Bigger. 2018. Rethinking the financialization of 'nature'. *Environment and Planning A: Economy and Space* 50(3). https://doi.org/10.1177/0308518X18755748.
Parés, M., H. March and D. Saurí. 2013. Atlantic gardens in Mediterranean climates: Understanding the production of suburban natures in Barcelona. *International Journal of Urban and Regional Research* 37(1): 328–47.
Peake, L., D. Patrick, R.N. Reddy, G. Sarp Tanyildiz, S. Ruddick and R. Tchoukaleyska. 2018. Placing planetary urbanization in other fields of vision. *Environment and Planning D: Society and Space* 36(3): 374–86.
Pickerill, J. 2018. Black and green: The future of Indigenous–environmentalist relations in Australia. *Environmental Politics* 27(6): 1122–45, DOI: 10.1080/09644016.2018.1466464.
Ranganathan, M. 2014. Paying for pipes, claiming citizenship: Political agency and water reforms at the urban periphery. *International Journal of Urban and Regional Research* 38(2): 590–608.
Ranganathan, M. and C. Balazs. 2015. Water marginalization at the urban fringe: Environmental justice and urban political ecology across the north–south divide. *Urban Geography* 36(3): 403–23.
Rice, J.L. 2014. An urban political ecology of climate change governance. *Geography Compass* 8(6): 381–94.
Rice, S. and J. Tyner. 2017. The rice cities of the Khmer Rouge: An urban political ecology of rural mass violence. *Transactions of the Institute of British Geographers* 42(4): 559–71.
Robbins, P. 2007. *Lawn people: How grasses, weeds, and chemicals make us who we are*. Philadelphia, PA: Temple University Press.
Robbins, P. 2020. Is less more … or is more less? Scaling the political ecologies of the future. *Political Geography* 76: 102018, https://doi.org/10.1016/j.polgeo.2019.04.010.
Roy, A. 2009. The 21st-century metropolis: New geographies of theory. *Regional Studies* 43(6): 819–30.
Saguin, K. 2017. Producing an urban hazardscape beyond the city. *Environment and Planning A: Economy and Space* 49(9): 1968–85.
Schmidt, D.H. 2017. Suburban wilderness in the Houston metropolitan landscape. *Journal of Political Ecology* 24(1): 167–85.
Schulz, K. 2017. Decolonizing political ecology: Ontology, technology and 'critical' enchantment. *Journal of Political Ecology* 24(1): 125–43.
Serna, J. 2019. 2018 was California's worst year of fire ever, federal report confirms. *Los Angeles Times*, 9 March.
Shields, R. 2012. Feral suburbs: Cultural topologies of social reproduction, Fort McMurray, Canada. *International Journal of Cultural Studies* 15(3): 205–15.
Sieverts, T. 2003. *Cities without cities: An interpretation of the Zwischenstadt*. London: Routledge.
Sieverts, T. 2017. Rurbane Landschaften: Vom Aufheben des Ländlichen in der Stadt auf dem Weg ins Anthropozän. Personal communication from author.
Silver, J. 2014. Incremental infrastructures: material improvisation and social collaboration across post-colonial Accra. *Urban Geography* 35: 788–804.

Silver, J. 2017. The climate crisis, carbon capital and urbanisation: An urban political ecology of low-carbon restructuring in Mbale. *Environment and Planning A: Economy and Space* 49(7): 1477–99.

Shillington, L. and Murnaghan, A.M. 2016 Urban Political Ecologies and children's geographies: Queering urban ecologies of childhood, *International Journal of Urban and Regional Research*. DOI:10.1111/1468-2427.12339.

Simone, A. 2004. People as infrastructure: Intersecting fragments in Johannesburg. *Public Culture* 16: 407–29.

Simone, A. 2019. Maximum exposure: Making sense in the background of extensive urbanization. *Environment and Planning D: Society and Space* 37(6): 990–1006. https://doi.org/10.1177/0263775819856351

Simpson, M. and J. Bagelman. 2018. Decolonizing urban political ecologies: The production of nature in settler colonial cities. *Annals of the American Association of Geographers* 108(2): 558–68.

Stavrakakis, Y. 1999. *Lacan and the political*. London: Routledge.

Stavrakakis, Y. 2007. Antinomies from space: From the representation of politics to a topology of the political. In BAVO (ed.), *Urban politics now: Re-imagining democracy in the neoliberal city*. Rotterdam: NAI Publishers, pp. 143–61.

Swyngedouw, E. 2004. *Social power and the urbanization of water: Flows of power*. Oxford: Oxford University Press.

Swyngedouw, E. 2006. Metabolic urbanization: The making of cyborg cities. In N. Heynen, M. Kaika, and E. Swyngedouw (eds.), *In the nature of cities: Urban political ecology and the politics of urban metabolism*. New York: Routledge, pp. 21–40.

Swyngedouw, E. and H. Erntson. 2018. Interrupting the Anthropo-obScene: Immuno-biopolitics and depoliticizing ontologies in the Anthropocene. *Theory, Culture & Society* 35(6): 3–30. https://doi.org/10.1177/0263276418757314

Swyngedouw, E. and M. Kaika. 2014. L'ecologia Política Urbana. Grans Promeses, Aturades... i Nous Inicis? [Urban political ecology. Great promises, deadlock... and new beginnings?]. *Documents d'Anàlisi Geogràfica* 60(3).

Swyngedouw, E., M. Kaika and E. Castro. 2022. Urban water: A political-ecology perspective. *Built Environment* 28(2): 124–37.

Taylor, L. 2011. No boundaries: Exurbia and the study of contemporary urban dispersion. *GeoJournal* 76(4): 323–39.

Taylor, K.Y. 2019. *Race for profit: How banks and the real estate industry undermined black homeownership*. Chapel Hill, NC: University of North Carolina Press.

Truelove, Y. 2011. (Re-)conceptualizing water inequality in Delhi, India through a feminist political ecology framework. *Geoforum* 42(2): 143–52.

Truelove, Y. 2016. Incongruent waterworlds: Situating the everyday practices and power of water in Delhi. *South Asia Multidisciplinary Academic Journal* 14.

Tsing, A.L. 1993. *In the realm of the diamond queen: Marginality in an out-of-the-way place*. Princeton, NJ: Princeton University Press.

Turner, V.K. and D.H. Kaplan. 2018. Geographic perspectives on urban sustainability: Past, current, and future research trajectories, *Urban Geography* 40(3): 267–78. DOI: 10.1080/02723638.2018.1475545.

Tzaninis, Y. 2020. Cosmopolitanism beyond the city: Discourses and experiences of young migrants in post-suburban Netherlands. *Urban Geography* 41(1): 143–61. DOI: 10.1080/ 02723638.2019.1637212.

Tzaninis, Y. and Boterman, W. 2018. Beyond the urban–suburban dichotomy: Shifting mobilities and the transformation of suburbia *City* 22(1): 43–62.

Valdivia, G. 2018. 'Wagering life' in the petro-city: Embodied ecologies of oil flow, capitalism, and justice in Esmeraldas, Ecuador. *Annals of the American Association of Geographers* 108(2): 549–57.

Velicu, I. and M. Kaika. 2017. Undoing environmental justice: Re-imagining equality in the Rosia Montana anti-mining movement. *Geoforum* 84: 305–15.

Velzeboer, L., M. Hordijk, and K. Schwartz. 2018. Water is life in a life without water: Power and everyday water practices in Lilongwe, Malawi. *Habitat International* 73: 119–28.

Veracini, L. 2012. Suburbia, settler colonialism and the world turned inside out. *Housing, Theory and Society* 29(4): 339–57. DOI: 10.1080/14036096.2011.638316.

Wachsmuth, D. and H. Angelo. 2018. Green and gray: New ideologies of nature in urban sustainability policy. *Annals of the American Association of Geographers* 108(4): 1038–56.

Wachsmuth, D., D. Aldana Cohen, and H. Angelo. 2016. Expand the frontiers of urban sustainability. *Nature* 536: 7617. DOI:10.1038/536391a.

Wang, J.Y., D. Snoeck, S. Van Vlierberghe, W. Verstraete, and N. De Belie. 2014. Application of hydrogel encapsulated carbonate precipitating bacteria for approaching a realistic self-healing in concrete. *Construction and Building Materials* 68: 110–19.

Wilderson, F. 2021. An Afropessimist on the year since George Floyd was murdered. *The Nation*, 27 May.

Wilson, D. and A.E.G. Jonas. 2018. Planetary urbanization: New perspectives on the debate. *Urban Geography* 39(10): 1576–80. DOI: 10.1080/02723638.2018.1481603.

Wu, F. and R. Keil. 2020. Changing the geographies of sub/urban theory: Asian perspectives. *Urban Geography* 41(7): 947–52. DOI: 10.1080/02723638.2020.1712115.

Wu, J. 2013. Landscape sustainability science: Ecosystem services and human well-being in changing landscapes. *Landscape Ecology* 28(6): 999–1023.

Wu, J. and R. Hobbs. 2002. Key issues and research priorities in landscape ecology: An idiosyncratic synthesis. *Landscape Ecology* 17(4): 355–65.

Wu, J., G.D. Jenerette, A. Buyantuyev, and C.L. Redman. 2011. Quantifying spatiotemporal patterns of urbanization: The case of the two fastest growing metropolitan regions in the United States. *Ecological Complexity* 8(1): 1–8.

Yiftachel, O. 2020. From displacement to displaceability. *City* 24(1–2): 151–65. DOI: 10.1080/13604813.2020.1739933.

Zimmer, A. 2010. Urban political ecology. Theoretical concepts, challenges, and suggested future directions. *Erdkunde* 64(4): 343–54.

Part I

Extended urbanisation: Moving UPE beyond the 'urbanisation of nature' thesis

1

Capital's natures: A critique of (urban) political ecology[1]

Erik Swyngedouw

> The question that now begins to gnaw at your mind is more anguished: outside Penthesilea does an outside exist? Or, no matter how far you go from the city, will you only pass from one limbo to another, never managing to leave it?
>
> (Calvino, 1974: 122)

> The capitalist system has proved infinitely more robust than its detractors – Marx as their head – thought ... Because it has discovered routes to its survival in critiques of it.
>
> (Boltanski and Chiapello, 2007: 27)

Urban political ecology has over the past few decades matured into a thriving and sophisticated perspective across academic disciplines, policy networks, and activist organisations. A wide range of complementary, and occasionally competing ontologies, epistemologies, and associated social and political ecological imaginaries have spurred a vibrant debate (see Angelo and Wachsmuth, 2014; Connolly, 2019; Ernstson and Swyngedouw, 2018a; Heynen, 2014, 2016, 2018; Heynen et al., 2006; Keil, 2003; Lawhon and Ernstson, 2014; Loftus, 2012, 2019a, 2019b; Tzaninis et al., 2020). Inspired by Marxist, feminist, postcolonial, psychoanalytical, Foucauldian, new materialist, more-than-human, and other perspectives, (urban) political ecology has recentred the role of non-humans in the assemblages of socio-ecological relations that animate the present urban condition and teased out the multiple and diverse socio-ecological power relations that quilt the making, unmaking, and remaking of these socio-natural constellations. Despite the heterogeneous theoretical frameworks that inform (urban) political ecology, there is nonetheless a shared assumption that considers political ecological perspectives to be inherently 'critical' and politically progressive by virtue of their focus on the performative presence of the non-human or the more-than-human in the structuring of everyday urban life (and thereby decentring the place of humans), on the theoretical and empirical analysis of the constitutive and conflicting socio-ecological power relations that animate socio-environmental relations, and on the activist-scholarly articulation with subaltern socio-ecological movements that informs much of the political-ecological research (Swyngedouw and Kaika, 2014).

However, in this chapter, I shall argue that there is nothing inherently critical or progressive about the current state of 'political ecology', urban or otherwise, neither as a practice nor as a theoretical perspective. I shall make a case for the need of a 'critique of (urban) political ecology'. This heading is of course freely borrowed from the title of Karl Marx's magnus opus *Capital: A critique of political economy*. It is, I maintain, through a 'critique of political ecology' that the intellectual gaze might shift to identifying the mechanisms through which new and progressive political-ecological configurations can be forged, something that is centrally important if we are really concerned with inflecting the infernal socio-ecological dynamics of the political ecology of present-day capitalism in a socially more equitable, politically more democratic, and ecologically more sensible direction. Indeed, the point is not, as Marx argued a long time ago, to insist on the need to embed our understanding of social life within wider socio-ecological metabolisms and their conflicting dynamics – this is already well-known and visible to all – but also to chart the contours that might permit a progressive and emancipatory transformation from within actually existing conditions and possibilities. The key signifiers for such progressive or emancipatory transformation are, of course, socialism or communism.

In other words, the political ecology of capitalism is clearly and indisputably predicated on deepening and widening its insertion in and entanglement with physical, chemical, and biological processes, organised through a social configuration marked by uneven relations of ownership of nature, an insatiable drive for accumulation, a global urbanisation process, and inserted with a system of generalised market exchange. These processes, in turn, are paralleled by combined and uneven socio-ecological conditions and by significant conflict and socio-ecological struggle, waged primarily by those who hold significant political or economic power positions. In addition, these material processes are sustained by and entwined with particular imaginaries and discourses of what Nature is and how it can or should be 'managed'. I argue that there is indeed an actually existing political ecology of capitalism through which capitalist socio-ecological relations are reproduced and deepened. A critique of this political ecology unearths the power relations, inconsistencies, systematic inequalities, and conflicts through which the political ecology of capitalism is sustained, whereby the point is not just to understand the world, but to change it! And this requires a critique of (urban) political ecology, one that relates the material to the imaginary and, in doing so, contributes to imagining and practising different urban futures.

The chapter is organised in two sections and four parts, followed by a conclusion. The first section focuses on a critique of the political ecology of capitalism as an urban socio-physical process. In the second section, the focus will shift to a critique of the discursive-imaginary configuration of the political ecology of capitalism. The conclusion will concentrate on the central importance of traversing the fantasies upon which both the material and imaginary sustainability of the infernal socio-ecological dynamics of capitalism are predicated and that inform much of contemporary environmental or ecological activism. Shifting the gaze in ways that radically reimagines our view of the socio-ecological situation we are in, I contend, is vital to configuring a strategy and forms of speaking and acting that are performative with respect to enacting progressive socio-ecological transformations.

Capital's natures: A critique of (urban) political ecology

There is an impressive genealogy of political economists that have in important ways contributed to understanding the processes that animate socio-economic change in general and capitalist dynamics in particular. Thomas Malthus, the Physiocrats, Adam Smith, and David Ricardo were early and crucial interlocutors, later joined by political economics like John Maynard Keynes, Elinor Ostrom, and a wide range of Marxist, institutional, and other heterodox economists. They all shared the view that economic processes (the social appropriation, socio-metabolic transformation, and distributive allocation of all sorts of natures in the form of commodified goods and services) are necessarily embedded within historically and geographically variable social and ecological relations and regulated by and through particular socio-legal and institutional forms (in particular, but not exclusively, the state). This socio-institutional embedding, in turn, co-determines (together with the state of technology, the physical geographical conditions and processes, socio-cultural preferences, and the like) the constellation and dynamics of socio-ecological processes. Many among them, albeit not all, took a keen and direct interest in the active role of 'external' physical and ecological conditions. This is particularly evident in the work of Malthus, the Physiocrats, Ricardo, and, much more recently, Ostrom. We could easily classify them under the umbrella of proto-political ecologists. The early political economists heavily influenced Karl Marx. His historical materialist perspective was also, and in a foundational manner, rooted in understanding the social within the material processes and biophysical relations through which non-human 'stuff' was appropriated, transformed, and distributed

(Swyngedouw, 2006). Marx's work can, therefore, be viewed as a precursor to what we define today as a 'critique of political ecology' (Burkett, 2014; Foster, 2000; McKenzie, 2016; Saito, 2017).

The simple (albeit theoretically complex) point that political ecology, since its inception in the 1980s, insisted on, and revolved around how to make nature and ecology, the non-human, enter our theorisations of social change such that non-humans are foregrounded as active and significant agents within the dynamics of socio-ecological change. The point is to render discernible how the non-human is always embedded within socio-economic processes on the one hand and how socio-ecological transformations are configured through a socio-ecological 'metabolic' process, despite the systematic disavowal of this truth, most notably in recurrent ideological attempts to separate the social from the natural (Foster et al., 2010). While the political ecology of capitalism is related to and insists on the possibility, if not necessity, of de-coupling the social or economic from the ecological, a critique of political ecology insists on the inevitable deepening and knotting together of human and non-human entanglements as the historical dynamics of capital unfold. In doing so, the non-human and more-than-human become an integral part of the tensions, contradictions, and crises that mark the trajectory of capitalist transformations (Smith, 1984; Swyngedouw, 2018a).

In a manner similar to understanding the 'economy', which is always a *political* economy, 'ecology' is always also inherently a *political* ecology, and in the present conjuncture, a capitalist and neoliberal one. There is, therefore, nothing foundationally radical or critical about (urban) political ecology. Decades of research have now firmly theoretically established and empirically verified that ecological relations and processes are intrinsically and intimately enmeshed with social, political, cultural, and technological processes. In other words, political ecologists have only affirmed, expanded, and reformulated classical political economic insights. What is now urgently required is a 'critique of (urban) political ecology' that opens up a terrain for the politicisation of 'Nature', and that is what I shall concentrate on in the remainder of this chapter. Indeed, while there is a wide and inspiring urban political ecology literature that critically dissects the power-laden and largely impotent acting of climate and other environmental policies and forms of activism, the question of political change and transformation remains somewhat ambiguous and elusive (with the possible exception of the degrowth movement) (D'Alisa et al., 2014).

The political struggle over 'Nature', I maintain, operates today along two interrelated axes. On the one hand, there are major conflicts raging over the material bases of life and the modalities of access, control, and reproduction of the non-human or more-than-human organic and inorganic matter, relations, and processes. On the other hand, major contestation unfolds over the meaning of 'Nature', i.e., the discursive configurations through which nature is imagined and symbolised (Fraser and Jaeggi, 2018). The former will be discussed in the next part of the chapter, while the latter will be the key theme of the second section of the chapter.

Planetary urbanisation, resource extraction, and the socio-ecological circulation of capital

In *Planetary mine*, Martín Arboleda (2020) excavates brilliantly the shifting territories, infrastructures, logistics, socio-economic dynamics, and conflicts that animate the extractive mobilisation of non-human matter upon which the expansion of global capital rests, the insertion of these materialities in sustaining the circulation and accumulation of capital, and their associated combined and uneven socio-ecological development. The continuous de-territorialisation of extractive matter re-territorialises as socio-ecologically metabolised commodities through the process of planetary urbanisation (Arboleda, 2016). Consider, for example, that China consumed in three years (2011–13) more concrete than the US used during the whole of the twentieth century (6.5 gigatons for China in three years against 4.5 gigatons for the US in a century), primarily to construct the country's megacities and support the logistical flows that assure its expansive 'sustainability'. Of course, similar data could be compiled for sand, water, aluminium, oil, avocado, soybeans, and many other 'resources'. Planetary capitalist urbanisation, a term already coined by Henri Lefebvre in 1989 (in English 2014), is a parallel process and made possible precisely by the expansion of planetary mining and globally organised circulations and metabolisms of organic matter such as food, fibres, oil, or wood. As David Harvey (1996) argued a long time ago, there is nothing unnatural about New York City. Urbanisation and city formation is indeed nothing else than the geographical imprint of the political-ecological dynamics of metabolising flows of matter on the one hand and the circulation of capital in the mad dance of accumulation that drives capitalism forward on the other (Harvey, 2017). In that sense, a critique of political ecology is necessarily a critique of urban political ecology, precisely because the circulation of money, bodies, and matter unfolds as a process of 'the urbanization of capital' as David Harvey (1985) called it.

Indeed, the flow of money-as-capital and the reverse flow of commodified matter (and its non-commodified excesses like pollution and waste (see Chapter 18 by Savini and Chapter 17 by Connolly and Muzaini in this volume) embedded in and supported by particular social and institutional configurations weld the social and the physical together in the production of both new socio-ecological constellations and ever-changing unequal socio-ecological landscapes, whereby the urbanisation process is both the pivot and the imprint. The continuous de- and re-territorialisation of transformed matter (what Marx called the metabolic rift), and the socially triaged and conflicting relations that push this forward produce a combined and uneven spatial configuration that reshuffles socio-material ecologies and manufactures both the landscapes of socio-ecological disintegration and the patterning of the urbanisation process. As capitalism is an urbanising process, so is the political ecology of capitalism inherently an urban political ecology. There cannot be a political ecology of, say, avocado or quinoa production in Latin America's agricultural landscapes without considering the urbanisation of avocado or quinoa in the 'sustainable' *woke* eco-consumption bars of Amsterdam, Toronto, or New Delhi.

A critique of political ecology, therefore, should foreground, both theoretically and empirically, the de- and re-territorialising flows through which socio-ecological transformations unfold and sediment to constitute the everyday matrix of the urban fabric. While (research on) ecological politics customarily focuses on territorially bounded processes (like, for example, greenhouse gas emissions, pollution, biodiversity loss, ecological gentrification), a critique of political ecology foregrounds the flow/fixity dialectic, and focuses on conflicts, struggles, contradictions, inconsistencies, and crises that symptomatically erupt both around the metabolic flow of matter and the conditions of its de- and re-territorialisation. Such a flow or flux-based perspective requires its particular methodology. The territorially, hence locally, configured socio-ecological assemblages (like wind turbines, cars, mines, dams, or skyscrapers) are always inserted within the flow of socio-ecological metabolic processes. A key focus for a critique of (urban) political ecology, therefore, is the development of flow-based methodologies that attempt to measure, chart, and index the combined and uneven geographical layering of the triaged socio-ecological patterning of planetary urbanisation (Blakey, 2019; Kenis and Lievens, 2017; Peters, 2008). Kiel Moe's great excavation of the socio-ecological footprint of New York's Empire State Building is an emblematic example of such an approach (Moe, 2017). Consider also, for example, how deeply everyday urban life is inserted in the IT-based cognitive economies of twenty-first-century capitalism. Yet, while co-constituting uneven socio-ecological relations within the city, these networks are also predicated upon, among others, sustaining the infernal ecologies of coltan mining in central Africa, deeply exploitative class relations that drive its transformation into semiconductors, the massive use of freshwater resources, and the ultimate return of the morally depreciated IT-commodities to the dystopian suburban wastelands of the 'recycling' enclaves in the Global South.

Similarly, the attempts undertaken by many cities to reduce their greenhouse gas emissions to mitigate climate change blissfully ignore the total flow-based carbon emissions of the matter that sustains the urban process. Consider, for example, that the greenhouse gas emissions of global internet and IT-use – at approximately 3.7 per cent of the total – are higher than those of the world's aviation industry (at about 2 per cent), while the aviation industry is (correctly) portrayed as a major climate polluter.[2] The production-based greenhouse gas emissions in most cities in the Global North are only a fraction of their consumption-based emissions; yet the latter are rarely, if ever (ac)counted (for).

Such excavation of the flow of circulating socio-ecological stuff that seeks to symbolise how the material and physical characteristics of non-human matter is enrolled and transformed (metabolised) through technologically and institutionally mediated social relations of production and reproduction foregrounds also how gender, racial, ethnic, and other identitarian inscriptions become mobilised and demarcated within the uneven and unequal patterning of this class-driven process and reveals the multiple conflicts, contestations, and ruptures that characterise the production and reproduction of these expanding circulatory flows. In other words, the spectral class dynamics of capital circulation and accumulation, with their twin forces of exploitation and expropriation, striate bodily social inscriptions in ways that render it socially unequally layered, gendered, and racialised, while producing unevenly distributed socio-physical constellations.

Of course, I am not arguing for a return to economic reductionism, but rather for an expansion of what is meant by 'capitalism'. As Max Horkheimer argued a long time ago, the problem of economic reductionism is based on a too narrow understanding of 'the economy' (Fraser and Jaeggi, 2018). Indeed, the key features of capitalist socio-ecological relations and dynamics are inherently predicated upon their insertion within particular institutional and regulatory regimes, within all manner of arrangements of social and ecological reproduction upon which the 'sustainability' of capitalism necessarily rests, and on a range of often inconsistent imaginaries and fantasies that support and legitimise its continuation. This includes the particular gendered and racialised private and collective practices through which labour is reproduced and the ecological dynamics through which the non-human conditions are reproduced (or not as the case may be) (Barca, 2020). And this is what I shall turn to next.

Putting neoliberalisation in its place

In a strange twist of intellectual obfuscation, much of critical urban political ecological literature has, not surprisingly, focused on the critical analysis of processes of neoliberalisation and their constitutive practices such as privatisation, deregulation, growing austerity, the commodification of pseudo-commodities like water, ecosystem services, or carbon, and the fetishisation of 'the market' as prime allocative and distributive arrangement (Heynen, 2007). Indeed, neoliberalisation has, with a few notable exceptions, discursively almost completely replaced signifiers like 'capitalism' or 'class struggle' (and even more so 'socialism' or 'communism') as if a particular state policy and near-hegemonic elite fantasy and discourse stands in for the totality of the historically and geographically variegated, dynamic, and contradictory permutations of the political-ecology of capitalism. Only after the twin crises of the post-2008 financial catastrophe and the 2020 COVID-19 pandemic did the signifier 'capitalism' return as the class dynamics through which many of the socio-ecological relations of the political-ecology of capitalism are patterned became more difficult to foreclose, repress, or disavow. In other words, the return of the Real of the socio-ecological situation terminally undermined the neoliberal fantasy script. The imaginary construction of neoliberalism as an inclusive, democratic, and efficient growth-oriented system collapsed when the realities of rising inequalities, class struggle, and socio-ecological triaging associated with neoliberal capitalism became impossible to disavow or repress (Swyngedouw, 2019).[3]

The critique of (urban) political ecology that I suggest would consider neoliberalisation as a more or less successful (for the elites), and geographically variegated, class strategy and tactics to impose a utopian imaginary vision of what kind of socio-ecological relations need to be sustained and how to organise these materially and institutionally within capitalist socio-ecological relations (Harvey, 2005). Neoliberalisation, therefore, is an elite strategy, focused on the control of the state and other governance arrangements, and becomes enacted as a set of multiscaled institutional and regulatory dispositives imposed to assure the smooth functioning of 'free' market exchange, to deepen the process of 'accumulation by dispossession' (Harvey, 2003), and to foster the enrolment of as much human and non-human 'matter' within the capital circulation process as the capital accumulation process can sustain. In doing so, neoliberalisation inaugurated a new socio-ecological mode of development – a combination of a particular regime of accumulation with a mode of regulation and associated socio-cultural inscriptions and prescriptions – that increasingly displaced, albeit by no means in a homogeneous and undifferentiated manner, the Fordist and Keynesian political-ecological model that animated much of the socio-ecological dynamics of twentieth-century capitalism (Brand and Wissen, 2018).

Neoliberalisation as a political class strategy is paralleled too by the restructuring of identity and desire and the consolidation of a new imaginary of emancipation, whereby the individual is elevated to the status of autonomous and responsible subject, capable of managing their life as an entrepreneur of the self, and operating under the injunction *to enjoy* (Swyngedouw, 2021). The drive for enjoyment – a combination of anxiety and excitement – coupled with self-responsibilisation, became the ideological glue through which neoliberal subjectivation proceeded (McGowan, 2016; Verhaeghe, 2014). The insatiable, since unquenchable, desire for private enjoyment displaced the search for a 'better' society. As such, the subject becomes caught within the Scylla of the fear of failing to become what one desires on the one hand and the Charybdis of unbearable, because never sufficient or fully satisfying, ethical, social, or ecological responsibility on the other. Such immunological dispositives, i.e., the sequestering of the individual from the social bond, the obligations and possibilities that mark life-in-common (Esposito, 2011), nurtures neuroses that can take the form of lingering depression and melancholia or obsessive, but mindless, acting-out (Ernstson and Swyngedouw, 2018b). A critique of political ecology insists on the intimate articulation between the political struggle over institutional arrangements on the one hand and the associated engineering of new forms of neoliberal subjectivity on the other, both of which point to a sustained disavowal of the pervasive class dynamic that animate these processes. In particular, what Nancy Fraser (2019) called progressive neoliberalism, whereby a leftist position became identified as embracing identitarian recognition within a meritocratic urban cosmopolitan market-based political economy, fuelled the hegemonic formation of neoliberal subjectivity that not only intensified further the disdain for, if not the silencing of, a more fundamental critique of the political ecology of capitalism but also foreclosed forging alternative post-capitalist imaginaries and discourses. Foregrounding neoliberalisation as a political strategy and a cultural condition waged within the contours of the class dynamics of capitalism permits inserting again the Real of Capital and its embedding within political and cultural processes and opens potentially new trajectories for performative political acting. Put simply, the class structuring of socio-ecological transformation striates the multiple socio-ecological tensions through which the political-ecology of capitalism unfolds.

Capital's natures reimagined: The Urbicene and the 'madness of economic reason'

Planetary urbanisation is the geographical imprint of what is now generically referred to as the Anthropocene (Swyngedouw, 2018b). The human forcing of socio-physical transformations finds indeed its material and socio-cultural expression in the urbanisation process. Perhaps *the Urbicene* is a more appropriate signifier to label the socio-material form the Anthropocene takes.

As Jason Moore (2016) asserts, the Anthropocene has never been 'the Age of Humans', but rather the age of the few, mainly men, through whom capital circulation was organised, nurtured, and deepened on a planetary scale. Moore appropriately calls this period the Capitalocene. Nurturing the process of planetary urbanisation was and is predicated upon intensifying proliferations of metabolic vehicles, in the form of techno-natural intermediaries that etch the transformation of non-human 'stuff' in myriad socio-ecological metabolic cyborgian relations that reorder human/non-human assemblages in radically uneven ways and with profound socio-ecological implications. Given the desperate socio-ecological condition the earth is in and recognising the pivotal role of the urbanisation process, the city is today customarily staged as the terrain for experimenting with new socio-technical and metabolic imbroglios that render the city not only 'smart' but also 'resilient' in the face of uncertainty and 'adaptive' to potentially disruptive processes of rapid socio-ecological change. The main objective of these socio-technical procedures is to assure that the ecological conditions remain fully within a matrix that permits the continuation of the political-ecology of capitalism. In other words, socio-technical arrangements have to change such that the dominant socio-ecological relations can continue. Sustaining the mad dance of capital accumulation, supported by the 'madness of economic reason' (Harvey, 2017), seems indeed to be the only game in town, despite recurrent, but politically impotent, critiques of such techno-material dispositives.

The proliferation of these prophylactic socio-technical assemblages to make the urban 'sustainable' and 'resilient' coincided with and, in part, required the emergence of a radical ontological shift that reframed and reimagined 'Nature' in ways more aligned with the requirements of a more ecologically reflexive capitalism. Indeed, theorists from both the social sciences and the humanities articulated new earthly cosmologies pioneered by Earth System scientists (such as the notions of radical uncertainty, non-linear dynamics, and complex non-deterministic feedback loops). Together with these complexity theories, the emergence of new materialist perspectives and more-than-human ontologies that point towards grasping worldly matters in a more symmetrical human/non-human, if not post-human, constellation have become an integral part of the proliferating techno-managerial efforts to sustain and support further the galloping process of capitalist planetary urbanisation (Ernstson and Swyngedouw, 2018a).

Nonetheless and despite its radical presumptions, we contend that this new cosmology also opens the spectre, albeit by no means necessarily so, for deepening particular capitalist forms of human–non-human entanglements and can be corralled to sustain the possibility for a hyper-accelerationist urban eco-modernist vision and practice in which science, geo-engineering, terraforming technologies, and big capital join and are presumed to be capable to save both earth and earthlings. The geo-sciences and, in particular, Earth

System experts discern in the advent of the Anthropocene the possibility, if not necessity, for the management and careful 'adaptive' and 'resilient' massaging of the totality of the Earth System. The recognition of the earth as an intricate intertwined socio-natural constellation and socio-ecological imbroglio inaugurates indeed the possibility that with loving supervision, intelligent crafting, reflexive calculation, and careful techno-natural nurturing and manicuring, the earth can be terraformed in 'sustainable' manners (Swyngedouw, 2018b). As Bruce Braun (2015) insisted in his careful dissection of the historiographies of the new materialisms, the parallel between non-deterministic geo-science, 'resilience' studies, neoliberalisation, and the varieties of new materialisms associated with a more-than-human ontology are not difficult to discern.

While in many nineteenth-century modernist accounts, non-human processes were considered to be recalcitrant, uncooperative, and prone to revengeful action when marshalled into capital's subordination and use, the recent turn to a symmetrical ontology permits – at least in discourse and imaginary – a potentially more benign, mutually supporting, sustainable, adaptive, and resilient assembling of human–non-human relations, a constellation that would, with some massaging, permit capitalism to propel forward to even greater heights of socio-ecological knotting while recognising both the acting and the incalculability of the non-human. This desire to produce a new terrestrial configuration unfolds through signifiers like 'Earth System governance' and 'planetary stewardship', and is translated on to the urban terrain as 'smart' urbanism, and 'resilient' city planning. To save the world and ourselves, we need not less capitalism, but a deeper, a more intense and radically reflexive form, one that revolves around reconstructing DNA and genetic material, mobilises the power of the nuclear to drive the economy, forces gas out of shale formations so it can be 'carbon-stored' elsewhere, and works to terraform earth in a mutually benign co-constitution, all this supported by a cosmopolitan and liberal, but decidedly meritocratic, professional elite that embraces the inclusion of everyone provided they sustain the modernising status quo and insert themselves in the mad dance of sustained capital accumulation (Ellis, 2011; Schellenberger and Nordhaus, 2011). Covering up the contradictions of capitalist eco-modernisation, the apparently revolutionary new material ontologies offer new storylines, new symbolisations of the earth's past and future that can be corralled to help perform the ideological groundwork required (Neyrat, 2019).

Traversing the fantasy: Towards a progressive (urban) political ecology

As argued above, foregrounding the political implies, among others, the transformation and re-symbolisation of the imaginary upon which the need and urgency of environmental action is legitimised and sustained. The hegemonic and symptomatic base upon which the legitimacy of the environmental discourse and practice of both mainstream and more activist climate movements is predicated rests upon two repressed traumas, both of which are displaced onto a phantasmagorical imaginary. Opening different political-ecological trajectories requires transgressing the fantasy that conceals these traumas. We shall explore and illustrate this through examining the fantasies that support the climate change narrative.

Living in catastrophic times

First, the climate emergency is articulated around the insistent construction of a dystopian, quasi-catastrophic future if no urgent and appropriate action is taken. This real catastrophic imaginary of an unliveable future reminiscent of the post-apocalyptic fantasy of the Mad Max movie series, is staged as the horizon that needs to be avoided or averted. In other words, insistent action is required today in order to deflect the unfolding of this possible (and very real) cataclysmic climate future. This argument sustains the view that it is not too late yet, that the forecasted future can still be changed or deflected if appropriate and determined action is taken. The climate condition is very close to irreversible transformation, but this dystopian condition can still be averted if the right measures are taken now. However, many people around the world already live in such a socio-ecological apocalypse, demonstrated by the large numbers of climate refugees and mounting socio-ecological problems in the poorest parts of the world or, rather, experienced by the poorest part of the world's population (Miller, 2017; Parenti, 2011). The apocalypse has already happened for them. The fear of the consequences of climate change in one place is paralleled by already really existing socio-ecological disintegration elsewhere. The promise of a catastrophe-to-come is one around which middle-class anxiety and elite desires (for a 'better' climate and fears of collapse) circulate. While the elites nurture an apocalyptic dystopia that can nonetheless be avoided (for them), the majority of the world already lives 'within the collapse of civilization' (Invisible Committee, 2009). The apocalypse is indeed a combined and uneven one, both in time and across space (Calder Williams, 2011; Harper, 2020). More importantly, the combined and uneven collapse implies that the costs and consequence of attempts to postpone the climate disaster for some people and places is increasingly decanted onto the poorest parts of the world's population.

I would argue that sustaining and nurturing catastrophic imageries are an integral and vital part of the new cultural politics of capitalism for which both the management of fear and the injunction to enjoy are a central leitmotif and provides part of the cultural support for a process of environmental-populist post-politicisation (Swyngedouw, 2019; see Loftus and Gort, Chapter 14 in this volume). At the symbolic level, apocalyptic imaginaries are extraordinarily powerful in disavowing or foreclosing social conflict and antagonisms. Or, in other words, the presentation of climate change as a global and universal humanitarian cause produces a thoroughly depoliticised imaginary, one that does not revolve around choosing one trajectory rather than another, or identifies clear adversaries in a political process; it is one that is not articulated with specific political programs or socio-ecological projects or transformations (Swyngedouw, 2018b).

Transgressing this fantasy cuts through this deadlock. To begin with, the revelatory promise of the apocalyptic narrative as well as the redemptive, but impotent, insistence on the key importance of behavioural and technomanagerial, more eco-sensitive, change have to be fully rejected. In the face of the dystopian imaginaries mobilised to assure that the apocalypse will *not* happen sometime in the future (if the right technomanagerial actions are taken), the only reasonable response is: 'Don't worry (eco-modernisers, King Charles III, COP-meetings, many environmental activists…), you are really right, the environmental catastrophe *will* not only happen, it is too late, *it is already here* in the actual present conditions of planetary life.' Many already live in the post-apocalyptic interstices of life, whereby the fusion of environmental transformation and social conditions, render life 'bare'. The fact that the socio-environmental imbroglio has already passed the point of no return for many people and places on earth has to be fully asserted. The socio-environmental ruin is already here for many. It is not some distant dystopian promised future mobilised to trigger response today. Water conflicts, struggles for food, environmental refugees, the extreme social triaging inflicted by the COVID-19 pandemic, etc., testify to the socio-ecological predicament that choreographs everyday life for the majority of the world's population, many of whom are living in urbanised environments. It is already too late; it has always already been too late. There is no Arcadian place, time, or environment to return to, no benign global socio-ecological past or ideal climate that needs to be reconstructed, maintained, or stabilised. It is only within the realisation of the apocalyptic reality of the now that a new politics might emerge. Directing the environmental gaze to the perspective of those who are already barely surviving within the collapse of the socio-ecological conditions opens a wide range of new ways of grappling with socio-ecological realities and a vast terrain of different political and socio-technical interventions other than the presently dominant ones.

There is no humanity!

Second, the consensual climate discourse is mobilised through insisting on the immanent dangers that climate change poses to the future of humanity. Humanity in this context is not just understood as the sum total of humans living on planet earth but rather as human civilisation, characterised by a range of shared and common beliefs, ethics, and principles (such as liberty, solidarity, social relationality, principled equality, and civic rights). As Maurice Blanchot already argued in the early 1960s, this view is predicated upon the fantasy that 'humanity' (in the civilising sense) actually exists, that there is a global human civilisation, that human history has demonstrated the making of a common 'humanity', one that requires or deserves salvation. However, the Real of the human presence on earth, of course, exposes the empty core of 'humanity' (Blanchot, 1971). There is no foundational core that produces the reality of humanity. The multiple tensions and conflicts, and the unspeakable violence inflected by humans on humans testify to this 'emptiness', despite occasional manifestations of a deep humanity shared by some humans.

It is precisely this emptiness that is denied; it is a repressed trauma, namely the disavowed knowledge that there is no such thing as humanity. The pervasive inequalities, the rampant uneven power relations, the continuous objective and subjective violence inflicted by some humans onto other humans (consider, for example, the genocide committed by the European Union on refugees drowning in the Mediterranean Sea or reduced to 'bare life' in North African concentration camps, or the infernal consequences of serial exclusion) demonstrate the radical antagonisms and conflicts that cut through the human collective and signal that a communitarian 'humanity' has never existed. It may never do unless a sustained political fidelity to the possible, if not necessity, of its making is inaugurated. The disavowal in the climate discourse of the barbarism that also characterises humanity is a classic form of traumatic repression. According to Blanchot (1971), the fundamental challenge is the choice between an apocalyptic future that speeds ahead precisely because of the absence of 'humanity' or the actual construction of a 'humanity' now that, in turn, would deflect the course of the future in a different and more benign direction. The issue is, therefore, not to assure the future of a non-existing humanity as we know it, but first and foremost the creation of a humanity. As Alenka Zupančič (2018: 19) insists:

> Blanchot isn't saying that the destruction of the world would be insignificant because there is no real (communal) world yet; he is not, that is, cynically saying, 'Let it all go to hell, the world such as it is is not worth the trouble anyway!' On the contrary, Blanchot is suggesting that, now that we have at

least an abstract idea of the world (humanity) as a whole, it is worth the trouble more than ever.

Indeed, a significant post-truth imaginary seeps into the dominant climate discourse, a phantasmagoria of an abstract and virtual, but nonetheless threatened, global humanity. In doing so, the Real of class and other antagonisms that cut through the semblance of humanity is considered irrelevant or at least subordinate. The fetishistic disavowal or foreclosure of the class and other antagonisms that form the matrix of the social assures that nothing will really change.[4] Traversing the present fantasy of a just climate transition through technomanagerial and (neo)liberal consumerist adjustments requires recognising the trauma of the non-existence of humanity and that it is precisely this non-existence, i.e., the class and other dimensions that cut through humanity, that has already caused the climate catastrophe. Traversing this fantasy is predicated upon reversing the dominant argument: recognising that is already too late – the apocalypse has already happened – and the only possible thing left to do is to engage in a process of constructing a real 'humanity', of producing a human world in the world (Swyngedouw, 2022a). As the Invisible Committee (2009: 138) put it:

> It's useless to wait – for a breakthrough, for the revolution, the nuclear apocalypse or a social movement. To go on waiting is madness. The catastrophe is not coming, it is here. We are already situated within the collapse of a civilisation. It is within this reality that we must choose sides.

The latter necessitates foregrounding radical politicisation. Or in other words, if we really want to take the ecological condition seriously, we have to displace the question of ecology onto the terrain of agonistic politicisation, animated by a sustained fidelity to what Alain Badiou calls a passion for the real possibility and necessity of an egalitarian common world. It is through such political project that a common and enabling climate might be constituted. First and foremost, we have to insist that indeed there is no alternative. It is at such moment that a critique of (urban) political ecology may find its politicising voice.

Notes

1 *A critique of political ecology* was, as far as I know, first used as the title for one of the founding contributions to political ecology by the German intellectual Hans Magnus Enzensberger (1974). While now largely forgotten, it remains a key and foundational contribution to political ecology, one that deserves to be read and re-read.
2 See www.climatecare.org/resources/news/infographic-carbon-footprint-internet/ – accessed 12 August 2022.

3 I draw here on the Lacanian conceptualisation of social reality. According to Lacan, social reality is structured as Borromean knot of three interrelated instances: the Symbolic, the Imaginary, and the Real. The Symbolic refers to the discourses, practices, rules, and institutions through which we live our everyday life and in which we find our role and place. The Symbolic constitutes the Law (or the big Other) that prescribes, prohibits, entices, lures, punishes, or rewards. This is a symbolic representation of something that is neither unified nor coherent, and utterly contingent.

The Imaginary refers to the fantasies that provide a sense of consistency, cohesion, purpose, identity, a sense of what to desire (and what not), etc.… for what we do. The Imaginary is the terrain of fantasy, of giving meaning. It offers a way to see and understand things and relations as common-sensical and self-evident. The Imaginary invariably covers up or conceals the gap, the void, the abyss between the Real and the Symbolic.

For Lacan, the world of the symbolic order is always lacking. It is an unstable, shifting, and necessarily incomplete register. There is always excess, a rem(a)inder, which cannot be symbolised or represented; a hard kernel that sticks to the world like a fishbone in the throat and exerts an unalienable scratch. This is what Lacan calls the Real, a complex, shifting spectral presence (Lacan, 1991: 66). The Real refers to what cannot be symbolised, that what is left out, repressed, disavowed, or foreclosed. The Real, therefore, reveals itself through symptoms that shatter the fantasy screen and that cannot be accounted for by the Symbolic (without fundamentally altering the Symbolic order). For example, the spectral class dynamics that drive the accumulation of capital and produce constitutive inequality or antagonisms, or the shattering effects of the truth of climate change can be understood as symptoms of the Real (see Pohl and Swyngedouw 2021a, 2021b; Swyngedouw 2022b).

4 'Fetishistic disavowal' is a notion coined by the psychoanalyst Octavio Mannoni (2003) and is captured well by the phrase 'I know very well, but all the same … I act if I do not know'. It can be illustrated with respect to the environmental or climate condition, and the genuine concerns of those who are worried about this. It is indeed generally accepted that climate change is largely caused by anthropogenic greenhouse gas emissions and has devastating effects on poor, subaltern, or marginalised communities and social groups. Most people know that it is the present dominant (capitalist) socio-ecological order that is responsible for this. Yet, the mainstream strategic focus is on dealing technically and institutionally with reducing, capturing, or substituting greenhouse gas emissions as if dealing with those climate symptoms would in themselves restore a benign environment and socio-ecologically just world. The underlying Real mechanisms that produced the problem in the first instance are repressed, disavowed, or foreclosed. CO_2 and other greenhouse gases are elevated to a fetish that stands in the place of the repressed Real that produces the problem. This repression is caused by the traumatic experience that dealing with those processes (and the consequences of doing so) unleashes: it is too big, too dangerous, too shattering, too horrifying, too daunting, or too anxiety-inducing

to be confronted directly. For example, everyone knows that recycling, vegetarianism, and assorted other individual actions undertaken in the name of the climate and ecological justice are not hitting the mark; nonetheless, most of us keep doing it as if it really matters, while shying away from engaging in really transformative action (see Swyngedouw, 2018a).

References

Angelo, H. and D. Wachsmuth. 2014. Urbanizing urban political ecology: A critique of methodological cityism. *International Journal of Urban and Regional Research* 39(1): 16–27.
Arboleda, M. 2016. In the nature of the non-city: Expanded infrastructural network and the political ecology of planetary urbanisation. *Antipode* 48(2): 233–51.
Arboleda, M. 2020. *Planetary mine: Territories of extraction under late capitalism*. London: Verso.
Barca, S. 2020. *Forces of reproduction: Notes for a counter-hegemonic Anthropocene*. Cambridge: Cambridge University Press.
Blakey, J. 2019. (Post)democratic carbon accounting: Creating the climate for disagreement. PhD Dissertation, Department of Geography, University of Manchester.
Blanchot, M. 1971. L'Apocalypse Deçoit. In M. Blanchot (ed.), *Amitié*. Paris: Gallimard.
Boltanski, L. and E. Chiapello. 2007. *The new spirit of capitalism*. London: Verso.
Brand, U. and M. Wissen. 2018. *Limits to capitalist nature: Theorizing and overcoming the imperial mode of living*. London: Rowman & Littlefield.
Braun, B. 2015. The 2013 antipode RGS-IBG lecture: New materialisms and neoliberal natures. *Antipode* 47(1): 1–14.
Burkett, P. 2014. *Marx and nature: A red and green perspective*. Chicago, IL: Haymarket Books.
Calder Williams, E. 2011. *Combined and uneven apocalypse*. Washington, DC: Zero Books.
Calvino, I. 1974. *Invisible cities*. London: Picador.
Connolly, C. 2019. Urban political ecology beyond methodological cityism. *International Journal of Urban and Regional Research* 43(1): 63–75.
D'Alisa, G., F. Demaria, and G. Kallis (eds.). 2014. *Degrowth: A vocabulary for a new era*. London: Routledge.
Ellis, E. 2011. The planet of no return: Human resilience on an artificial earth. *The Breakthrough Journal* 2(2): 37–44.
Enzensberger, H.M. 1974. A critique of political ecology. *New Left Review* 84: 3–31.
Ernstson, H. and E. Swyngedouw (eds.). 2018a. *Urban political ecology in the Anthropo-Obscene: Political interruptions and possibilities*. London: Routledge.
Ernstson, H. and E. Swyngedouw. 2018b. Interrupting the Anthropo-obScene: Immuno-biopolitics and depoliticising ontologies in the Anthropocene. *Theory, Culture, Society* 35(6): 3–30.
Esposito, R. 2011. *Immunitas*. Cambridge: Polity Press.
Foster, J.B. 2000. *Marx's ecology: Materialism and nature*. New York: Monthly Review Press.

Foster, J.B., B. Clark, and R. York. 2010. *The ecological rift: Capitalism's war on the earth*. New York: Monthly Review Press.
Fraser, N. 2019. *The old is dying and the new cannot be born: From progressive neoliberalism to Trump and beyond*. London: Verso.
Fraser, N. and R. Jaeggi. 2018. *Capitalism: A conversation in critical theory*. Cambridge: Polity Press.
Harper, E.T. 2020. Ecological gentrification in response to apocalyptic narratives of climate change: The production of an immune-political fantasy. *International Journal of Urban and Regional Research* 44(1): 55–71.
Harvey, D. 1985. *The urbanization of capital*. Oxford: Blackwell.
Harvey, D. 1996. *Justice, nature and the geography of difference*. Blackwell: Oxford.
Harvey, D. 2003. *The new imperialism*. Oxford: Oxford University Press.
Harvey, D. 2005. *Neoliberalism: A short history*. Oxford: Oxford University Press.
Harvey, D. 2017. *Marx, capital and the madness of economic reason*. New York: Oxford University Press.
Heynen, N. 2007. *Neoliberal environments: false promises and unnatural consequences*. Abingdon, Oxon: Routledge.
Heynen, N. 2014. Urban political ecology I: The urban century. *Progress in Human Geography* 38(4): 598–604.
Heynen, N. 2016. Urban political ecology II: The abolitionist century. *Progress in Human Geography* 40(6): 839–45.
Heynen, N. 2018. Urban political ecology III: The feminist and queer century. *Progress in Human Geography* 42(3): 446–52.
Heynen, N., M. Kaika, and E. Swyngedouw (eds.). 2006. *In the nature of cities: Urban political ecology and the metabolism of urban environments*. London: Routledge.
Invisible Committee. 2009. *The coming insurrection*. Cambridge, MA: MIT Press.
Keil, R. 2003. Urban political ecology 1. *Urban Geography* 24(8): 723–38.
Kenis, A. and M. Lievens. 2017. Imagining the carbon neutral city: The (post) politics of time and space. *Environment and Planning A: Economy and Space* 49(8): 1762–78.
Lacan, J. 1991. *Le Seminaire, Livre XVII: L'Envers de la Psychanalyse*. Paris: Seuil.
Lawhon, M. and H. Ernstson. 2014. Provincializing urban political ecology: Towards a situated UPE through African urbanism. *Antipode* 46(2): 497–516.
Lefebvre, H. 2014. Dissolving city, planetary metamorphosis. *Environment and Planning D: Society and Space* 32(2): 203–5. https://doi.org/10.1068/d3202tra
Loftus, A. 2012. *Everyday environmentalism: Creating an urban political ecology*. Minneapolis, MN: University of Minnesota Press.
Loftus, A. 2019a. Political ecology I: Where is political ecology? *Progress in Human Geography* 43(1): 172–82.
Loftus, A. 2019b. Political ecology III: Who are 'the people'? *Progress in Human Geography* 44(5): 981–90. https://doi.org/10.1177/0309132519884632
Mannoni, O. 2003. I know well, but all the same ... (Je sais bien mais quand même [1968]). In M.A. Rothenberg, D.A. Foster, and S. Žižek (eds.), *Perversion and the social relation*. Durham: Duke University Press, pp. 68–92.
McGowan, T. 2016. *Capitalism and desire: The psychic cost of free markets*. New York: Columbia University Press.
McKenzie, W. 2016. *Molecular red: Theory for the Anthropocene*. London: Verso.
Miller, T. 2017. *Storming the wall: Climate change, migration, and homeland security*. San Francisco: City Lights Books.
Moe, K. 2017. *Empire, state & building*. Barcelona: Actar Publishing.

Moore, J. (ed.). 2016. *Anthropocene or Capitalocene? Nature, history and the crisis of capitalism.* Oakland, CA: PM Press.
Neyrat, F. 2019. *The unconstructable earth: An ecology of separation.* New York: Fordham University Press.
Parenti, C. 2011. *Tropic of chaos: Climate change and the new geography of violence.* New York: Bold Type Books.
Peters, G.P. 2008. From territorial-based to consumption-based national emission inventories. *Ecological Economics* 65(1): 13–23.
Pohl, L. and E. Swyngedouw. 2021a. The world and the real: Space and the political after Lacan. In F. Landau, L. Pohl, and N. Roskamm (eds.), *(Un)grounding: Post-foundational interventions in space* [transcript]. Berlin, pp. 43–62.
Pohl, L. and E. Swyngedouw 2021b. 'What does not work in the world': The specter of Lacan in critical political theory. *Distinktion: Journal of Social Theory.* https://doi.org/10.1080/1600910X.2021.1872667
Saito, K. 2017. *Karl Marx's ecosocialism: Capital, nature, and the unfinished critique of political economy.* New York: Monthly Review Press.
Schellenberger, M. and T. Nordhaus (eds.). 2011. *Love your monsters: Postenvironmentalism and the Anthropocene.* Oakland, CA: The Breakthrough Institute.
Smith, N. 1984. *Uneven development: Nature, capital and the production of space.* Oxford: Blackwell.
Swyngedouw, E. 2006. Circulations and metabolisms: (Hybrid) natures and (cyborg) cities. *Science as Culture* 15(2): 105–21.
Swyngedouw, E. 2018a. *Promises of the political: Insurgent cities in a post-democratic environment.* Cambridge, MA: MIT Press.
Swyngedouw, E. 2018b. More-than-human constellations as immuno-biopolitical fantasy in the Urbicene. *New Geographies* 9: 18–23.
Swyngedouw, E. 2019. The perverse lure of autocratic post-democracy. *South Atlantic Quarterly* 118(2): 267–86.
Swyngedouw, E. 2021. Illiberalism and the democratic paradox: The infernal dialectic of neoliberal emancipation. *European Journal of Social Theory.* https://doi.org/10.1177/13684310211027079
Swyngedouw, E. 2022a. Climate change consensus: A depoliticized deadlock. In L. Pellizzoni, E. Leonardi, and V. Asara (eds.), *Handbook of critical environmental politics.* London: Edward Elgar.
Swyngedouw, E. 2022b. The unbearable lightness of climate populism. *Environmental Politics* (submitted).
Swyngedouw, E. and M. Kaika. 2014. Urban political ecology: Great promises, deadlock ... and new beginnings? *Documents d'Anàlisi Geogràfica* 60(3): 459–81.
Tzaninis, Y., T. Mandler, M. Kaika, and R. Keil. 2021. Moving urban political ecology beyond the 'urbanization of nature'. *Progress in Human Geography* 45(2): 229–52.
Verhaeghe, P. 2014. *What about me? The struggle for identity in a market-based society.* London: Scribe Publications.
Zupančič, A. 2018. The apocalypse is (still) disappointing. *S: Journal of the Circle for Lacanian Ideology Critique* 10–11(16–20).

2

Urban political ecology versus ecological urbanism

Matthew Gandy

> For the city of the future, the concept of the balanced, stable and diverse city ecosystem needs to be recognized as a goal and planned in both strategic and detailed policies.
>
> (Laurie 1979: xviii)

This interesting call from the landscape designer Ian Laurie is contained in his introduction to a pathbreaking essay collection emerging from a symposium held at the University of Manchester in 1974 that served in many ways as a European counterpart to an earlier conference on the theme of urban nature held in Washington, DC in 1968. Many of the contributors to the Manchester symposium were connected to the nascent scientific sphere of urban ecology and also with established disciplinary domains such as botany, zoology, and landscape architecture. Underpinning the thinking of Laurie and his contemporaries was an interest in how ecological ideas might enhance the liveability and long-term viability of cities. An emphasis on the centrality of nature and ecological processes to the design of better cities has a long history, predating the emergence of ecology itself as a sub-field of the biological sciences, and encompassing various attempts to modify or refashion the human environment through the inclusion of parks, gardens, and elaborate infrastructure systems.

The recent interest in 'ecological urbanism' marks the expanding scope of ecological ideas in architecture, urban planning, and landscape design but also holds significant continuities with these earlier interventions. The idea of nature serving as some kind of blueprint for addressing environmental problems has become an increasingly prominent element in urban sustainability discourse. In many ways Laurie's essay collection highlights an enduring tension in the field of urban ecology and landscape design: on the one hand, many contributors look to patterns and models derived from nature as a way of conceptualising urban form, yet on the other hand, it is clear that much of the reflection from these authors is largely curiosity-driven, and simply rooted in the cultural and scientific fascination of the subject matter. It is arguably in Laurie's own essay on 'urban commons' that this disjuncture becomes most strikingly apparent: here we encounter the contested histories of urban land use that 'has been kept open by and for the people' in the face of multiple threats (Laurie, 1979: 231). An ecological sensibility, and the possibility of creating what Laurie terms 'nature parks' in urban areas, is clearly rooted in specific cultures of nature derived in part from the ecological sciences but is also connected with facets of urban history and attempts to protect vernacular spaces of nature from erasure. In this chapter I want to reflect further on the role, status, and meaning of ecology in urban environmental discourse. In particular I will draw a contrast between an emerging coalescence of scientifically inflected approaches to landscape design under the umbrella term 'ecological urbanism' and the alternative field of 'urban political ecology' that marks an ongoing critical reformulation of relational and structuralist accounts of nature–society relations under capitalist urbanisation. If the former perspective aims to both naturalise and ecologise the urban process, the latter brings the question of nature back within the realm of historical agency and the political parameters of human intentionality.

The origins of urban ecology

The term 'ecology' is now almost ubiquitous in urban environmental discourse, especially in the post-Rio context, with different elements of ecological thinking woven into a wide range of public policy concerns ranging from the protection of biodiversity to the shaping of zero carbon cities. The conceptualisation of urban space as an interdependent set of socio-ecological relationships has now permeated a broad spectrum of professional and scientific domains. Yet the idea of ecology holds a series of different connotations in an urban context: the functionalist reading of ecosystem dynamics has permeated organicist conceptions of urban space at a variety of spatial scales; the epistemological contours of systems-based urban ecology have driven various attempts to produce overarching analytical frameworks for both social and environmental processes; the influence of conservation biology within land-use planning and other fields marks the rise of specific concerns with urban biodiversity; the articulation of critical readings of ecology has opened up new insights into relations between politics and science, that has contributed to the emergence of urban political ecology; and most recently, an emerging interest in posthumanism and the 'multispecies city'. The advent of 'ecological urbanism,' as a design-led intellectual agenda exemplifies the steady diffusion of an 'ecological sensibility' through a succession of professional fields engaged with the shaping of human environments. As the geographer James Evans (2019) emphasises, the rising significance of urban ecology marks the transformation of a previously marginal scientific field into a vibrant focus of debate spanning several interrelated spheres of concern such as biodiversity, infrastructure, resilience, and sustainability. But what is implied by the growing significance of ecology in urban policy and politics? Where did a distinctively ecological conception of urban space originate?

The origins of the modern term 'ecology' lie within the work of the German zoologist Ernst Haeckel, who first used the word in 1866 to refer to environmental influences on the development of individual organisms, yet Haeckel's interest in the interaction between organisms and their environment certainly has earlier roots, especially in the pattern-oriented botanical studies of Alexander von Humboldt and the transformation of natural history into what would become the natural sciences (see Dettelbach, 1996; Krausse, 1987). Humboldt's interest in 'plant sociology', later elaborated by the Swiss botanist Josias Braun-Blanquet and others, provides an intellectual lineage between cartographic techniques such as isometric mapping and the eventual emergence of urban ecology as a distinctive sub-field within both the biological and social sciences. There was always a tension between the emergence of ecology as a field science, in the service of colonial acquisition of territory and resources, and a more curiosity-driven impetus towards the study of relations between organisms in any setting, including urban and industrial areas. At a global scale, for example, the historian Daniela Bleichmar shows how the economic and taxonomic dimensions to imperial botany evolved in tandem, with the European cataloguing of specimens following in the wake of violence and destruction elsewhere (see, for example, Bleichmar, 2018). During the twentieth century the scope of ecology within the biological sciences expanded to acquire a more clearly defined spatial connotation through related terms such as the ecosystem, ecotope, and ecological zone. Under the influence of Frederic Clements, Arthur Tansley, and others, the focus of ecology gradually moved towards various forms of 'human ecology' that have been in consistent tension with alternative vantage points concerned with the functional dynamics of 'natural ecosystems'. Indeed, the recent interventions of the geographer Erle Ellis, in the context of the Anthropocene debate, stem precisely from this sense that the ecological sciences need a radical reorientation towards human modified landscapes (see Ellis et al., 2013).

The use of ecology as an analytical tool for understanding capitalist urbanisation was extended significantly through the work of the Chicago School of urban sociology before its gradual demise from the late 1930s onwards (see Gaziano, 1996). Ideas drawn from vegetation dynamics, and in particular the emphasis on processes of plant invasion and succession, were used to develop a neo-Darwinian model of urban change driven by the competitive outcomes of individual decision-making. It is fair to say, however, that this body of work had little in common with the emerging practice of ecology as a scientific sub-field and also made little contribution to the study of socio-ecological dimensions to urban space. The concept of ecology utilised by the Chicago School rested on a dualistic distinction between society and nature within which models of 'nature' and the presence of 'natural areas' originated outside the urban process as part of a naturalistic framework of analysis (see Wolch et al., 2002). By the 1960s and 1970s the emergence of terms such as 'ecological studies', though related to the Chicago School, marked a more elaborate engagement with quantifiable variables that could be correlated across urban space (see Berry and Kasarda, 1977). Interest in measurement and quantification provided a segue into systems-based models of urban ecology including influential recent contributions such as the Baltimore Ecosystem Study and other metropolitan research programmes. The cartographic impetus behind the modification of ecological approaches within spatial science began to edge closer towards incipient trends within urban ecology as a scientific field, focused on the spatial and ecological dynamics of non-human nature in cities. The growing interest in population dynamics rather than crudely atomistic interpretations of human behaviour also connected with an emerging focus on human ecology, self-regulatory homeostatic systems, and attempts to develop more sophisticated models for the analysis of urban environmental change.

Emerging in parallel with the more abstract concept of ecology, the emphasis on 'urban field science' and the observational paradigms of natural history began to flourish from the nineteenth century onwards. Interest in the distinctive characteristics of urban flora and fauna laid the basis for an ongoing fascination with cities as 'open laboratories' for the study of unusual socio-ecological assemblages and also intimations of a future nature. New insights into urban botany, for example, clearly differed from the emphasis of 'plant sociology' on naturally occurring ecological assemblages that corresponded to either a lack of human influence or to a narrow range of non-metropolitan landscapes. Some botanists, such as Paul Jovet, devoted their research to the ecological characteristics of modern cities while others, such as Paul Duvigneaud, switched emphasis towards urban environments. Duvigneaud, for example, applied insights derived from the study of biomass production in tropical rainforests to the city of Brussels in the 1970s (see Duvigneaud, 1974). Of particular interest in a policy context is Duvigneaud's promotion of a regional ecological imaginary as a means to articulate an environmental rationale for the enhanced status of the Brussels metropolitan agglomeration within the Belgian state (see Danneels, 2021). A contrasting example is provided by the botanist Herbert Sukopp and his colleagues who worked in post-war Berlin, challenging the limitations of plant sociology by exploring the full complexity of urban nature, including the presence of so-called 'weeds' and non-native species. Rather than a focus on biomass, the emphasis of Sukopp and other Berlin-based botanists was on urban biodiversity and the many interesting species that flourished in unusual urban biotopes produced by wartime destruction and geopolitical separation (see Sukopp, 1990). Instead of a regional orientation à la Duvigneaud, the emphasis of Sukopp was on the protection of specific sites of scientific interest as part of the shifting politics of land-use planning away from narrowly technocratic goals such as highway construction or urban renewal. The brief impact of what Jens Lachmund (2013) has referred to as a 'biotope-protection regime' in West Berlin, building on the conceptual insights of Arturo Escobar, marks a unique conjunction between urban ecology, as a methodologically distinctive branch of the biological sciences, and a wider grassroots challenge towards technocratic or narrowly utilitarian forms of urban policymaking. The interface between ecology and urban politics is different in these two examples: for Duvigneaud we could say that the question rested on an enhanced role for science in the management of urban space, not unlike contemporary interest in resilience discourse, whereas for Sukopp the emphasis is only obliquely utilitarian, and is oriented more towards discourses of ecological endangerment and site vulnerability. Or as Jens Lachmund (2020: 27) suggests, 'Duvigneaud was much more assertive than Sukopp in linking his ecology to a broader moral and political vision'. In both cases, however, we contend with an essentially expert-led vision for alternative conceptualisations of urban nature, except that Duvigneaud is oriented towards the generic and quantifiable parameters of a putative urban ecosystem while Sukopp is focused on the relational ecologies of specific organisms (and especially plants).

Despite the direct engagement of Duvigneaud, Sukopp, and other ecologists with aspects of policymaking in the urban arena there were a number of methodological and political uncertainties surrounding the interface between science and politics. The ecological models never strayed far from a largely positivist (or at least empiricist) conception of socio-ecological relations within which the political context for environmental degradation and the role of human agency in the production of space remained ill-defined. The emphasis on metabolic or systems-based conceptions of the urban environmental field has if anything become more dominant since the 1970s and 1980s. A pluralist conception of urban political discourse as a melee of competing 'stakeholders' now predominates much of the policy-oriented or practice-based literature. The earlier fascination with the measurement of biomass or flows has been radically extended as part of a quantitative ecological paradigm that aligns with a range of comparative indices to track the progress of individual municipalities towards a post-carbon future.

The rise of urban political ecology

An alternative intellectual lineage to the dominance of systems-based conceptualisations of urban ecology is to be found in the body of work widely referred to as 'urban political ecology' that began to take shape during the 1990s. Although urban political ecology shares significant conceptual roots with the emergence of neo-Marxian approaches to political ecology in the Global South there are other important elements including Frankfurt School-inspired critiques of bourgeois environmentalism and radical strands of urban history (see, for example, Gandy, 2022; Görg, 2011; Trepl, 1996). Early contributions to urban political ecology stressed the co-evolutionary dynamics of capital circulation and the production of the built environment. In the influential essay collection *In the nature of cities: Urban political ecology and the politics of urban metabolism*, published in 2006, for example, the editors Nik Heynen, Maria Kaika, and Erik Swyngedouw set out a 'manifesto' for urban political ecology comprising several key elements: an emphasis on the co-evolutionary dimensions to social and environmental change; a relational conception of nature that drew in particular from the critique of nature–culture dualisms; an expanded conception of urban metabolism and the circulatory dynamics of urban space, that contrasted with organicist or systems-based formulations; an engagement with the intersections between power and social difference within the urban arena, including connections with the nascent field of environmental justice; an expanded critique of technocratic policy discourse; and an emphasis on the democratisation of environmental policymaking (see Heynen et al., 2006). Yet what is striking about this definition of the field, published more than 15 years ago, is that the science of ecology itself plays a relatively minor role (see Gandy, 2022). The interdisciplinary impetus of urban political ecology from this earlier wave of work did not come from the biophysical sciences, apart from important exceptions in fields such as urban epidemiology. In particular S. Harris Ali and Roger Keil (2008: 10) stressed the 'dialectical interaction' of globalisation and urbanisation in the wake of the SARS outbreak of 2003, and raised a series of prescient observations about new and emerging diseases, including zoonotic dangers from the extractive frontiers of global capital. Roger Keil, for example, drawing on his public health research, developed the notion of post-Westphalian or 'transnational urbanism' in relation to 'a new global urban political ecology' (Keil, 2011: 720).

Another interesting contribution to the urban political ecology literature at this time is the careful delineation of the 'turfgrass subject' by Paul Robbins and Julie Sharp as a situated investigation into lawns, consumption, and non-sustainable urbanism. Their study of the political economy of the lawn chemical industry segues into a reflection on the agency of lawns influenced in part by actor–network theory and wider reflections on the 'active role of natural objects in capitalized ecosystems' (Robbins and Sharp, 2006: 123). The work of Robbins and Sharp prefigures elements of the neo-vitalist challenge to human subjectivities but holds onto the social and historical specificities of power.

Unity and dissonance in urban ecological discourse

Since the contours of urban political ecology first became apparent in the 1990s the wider field of urban ecology has developed significantly, including an increasing role for ethology, evolutionary biology, and ever more ambitious attempts to articulate some form of epistemological unity across the social and biophysical sciences. The term ecology has multiplied in terms of its rhetorical and analytical associations. The combined challenges of climate change and the sixth mass extinction have heralded a radical extension of ecological discourse within the urban arena as specific targets for biodiversity, carbon emissions, and other goals have become woven into legislative and political objectives for policy and design.

The recent emergence of 'ecological urbanism' within landscape design discourse is indicative of an expanded discursive field for contemporary ecology. By way of intellectual bricolage, for example, the architectural theorist and former Dean of Harvard's Graduate School of Design, Mohsen Mostafavi, presents a case for ecological urbanism as an expanded design programme based on new levels of flexibility and responsiveness. At a conceptual level Mostafavi presents ecological urbanism as a natural outgrowth of the 'ecosophic problematic' of Félix Guattari and his elaboration of Gregory Bateson's critique of neo-Darwinian thinking. There is a radical interdisciplinarity in play that is marked by an emphasis on 'the articulation of the interface, the liminal space, between the urban and the political' (Mostafavi, 2010: 48). The conceptual agenda for ecological urbanism shares significant conceptual and institutional continuities with the earlier emergence of 'landscape urbanism' as a synthesis between landscape and urban design (see Mostafavi, 2010; Steiner, 2011). Other significant influences include the 'landscape ecology' programme initiated by Richard T.T. Forman with his emphasis on 'patch dynamics' and the Baltimore Ecosystem

Study, which is strongly rooted in earlier systems-based approaches to urban ecology (see Grove et al., 2015). For the urban designer Anne Whiston Spirn (2014: 557), who aligns 'ecological urbanism' with her own previous work, this emerging paradigm 'weds the theory and practice of urban design and planning, as a means of adaptation, with the insights of ecology and other environmental disciplines'. Spirn (2014: 557) emphasises that the adoption of this framework is 'critical to the future of the city' in order to tackle the twin challenges of climate change and environmental justice. Yet Spirn's avowedly Eurocentric framing of the field – connecting with Vitruvius, Alberti, and Olmsted among others – belies an uncertainty about the political parameters of capitalist urbanisation. As a result, we are confronted with a naturalisation of the urban process that requires the adaptation of 'urban form to natural process' rather than an emphasis on structural change in human societies (Spirn, 2014: 569). In defining the city as an ecosystem there is a radical disjuncture between urban space and human history. By supplanting politics by design the urban arena is reduced to a series of intersecting flows, cycles, and material elements. The programmatic aims of ecological urbanism are clearly geared towards the alignment of design, and landscape design in particular, with the emerging emphasis on resilience discourse under the 'adaptive Anthropocene'.

Ecological urbanism presents an interdisciplinary agenda for future cities that is marked by a degree of epistemological convergence between fields such as ecology, economics, engineering, social psychology, and other forms of knowledge that lie broadly outside the domain of critical theory. In keeping with the wider insistence on the need for a form of radical interdisciplinarity exemplified by the entomologist E.O. Wilson's use of the term 'consilience' there is a palpable sense of impatience with forms of nuance or complexity that might challenge 'self-evident' dimensions to urban environmental discourse. This is, above all, a client-oriented ecological discourse that is more revealing about the institutional context for landscape design than it is about the environmental phenomena under investigation.

The emphasis on urban resilience has emerged out of attempts to effectively depoliticise capitalist urbanisation. The question of design has become a focal point for reframing political questions as a series of technical challenges. The difficulty, however, is that despite yearly conferences held under the United Nations Framework Convention on Climate Change, including Kyoto in 1997, Copenhagen in 2009, and Paris in 2016, the pace of environmental degradation has markedly worsened. The emerging emphasis on the adaptive Anthropocene merely resituates the global environmental crisis as a matter for enhanced forms of human ingenuity, the need for 'smart' changes in land use, or the construction of vast geo-engineering projects.

Conclusions

There is a growing sense of anticipation that cities will make a major contribution to achieving global environmental policy goals. In particular, there is an expectation that international networks of cities, spearheaded by charismatic mayors, might take on nation-states, the fossil fuel industry, and successfully transform patterns of consumption and everyday life. Yet this network-based conceptualisation of urban environmental discourse, which emphasises forms of policy innovation, tends to overlook the historical dynamics of urban political mobilisation. The sharing of 'best practice' in the field of design, for example, is a very different kind of policy legacy to that offered by urban social movements, campaigns for environmental justice, and other forms of grassroots intervention.

The COVID-19 public health crisis has again exposed the tensions between a design-oriented urban discourse and the political parameters of structural health inequalities and corporeal vulnerabilities. Speculation over the possible characteristics of the 'post-COVID city' has highlighted themes such as walkability, homeworking, and the enhancement of green spaces but there has been much less emphasis on the networked dimensions to urbanisation that connect with capitalist agriculture or extractive frontiers where zoonotic 'spillover events' may occur. The 'COVID mirage' of tranquil cities under lockdown has instilled a renewed confidence in the possibilities for ecological design. Similarly, reduced levels of international travel have contributed to a temporary dip in global fossil fuel emissions. At the same time, however, the COVID-19 pandemic has swept through community after community, especially in the Global South, exposing pre-existing patterns of poverty and ill health. The fetishisation of the 'ecological city' and its cultural modalities of aesthetics and design works against an understanding of global health threats.

The tension between varieties of ecological urbanism and the ongoing development of urban political ecology is illuminating. A recourse to design as the focal point for urban policymaking cannot advance beyond various forms of behavioural, organisational, or technological change that effectively obscure the underlying dynamics of environmental degradation. Nineteenth-century concerns with 'urban beautification' and the ameliorative effects of contact with nature are alive and well. The figure of the expert – whether scientist or designer – remains pre-eminent in a wider choreography of ecologically framed spatial interventions. What urban political ecology offers in contrast is a focus on the power relations and historical contingencies that underpin the dynamics of capitalist urbanisation. The use of ecology as a cultural resource for political mobilisation is problematised rather than valorised.

References

Ali, S.H. and R. Keil. 2008. Introduction. In S.H. Ali and R. Keil (eds.), *Networked disease: Emerging infections in the global city*. Oxford: Wiley-Blackwell, pp. 10–12.
Berry, B.J.L. and J.D. Kasarda. 1977 *Contemporary urban ecology*. New York: Macmillan.
Bleichmar, D. 2018. Botanical conquistadors. In H.A. Curry, N. Jardine, J.A. Secord, and E.C. Spary (eds.), *Worlds of natural history*. Cambridge: Cambridge University Press, pp. 236–54.
Danneels, K. 2021. *From sociobiology to urban metabolism: The interaction of urbanism, science, and politics in Brussels (1900–1978)*. PhD Thesis, University of Antwerp and KU Leuven.
Dettelbach, M. 1996. Humboldtian science, in N. Jardine, A. Secord, and E.C. Spary (eds.), *Cultures of natural history*. Cambridge: Cambridge University Press, pp. 287–384.
Duvigneaud, P. 1974. Étude écologique de l'écosystème urbain bruxellois: 1. L'écosystème 'urbs'. *Mémoires de la Société Royale de Botanique de Belgique* 6: 5–35.
Ellis, E.C., J.O. Kaplan, D.Q. Fuller, S. Vavrus, K.K. Goldewijk, and P.H. Verburg. 2013. Used planet: A global history. *Proceedings of the National Academy of Sciences* 110(20): 7978–85.
Evans, J. 2019. Ecology in the urban century: Power, place, and the abstraction of nature. In H. Ernston and S. Sörlin (eds.), *Grounding urban natures: Histories and futures of urban ecologies*. Cambridge: MIT Press, pp. 303–22.
Gandy, M. 2022. Urban political ecology: A critical reconfiguration. *Progress in Human Geography* 46(1): 21–43.
Gaziano, E. 1996. Ecological metaphors as scientific boundary work: innovation and authority in interwar sociology and biology. *American Journal of Sociology* 101(4): 874–907.
Görg, C. 2011. Societal relationships with nature: A dialectical approach to environmental politics. In A. Biro (ed.), *Critical ecologies: The Frankfurt School and contemporary environmental crisis*. Toronto: University of Toronto Press, pp. 43–72.
Grove, J.M., M.L. Cadenasso, S.T. Pickett, G.E. Machlis, and W.R. Burch. 2015. *The Baltimore school of urban ecology: Space, scale, and time for the study of cities*. New Haven, CT: Yale University Press.
Heynen, N., M. Kaika, and E. Swyngedouw (eds.). 2006. *In the nature of cities: Urban political ecology and the politics of urban metabolism*. London: Routledge.
Keil, R. 2011. Transnational urban political ecology: Health and infrastructure in the unbounded city. In G. Bridge and S. Watson (eds.), *The new Blackwell companion to the city*. Oxford: Wiley-Blackwell, pp. 713–25.
Krausse, E. 1987. *Ernst Haeckel*. Leipzig: B.G. Teubner.
Lachmund, J. 2013. *Greening Berlin: The co-production of science, politics, and urban nature*. Cambridge, MA: MIT Press.
Lachmund, J. 2020. The metabolic city and the city of biotopes: Paul Duvigneaud and Herbert Sukopp. In M. Gandy and S. Jasper (eds.), *The botanical city*. Berlin: Jovis, pp. 22–9.
Laurie, I.C. (ed.) 1979. *Nature in cities: The natural environment in the design and development of green space*. Chichester: John Wiley, 1979.

Mostafavi, M. 2010. Why ecological urbanism? Why now? In M. Mostafavi and G. Doherty (eds.), *Ecological urbanism*. Basel: Lars Müller Publishers, pp. 12–55.

Robbins, P. and J. Sharp. 2006. Turfgrass subjects: The political economy of urban monoculture. In N. Heynen, M. Kaika, and E. Swyngedouw (eds.), *In the nature of cities: Urban political ecology and the politics of urban metabolism*. London: Routledge, pp. 110–28.

Spirn, A.W. 2014. Ecological urbanism: A framework for the design of resilient cities. In F.O. Ndubisi (ed.), *The ecological design and planning reader*. Washington, DC: Island Press, pp. 557–71.

Steiner, F. 2011. Landscape ecological urbanism: origins and trajectories. *Landscape and Urban Planning* 100: 333–7.

Sukopp, H. (ed.). 1990. *Stadtökologie*. Berlin: Dietrich Reimer.

Trepl, L. 1996. City and ecology. *Capitalism, nature, socialism* 7(2): 85–94.

Wolch, J., S. Pincetl, and L. Pulido. 2002. Urban nature and the nature of urbanism. In M. Dear (ed.), *From Chicago to LA: Making sense of urban theory*. Thousand Oaks, CA: Sage, pp. 369–402.

3

Towards the urban-natural: Notes on urban utopias from the decolonial turn

Roberto Luís Monte-Mór and Ester Limonad

> If money, according to Angier (1842), 'comes into the world with a congenital blood-stain on one cheek,' capital comes dripping from head to foot, from every pore, with blood and dirt.
>
> (Marx, 1990 [1867]: 656)

In the present world scenario, Marx's statement remains sharply actual, highlighting the urgency of advancing a human emancipation project that strengthens social solidarity, grassroots, other economies, other social relations of production, other forms of producing social (and differential) space, and mainly other forms of everyday life capable of confronting destructive capitalist accumulation.

Imagining emancipatory alternatives is crucial to giving up dogmatic and ideological postulates that legitimate domination and exploitation without contemplating social needs and hindering changes. However, any project addressing social transformation must strive for utopia,[1] now more than ever. But not any utopia, since only a utopia free of myths may serve as an orientation for other socio-spatial practices, enabling a move towards another society and a differential space (Lefebvre, 1991).

Bloch's (2004) concrete utopia[2] has its base on social life with an immanent referential in the reality of the present, in the here and now, in the perspective of building another society, where the utopian future glimpsed never materialises but is in permanent re-elaboration. So, only the unfinished dream can be rigorously designated as utopia once 'in its conciseness and new rigor this expression means as much as a methodical tool for the novelty, an objective condensation of what is to come' (Bloch, 2004: 196). Hence, utopia gains a political dimension and a different meaning, allowing it to become something more complex, as a north for social action, neither as a determinant nor as a plan, nor even as a prescription of pre-established goals. The path towards what is to come is to be built during its course, and not *ex ante*.

Indeed, what seems impossible and utopian today might be reinterpreted as possible, concrete, and experimental, and eventually become an instrumental response to the present societal planetary crises. Lefebvre proposes to turn the impossible into the possible since

> theory explores the possible/impossible and declares that 'one must' (a theoretical imperative, not an ethical one) want the impossible in order to realize the possible. Nothing closer to and nothing further from the possible. Utopia therefore assumes an urgent character. Urgent utopia defines a style of thinking turned toward the possible in all areas.
>
> (Lefebvre, 2009: 287–8)

Following Bloch's (2004) and Lefebvre's (2000) propositions, an open, bottom-up utopian project to disclose a path into a possible future is mandatory, demanding other spatial practices to overcome the society–nature rupture imposed by Western European modernity.

Utopian proposals forage the ground with social transformation seeds full of new possibilities. From such a reasoning, a concrete urban-natural tissue, superseding and redefining the current urban-industrial tissue, emerges as an urban utopia and as a possibility of experimentation and transformation of everyday life, as an ongoing citizen training, a social awareness experimentation process that concerns spatial practices, subversion, and instrumentalisation (Randolph, 2015, 2016) in order to allow a differential space to come to life (Lefebvre, 1991).

From these perspectives, our intention is to talk about an urban-natural virtuality as a breakthrough from the present hegemonic urban-industrial society, moving towards the urban utopia envisioned by Lefebvre in close relation to Bloch's concrete utopias. Moving forward towards an urban-natural possible future calls both for spatial and social justice, as well as a continuing critical theory effort to offer some possible answers following the trail opened by Swyngedouw (1996), Heynen et al. (2006), Keil et al. (1998), Keil and Graham (1998), Desfor and Keil (2004), among many others.

Hence, we will perform here a theoretical exercise to imagine and elaborate on some current urban-natural seeds capable of pointing towards alternative society–nature relations aiming to construct more just societal utopian projects.

Assuming the urban-natural as a necessary step towards urban utopia, as a starter, we must clarify where it comes from. The urban-natural idea comes to mind first as an 'extended naturalisation' idea, taken to be a necessary complement to an 'extended urbanisation' that redefines life space itself (Monte-Mór, 2014a [1994], 2018a). Therefore, the urban-natural should be seen, initially, as an outcome of the centripetal movement of nature coming to meet along its own ways, dialectically, the urban-industrial tissue centrifugal movement onto the countryside, virtually encompassing the totality of social space – and natural space as a whole. The increasing blurring of the city's and the countryside's boundaries and characteristics, as extended urbanisation develops in space, seems to express those various and diverse encounters.

Extended urbanisation, as it encounters and reorganises social space in multiple ways, also appears as a terrain of possibilities for post-capitalist transition. The urban tissue and its inherent urban-industrial relations go beyond the city's agglomeration, taking over the territory and making room for the emergence of urban-natural socio-spatial forms and processes that stem from suppressing and overcoming the town-and-country dichotomy. Tzaninis et al. (2021) contend that there are many avenues for understanding urban political ecology in relation to the various new urban forms and processes of extended sub/urbanisation (Limonad, 2002, 2005).

Difference, diversity, and dispersion, as well as the proliferation of various urban centralities, are significant features of extended urbanisation. They embrace urban archipelagos and metropolitan suburbs extending onto the countryside, from forests and savannahs to towns, villages and multiple centralities (Monte-Mór, 1988, 2014b; Limonad, 1991). All of them contain today, in varying ways, degrees, grades and intensities, the seeds of the urban interacting with nature – as a quality, as a social relation (Lefebvre, 2000; Limonad, 2010; Limonad and Monte-Mór, 2015).

Following Lefebvre's (2009:179) proposition that 'there is today, especially in the domain that concerns us, no theory without utopia', together with Bloch's (2004) conception of concrete utopia as an engine of social transformation, we understand that the production of another social space, a differential space (Lefebvre, 1991), demands other conceptions (representations of space) and social imaginaries (spaces of representation) embedded in other spatial practices.

From a contemporary Latin American angle, issues related to urban utopias and urban-natural possibilities should be approached from a critical perspective concerning modernity and coloniality. The current 'decolonial turn' has brought an awareness and a sense of urgency to deconstruct colonial forms of domination, of power, of thoughts and representations of the world we live in. It opens a horizon of emancipation from previous colonialism, distinguishing it from the present coloniality of power, social existence, and knowledge, offering a rich ensemble of approaches (Escobar, 1995, 1997; Mignolo, 2000; Maldonado-Torres, 2007; Grosfoguel, 2008; Ballestrin, 2013; Acosta, 2016; Coraggio, 2018, among others). Yet, our attention will focus mainly on Walsh's (2005a, 2005b, 2010) and Quijano's (2000, 2014) contributions. Walsh's (2005a: 24) interculturality looms within the decolonial turn as a non-institutionalised bottom-up social practice.

As such, it constitutes a means of creating radically different conditions of existence, knowledge, and power (Quijano, 2000). It could also contribute to building gradually distinct societies and breaking the 'vicious infernal circle' (Lefebvre, 1991: 82) imposed by capital over spaces, bodies, and daily life rhythms.

From this standpoint, Quijano's (2000) decolonial turn and Walsh's (2005a, 2005b, 2010) approach to interculturality kind of converge towards Lefebvre's and Bloch's conceptions of utopia. Such convergence allows us to comprehend interculturality as an alternate spatial practice in construction, as a virtuality and part of an utopian project that may lead to enhancing and strengthening urban-natural spatial practices and, at last, a differential space.

Moving further into the search for the urban-natural and virtual urban utopias entails at least some steps. A first one leads to utopia, urban utopias, the urban-natural, and nature itself. A second one relates to Western modernity's illusion and other conceptions, and a third one enhances the transforming role of everyday life alongside alternative ways of producing material life and social existence. A dialogue between Lefebvre and the decolonial turn, bridging interculturality and differential space, taken from Limonad (2021), appears as an intriguing option for the second step since the decolonial turn has a complementary 'natural-colonial turn' that attempts 'to read and narrate the epic of modernity through its obverse, from its silenced dimensions' (Alimonda, 2019: 118). Moreover, the decolonial turn allows surpassing the ideologisation and reduction of nature to land and resources, once essential to capitalism and the European modernity project of colonising other countries and worlds as if they had no former history and past (Said, 1980). As there is a match between Quijano's approach, Walsh's interculturality, and Lefebvre's differential space, it may highlight everyday life and other ways of producing it that may make possible the society–nature (re)encounter towards an utopian urban-natural project.

Introducing the urban-natural

Talking about the urban-natural means exploring a terrain of possible transformative social relations, standing out as experimental and concrete utopia seeds. Initially, this endeavour demands some methodological demarcations to clarify our understanding of urban-natural meanings and their implications.

The urban-natural equation may comprise three terms (urban, rural, and natural) and include mediations among town, country, and nature. But it implies a transformed and produced nature, for nature as such escapes the hold of rationality pursued action, as well as from domination and appropriation. More precisely, it remains outside of these influences: it 'is' what flees: it is reached by the imaginary [...] The countryside is the place of production and *oeuvres*.

(Lefebvre, 2000: 118)

The urban-natural as a virtuality implies neither a merge nor an effective synthesis but a convergence where the three terms (town, country and nature) meet, mediated by the urban tissue. Following Lefebvre (1996: 165),

> a virtuality which is outlined but realized only at the *limit*. This limit is not somewhere in the infinite, and yet it can be reached by successive leaps and bounds. It is impossible to settle in it and to establish it as an accomplished reality.

Thus, the urban-natural concerns the slow construction of a virtual object that manifests through alternate spatial practices (mediations), which to different degrees integrate the three terms of the equation (urban, rural, and natural).

Then, where do the rural and the countryside stand in the urban-natural equation? While nature resists, here and there, pervading social spaces, what about the countryside and the rural? The urban-industrial fabric has colonised both. The countryside lost the rural and peasant quality, it has been ravaged by the urban. For Lefebvre (2000: 158) 'this urbanized countryside opposes itself to a dispossessed rurality, the extreme case of the deep misery of the inhabitant, the habitat, of to inhabit. Are the rights to nature and to the countryside not destroying themselves?'

Indeed, there is no more a coincidence among urban and rural as qualities (essence) with the landscapes (forms) city and countryside (Limonad, 2010; Limonad and Monte-Mór, 2015), the urban pervades the countryside, and the rural pervades the city. Therefore,

> there is no more question of isolating the points of space and time, of considering separately activities and functions, or of studying apart from each other behaviours or images, distributions and relations. These various aspects of social production, that of the city and urban society, are situated in relation to a framework of explanation and forecasting.

(Lefebvre, 2000: 174–5)

About urban utopias and the urban-natural

It may be worth clarifying that we conceive of the urban-natural as a set of transformative alternatives (spatial practices) to overcome the urban-industrial, towards an equitable society and a differential space, following Lefebvre's and Bloch's assumptions. The urban-natural as such is neither plainly urban nor utterly natural. Rather, it implies a social appropriation of nature within urbanised space in opposition to capitalist domination. It thus also implies the rescuing of use value within everyday life as opposed to the current overall domination of exchange value that characterises abstract space. It also implies the emergence of the urban era, following the industrial era, in which the central focus on economic growth and capital accumulation gives room to a focus on everyday life and collective reproduction (Lefebvre, 1999; Monte-Mór, 2018a). Therefore, it comprises several spatial practices, which could be viewed as a possible mediation for transforming daily life, thereby creating the conditions for the emergence of another space, a differential space, and a transformative society.

An alternative path to urban utopias – including the urban-natural – must overcome the colonisation of social life, knowledge and techniques, and thus surpass hegemonic ideologies and idealisations proper to the industrial period. It equally requires looking for answers from already existing alternative ways of producing material life and spatial practices supported by other society–nature relationships embedded in everyday life, despite the worldwide encompassing expansion of capitalism that tends to subsume all and everything.

Such germs of interaction, named here urban-natural, herald a (re)encounter of society and nature, a (re)encounter that must be supported by other social relations, other social organisations, other economies, fostering social solidarity and promoting collective life commonness.

However, nowadays we could say that not even a pristine natural nature exists.[3] But then, what can nature be for us? Is it totality itself, something that encompasses the whole world and in which we are embedded as an integral part of it, as several traditional cosmologies understand it to be?

From a bioecological standpoint, nature encompasses all elements necessary to maintain life and how human (and non-human) beings live, inhabit, eat, and produce all material life. All we do and are has to do with nature. Theoretically, nature is a social construct, a social conception, a representation conceived and imagined whose meaning changes in time and space (Limonad, 2004). As each society produces its own space and representations of space (Lefebvre, 1991), it also produces its representations of nature (hegemonic and subaltern) founded on its spatial practices and in the living social imaginary (spaces of representations), and such representations shape society–nature relations across time and space. Nevertheless, different conceptions of nature involve distinctive relationships between society and nature, as well as between humanity and nature, entailing different rankings among them. With Kaika and Swyngedouw (2014), we must now think of an 'urbanisation of nature itself', wherein humans and non-humans are connected by a myriad of elements, from water to chemicals and viruses. Dialectically, however, we must also think of a 'naturalisation of the urban itself', through which everyday life space becomes (re)embedded in nature in its many manifestations. Silva (2017), for example, argues that to better envision Amazonia's development alternatives one must think of a process of 'socialisation of nature'. Many more citations and theoretical proposals could be mentioned to demonstrate how widespread and diverse current concerns about the relationship between the urban (and the regional) and nature are asking to become in contemporary days.

Productive forces development and the complexification of social organisation change the ways of appropriation and domination of nature. The theological vein stretches from a magical understanding of nature to a divine one represented by a pantheon of natural elements and forces' deities. From that followed a conception of humanity and nature as an abstract deity creation, within which humans were always a part of, or subsumed into, nature. Natural rhythms thus regulated daily social life. Finally, Western Enlightenment and Modernity gave birth to an anthropocentric vision of nature as a resource to be conquered, subsuming it to humankind's power and will, changing the relationship between society and nature in space and time, and forcing them apart.

Thus, progressively, nature became alien to daily life, transformed from common good into commodities to respond to market needs.

Notwithstanding, nature is seemingly apart from daily life, and it remains within social spaces often reduced to one of its features (land, water, air, fauna, or flora) or unidentified as such, since it is commodified and/or degraded. Kaika (2005: 24) remarks that 'the proliferation of entities of ambiguous nature that are neither purely "natural" nor purely "nonnatural" becomes more and more the "normal" outcome of modernity's production processes'. For, as a commodity, nature integrates modern social life and after being consumed and processed, it is often externalised and discarded as dirt, unnatural and evil.

Once everything is also a part of the (urban-industrial) built environment production, which intermingles both natural and social elements, why should even a degraded nature, comprising contaminated brownfield soils, rivers converted into sewage, and everything else, not be seen as nature (Limonad, 2004)?

Santos (2021 [1996]) gives us a clue when he talks about a changing produced milieu. A technical, scientific (and today, informational) milieu resulting from the social relations of production and technical development implies accordingly a transformed natural nature that renews itself as a diversified, socialised, and produced nature, where each diversification ensues another one, in a dialectical move where human action intervenes and whose result is a social and natural space. Such produced nature comprises all kinds of nature.

Hence, if the urban – stemming here from the adjective for the city[4] – also encompasses a produced nature, although it is seemingly apart from nature, then it is admissible to say that a produced nature has endured within social spaces, in cities and in the countryside, in many modified forms. Nevertheless, why does such produced nature seem invisible and apart from the social space, as if there were no connections between them? According to Polanyi (2001: 187), economic life organisation relies upon factors of production indistinguishable from human and nature relationship, 'and yet to separate land from man and to organize society in such a way as to satisfy the requirements of a real-estate market was a vital part of the Utopian concept of a market economy'. Consequently, this produced nature (even degraded) becomes apparently invisible inasmuch as it is not recognised by many as nature (Limonad, 2004). Then (re)encountering the urban-natural presumes to rescue the many forms and manifestations of the transformed produced nature within the urban as a whole. Furthermore, such a step demands decolonising the reflection on nature, as well as the search for other society–nature relationships beyond economic development and Western modernity illusions (Monte-Mór and Ray, 1995).

To conceive of an urban-natural tissue that redefines or supersedes the urban-industrial tissue also implies embracing other society–nature relations, a more human and equitable development (Limonad, 2004, 2021; Monte-Mór, 2018a, 2018b). It also requires overcoming the paradigm based on the 'universal and dominant regime of the market as the measure of all things, as the organizing principle of the globalized world and the very meaning of human existence' (Leff, 2008: 33). It entails going beyond the improvement of the population's living conditions and increasing accessibility to goods, equipment, and services. Therefore, another development and another paradigm require the recognition and appraisal of social diversity, territorial specificities, difference and identity affirmations, a non-colonial society–nature relationship, and a more profound and more respectful attitude toward different social forms of existence, knowledge, and know-how (Limonad, 2021).

Thus, to deal with the urban-natural it is imperative to understand it as a concrete utopia with several experimental manifestations. Following Bloch's conception of a changing concrete utopia, the urban-natural ought not to be defined now and be frozen as a concept for a possible future, since it must be (re)elaborated every now and then, nor should it be plastered into a closed theoretical conception, since concepts usually stifle and restrain social spatial practices within a straightjacket, often resulting in an estrangement between concepts and practices (as in coloniality). Following Gramsci's idea (1994: 20) that 'in order to act, man needs to be able to predict things, at least in part', they must have an aim to guide their actions; and he adds further:

> it can only be an idea, or moral principle. The inherent defect of utopias is this: believing that a vision of future can be a vision of factual details, whereas it can only be a vision of principles, or of juridical maxims.

So, to move towards the urban-natural, we must deal with notions and ideas to guide spatial practices. Notions, taken as systematised ideas, must guide and also emerge from concrete needs and practices related to everyday urban life. These ideas (and notions) may change, as do everyday life and spatial practices. As it happens, what should be a possible urban-natural embedded in these novel spaces of representation is (re)defined at each moment.

Furthermore, the urban-natural that emerges from spatial practices and social life as an experimental and concrete utopia, intermingling Lefebvre's idea of an experimental utopia with Bloch's out of reach concrete utopia, must be understood as an encounter of differences, of distinctive qualities, times, rhythms, and cultures. Thus, in order to grasp the urban-natural complexity, it is essential to decolonise our minds to overcome colonial illusions that turn invisible current expressions of the urban-natural that endure amid capitalism and extended urbanisation.

Approaching urban-natural alternative paths

To think about urban-natural alternatives concerns envisioning other society–nature relations and a more equitable society that contemplates difference. Such a task requires decolonising daily life and overcoming present coloniality. It also involves imagining other modernities and developments, beyond the crystallised Western bourgeois model (Monte-Mór and Ray, 1995). For Quijano (2000), if the idea of modernity comes from novelty, rational, scientific, and secular advance with all its unfoldings, then it would be an immanent phenomenon in any society at any time. Henceforth, it seems essential to make an effort to combine different points of view, to reach new levels of understanding, and to explore in-depth alternative proposals that are embedded in daily life practices, especially practices that may enable us to bring forth changes towards more progressive, democratic, alternative, and egalitarian futures. Anyway, this should be done from a critical perspective because 'everyday life under capitalism is permeated with utopian possibilities and strivings, of both reactionary and progressive variants and with foreboding, benign or emancipatory ramifications' (Brenner, 2001: 802).

Now, the decolonisation of everyday life is pressing, for 'the State unifies all forms, that of exchange and of the commodity, that of contracts, that of laws. Homogenising, identitarian, the State crushes that which resists it; it makes differences disappear' (Lefebvre, 2001: 774), as simultaneously it covers up and masks social classes. However, alongside the State is the media, institutions, and corporations, which extend their representations and power, deeply penetrating daily life on various scales. For Lefebvre (2001: 774):

> Once constituted, this State functions as a system. It reproduces itself in reproducing the relations of domination; it has at its disposal an unlimited power to constrain its citizens; it can therefore paralyze all their initiatives. Such is the danger that menaces the modern world and against which it is necessary to struggle at all costs. There is no 'good State'; today there is no State that can avoid moving towards this logical outcome: the State Mode of Production; that's why the only criterion of democracy is the prevention of such an outcome.

Nevertheless, there is hope to avoid such a dystopian outcome. During the last two decades, in countless countries of the Global South, several alternative proposals[5] have emerged that, besides sharing a criticism on the various aspects of economic development, favour the social character of development to encourage and strengthen human potentialities, capacities, and needs regarding their relations with nature, characterised by some as sustainable human development. Although some contribute to citizen emancipation by offering alternatives for self-managed production, most of them remain linked to the capitalist logic without reaching its fundamental contradictions. Furthermore, as these alternatives are institutionalised by the State and imposed on society as a whole, they become associated to alien ideas turning them, as with 'buen vivir', into 'another discursive tool and co-opted term, functional to the State and its structures and with little significance for real intercultural, interepistemic, and plurinational transformation' (Walsh, 2010: 20).

Here, Walsh's (2005b, 2010) interculturality approach stands out, as it refers to a complex framework of equitable interactions in multiple ways, involving social relations, negotiations, and cultural exchanges, without reifying, mystifying, or seeing identities as unshakeable ethnic attributes. Interculturality's main feature is its alternate, permanent under-construction procedural character, not constituting a product in itself, but rather a bottom-up practice of another way of being, thinking, and acting, which is built in the political game, little by little, within the daily practices of non-hegemonic groups, standing against its institutionalisation by the State. In addition, as interculturality questions consecrated hegemonic premises, it may be feasible to reconstruct and make visible other logics and ways of thinking that the dominant power seeks to render invisible, crush, eliminate, control, and hide. Furthermore, as an ethnic, strategic, and political confrontation with the hegemonic production of knowledge, interculturality is kind of an expression of a war of position (Gramsci, 1971). So, it might have the potential to create conditions for the emergence of an urban-natural related to other knowledges, other ways of living and other society–nature relationships, allowing for the production of a differential space, which demands other spatial representations and practices (Lefebvre, 1991) with the permanent (re)formulation of a project for another society, founded in the here and now (Bloch, 2004).

Interculturality must be considered, together with the 'buen vivir' original paradigm, as a non-institutionalised practice insofar as it bears a different ethical posture, comprehending nature as part of social life, which goes against the current society–nature relationship, based on its plundering and dilapidation on a global industrial scale. In its original conception,

> buen vivir denotes, organizes, and constructs a system of knowledge and living based on the communion of humans and nature and on the spatial-temporal-harmonious totality of existence. That is, on the necessary interrelation of beings, knowledges, logics, and rationalities of thought, action, existence, and living.
>
> (Walsh, 2010: 18)

The interaction 'buen vivir' – interculturality, as a spatial practice under construction – is an exciting perspective to elaborate on other spatial practices and empower non-hegemonic social groups since it can allow changes in social and political relations and forward an alternate paradigm of human development and sustainability. A paradigm capable of contributing to the production of other representations of space and differential space. Due to its feature as a lived practice of socio-ecological transformation, 'buen vivir' is not only a movement to take back the economy and economic development in alternative ways, but it also promotes, encourages, and connects with solidarity and joint movements on different scales (Sparn, 2019).

On the colonisation of knowledge, everyday life, and the society–nature relation

Each society's representations of space and nature, hegemonic and/or subversive, pervade spatial practices, mediating the relations that humans establish among themselves and with nature to ensure their material reproduction

(Limonad, 2004). Likewise, such representations embed know-how, the social imaginary, and the very production of knowledge, colonising social space with artefacts as an explicit manifestation of power to meet certain strategic ends (Lacoste, 1975: 198).

From a historical angle, confronting different world conceptions and cultures denotes a struggle for hegemony, endowing a nation's dominance over others, imposing an alien way of social existence, doing, and thinking, obliterating languages, world conceptions, and native cultures (Gramsci, 1971). Western European modernity has its roots in Latin American coloniality, it is argued today (Mignolo, 2000; Maldonado-Torres, 2007). Though emerging as a horizon for overcoming coloniality (present and past), Western modernity promises also to fulfil capitalism's demands to maintain the exploitation structures that warrant its primitive accumulation conditions (Luxemburg, 2015). The modernity project pursued in capitalism is dialectical, contradictory, and often incomplete (Habermas, 1990; Ianni, 1989; Santos, 2021 [1996]). Insofar as its intrinsic coloniality renders it unfeasible, it must remain an unaccomplished promise to uphold social hopes of progress and ensure neocolonial structures of domination following capital's creed (Limonad, 2021).

New coloniality replaces old colonialism. Capital colonises everything, all instances of social life included, bringing about a neo-colonisation with other forms of domination, founded on spatial differences and heterogeneous stages of development, engendering a centre–periphery relation of power on a world scale (Lefebvre, 1978: 174; Escobar, 1995, 1997). As such, this neo-colonisation produces hierarchical territorial relations that are not limited to a country's past events or periods; furthermore, it helps articulate globally hegemonic states and international multilateral organisations to subsume non-hegemonic countries (Lefebvre, 1978: 170–1; Escobar, 1995, 1997). Present coloniality is partially an outcome of capital colonisation combined with previous enduring forms of coloniality. Consequently, coloniality comprehends an unceasing structure with new changing forms, pervading and underlying what we have been and what we are now. For Limonad (2021), coloniality endures as a quality, as part of a spatial roughness (*rugosidade*), an idea formerly elaborated by Santos (2021 [1996]) to characterise persisting material features in space and time. As a spatial roughness, coloniality encompasses distinctive overlapping colonial manifestations, combining past and present coloniality, also paving the road for the future. Surmounting modern coloniality demands going beyond economic facts and political domination. In order to grasp its complexity, modern coloniality must be understood in articulation with other dimensions of social life, accompanied by a search for alternatives to move towards another society.

For Quijano (2014: 285), coloniality is one of the specific elements constitutive of the world pattern of capitalist power. Founded on the imposition of a racial/ethnic classification, it operates in the material and subjective planes, spheres and dimensions, of everyday social existence, thus marking both knowledge and power. Moreover, coloniality supports the patriarchy's maintenance, the continuous dispossession of land and natural resources, the lack of access to land, the elites' control over decision-making, the despoliation of nature, the limitless extraction of natural resources, and, principally, the disrespect for native cultures, in addition to racial prejudices and discriminatory social conventions towards the other, to the different. For Lacoste (1988), it is not only a matter of annihilating or transforming ecological relations, but of a much more extensive change in the situation in which thousands live.

Insofar as Quijano's (2000: 540–1) coloniality conception intertwines with Lefebvre's (1991) spatial triad, it highlights the complex and general character of contemporary coloniality comprehending the subsumption of the hegemonic representations of space, power, and knowledge, as well as the spaces of representation subsuming the colonised individuals' social existence (dehumanisation, social-racial differentiation, and repression of symbolic meanings and native forms of subjectivity). The outcome is the subsumption of culture, knowledge, and know-how to an imposing dominant alien culture's spatial practices (domain of the perceived) in a valuable way to maintain domination, starting with religion, society–nature relationships, and often language itself.

The colonisation of everyday life, social existence, and social space production and appropriation unfolds in the colonisation of the forms of representation of space and spatial practices, resulting in multiple representations and spatial practices seemingly dissociated from and meaningless to everyday life, but valuable for capitalist accumulation. Furthermore, the social appropriation of space, now transformed into the abstract space of capital, becomes more difficult. The colonisation of a country and its society happens within the distant spatial order, concerning the means of production, the State, institutions, churches, and representations of space themselves. Likewise, it also happens in the immediate spatial order concerning family, workforce, everyday life, and the reproduction of spaces of representation. The colonised society tends to no longer produce its own social space but to mimic the new coloniser (capital) hegemonic social production of space, reproducing and following its prevailing hegemonic conceptions and representations (Limonad, 2021). Such colonisation commanded by capital needs interferes with lived, perceived, and conceived space, hinders local specificities, and suppresses social identities.

Hence, following Lefebvre (2014: 205) a transformative path should consider that 'the right to the city implies nothing less than a revolutionary concept of citizenship' and alternate spatial practices. Thus, according to the author, 'the question then is to know if social and political action can be formulated and rearticulated in relation to specific problems that, even if they are concrete, concern all dimensions of everyday life'.

In search of the urban natural: Towards urban utopias

A new society, a new space, a differential space (Lefebvre, 1991) demands other spatial practices that should be permanently (re)elaborated. It requires a different society–nature relationship, a different social division of labour within 'domestic units' (Coraggio, 1994), territories and society. Moreover, it demands the recognition and respect of race, gender, and class differences, considering that racial differentiation constitutes an essential element of colonial power and a means of legitimising relations of domination, superiority, and inferiority between the dominant and the dominated (Quijano, 2000; Fanon, 2004 [1961]; Maldonado-Torres, 2007). Such differentiation materialises spatially through the constitution of segregated spaces. Thus, building another society and another space demand decolonising everyday life, spatial practices, and, mainly, the realm of the imaginary – the spaces of representation (Lefebvre, 1991).

Therefore, it is imperative to find a path of reconciliation, not only political, social, and environmental, but also epistemological (and even ontological), between society and nature (Alimonda, 2019). In order to conceive an urban-natural space beyond capitalism, and (re)considering humans and nature as a unity, it also requires understanding that capitalism has colonised all spheres of social life, including daily life, to impose its own representations of space and nature. Thus, a search for the urban-natural shall look where it endures as an alternative spatial practice today, and to succeed it must, according to Lefebvre (1976: 126), go beyond the terrain and terms defined by capitalism and the State. Mainly, if we consider that

> Soon, only islands of agricultural production and concrete deserts will remain at the Earth's surface. Hence the importance of ecological questions: it is correct to assert that the milieu of life and the quality of the environment have acquired an urgent, politically central status. Inasmuch as one accepts such an analysis, the prospects for action are profoundly transformed. Several well-known but somewhat neglected forms – such as associative life or grassroots democracy (autogestion) – must be reinstated as key priorities; they assume new meanings when applied to the urban.
>
> (Lefebvre, 2014: 205)

Finally, it seems clear by now that the possible contemporary revolution will be centred on everyday life, in efforts connected to collective (re)production and life space, and in which the economies will be more related to their original 'substantive' meaning, i.e., the management of the household, and life space itself. A dialectical process, wherein quantity is transformed into quality with incremental changes, as in previous societal transformations that took place from within, resulting in gradual changes that question the hegemony or current social relations of production. The rising urban era announced by Lefebvre, superseding the industrial one, moves basic concerns from production and accumulation into concerns about the 'amplified reproduction of life' (Coraggio, 1994), driven by the understanding of a planetary crisis that sets human survival at the very centre of our concerns.

In this context, the urban-natural is understood as a vital transformation, already in course, from the urban-industrial society towards different forms of socio-spatial organisation in search for the virtual urban utopia that should characterise the urban era. This transformative process contains multiple difficulties, limitations, and contradictions but it seems that there is no point of return, apart from the many dystopias presented to us by current capitalist perspectives.

The manifestations of a resurgence of contemporary concerns with nature and its renewed insertion into our everyday lives can be noticed in many and various ways, and it would be impossible to list or even to categorise them as they appear all around the world, from the richest to the poorest environments. They are present in wealthy and futuristic cities as well as in poor metropolitan peripheries, or else in the countryside, in forests, savannahs, etc. Notwithstanding their implicit contradictions, all of them seem to carry the seeds of a transformative critical process.

In Latin America, the actions and practices of popular social movements, meaning the rescuing and reinvention of society–nature relations, are often linked to the understanding that resistance to capitalism is also a matter of daily life survival (Silva and Maciel, 2021). There is a myriad of interactions and social appropriations of nature, of the social production of space and territories' occupation. Such experiences must be seen as ongoing processes that contemplate sustainability and respect for the environment, understood as the need to rescue natural space and guarantee its centrality within an urbanised society. They embrace a rich ensemble of popular spatial practices, which are constitutive and expanded processes of this daily survival, encompassing, among many others, popular organisation towards occupying official decision-making spaces, such as municipal councils, to guarantee the maintenance of natural commons and prevent the expansion of abstract space,[6] planting and maintenance of urban gardens,[7] alternate territorial planning initiatives building spaces of legitimacy by proposing popular policies and laws,[8] traditional people's territories networks committed to the preservation of their costumes and living spaces,[9] and social community networks promoting popular and solidaristic economies dedicated to generating employment and basic income.[10]

In their development, these experiences contribute to promoting citizen awareness and integrating spaces for community participation, communication, culture, and education, as they build up social cartographies with the potential to construct other spatial practices that may lead to differential spaces.

Therefore, the transformation of the urban-industrial tissue into an urban-natural tissue does not entail the end of an era (industrial era) and the beginning of another one (urban era), just as the agrarian era did not entirely end (we are actually excavating its resilient remains). Instead, it should be constructed from within, from the contradictions of everyday life and their manifestations in our current societal crisis. It also emphasises Lefebvre's idea of urban utopia, understood as the achievement of 'urban society' and, in this sense, the right to the city itself is to be understood as the right to urban society. Busquet (2012–13: 8) emphasises:

> This 'utopia' defended by the author (Lefebvre) is in no way, however, intended to serve as a 'model'. By determining the 'possibles-impossibles' of the 'reality' – that which Lefebvre calls 'transduction' – this utopia only makes it possible to make knowledge of the urban evolve at the theoretical level, among other things, and then, to open, it could be said, to a better spatial planning that does not go against social practices, the 'desires', or freedom. This is an 'experimental utopia', 'studying utopia's implications and consequences on the ground' (Lefebvre, 2000 [1968]: 112) [...] Thus, when Lefebvre states that society can only develop in the urban, he is implying generalized urbanisation.

The dialectical interaction between extended urbanisation and extended naturalisation, as previously proposed, involves rescuing the urban-natural that endures in both city and countryside, and in its diverse (and virtual) manifestations in the urban itself (taken here as a noun, not as an adjective to the city[11]). The urban society proposed by Lefebvre now demands another element, nature and natural space, that, although implicit in his proposal, have become crucial to confronting our current threats and illuminating our very understanding of contemporary everyday life.

Urban society also implies a world of differences, of which Lefebvre's differential spaces must be an integral part. Urban centralities, the nodes within extended urbanisation, are certainly the locales where those synergies emerging from urban life shall flourish, where *'synekism'* (Soja, 2000) might recreate and redefine town-and-country intermingled relations, and thus make room for the urban society.

We take the urban-natural as the notion or idea that reunites contemporary concerns and spatial practices within everyday life, today present in countless manifestations and concerns in most parts of the world, that will metaphorically represent the transformation from the industrial era into the urban era. An insufficient but necessary step towards urban utopia.

Notes

1 To this end, we draw here on Limonad's (2016) approach to utopia based on Bloch (2004), Lefebvre (1976, 1978, 1991, 2000, 2001, 2009), and Heller and Feher (1985).
2 Bloch (2004) elected utopia as the leading transforming concept in the twentieth century, stressing the distinction between abstract and concrete utopias, as well as between utopic and utopian thought. Following Bloch (2004), Limonad (2016) understands that utopic thought would refer to blueprint elaborations of ideal 'milk and honey' future societies, like Thomas More's *Utopia*. In contrast, utopian thought should offer perspectives for other societies, other worlds, where nothing is previously defined. Instead, everything should be outlined at each concrete moment. Since, according to Bloch (2004), to deserve its name, 'utopia' must be permanently re-elaborated, with its feet founded in the here and now, in constant non-stop change, since the future is always to come, although not yet (*noch-nicht*).
3 For a radical critique of the 'modern myth of untouched nature' imported from the United States parks paradigm and the emergence of the concern with traditional peoples and their territories in Brazil, see Diegues (1998).
4 For a discussion about 'the urban' as either an adjective or a noun, see Monte-Mór (2007).
5 Such initiatives include popular and solidary economies (Coraggio, 2007, 2018), well-being (Keyes, 2002), *ubuntu* (Amaro, 2017; Alcantara and Sampaio, 2017), gross internal happiness (UN, 2011), 'buen vivir' (Acosta, 2016), and interculturality (Walsh, 2005b). Most of them are either institutionalised to varying degrees and intensities or swallowed by the State or multilateral organisations.
6 Grassroots movements, opposing real-estate endeavours, restore and defend urban natural parks as meeting places, leisure spaces, and places for interaction with nature. The Costanera Sur Ecological Park, with 350 hectares, stands in Buenos Aires's popular low-income southern area, on the riverbanks of the Rio de La Plata. It started with a landfill and debris dumping from 1978 to 1984. Afterwards, gradually, several native plants developed, providing refuge and food for diverse animal species to settle in. The former landfill became an example of how natural dynamics can take back a degraded area. Buenos Aires's inhabitants began to visit, and it became a leisure area and meeting point. In 1986, the Buenos Aires town hall transformed it into an official ecological reserve. Since 2001, many attempts have been made to connect the park with the high-income area of Puerto Madero. These attempts have been unsuccessful due to the strong citizen movement and environmental awareness.

The last one was the Ciudad Deportiva de Boca with 24 hectares on the banks of the Río de la Plata alongside the Costanera Sur Ecological Reserve. With the support of many professional and academic institutions, organised grassroots movements defend the fact that green spaces are alive and well even in the absence of human settlements. After many town hall audiences, the project was rejected due to its environmental impact (insofar as the towers would prevent breezes from the wetlands from entering the city) and its contribution to deepening the housing crisis, as it would increase the value of housing. See:www.telam.com.ar/notas/202110/572648-costanera-sur-audiencia-publica-ex-ciudad-deportiva-boca-convenio-urbanistico.html; www.agenciacma.com.br/esp/mayoria-en-audiencia-publica-rechaza-construccion-de-torres-de-irsa-en-costanera-sur-de-buenos-aires/; www.pagina12.com.ar/380569-costanera-sur-termino-la-audiencia-publica-con-un-fuerte-rec, accessed 12 August 2022.

7 Neighbourhood associations and slum community protection of springs and risk areas in Rio de Janeiro: a) Parque da Alice, Laranjeiras, Rio de Janeiro, on a Tijuca massif slope with more than 40 degrees of inclination, between Julio Ottoni and Vila Pereira da Silva. Originally, this was a private, *non edificandi* area of a residential complex, which was part of an Environmental Protection Area (APA). In 1992, the first 39 houses of the Vila Alice slum were installed there. In 2002, environmental protection limits were defined, which were not respected. In 2005, the Rio de Janeiro City Hall, following a court order, expropriated the land and a project to keep the families in the area was elaborated. However, in 2006, a new court order determined the reintegration of the former environmental area, the indemnity and eviction of the 93 families that lived there, whose majority moved to a neighbouring community. The Environmental Protection Area was reconstituted and the implementation of a community park began. The park is under construction through the direct action of the neighbourhood association (AMARALICE) with support from the South Zone Subprefecture of Rio de Janeiro and the Municipal Environment Secretariat. See: www.bairrodaslaranjeiras.com.br/gente/noticias250306.shtml: www2.senado.leg.br/bdsf/bitstream/handle/id/394341/noticia.htm?sequence, accessed 12 August 2022.

b) The Guararapes community is a communal territory autogestion experience located on the Tijuca massif's slope, on the way up to Corcovado, between the Tijuca National Park's forests and the city. The Carioca River runs through its streets and alleys. The occupation began in 1930, and has resisted several removal attempts. In 1967, after a long-running lawsuit, the Guararapes Residents' Association bought the 3.4-hectare land. Since 1978, the community, together with other communities and various social players, collaborates in the maintenance of the Carioca River and neighbouring forested areas and helps the reorganisation of visitor-driving activities through support for educational activities, citizenship education, environmental education workshops, community organisation and formal education. These activities contribute to building a closer community and increasing citizen awareness of the National Park. See https://anfitrioesdocosmevelho.loguei.com/comunidade-guararapes; www.youtube.com/watch?v=Nx035jhvxwk, accessed 12 August 2022.

8 Actions in metropolitan and urban planning: In many cases, it also implies the development of popular and solidarity local economies based on agroecological production, local fairs, ecotourism and sports, among other social and economic practices combining an urban-natural and the urban-industrial tissue. Drawing from an experience of a *Trame Verte et Bleue* (green and blue weft) in the Nord Pas-de-Calais former mining region surrounding Lille's metropolitan region, in Northern France, and from other examples around the world, the Metropolitan Plan of Belo Horizonte (Minas Gerais state capital) proposed the re-structuring of the metropolitan region on a basis of a *Trama Verde e Azul (TVA)*, both at the metropolitan and the municipal levels. However, the proposed TVA went beyond the French ecological approach to include a Lefebvrian urban utopian approach, meaning the inclusion of natural and cultural heritage elements and their related spatial practices that may produce a metropolitan space (and municipal territories) based on the urban-natural tissue (Monte-Mór et al., 2016; Costa et al., 2020). The responses from the communities were quite enthusiastic, making it clear that the population is eager for such actions, concerns, and public policies.

Further actions conducted by the university, together with metropolitan communities, show that the demands for environmental protection and strengthening, the creation of ecological parks and of areas to enjoy natural spaces are growing in importance.

9 Traditional peoples' territories networks. Brazilian Natives' territories, as well as various other traditional peoples' (Afro-Brazilian *quilombolas*; riverine traditional populations; peasants in the countryside; nuts, fruits and spices collectors, among many others) that managed to survive intense capitalist industrial destruction are each day more vocal and socio-politically organised, pushing their radical approaches toward nature into the national (and international) debates. They gained ample visibility and have been rather successful in influencing peoples both in the countryside and in metropolitan areas, not only in Brazil, but also in several countries in Latin America, as the buen vivir experience has shown. In Minas Gerais, there are now ten native Indigenous groups recognised, whereas before there were four. Self-recognition is spreading among traditional populations along with extended urbanisation and the politicisation of social space. The Indigenous Xakriabá group is becoming more integrated into the technological, scientific and informational milieu (Santos, 2021 [1996]). While their territory is being transformed by extended urbanisation, their social and cultural practices are being rebuilt and their voices are being amplified (Monte-Mór and Gomes, 2020). In Amazonia, the number of new groups claiming their Indigenous identities has also grown in these past years. In all these cases, their relations to nature and to the urban-industrial tissue are being transformed towards a certain sacralisation of their life-spaces (Monte-Mór, 2018b).

10 Artisanal fishing colonies in major cities, comprising artisanal fishermen and shellfish gatherers, who resist the advance of industrial urbanisation, remain and reside in marine areas in several Brazilian metropolitan regions. In the state of Rio de Janeiro, several projects have been developed to support these

colonies through the exchange of knowledge, the encouragement of sustainable fishing, the adoption of principles of the solidarity economy, and the strengthening of community organisations, production and marketing spaces for artisanal fisheries and shellfish gatherers. Among these projects, the 'Eastern Tide Shaking up the Territories with knowledge exchange, generating income and environmental sustainability in Fishing Communities' looms. This project receives funds from the Conduct Adjustment Agreement (TAC) signed by the Federal Public Ministry (MPF) with Chevron Brazil, Chevron Latin America and Transocean Brazil, responsible for the oil spills at sea in the Campos Basin, which occurred between 2011 and 2012, and is coordinated by the National Commission for the Strengthening of Extractive Reserves, Coastal and Marine Extractive Peoples and Traditional Communities (CONFREM Brazil) with the support of FUNBIO (Brazilian Biodiversity Fund) and the Federal Universities in Rio de Janeiro, among other bodies. See www.funbio.org.br/programas_e_projetos/educacao-ambiental/, accessed 12 August 2022. The CONFREM congregates around 100,000 families of Coastal and Marine Extractive Peoples and Traditional Communities in 18 Brazilian states. See https://confrem.wordpress.com, accesed 12 August 2022.

11 Following Lefebvre's 'dialectic of the triad', Monte-Mór (2007) proposes taking the urban as the third term in the dialectical city-and-country dichotomy.

References

Acosta, A. 2016. *O Bem Viver: Uma oportunidade para imaginar outros mundos*. São Paulo: Elefante.

Alcantara, L.C.S. and C.A.C. Sampaio. 2017. Bem Viver como paradigma de desenvolvimento: utopia ou alternativa possível? *Desenvolvimento e Meio Ambiente* 40: 231–51. http://dx.doi.org/10.5380/dma.v40i0.48566

Alimonda, H. 2019. The coloniality of nature: An approach to Latin American political ecology. *Alternautas (Re)Searching Development: The Abya Yala Chapter* 6(2): 102–42.

Amaro, R.R. 2017. Desenvolvimento ou Pós-Desenvolvimento? Des-Envolvimento e... Noflay! *Cadernos de Estudos Africanos* 34: 75–111. https://doi.org/10.4000/cea.2335

Ballestrin, L. 2013. América Latina e o giro decolonial [Decolonial turn and Latin America]. *Revista Brasileira Ciência Política* 11: 89–117. https://doi.org/10.1590/S0103-33522013000200004

Bloch, E. 2004. *El principio esperanza*. Madrid: Trotta.

Brenner, N. 2001. State theory in the political conjuncture: Henri Lefebvre's 'Comments on a new state form'. *Antipode* 33(5): 783–808. http://dx.doi.org/10.1111/1467-8330.00217

Busquet, G. 2012–13. L'espace politique chez Henri Lefebvre: l'idéologie et l'utopie [Political space in the work of Henri Lefebvre: Ideology and utopia, translation: Sharon Moren]. *Justice Spatiale/Spatial Justice* 5. www.jssj.org/article/lespace-politique-chez-henri-lefebvre-lideologie-et-lutopie/, accessed 12 August 2022.

Coraggio, J.L. 1994. *Economia urbana: La perspectiva popular*. Quito: Instituto Fronesis.

Coraggio, J.L. 2007. La economía social y la búsqueda de un programa socialista para el siglo XXI. *Revista Foro* 62: 37–64.

Coraggio, J.L. 2018. Potenciar la Economía Popular Solidaria: una respuesta al neoliberalismo. *Otra Economía* 11(20): 4–18.

Costa, H., R. Monte-Mór, and G. Costa. 2020. La trame verte et bleue, matrice du renouvellement de la planification métropolitaine au Brésil. Réflexions à partir de l'expérience de Belo Horizonte. *Risco. Revista de Pesquisa em Arquitetura e Urbanismo* 18: 119–137. www.revistas.usp.br/risco/article/view/170564/163218, accessed 12 August 2022.

Desfor, G. and R. Keil. 2004. *Nature and the city: Making environmental policy in Toronto and Los Angeles.* Tucson: University of Arizona Press.

Diegues, A.C. 1998. *The myth of untamed nature in the Brazilian rainforest.* São Paulo: NUPAUB-Universidade de São Paulo. www.ethnographic.org/images/myth.pdf, accessed 12 August 2022.

Escobar, A. 1995. *Encountering development.* Princeton, NJ: Princeton University Press.

Escobar, A. 1997. The making and unmaking of the Third World through development. In M. Rahnema and V. Bawtree (eds.), *The post-development reader.* London: Zed Books, pp. 85–93.

Fanon, F. 2004 [1961]. *The wretched of the earth.* New York: Grove Press.

Gramsci, A. 1971. *Selections from the prison notebooks.* New York: International Publishers.

Gramsci, A. 1994. *Pre-prison writings.* Cambridge: Cambridge University Press.

Grosfoguel, R. 2008. Para descolonizar os estudos de economia política e os estudos pós-coloniais: Transmodernidade, pensamento de fronteira e colonialidade global [Decolonizing Political-economy and Postcolonial Studies: Transmodernity, Border Thinking, and Global Coloniality]. *Revista Crítica de Ciências Sociais* 80: 115–47. https://doi.org/10.4000/rccs.697

Habermas, J. 1990. *The philosophical discourse of modernity.* Cambridge, MA: MIT Press.

Heller, A. and F. Fehér. 1985. *Anatomía de la Izquierda Occidental.* Barcelona: Península. http://biblioteca.clacso.edu.ar/clacso/se/20140424014720/Cuestionesyhorizontes.pdf, accessed 12 August 2022.

Heynen, N., M. Kaika and E. Swyngedouw (eds.). 2006. *In the nature of cities: Urban political ecology and the politics of urban metabolism.* New York: Routledge.

Ianni, O. 1989. A Sociologia e o mundo moderno. *Tempo Social* 1(1): 7–27. https://doi.org/10.1590/ts.v1i1.83315.

Kaika, M. 2005. *City of flows: Modernity, nature, and the city.* New York: Routledge.

Kaika, M. and E. Swyngedouw. 2014. Radical urban political-ecological imaginaries: Planetary urbanization and politicizing nature. *Eurozine.* www.eurozine.com/radical-urban-politicalecological-imaginaries/, accessed 12 August 2022.

Keil, R. and J. Graham. 1998. Reasserting nature: Constructing urban environments after Fordism. In B. Braun and N. Castree (eds.), *Remaking reality: Nature at the millennium.* London: Routledge, pp. 100–25.

Keil, R., D.V.J. Bell, P. Penz, and L. Fawcett (eds.). 1998. *Political ecology: Global and local.* London: Routledge.

Keyes, C.L. 2002. The mental health continuum: From languishing to flourishing in life. *Journal of Health and Social Behavior* 43(2): 207–22. https://doi.org/10.2307/3090197

Lacoste, Y. 1975. *Geografia do subdesenvolvimento.* São Paulo: Difel.

Lacoste, Y. 1988. *A Geografia isso serve, em primeiro lugar, para fazer a guerra*. Campinas: Papirus.
Lefebvre, H. 1976. *The survival of capitalism: Reproduction of the relations of production*. New York: St Martin's Press.
Lefebvre, H. 1978. *De L'État*. v. 4. Paris: Union Générale des éditions.
Lefebvre, H. 1991. *The production of space*. London: Blackwell.
Lefebvre, H. 1996. *Writings on cities*. Selected, translated, and introduced by E. Kofman and E. Lebas. Oxford: Blackwell.
Lefebvre, H. 1999. *A Revolução Urbana*. Belo Horizonte: Editora UFMG. Translated by S. Martins from Lefebvre, H. 1970. *La Révolution Urbaine*. Paris: Galimard.
Lefebvre, H. 2000. *Writings on cities*. London: Blackwell. Translated by E. Kofman and E. Lebas from Lefebvre, H. 1968. *Le Droit à la ville*. Paris: Seuil.
Lefebvre, H. 2001. Comments on a new state form. *Antipode* 33(5): 769–82. https://doi.org/10.1111/1467-8330.00216
Lefebvre, H. 2009. *State, space, world: Selected essays*. Minneapolis, MN: University of Minnesota Press.
Lefebvre, H. 2014. Dissolving city, planetary metamorphosis. *Environment and Planning D: Society and Space* 32: 203–5. https://doi.org/10.1068/d3202tra
Leff, E. 2008. *Discursos Sustentables*. Mexico: Siglo XXI.
Limonad, E. 1991. Así camina lo urbano. *Revista de la SIAP: Sociedad Interamericana de Planificación, Guatemala* 24(95): 96–115. https://doi.org/10.22409/GEOgraphia2000.v2i3.a13376
Limonad, E. 2002. Multipolar urbanisation patterns in south Rio de Janeiro: From competition or cooperation to coopetition. In T. Markowski and T. Marszal (eds.), *Polycentric metropolitan regions: New concepts and experiences*. Warsaw: Polish Academy of Sciences, Committee for Space Economy and Regional Planning, vol. 11, pp. 143–58.
Limonad, E. 2004. Questões ambientais contemporâneas, uma contribuição ao debate. In *Conference Proceedings of the Associação Nacional de Pesquisa e Pós-Graduação em Ambiente e Sociedade*. Campinas. www.researchgate.net/publication/303895885_Questoes_ambientais_contemporaneas_uma_contribuicao_ao_debate, accessed 12 August 2022.
Limonad, E. 2005. Entre a Urbanização e a Sub-Urbanização do Território. In: *Conference Proceedings of the XI Encontro Nacional da Associação Nacional de Pesquisa e Pós-Graduação em Planejamento Urbano e Regional*, Salvador. Planejamento, Soberania e Solidariedade: perspectivas para o território e a cidade. UFBA/ANPUR, vol. 1, pp. 1–18.
Limonad, E. 2010. Regiões Reticulares: algumas considerações metodológicas para a compreensão de novas formas urbanas. *Cidades* (Presidente Prudente) 7: 1–15.
Limonad, E. 2016. Utopias urbanas, sonhos ou pesadelos? Cortando as cabeças da Hidra de Lerna. In N. Benach, M.H. Zaar, and P.M. Vasconcelos (eds.), *Las utopías y la construcción de la sociedad del futuro*. Universidad de Barcelona. www.ub.edu/geocrit/xiv-coloquio/EsterLimonad.pdf
Limonad, E. 2021. Por uma outra sustentabilidade: um diálogo entre Lefebvre e o pensamento decolonial [Towards another sustainability: a dialogue between Lefebvre and the decolonial thought]. *Boletim Goiano de Geografia* 41: e70787. https://revistas.ufg.br/bgg/article/view/70787/37644, accessed 12 August 2022.
Limonad, E. and R.L. Monte-Mór. 2015. Beyond the right to the city: Between the rural and the urban. *Urbia* 13(17): 103–15. www.unil.ch/ouvdd/files/live/sites/ouvdd/files/shared/URBIA/Urbia_no_17/Decoupe_7.pdf, accessed 12 August 2022.

Luxemburg, R. 2015. *The accumulation of capital*. London: Routledge.
Maldonado-Torres, N. 2007. On the coloniality of being. *Cultural Studies* 21(2–3): 240–70. https://doi.org/10.1080/09502380601162548
Marx, K. 1990 [1867]. *Capital (unabridged). Vol. 1: A critic of political economy*. London: Penguin Classics.
Mignolo, W. 2000. Diferencia colonial y razón pos occidental. In S. Castro-Gómes (ed.), *Reestructuración de las ciencias sociales en América Latina*. Bogotá: Centro Editorial Javeriano, pp. 3–28.
Monte-Mór, R.L. 1988, August. Urbanization, colonization and the production of regional space in the Brazilian *Amazon*. Conference presentation, 16th Interamerican Congress of Planning (SIAP – Sociedad Interamericana de Planificación), San Juan, Puerto Rico.
Monte-Mór, R.L. 2007. Cidade e campo, urbano e rural: o substantivo e o adjetivo. In S. Feldman and A. Fernandes (eds.), *O urbano e o regional no Brasil contemporâneo: mutações, tensões, desafios*. Salvador, Bahia: EDUFBA, pp. 93–114
Monte-Mór, R.L. 2014a [1994]. Extended urbanization and settlement patterns in Brazil: An environmental approach. In N. Brenner (ed.), *Implosions/explosions: Towards a study of planetary urbanization*. Berlin: Jovis Verlag, pp. 109–20.
Monte-Mór, R.L. 2014b. What is the urban in the contemporary world? In N. Brenner (ed.), *Implosions/explosions: Towards a study of planetary urbanization*. Berlin: Jovis Verlag, pp. 260–75.
Monte-Mór, R.L. 2018a. Urbanization, sustainability, development: Contemporary complexities and diversities in the production of urban space. In P. Horn, P. Alfaro, and A.C. Cardoso (eds.), *Emerging urban spaces: a planetary perspective*. Springer ebook, pp. 201–15. https://doi.org/10.1007/978-3-319-57816-3_10
Monte-Mór, R.L. 2018b. Utopias urbanas e outras economias. In M. Viegas and E. Albuquerque (eds.), *Alternativas para uma crise de múltiplas dimensões*. EbookCedeplar/Face/UFMG.https://cedeplar.ufmg.br/wp-content/uploads/2021/06/Alternativas-para-uma-crise-de-multiplas-dimensoes.pdf, accessed 12 August 2022.
Monte-Mór, R.L. and A.M.R. Gomes. 2020. Duas décadas de pesquisa com os Xakriabá do Norte de Minas: Do diagnóstico da economia ao monitoramento da pandemia da COVID-19. *Nova Economia* 30(3): 747–69. http://dx.doi.org/10.1590/0103-6351/6509
Monte-Mór, R.L. and S. Ray. 1995. Post-*.ism & the Third World: A theoretical reassessment and fragments from Brazil and India. *Nova Economia* 5(1): 177–208.
Monte-Mór, R.L., G. Costa, H. Costa, and M. Melo. 2016. The university and metropolitan planning: An innovative experience. *Nova Economia* 26: 1133–56. http://dx.doi.org/10.1590/0103–6351/3952
Polanyi, K. 2001. *Great transformation: The political and economic origins of our time*. Boston: Beacon Press.
Quijano, A. 2000. Coloniality of power, Eurocentrism, and Latin America. *Nepantla: Views from South* 1(3): 533–80. http://muse.jhu.edu/journals/nep/summary/v001/1.3quijano.html, accessed 12 August 2022.
Quijano, A. 2014. Colonialidad del poder y clasificación social. In *Cuestiones y Horizontes*. Buenos Aires: CLACSO, pp. 285–326.
Randolph, R. 2015. A origem estrutural da subversão em sociedades capitalistas contemporâneas, suas práticas baseadas na vivência cotidiana e um novo paradigma de um contra planejamento. In G.M. Costa, H.S.M. Costa, and

R.L. Monte-Mór (eds.), *Teorias e Práticas Urbanas: condições para a sociedade urbana*. Belo Horizonte: C/Arte, pp. 71–102

Randolph, R. 2016. A utopia do planejamento e o planejamento da utopia: o longo caminho de uma contra-planejamento até o alcance da justiça social. In N. Benach, M.H. Zaar, and P.M. Vasconcelos (eds.), *Las utopías y la construcción de la sociedad del futuro*. Universidad de Barcelona. www.ub.edu/geocrit/xiv-coloquio/RainerRandolph.pdf, accessed 12 August 2022.

Said, E.W. 1980. *Orientalism*. London and Henley: Routledge & Kegan Paul.

Santos, M. 2021 [1996]. *The nature of space*. Durham: Duke University Press. Translated from Santos, M. 1996. *A Natureza do Espaço*. São Paulo: Loyola.

Silva, H. 2017. Socialização da natureza e alternativas de desenvolvimento na Amazônia Brasileira. PhD Dissertation in Economics. Belo Horizonte: Cedeplar/UFMG.

Silva, F.F.A.E. and L. Maciel. 2021. Decolonizando o planejamento a experiência dos conflitos urbanos em cidades latino-americanas. In E. Limonad, J.C. Monteiro, and P. Mansilla (eds.), *Planejamento territorial: Reflexões críticas e perspectivas*. São Paulo: Editora Max Limonad, pp. 185–219. www.researchgate.net/publication/353742264_Planejamento_Territorial_reflexoes_criticas_e_perspectivas, accessed 12 August 2022.

Soja, E.W. 2000. *Postmetropolis: Critical studies of cities and regions*. Oxford/Malden: Blackwell Publishers.

Sparn, J.O.W. 2019. (Re)imagining sustainable futures: A discussion between degrowth and buen vivir. PhD Dissertation in Economics. Belo Horizonte, Cedeplar/UFMG.

Swyngedouw, E. 1996. The city as a hybrid: On nature, society and cyborg urbanization. *Capitalism Nature Socialism* 7(2): 65–80.

Tzaninis, Y., T. Mandler, M. Kaika, and R. Keil. 2021. Moving urban political ecology beyond the 'urbanization of nature'. *Progress in Human Geography* 45(2): 229–52.

UN (United Nations). 2011. Happiness: Towards a holistic approach to development: Resolution / adopted by the General Assembly. https://digitallibrary.un.org/record/715187?ln=en, accessed 12 August 2022.

Walsh, C. 2005a. (Re)pensamiento crítico y (De)colonialidad. In C. Walsh (ed.), *Pensamiento crítico y matriz (de)colonial. Reflexiones latinoamericanas*. Quito: Abya-Yala, pp. 13–35.

Walsh, C. 2005b. Interculturalidad, conocimientos y decolonialidad. *Signo y Pensamiento* 24(46): 39–50.

Walsh, C. 2010. Development as *buen vivir*: Institutional arrangements and (de)colonial entanglements. *Development* 53(1): 15–21. https://doi.org/10.1057/dev.2009.93

4

Circuits of extraction and the metabolism of urbanisation[1]

Martín Arboleda

Introduction

The research programme of what is usually referred to as 'extractivism' emerged in the context of struggles against large-scale resource extraction in Latin America. In their preliminary phase, studies of extractivism laid out the dynamics of monopoly control, extra-economic force, and rentiership that underlined globalised forms of primary commodity production in the region. More recently, a second phase of theoretical development in this tradition has advanced towards *an expanded conception of extractivism* premised on the fact that primary commodity production extends far beyond sites of extraction and becomes densely imbricated with finance capital, logistical infrastructure, digital technology, and urbanisation (see Gago and Mezzadra, 2017; Mezzadra and Neilson, 2017; Arboleda, 2020; Ye et al., 2020). In this way, an expanded conception of extractivism resonates with urban political ecology's (UPE) theorisation of the ways in which extra-human natures become severed from their raw state in order to be commodified and integrated to the city through complex socio-technical systems (see Kaika and Swyngedouw, 2000; Heynen et al., 2006; Tzaninis et al., 2021).

Although studies of extractivism and of UPE have so far developed separately, the current climate emergency has raised the stakes of each of these research agendas, thereby demanding productive articulations between them. The extraction and primary processing of metals and other minerals are responsible for 90 per cent of biodiversity loss and 26 per cent of global carbon emissions, while the production and circulation of food accounts for 34 per cent of all global anthropogenic emissions (Crippa et al., 2021; Riofrancos, 2021). These escalating levels of carbon intensity, according to recent reports on the global climate crisis, are to a considerable extent the result of 'telecoupling' dynamics that link together remote ecosystems and densely populated cities through complex, transnational commodity chains (IPCC, 2019; IPBES, 2019). For this reason, it has been argued that any substantive energy transition that can be able to stabilise the climate and to also confront extreme social inequality, should also simultaneously be a *post-extractive transition* (see War on Want and London Mining Network, 2020; Riofrancos, 2021).

This chapter suggests that an engagement with a critical theorisation of the circulation of capital – as laid out by Marx (1992 [1885]; see also Marx, 1973 [1939]) in Volume II of *Capital* – can contribute to the agenda of developing an expanded conception of extractivism that lays bare the actual interdependencies, crisis-tendencies, and points of intersection between the space-economy of extraction and the process of capitalist urbanisation. In this way, this approach can also contribute to UPE's renewed aspiration to develop an integrated agenda for understanding and confronting the sociometabolic foundations of global warming (Tzaninis et al., Introduction in this volume). By positing the reproduction of capital in terms of three interrelated circulatory systems (money capital, productive capital, and commodity capital), Marx sought to supersede compartmentalised understandings of production, circulation, exchange, and distribution, and grasp the capitalist economy as a differentiated unity (see Arthur and Reuten, 1998; Fine and Saad-Filho, 2016; Harvey, 2013). On this basis this chapter proposes a relational understanding of primary-commodity production in terms of three contradictory and yet integrated circuits of extraction:

First, a *productive circuit of extraction*, which encompasses the actual territoriality and the material process of raw materials production – shafts, pits, wells, processing facilities, and agroindustrial hinterlands, among others;

Second, a *commodity circuit of extraction*, formed by all the webs of infrastructural and logistical connectivity that enable the journey of raw materials from sites of extraction to their realisation in the market – ports, dry-bulk carriers, railways, pipelines, and highways;

Third, a *money circuit of extraction*, which entails all the financial actors, instruments, and institutional systems that mediate the activity of resource-based industries at multiple spatial scales.

At stake in the notion of circuits of extraction is not only the aspiration to contribute to the challenge of developing an expanded conception of extractivism; it is also to shed light on the modes of socio-spatial interdependence that emerge as processes of industrial upgrading in the so-called Global South – and especially in East Asian economies – give rise to one of the most persistent and wide-ranging commodity supercycles in recent history. These distinct yet interrelated world-historical transformations, as this chapter shows, have brought together natural resources and built environments, as well as city and non-city space, into novel and ever-more intricate configurations. In the first three sections, the chapter explores the aforementioned circuits of extraction. Each of the three circuits is assessed in terms of the role it performs in broader processes of metabolic urbanisation and global capital accumulation. In the final section the chapter explores the dynamics of expanded reproduction that emerge from the combined movement of the three circuits. Considering extractive economies in terms of their expanded reproduction, I suggest, enables understanding how resource economies are also pushing the frontier of capitalist commodification and of anthropogenic carbon emissions to an unprecedented degree.

Productive circuit of extraction

The productive circuit of extraction is circumscribed to the moment of value production when fixed and variable capitals are expended in order to yield minerals, oil, or foodstuffs. This circuit usually encompasses all the processes and territorialities that form the object of analysis of traditional studies of extractivism. In recent decades the physical organisation of this circuit has become reconfigured in order to boost productivity, especially in the face of declining mineral grades and of escalating demand from rapidly industrialising 'Asian Tigers'. Bunker and Ciccantell's (2003, 2005) study of new resource frontiers reveals that it was the ship-building and steel-making capacity that emerged from processes of industrial upgrading in East Asia that set the economies of Japan, South Korea, and China, on the path to become the world's largest importers of raw materials. These processes of late industrialisation, it is worth pointing out, have underpinned a long-standing commodity supercycle in Latin America, starkly evidenced in the expansion of the balance of trade between China and Latin America, which went from $15 billion in 2009 to a staggering $200 billion in 2011 (Valdez Mingramm, 2013: 32).

This emerging transpacific landscape of mineral trade has pushed the extractive industries towards a greater degree of functional integration, not only between the various phases of the production process – exploration, blasting, crushing, haulage – but also between the port and shipping industries. Efforts to implement technologies for mineral traceability and supply chain mapping in order to reduce asymmetries of information between the different phases of production have been contingent on the standardisation of operations across the supply chain (Arboleda, 2018).[2] Moreover, increasing complexity in the technical division of labour has also favoured the emergence of large-scale contractors in a manner akin to that of the 'Wintelist' or Modular Production Networks that tend to predominate in the electronics industry – characterised by a sharp division between design and execution, and by vertical reintegration of manufacturing activity. The tasks initially outsourced in the mining industry were labour-intensive and marginal to the core operation, such as catering, hostels, and shaft sinking, but gradually shifted towards a constellation of more complex services such as mineral forecasting, geological modelling, and process engineering. The trend toward a larger degree of diversification of functions seems to have taken off in the South African mining industry during the 1990s, when whole shafts began to be outsourced to third parties (Kenny and Bezuidenhout, 1999). In Latin America the rescaling and specialisation of contractors has evolved to the extent that large transnational corporations such as Komatsu, Siemens, Atlas Copco, and Cat-Finning now commonly operate alongside extractive corporations in shafts, pits, and industrial facilities for mineral processing (Innovum/Fundación Chile, 2014).

Processes of organisational restructuring of this sort have enabled quantum leaps in labour productivity, but they have also triggered new forms of socio-spatial inequality as a result of a workforce that is increasingly polarised not only in terms of gender, race, and citizenship, but also in terms of the productive attributes that it embodies (Arboleda, 2020). During the national-developmentalist phase of capitalist development, settlement space in resource geographies was structured around relatively equitable and socially homogeneous 'company towns' for the salaried workers of mining and oil firms. The commodification of labour-powers of heterogeneous complexity that technological upgrading in the mining industry requires has brought overspecialisation among intellectual workers (geologists, engineers, geophysicists), as well as deskilling and labour insecurity among industrial and manual operators. The proliferation of networks of subcontracted, temporary, and piecemeal labour has therefore heralded a shift to a 'far west', ephemeral paradigm of resource urbanism structured on the basis of boom towns, agropolises, and campsites (see Canales, 2012; Gordillo, 2019; for resource extraction urbanism in sub-Saharan Africa see Kirshner and Power, 2015). Moreover, recent reconfigurations in the productive circuit of extraction have also become manifested in encroaching environmental plunder, soil depletion, land-use change, and water pollution, leading to a veritable exodus of rural populations towards the outskirts of both intermediate and large cities across Latin America. This new iteration of resource-driven global depeasantisation is well documented in the literature (see for example Ruiz et al., 2016; Vásquez Duplat, 2017).

Commodity circuit of extraction

The commodity circuit of extraction encompasses all the physical and social infrastructures that are put in place in order to facilitate the swift movement of primary commodities from the point of production to their subsequent realisation in the market. Reducing the time that it takes for capital to transition from its determination as commodity-form, to the point when it becomes realised in its money-form and returns to the capitalist as profits to be reinvested – its *turnover time* – has consistently figured as a key driver for inter-capitalist competition in modern society. It is therefore unsurprising, as Marx (1992 [1885]) argues, that the ongoing reproduction of capital is contingent upon the constant development and concentration (i.e., scaling-up) of means of transport and communication. As he puts it in the *Grundrisse*, 'the creation by capital of *absolute surplus value* – more objectified labour – is conditional upon an expansion, specifically a constant expansion, of the sphere of circulation' (Marx, 1973 [1939]: 407, emphasis in the original). For Bunker and Ciccantell (2003, 2005), it is the drive to access ever-more remote resource peripheries that has triggered the types of technological breakthroughs in the means of transportation that have come to define historical cycles of accumulation proper. Notable examples in this regard are perhaps the *bergantines* that Spain used to carry gold and silver across the Atlantic in the sixteenth century, the motorised ships that the British Empire devised to gain access to guano and rubber in the Amazon, and the *Valemax*, the largest dry bulk vessel ship ever built, which carries iron ore from Brazil to China across the Pacific Ocean.

The tendency to constantly modernise and overhaul infrastructures of circulation has been the hallmark of industrial capitalism since its inception. However, it is in the context of the logistics revolution that the productive circuit and the commodity circuits of extraction have reached a more advanced degree of functional integration. It has been argued that one of the central features of the logistics revolution is that in the interests of speed, connectivity, and homeostasis, it has blurred the boundaries between transport and other forms of productive labour (Cowen, 2014; Toscano, 2014). As the previous section explained, technologies for supply chain mapping and mineral traceability implemented in the mining industry have deliberately shifted the emphasis from extraction sites individually considered, to the supply chain understood as a total system. The implications of the logistics revolution in the geography of extraction are also evinced in the geoeconomic shift that enabled Japan and South Korea to achieve a tenfold increase in the number of dry-bulk carriers between 1961 and 1992, going from 471 to 4,846 (Ciccantell, 2009: 117). In 1995 China became the world's largest steel producer, a landmark shift that later enabled it to become the main importer of raw materials and develop the largest merchant marine fleet in the world.

The increasing relevance that the commodity circuit of extraction has acquired in the context of the entire geography of primary-commodity production has led to novel expressions of socio-political protest and unrest. In other words, the enlargement of the sphere of circulation has evolved alongside its concomitant politicisation. And indeed, Mezzadra and Neilson (2017) argue that an understanding of extraction in a narrow sense has ended up by obfuscating emerging forms of contestation and revolt that take place beyond extractive sites but still have direct incidence on them. This is patently manifested in the context of the logistics revolution, which has elevated the 'chokepoints' of global supply chains into key sites of political struggle and labour insurgency across the global economy. Indeed, technical sabotage in ports, railways, and road infrastructure, has become one of the staple tactics of socio-political movements involved in territorial struggles concerning natural resource governance and circulation (see Arboleda, 2018; Cuevas Valenzuela and Budrovich Sáez, 2018; Khanna, 2016). The effectiveness of these forms of socio-political contestation stem from the fact that their disruptive effects are not exclusively confined to the commodity circuit. In fact, they often spill over to the productive circuit of extraction.

Money circuit of extraction

Mediating the combined movement of the commodity circuit and the production circuit we find the money circuit of extraction, personified in the figure of financial institutions, bankers, debt instruments, regulatory policy frameworks, and so forth. For Marx, the circuit of money capital is of fundamental relevance because it manages the existing contradictions between production and realisation through the extension of credit, which provides liquidity to material operations in advance of real accumulation (Fine and Saad-Filho, 2016; Harvey, [1982] 2006, 2013; Heinrich, 2012). Through an elaborate array of debt instruments – bonds, mortgages and corporate stock – the financial system has historically furthered the momentum for the technological innovations in transport systems, as well as for the construction of infrastructural developments across resource-rich countries (Bunker and Ciccantell, 2005). In fact, the very possibility for the mining industry to become increasingly capital-intensive, smart, horizontally integrated, and autonomous has been directly contingent upon the mediations of a complex network of financial actors, practices, and instruments. Findings from the 2019 *Banking on Climate Change* report, for example, reveal that financial institutions such as JP Morgan Chase, Barclays, the Bank of China, and the Japanese MUFG, have furnished the fossil fuel industry with USD 1.9 trillion since the Paris Agreement was adopted in 2016.

Far from subordinating industrial production to the financial system – as mainstream readings of financialisation assume – it has been argued that the financialisation of investment strategies has in fact served as a lever to expand material operations across extraction sites. This, in turn, has increased the organic composition of capital at points of production and intensified the antagonism between capital and living labour (Labban, 2010, 2014; Kaika and Ruggiero, 2015, 2016). In specific terms, the relation between the money circuit of extraction and the productive circuit of extraction can be disaggregated into three different scales or domains of socio-spatial intervention. First, sovereign debt has historically functioned as a key mechanism by which nation-states can finance the mega-infrastructural systems required to attract foreign direct investment for primary commodity production such as ports, power plants, dams, highways, railways, airports, etc. The rise of East Asian economies as the main creditor nations is indicative of how the financial system dovetails with the geographical relocation of large-scale industry. Several studies have concluded that Latin American states have become increasingly indebted to international financial institutions, and more recently to East Asian economies and multilateral banks (Bunker and Ciccantell, 2005; Schmalz, 2016; Stanley, 2016). Second, physical producers in the extractive industries – mining, oil and energy firms – have also developed systematic engagements with the credit system, as well as reoriented their corporate behaviour and strategies towards financial and/or speculative operations (see for example De Los Reyes, 2017; Labban, 2010, 2014). Publicly traded mining and oil companies, for example, tend to exaggerate the size of their reserves, because in so doing they also manage to inflate and distort the price of their shares in stock markets (Labban, 2010; Tsing, 2005).

Third, geographies of consumer debt have increasingly asserted themselves as one of the foremost sources of financial liquidity for primary-commodity production, especially as institutional investors systematically reoriented investment flows towards land and natural resources in the aftermath of the 2008 financial crisis (see Sassen, 2014). The ways in which the variegated revenue streams extracted from households and workers are channelled by institutional investors towards the extractive industries (De Los Reyes, 2017; Tsing, 2005), and towards territorial and environmental infrastructures in general (Christophers, 2011; Purcell et al., 2019), is adequately documented in the literature. It is in its continuous expansion of the frontiers of profit-making towards new realms of social and ecological existence that the financial system has been recently paralleled to an extractive industry (Mezzadra and Neilson, 2017; Sassen, 2017). In the section that follows we begin to frame the question of frontier-making through an exploration of the expanded reproduction of what Marx terms the circuit of 'industrial capital'.

Expanded reproduction and the mine/city nexus

In his introduction to the 1978 edition of Volume II of *Capital*, Ernest Mandel (in Marx, 1992 [1885]: 61) explains that conceptualising the movement of capital in terms of three integrated circuits enabled Marx to point out how money capital becomes recurrently expelled from the process of value production and is mobilised to increase the scale of the circuit as a whole – a phenomenon that he termed 'expanded reproduction'. As is well-known, Marx's insights on this question were left only partially developed, and it was actually Rosa Luxemburg who first developed a systematic theorisation of expanded reproduction as an instance – if not *the* instance – of crisis-formation within capitalism (Luxemburg, 2003 [1913]). Gago and Mezzadra (2017), for example, build upon Luxemburg's work to frame extractivism as the continuous appropriation of the non-commodified outside. Although the question of appropriation is without a doubt fundamental for understanding the extractive nature of capital's motion of self-expansion, it is worth pointing out that Luxemburg's notion of expanded reproduction is also, crucially, an *economic theory* of overaccumulation, and not merely a *political theory* of imperialism. By positing expanded reproduction as a problem of surplus money capitals that become *realised* elsewhere, Luxemburg (2003 [1913]: 332–3) offers important elements for grasping the nature of accumulation as a contradictory unity of production and realisation.

The socio-spatial and urban implications that underpin the realisation of overaccumulated capitals under conditions of enlarged reproduction are notably theorised by David Harvey (1985, 2006 [1982]) through the notion of 'capital switching'. Specifically, Harvey (1985) claims that crisis tendencies emerge when overaccumulation in a 'primary circuit' yield surplus that cannot be reabsorbed in the productive process. As a result, money capital becomes periodically reoriented towards a 'secondary circuit', which is formed by a physical framework for investment in the built environment, and which entails the creation of the spatial arrangements for production, circulation, transportation, and consumption that are most patently embodied in the city. The transformation of the urban landscape as a result of surpluses that originate in primary-commodity production and are later jettisoned outwards to the secondary circuit has been an overarching trend in the historical evolution of extractive industries, and has also been central in the development of the field of urban political ecology. Gray Brechin's (2006) landmark historiographical study suggests that it was precisely the vast material wealth springing from the silver and gold rushes of the Nevada and California mines during the mid-nineteenth century that fuelled similar construction and real estate speculation booms in the city of San Francisco. Joe Feagin's (1990) comparative study of the oil boom of the post-war period concludes that Aberdeen and Houston were reconfigured through similar dynamics of capital circulation and investment in the built environment.

The scale at which these capital-switching strategies operate, however, has been redefined by the combined world-historical tendency towards the intensification of monopoly power, the globalisation of production, and the pervasiveness of social and ecological crises. The pervasiveness and magnitude of contemporary investment strategies in the built environment are hinted at in Khanna's claim that 'China is not "buying the world" per se but *building it* in exchange for natural resources' (2016: 95, emphasis in original). Moreover, recent studies show that export booms in the Chilean mining industry under the commodity supercycle have tended to further vast surpluses of financial liquidity that are consistently reabsorbed by the real estate sector, either through direct construction of housing and infrastructure, or through the expansion of credit via the mortgage system and other forms of personal debt (see Rehner and Rodríguez-Leiva, 2017; Rehner and Vergara, 2014; Vergara-Perucich, 2018).

Also, it is estimated that the dramatic growth of transgenic soybean production in Argentina has metastasised into large-scale urban redevelopment projects and speculation, thereby triggering gentrification, environmental degradation, and the enclosure of urban space across several cities under the rubric of what is termed 'urban extractivism' (see Vásquez Duplat, 2017; Viale, 2017). It is precisely in the interlinkages between the process of extraction and the process of urbanisation that, according to recent findings of intergovernmental panels of climate science, the thrust of anthropogenically driven global warming is to be found (see IPCC, 2019; IPBES, 2019).

Moreover, processes of capital switching from resource-based industries towards a tertiary circuit – in Harvey's formulation – reveal how the productive circuit of extraction also extends outwards to directly shape general research on social science, natural science, investment banking, and public policy broadly considered. John Urry (2014), for example, documents the elaborate switching dynamics that fossil fuel companies set into motion in order to reorient profits towards tax havens, thus giving momentum to the 'chains of concealment' that, in the author's view, lie at the heart of the transnational financial system. As Oreskes and Conway's (2011) landmark work shows, the fossil fuel industry has also funded the think tanks and scientists that have been notorious for casting doubt on the scientific evidence of climate change with unsubstantiated research and information. Endowments and donations from resource extraction firms to prestigious universities have also spurred concerns over the potential loss of scholarly autonomy and independence.

Conclusions

The notion of *extractivism* is often mobilised as a slogan and rallying cry against evolving forms of enclosure and dispossession taking place in primary commodity frontiers, and also recently in urban, financial, and digital realms of social life. By framing the organisation of resource-based industries in terms of three distinct yet overlapping circulatory systems – i.e., the productive circuit of extraction, the commodity circuit of extraction, and the money circuit of extraction – this chapter has intended to shed light into the magnitude and dynamism at which resource economies are reconfiguring the financial system, knowledge production, scientific and technological innovation, socio-political mobilisation, and planetary urban landscapes. A wide array of infrastructural developments has been put into place in order to reduce the turnover times of capital, as well as to seamlessly integrate resource extraction with the port and transport industries under the aegis of a logistics revolution. In this way, the deployment of circuits of extraction has given momentum to the telecoupling dynamics that open up remote and biodiverse resource geographies across the world to extreme and socio-ecologically destructive forms of capitalist appropriation. For this reason, any visions of mass decarbonisation that do not take into account the origins of the climate emergency in resource peripheries will be ill-equipped to stabilise the climate and to reduce the carbon intensity of modern urban life.

For the above reasons, an analysis of the extractive industries through the standpoint of the circulation of capital is much more than just a question of analytically grasping the movement of raw materials in space; chiefly, it also hints at how surplus capitals produced in the primary sector are being systematically projected or 'switched' outwards in a movement of *expanded reproduction*, thereby giving rise to speculative booms, new forms of enclosure across the wider urban system, and most importantly, to a staggering increase in global carbon emissions. Accordingly, an approach that shifts the gaze of analysis from *spaces* towards *circuits* of extraction can provide fruitful theoretical and methodological insights for understanding the ways in which the extractive industries shape the metabolism of urbanisation in historically and geographically specific ways. For this reason, it can productively complement UPE's longstanding aspiration to decentre the city and to reflect on the ways in which the periphery (in this case, the extractive industries) drive the process of urbanisation towards what is an ostensibly more unstable, ecologically destructive, and crisis-prone configuration.

Notes

1 This chapter is a revised and abridged version of a longer article published in *Capitalism Nature Socialism*.
2 Although mineral traceability began as a private initiative by mineral buyers in Asian markets to reduce costs, it has recently been embraced by civil society and multilateral organisations such as the OECD and the UN as a way to increase transparency and avoid human rights violations, especially with respect to conflict minerals such as coltan, tin, tungsten, and gold.

References

Arboleda, M. 2018. Extracción en movimiento: circulación del capital, poder estatal, y urbanización logística en el norte minero de Chile. [Extraction in motion: Circulation of capital, state power, and logistical urbanization in northern Chile's mining regions]. *Investigaciones Geográficas* 56: 3–26.
Arboleda, M. 2020. *Planetary mine: Territories of extraction under late capitalism*. London and New York: Verso.
Arthur, C. and G. Reuten (eds.). 1998. *The circulation of capital: Essays on volume two of Marx's Capital*. London: Macmillan.
Brechin, G. 2006. *Imperial San Francisco: Urban power, earthly ruin*. Berkeley: University of California Press.
Bunker, S. and P. Ciccantell. 2003. Generative sectors and the new historical materialism: Economic ascent and the cumulatively sequential restructuring of the world economy. *Studies in Comparative International Development* 37(4): 3–30.
Bunker, S. and P. Ciccantell. 2005. *Globalization and the race for resources*. Baltimore: Johns Hopkins University Press.
Canales, M. 2012. De la metropolización a las agrópolis: el nuevo poblamiento urbano en el Chile actual [From metropolization to the agropolis: The new urban settlements in contemporary Chile]. *Polis* 34: 1–23.
Christophers, B. 2011. Revisiting the urbanization of capital. *Annals of the Association of American Geographers* 101(6): 1347–64.
Ciccantell, P. 2009. China's economic ascent and Japan's raw-material peripheries. In H.-F. Hung (ed.), *China and the transformation of global capitalism*. Baltimore: Johns Hopkins University Press, pp. 109–29.
Cowen, D. 2014. *The deadly life of logistics: Mapping violence in global trade*. Minneapolis, MN: University of Minnesota Press.
Crippa, M., E. Solazzo, D. Guizzardi, F. Monforti-Ferrario, F.N. Tubiello, and A. Leip. 2021. Food systems are responsible for a third of global anthropogenic GHC emissions. *Nature Food* 2: 198–209.
Cuevas Valenzuela, H. and Budrovich Sáez, J. 2018. Contested logistics? Neoliberal modernization and resistance in the port of Valparaíso. In J.A. Wilson and I. Ness (eds.), *Choke points: Logistics workers disrupting the global supply chain*. London: Pluto Press, pp. 162–78.
De Los Reyes, J.A. 2017. Mining shareholder value: Institutional shareholders, transnational corporations, and the geography of gold mining. *Geoforum* 84: 251–64.
Feagin, J. 1990. Extractive regions in developed countries: A comparative analysis of the oil capitals, Houston and Aberdeen. *Urban Affairs Review* 25(4): 591–619.
Fine, B. and A. Saad-Filho. 2016. *Marx's 'Capital'*. London: Pluto Press.
Gago, V. and S. Mezzadra. 2017. A critique of the extractive operations of capital: Toward an expanded conception of extractivism. *Rethinking Marxism* 29(4): 574–91.
Gordillo, G. 2019. The metropolis: The infrastructure of the Anthropocene. In K. Hetherington (ed.), *Infrastructures, environment and life in the Anthropocene*. Durham: Duke University Press, pp. 66–94.
Harvey, D. 1985. *The urbanization of capital*. Baltimore: Johns Hopkins University Press.
Harvey, D. 2006 [1982]. *Limits to capital*. London and New York: Verso.
Harvey, D. 2013. *A companion to Marx's Capital, volume 2*. London and New York: Verso.

Heinrich, M. 2012. *An introduction to the three volumes of Marx's* Capital. New York: Monthly Review Press.

Heynen, N., M. Kaika, and E. Swyngedouw (eds.). 2006. *In the nature of cities: Urban political ecology and the nature of urban metabolisms*. New York: Routledge.

Innovum/Fundación Chile. 2014. *Proveedores de la minería chilena: Estudio de caracterización 2014* [*Suppliers of the mining industry: A profile study 2014*]. Santiago de Chile: Fundación Chile.

Intergovernmental Panel on Biodiversity and Ecosystem Services (IPBES). 2019. *Global Assessment Report on Biodiversity and Ecosystem Services*. Bonn, Germany: IPBES Secretariat.

Intergovernmental Panel on Climate Change (IPCC). 2019. *Climate change and land: An IPCC special report on climate change, desertification, land degradation, sustainable land management, food security, and greenhouse gas fluxes in terrestrial ecosystems*. Geneva: IPCC Secretariat.

Kaika, M. and L. Ruggiero. 2015. Class meets land: The social mobilization of land as catalyst for urban change. *Antipode* 47(3): 708–29.

Kaika, M. and L. Ruggiero. 2016. Land financialization as a 'lived' process: The transformation of Milan's Bicocca by Pirelli. *European Urban and Regional Studies* 23(1): 3–22.

Kaika, M. and E. Swyngedouw. 2000. Fetishizing the modern city: The phantasmagoria of urban technological networks. *International Journal of Urban and Regional Research* 24(1): 120–38.

Kenny, B. and A. Bezuidenhout. 1999. Changing nature of subcontracting in the South African mining industry. *Journal of the South African Institute of Mining and Metallurgy* (July/August): 185–92.

Kirshner, J. and M. Power. 2015. Mining and extractive urbanism: Postdevelopment in a Mozambican boomtown. *Geoforum* 61: 67–78.

Khanna, P. 2016. *Connectography: Mapping the global network revolution*. London: Weidenfeld & Nicolson.

Labban, M. 2010. Oil in parallax: Scarcity, markets and the financialization of accumulation. *Geoforum* 41: 541–52.

Labban, M. 2014. Against shareholder value: Accumulation in the oil industry and the biopolitics of labour under finance. *Antipode* 46(2): 477–96.

Luxemburg, R. 2003 [1913]. *The accumulation of capital*. Translated by A. Schwarzschild. New York: Routledge Classics.

Marx, K. 1973 [1939]. *Grundrisse: Foundations of the critique of political economy*. New York: Penguin Books.

Marx, K. 1992 [1885]. *Capital: A Critique of Political Economy, Vol. 2*. New York: Penguin Books.

Mezzadra, S. and B. Neilson. 2017. On the multiple frontiers of extraction: Excavating contemporary capitalism. *Cultural Studies* 31(2–3): 185–204.

Oreskes, N. and E. Conway. 2011. *Merchants of doubt: How a handful of scientists obscured the truth on issues from tobacco smoke to global warming*. New York: Bloomsbury Press.

Purcell, T., A. Loftus, and H. March. 2019. Value-rent-finance. *Progress in Human Geography*. https://doi.org/10.1177/0309132519838064

Rehner, J. and S. Rodríguez-Leiva. 2017. Inversión inmobiliaria en tiempos de auge y crisis: es la ciudad un producto minero o derivado financiero? [Real estate investment in times of boom and crisis: Is the city a mining product or a financial derivative?]. *Revista de Geografía Norte Grande* 67: 183–210.

Rehner, J. and F. Vergara. 2014. Efectos recientes de la actividad exportadora sobre la reestructuración económica urbana en Chile [Recent Effects of Export Activity on Economic Restructuring in Chile]. *Revista de Geografía Norte Grande* 59: 83–103.
Riofrancos, T. 2021. The rush to 'go electric' comes with a hidden cost: Destructive lithium mining. *The Guardian*, 14 June. www.theguardian.com/commentisfree/2021/jun/14/electric-cost-lithium-mining-decarbonasation-salt-flats-chile?fbclid=IwAR0mD94pIuY5wsZBV8GKYLKpPEkVQnO5qfokOVyI073ZbqYkOPsQsBFLioI.
Ruiz R., N. Yaneth, and L.D.S. Rivas. 2016. La nueva geografía de la explotación minero-energética y la acumulación por desposesión en Colombia entre 1997 y 2012 [The new geography of mining-energy production and accumulation by dispossession in Colombia in the 1997–2012 period]. *Notas de Población* 102: 249–77.
Sassen, S. 2014. *Expulsions: Complexity and brutality in the global economy*. Cambridge, MA: Harvard University Press.
Sassen, S. 2017. Predatory formations dressed in wall street suits and algorithmic math. *Science, Technology & Society* 22(1): 1–15.
Schmalz, S. 2016. El ascenso de China en el sistema mundial: Consecuencias en la economía política de sudamérica [The ascent of China in the world system: Consequences for the political economy of South America]. *Pléyade* 18: 159–92.
Stanley, L. 2016. El proceso de internacionalización del RMB y el nuevo protagonismo del sistema financiero chino [The internationalization of the RMB and the new protagonism of the Chinese financial system]. In E.D. Peters (ed.), *América Latina y el Caribe-China: Economía, Comercio e Inversiones* [*Latin America and the Caribbean and China: Economy, trade and investment*]. Mexico: Unión de Universidades de América Latina y el Caribe, pp. 147–70.
Toscano, A. 2014. Lineaments of the logistical state. *Viewpoint Magazine*. www.viewpointmag.com/2014/09/28/lineaments-of-the-logistical-state/, accessed 12 August 2022.
Tsing, A. 2005. *Friction: An ethnography of global connection*. Oxford: Princeton University Press.
Tzaninis, Y., T. Mandler, M. Kaika, and R. Keil. 2021. Moving urban political ecology beyond the 'urbanization of nature'. *Progress in Human Geography* 45(2): 229–52.
Urry, J. 2014. *Offshoring*. London: Polity.
Valdez Mingramm, R. 2013. China y América Latina hacia el 2030, colaboración estratégica y colaboración energética [China and Latin America towards 2030: Strategic Partnership and energy partnership]. In Y.T. Delfín (ed.), *América Latina y el Caribe-China: Recursos Naturales y Medio Ambiente* [*Latin America and the Caribbean and China: Natural resources and the environment*]. Mexico: Unión de Universidades de América Latina y el Caribe, pp. 31–42.
Vásquez Duplat, A.M. 2017. Extractivismo urbano y feminismo: Dos claves para el estudio de las ciudades [Urban extractivism and feminism: Two elements for the study of cities]. In A.M. Vásquez Duplat (ed.), *Extractivismo Urbano: Debate para una Construcción Colectiva de las Ciudades* [*Urban extractivism: Debate for the collective construction of cities*]. Buenos Aires: Editorial El Colectivo, pp. 98–108.
Vergara-Perucich, J.F. 2018. Aplicaciones de la teoría implosión/explosión: relación entre la Región Metropolitana de Santiago de Chile y los territorios productivos

regionales [Usages of the theory of implosion/explosion: Relation between the Santiago metropolitan region and the regional productive territories]. *EURE* 44(133): 77–96.

Viale, E. 2017. El Extractivismo Urbano [Urban extractivism]. In A.M. Vásquez Duplat (ed.), *Extractivismo Urbano: Debate para una Construcción Colectiva de las Ciudades* [*Urban extractivism: Debate for the collective construction of cities*]. Buenos Aires: Editorial El Colectivo, pp. 15–24.

War on Want and London Mining Network. 2020. *A just(ice) transition is a post-extractive transition: Centering the extractive frontier in climate justice*. London: War on Want and London Mining Network.

Ye, J., J.D. van der Ploeg, S. Schneider, and T. Shanin. 2020. The incursions of extractivism: Moving from dispersed places to global capitalism. *Journal of Peasant Studies* 47(1): 155–83.

5

Hinterlands of the Capitalocene[1]

Neil Brenner and Nikos Katsikis

Contemporary conceptualisations of the urban condition emphasise the specific geographies, dynamics, and consequences of city-building processes, whether in specific regional contexts, or as a national, continental, or global aggregation. Such conceptualisations have been pervasive in recent debates on the global urban age and global urbanism, which treat 'the city' as the key arena for the major political-economic and ecological transformations of our time. Major disagreements abound regarding how best to understand cities, their spatial patterns, their developmental dynamics, their crisis tendencies, and their future potentialities. Nonetheless, from the resurgent universalism of contemporary agglomeration economics and the new 'science of cities' to the more contextually embedded explorations of postcolonial, Southern, and assemblage-theoretical approaches, there is an underlying consensus regarding the basic parameters of the urban question. This consensus can be concisely captured in the following formulas:

urban = city
urbanisation = city growth

Today, this methodologically cityist framing of the urban question appears nearly all-pervasive, even among critically reflexive accounts that reject inherited technoscientific, Eurocentric, and economistic models, that insist on the situatedness, provisionality, and ideological overdetermination of urban epistemologies, and that emphasise the uneven, crisis-riven character of urban development. The urban is conceived, at core, with reference to the conditions, morphologies, and transformations of the city, a specific type of human settlement or techno-infrastructure that is contrasted to other, putatively non-urban (suburban, rural, or wilderness) spaces (Brenner and Schmid, 2013; Angelo and Wachsmuth, 2015).

In our recent work, in collaboration with Christian Schmid and other scholars of planetary urbanisation, we have questioned this inherited epistemology of the urban (Brenner and Schmid, 2015; Brenner, 2016; Katsikis, 2018). We do not deny the fundamental connection between urbanisation and the power of agglomeration (and thus, with spaces that have been labelled as 'cities'). We argue, however, that the urbanisation/city nexus is not logically self-evident. Unlike an analytical statement whose subject and predicate mutually contain one another (for example, 'a triangle is a three-sided figure'), the assumption that 'urbanisation entails city growth' requires careful theoretical clarification and comparative historical-geographical investigation: it is not a logical truism but a *synthetic* proposition whose content must be systematically explicated. From this perspective, the connection between urbanisation and city-building is not a definitionally pregiven premise for urban research, but one of its core *problematiques*. Rather than presupposing the outcome (the growth of 'the city') of the process under investigation (urbanisation) as a logical requirement or definitional necessity, this approach to urban studies asks: how, why, and with what consequences do determinate patterns and pathways of city-building flow from historically and geographically specific forms of urbanisation? This reframing of the urban question requires not only the interrogation of its historically specific manifestations across spatio-temporal contexts, but a reflexively multiscalar analytic framework that embeds city-building processes within the broader political-economic and environmental geographies that at once support and result from them.

While the notion of the city is likely to remain useful and even necessary as a generic shorthand reference to zones of spatial concentration, densification and intensification (and their juridical expressions in municipal governmental apparatuses), its deployment as a social science concept requires considerable caution, precision, specificity, and reflexivity. Too often, folk concepts of the city have been naturalised in the social sciences, in part due to their pervasive deployment by state institutions, corporate alliances, and growth coalitions to promote projects of territorial regulation, biopolitical management, and economic development. This widespread conflation of categories of practice with categories of analysis has undermined the capacity of urban scholars to interrogate the specific processes and (geo)political strategies through which apparently 'city-like' spaces are produced and transformed across time and space. The concept of *concentrated urbanisation* breaks from the long entrenched, *a priori* assumption that urbanisation processes result in formally identical, city-like spatial units, directing attention instead to the patterned diversity of such processes, their contextually specific causes, their variegated spatial expressions and their wide-ranging consequences.

This epistemological reorientation is closely connected to a second core research agenda among scholars of planetary urbanisation – namely, to consider processes of city-building as being intermeshed with massive transformations of socio-spatial and political-ecological relations beyond the city, across diverse territories and landscapes. While such 'hinterland' spaces may not assume city-like morphologies or demographics, their socio-spatial relations, land-use arrangements, infrastructural configurations, and biogeophysical dynamics are fundamentally shaped and reshaped through their evolving connections to city-building processes, networks, and systems. From this point of view, the preconditions and consequences of city-building stretch far beyond the city's immediate environs, at once in political-economic, infrastructural, and metabolic terms. The term 'hinterland' is used here to demarcate the variegated non-city spaces that are thereby swept into the maelstrom of urbanisation, whether as supply zones, logistical corridors, impact zones, sacrifice zones, or otherwise. Such spaces include human settlements (cities, towns, villages), land-use configurations (industrial, agrarian, extractive), and non-human ecologies (terrestrial, oceanic, subterranean, atmospheric). We refer to explorations of such spaces, and their role in urbanisation processes, as engagements with 'the hinterland question'.

The concept of *extended urbanisation* refers to the co-evolution of hinterland zones with metropolitan centres and, more generally, in relation to ongoing processes of concentrated urbanisation. Within this expanded conceptualisation of the urban question, the non-city preconditions and consequences of city-building are essential and intrinsic, not secondary or extrinsic, dimensions of the urbanisation process. Here, urbanisation is conceived as a dialectic of implosion-explosion: it encompasses not only the moment of spatial concentration (city-building), but equally, the making and remaking of extra-city geographies and political ecologies in direct relation to the latter (Lefebvre, 2003 [1970]); Brenner, 2013, 2019). Thus conceived, city/hinterland dynamics are not a merely contingent articulation among distinct, externally related sites or spaces, but represent mutually co-constitutive, dialectically interlinked moments of the urbanisation process (Arboleda, 2015, 2016).

Against the background of these epistemological realignments and conceptual proposals, this chapter revisits the *problematique* of the hinterland question, especially since the accelerated industrialisation of capital in the mid-nineteenth century. Across the urban social sciences and design disciplines, the hinterland question is today largely considered secondary or irrelevant to the study of urbanisation. The city, its dense socio-economic networks, and its powerful agglomeration economies occupy centre stage. We consider this position untenable: from our perspective, the dialectic of city/hinterland relations lies at the heart of the urban *problematique*. And yet, these relations are today undergoing mutations that necessitate not only a repositioning of the hinterland question into the core of urban research and practice, but its radical reconceptualisation as such.

Cities without hinterlands?

Prior to the 1970s, the field of urban studies devoted extensive attention to the role of non-city landscapes in the urbanisation process. From Johann Heinrich von Thünen's early nineteenth-century model of the relationship between an isolated city and land-use differentiation in its agrarian hinterland, through the early twentieth-century writings of Patrick Geddes, Lewis Mumford, and Benton MacKaye on ecological regionalism, up through post-Second World War explorations of central place hierarchies and polarised regional development, city/hinterland relations were widely regarded as constitutive dimensions of the urban *problematique* (Katsikis, 2016).

However, during the last half-century, the hinterland has largely disappeared from urban theoretical discourse, or has been relegated to mere background status. Under conditions of accelerated geoeconomic integration, splintering national economies, the rollout of neoliberal austerity programs, cascading social, financial, and ecological crises, and proliferating local growth initiatives, cities are increasingly viewed as self-propelled economic engines. Within this post-1980s approach to the urban question, the major emphasis is on the internal preconditions, dynamics, and consequences of agglomeration. Urbanisation is understood as city growth *tout court* – in effect, as *city*isation – rather than as a process that is actively supported by non-city spaces (Soja, 2000).

The empty, desolate, and isolated condition to which the planet's non-city spaces are thereby consigned is starkly illustrated in the iconic image of the world's night-time lights, in which brightness is treated as a proxy for cityness. This excision of the hinterland's role in urbanisation is even more starkly spatialised in the influential concept of the 'spiky world', developed by urbanist Richard Florida (2005). Here, cities are viewed as the nodal concentration points of global GDP. In both visualisations, non-city spaces appear as barren, depopulated, shapeless voids.

While the roots of this conceptualisation predate the 1970s, it was consolidated into a broadly shared episteme of urban studies following the erosion of Fordist-Keynesian, national-developmentalist capitalism. Debates on industrial clusters in the 1980s, global cities in the 1990s, postcolonial cities in the 2000s, and more recent assertions of a majority-urban world or 'urban age' represent but variations on an underlying vision of cities without hinterlands.

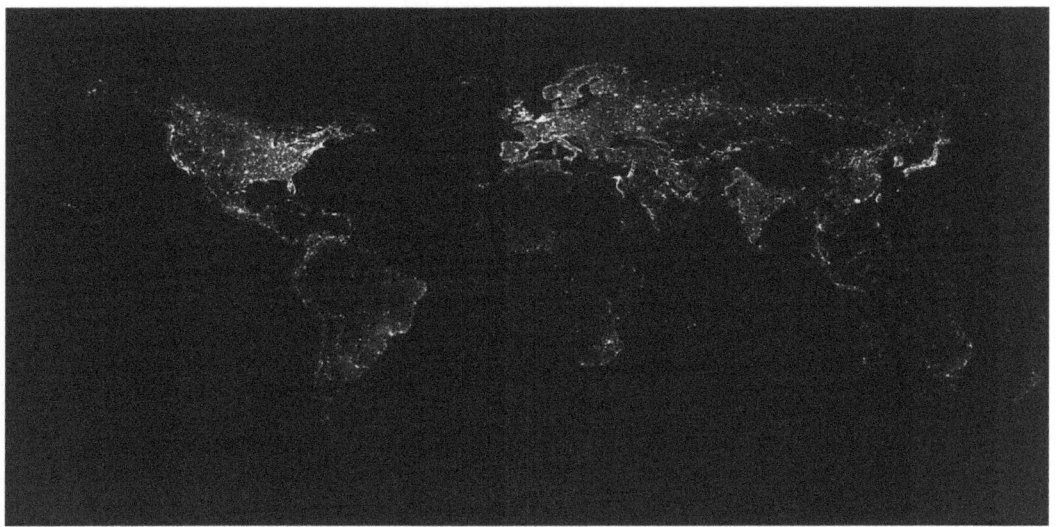

Figure 5.1 Night-time lights of the world. Few images have had a greater impact on contemporary metanarratives of global urbanisation than the 'night-time lights of the world' series, initially synthesised during the 1990s in the National Geophysical Data Center (NGDC) in Boulder, Colorado, and subsequently improved through NASA's remote sensing networks.

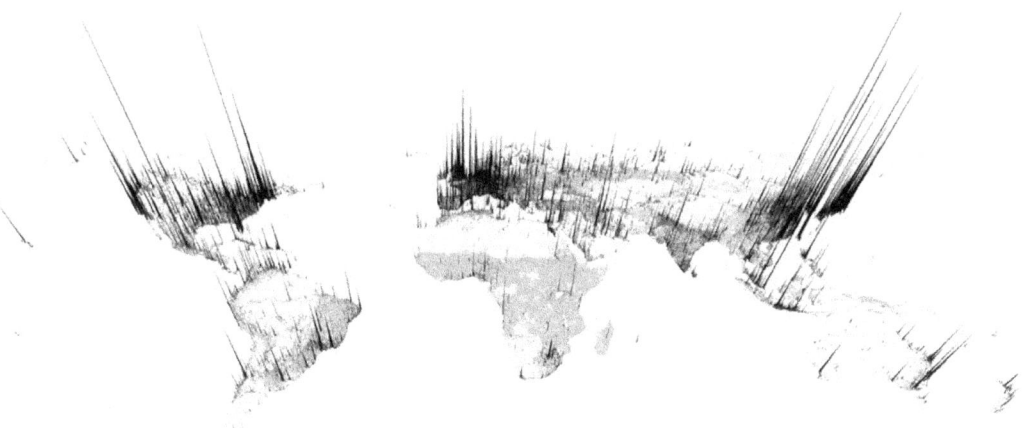

Figure 5.2 Spiky world: Geographical distribution of global GDP in a three-dimensional perspective. Based on a disaggregation of national GDP data, this visualisation represents cities and metropolitan regions as the 'spiky' concentration points for major economic activities, reflecting an approach popularised by Richard Florida. Hinterlands – the world's non-city spaces – are correspondingly represented as empty, barren, and, by implication, economically marginal.

Counterpoint: Metabolic urbanisation

The major contemporary counterpoints to this hegemonic, city-centric approach to urban studies are associated with various streams of urban ecological thought. Despite their otherwise divergent agendas, these dissident approaches conceive urbanisation as a socio-metabolic process. From this point of view, cities are supported by diverse metabolic inputs (labour, materials, fuel, water, and food), the vast majority of which are produced within non-city zones and, eventually, absorbed back into them as metabolic by-products (waste, pollution, carbon emissions). Such approaches embrace a multiscalar understanding of urbanisation that encompasses not only cities and metropolitan regions, but extended landscapes of primary commodity production, logistics and waste management. Metabolic approaches to urbanisation thus seek to connect the dynamics of agglomeration to a panoply of non-city geographies – for instance, of land enclosure, population displacement, deforestation, industrial agriculture, extraction, energetics, logistics, waste processing, and ecological load displacement.[2]

The contemporary vibrancy of metabolic approaches to urbanisation underscores the continued centrality of hinterland questions to early twenty-first-century urban studies. These research traditions have contributed fundamental insights that unsettle the myopic narrowing of urban investigations to cities and intercity relations, while illuminating the myriad socio-material processes through which city development is supported by, and actively coevolves with, non-city spaces. Thus understood, cities are *not* self-propelled. The urban process is materialised within city spaces while invariably exceeding them. City and non-city landscapes are thus dialectically *coproduced* under modern capitalism. The urban *problematique* can only be deciphered adequately through an approach that dialectically connects them, at once in social, political, material, infrastructural, and ecological terms.

The hinterland enigma

Despite its role in offering powerful scholarly counterpoints to the ideology of the self-propelled city, the bulk of contemporary urban ecological scholarship has confronted the hinterland question only indirectly. While studies of urban metabolism have exhaustively quantified the material and energetic flows that mediate city/hinterland relations, they have tended to by-pass the question of how non-city spaces are reconfigured through these mediations. Consequently, the hinterland itself has remained something of a 'black box': metabolic flows move in and out, but what actually happens 'inside' the box, and how the latter has itself evolved, are not interrogated.

The hinterland's internal political-economic operations, land-use matrices, property relations, spatio-temporal dynamics and socio-ecological crisis-tendencies thus remain enigmatic.

Many contemporary urban researchers appear to presuppose a conception of the hinterland that is derived from the mercantile period of capitalist development in which von Thünen constructed his famous account of the 'isolated state' (1966 [1826]). Here, the hinterland is territorially contiguous and directly linked to the city, which in turn serves as its market outlet and its manufacturing centre. Although commodity production is generalised, there is no structural impulse to enhance labour productivity or to maximise crop yields. In this model, the non-city zone is, by definition, non-industrial; land-use sorting occurs due to differential transport costs.

The point here is not to assert that contemporary urbanists self-consciously embrace von Thünen's conception of a contiguous, nonindustrial hinterland, but to suggest that some version of this nineteenth-century model continues to shape our collective imagination of non-city landscapes, which are thereby reduced to what Gavin Bridge (2001: 2154) has aptly characterised as an amorphous 'ghost acreage' of 'emptied spaces, homogeneous blanks yet to be inscribed by human history'. To some degree, this tendency to 'black-box' spaces beyond the metropolis, or to treat them as a secondary expression or subsidiary consequence of urbanisation, remains a widely pervasive habit of mind in significant streams of urban political ecology (UPE). Indeed, despite its broadly effective transcendence of the city/nature divide and its consistent embrace of a relational conception of scale, key streams of UPE research have been framed in ways that equate the urban with processes of socio-spatial concentration *tout court*. Consequently, the broader implications of a UPE approach for rethinking the variegated, uneven geographies of urbanisation under capitalism have only just begun to be systematically explored (for further elaborations on this problem, see Angelo and Wachsmuth, 2015; and Tzaninis et al., Introduction to this volume).

In sum, critical urban scholars have only rarely sought to decipher the specific patterns and pathways through which hinterlands – variegated non-city zones across the planet – have been enclosed, colonised and creatively destroyed since the 1850s, even though such transformations have been as far-reaching as those that are commonly ascribed to the crisis-riven remaking of cities' own built environments during the same period. Investigating such mutations will require new conceptualisations of city/hinterland matrices in relation to historical, contemporary, and emergent geographies and political ecologies of planetary urbanisation (this framework of analysis is further elaborated in Brenner and Schmid, 2015; Katsikis, 2016; Sevilla-Buitrago, 2013; Brenner and Ghosh, 2022).

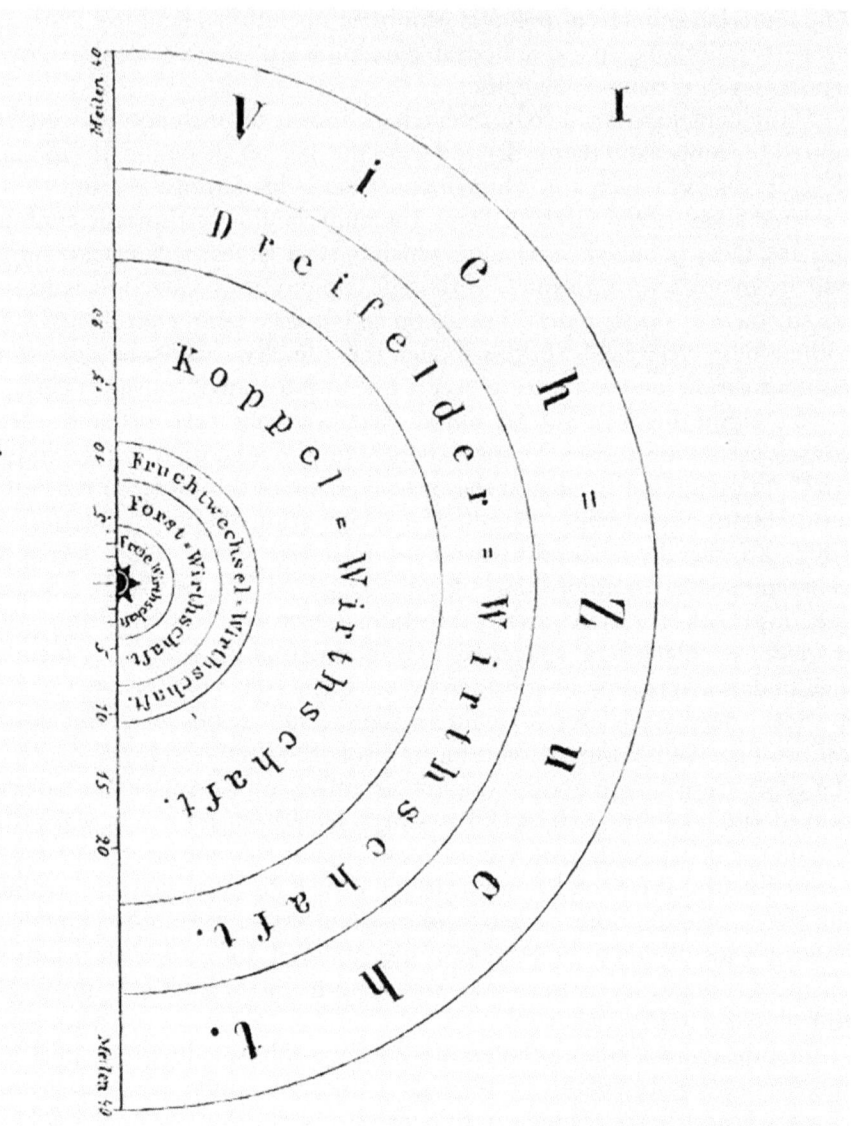

Figure 5.3 The hinterland of the 'isolated state': Von Thünen's visualisation (1826). Johann Heinrich von Thünen's model of city/hinterland relations under mercantile capitalism shaped many subsequent generations of scholarship in urban economic geography. However, except in a few limit-cases of continued, dense metabolic interchange between settlements and their immediately contiguous supply zones, its basic assumptions have been superseded through the forward-motion of capitalist industrialisation.

Hinterlands of the Capitalocene

How, then, to decipher the role of hinterlands in supporting and buffering the metabolic dynamics, rifts, and crisis-tendencies of urbanisation under capitalism? This challenge is, on the one hand, a conceptual one insofar as it requires us to rethink the very nature of hinterlands in the age of capital, or 'Capitalocene' (Moore, 2018). The hinterland concept is not only a technical term of art within economic geography, but has been thoroughly intermeshed with racialised historical geographies of colonisation, land grabbing, enclosure, territorial dispossession, and institutionalised violence against Indigenous people, enslaved Africans, and other subordinated, displaced, and 'surplus' populations.[3] The exploration of such issues will require rigorously historical analysis, since the social, infrastructural, institutional, and environmental geographies of 'hinterlandised' regions have been dramatically transformed during the process of capitalist industrial development, in close connection to state spatial strategies to shape and reshape patterns of spatial inequality within and beyond their territories. Indeed, much like the term 'city', the inherited notion of the hinterland implies a static, context-transcendent universalism that belies the extraordinary variegation and dynamism of the spaces it purports to demarcate, while occluding the relations of imperial power, racial domination, and unequal ecological exchange through which they are constituted. As such, even within the definitionally specific parameters demarcated above, the hinterland concept should be used only with utmost reflexivity and precision, and as no more than a 'first cut' towards a broader inquiry into the *problematique* of extended urbanisation.

Investigating the hinterlands of the Capitalocene will also require a systematic re-engagement with classic questions about cities and empire. Much of the inherited scholarship on such issues emphasises the role of cities as 'spearheads' for colonial territorial conquest, plunder of resources, and ideological domination.[4] While our approach affirms the contributions of this classical line of analysis, it also directs attention to the intrinsic connection between accelerated city-building processes under capitalism and what we might think of as the 'hinterlandisation' of the world – that is, the large-scale enclosure, colonisation, and operationalisation of non-city zones, within and beyond capital's Euro-American heartlands, into subordinate zones of extraction through which successive historical 'cheap natures' are appropriated.[5] From this expanded point of view, urbanisation involves not only the role of city-building in grounding imperial projects of territorial expansion, but variegated processes of hinterlandisation through which non-city zones are operationalised, both economically and ecologically, to support agglomeration-centric processes of geographical transfer of value in both metropole and colony alike.[6] In this sense, the project of superseding narrowly Eurocentric formations of the urban question must not only explore the decidedly *non*-derivative theoretical significance of urbanisms beyond the West, but the *coloniality of urbanisation* itself – that is, the multiscalar, intercontinental force fields of extraction, surplus value transfer, and thermodynamic imperialism that underpin, animate, and result from city-building processes under modern capitalism.[7]

Confronting the hinterland enigma is, finally, a challenge that will require critical appropriations of newly available sources of geospatial data, which may offer a powerful basis for investigating the historical and contemporary rearticulation of land uses, built and unbuilt environments, and political ecologies around the world (Bergmann and Holmberg, 2016; Katsikis et al., forthcoming). It is not sufficient simply to posit that such non-city 'outsides' are constitutively important for city-building processes, or to focus on measuring the role of such spaces as 'taps' and 'sinks' for the metabolic dynamics of capitalist urbanisation. While this vast planetary hinterland covers nearly 70 per cent of the earth's terrestrial surface, and is densely layered with productive, extractive, circulatory, and informational infrastructure, it has remained an obscure background to the study of contemporary urbanisation. It is precisely in this sense that the 'black box' of the hinterland must be opened and systematically rearticulated to the central agendas of urban studies. What

Figure 5.4 Agglomerations and the 'used area' of the planet in the early twenty-first century. This map juxtaposes a demarcation of the world's metropolitan agglomerations onto a rendering of the total 'used area' of the entire planet. Agglomeration zones constitute only a miniscule percentage of the planet's operationalised landscapes, which are mostly devoted to primary commodity production (agricultural cultivation, grazing, forestry), resource extraction, logistics, and waste disposal.

is required is a framework that can connect historically and geographically specific forms of city and non-city space (and associated relations of domination) as coproduced, coevolving moments within the combined, uneven, variegated, and crisis-riven world-ecologies of capitalist urbanisation.

The development of such a framework requires systematic elaboration elsewhere. Here, it must suffice to offer some initial generalisations regarding four key mutations of city/hinterland relations that have been particularly pronounced during the past half-century. These relatively abstract propositions are not intended to foreclose more contextually embedded, historically specific lines of inquiry, but to stimulate further reflection, investigation, and debate regarding the restlessly churning dynamics of planetary urbanisation. We aim not to subsume all aspects of social life in non-city zones under the latter rubric, but rather to mobilise the methodological tactics proposed here as a basis for investigating historically and geographically specific processes of hinterlandisation, and their far-reaching implications for the political-economic and environmental geographies of capital. For present purposes, we continue to deploy the term hinterland, even as our analysis demarcates various ways in which its analytic usefulness has been ever-more narrowly circumscribed through the vicissitudes of capitalist uneven spatial development.

Enclosure, distanciation, and infrastructuralisation

First, primary commodity production has been globalised and specialised, causing local, contiguous hinterlands to be enmeshed within export-oriented transnational production networks. Contiguous hinterlands remain important, but are no longer the norm, either in the older industrialised world or in most Southern megacities. This implosion-explosion of hinterland zones has been animated by capital's drive to increase labour productivity, to extend interspatial connectivity, and to appropriate ecological surpluses, all of which entail the construction of large-scale infrastructural configurations for extraction, production, and circulation, and the concomitant expropriation of peasant populations from their historic means of subsistence. While such strategies may temporarily boost profits, they also increase the organic composition of capital, as living labour is replaced by machinery, equipment, and infrastructure. This leads to the precipitous decline of the non-city workforce ('depeasantisation'), the dispossession of formerly agrarian laborers from non-market means of social reproduction, and their mass expulsion into the squatter settlements, or 'slums', of expanding megacities, where they forge informal economies of survival as a proletarianised, migratory reserve army of 'surplus labour'.[8] This demographic 'emptying of the world's countryside' has been inextricably linked to strategies to hollow out, enclose, and operationalise the spaces of erstwhile rural life – manifested,

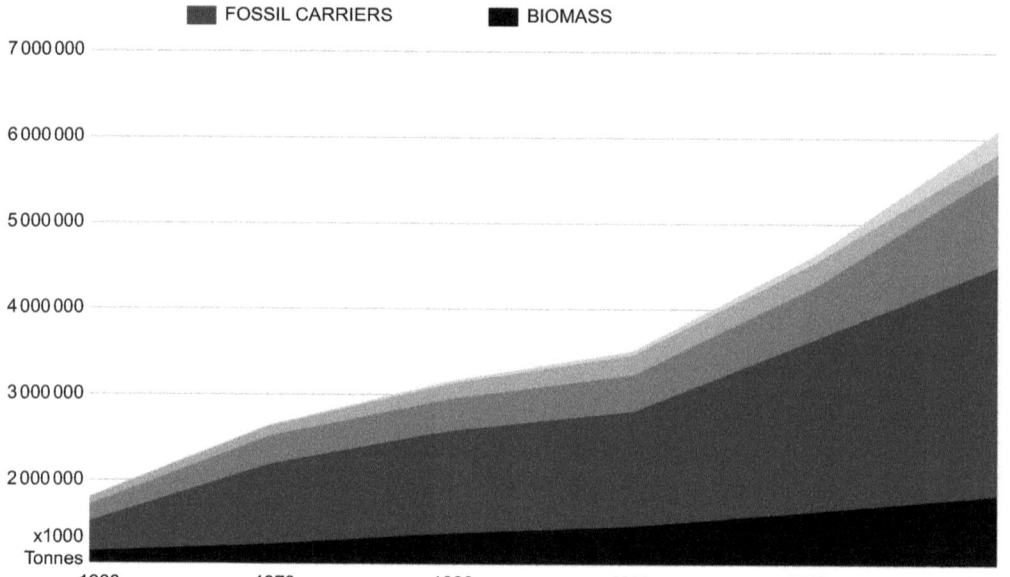

Figure 5.5 Growth in global trade of basic materials, 1960–2010. Over the past decade, the global trade in primary commodities – such as agricultural and forestry products (biomass), fossil fuels, industrial minerals, metals, and construction materials – has increased more than threefold. This reflects the increasing globalisation of hinterland economies.

for example, in the differential integration of smallholders into cash-crop based commercial networks, the progressive concentration of agrarian property regimes, the resurgence of plantation agriculture, the large-scale conversion of arable land into enclosed livestock pasture, the establishment of robotised, monofunctional, and export-oriented agribusiness landscapes, and massive ecological devastation, as significant territories are transformed into 'sacrifice zones' for capital's spatially externalised impacts.[9]

Hinterlands of hinterlands

Second, as they are embedded within global supply chains, inherited hinterlands lose their directional articulation to specific zones of consumption, metropolitan or otherwise. The linear directionality of von Thünen's classic model – in which each hinterland has 'its' city, and each city 'its' hinterland – is thus no longer a reliable guide. The point is not simply that contemporary cities' hinterlands are more distanciated than previously, but that their operational logics, infrastructural configuration, metabolic relays, and developmental dynamics have been qualitatively transformed. On the one hand, most of the world's most productive, specialised, and export-oriented

Figure 5.6 Worlds of specialised agricultural production, 2000. This map series depicts the geographical distribution of production sites for the five most globally traded agricultural commodities as of 2000. The grayscale gradient on the maps corresponds to production areas (arranged, respectively, from top to bottom) for corn, soybeans, wheat, palm oil, and cotton.

hinterlands now circulate their outputs to a multitude of metropolitan agglomerations and across the global metropolitan network as a whole. Just as importantly, many zones of primary commodity production are now most directly articulated not to major cities and metropolitan regions, but to other operational landscapes of extraction, cultivation, processing, and distribution, which are in turn embedded and intermeshed within an intercontinental logistics space. This situation is exemplified in the monocrop soybean landscapes of Amazonia, whose outputs are mostly exported as cattle feed to Chinese livestock hinterlands; in the export of phosphate fertiliser from Central Florida to Brazilian agro-industrial hinterlands; or in the use of hydroelectric dams to power the extractive hinterlands of northern Chile. In this sense, the hinterlands of the Capitalocene are now more tightly articulated to transnational production matrices than to localised relays of consumption (Bergmann and Holmberg, 2016).

From formal to real subsumption

Third, most forms of primary commodity production have remained heavily contingent upon the extra-human geographies of the earth system (for instance, soil and weather conditions, water availability, or resource deposits) that can only be modified through significant industrial investment (for instance, in fertiliser, greenhouses, irrigation systems, biotechnology, and other socio-technical fixes). Historically, therefore, the industrial operationalisation of hinterland spaces has occurred through strategies to establish new resource frontiers and, as the latter are exhausted, through compensatory efforts to intensify techno-extractive logics. In both moments of this process, new industrial infrastructures are established and intensively operationalised before being superseded as successive regimes of accumulation are exhausted. Many contemporary hinterlands, therefore, are no longer zones of mere 'formal subsumption' in which inherited socio-ecological resource matrices and regimes of cheap nature are directly appropriated as commodities for external market exchange. Insofar as the geographies and ecologies of non-city zones are themselves systematically re-engineered to maximise surplus value extraction and accelerate capital accumulation, a 'real subsumption' of hinterland spaces appears to be under way: nature is itself increasingly capitalised in a profit-driven terraforming process.[10] In this manner, many erstwhile hinterlands, or parts thereof, are transformed into configurations of large-scale territorial-ecological machinery: capital-intensive, more-than-human infrastructural assemblages oriented towards capital accumulation within a planet-encompassing profit-matrix.

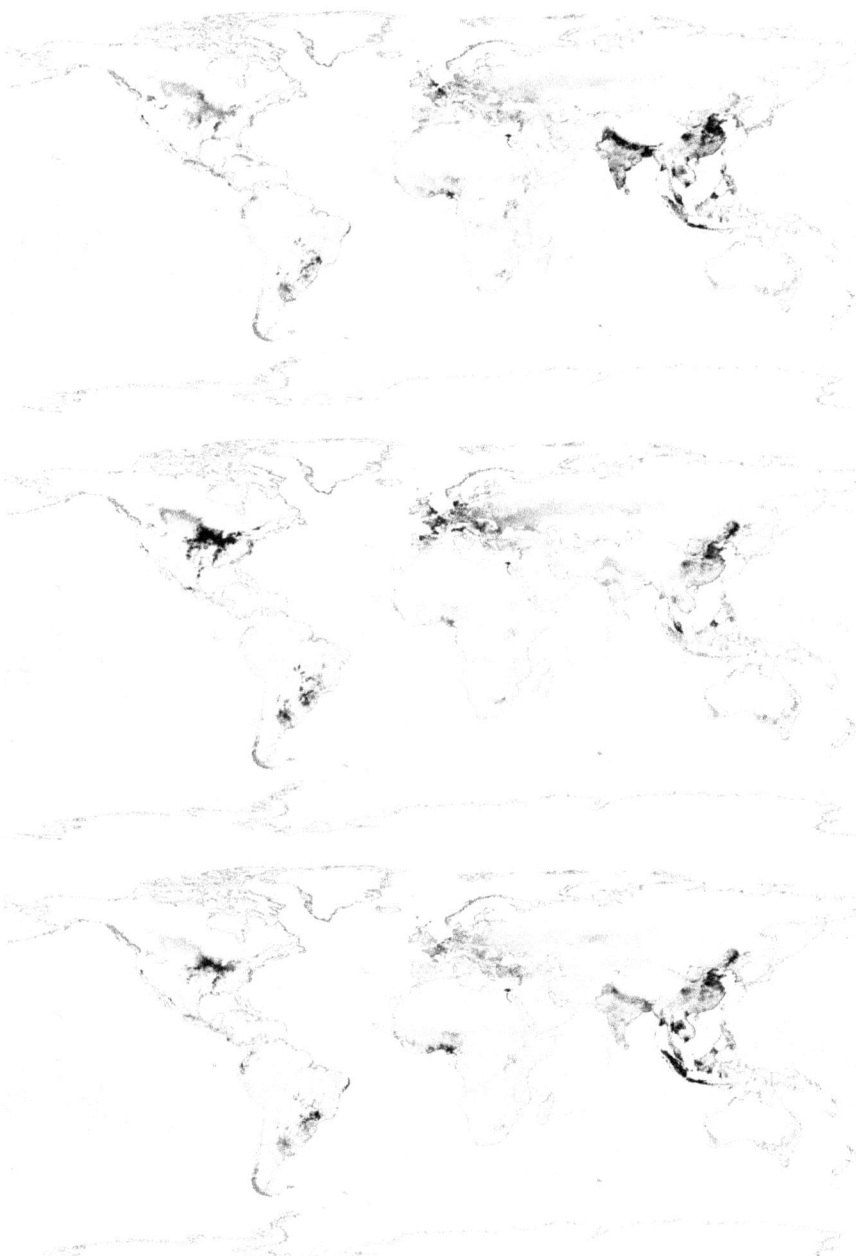

Figure 5.7 Hinterlands of hinterlands, 2000. This map series depicts the geographical distribution of cropland areas (arranged, respectively, from top to bottom) dedicated to food, feed, or non-food uses (such as energy and industrial inputs). The bottom two maps can be conceived as representations of hinterlands of hinterlands, insofar as they depict the supply of specific industrial inputs to other hinterlands (for example, cattle feed to livestock production zones, or biofuel to the energy sector).

Metabolic rifts and cycles of creative destruction

The proliferation of specialised, globally interdependent zones of primary commodity production reveals not only the ways in which inherited human and non-human landscapes have been commodified, infrastructuralised, capitalised, and terraformed, but the progressive depletion of their capacity to contribute ecological surpluses to sustain the accumulation process as they are subjected to overcultivation, overgrazing, deforestation, and generalised toxic contamination. The proliferation of such metabolic rifts further accelerates capital's drive to redesign, terraform, and mechanise hinterland geographies, at once through the substitution of manufactured, biotechnological inputs into production and through the construction of colossal techno-infrastructural configurations (Moore, 2015; Araghi, 2009). The hinterlands of the Capitalocene are, therefore, chronically unstable. As the capitalisation

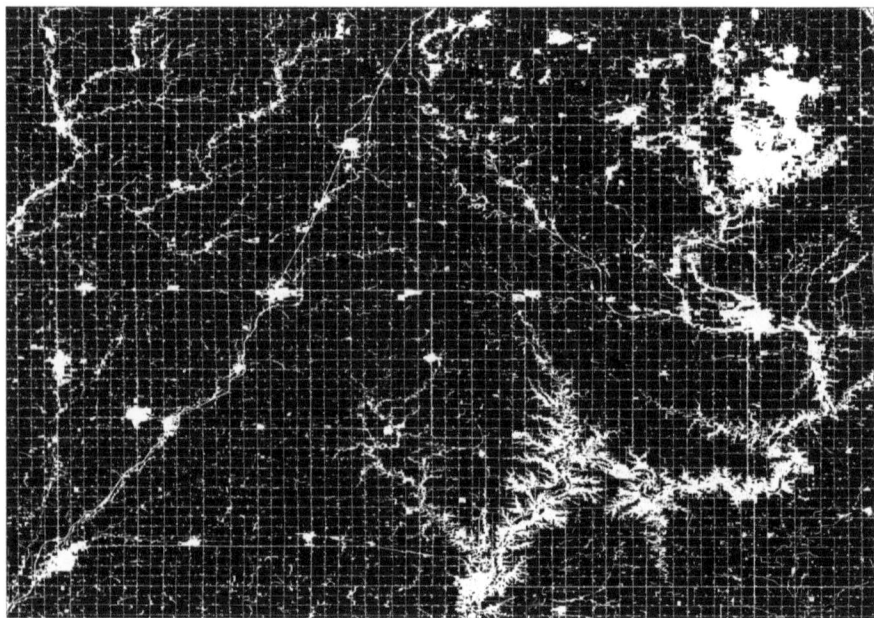

Figure 5.8 Mechanised, monoculture landscapes of corn and soybean production in the US Midwest, 2018. Capital-intensive, highly industrialised, and densely equipped landscapes of cash-crop monocultures dominate the US Cornbelt, where more than 80 per cent of all land is dedicated to the cultivation of corn and soybeans. The zone of corn and soybean production (depicted in black) is configured among one-mile tiles within a Jeffersonian grid pattern. This permits the maximally efficient operation of agro-industrial machinery. Beneath this terrestrial surface is an extensive subterranean drainage system that supports soil tilling.

Figure 5.9 Intensity of synthetic fertiliser application (nitrogen) over the global croplands, 2000. This map depicts annual levels and locations of nitrogen fertiliser use through a black-dotted gradient pattern. Since 1950, fertiliser use has increased ninefold, while total cropland area has expanded by less than 30 per cent.

of nature proceeds apace and ecological surpluses are exhausted, the resultant metabolic rifts severely destabilise prevalent regimes of accumulation, leaving vast tracts of 'dead land, dead water' in which not only economic activity, but life itself, are largely expunged (Sassen, 2015). Consequently, established hinterland infrastructural configurations and political ecologies are rendered obsolete, even though their socio-technical capacities and resource stocks may have been only partially amortised. This leads to intense struggles over the choreography, form, socio-ecological impacts, and future pathways of territorial transformation, across the global metropolitan network and throughout the interconnected landscapes of extraction, production, and circulation that underpin transnational production systems. For this reason, any contemporary approach to the hinterland question must consider the systemic political-economic *and* political-ecological vulnerabilities of those non-city spaces that have been forged to support the globalising, profit-maximising dynamics of supply-chain capitalism and its coordinating centres in the global metropolitan network.

The hinterland question reframed

Under contemporary conditions, there is no singular hinterland of 'the' city. Instead, non-city productive landscapes have become more specialised, infrastructurally dense, and industrially intensive, and they are intermeshed with one another through extended material, operational, and informational linkages, as well as through their continuous, but largely indirect exchanges with (strategic nodes within) the global metropolitan network. However, the operational landscapes of planetary urbanisation are hardly a stable foundation for territorial development, social reproduction, or political-ecological security. Indeed, even as they support (unevenly distributed bursts of) enhanced industrial productivity and the (crisis-riven) accelerated, long-distance circulation of commodities, the hinterlands of the Capitalocene expose local territories and communities to increasing turbulence, risk, and precarity, while systematically degrading the ecological preconditions of both human and non-human life on a planetary scale.

How, and by whom, has this planetary fabric of urbanisation been forged? What are its social, political, institutional, regulatory, and ecological preconditions? What are its major contradictions, crisis-tendencies, and vulnerabilities? Can the massive socio-technical capacities it has unleashed somehow be harnessed to support more just, democratic, non-violent, culturally vibrant, and ecologically sane forms of collective existence? Are there alternative forms of urbanisation, planetary or otherwise, and can their socio-metabolic dynamics be reflexively designed, negotiated, and institutionalised through political agency? Or, will the violent, exclusionary, and relentlessly profit-driven illogics of planetary urbanisation continue to degrade, erode, and destroy the web of life? These are among the most urgent dimensions of the hinterland question in the Capitalocene. They are essential for any critical approach to the political ecologies of contemporary urbanisation.

Notes

1 An earlier version of this chapter appeared in Michele Lancione and Colin McFarlane (eds.), 2021, *Global urbanism: Knowledge, power and the city*. New York: Routledge, pp. 34–48. © N. Brenner and N. Katsikis.

2 The most significant contemporary streams include, among others, historical investigations of city/hinterland relations, such as William Cronon's (1991) study of Chicago and the US Midwest in *Nature's metropolis*, or Gray Brechin's (1999) investigation of urbanising California in *Imperial San Francisco*; approaches to materials flow analysis by Marina Fischer-Kowalski, Helmut Haberl and their colleagues in the Institute of Social Ecology at Klagenfurt University (www.aau.at/en/social-ecology/, accessed 12 August 2022); the investigation of 'teleconnections' through which land use transformations in cities impact land-use change elsewhere developed by Karen Seto and her colleagues at Yale University (https://urban.yale.edu/, accessed 12 August 2022); the analysis of urban ecological footprints developed by William Rees, Mathis Wackernagel, and their collaborators (www.footprintnetwork.org/our-work/cities/, accessed 12 August 2022); as well as the wide-ranging field of urban

political ecology (UPE) research that was consolidated in the early 2000s through the pioneering work of, among other authors, Matthew Gandy, Nik Heynen, Maria Kaika, Roger Keil, and Erik Swyngedouw. For overviews and detailed citations to these literatures, see Katsikis (2016).

3 The link between hinterlandisation – the subordination of non-city space into a production and supply zone for city-based economic operations – and the violent seizure and enclosure of land is evident, albeit not centrally theorised, in Cronon's (1991) classic account of Chicago and the 'Great West'. On the genealogy of the hinterland concept within the study of ports, trade routes, and 'remote' zones by economic geographers, see van Cleef (1941).

4 On cities as 'spearheads' for empire, King (1990). In King's work, this conception is closely connected to a world-systems conception of spatial polarisation under capitalism, in which the world economy is coherently divided among core, semi-peripheral, and peripheral zones, with each defined as a more-or-less bounded territorial whole. Cities form the mediating links between such zones, the nodes of connectivity through which world-systemic relations of domination are articulated.

5 The concept of extraction is used here in a broad sense, not simply with reference to mining, but as a more general characterisation of capital's relentlessly expansionary transformation/appropriation of social and ecological relations to fuel its accumulation process. See Mezzadra and Neilson (2017). On the appropriation and capitalisation of cheap natures during successive world-ecological revolutions under capitalism, see Jason Moore's seminal account in *Capitalism and the web of life* (2015).

6 This formulation provides a basis on which to revisit some of the classic Marxian formulations on the city and the countryside, from Marx and Engels' *German ideology* (1845) and Antonio Gramsci's (2005 [1926]) account of the 'Southern Question' to Raymond Williams's *The country and the city* (1973), which explicitly connect intra-national city/countryside divides to broader geographies of worldwide imperialism. For further elaborations, see Brennan (2015), Ekers et al. (2013), and Goonewardena (2013). This approach also productively destabilises traditional, methodologically territorialist models of the capitalist world-system as involving a neat division among core, semi-peripheral, and peripheral zones. For a critique of the latter in the context of post-1980s patterns of geoeconomic restructuring, state rescaling, and urban redevelopment, see Brenner (1999).

7 Many intellectual resources for such an inquiry can be gleaned from established literatures – for instance, on race, territory, and empire; on agrarian environments, deruralisation, and depeasantisation; on the neoliberalisation of nature; and on the geographies and spatial politics of extractivism, forestry, fishing, and energy. However, their appropriation for the lines of inquiry proposed here is constrained by the continued intellectual parcelisation of research among distinct, city-centered, or rural- or nature-centered fields of scholarship that are only rarely connected, either in theoretical-epistemological or historical-empirical terms. For a critical reflection on this problem with reference to important links between accounts of extended urbanisation and Marxian

agrarian studies, see Ghosh and Meer (2021). For exceptions to this generalisation with reference to the study of urbanisation and the contemporary global land rush see Zoomers et al. (2017) and Leon (2015). For a pioneering urbanisation-theoretical approach to wood and forestry, see Ibañez et al. (2020).

8 On the link between depeasantisation and slum formation in Southern megacities, see Araghi (1995, 2000); and Davis (2005).
9 On the 'emptying' of the global countryside and the various pathways of peasant displacement and dispossession, see Araghi (2009).
10 On the application of the Marxian distinction between formal and real subsumption to biogeophysical processes, see Boyd et al. (2001). On the capitalisation of nature, see Moore (2015). For a reflection on terraforming in the Anthropocene, via a discussion of Kim Stanley Robinson's *Mars trilogy*, see Wark (2015).

References

Angelo, H. and D. Wachsmuth. 2015. Urbanizing urban political ecology: A critique of methodological cityism. *International Journal of Urban and Regional Research* 39(1): 16–27.
Araghi, F. 1995. Global depeasantization, 1945–1990. *Sociological Quarterly* 36(2): 337–68.
Araghi, F. 2000. The great global enclosure of our times: Peasants and the agrarian question at the end of the twentieth century. In F. Buttel, F. Magdoff and J.B. Foster (eds.), *Hungry for profit: The agri-business threat to farmers*. New York: Monthly Review Press, pp. 145–60.
Araghi, F. 2009. Accumulation by displacement: Global enclosures, food crisis and the ecological contradictions of capitalism. *Review* 32(1): 113–46.
Arboleda, M. 2015. Financialization, totality and planetary urbanization in the Chilean Andes. *Geoforum* 67: 4–13.
Arboleda, M. 2016. Spaces of extraction, metropolitan explosions: Planetary urbanization and the commodity boom in Latin America. *International Journal of Urban and Regional Research* 40(1): 360–78.
Bergmann, L. and M. Holmberg. 2016. Land in motion. *Annals of the American Association of Geographers* 106(4): 932–56.
Boyd, W., S. Prudham, and R. Shurman. 2001. Industrial dynamics and the problem of nature. *Society and Natural Resources* 14(7): 555–70.
Brechin, G. 1999. *Imperial San Francisco*. Berkeley and Los Angeles: University of California Press.
Brennan, T. 2015. On the image of the country and the city. *Antipode* 49(1): 34–51.
Brenner, N. 1999. Beyond state-centrism: Space, territoriality and geographical scale in globalization studies. *Theory and Society* 28(1): 39–78.
Brenner, N. (ed.). 2013. *Implosions/explosions: Towards a study of planetary urbanization*. Berlin, Jovis.
Brenner, N. 2016. *Critique of urbanization: Selected essays*. Basel: Bauwelt Fundamente/Birkhäuser Verlag.

Brenner, N. 2019. *New urban spaces: Urban theory and the scale question*. New York: Oxford University Press.
Brenner, N. and S. Ghosh. 2022. Between the colossal and the catastrophic: Planetary urbanization and the political ecologies of emergent infectious disease. *Environment and Planning A: Economy and Space*. DOI: 10.1177/0308518X221084313.
Brenner, N. and C. Schmid. 2013. The 'urban age' in question. *International Journal of Urban and Regional Research* 38(3): 731–55.
Brenner, N. and C. Schmid. 2015. Towards a new epistemology of the urban? *City* 19(2–3): 151–82.
Bridge, G. 2001. Resource triumphalism: Postindustrial narratives of primary commodity production. *Environment and Planning A* 33: 2154.
Cassidy, E., P. West, J. Gerber, and J. Foley. 2013. Redefining agricultural yields: From tonnes to people nourished per hectare. *Environmental Research Letters* 8(3): 034015.
Cronon, W. 1991. *Nature's metropolis*. New York, Norton.
Davis, M. 2005. *Planet of slums*. London: Verso.
Ekers, M., G. Hart, S. Kipfer, and A. Loftus. 2013. *Gramsci: Space, nature, politics*. Malden, MA: John Wiley & Sons.
Erb, K.-H., V. Gaube, F. Kruasmann, C. Plutzar, A. Bondeau, and H. Haberl. 2007. A comprehensive global 5 min resolution land-use dataset for the year 2000 consistent with national census data. *Journal of Land Use Science* 2(3): 191–224.
Florida, R. 2005. The world is spiky. *The Atlantic Monthly*, October: 48–51.
Ghosh, S. and A. Meer. 2021. Extended urbanization and the agrarian question: Convergences, divergences and openings. *Urban Studies* 58(6): 1097–119.
Goonewardena, K. 2013. The country and the city in the urban revolution. In N. Brenner (ed.), *Implosions/explosions: Towards a study of planetary urbanization*. Berlin: Jovis, pp. 218–31.
Gramsci, A. 2005 [1926]. *The southern question*. Toronto: Guernica.
Ibañez, D., J. Hutton, and K. Moe. 2020. *Wood urbanism: From the molecular to the territorial*. Barcelona: Actar.
Katsikis, N. 2016. From hinterland to hinterglobe: Urbanization as geographical organization. Doctor of Design (DDes) thesis. Graduate School of Design (GSD), Harvard University.
Katsikis, N. 2018. The 'other' horizontal metropolis: Landscapes of urban interdependence. In Paola Vigano (ed.), *The horizontal metropolis between urbanism and urbanization*. Berlin: Springer, pp. 23–46.
Katsikis, N., N. Brenner, and G. Basic. Forthcoming. *Is the world urban? Towards a critique of geospatial ideology*. Barcelona: Actar.
King, A.D. 1990. *Urbanism, colonialism and the world-economy*. London: Routledge.
Krausmann, F., N., Gingrich, N. Eisenmenger, K.-H. Erb, H. Haberl, and M. Fischer-Kowalski. 2009. Growth in global materials use, GDP and population during the 20th century. *Ecological Economics* 68(10): 2696–705.
Lefebvre, H. 2003 [1970]. *The urban revolution*. Translated by R. Bononno. Minneapolis, MN: University of Minnesota Press.
Leon, J. 2015. The role of cities in land grabs. *Third World Quarterly* 36(2): 257–73.
Marx, K. and F. Engels. 1845. *The German ideology*. www.marxists.org/archive/marx/works/1845/german-ideology/, accessed 12 August 2022.

Mezzadra, S. and B. Neilson. 2017. On the multiple frontiers of extraction: Excavating contemporary capitalism. *Cultural Studies* 31(2–3): 185–204.
Monfreda, C., N. Ramankutty, and J. Foley. 2009. Farming the planet 2: Geographic distribution of crop areas, yields, physiological types, and net primary production in the year 2000. *Global Biogeochemical Cycles* 22(1): GB1022.
Moore, J.W. 2015. *Capitalism and the web of life: Ecology and the accumulation of capital*. New York: Verso.
Moore, J.W. (ed.). 2018. *Anthropocene or Capitalocene?* Oakland: PM Press.
Potter, P., N. Ramankutty, E.M. Bennett, and S.D. Donner. 2012. *Global fertilizer and manure, version 1: Nitrogen fertilizer application*. Palisades, NY: SEDAC.
Ramankutty, N., A.T. Evan, C. Monfreda, and J.A. Foley. 2010. *Global agricultural lands: Croplands, 2000*. Palisades, NY: SEDAC.
Sassen, S. 2015. *Expulsions: Brutality and complexity in the global economy*. Cambridge, MA: Harvard University Press.
Sevilla-Buitrago, A. 2013. *Urbs in rure*: Historical enclosure and the extended urbanization of the countryside. In N. Brenner (ed.), *Implosions/explosions: Towards a study of planetary urbanization*. Berlin: Jovis, pp. 236–59.
Soja, E. 2000. *Postmetropolis*. Oxford: Blackwell.
Tzaninis, Y., T. Mandler, M. Kaika, and R. Keil. 2021. Moving urban political ecology beyond the 'urbanization of nature'. *Progress in Human Geography* 45(2): 229–52.
van Cleef, E. 1941. Hinterland and umland. *Geographical Review* 31(2): 308–11.
von Thünen, J. 1996 [1826]. *Von Thünen's isolated state*. Translated by C.M. Wartenberg, edited by P. Hall. Oxford: Pergamon Press.
Wark, M. 2015. Molecular red: Theory for the Anthropocene. *E-flux* 63.
Williams, R. 1973. *The country and the city*. London: Oxford University Press.
Zoomers, A., F. Noorloos, K. Otsuki, G. Steel, and G. Westen. 2017. The rush for land in an urbanizing world: From land grabbing toward developing safe, resilient and sustainable cities and landscapes. *World Development* 92: 242–52.

Part II

Situated urban political ecologies

6

The case for reparations, urban political ecology, and the Black right to urban life

Nik Heynen and Nikki Luke

Introduction

In the 5 June 1886 issue of *The Electrical World*, Bishop Henry McNeal Turner made a prophetic argument. Turner played an important role in organising the Union Army's First Regiment of US Colored Troops during the US Civil War and later establishing the African Methodist Episcopal Church across the South after the War. Given his accomplishments, he wielded significant power during Reconstruction across Black and white political spheres. The reporting suggested that, 'While admiring the invention of the white man in controlling electricity, he [Turner] claims that the subjection of God's agent is carried too far in making it light the world' (1886: 257). Turner predicted

> that the unbalancing of the air currents which electrics are causing will in a few years, if they increase in numbers as fast as in the past five years, cause whole cities to be blown away at a time, and floods unlike any save Noah's.

He concluded: 'All the floods, hurricanes, cyclones and other atmospheric disturbances taking place in the heavens and upon earth are due to the work of electric lighting companies.' Turner's prophecy of impending urban climate change as a result of increasing fossil fuel use to power electrification came in a moment when electric generation companies were also using their political and economic might to transform the urban landscape through streetcars and electric lighting. In the US South, these corporate visions of an electrified *New South* in the post-war era remained wedded to white supremacy (Cater, 2019; Luke, 2021). During the Civil War, a different demand for the future of the South emerged in the uprising of enslaved people against the plantocracy, the term often used as shorthand for the South's political order as governed by plantation owners. In response, General William Tecumseh Sherman issued *Special Field Order 15* in 1865, which is regarded as one of the most important statements on

US reparations for chattel slavery. It is this document that allocated 40,000 acres in forty-acre plots to those previously enslaved to start a new life, culture, and society along the US Southeastern Coast. Here, taking these contradictory moments together we start to uncover and connect histories, prophecies, visions, and political demands little recognised within urban political ecology.

Uncovering contradictions buried within the interdependent, yet highly uneven constellations of socio-natural relations has been a primary objective of urban political ecology (UPE). In an effort to account for the ways nature and the city congeal through power and oppression, scholars have insisted that we continue to complicate, as opposed to simplify, how we understand the city across all its myriad forms, scales, and configurations of injustice as a means of building more just cities. To date, this push to understand urban political ecologies has most frequently drawn upon canonical urban theory. The slow pace of engagement with questions of white supremacy within UPE has arrested the explanatory power of this literature, cross-disciplinary collaborations, and by the same token, the audiences and authorship it engages. In this chapter we work toward a new register, with the goal of further complicating how we understand the co-dependent ways climate change is shaping cities through the logics of racial capitalism. Perhaps more centrally though, we are focused on concrete policy mechanisms that already exist and could be linked to reparative politics through more deliberate and concerted organising efforts in which we understand that academics have a role to play.

In his *Between the world and me*, Ta-Nehisi Coates (2015) shares an intimate accounting of the white supremacist logics that ground the 'American Dream' and the 'Dreamers' who have produced its reality; a reality embedded in the cascading problems seared into the intersections of city/nature/climate. Coates offers a generative method for reparative change in deconstructing how utopian visions often become reality and in turn tracing how these realities can become nightmares. Coates writes (2015: 150),

> Once the Dream's [hetero-patriarchal white supremist capitalist] parameters were caged by technology and the limits of horsepower and wind. But the Dreamers have improved themselves, and the damming of seas for voltage, the extraction of coal, the transmuting of oil into food, have enabled an expansion in plunder with no known precedent.

Coates conveys the magnitude of these technological advances driving climate change by suggesting that 'this revolution has freed the Dreamers to plunder not just the bodies of humans but the body of the Earth itself'. Connecting Turner's prophecy and Coates's method points to new ways to mobilise UPE. For just as Coates pronounces this damnation, he is clear about where much of the power to bring about emancipatory change rests:

> The Dreamers will have to learn to struggle themselves, to understand that the field for their Dream, the stage where they painted themselves white, is the deathbed of us all. The Dream is the same habit that endangers the planet, the same habit that sees our bodies stowed away in prison and ghettos.
>
> (2015: 151)

A critical and reflexive practice of UPE can contribute to transformative change in investigating the intersections of colonial, racialised, and gendered power relations that shape urban space and interrogating the ideologies, plans, and theories through which we know and account for cities in an effort to disrupt these hegemonic practices.

Drawing on Bittker's (2003) *The case for Black reparations*, in 2014 Coates offered his own account of US public and private institutions that benefited either directly or indirectly by extracting wealth and resources out of African-American communities. Coates builds a case for reparations in the historical production of urban space and links the theft of Black labour, rural land, and urban property, including through mortgage markets, to white wealth accumulation through property and asset inflation. Where the wealth gap between white and Black Americans 'illustrates the enduring legacy of our country's shameful history of treating black people as sub-citizens, sub-Americans, and sub-humans', Coates (2014) envisions that 'Reparations would seek to close this chasm'. The legacies of urban renewal and ongoing anti-Black violence that characterise US cities cannot be addressed through reparations alone and are situated as part of a suite of necessary changes to public and private institutions in the multi-pronged *Vision for Black Lives* (2020) platform. As Coates also notes, working to broker cooperation at all levels of society for reparations would herald a change in US governance. Through the lens of UPE, we argue that acknowledgement of and effort to repair harms can be incorporated into a range of policies and are vital to consider alongside potential urban planning, investment, and land-use decisions when incorporating climate change scenarios.

Herein lies a series of clear challenges if we approach questions of climate change and urban nature from a Black geographic perspective that also insists white people have to do more to think through the issues white supremacy has created. What can the connective logics of urban political ecology contribute to ongoing policy experimentation that embeds racial justice and could offer reparations? Perhaps most crucially, how can these literatures be in solidarity to hold up a Black right to urban life?

Reparations, climate change, and the city

Bringing Black lives, Black ideas, and Black political logics into conversation with the largely Anglo-American and Eurocentric literature on urban political ecology does not need to mean expunging theoretical frames that have been central to the approach. Rather, as McKittrick and Woods (2007: 5) suggest, 'Inserting black geographies into our worldview and our understanding of spatial liberation and other emancipatory strategies can perhaps move us away from the territoriality, the normative practice of staking a claim to a place' (see also Simone, 2010). Moving away from this colonial practice and place-specific case studies has been a longstanding critique of UPE (see Angelo and Wachsmuth, 2015). McKittrick (2021) proposes an embodied methodology to begin from a Black sense of place attentive to the creative and collaborative labour of Black people living within plantocratic and colonial logics. Her analysis generatively expands geographic theory on the production of space, which has been central to UPE. Opening a conversation between these literatures opens space to understand and engage in contemporary urban struggle.

Urban nature–society scholars draw especially on Lefebvre's work to consider existing and potential urban practices. As Lefebvre argued in *The right to the city*: 'Utopia is to be considered experimentally by studying its implications and consequences on the ground' (Lefebvre and Kofman, 1996: 151). Recent international uprisings for Black lives and against anti-Black police brutality provide utopian visions of ongoing abolitionist struggles for freedom from oppression. These grassroots movements that emerged from and have given new fuel to abolitionist organising are taking on local school boards, universities, city councils, and the US Congress in seeking policy to end policing and incarceration. Community reading groups that emerged to engage abolitionist and decolonial texts such as Angela Davis's *Are prisons obsolete?*, Nick Estes's *Our history is the future*, and Ruth Wilson Gilmore's *Golden gulag* evidence the dialogue between theory and organising that shapes emergent and intersectional demands for urban space. As Lefebvre goes on to argue, 'The *right to the city* cannot be conceived of as a simple visiting right or as a return to traditional cities. It can only be formulated as a transformed and renewed *right to urban life*' (Lefebvre and Kofman, 1996: 158, emphasis in original). At their core, reparational politics are about the Black right to urban life.

The centrality of radical praxis and the aspirational synthesis of theoretical arguments and grassroots organising has driven meaningful development of UPE and together are core to any advancement of linking UPE and reparational politics. We can see this in the ways Gilmore's work has been taken up, as well as how Lefebvre's provocations about the right to the city manifested the Right to the City Alliance (RTTC) which formed in the US in 2007 as a grassroots mobilisation against uneven urban development based in gentrification. The proliferation of organising around the displacement of low-income people, Black, Indigenous, People of Colour (BIPOC), and lesbian, gay, bisexual, transgender, and queer or questioning (LGBTQ) communities helped foster solidarities across racial, economic, and environmental justice organisations. While RTTC organisers have argued for an array of emancipatory issues, most revolve around redress associated with the ongoing ways white supremacist planning in the US has shaped cities. The RTTC platform embeds two claims for reparations in their demand for environmental justice and 'reparations for the legacy of toxic abuses such as brown fields, cancer clusters, and superfund sites'. Additionally, RTTC make a broader claim for reparations in arguing for 'the right of working class communities of color to economic reciprocity and restoration from all local, nation and transnational institutions that have exploited and/or displaced the local economy'.

While the language and logics of racial capitalist dynamics has not figured prominently into urban political ecological scholarship yet, there is abundant writing that offers a foundation for broader connections (see Gilmore 2007; 2017; Bledsoe et al., 2017; Wright, 2018). At the same time, there is increasingly more work being done that takes Black emancipatory objectives as core to political ecological concerns (Pellow, 2021). These political ideas can be put into practice through policy. To this end, Gilmore (2011: 264) suggests, 'Policy is the new theory. Policy is to politics what method is to research. It's a script for enlivening some future possibility – an experiment.' Gilmore situates this discussion in the ethos of abolitionist organising. In this vein, we endeavour to connect historically embedded questions of reparations to new policy approaches. We turn to two brief case studies from Atlanta, Georgia and New Orleans, Louisiana to bring reparational policy into deeper conversation with UPE and that offer a deliberate response to the case for reparations from a UPE perspective in the face of climate change.

Atlanta land banking, the 'land question', and climate change

First, we will discuss how an abolitionist framing of Atlanta's land bank opens up new questions about property-based reparative politics, climate change, and ongoing struggles for self-determination. Atlanta has received increasing international attention given its meteoric growth following the 1996 Olympics and its changing political landscape. Stacey Abrams – the 2018 Democratic candidate for governor who nearly won amidst claims of election impropriety by the ultimate winner and then Secretary of State in charge of election administration, Brian Kemp – has been a leading representative of the city's changing political environment. In 2018, she endorsed reparations for both Black and Indigenous people saying, 'We are the two communities who were legally disenfranchised from the inception of this country ... [such] that our ability to achieve and access opportunity at a level that was commensurate with the rest of America was just not available' (see Starr, 2019). These histories converge in Atlanta's founding in the aftermath of the Trail of Tears that violently removed and dispossessed the Muscogee Creek and Cherokee people, on whose land the city now sits, from the region. Prior to the US Civil War very few Black residents owned property in land, and many were claimed as property under conditions of slavery. For a brief moment after Emancipation, *Special Field Order 15* created a large swath of coastal Georgia and North and South Carolina for freed people to own property and create new societal possibilities. However, in the wake of the assassination of President Lincoln, President Andrew Johnson rescinded *Special Field Order 15* and freed people lost access to the 40,000 acres of land they had been allocated. The political theory of reparations in the US context is most widely associated with the unrealised promise of *Special Field Order 15*. These events are important for understanding the politics of property in land but also their centrality to arguments for reparations in the urban context.

Contemporarily, the question of land and the Black right to urban life has emerged in Atlanta in the crisis of affordable housing. In June 2019, Atlanta's Mayor, Keisha Lance Bottoms, who ran on a platform to making housing in the city more affordable, released *Atlanta's Housing Affordability Action Plan*. While there is much in the plan that echoes other cities' campaigns to grapple with housing justice, something unique, if barely mentioned, is Atlanta's plan to 'Expedite the development of affordable housing on vacant publicly owned land' given that the city government and quasi-public agencies including the housing authority, the economic development authority, Invest Atlanta, Atlanta Beltline Inc., and the Fulton County Land Bank hold more than 1,300 acres of vacant land (One Atlanta, 2019: 11).

The incorporation of the land bank to reimagine vacant property is of special note given the historical connection between land banking and Black radical calls for reparations for slavery in the US. To this end, one of the earliest mentions of land banking comes from the *Black manifesto* in which James Forman, who played an important leadership role in the Student Nonviolent Coordinating Committee (SNCC), and other Black radical leaders, made a series of demands relating to reparations for slavery. Forman (1969: 22) specifically argued:

> We call for the establishment of a Southern land bank to help our brothers and sisters who have to leave their land because of racist pressure for people who want to establish cooperative farms, but who have no funds. We have seen too many farmers evicted from their homes because they have dared to defy the white racism of this country. We need money for land. We must fight for massive sums of money for this Southern Land Bank. We call for $200,000,000 to implement this program.

In addition to SNCC-inspired thinking about land banking as represented in the *Black manifesto*, David Hilliard, former Chief of Staff for the Black Panther Party (BPP), described that the BPP also incorporated political demands about land banking as a way to accumulate land for Black communities within their programmatic 'survival programs'. Hilliard (2010: 44) writes,

> First, where's the land? In a crowded inner city, where does one find or create open space? The immediate and most obvious answer is perhaps seldom considered or seen for its potential use-the blighted, unsightly vacant lots that dot our cities. These lots can be acquired from their absentee landlords and developed into much-needed miniparks, tot lots, community gardens, and cultural or recreation centers.

Following these scholar-activists in the Black Radical Tradition who envision land banking as a way to acquire properties for community purposes, we ask whether the land bank can be mobilised in reparative ways to advance the city of Atlanta's existing affordable housing plan and to envision sustainable housing solutions for a possible influx of residents from the coastal US Southeast?

According to Alexander (2004), land banks were initially created as a public administrative mechanism to acquire vacant, abandoned, and tax-delinquent properties for reuse or development. Many cities recognised that the growing number of vacant homes and land were spatially concentrated and dispersed in patterns that challenged traditional approaches of property redevelopment. Within the matrix of public and private ownership, these parcels are difficult to repurpose given tax obligations and legal and financial obstacles that impeded cities' abilities to repossess and return vacant parcels into use.

Atlanta's land bank, founded in 1991, emerged from a suggestion of the Housing Forum, which was a coalition of public and community groups that met regularly at the Atlanta Food Bank. Two of the principal partners who helped to create the land bank were Bill Bolling of the Atlanta Community Food Bank and John Abercrombie, an affordable housing advocate, who were interested in making it possible for the Atlanta-based non-profit Habitat for Humanity to gain control of abandoned homes that had fallen into disrepair. The idea was to create a policy mechanism whereby the owners could donate their property to the city government, which could then extinguish the tax obligation on a site so that it could be used to house low and fixed-income residents in Atlanta. Alexander, who would go on to write the land banking legislation for many US cities, was central to formulating the policy language and developing the structure of the Atlanta land bank. Atlanta was among the first generation of land banks established in the US and remains unique in having a mandate to use the properties it acquires to develop market-rate and affordable housing.

Whether it can or will incorporate reparative logics to organise against destructive market forces of ongoing enclosure for profit and private gain requires a deeper interrogation of historical-geographical processes that have exacerbated displacement and gentrification in Atlanta's historically Black communities. Understanding these processes illuminates longstanding needs for the land bank to consider, such as whether it could work with Black residents facing foreclosure so that they can stay in their homes; how the land bank defines market-rate and affordable to secure Black land ownership or stewardship; and how, as the city moves to address urban sustainability, the land bank can stem ecological gentrification. The latter is of particular concern in predominately Black neighbourhoods of the southwest where the Beltline – a walking and biking trail that circumnavigates the City – parks, and green infrastructure designed to manage storm water overflow and flooding have contributed to speculation.

Examining these socio-ecological relations that have emerged through the racialised uneven development of Atlanta (see McCreary and Milligan, 2021) illuminates new and emerging concerns for the land bank's stewardship of public land, which will only grow as Atlanta faces increased risk of flooding, fire, and heat waves from climate change. Further, according to demographic forecasts, Atlanta could see more than 250,000 previously unanticipated migrants move into the city as a result of sea level rise (SLR) on the US Southeastern coast (see Hauer, 2017). The political ecological ramifications of this could be dire and would certainly exacerbate existing affordable housing shortages. Furthermore, this influx of 'SLR migrants' into Atlanta, beyond placing more pressure on the housing market, would stress virtually all other urban infrastructure from sanitation to roads and the electric grid. The land bank is a malleable institution that can enable developmentalist or community objectives. Securing land reparations through policy means that addressing the socio-ecological power relations that enable past and ongoing land loss must become a political priority in line with Abrams's sentiments to secure the Black right to urban life.

New Orleans energy reparations

Our discussion of the possibilities for land banking in Atlanta points to the centrality of land to historical claims for reparations. However, other resources, subject to intertwined histories of white supremacist monopolisation and dispossession, also elicit claims for reparations and simultaneously open up important questions related to UPE and climate change. Of particular concern is control and ownership of the energy system. Marable (1981: 8) writes,

> Energy – the technology to develop property efficiently and productively, access to cheap and renewable supplies of electricity, natural gas, petroleum, etc. becomes vital as more Black people leave the land and become dependent upon non-agricultural employment as salaried workers.

To ensure the sustainability of Black urban residents, Marable insists on bringing 'the question of energy' in closer relation to 'the land question' to counteract control of white supremacist financial institutions and utilities that profit as people of colour face disproportionately burdensome household energy costs. Elsewhere and in greater detail, we analyse the corporate control of energy within the framework of 'petro-racial capitalism', an accumulation strategy that has 'relied on the production, distribution, and consumption of petroleum that both requires and perpetuates colonial dispossession and racialized accumulation enacted through processes of slavery, patriarchy, imperialism, and genocide' (Luke and Heynen, 2020: 604). We are interested in understanding how energy reparations could disrupt these uneven, socio-ecological power relations that are concretised in energy infrastructure in New Orleans.

Like Atlanta, New Orleans is an important site in the US South to understand the generative ways UPE could contribute to reparative politics and to what Clyde Woods terms 'sustainable development' rooted in a blues epistemology and ontology. While not in reference to the theory of UPE, Woods (2017) provides a rich account of the ways in which energy, housing, and climate change, through processes we identify as petro-racial capitalism, made New Orleans defenceless against Hurricane Katrina. Policy shifts after Katrina replicated 'asset stripping' and propertied accumulation at the expensive of Black, migrant, and working-class residents of New Orleans. Thinking about 'petro-racial capitalism' through Woods' urban political ecological analysis builds other connections to the Black Radical Tradition and Robinson's theorisation of capitalism in *Black Marxism* (2000) as a political economic system that is predicated upon the logics of racialised difference, exploitation, and oppression. Connecting these ideas requires examining the political and planning decisions that contributed to uneven energy geographies and that fuel the racialised and gendered disparities that result from socio-natural crises. Making space for this complexity also allows for new ways to imagine abolitionist organising toward more emancipatory models to combat climate change and repair the damage of petro-racial capitalism more generally. As Gilmore (2020) argues, 'abolition really does require we change one thing which is everything', therefore including the sites of urban and energy investment. Incorporating the *longue durée* of Indigenous and abolitionist politics into UPE analysis that has long been central in the environmental justice movement further connects reparations to climate justice.

In the aftermath of Katrina, Louisiana offered generous property tax credits for home restoration, including residential solar energy installation, that was funded in part through severance and excise taxes on oil and regressive sales taxes. The growth of solar energy became another moment of redistribution and asset-stripping as the public subsidised residential solar for homeowners. In a June 2019 interview on New Orleans' WHIV community radio, Logan Burke, executive director of the Louisiana Alliance for Affordable Energy, opened the door for theorising these political ecological contradictions and organising energy policy to benefit all urban residents. She detailed the New Orleans City Council effort to authorise 'community solar', which means 'that rather than depending on the utility itself to procure renewables, a community can invest in and own solar resources and other renewable resources and reduce their bills, lock[ing] in the cost of that energy over time'. Further, the developments in New Orleans bring policy innovations that work toward energy equity to the US South given that the rule is 'the first community solar opportunity that anybody has seen in our region' (Burke and Hilton, 2019).

Community solar programmes focused on low-income communities work to ameliorate energy insecurity by eliminating financial and infrastructural impediments for renters, as well as other customers lacking adequate infrastructure or the financial means to acquire residential solar, to have their energy usage provided by solar panels installed in their community at alternative locations beyond their homes. Residents who purchase a share of a community-owned solar array receive credit on their electric bills for the power their panels produce. Given the history of racial discrimination in home mortgage lending that Coates analyses in *The case for reparations*, and continued disparities in home ownership across racial groups in New Orleans that widened after Katrina, community solar is 'a concrete policy intervention' to reduce racialised disparities in energy costs linked to historical disparities in home ownership. Distributing the means to produce electricity in ways that are affordable and accessible also 'confronts the power relations that sustain petro-racial capitalism in New Orleans' (Luke and Heynen, 2020: 603).

The political ecological dimensions of Woods's (2017) and Gilmore's (2007) analyses identify the abuse and transformation of natural resources through hegemonic and racial capitalist systems and the political possibilities inherent in collective response to seize state power and resist dispossession. Community solar in New Orleans can be understood within the abolitionist politics that have come before, beginning with the demands for reparations. In addition to raising land banking as an aspect of reparational politics in his *Black manifesto* in 1969, Forman argued for an extensive list of other demands from investments in Black-controlled publishing, media, skill training, research centres, welfare, and the national Black labour strike and defence funds. While Forman did not name energy explicitly in the *Manifesto*, energy has long been recognised as core to the urban infrastructure that supported the subjugation of Black communities and is an increasingly important aspect of determining community responses to mitigate and adapt to climate change. The white supremacist, petro-plantation political bloc has always been the target of political organising and confrontation from Black, working-class organic intellectuals. To this end, Woods narrates, according to Camp and Pulido (2017: xxvi) the dialectical tensions that have produced 'a way of knowing rooted in the historic redistributive agenda of freedom and labor struggles'. Gilmore (2011: 258) helps identify these liberatory ways of knowing and organising, to be the longstanding model of abolitionist praxis.

New distributive logics directing community solar in New Orleans can inform policy to address the role of the energy sector in fuelling racial capitalism. At least nineteen states in the US have adopted aspects of community solar as a way to expand access to solar energy. Community solar has the possibility of both creating new institutional networks to build assets through the logic of energy reparations as well as undermining the economic and ecological control of petro-racial capitalism. Scholars engaged in UPE can contribute our voices through research that adds to the case for reparations through diverse housing, energy, and infrastructure policies that safeguard and centre the Black right to urban life as a central tenant.

Conclusion

Making the case for reparations and UPE to work together theoretically and in solidarity with the Black right to urban life is one thing; and there is important potential and historical context in making these arguments. It is something else, however, to harness the praxis inherent to both the Black

Radical Tradition and the underlying political commitments in the origin stories of UPE to build upon (or co-opt if necessary) contemporary policy initiatives that can ensure a Black right to urban life amid climate change and the other interdependent forces that produce space. This move forces us to grapple with the legacies of white supremist urbanism, including colourblind urban theory. We must also recognise that varieties of Anglo-American and Eurocentric theory are central to the production of considerable suffering, and demands, as Coates's calls for that 'The Dreamers will have to learn to struggle themselves' and to analyse critically 'the field for their Dream, the stage where they painted themselves white'. For Coates (2014), reparations mean 'the full acceptance of our collective biography and its consequences – is the price we must pay to see ourselves squarely'. The utopian realm of theory has something to contribute but must be accountable to history and visions of organisers and communities in multiple realms of implementation including through praxis and policy.

Hawthorne (2019) helps paint a larger realm of intellectual solidarity and the ways UPE can build upon both the Black Radical Tradition and the Black geographic tradition when she says that scholars engaging 'insurgent practices of Black political ecology, community formation, political action, and artistic reappropriation … also show the richness of Black urban spatial imaginaries'. Land banking in Atlanta and community solar in New Orleans both offer concrete potential for emplacing reparative politics in US Southern cities produced both through white supremacist and colourblind urban planning as well as Black spatial imaginaries. The cascading harms of climate change threaten to impart the greatest suffering on those without property or wealth. However, if we put Turner's prophetic vision into conversation with Forman's and Coates's thinking on reparations and the generative power of Black geographic thought, we can be just as certain that there are important ideas, histories, and legacies that can enliven ongoing political struggle over land, infrastructure, energy, and water that have informed UPE and can continue to do so toward the Black right to urban life.

References

Alexander, F.S. 2004. Land bank strategies for renewing urban land. *Journal of Affordable Housing. & Community Development Law* 14: 140.

Angelo, H. and D. Wachsmuth. 2015. Urbanizing urban political ecology: A critique of methodological cityism. *International Journal of Urban and Regional Research* 39(1): 16–27.

Bittker, B.I. 2003. *The case for Black reparations*. Boston, MA: Beacon Press.

Bledsoe, A., L.E. Eaves, and B. Williams. 2017. Introduction: Black geographies in and of the United States South. *Southeastern Geographer* 57(1): 6–11.
Burke, L. and T. Hilton. 2019. In the movement: Logan Burke / Alliance for Affordable Energy. *News and Views, WTUL 91.5*, New Orleans, LA, June 12. https://soundcloud.com/cruisinrecs/interview-with-logan-atkinson-burke-from-the-alliance-for-affordable-energy, accessed 12 August 2022.
Camp, J.T. and L. Pulido. 2017. The dialectics of bourbonism and the blues. In C. Woods, *Development drowned and reborn: The Blues and bourbon restorations in post-Katrina New Orleans*. Athens, GA: University of Georgia Press, pp. xxi–xxix.
Cater, C. 2019. *Regenerating Dixie: Electric energy and the modern South*. Pittsburgh, PA: University of Pittsburgh Press.
Coates, T.-N. 2014. The case for reparations. *Atlantic*. www.theatlantic.com/magazine/archive/2014/06/the-case-for-reparations/361631/, accessed 12 August 2022.
Coates, T.-N. 2015. *Between the world and me*. New York: Penguin Random House.
The Electricial World, 5 June 1886, 257.
Forman, J. 1969. The Black manifesto. *Africa Today* 16(4): 21–4.
Gilmore, R.W. 2007. *Golden gulag: Prisons, surplus, crisis, and opposition in globalizing California*. Berkeley, CA: University of California Press.
Gilmore, R.W. 2011. What is to be done? *American Quarterly* 63(2): 245–65.
Gilmore, R.W. 2017. Abolition geography and the problem of innocence. In G.T. Johnson and A. Lubin (eds.), *Futures of Black radicalism*. London: Verso, pp. 226–40.
Gilmore, R.W. 2020. Ruth Wilson Gilmore on COVID-19, decarceration, and abolition: Interview by Naomi Murakawa. Video from Haymarket Books. www.haymarketbooks.org/blogs/128-ruth-wilson-gilmore-on-covid-19-decarceration-and-abolition, accessed 12 August 2022.
Hauer, M. 2017. Migration induced by sea-level rise could reshape the US population landscape. *Nature Climate Change* 7(5): 321–5.
Hawthorne, C. 2019. Black matters are spatial matters: Black geographies for the twenty-first century. *Geography Compass* 13(11): e12468.
Hilliard, D. 2010. *The Black Panther Party: Service to the people programs*. Albuquerque, NM: University of New Mexico Press.
Lefebvre, H. and E. Kofman. 1996. *Writings on cities*. Oxford: Blackwell.
Luke, N. 2021. Powering racial capitalism: Electricity, rate-making, and the uneven energy geographies of Atlanta. *Environment and Planning E: Nature and Space*. https://doi.org/10.1177/25148486211016736
Luke, N. and N. Heynen. 2020. Community solar as energy reparations: Abolishing petro-racial capitalism in New Orleans. *American Quarterly* 72(3): 603–25.
Marable, M. 1981. Power to the people? Energy and economic underdevelopment of Black people in the 'New South'. *Black Books Bulletin* 7(3): 8–13.
McCreary, T. and R. Milligan. 2021. The limits of liberal recognition: Racial Capitalism, settler colonialism, and environmental governance in Vancouver and Atlanta. *Antipode* 53(3): 724–44.
McKittrick, K. 2021. *Dear science and other stories*. Durham, NC: Duke University Press.
McKittrick, K. and C. Woods. 2007. No one knows the mysteries at the bottom of the ocean. In K. McKittrick and C. Woods (eds.), *Black geographies and the politics of place*. Toronto: Between the Lines, pp. 1–13.

One Atlanta. 2019. Housing Affordability Action Plan. City of Atlanta. www.atlantaga.gov/home/showdocument?id=42220, accessed 12 August 2022.

Pellow, D.N. 2021. Struggles for environmental justice in US prisons and jails. *Antipode* 53(1): 56–73.

Robinson, C. 2000. *Black Marxism: The making of the Black Radical Tradition*. Chapel Hill: University of North Carolina Press.

Simone, A.M. 2010. *City life from Jakarta to Dakar: Movements at the crossroads*. London and New York: Routledge.

Starr, T.J. 2019. Stacey Abrams says there was 'incompetence' in media coverage of her campaign, will announce her future political plans in the coming weeks. *The Root*, 15 April. www.theroot.com/stacey-abrams-says-there-was-incompetence-in-media-cove-1834048304, accessed 12 August 2022.

Woods, C. 2017. *Development drowned and reborn: The blues and bourbon restorations in post-Katrina New Orleans*. Athens: University of Georgia Press.

Wright, W.J. 2018. As above, so below: Anti-Black violence as environmental racism. *Antipode* 53(3): 791–809.

7

Urban climate change and feminist political ecology

Andrea J. Nightingale

Urban political ecology has placed firmly on the agenda questions of how cities reflect the materialisation of capital flows, social political relations, and the metabolism of the more-than-human (Tzaninis et al., Introduction in this volume). Within this work, the urban is understood as a relational sphere, one wherein socio-natural relations that span time and space consolidate and allow for an analysis of political, material, policy, and cultural change simultaneously (Tzaninis et al., 2021). In this chapter, I take up the idea that material relations are co-emergent with social political dynamics and use this framing to look at risks from climate change, and also how to create new openings for deliberative politics around adjusting to a changing world.[1] This framing recognises the city as a scale wherein certain kinds of governance and social relations are organised by jurisdictional powers but also by everyday interactions and associations that span the human and non-human, relations that can be the key to transformational change.

This distinction is important for climate change adaptation processes because challenges for urban areas may not map cleanly onto the kinds of responsibilities and actions that cities as municipal units have. Given this, it is interesting to see how cities are emerging at the vanguard of formal climate change adaptation innovations (Angelo and Wachsmuth, 2020; Broto and Bulkeley, 2013), and some are forming support networks to promote zero carbon urban areas (CNCA, 2021a). These are purported responses to stagnation within global agreements and national level programmes when confronted with the realities of political economic relationships and infrastructures that support the status quo (Nightingale et al., 2020; Lawhon et al., 2017). Policymakers find themselves needing to balance immediate demands of the present with predictions of significant long-term change not only for their areas, but for others as well. In this context, many cities have presented bold adaptation initiatives to radically reduce carbon emissions and overall consumption, attempting to pioneer new practices for transforming the environment–society nexus (Broto and Bulkeley, 2013). Some of these efforts contain a climate justice element, recognising that social exclusions – including those shaped by gender, race, caste, ethnicity, and age – can be exacerbated by climate change effects. But these efforts fail to account for how existing social exclusions are not just exacerbated by climate change; they are also constitutive of who, how, and what is done to respond to climate change (Kaika, 2017). In this chapter I ask two key questions: how do processes of social inclusion and exclusion reshape urban climate change adaptation; and how are these social inequalities shaped by but also shape the knowledge politics that emerge around adaptation questions?

Drawing from feminist political ecology and critical socio-natures scholarship, I develop an analysis for thinking through urban climate change adaptation struggles that place an understanding of intersectional social inequalities and knowledge politics at the centre of policy debates. Efforts to guide change can never be politically neutral. They reflect the contexts from which they emerge, including intersectional differences fractured along caste, class, race, ethnicity, nationality, and age, among other social-political inequalities (Nightingale, 2006; Tschakert et al., 2016; Truelove, 2011). Adaptation processes therefore cannot be conceived separately from politics: they need to be recognised as developing and unfolding within already-politicised relationships and networks (Broto and Bulkeley, 2013; Swyngedouw and Kaika, 2014; Tzaninis et al., 2021).

In this chapter I argue that these politics are not inconvenient side-effects, or relationships that need to be managed after policies are in place. Rather, they in part constitute the types of knowledges which are used to assess needs, consider measures, choose the people who become involved in efforts, and affect the final outcomes.

Underpinning a feminist political ecology analysis is an implicit emphasis on socio-natures, or the ways 'through which all types of nature are socially mobilized, economically incorporated (commodified), and physically metabolized/ transformed in order to support the urbanization process' (Swyngedouw and Kaika, 2014: 462). In addition, I will emphasise here how intersectional social relations and knowledge politics play out to shape adaptation programs (Tschakert et al., 2016) by presenting two examples to help illustrate how to use these concepts within an analysis of adaptation. The first example is of a water scheme in an urbanising market and administrative centre in eastern Nepal; the second of the Carbon Neutral City Alliance, an international network of cities working together to promote zero carbon urban areas. I conclude by suggesting that many current approaches to planning are too static to allow the kinds of renegotiations that are required to address social inequalities within the core of adaptation programmes. Rather there is a need for deliberative, democratic practices that hold the politics of exclusion and multiple ways of knowing in the centre of adaptation processes in order to better respond to uncertainty and change.

A feminist political ecology framework: Power and intersectional subjectivities

Making sense of social exclusions and knowledge politics within multiscalar and complex socio-environmental contexts is not so simple as categorising the people involved and the knowledges used. Feminist political ecologists focus not just on how women are more vulnerable to climate change; they also ask questions about how social inequalities combine into intersectional subjectivities (Butler, 1997; Crenshaw, 2017) and create uneven vulnerabilities and capabilities (Tschakert et al., 2016). Feminist political ecologists use intersectionality (broadly understood as the interlocking social differences that combine to create inequalities) to explore questions around: how power operates within transitions and environmental change; who is authorised to govern change; whose interests and voices are prioritised; and how power operates to privilege some groups and some knowledges over others (Ahlborg and Nightingale, 2018; Nightingale, 2017; Doshi, 2017; Elmhirst, 2011; Tschakert et al., 2016).

Many feminists use the concept of subjectivity instead of identity to understand intersectionality because it offers a more dynamic understanding of how power operates in and through social differences. Subjectivity refers to the internalisation and resistance of power, usually understood through various aspects of identity, gender, race, class, and other social difference. As power is exercised – whether that be dominating or enabling power – the subject internalises but never fully accepts its subjection; there is always some resistance. The result is known as subjectivity, understood to be fluid and dynamic. Since subjectivity is performative, it emerges out of everyday practices. Here it is important not to conflate the subject with the individual. A given individual is subjected in multiple ways, meaning everyone has multiple (dynamic, intersectional) subjectivities (Crenshaw, 2017). My own formulation of subjectivity includes how subjectivities arise out of relations with both humans and non-humans such that the operation of power extends into and from nature (Nightingale, 2006, 2013). Subjectivity can also help to explain collectives such as 'climate activists', 'village women', 'city dwellers' – the subjects of many adaptation efforts – which are similarly dynamic and performed in the everyday through which collective identities emerge (Nightingale, 2013; Singh, 2017). By thinking of these collectives as the outcome of the exercise and internalisation of power, it gives them agency and helps to explain why sometimes their effects are ambivalent or contradictory (Ahlborg and Nightingale, 2018). Subjectivity is thus useful for understanding the dynamic interplay between efforts at promoting particular kinds of climate actions and the sorts of acceptances and resistances to those actions as they unfold.

In relation to climate change, feminists have taken two main approaches to the climate problem. Many have probed how patriarchy operates to place (some) women more at risk than others, or to exclude women from decision-making authority, using gender relations as an entry point into understanding how climate change impacts are uneven for a population (MacGregor, 2010). Here, gender relations are used to show that existing social inequalities can be compounded by environmental stresses and long-term change. An intersectional subjectivities approach, however, takes such analyses further by using a more nuanced understanding of the operation of power to explain not only vulnerability, but also abilities to access the benefits of adaptation (Bee et al., 2015; Tschakert et al., 2016). But this kind of analysis tells only part of the story (Arora-Jonsson, 2011). It is not just that patriarchy shapes how vulnerabilities unfold. Feminists have also sought to understand how the operation of power through social difference shapes adaptation itself. These kinds of analyses show the ways in which gender, race, and class relations shape how adaptation problems are framed in the first place and which policies are developed to implement them (Nightingale, 2017; Gonda, 2019).

My analysis builds from the body of work outlined above, by using feminist theory to explain how gender, other social relations, and changing socio-natures can serve to create vulnerabilities *and* serve as a point of friction through which resources are struggled over. Thus, intersectional social relations are not simply impacted by environmental change, they can constitute the kinds of struggles over resources that unfold. This analysis draws out the multi-scalar and multi-dimensional aspects of adaptation processes. Such a conceptualisation demands that attention is paid to social justice, not because of disproportionate impacts on women, but because it is impossible to produce durable adaptation programmes without accounting for the uneven knowledge politics and power relations that shape outcomes. Thus, a feminist approach attends to more than simply gendered impacts of climate change, but rather seeks to capture how adaptation is conceived, implemented, and enacted on the ground (Nightingale, 2017).

In order to understand these dynamics of socio-natural change in relation to the climate crisis, I probe how climate 'adaptation' comes to be constituted through particular everyday practices. Assumptions about how people behave or which groups are vulnerable are at the centre of evaluations over what and when adaptation efforts should be implemented. But these assumptions themselves are complicit in producing vulnerabilities, as the example of an urban water scheme below elaborates. These practices are key arenas wherein contestations, alliances, and desires to be recognised by policy and governments are played out with significant material and political consequences for what will come in future.

Adaptation efforts are also normally informed by knowledge that is often produced outside the locality where programmes are targeted. Such knowledge is generated through computer models or analyses done by outside experts which rarely take into consideration observations and experiential knowledge of locally based people (see also Gururani and Vandergeest, 2014). On a theoretical level, this points to the need to understand how local responses are embedded within global political economies, policies and knowledge practices which in themselves serve to make some areas more vulnerable than others. When brought together with a feminist conceptualisation of the operation of power, it helps to understand how such struggles are linked across scales. One empirical outcome of these dynamics are national-level policies which can actually inhibit local adaptation initiatives (Eriksen and Selboe, 2013), or exacerbate local inequalities. In this way, knowledge politics and intersectionality come together to shape the trajectory of change, moving beyond conceptualisations of the urban that sees them as somehow islands or separated from socio-natural processes, to ones that extend from the local to the global (Tzaninis et al., 2021).

I have argued elsewhere that knowledge politics lie at the heart of the climate crisis: all policy reactions are underpinned by what the problem is understood to be (Nightingale et al., 2020). While I do not discount the excellent biophysical science of climate change, I do question the framing of it. Climate change adaptation efforts are never simply responses to biophysical change; adaptation efforts always entwine with social and political processes that create new networks of natures, peoples, and bureaucracies across scales. These networks determine what knowledge counts as valid, who is included, who is excluded, and what solutions are proposed.

My feminist political ecology analysis therefore advocates for an approach to climate problems that seeks to ask critical questions about these normative, political and ultimately contested processes of knowledge production (Tschakert et al., 2016). Feminist scholars have advocated for situated knowledges, a stance which embraces the contexts of knowledge production and mobilisation along with the facts themselves. Objectivity emerges out of taking accountability for 'how we learn to see' (Haraway, 1988) and thinking about how the situatedness of knowledge claims generates a particular politics around them (Jasanoff, 2013; Lawhon et al., 2017; Tzaninis et al., 2021). Such a view demands that other ways of knowing are also brought to the table as equally valid alongside climate science. Demands which could well lead to re-evaluating the dominance of current efforts at prediction, adaptation, and mitigation in favour of other approaches that carry more possibilities for new political and social coalitions.

This is one area where local initiatives can have widespread influence. Rather than trying to scale up specific solutions, a focus on the practices through which different kinds of knowledges generate creative frictions within problem-solving processes is needed. Here the emphasis shifts to developing deliberative, democratic practices that embrace uncertainty and change, multiple ways of framing the same problem, drawing on diverse knowledges, and freeing our imagination. The role of science becomes one of 'sparking debates' rather than settling them.

A tale of two cities: Examples of urban possibilities

I now turn to two examples to help show how an analysis of intersectional social relations and knowledge politics opens up space for engaging in deliberative politics.

The first is a case about a bajaar (market) town in Nepal which draws out well how intersectional relations shape an infrastructure project. This rapidly urbanising area is also experiencing a drying climate, which exacerbates long-term challenges for adequate water supply to the bajaar. The response to water access issues reveals the intersectional politics of water governance shaped around issues of political authority, ethnicity, gender, upstream/downstream, and urban–rural territories. When water schemes come in with a focus on increasing water quantity, they miss how intersectional social relations and knowledge politics shape who will actually have access to water once the project is completed.

The second is the case of the Carbon Neutral Cities Alliance (CNCA), a private foundation-funded global network of urban municipalities committed to 'radical, transformative changes to core city systems' (CNCA, 2021a) to achieve carbon neutrality. This case draws out sharply how knowledge politics shape adaptation efforts and outcomes. The network is composed of self-proclaimed vanguard cities that have adequate financial and political resources to promote cutting-edge technologies and infrastructural transformations. These cities see themselves as leading both by experimentation, with new technologies that can then be taken up elsewhere, and by assisting transitions in other places. They are partnered with cities which face bigger carbon neutrality challenges and seek to support them both by leveraging private donations and through knowledge exchange. The Alliance has a strong commitment to climate justice and their promotional materials discuss extensively intersectional social exclusion issues, yet their interventions remain largely within technical and infrastructural spheres. The Alliance shows possibilities that open up when traditional scalar networks of power are by-passed (cities aligning together directly rather than going through their national governments) and also the real challenges in putting intersectional social relations into centre frame.

Urbanisation and the politics of exclusion

The market town in eastern Nepal, which I will name Pani Bajaar (water market) to protect anonymity, reflects the challenges faced by many urbanising areas in the Global South. On the one hand, the growing market offers possibilities for diversifying income away from a reliance on subsistence agriculture, not only for town residents, but also for far-flung farmers who sell produce, forest products, and services to the bajaar. Income diversification is usually considered an adaptation outcome in itself. On the other hand, demands for fresh drinking and washing water are escalating. Town planners and internationally supported development projects have their eyes on springs in the surrounding hills to ensure an adequate supply of water to the bajaar area. Our research team[2] took a closer look at an Asian Development Bank (ADB) supported scheme operating in this town.

The evaluation of water supply in rural Nepal took into consideration two main factors: availability and flow rates of water sources; and land ownership patterns and related possibilities to make a claim on water sources. The ADB water supply project, however, was also caught up in the local political transition. Nepal's government has been radically restructured since 2017 meaning that local municipalities have more political power and resources as well as newly elected leaders. New leaders lack institutional memory, and in a pattern that began after the civil war (1996–2006), local leaders, civil society groups, and political parties compete for authority precisely around projects like the ADB one (Nightingale, 2017).

The politics of knowledge are subtle but significant here. In this part of Nepal, springs are the property of landowners or community forestry groups (CFUGs), but many have associated traditional use rights for surrounding residents. These rights often do not extend to the bajaar area. When 'water supply' is thought of in terms of where it is, how to move it, and how to pay for it (i.e., lease or buy it from land owners/CFUGs) as in the ADB project, it privileges narrow understandings of water access, derived only from how much flows and from where, over more complex understandings of water, taking into account how water flows are tied into everyday life. These ties include the socio-natural production of subjectivities (who carries or has access to water, when, for what purpose, is bound up in social hierarchies), as well as prestige associated with 'bringing new projects' for local politicians, leaders, and facilitators (often the 'social mobilisers' of development projects). A narrow biophysical vision of water supply thus collides with the aspirations of local politicians and civic leaders who have a vested interest in serving their constituents – which is usually interpreted along political party lines rather than residence. But perhaps even more striking is the failure to account for climate change. The water project is focused exclusively on water supply in the present, rather than water supply in the upcoming 10 to 20 years.

A requirement of the ADB's support is that local water user groups are formed and together with municipality leaders, secure access to a predefined metres per second of water supply from the surrounding hills. Only once the supply is secured will the donor get involved with implementation. Precisely how that plays out on the ground is highly localised, but the fault-lines are telling: ethnicity and caste shape which groups are able to best advocate for their interests, CFUGs have proven adept at negotiating for their members, gender shapes who is involved in planning versus who is responsible for daily household water management, and political parties use water as a way to compete for supporters. The ADB water supply project failed to account for these more complex intersectional relations linked to water access and distribution by pushing responsibility for securing metres per second to the municipality.

In Pani Bajaar the way that power operates to shape adaptation projects is already evident. In January 2020, the Mayor of the town (elected in 2017) proudly stated that, 'everyone is happy now and all grievances have been fully addressed'. The bajaar water user groups were able to secure the total water flow they required by the ADB project for it to go ahead. But exactly how these sources were secured and whether landowners really gave consent is in question. One city water leader told the research team, 'we used *sam, dam, danda bhed niti*[3] [coercion, money, physical intimation, and ostracism] to make the deal'.

Landowners who have spring sources on their land overwhelmingly come from an ethnic group that is underrepresented in political positions and has a scant residential presence in the bajaar. Yet in an interesting twist, local ethnic leaders are trying to claim exclusive rights to water resources under International Labour Organization (ILO) 169, which gives Indigenous people exclusive rights to resources, signed by Nepal in 2007. Overall, their ethnicity intersects with class (wealth and occupation) to place them in weaker bargaining positions when it comes to negotiating whether they are willing to lease or sell their springs, but ILO 169 has helped them exert a bit more power. This does not mean they have given consent, however. Our research team found many landowners and CFUGs were focused on their own long-term water needs and the desire for their own area to develop in the future. One elderly man told the research team: 'We want road and *bikas* [development] in our own area and we need to keep our water with ourselves to support our future needs.' Nevertheless, many were lured by short-term financial gains by selling water access, or were persuaded by '*sam, dam, danda bhed niti*'.

The wider context within which people are asked to sell or lease their water source along with intersectional gender and age relations, are paramount in terms of how power operates to shape who has long-term water security and who does not. Almost exclusively, men negotiate with planners and project representatives and control household cash income, while women, even those with jobs or shops, collect and manage daily household water supply. As a result, water decisions impact upon household members in uneven ways and serve to shape subjectivities. What might be a significant increase in so-called adaptative capacity for senior men in the household can lead to increased precarity and higher work burdens for women of all ages. This is true in both the bajaar and water supplying areas. In these ways, climate change adaptation projects are changing how – and which – households are incorporated into managerial logics and burgeoning capitalist relations around the fulfilment of everyday needs for water.

So far, my telling of this story is a cautionary one. Failure to account for how power operates through knowledge politics and intersectional social relations can doom well-intentioned projects before they come on-line. Politics shape which knowledges and which short- and long-term considerations frame how much water is needed where. Our fieldwork was riddled with accounts of women getting into violent fights at public water taps, or needing to wait in lengthy lines at unsociable hours to secure water before this project was up for consideration. It is noteworthy that while gender relations are considered significant in other domains (especially forest governance), in this water project my research team saw little recognition of the need to ensure women and men had equal representation in decision-making forums. Not only does this mean water may not be available when, where, and how it is needed for daily subsistence, but it also means that projects are likely to have bigger problems with leakage and waste. Thus, a project intended to be adaptive can have significant mal-adaptive outcomes for people impacted by it (Eriksen et al., 2021).

But the Pani Bajaar story offers an optimistic tale as well. While negotiations over water allocation are rife with the kinds of intersectional caste, ethnicity, and political party dynamics I described above, the importance of water to everyday life also means that leaders authorised to negotiate for water on their behalf will be held to account. This simultaneously recognises the new municipal system (Nightingale, 2017), helping to mitigate other kinds of competition for power that have occurred as civil servants adjust to different roles under the new regime, and opens up some deliberative space around local infrastructural needs. Furthermore, the case offers possibilities for taking account of intersectional social relations within adaptation projects. Leaders of ethnic organisations, water user-group chairpersons, and even the municipality itself is unable to successfully negotiate without recognising that some groups are more disadvantaged than others. They form alliances based on caste and ethnicity, and their intersection with political parties, but they also work for compromise across those differences and a complete neglect of the poor is socially and politically unacceptable.

Cities at the vanguard: Alliances and innovation

The Carbon Neutral Cities Alliance (henceforth CNCA) is a radically different case in terms of its agenda and the kind of municipal areas it is trying to link together – Pani Bajaar would not be a 'city' under their rubric, being too small and remote – but it nevertheless also points to the importance of knowledge politics and intersectional social relations when taking account of urban climate change (Tzaninis et al., 2021). The Alliance consists of cities of different sizes and vastly different adaptation challenges located both in the Global North and South. My analysis of the alliance is limited to information obtained from their web sites and 2021–23 Strategy document (CNCA, 2020).

Knowledge politics drove the formation of the Alliance. The CNCA was a response to the perception that many national-level policies are unable to react quickly enough to the challenges posed by climate change for cities. Some are bastions of environmental and progressive politics within wider national contexts that have a more tentative commitment to such ideals. They work collectively at scales beyond their current governance mandates, to 'communicat[e] effectively with the stakeholders [cities] are trying to influence so they can implement the game changing policies necessary for achieving their ambitious goals' (CNCA, 2020: 10).

Here the politics of scale and the politics of knowledge come together to shape the CNCA agenda in two ways. First by mobilising the alliance to by-pass large-scale institutions like national governments and international bodies in order to take action on the ground, they argue that the scale of the city is ideal for innovation. Their model is to support new technologies in cities like Amsterdam, Oslo, and Adelaide to pioneer green roofs, community gardening, new building materials and techniques, car-free inner cities, and other energy (carbon)-saving technologies (for a critique of this kind of infrastructural approach see Kaika, 2017). These cities have the resources and interested populations to experiment with technologies that can be transferred to areas less fortunate, if proven successful. Yet whether this in itself can contribute to their overall climate justice and innovation goals is unclear. It is telling that carbon budgets and climate justice both appear under 'governance' in the strategy document and are always listed together.

Second, local and scientific knowledges continue to be held separate. They refer to communities historically excluded as 'priority communities' which are defined as 'low-income people, Indigenous Peoples, communities of colour, immigrants and refugees and other historically marginalized communities' (CNCA, 2021a). Non-scientific knowledges are assumed to reside with Indigenous people: 'through their connection to the land, traditions, and perspectives rooted in their history and culture, Indigenous Peoples have unique knowledge vital to creating a more sustainable future' (CNCA, 2020: 12). And the network 'value[s] the insights of people, especially priority communities, as much or more than traditional data sources' (CNCA, 2020: 13). These commitments, however, sit uneasily alongside their assertion of science underpinning their activities, 'science is a necessary foundation of our understanding of climate change and the resulting disproportionate burdens, and the design of effective climate action' (CNCA, 2020: 13). While perhaps not surprising in a public strategy document, it does point to the need to dig deeper into how intersectional social relations shape the underlying knowledge politics of the CNCA (Lawhon et al., 2017). On the one hand, the need to assert the salience of science is one reaction to climate denialism, but of more interest to me is how science and Indigenous knowledges are cast as separate. A feminist political ecology approach unpacks this separation and explores how, when, where, and by whom different knowledge claims are made and accepted as authoritative (Nightingale, 2017). Further research into the Alliance should focus around how these presumably incommensurate knowledges are considered when making decisions (Klenk et al., 2017).

The Alliance also has programmes targeted at their priority communities, including Minneapolis's Southside green zone, located in neighbourhoods with a high proportion of priority households (near where George Floyd was killed in 2020). Yet this programme is again infrastructure-oriented with grants that support air and soil, energy efficiency, economic growth, and addressing problems of environmental pollutants. Further research needs to probe how such programmes were identified and whether the Alliance was able to live up to its commitment to ensure input by priority communities into what they need. Promotional videos on the website spotlight the voices of Indigenous and immigrant communities and their concerns over environmental pollution, yet in one video, a programme employee prompts a local respondent when she stumbles over an answer (CNCA, 2021b). Community consultations are notoriously fraught, and in this case where there is a direct acknowledgement of highly uneven power relations, exploring intersectional power dynamics and knowledge politics that serve in subtle, difficult to shift ways to reproduce social and political inequalities is crucial.

The strategy planning document is somewhat reflexive, acknowledging the overemphasis on infrastructure in activities undertaken so far. 'Cities have been focused on the "what", "when" and "how" of carbon neutrality work. We've found that a key missing piece is the "who"' (CNCA, 2020: 9). But simply recognising the importance of 'who' will not overturn entrenched politics. Their own materials are illustrative. That current efforts have fallen short is reflected in their bullet point to 'increase priority community representation in CNCA and the field through fellowships and participation in CNCA activities' (CNCA, 2020: 11), and in the photos chosen for each strategy subheading: 'exert collective influence' depicts white men and one white woman; 'peer-learning' shows all white men and one white woman; the 'transformational leadership' photo is more diverse by gender, but has only one woman of colour (no men of colour). It is admirable that the CNCA is placing such a high rhetorical emphasis on climate justice, but more research is needed to understand how such efforts play out in practice. A feminist political ecology analysis looks to how social inclusions and exclusions are generated through the socio-natures of adaptation projects: changing infrastructures not only requires understanding 'who', it also requires understanding how subjectivities shift as socio-natural entanglements change and the urban landscape takes on new forms, meanings and possibilities (see also Kaika, 2017).

While here I have looked at the politics of knowledge within a well-intentioned network like the CNCA, it is also important to flag the potentials. Placing climate justice questions at the centre of the Alliance is promising. It helps to direct activities towards those communities and give them space to become more closely involved. Second, it offers an interesting model: using private foundation funding and collective action from the city level where politicians and civil servants are closer to the people to exert global political clout has the potential to help undercut some of the national-level resistances to major change.

Conclusion

The two stories of adaptation efforts within cities in the Global South and the Global North that this chapter presented bring us back to the questions I raised at the beginning of this piece: how do processes of social inclusion and exclusion reshape adaptation; and how can the politics of knowledge production and feminist urban political ecology scholarship in particular help reshape adaptation? While IPCC definitions – and associated funding – are tied to understanding biophysical climate impacts, my examples show how climate change combines with social, economic, and political dynamics to create the adaptation challenges that unfold.

Feminist political ecology offers a framework for working through these dynamics to show how climate change adaptation processes create uneven outcomes for people from different walks of life. It is at the level of the everyday, the contradictions that emerge when decisions are made by people different than those impacted, when climate injustices become most pronounced, as the case of Pani Bajaar shows. There, new dynamics of gender, caste, age, and geography are changing who is vulnerable to what under a drying climate scenario. As a water scheme focuses on metres per second, from where and delivered to where, it leaves unaddressed the aspirations of people in upstream areas, the burdens for water management that are made invisible within households, and the hardships of those who fall between upstream springs and downstream water taps. While it is tempting to assume that including women, people of colour and Indigenous people will solve problems, my analysis shows why such an approach to intersectional social relations is inadequate. Yet in the CNCA case, these categories stand in for a real analysis of climate justice issues; issues that need to be fully considered not only at the moment of project implementation, but from the design stage (Ahlborg, 2017; Lawhon and Murphy, 2012). Such an approach would see the investments of the CNCA move away from their overemphasis on infrastructure and give more attention to the how, who, and when questions that are at the centre of climate justice concerns.

But my purpose in highlighting the influence of intersectional social relations and knowledge politics in adaptation processes is not to present another story of exclusion and mis-development. Rather, the analysis lends insights into both who is most at risk from climate change, and how climate change can become an opportunity for social change. If the context of rapidly shifting resources can be used to foster greater deliberation, inclusion, and realistic democratic processes that take inequality as a starting point rather than an externality that requires management, there is hope for cities to truly be at the vanguard. Current approaches to climate change research and planning are too static and have inadequate provision to place social inequalities within the centre of adaptation processes. The CNCA network and the political mobilisation of newly elected leaders in Pani Bajaar demonstrate the great potential the city scale offers for innovation and grassroots politics. While in the latter case, *sam, dam, danda bhed niti* (coercion, money, physical intimation, and ostracism) was used, perhaps next time citizen forums that debate knowledge claims, that use various approaches to fellowship, mentoring, and recognition of inherent power dynamics, such as those promoted on paper by the CNCA, can replace these means. Whether 'adaptation' occurs or not will be the outcome of contestations over such relations and knowledge politics, regardless of how well the plans are formulated. Taking a feminist political ecology approach suggests the adaptation 'priority areas' are questions of politics, power, and the *means* through which socio-natural and political reproduction occurs.

Notes

1 Climate change adaptation is emerging as a central issue for urban areas. Adaptation here draws from the well-established 2014 Intergovernmental Panel on Climate Change (IPCC) definition as desires to minimise impacts or capitalise upon benefits from a changing environment (IPCC, 2014). While many critical scholars have challenged the premises of adaptation, millions of dollars and hundreds of thousands of projects have proliferated across the globe in both formal and informal ways in the name of adjusting to climate change. It is this latter process which interests me here.
2 The work in Pani Bajaar was done under Swedish Research Council (VR) Grant number 2018–05866 of which I am the lead investigator. The data used for this chapter was part of our ongoing collaborative work. The fieldwork was led by Dr Hemant Ojha (University of Canberra) and Dr Dil Khatri (Southasia Institute of Advanced Studies in Kathmandu (SIAS)), the data collection team also included Gyanu Maskey, Pema Norbhu Lama Tsumpa, Ankita Shrestha, Kaustuv Raj Neupane, all from SIAS, and myself. I am grateful to the team for allowing me to use our data here and their useful comments on earlier drafts.
3 A Hindi-Nepali expression used to confer the extra-legal ways in which political authority is asserted in the Subcontinent. The implication here is that all means – including arguments, laws, bribes, violence, intimidation, and ostracism – are used to secure compliance.

References

Ahlborg, H. 2017. Towards a conceptualization of power in energy transitions. *Environmental Innovation and Societal Transitions* 25: 122–41. https://doi.org/10.1016/j.eist.2017.01.004.

Ahlborg, H. and A.J. Nightingale. 2018. Theorizing power in political ecology: The where of power in resource governance projects. *Journal of Political Ecology* 25(1): 1–21.

Angelo, H. and D. Wachsmuth. 2020. Why does everyone think cities can save the planet? *Urban Studies* 57(11): 2201–21. DOI: 10.1177/0042098020919081.

Arora-Jonsson, S. 2011. Virtue and vulnerability: Discourses on women, gender and climate change. *Global Environmental Change* 21(2): 744–51. http://dx.doi.org/10.1016/j.gloenvcha.2011.01.005

Bee, B.A., J. Rice, and A. Trauger. 2015. A feminist approach to climate change governance: Everyday and intimate politics. *Geography Compass* 9(6): 339–50. DOI: 10.1111/gec3.12218.

Broto, V.C. and H. Bulkeley. 2013. Maintaining climate change experiments: Urban political ecology and the everyday reconfiguration of urban infrastructure. *International Journal of Urban and Regional Research* 37(6): 1934–48. https://doi.org/10.1111/1468-2427.12050

Butler, J. 1997. *The psychic life of power: Theories in subjection.* Stanford, CA: Stanford University Press.

CNCA (Carbon Neutral Cities Alliance). 2020. *Mobilizing transformative climate action in cities: Strategic plan 2021–2023*. Copenhagen: Carbon Neutral Cities Alliance.
CNCA (Carbon Neutral Cities Alliance). 2021a. About us. https://carbonneutralcities.org/about/, accessed 12 August 2022.
CNCA (Carbon Neutral Cities Alliance). 2021b. Southside Green Zone – self determination and accountability. https://carbonneutralcities.org/cities/minneapolis/, accessed 12 August 2022.
Crenshaw, K.W. 2017. *On intersectionality: Essential writings*. New York: The New Press.
Doshi, S. 2017. Embodied urban political ecology: Five propositions. *Area* 49(1): 125–8. https://doi.org/10.1111/area.12293
Elmhirst, R. 2011. Introducing new feminist political ecologies. *Geoforum* 42(2): 129–32. https://doi.org/10.1016/j.geoforum.2011.01.006
Eriksen, S. and E. Selboe. 2013. Towards sustainable adaptation or paradoxical development pathways? Contrasting understandings and local actions in Øystre Slidre, Norway. In K. O'Brien and E. Selboe (eds.), *The adaptative challenge of climate change*. Cambridge: Cambridge University Press.
Eriksen, S. et al. 2021. Adaptation interventions and their effect on vulnerability in developing countries: Help, hindrance or irrelevance? *World Development* 141: 105383. https://doi.org/10.1016/j.worlddev.2020.105383
Gonda, N. 2019. Re-politicizing the gender and climate change debate: The potential of feminist political ecology to engage with power in action in adaptation policies and projects in Nicaragua. *Geoforum* 106: 87–96. https://doi.org/10.1016/j.geoforum.2019.07.020
Gururani, S. and P. Vandergeest. 2014. Introduction: New frontiers of ecological knowledge: Co-producing knowledge and governance in Asia. *Conservation and Society* 12(4): 343–51.
Haraway, D. 1988. Situated knowledges: The science question in feminism and the privilege of partial perspective. *Feminist Studies* 14(3): 575–99. DOI: 10.2307/3178066.
IPCC. 2014. Summary for policymakers. In C. B. Field et al. (eds.), *Climate change 2014: Impacts, adaptation, and vulnerability. Part A: Global and sectoral aspects. Contribution of Working Group II to the Fifth Assessment Report of the Intergovernmental Panel on Climate Change*. Cambridge and New York: Cambridge University Press, pp. 1–32.
Jasanoff, S. 2013. *States of knowledge: The co-production of science and the social order*. London and New York: Routledge.
Kaika, M. 2017. 'Don't call me resilient again!': The new urban agenda as immunology or what happens when communities refuse to be vaccinated with 'smart cities' and indicators. *Environment and Urbanization* 29(1): 89–102. DOI: 10.1177/0956247816684763.
Klenk, N., A. Fiume, K. Meehan, and C. Gibbes. 2017. Local knowledge in climate adaptation research: Moving knowledge frameworks from extraction to co-production. *Wiley Interdisciplinary Reviews: Climate Change* 8(5): e475. DOI: 10.1002/wcc.475.
Lawhon, M. and J.T. Murphy. 2012. Socio-technical regimes and sustainability transitions: Insights from political ecology. *Progress in Human Geography* 36(3): 354–78. DOI: 10.1177/0309132511427960.

Lawhon, M., D. Nilsson, J. Silver, H. Ernstson, and S. Lwasa. 2017. Thinking through heterogeneous infrastructure configurations. *Urban Studies* 55(4): 720–32. DOI: 10.1177/0042098017720149.

MacGregor, S. 2010. Gender and climate change: From impacts to discourses. *Journal of the Indian Ocean Region* 6(2): 223–38. DOI: 10.1080/19480881.2010.536669.

Nightingale, A.J. 2006. The nature of gender: Work, gender and environment. *Environment and Planning D: Society and Space* 24(2): 165–85.

Nightingale, A.J. 2013. Fishing for nature: The politics of subjectivity and emotion in Scottish inshore fisheries management. *Environment and Planning A* 45(10): 2362–78.

Nightingale, A.J. 2017. Power and politics in climate change adaptation efforts: Struggles over authority and recognition in the context of political instability. *Geoforum* 84: 11–20. https://doi.org/10.1016/j.geoforum.2017.05.011

Nightingale, A.J. et al. 2020. Beyond technical fixes: Climate solutions and the great derangement. *Climate and Development* 12(4): 343–52. DOI: 10.1080/17565529.2019.1624495.

Singh, N.M. 2017. Becoming a commoner: The commons as sites for affective socio-nature encounters and co-becomings. *Ephemera: Theory and Politics in Organisation* 17(4): 751–76.

Swyngedouw, E. and M. Kaika. 2014. L'ecologia política urbana. Grans promeses, aturades ... i nous inicis? [Urban political ecology: Great promises, deadlock ... and new beginnings?]. *Documents d'Anàlisi Geogràfica* 60(3): 459–81.

Tschakert, P., P.J. Das, N. Shrestha Pradhan, M. Machado, A. Lamadrid, M. Buragohain, and M.A. Hazarika. 2016. Micropolitics in collective learning spaces for adaptive decision making. *Global Environmental Change* 40: 182–94. http://dx.doi.org/10.1016/j.gloenvcha.2016.07.004

Truelove, Y. 2011. (Re-)conceptualizing water inequality in Delhi, India through a feminist political ecology framework. *Geoforum* 42(2): 143–52. DOI: 10.1016/j.geoforum.2011.01.004.

Tzaninis, Y., T. Mandler, M. Kaika, and R. Keil. 2021. Moving urban political ecology beyond the 'urbanization of nature'. *Progress in Human Geography* 45(2): 229–52.

8

Nairobi's bad natures

Wangui Kimari

Introduction

For those who see it from one of its higher vantage points, Mathare is a mosaic of dins, architectures, and enterprises. Colourful, noisy, tragic, and also enterprising, it is a veritable city within a city where situated norms are established and where, for example, a halo of smoke can signal any number of things: from cooking, a burning house, or the impressive chemical reactions engineered by the constant brewing of *chang'aa* – the criminalised brew that is its cash crop. It is also a province of many chromatic dreams both deferred and desired. For nearly a century this poor city habitation has produced many of Nairobi's African urban (and female) pioneers; it is the home of intersecting histories – political, ecological, social, and economic – that are threaded together by a multitude of unwritten but powerful tragic comedy tales of colonial and postcolonial existences. Together, the combined sentiences of these many presences collide and condense together, bringing about the embers of a situated community fire that has enabled this 'illegal' settlement to remain for close to a century.

But this remainder is constantly jeopardised. Though residents have been able to resist, often tragically (Kimari, 2021), the crossfires of the state for generations – evictions, police killings, and the absence of basic services, for example – more unpredictable disasters brought about by the co-territorialisation of structural violence and a changing climate make this remainder increasingly harder to do. And even as Shisanya and Khayesi (2007) argue that as a priority in Nairobi lives, climate change is vastly overshadowed by the prevailing realities of poverty and all of its manifestations, it is undeniable that climate change and poverty come together in many grave ways in this city. Certainly, pronounced Anthropocenic signatures intersect with a necrotic urban governance to further jeopardise the lives of those already at the margins.

Expressing this in an unsolicited and visceral declaration, one interlocutor asked: 'Why is it we are being shot and we go and steal again? It is a question of ecological justice.' In this unexpected association, a young man from Mathare can be highlighting any number of scenarios: that a lack of food from the lack of rain, or the reality that a house may have been swept away by the flooded river that intersects this settlement, can be part of the causal linkages that catalyse petty theft, which, for those who live in this geography, can prompt, not court, a police bullseye on their backs.

Informed by these community connections, which external observers may perceive as Nairobi's bad natures – that the internal landscapes considered immanent to Mathare residents and that are thought to programme them to steal merge and reflect an uneven environment prone to disaster, this chapter aims to show how these natures, of which Mathare is symbolic, are reproduced through a colonial metabolic process territorialised in the discursive and material practices of the city's urban spatial management. This governance, that intentionally conjoins particular socio-physical environments and their people, embodied ecologies (Doshi, 2017), reaffirms, through various sinister effects, the marginality of places like Mathare. Because of this its natures – in the dual sense of the term – suffer elevated states of crisis exacerbated by worsening poverty and climate emergencies, enabling, as our interlocutor affirmed deliberately, an urgent 'question of ecological justice'.

Building on urban political ecology (UPE), here I map how both subjects and their environment continue to represent the city's biophysical and socio-political profanities. In my work in Nairobi, urban political ecology has been a useful bridge to relate the 'natural' environment to other dynamics implicit within the making of this city, and how they all come together to render an urban nature of grave inequity (Lawhon et al., 2014: 500). Prompted by the associations Mathare residents themselves make – for example, between petty theft and ecological justice – I connect events as disparate as cholera and teenage pregnancies in this geography, to detail how inequality condenses here, and its (re)production within a colonial urban planning (Kimari, 2017). These seemingly unrelated connections are theorised with the help of an UPE that 'mobilizes a multitude of things, discourses, and people – into hybrids, assemblages or quasi-objects – to stabilize infrastructures, modes of governing, and problem definition' (Lawhon et al., 2014: 501). Certainly, assembling local events, artefacts, and stories has enabled me to excavate the 'deep historical spatial logics of [this] "ghetto"' (Heynen, 2016: 840), and how its 'power geometries' (Heynen et al., 2006) engender uneven urban lives, distinguishing between, 'core' and 'periphery' (Tzaninis et al., 2021), 'good' and 'bad' natures.

In my work, both the outcomes and the co-constitutive political processes that create these 'bad' natures and subjects are captured by the term 'ecology of exclusion'. I use this phrase to show how all of the situated spatial conditions and circulated subjectivities (for example, crime/criminals, cholera, overcrowding, bedbugs, monster rats, fetid and toxic sewage, and sexual violence) are naturalised in this environment through processes that legitimate both Mathare's hypervisibility and invisibility, while concomitantly seeking to de-naturalise them. With ecology of exclusion, I would like to register the following: that sites of 'bad natures' (in all senses) are intentionally produced through interconnected ecological, political, economic, and social processes sanctioned by the state, and that have imperial origins. Drawing attention to these forces that come together to produce related but seemingly disparate grave ecological and socio-spatial circumstances is an intentional act: one that challenges their normalisation and traces their genealogies not within Mathare, but to the very urban governance practices that claim to, discursively and physically, rally against these 'bad natures'.

Bad natures

Urban political ecology seeks to rupture the idea that cities are 'ontological entities separate from "nature" (Tzaninis et al., 2021: 229). Extending this ontological connectedness between nature and its inhabitants, the environment of particular urban spaces is often thought to represent, in a total way, the internal landscapes of their residents. In this regard, in discussing the 'spatialization of virtue' implicit in the governance of European cities in the nineteenth century, Osborne and Rose (1999: 743) convey how the diagrammers of the city believed that

> There seems to be a negative spiral of interaction between milieu and character. Poor character, which may be inherited from one's forbears, led not only to conduct and ways of living that degraded ones' surrounding milieu; it also led one to gravitate towards a certain kind of milieu, which itself has an effect upon character – an effect which, in turn, might be passed down to future generations through a weakened constitution, and through the ways in which one rears one's children and the habits one inculcates in them.

Undoubtedly, the perceived symbiosis between character and milieu in Mathare – the connection between a 'weakened constitution' and 'one's surroundings' – owes some provenance to these nineteenth-century beliefs imprinted in European cities. However, added to these enduring global tropes are situational nuances that layer pre-established notions of 'slums' and their inhabitants.

Davis (2006: 122) states that slums begin with 'bad geology'. And true to this statement, Mathare's disembowelled landscape and uneven terrain speak to its initial life as a low-lying floodplain, and subsequent history as a colonial stone quarry. Regarding this more recent commercial metabolic experience, since at least 1921 and up to the late 1940s, it was used as a stone mine and its products were put towards the concrete machinations of a growing colonial city (Chiuri, 1978). These raw materials are said to have contributed to key city infrastructures, shaping city space beyond the 3km^2 of this settlement, and it is suggested that some of its rocks breathed life into the brick and mortar of the Supreme Court, ambassadorial neighbourhoods such as Muthaiga, and even the infamous Kamiti Maximum Security Prison.

Despite the vitality of life in this area, and the collective resolution that has enabled this place – one of the harshest environments in Eastern Africa (Muungano Support Trust, 2012) – to endure for almost a century, Mathare has always been considered a place of bad natures. And nature in all senses: its people, their practices, their place. Conjured, like those from other poor areas in the east of Nairobi, as the outlaws of the city living in a degenerate and crime-ridden headquarters, their home becomes all that is taken as the 'problem' in the city; the habitations that prevent it from being 'world-class', 'smart', and modern. This characterisation, of both the external and internal landscapes of this settlement, stems from a conjunction of histories briefly attended to below.

It is important to note that nature, in a variety of forms, is consistently referenced by Mathare interlocutors. Whether it is included in descriptions of the garbage and other forms of waste that make many tributaries throughout this geography, or in the unsolicited parables of environmental decay expressed to index changes in individual and collective experiences of life, nature is a key part of the texture of residents' stories of community and space. Interestingly, much academic writing on Mathare, or Nairobi broadly, does not foreground nature in its analyses (see Hake, 1977; Médard, 2010; Van Stapele, 2015). While the extensive environmental pollution in Mathare is affirmed in these academic discussions, with the exception of Otiso (2005), scholars do not appear to pay due attention to the particular human–nature metabolisms that brought forth this specific urban environment, nor connect it to the residents whose subjectivities are often understood as symbiotic to their home environment.

By off-staging nature, earlier scholarship on Mathare enables what many urban political ecology scholars discern as the false dichotomy that separates the city from nature in studies that focus on urban areas. Correspondingly, this has prevented paying more attention to how the majority of city dwellers are envisioned as a self-evident reflection of their intentionally abandoned geographies – a 'slum' identity as representative of a degenerate personhood, even as the valuation of land in Nairobi was determined within nineteenth-century colonial spatial bargains catalysed by racialised imperial political, ecologic, social, and economic determinations.

Let us look at the histories that created the conditions of possibility for the production of such an environment, an ecology of exclusion. In order to ensure British dominance in East Africa during the 'scramble for Africa', a Kenya-Uganda railway was proposed and built between 1896 and 1901. Following the arrival of the railhead in *Enkare Nyrobi* – the site that would later become Nairobi – efforts were soon directed towards making this savannah landscape legible for empire. By virtue of its status as a railway town, an important node in Britain's extraction efforts in East Africa, one of the first contributions to Nairobi's built environment was the railway headquarters that stands to this day (Amutabi, 2012: 327; Hake, 1977).

Following the construction of the Kenya-Uganda locomotive, European settlement in Kenya was encouraged by this 'colony's' second commissioner, Sir Charles Eliot (1901–4), since Britain was anxious to repay debt accrued from the building costs of the railway. What's more, it was also imperative that this new British outpost became self-sustaining (White, 1990: 35). Correspondingly, protectorate-sanctioned narratives, of a 'white man's country' of abandon and lordship over natives and a vast savannah full of wildlife, were launched and did much to encourage European settlement in Kenya (Amutabi, 2012: 334; Jackson, 2011; Robertson, 1997: 16). More locally, Nairobi's population growth also coincided with rural disasters, specifically rinderpest (cattle plague) and famine, which compelled many of those impacted to come to the city to find the monies needed to replenish agricultural stocks and households, as well as to pay the hut tax that had recently been imposed on them by the colonial administration.

Occurring in tandem with its expansion were efforts to make Nairobi more functional for the imperial enterprise. This facilitated the emergence of a more intentional socio-spatial engineering that inserted racialisation into all vital urban processes. As part of these developments, myths about contagion attached to certain 'races' abounded and were mapped onto geography: for example, Africans were synonymous with conditions that emerged from living in conditions of 'squalor' and even 'excess' – from skin diseases to syphilis – while South Asian descendants were, in the early twentieth century, associated with the plague.

The circulation of these bio-medical tropes reflected global trends (see, as but one example, Caldeira, 2000, for this in Brazil), and it was the Simpson Report of 1913 that, in rallying disease as a sufficient motivator, called explicitly for racial separation in both residential and commercial areas in Nairobi (Hake, 1977: 39). This fear of biological contamination was also firmly anchored within a moral economy that sought to prevent the coexistence of Africans and 'lower-class Asiatics', who had been brought from India in the late nineteenth century, primarily to help build the railway, in order to foil the possibility of socio-sexual transgressions against the colour line (White, 1990: 46; Hake, 1977) Undoubtedly, these anxieties were also anchored in the historical pathologisations of the African subject.

Though the racial zoning of the city was an active practice of city managers soon after the designation of Enkare Nyrobi as a railway town, the outcome of the Simpson Report and subsequent legislation was that non-white residents were more vehemently confined to geographies that, according to the colonial administration, were reflective of their natures. Europeans took the elevated land with better drainage, seen to be free of malaria, while 'Asiatics' were emplaced between Europeans and the low-lying flood plains designated for Africans. The result was that

> the large area of high ground and ridges (on which building costs were cheaper and drainage healthier) between the streams to the west and north had been chosen for the building of estates reserved by covenant or otherwise for European occupation. Plots were normally one acre, but in some cases half an acre. The 10,400 Europeans lived at so low a density that the figure for the whole town was 4.8 persons per acre, for a total population (1944) of 108,900. To the north-east, the estates in which the town's 34,300 Asians lived were laid out with from two to twelve houses to the acre. To the south-east, the small area reserved for 'natives' sheltered many of the town's 64,200 Africans.
> (Hake, 1977: 57)

Because of these spatialised covenants, Nairobi's African population was confined to the 'inferior' geographies of the city, and the concomitant colonial pathologisation of African subjects meant that *naturally* 'squalid and crime infested, Eastlands was for Africans [and] it has been this way since the early 1900s' (Anderson, 2005: 182). As is evident from the formal merger of imposed home and habitus, perceived subject and spatial natures in Mathare produced and continue to reproduce what White (1990: 97) describes as 'a squatter settlement with no legitimacy at all'.

Inevitably, the imposed coalescence of subjects and their space leads to particular spatial languages about poor urban sites like Mathare. Its environment is often conjured as a place of waste and a graveyard of nature, while its residents are similarly viewed as, 'criminals and prostitutes' (in the words of a former member of parliament for the area). Both residents and outsiders alike use the term 'slum', perhaps with differing motives, to evoke pervasive images of decaying uneven landscapes and informal infrastructures of 'autoconstruction' (Holston, 2009). What is evident from these imaginings of Mathare's nature is that its iconicity is always a biophysicality of overflowing, rotting excess: a filthy wasteland (Wa Mungai, 2013: 175). And the prevailing narratives about this community – of criminals unwanted subjects, and outlaws – is evident in public and archival media discourses featuring Mathare over the past seven decades.

Fanon (1961) wrote about these most impoverished and stigmatised sections, the former *cite indigenes* of the compartmentalised colonial geographies. These continue to be the labour heartbeat of all Nairobi's operations but are the parts that formal urban governance regimes intentionally forget. They become more and more overcrowded, underserviced, and abandoned to high incidences of alarming health statistics, political turbulence, and grave pollution levels. Currently, against the recurrent flooding, disease, and water absence (see Kithiia and Dowling, 2010), as but a few examples of the effects of climate change in the country, Mathare remains one of the most infamous exemplars of these conditions.

Both then and now, most of Nairobi's population continue to live in the *cite indigenes*, and, as in the colonial period, a violent police force staffs and surveils the socio-ecological borders between the rich and poor, also embodied ecologies (Doshi, 2017). More than half of Nairobi's residents, over 2.5 million people, lives in these spaces of bad natures that account for roughly 5 per cent of the city's surface area. And the conditions in the former native city have only worsened over the years. The population has grown, but service provision has not increased commensurately – as postcolonial urban governance took on the same imperatives as those of colonial Nairobi – it continues to be a planning of force and neglect for those living in ecologies of exclusion. Certainly, after independence, the African cities within Nairobi became habitations for a large urban poor population who were incorporated into the city by their effective disincorporation. This time, segregation took place not primarily through race, but through a discursive stigma inherited from colonial practices that built on class, and informed an urban exclusion articulated through a lack of basic services (water, sanitation, housing), tenure insecurity and evictions (Hake, 1977; Owuor and Mbatia, 2008).

Irrespective of some equalising interventions proposed in planning documents since the 1970s[1] it is in the more prosperous parts of the city where infrastructural improvements are actually made, and where, perhaps, innovation in the face of changing climatic conditions are launched; undoubtedly class interests, conjoined with former racialised priorities, now orient the city. The urban majority, as before, are, for the most part, left to their own devices.

As a result of this abandonment, Mathare and places like it, embody frightening 'natural' conditions, including: a high incidence of ailments as a result of chronic air pollution exacerbated by climatic changes – 46 per cent of women have respiratory illness or cough (Corburn and Hildebrand, 2015); less than 20 per cent of households have access to reliable, affordable, and clean piped water (Mathare Social Justice Centre, 2019), while all households can also go up to five days without this service (Kamau and Njiru, 2018); and Mathare also has the 'lowest average elevation' of all 'slums' in Nairobi, making it highly vulnerable to flooding (MSPARC, 2020). The dire living conditions within this settlement are then coupled with high levels of intra-community crime and excessive policing, which led to another interlocutor to affirm, 'here it is not only the police that will kill you, but the environment can kill you as well' (Murogi, personal communication).

Through the interplay of these phenomena across social, political, economic, and ecological registers, Mathare is reinscribed as a place of, simultaneously, a 'bad' environment and 'bad' subjects. The reproduction of bad natures, as I discussed above, is intentionally (materially and discursively) territorialised in this geography, normalising all of the marginalisations that come together in this space, as if it had always been, *naturally*, an ecology of exclusion (Kimari, 2017). Building on the brief historicisation of the dynamics that have laid the foundation for Mathare's bad natures, in the following section I conclude by discussing how its subjects appropriate and contest their bad natures, even as both are increasingly imperilled by worsening Anthropocenic outcomes.

Conclusion

Mathare, across its century-long existence, is always constructed as a place of bad natures. This status is perpetuated by practices and discourses that, I argue, derive from the uneven and segregatory colonial and postcolonial governance histories of Nairobi (Kimari, 2017). Certainly, imperial logics territorialise the city both tangibly and discursively: materialising the coalescence of colonial factors in this space over time that have produced and keep producing Mathare as an ecology of exclusion. Material and immaterial attention to natures helps excavate the multiple modes and nodes of formal urban governance practices, which violently entrench and sustain Mathare as a 'slum' of degenerate subjects. At the same time, extending natures to ideas about personhood and registering events such as police killings as ecological effects helps elaborate the conditions through which natures are established and used to reinforce exclusion.

Without a doubt, the external representations of Mathare make evident how it is persistently conjured as a place of decay. Grave depictions of this space – as rife with illegality, waste, and criminality – inform popular imaginaries constructed by weaving together historical economic, social, political, and ecological registers. Here, particular biographies come alive, enabling the interplay of stigmatisation and segregation that legitimates formal city neglect and hyper-policing.

But despite these conditions, its bad natures are also mobilised as fronts through which people can spearhead their bids for abolition – it offers 'multiple loci of enunciation' (Schulz, 2017: 139) – to resist and reclaim the 'hidden virtues of the troublesome' (Ralph, 2014, 49). That multiple interlocutors gestured towards the need to demand an end to police bullets as an 'ecological question' highlights the everyday connections made: the community articulation that the 'bad' internal landscapes that prompt petty theft can be explained and remedied by a need to pursue a city that demands abolition for its ecologies – a governance of space free from colonial regimes. And it is part of the effrontery to make these associations that keeps Mathare dwellers here; it builds on a situated community fire described earlier, which insists that they remain even against the constant de- and recomposition of this geography, the never-ending violence across colonial and postcolonial moments that reproduce its bad natures.

Note

1 Such as the 1973 Nairobi Metropolitan Growth Strategy and the 2014 Nairobi Integrated Urban Development Master Plan 2014–2030.

References

Anderson, D. 2005. *Histories of the hanged: The dirty war in Kenya and the end of empire*. New York: W.W. Norton & Company.
Amutabi, M. 2012. Buildings as symbols and metaphors of colonial hegemony: Interrogating colonial buildings and architecture in Kenya's urban spaces. In F. Demissie (ed.), *Colonial architecture and urbanism in Africa: Intertwined histories*. Surrey, UK: Ashgate, pp. 325–46.
Caldeira, T. 2000. *City of walls: Crime, segregation, and citizenship in São Paolo*. Berkeley: University of California Press.
Chiuri, W. 1978. *Mathare Valley: A squatter settlement in Nairobi: A case study*. Nairobi: United Nations International Children's Emergency Fund (UNICEF).
Corburn, J. and C. Hildebrand. 2015. Slum sanitation and the social determinants of women's health in Nairobi, Kenya. *Journal of Environmental and Public Health*. https://doi.org/10.1155/2015/209505
Davis, M. 2006. *Planet of slums*. London: Verso.
Doshi, S. 2017. Embodied urban political ecology: Five propositions. *Area* 49(1): 125–8.
Fanon, F. 1961. *The wretched of the earth*. New York: Grove Press.
Hake, A. 1977. *African metropolis: Nairobi's self-help city*. New York: St Martin's Press.
Heynen, N. 2016. Urban political ecology II: The abolitionist century. *Progress in Human Geography* 40(6): 839–45.
Heynen, N., M. Kaika, and E. Swyngedouw (eds.). 2006. *In the nature of cities: Urban political ecology and the politics of urban metabolism*. London: Routledge.
Holston, J. 2009. Insurgent citizenship in an era of global urban peripheries. *City & Society* 21(2): 245–67.

Jackson, W. 2011. White man's country: Kenya colony and the making of a myth. *Journal of Eastern African Studies* 5(2): 344–68.

Kamau, N. and H. Njiru. 2018. Water, sanitation and hygiene situation in Kenya's urban slums. *Journal of Health Care for the Poor and Underserved* 29(1): 321–36.

Kimari, W. 2017. 'Nai-rob-me' 'Nai-beg-me' 'Nai-shanty': Historicizing space-subjectivity connections in Nairobi from its ruins. Unpublished doctoral dissertation. York University, Toronto.

Kimari, W. 2021. The story of a pump: Life, death and afterlives within an urban planning of 'divide and rule' in Nairobi, Kenya. *Urban Geography* 42(2): 141–60.

Kithiia, J. and R. Dowling. 2010. An integrated city-level planning process to address the impacts of climate change in Kenya: The case of Mombasa. *Cities* 27(6): 466–75.

Lawhon, M., H. Ernstson, and J. Silver. 2014. Provincializing urban political ecology: Towards a situated UPE through African urbanism. *Antipode* 46(2): 497–516.

Mathare Social Justice Centre. 2019. *Maji ni Haki: Haki ni Maji. Eastlands residents demand their right to water: A participatory report*. Nairobi: Mathare Social Justice Centre.

Médard, C. 2010. City planning in Nairobi: The stakes, the people, the sidetracking. In H. Charton-Bigot and D. Rodriguez-Torres (eds.), *Nairobi today: The paradox of a fragmented city*. Nairobi: IFRA, pp. 25–60.

MSPARC (Mathare Special Planning Area Research Collective). 2020. *Draft research situation and gap analysis*. Nairobi: MSPARC Technical Committee.

Muungano Support Trust. 2012. *Mathare Support Trust*. Nairobi and Berkeley: University of Nairobi and University of California.

Osborne, T. and N. Rose. 1999. Governing cities: Notes on the spatialisation of virtue. *Environment and Planning D: Society and Space* 17(6): 737–60.

Otiso, K.M. 2005. Colonial urbanisation and urban management in Kenya. In S.J. Salm and T. Falola (eds.), *African urban spaces in historical perspective*. Rochester, NY: University of Rochester Press, pp. 73–95.

Owuor, S. and T. Mbatia. 2008. *Post-independence development of Nairobi City, Kenya*. Paper presented at Workshop on African Capital Cities, Dakar, Senegal, 22–23 September.

Ralph, L. 2014. *Renegade dreams: Living through injury in gangland Chicago*. Chicago: University of Chicago Press.

Robertson, C.C. 1997. *Trouble showed the way: Women, men, and trade in the Nairobi area, 1890–1990*. Bloomington: Indiana University Press.

Shisanya, C.A. and M. Khayesi. 2007. How is climate change perceived in relation to other socioeconomic and environmental threats in Nairobi, Kenya? *Climatic Change* 85(3): 271–84.

Schulz, K. 2017. Decolonizing political ecology: Ontology, technology and 'critical' enchantment. *Journal of Political Ecology* 24(1): 125–43.

Tzaninis, Y., T. Mandler, M. Kaika, and R. Keil. 2021. Moving urban political ecology beyond the 'urbanization of nature'. *Progress in Human Geography* 45(2): 229–52.

Van Stapele, N. 2015. Respectable 'illegality': Gangs, masculinities and belonging in a Nairobi ghetto. PhD dissertation, University of Amsterdam.

Wa Mungai, M. 2013. *Nairobi's 'Matatu Men': Portrait of a subculture*. Nairobi: Contact Zones.

White, L. 1990. *The comforts of home*. Chicago: University of Chicago Press.

9

Situating suburban ecologies in the Global South: Notes from India's urban periphery[1]

Shubhra Gururani

On a sunny December morning, Kushal Singh,[2] a Gujjar elder,[3] sitting in front of his small grocery store, pointed his finger to the dried-up area of the Ghata Lake and said to me,

> This entire region is very uneven, rocky, it is full of deep ditches, craters, and trenches ... There are five small *jhors* [ponds] in the village and then there was the Ghata *jheel* [lake]. When it rained the entire area used to fill up with water. The British built a dam more than a hundred years back, it is still there and until recently it was regularly maintained. There was a passage [*mori*] for the water, which was closed in June to collect all the rainwater, and then drained after Diwali in October ... water came down from Mehrauli to Mandi Gaon to Gwal Pahari to Bandhwari and then to Ghata ... The rains would feed the water level of the *jheel* and we would dig holes in our land and they would fill up with water which we would keep for drinking. Similarly, we would dig holes for our animals as well; there are separate ditches for our animals and us near the bundh down there ... There was a lot of rain in 1972 and the lake filled up in 1977, but since then the rains have diminished and it has barely filled up. You can go even 200ft [deep] there is nothing, borewells have sucked all the water.
>
> (Interview, December 2018)

Kushal Singh was describing the life and death of Ghata Jheel, an old lake, one of the largest and deepest waterbodies in the city of Gurgaon, that has now disappeared. According to a recent survey, in Gurgaon District alone, as many as 389 waterbodies have disappeared in the past 60 years,[4] including some fairly old lakes, that have dried out to make room for India's millennial city.[5] These waterbodies were crucial to maintaining the regional hydrology that would seasonally liven up the arid landscape. They saturated the parched lakebeds, nourished the soil for crops, vegetables, and pasture for local residents to make a living, and channelled the rainwater into the Najafgarh Basin and prevented flooding. But, since the mid-1980s with the liberalisation of India's economy, vast tracts of agro-pastoral lands have been acquired by private developers and state authorities to build housing, highways, shopping malls, corporate offices, and special economic zones. In this moment of land rush, the soaring prices of land and speculation have meant that the vast network of drains, ditches, wells, canals, ponds, and creeks has been covered up, blocked, and virtually erased for the city yet to come. Not only have hundreds of waterbodies been covered up, concretised, or overlooked, many have also disappeared from governmental maps and plans and certainly from the gaze of most private developers and new residents who have come to live and work in the new Gurgaon.

The changes in the rhythms of land and water in the context of urbanisation are by no means new, nor are they unique to Gurgaon. The Centre of Science and Environment, in their report *Why urban India floods?* (2016), has drawn attention to the increased risk of urban flooding due to climate change. With global warming, the weather patterns have changed, and the frequency of extreme weather events, like heavy rainfalls and flooding, are on the rise in large parts of India. Amid these climatic changes, rapid and often indiscriminate urban expansion on erstwhile waterbodies, wetlands, drains, and channels have transformed local landscapes and exposed them to significant ecological harm. The disappearance of lakes in Bangalore (see Ranganathan, 2015), or the making of colonial Calcutta (see Bhattacharya, 2019), or of Hong Kong, Kathmandu (see Rademacher, 2011), or Beijing are some of the many examples that tell a compelling story of how the boundaries between land and water are blurred, or ignored, to pave the way for suburban geographies to unfold. While the regional dynamics vary, in each instance the changing ecologies reveal how and why 'certain ecological logics [a]re made legible, powerful, and active' (Rademacher, 2011: 176), and how local relations of power articulate with the unfolding geography of value, land, property-making, and speculation (see Bhattacharya, 2019; Cronon, 1991; Rademacher, 2011).

In an attempt to push urban political ecology beyond its city-centric focus, the editors of this volume have argued that it is critical to not only interrogate and dismantle the familiar binaries of city and suburb, inside and outside, core and periphery, but it is equally crucial to attend to how the suburb or the periphery may dictate and coproduce the logics and social-spatial dynamics of the city. The constitutive role of the periphery, as the Global Suburbanisms project[6] has convincingly made evident, is central to understanding the dynamics of contemporary urban sprawl and climate change. While suburban sprawl is more of a norm than an exception in the contemporary moment, the role of the periphery is ever-more pronounced in the postcolonial contexts where the teleologies of economic growth and development have not exactly followed the familiar lines of industrialisation, de-industrialisation, and suburbanisation as in the case of Europe and North America. In the Global South, for instance, the rural and the agrarian do not represent a spatially or temporally distant past, or a faraway hinterland that is waiting to be encroached upon or assimilated.[7] Instead, the rural and the agrarian jostle with the city and the urban, coproduce it, and in many respects make the city and the urban possible.[8] I have described the constitutive role of agrarian dynamics in contemporary urbanisation in places like India, which are predominantly rural, as *agrarian urbanism* (Gururani, 2020). Agrarian urbanism is one of the dominant modalities of suburbanisation in India that describes how the boundaries of the city stretch far beyond the urban and into the rural and agrarian. The suburban in such agrarian urban landscapes is not a site of industrial monocultures of Monsanto crops, de-industrial ruins, or swathes of 'empty' nature but agro-pastoral landscapes mired in a fraught legacy of colonial land and property laws. The suburban in the south is composed of the village, the rural and agrarian, and is a complex social-spatial amalgamation of urban and agrarian that is ensconced in everyday practices of caste, gender, accumulation, dispossession, and exclusion. I have argued that the changing geographies of agrarian land and caste sustain the unfolding city and incrementally reconfigure the existing register of value as well as the incumbent caste dynamics. The processes of social-ecological transformations in such suburban landscapes transcend the manufactured boundaries of the city and inevitably collide with regional agrarian dynamics. These ecological changes pivot around land, but they are also, as I show below, entangled with water. In the case of Gurgaon, it is the peculiar interplay of land and water that contours the politics of ecology amid extended urbanisation and climate change. By focusing on the politics of land and water simultaneously and weaving it with ethnographic sensibilities of place, this chapter suggests that to understand the ecology of urbanisation in the Global South it is imperative to situate suburban ecologies in everyday relations of land and its titles, property and property-making, and critically in the crucible of caste and gender politics and consider ecological politics through the lens of property, tenure, and livelihoods (Lawhon et al., 2014). Such an anthropological inquiry is crucial for grasping the impact of rapid urbanisation on fragile ecologies and those who depend on them, but it is equally urgent in the context of changing patterns of rainfall, widespread extreme rain events that fluctuate between floods and droughts, and significant climatic shifts amid global warming.[9] To explore the changing suburban ecologies in a volatile frontier of speculation and accumulation in India, in the section below I turn my attention to the Ghata Jheel, which is no more.

Life and death of Ghata Jheel

The Ghata Jheel finds mention in the archives. It was described in the 1910 District Gazetteer of Gurgaon as part of a rather extensive drainage system referred to as the North Gurgaon drainage system that was carefully secured by an embankment (*bundh*) built around 1889. *Ghata* in Hindi and Haryanavi (the local dialect) refers to a gap, or loss, and describes the 1.5km long low-lying stretch between the two villages of Ghata and Behrampur that served as a conduit for carrying the rainwater from the Kaderpur-Mehrauli ridge and draining it through the Badshahpur drain into the Najafgarh drain, which is the only waterway to drain water onto the Yamuna river. The area of the lake is estimated to be close to 300 acres, but it has a vast catchment area upstream of 33,000 acres, of which 10,000 acres lies in the eight villages in Haryana and the rest is in Delhi. In the wake of extensive urban development, even though Ghata Lake exists in the minds and memories of local rural residents, it has almost disappeared, and only the Ghata bundh survives as an 800m long structure.

The defacement of Ghata and other waterbodies can be located at the intersection of multi-scalar processes of speculation, urban planning, property-making, ecological restoration, and, importantly, caste. In the context of soaring prices and volatile land markets, Goldman has described the intense real estate speculation and an unprecedented land frenzy in the case of Bangalore as *speculative urbanism* (2011). Embedded in the anticipatory telos of an urban future, speculation bolsters the aspirations of a growing middle class and conjures the dreams of modern living, homeownership, luxury, and aesthetics. It also recruits a powerful ecological imaginary of lush landscapes, sustainability, and natural heritage, an imaginary that not so surprisingly values landed property over watery one. As the city stretches out, all watery bodies, ponds, ridges, ditches, depressions, and wastelands, as Bhattacharyya has argued, come to be viewed as 'land-in-waiting for property development' (2018: 169); a watery terrain that can be and should be solidified and assetised.

Turning ponds and lakes into land is a convoluted process. It is a process that is not just about reckless urban development, which it is to some extent, or an act greed or profiteering, which it is too. But, the act of making new urban natures in the context of speculative urbanisms entails erasing boundaries between land and water, reconfiguring existing regimes and practices of property, manipulating local histories, and introducing a new lexicon of financialisation and assetisation of land, and risk and uncertainty. It involves a range of practices that work with and produce an 'instability of value' and generates a productive obscurity that paves the way for new social–ecological relations and with it new social and ecological imaginaries (Bear et al.,

2015: 387). The 'instability of value' is critical as it undergirds and propels speculation in agrarian-urban landscapes. The careful machination of value relies on the allegiance and support of dominant caste groups and political elites, who mobilise their caste-based authority and power to consolidate their status further and actively change the rhythms and rules of land and water. As speculation introduces new registers of value, aesthetics, and sociality, the situated (agrarian) ecologies and with it the everyday practices of land, property, and livelihood are slowly but surely obscured. In promoting a hegemonic vision of 'urban nature', the new discourses of greening generate what Raymond Williams has identified as a 'pleasing prospect'; a prospect invented for crafting a clean, green, and investible periphery (see Mozingo, 2011). Such emergent ecological imaginaries foreground how ideas of nature are enrolled in this moment of suburbanisation and the political and ideological work they perform to produce new registers of value and meaning (Rademacher, 2011).

In tracking the life of lost lakes, it is critical to ask what precisely the urban vision of the future is. What is at stake in building or expanding cities like New Delhi in arid ecologies of droughts and water shortages? Is ecological sustainability even possible in an uneven world? How can cities respond to climate change? What are the everyday practices of exclusion and dispossession, how does the politics of land and caste intersect in suburbanising landscapes? These questions are not new to urban political ecology scholarship, but they have gained renewed urgency, and they compel us to attend to the deeply splintered terrain of suburbanisation in the south under the context of the climate change emergency and support local environmentalists who strive to contest ecological loss and create possible avenues that can reconcile, as much as possible, capitalist urbanisation with ecological sustainability and social justice.

What is a waterbody and why does it matter in urbanising frontiers?

In an arid landscape, where water comes and goes seasonally, it is pertinent to ask – what qualifies as a waterbody? What are the attributes of this supposedly watery or not-so-watery mass? Must there be water to qualify as a waterbody? Is a dried-up lake still a lake? How can it be reckoned, and by whom? These were some of the questions that came up very early on in the fieldwork, and I worked with a GIS student to help me track the contours of Ghata Lake over the last two decades and develop land classification maps of the lake and its surroundings. It was an interesting exercise, and we went back and forth, only to soon realise that mapping land and water is tricky. For instance, even though we had read the reports that the lake had dried up, when we created land classification images, the same area of the lake was larger in 2014 than it was in 2003. This was puzzling, but the simple exercise urged us to reflect on our positivist assumptions and reconsider waterbodies as temporal entities attuned to seasonality, precarities of weather, rainfall, and temperature. We had to consider the rhythms of land and water and consider if and when the extensive but tenuous hydrological network that underlay the rocky terrain would be soaked or not.

The local agro-pastoralists who made a living in this rugged landscape by tending cattle, cultivating crops and vegetables, collecting stones and rocks were acutely aware of the unreliable nexus of land and water. Even when I asked about land and its transformation, my interlocutors would inevitably turn to talk about the precarity of water, the fluctuations of rain, the direction of flow, the levels of the water table, the slope of the land and the sites of water reservoirs. Not surprisingly, there is a vast vocabulary that indexes the degrees of aridity, irrigation, practices of cropping, usufruct, and property. For instance, *chahi* is the irrigated land, while *banjar kadim* refers to long fallow, *banjar jadid* refers to short fallow, and *gair mumkin* is uncultivable, and *pahadi* is the rocky terrain. While the short foray into mapping land-water was not particularly helpful in the end, it unravelled the boundary work that is entailed in generating a morphology of water-land and urged us to attend to the vicissitudes of land and water simultaneously and to grapple with ecologies in all their social-material complexity. We then turned to more precise geological and meteorological details like the seasonal cycles, the time of the year, amount of rainfall, length of the monsoon, floods, and droughts, which allowed us to acknowledge the limitations of the map and of the potentialities of an arid landscape. Attending to the ecological attributes of water-land meant that I slowly became cognizant of the grammar of cultivability, fertility, life, and livelihood, which in an arid landscape is contingent and contested.

The challenge of identifying and demarcating a waterbody also dogged the Haryana state authorities, who set out to identify all waterbodies. The Gurugram Metropolitan Development Authority (GMDA), with the support of environmentalists like Chetan Agarwal, surveyed all waterbodies and created an exemplary inventory of ponds and lakes and assigned unique identification designations (UID) to all of them but the attempt to record the number of waterbodies and assign them UIDs faced a significant challenge. It was not easy to catalogue the number of waterbodies. They had to rely on three different sources – the Revenue Record of 1956, the Survey of India Report of 1976, and the World View satellite imagery of 2011–12. The number of water bodies varied significantly – 640 water bodies were identified in the first record, 519 in the second, and 647 in the third (GMDA, 2019).

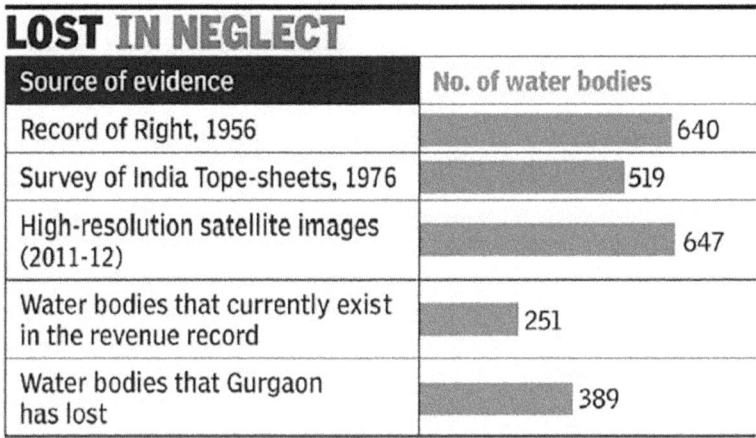

Figure 9.1 Number of water bodies lost in the Gugugram region of India over 60 years.

With such significant variation, the National Green Tribunal noted that only 123 waterbodies were common in all these numbers and should be the focus of their restoration project. In preparing the inventory of waterbodies, Agarwal noted,

> We consulted the revenue reports. Some waterbodies may not be in the revenue record but may be mentioned in the Survey of India's topographical map. So, we acknowledged these sources, but then we come to the third fuzzy part where a waterbody is not mentioned in any record, yet there is water when you go on the ground. Then you have to take a call on whether it is a regular waterbody that got left out or is it just some low-lying area where some water has collected or is it sewage.
>
> (Interview, 27 February 2020)

In other words, there is a fair bit of uncertainty about how to demarcate the boundaries of waterbodies and even what counts as a waterbody but this social-ecological confusion, as I discuss below, proved to be lucrative in an urbanising frontier. Amid speculation and property-making, the amphibious submergence areas, lakebeds, seasonal lakes, and wetlands that were crucial for maintaining regional hydrologies could be easily overlooked, encroached upon, solidified, and deemed to be land waiting for development.

In recent years, an impressive body of work on coasts, deltas, and riverscapes has drawn attention to the entangled land–water relations and to the notions of fluidity, sponginess, or permeability that animate such watery terrains (see Amrith, 2018; Bhattacharya, 2019; Krause, 2013; Lahiri-Dutt, 2014; Loftus, 2019; Rademacher, 2011).[10] The wet ecologies of riverbeds, bays, and oceans lend themselves to such a relationality, but inspired by this scholarship I would suggest that arid ecologies of hardy rocks and ridges too have to contend with the friction of land and water and acknowledge their delicate imbrication and seasonal coproduction. The rocky topography of Gurgaon is anthropogenically produced at the cusp of colonial calculations, irrigation networks, developmentalist dreams, agricultural improvement, and now urban transformation (see Gururani, 2021). There is nothing natural about urban ecologies. But, to materialise the urban vision, speculators and developers have to demarcate property, for which the boundaries between land and water have to be stabilised, lakes and ponds dried up, rocks chiselled and flattened, ditches and depressions filled up, forests cut for the work of property and value to take place. This precisely is the boundary work, the act of consolidating, categorising, and stabilising that reifies the distinction of nature and society, land and water, rural and urban, private and commons, legal and illegal, planned and unplanned, and describes how suburban ecologies are remade in the thorny politics of speculation, planning, and property-making, all of which are entwined with regional histories of caste and land.

City in waiting: Assetising land and water

Like most urban peripheries in India, Gurgaon is a frontier of accumulation, charged with anticipation, volatility, and hope, but also fear (see Gururani and Dasgupta, 2018). Starting in the mid-1980s, with the liberalisation of India's economy, urbanisation and commercialisation of agrarian hinterlands was identified as one of the key strategies to attract global investment and set up business processing offices, special economic zones, highways and expressways, and housing for a growing middle class. In 1985, to make room for the new city, the territorial boundary of the National Capital Territory was extended from 42.7km^2 to 1,484km^2 to create a National Capital Region (NCR). The NCR, which has since grown considerably, incorporated vast stretches of land in the neighbouring states of Haryana and Uttar Pradesh. In Haryana, seven out of 19 districts, including a third of its villages and towns, and about 40 per cent of the state's population were included in the NCR.[11] Due to its proximity to the international airport, Gurgaon soon became a desirable destination, and the price of land went up several-fold. In this land rush, Haryana opened its doors to private developers, and developers like the DLF, Ansals, and Unitech were the first to jump into the land bonanza.[12]

With full cognizance and even support of the state, the powerful nexus of local politicians, developers, brokers, real estate companies, and agrarian capitalists, mostly from the landowning castes of Jats and Yadavs, worked together to purchase land from farmers directly and put it in the property market. The dominant caste, namely the Jats, brazenly flouted land laws planning codes, tempered revenue records, forged land titles, fought countless court cases, converted agricultural zones to residential or commercial, turned water into land, and land into gold. In addition, they mobilised their traditional authority and political clout to encroach commons and the smallholdings that belonged to the Dalits or Other Backward Classes (OBCs).

After this initial frenzy, the next round of extended urbanisation began in the early 2000s, and an urbanisable territory was demarcated for a 'New Gurgaon' that stretched further into the hinterlands. Not surprisingly, two key social-spatial technologies of master planning and un-commoning (the village commons) came in handy as they not only worked to extend the ever-expanding urban frontier but they also manipulated existing regimes of the commons and worked to privatise non-private property. Through creative manoeuvring of legal, infrastructural, and financial processes, the urban planning manifesto reconfigured the commons by fragmenting and privatising them, and with it the practices of livelihood and made land a fungible asset. But, to re-inscribe the nature of land and property and assimilate it in a regime of private property, the lines and strokes of a planner demand a firm landing that can materialise the dreams and desires of speculation and accumulation and result in turning water into landed (private) property (see Bhattacharya, 2019: 23–31).

Through the 1980s and 1990s, Gurgaon evolved in the absence of a master plan and was largely subsumed by the dictates of the NCR. The Chief Minister of Haryana served as the Director of Haryana Urban Development Authority, Town and Country Planning, and Haryana State Industrial and Infrastructural Development Corporation, and administered all land transactions. Between 1981 and 2012, different Chief Ministers of Haryana granted licences for developing a total of 8,550.32 acres, but during Bhupinder Singh Hooda's tenure of seven years from 2005 to 2012, licences for a staggering 54,000 acres of land were granted – an increase of nearly 150 per cent.[13] This massive land grab was made possible by the familiar instrument of master planning. Typically, city plans and planning have a horizon of ten, 20, or more years, but not in Gurgaon. Under Hooda, three plans were drafted between 2005 and 2012. In July 2006, Gurgaon released its first draft of the Master Plan 2021 (DP, 2021), which was notified shortly after, in February 2007. Under Section 4 of the Land Acquisition Act of 1894, the Draft Plan is a necessary precursor to the Master Plan. It makes public the intent of the state to acquire land for public purposes; it seeks input and acknowledges claims. The period between Draft and Master Plans usually takes a few years and is usually a frenzied time of real estate activity as the price of land changes with change in land use. Rumours begin to fly about which zones have been earmarked for acquisition by the state and of how land can be sold to private developers before the final notification. The 2021 Draft Plan was, however, notified within a very short period of six months; as the journalist Shalini Singh notes, the Master Plan 2021 'reflected a dramatic shift from the draft plan, with the land use of as many as 11 sectors changed from public and semi-public/ public utility/ open space/ industrial to residential and commercial'.[14] With unseen kickbacks built in and soaring land prices, land became unbelievably valuable. After only four years, in October 2010, another draft of the Master Plan 2025 was released and was notified promptly in May 2011 and once again, between the two Master Plans MP2021 and MP2025, the State government further converted roughly 500 acres of agricultural land and forests into residential land use. Soon after, in November 2012, just a year later, a third draft Master Plan 2031 was released and notified in September 2013. In the 2031 Master Plans, 60 new sectors were added, and amid intense speculation and anticipation, the Department of Town and Country issued several licences to developers to urbanise land and classified the hitherto agriculture lands as urbanisable.

In tracing the history of city-making through the *chars* (marshes) of colonial Calcutta, Bhattacharyya in her book, *Empire and ecology in the Bengal delta*, considers property as a process, 'a form to frame our thinking about land, as a language to express the division between land and water and as a legal technology to demarcate land, marsh, accretion and water' (2018: 23). In thinking with Bhattacharyya in a very different topographical context, I would suggest that as the urban frontier stretched out, ponds, ditches, and lakes too came to be seen as 'land-in-waiting for property development' (Bhattacharyya, 2018: 169). Instead of seeing them as 'impediments' that thwarted suburban expansion, in MP 2021, the lakebed of Ghata Jheel was rezoned and designated as an urbanisable residential sector number 58. Several developers like BPTP, Vatika, Ansals, DLF, Emaar-MGF, IREO, and their corporate subsidiaries purchased licences, of which 651 acres of land was licensed to IREO, half of which was Ghata Jheel's lakebed and submergence area. In this transaction, from a relatively small player, IREO emerged as a recognisable brand name almost overnight. It has since built a state-of-the-art gated residential enclave called the Grand Arch. In an infrastructural feat involving heavy machinery, the vast submergence area of the *jheel* that stretched over a kilometre and covered roughly 300 acres was re-engineered, covered up, erased, or flattened, licensed for development, and turned into solid property/land for the city to rise. The lines between land and water were blurred and evacuated of historically sedimented meanings and practices of land and water, undoing the agrarian relations of land and livelihood to usher in a new urban sociality.

While the planners and engineers reworked the boundaries of land and water, they had to contend with the deeply entrenched practices of property, especially of the commons (*shamalat*) and create a privatised notion of property in its place. Space does not permit a detailed discussion here, but the property rights in colonial Punjab, of which Haryana was a part, have a complex history that, as the historian, Neeladri Bhattacharya (2019) has argued, made it hard to singularise and categorise. Yet, over time, caught between the colonial regimes of revenue, tenure, shares, tenancy, and customary practice, a system of property rights and obligation was created that vested authority in the village proprietary body (*malikan deh*), which not surprisingly was always the dominant caste of Jats. Even though the proprietary rights were consolidated in favour of the dominant castes, all villagers maintained their user rights in the commons for pasture, fodder, and cattle. Tensions prevailed between the proprietors and the non-proprietors but by and large in Ghata the lakebed was used for common purposes.

In the post-independence period, two important pieces of legislation – the Land Reform Act of 1954 and the Punjab Village Common Land Act of 1961– made important legal interventions as they vested the authority of the

Figure 9.2 Ghata lakebed used as a dumpsite and as settlement area for migrant workers.

commons in a *panchayat* (council) and took away the right to partition land and privatise the commons from the proprietors (see Kumar et al., 2000). Yet, through creative interpretation of competing legal regimes, parts of the Ghata lakebed were designated as 'private', and landholders, mostly from dominant castes, partitioned it and sold it to the private developers. As one local environmentalist pointed out, 'once it is deemed private, it is removed from the governmental register of revenue. If it is not in the revenue register, then it is also not on the map, and if there is no documentary record, then a waterbody ceases to exist. It is gone, disappeared!' (Interview, January 2020). There is currently a court case going on between the two proprietors and the village proprietary body.[15] In the crucible of master planning, speculation, the complicated colonial legacy of property regimes, village and caste politics, the watery body of the Ghata Jheel came to be erased, flattened, hardened, partitioned, and turned into land, assetised to usher in the city of tomorrow.

Speculating sustainability: Lush landscape of water and steel

Ghata Lake, as mentioned above, is not the only lake that has disappeared in this conjuncture of speculative urbanism. Over 100 lakes have gone missing in Haryana alone, and a similar story of disappearing lakes seems to repeat in the peripheries of most metropolitan cities like Mumbai, Bengaluru,[16] and Chennai.[17] In response to the growing concern over the environmental threats posed by diminishing or disappearing waterbodies, the National Green Tribunal (NGT) directed governmental authorities to monitor the state of water bodies and file a report. In addition, residents and environmental groups too have galvanised to challenge the environmental harm done to local forests and wetlands. In Gurgaon, Lt. Col. S.S. Oberoi filed an application before the NGT,[18] demanding that the Ghata Lake be restored and that no further permission be granted to develop over water bodies their catchment area. It also sought direction to restore 214 other waterbodies and natural channels in Gurgaon District and similar waterbodies in Faridabad District.[19] The NGT directive resulted in the passing of the Haryana Pond and Waste Water Management Authority Act to create the Haryana Pond and Waste Water Management Authority.[20] The Pond Authority through a painstaking exercise has compiled data over the last several decades and prepared an impressive report on the waterbodies of Gurugram (GMDA, 2019). While the steps to document and record the boundaries of water and land must be applauded, the task of enumerating also raises questions about the challenges of counting and stabilising the dynamic ecological processes and of the possible erasures and oversights such an exercise may entail, but they are beyond the scope of this discussion.

The report, among a list of recommendations, notes,

> if the bundh submergence area or 'lake' is to be revived, there will be a need to restore the streams or creeks that brought water to the erstwhile 'lake' bed. Along with this, the downstream creek will also need to be protected and restored. A minimum area behind the lake will need to be identified and put under the category of 'waterbody'.
>
> (GMDA, 2019: 15)

With the setting up of the Pond Authority, there seems to be a commitment to restore and regenerate waterbodies, but caught up between different administrative departments – the forest department, the irrigation department, the urban development authority – with overlapping and sometimes conflicting authority over the same piece of highly valuable land, the boundaries of the waterbody remain in question, and thus far no steps have been taken to revive or restore the Ghata Lake.

Instead, the Pond Authority has proudly embarked on an ambitious project to develop 18 model lakes with the aim of beautification, conservation, and irrigation, and to compensate for the lost nature. Claiming to be a pioneer in urban sustainability, Haryana is now set to carve one model lake in each of its districts.[21] And, to compensate for the lost Ghata Jheel, according to the Regional Officer of the Haryana State Pollution Control Board (HSPCB), 'We are ... building a lake near Sector 72 that will be a large lake, it will be a modern lake that will work like other natural lakes and help address Gurgaon's water problem' (Interview, 17 December 2018). Relying on a standard repertoire of images and a global discourse of sustainability, adaptation, and ecological futurity, the Pond Authority has embarked on beautifying and restoring natural heritage as its key goals in manufacturing new ponds. Despite the climatic challenges facing the region, the Pond Authority continues to keep the social-ecological entanglements of land and water, society and nature, and rural and urban conceptually and materially apart. In crafting new ponds and new pleasing prospects, the space of nature for the Pond Authority is just a matter of fact; as Latour would put it, a techno-managerial feat that can pave the way for such spectacles of nature.

It is not only the state that has embraced the discourse of sustainability, harmony, and greenness; the developers, too, have responded to the green call. The real estate developer IREO, who incorporated parts of the Ghata Jheel and built an 'iconic' state-of-the-art luxury residential enclave and is currently developing an IREO city, offers 'lush landscapes' and 'acres of carefully designed landscape [that] will complement the glorious natural surroundings that encircle the Grand Arch'.[22] In their ode to ecological concerns, the centrepiece of the Grand Arch is a 22ft high metal tree, called the Dada Tree, that the famous artist Subodh Gupta has designed.[23] The tree resembles a banyan tree and is constructed out of polished, hyper-reflective steel, with curvy branches, and has clusters of utensils as leaves. Leaving aside the fact that the tree is a brash embodiment of patriarchy, male inheritance (*dada lai*) and masculinity, what such arteacts of nature, materially and discursively, accomplish is that they bolster the developmentalist agenda in the cities of the south, generate consensus, and conceal the contested terrain of land and water on which they stand. The tree of metal and the model ponds not only script a new ecological imaginary and stage a new grammar of urban ecologies, albeit ungrounded and superficial, but such artifacts of nature also, symbolically and materially, undermine and erase rurality and agrarian histories of the land and livelihoods that surround them.

In invoking the discourse of ecological restoration and natural heritage, the project of city-making boldly and unabashedly erases sedimented social-ecologies, their agrarian entanglements, temporalises space, overlooks the fragile embrace of land and water, and works to commodify nature, assetise land, and privatise property. Yet, the force of flood belies such valiant attempts and urges us to remember as Kushal Singh said,

> in place of a village, they can build buildings and make a city, but a flood does not distinguish, you can try and stop [water's] course (but) we cannot ignore its fury. This is nature's game, this is life, and it is up to us to acknowledge it or get washed away.
>
> (Personal communication, December 2018)

If we were to take Kushal Singh's comments seriously and not ignore nature's game, it is urgent that we gain an understanding of how the politics and practices of suburban ecologies in the Global South are entangled with messy politics of land, speculation, and property-making. In describing the life and death of Ghata Jheel at the height of a real estate of boom, I have drawn attention to the entanglements of land and water and the politics of property making embedded in regional histories of caste. Even as new ecological imaginaries are crafted and new futures planned, the uneven sedimentations of property and caste come to inscribe the scriptures of capitalist urbanisation. In situating urban ecologies in the context of extended urbanisation and extreme weather events, this chapter directs its attention to the politics of ecology that exceeds the confines of the city. By focusing on one of India's peripheries, the chapter shows that, first, it is imperative to acknowledge the imbrications of urban and agrarian dynamics in primarily agrarian countries like India and attend to the micropolitics of power that are firmly intertwined with the social relations of land, water, and caste. Second, in presenting the account of disappearing waterbodies, the chapter argues that to address the imminent climatic challenges facing cities and their peripheries, it is critical to pay close ethnographic attention to the social and material processes through which 'nature' comes to be simultaneously assetised and urbanised and track how long histories of exclusion and marginalisation are recast in this political-economic moment. For cities to be sustainable and withstand climate emergencies, it is urgent to rethink the precepts that have historically guided urban planning and governance, undo the entrenched boundaries that separate 'nature' from urban, and highlight their intimate and constitutive entanglements. Any calls to protect or restore lakes or waterbodies can be meaningful only, as the vast urban political ecology scholarship has argued, if we consider ecology, not as an object outside of the social that can be managed through adaptation or eco-restoration, but instead, consider ecology as a relationally constituted and constitutive of social-political-material dynamics.

Notes

1. This chapter is an abridged and modified version of Gururani (2021).
2. Names of all the participants have been anonymised to protect their identity, although the caste and names of the village have been retained.
3. Gujjars are a heterogenous ethnic group in North India that has historically been pastoralists and smallholders and designated as Other Backward Class (OBC) in the state of Haryana.
4. https://timesofindia.indiatimes.com/city/gurgaon/gurgaon-lost-389-water-bodies-in-60yrs-study/articleshow/62610956.cms, accessed 12 August 2022.
5. www.thehindu.com/todays-paper/tp-national/tp-newdelhi/137-water-bodies-have-dried-up-in-gurgaon/article12558240.ece, accessed 12 August 2022.
6. SSHRC-funded Major Collaborative Research Initiative on 'Global Suburbanisms: Governance, Land, and Infrastructure in the Twenty-First Century', York University, Canada.
7. I am using agrarian, village, and rural rather loosely to refer to the social-spatial dynamics that are entangled with agrarian relation of land and property.
8. In India, agricultural land, rural to urban labour migration, and infrastructure are some of the key elements that pivot contemporary urbanisation.
9. www.nature.com/articles/s41467-017-00744-9, accessed 12 August 2022.
10. Lahiri-Dutt (2014: 3) has urged scholars to move beyond the notion of permanence in land or a 'hard edge' and proposed the concept of 'wet theory', a theory that hybridises assemblages of land and water, and 'brings to the fore the constant negotiations between the land and waters – the seas, rivers, and lakes that geographers have long constituted as lying outside the terra firma'.
11. There are now 22 districts in Haryana, of which 13 are in NCR.
12. DLF is the acronym for Delhi Land and Finance (see Gururani, 2013).
13. www.thehindu.com/news/national/behind-haryana-land-boom-the-midas-touch-of-hooda/article4048394.ece, accessed 12 August 2022.
14. www.thehindu.com/news/national/builder-profits-soar-as-master-plans-proliferate-in-gurgaon/article4753735.ece, accessed 12 August 2022.

15 Punjab and Haryana High Court Case No. 6590. Gram Panchayat Ghata v/s State of Haryana related to ownership of common lands.
16 www.thehindu.com/news/cities/bangalore/restore-19-disappeared-lakes-or-create-artificial-ones-to-compensate-for-loss-hc/article29096483.ece, accessed 12 August 2022.
17 www.deccanherald.com/science-and-environment/pandemic-taking-toll-on-weather-and-climate-watch-un-834661.html, accessed 12 August 2022.
18 Original Application. No. 325/2015: Lt. Col. Sarvadaman Singh Oberoi vs. Union of India & Others National Green Tribunal Order dated 20 July 2018.
19 The local Civil Judge, Senior Division recently served notices to several municipal authorities including the Director General, Town of Country Planning; Regional Director, Central Ground Water Board; Deputy Commissioner, Gurgaon; and IREO Builders.
20 http://hpwwma.org.in/index.aspx, accessed 12 August 2022.
21 www.prharyana.gov.in/en/haryana-pond-and-waste-water-management-authority-will-develop-18-model-ponds-on-a-pilot-project, accessed 12 August 2022.
22 https://gurgaonpropertyjunction.com/project_folder/brochure/2035733926brochure-2.pdf, accessed 12 August 2022.
23 According to Gupta, the Dada Tree symbolises Indian heritage and familial ties, as connoted by the kin term dada, which in Hindi means grandfather but, in another iteration, dada also means a bully, and can express patriarchal assertion and authority.

References

Amrith, S. 2018. *Unruly waters: How mountain rivers and monsoons have shaped South Asia's history.* London: Penguin.
Bear, L., R. Birla, and S. Puri. 2015. Speculation: India, uncertainty and new economic imaginaries. *Comparative Studies of South Asia, Africa and the Middle East* 35(3): 387–91.
Bhattacharya, N. 2019. *The great agrarian conquest: The colonial reshaping of a rural world.* Ranikhet, India: Permanent Black.
Bhattacharyya, D. 2018. *Empire and ecology in the Bengal delta: The making of Calcutta.* Cambridge: Cambridge University Press.
Centre for Science and Environment. 2016. *Why urban India floods?* New Delhi: CSE.
Cronon, W. 1991. *Nature's metropolis: Chicago and the great west.* New York: W.W. Norton and Co.
Department of Town and Country Planning (DP). 2021. https://tcpharyana.gov.in, accessed 12 August 2022.
Goldman, M. 2011. Speculative urbanism and the making of the next world city. *International Journal of Urban and Regional Research* 35(3): 555–81. DOI: 10.1111/j.1468-2427.2010.01001.x.

Gurugram Metropolitan Development Authority (GMDA) 2019. Water bodies of Gurugram: A report. www.indiaenvironmentportal.org.in/content/463595/report-on-waterbodies-of-gurugram-district/, accessed 12 August 2022.

Gururani, S. 2013. Flexible planning: The making of India's 'Millennium city', Gurgaon. In A. Rademacher and K. Sivaramakrishnan (eds.), *Ecologies of urbanism in India: Metropolitan civility and sustainability*. Hong Kong: Hong Kong University Press, pp. 119–43.

Gururani, S. 2020. Cities in a world of villages: agrarian urbanism and the making of India's urbanizing frontiers. *Urban Geography* 41(7): 971–89. https://doi.org/10.1080/02723638.2019.167056

Gururani, S. 2021. Making land out of water: Ecologies of urbanism, property, and loss. In A. Rademacher and K. Sivaramakrishnan (eds.), *Death and life of nature in Asian Cities*. Hong Kong: Hong Kong University Press, pp. 138–58.

Gururani, S. and R. Dasgupta. 2018. Frontier urbanism: Urbanisation beyond cities in South Asia. *Economic and Political Weekly* 53(12): 41–5.

Krause, F. 2013. Seasons as rhythms on the Kemi River in Finnish Lapland. *Ethnos* 78(1): 23–46.

Kumar, A., L. Bren, and I. Ferguson. 2000. The use and management of common lands of the Aravalli, India. *International Forestry Review* 2(2): 97–104.

Lahiri-Dutt, K. 2014. Beyond the water–land binary in geography: Water/lands of Bengal re-visioning hybridity. *ACME: An International E-Journal for Critical Geographies* 13(3): 505–29.

Lawhon, M., H. Ernstson, and J. Silver. 2014. Provincializing urban political ecology: Towards a situated UPE through African urbanism. *Antipode* 46(2): 497–516.

Loftus, A. 2019. Political ecology I: Where is political ecology? *Progress in Human Geography* 43(1): 172–82.

Mozingo, L.A. 2011. *Pastoral capitalism: A history of suburban corporate landscapes*. Cambridge, MA: MIT Press.

Rademacher, A. 2011. *Reigning the river: Urban ecologies and political transformation in Kathmandu*. Durham: Duke University Press.

Ranganathan, M. 2015. Storm drains as assemblages: The political ecology of flood risk in post-colonial Bangalore. *Antipode* 47(5): 1300–20.

Tzaninis, Y., T. Mandler, M. Kaika, and R. Keil. 2021. Moving urban political ecology beyond the 'urbanization of nature'. *Progress in Human Geography* 45(2): 229–52.

Williams, R. 1973. *The country and the city*. London: Oxford University Press.

10

Infrastructure beyond the modern ideal: Thinking through heterogeneity, serendipity, and autonomy in African cities

Mary Lawhon, Anesu Makina, and Gloria Nsangi Nakyagaba

Infrastructure has long been described as a black box to users: it is the stuff that brings what people need and want. It makes lives easier, safer, and more comfortable. Scholars of infrastructure have long observed that users like it this way; they primarily attend to infrastructure when it does not work (Kaika, 2004; Kaika and Swyngedouw, 2000; Star, 1999).

Yet in this time of political and ecological change, it has become harder to keep the lights on, to ignore where the waste goes, to stay safe when some have no clean water. Climate change and the novel coronavirus challenge our collective narratives of progress and technology, have made us question whether we really can know, control, and improve.

This is a moment when it seems possible that long-critiqued modernist conceits may finally be laid aside, and that we may be able to shift political ecological scholarship away from producing more critique (useful as this is) and towards envisioning and enacting alternatives (while still doing so with critical eyes, see Robbins, 2020; Lawhon et al., 2021). Such alternatives accept that we cannot black box our material flows, control nature, and predict each other. What this means for the lights and the waste and the water remains unclear, for the thing we seek is not a return to a premodern world of rivers, clay pots, and fire, nor do the abstractions of postmodernism offer us much to build on when it comes to the nuts and bolts, the pipes and wires of infrastructure. Nor does this tell us much about the visions and social relations that might enable and support such infrastructures.

In this moment when our collective futures seem more tightly bound than ever before, we begin tracing what it might mean to let go of faith in modernist infrastructure without accepting a world where some have adequate services and others do not. In this chapter, we first outline the modern infrastructure ideal, then make explicit what is *modern* about the modern infrastructure ideal by identifying the expectations of users, nature, technology, and labourers that underpin this ideal. Next, we use examples from our work on heterogeneous configurations of waste and sanitation to begin articulating a different mode of infrastructural provision and a different infrastructural imaginary. Thinking about heterogeneity, serendipity, and autonomy, we suggest, might provide possibilities that better accord with the dynamic and uncertain world we have.

While our examples below draw from infrastructures in Uganda and South Africa, our concerns with modernity are relevant across the Global North and South. Modern infrastructure in the Global North reaches more users, but urban infrastructures create ongoing social and ecological injustices both within and beyond cities. Awareness of the limits of modernity have prompted non-modern infrastructural practices in a variety of different cities, although the history and motivations for such practices vary across spaces. Our intention here is to generate political ecological conversations about such infrastructures, and to point such conversations beyond empirical analysis of what is there towards conceptualisations of what might be (see Lawhon et al., 2021, forthcoming).

The emergence of the modern infrastructure ideal

Twenty years ago, Graham and Marvin (2001) traced the emergence of a particular way of thinking about infrastructure: the modern infrastructure ideal. They describe how the socio-political goal of universal, uniform infrastructure was developed and spread globally. This ideal was initially typically motivated by concerns over public health rather than social justice, but often resulted in financial subsidies for the infrastructure provided to lower-income residents.

Graham and Marvin's text is largely analytical rather than normative, but it is hard to read their description of the end of the modern infrastructure ideal – the splintering of the urban – as anything but a lament. They conclude their book with a caution about romanticising the modern infrastructure ideal, and do not specifically call for a reunification of the city in the text, but many critical scholars before and after have provided even more explicitly political and interventionist agendas. Political ecologists have interrogated, for example, who owns infrastructure, who accesses it and who pays for it. Many have exposed the politics of infrastructure and, following political ecology more broadly, identified the winners and losers in different arrangements (Budds, 2004; K'Akumu, 2007; Loftus and McDonald, 2001). Often implicit, although at times drawn out more clearly, are normative, moral, and ethical questions: they have engaged in debates about who *should* own, access, and pay for infrastructure and its use (Bresnihan, 2017; McDonald and Ruiters, 2012). While much scholarship has focused on engineers and experts as well as users, there is also a growing body of work emphasising the importance of infrastructural labour and the need for regular, safe, well-paid jobs (Fredericks, 2018; Miraftab, 2004; Millington et al., 2022).

We read most political demands for infrastructure (within and beyond political ecology and the academy) as premised on a normative assertion about the merits of the modern infrastructure ideal: although not always by name, they argue for universal, uniform, state-owned services provided below-cost to residents and operated by state employees with permanent jobs and well-defined roles.[1] Many on the political left seem to attribute the failure to achieve this modernist vision to a lack of will: states could, if pressured in the right way, provide modern services to everyone (Bond, 1998; Robins, 2014). Such analyses are logically followed by calls to organise, pressure, try new ownership structures, and attempt to wrest control from those in power.

We are deeply sympathetic to this wider infrastructural narrative. The creation of large technical systems has created path dependencies that are hard to overcome: there are both artefacts on the ground and ways of thinking that have long constrained our imaginations. And yet, with our roots in environmental and development studies, writing in a time of political and ecological crisis, we are unconvinced. Mindful that progress towards providing infrastructure for all has clearly been made in the past 50 years, we have doubts about whether linear systems of sewer-connected flush toilets and grid-connected electricity can be provided to every household (Lawhon et al., 2018a). Rather than see the failure of the modern infrastructure ideal as a lack of political-economic will, we argue that there is something inherently flawed in the socio-technical imaginary that produced the *modern* infrastructure ideal. We tread carefully here and emphasise that this is not opposition to a political goal of services for all. Instead, we work to name and interrogate the fundamental assumptions of the predominant imaginary – modernist infrastructure – and separate the *modern mode of infrastructure provision* from the underlying goal of safe and dignified services for all. We also work to begin developing different imaginaries that are underpinned by ontologies that better accord with the world we have.

What is 'modern' about the modern infrastructure ideal?

Here, we work to make explicit a crucial component of the modern infrastructure ideal that Graham and Marvin (2001) attend to less overtly. While their book is about infrastructure and they are clear about what an 'ideal' is, their use of the term 'modern' is less clearly explained. Yet we believe it is critical to identify what exactly is *modern* about the modern infrastructure ideal. We draw on postcolonial and political ecological scholarship to point towards ongoing debates over the meaning of a modernity, including its accuracy as a framework through which to understand the world and its desirability as a world we seek to build. In providing a more explicit articulation of the modernist underpinnings of the modern infrastructure ideal, we hope to focus attention on the question of which parts we might reject, and which parts might be reworked, as we develop new infrastructural imaginaries (see Lawhon et al., forthcoming).

Political ecologists, as is true more broadly, use the term modern (and derivatives such as modernity and modernisation) in many ways. We do not use it as an indicator of a time period, but as a particular imaginary of what is and ought to be. In clarifying what we rework and reject of the modern gaze, we are compelled neither by modifiers (pre/post/anti) nor multipliers (varieties/alternatives) as appropriate labels (Lawhon, 2020). Instead, we contribute to opening a space for something beyond the modern, something defined through its positive attributes, not through opposition. Elsewhere, we have called this emergent imaginary which draws on an eclectic set of old and new non-modern ideas a 'modest' imaginary (Lawhon et al. 2021; forthcoming).

Modernity in its conjunctions – capitalist modernity and colonial modernity – are widely seen as causes of our ongoing socio-ecological crisis (Escobar, 2006; Rodríguez and Inturias, 2018). And modernity – in its many guises – has always been recognised as a partial project, emergent and struggling, failing to ever achieve completion (Kaika, 2006; Kaika and Swyngedouw, 2000; Latour, 2012 [1991]). Yet the implications of these shortcomings are not quite clear; we as political ecologists have yet to quite let go of modernity. We continue to debate what to do with such critiques, including whether to double down on, or reject, modernity (Keil 2007; Neimark et al., 2019). Ongoing debates between eco-socialist moderns and degrowth activists are but one lens through which we might examine an underlying, as yet unresolved tension over the modernist imaginary in critical environmental scholarship (Robbins, 2020).

Urban political ecologists have analysed several aspects of modernity and we point to a few as indicative rather than an exhaustive list of entry points. The first is the ontological dualism of nature and society. This dualism has been widely and is now routinely rejected (Gunn and Owens, 2006), but scholars continue to productively examine how this imaginary continues to inform policy and practices (Huber and Currie, 2007). The widely accepted rejection of the nature–society binary demonstrates the ambivalence and malleability of modernity: we can – have been able to – collectively reject the binary while still wrestling with the fallout from this longstanding view. This conceptual dualism in reinforced by modern infrastructure in which 'nature' moves into the city, to be processed, and waste moves out of the city (see in the discussion of circular and regional waste ecologies in Connolly and Muzaini, Chapter 17, and Savini, Chapter 18, in this volume). Many have overturned the binaries in such assumptions, focusing on socio-nature in the city (Swyngedouw, 1996; Zimmer et al., 2017), yet as Tzaninis et al. (2021) suggest, this separation also informs some urban political ecological work that focuses on what happens in the city, rather than examining flows across these divides.

Translating new ontologies of socio-nature into the doing of infrastructure, however, remains difficult. For as important as it is to see cities as hybrids, socio-material flows, as cyborgs and comprised of humans and non-humans (Gandy, 2005; Swyngedouw, 1996; Tzaninis et al., 2021), it is hard to envision what exactly this means for the pipes and wires of infrastructure and the social relations that enable them. Analytically, it might mean studying flows across the urban/rural divide, but it also might mean rethinking the spatiality of infrastructure. While it may be difficult to imagine cities that do not rely extensively on hinterlands for 'raw materials' and management of urban waste (Arboleda, 2016), rejecting modernist binaries might also mean reworking infrastructural flows away from the usual patterns of 'nature' in and 'waste' out (see Connolly and Muzaini, Chapter 17, and Savini, Chapter 18, in this volume).

A second, equally well-established component of modernity that political ecologists have engaged with is the assumption that we can know the world through science. This knowledge is important in itself, but there are also pragmatic implications of this: if 'nature' is knowable and predictable, then we can identify patterns and laws of nature. This knowledge is then what enables us to control nature, to build and rebuild nature to be and become the world we want; progress is ongoing and things are always getting better (Kaika, 2006; Worster, 1977). This perspective has also been resoundingly rejected across the natural and social sciences, but equally continues to underpin much human activity.[2]

Both of these ontological perspectives – that nature is separate and controllable through science – underpin modernist infrastructural practice. In what follows, we focus on two additional albeit related aspects of modernity that have been less explicitly attended to, but inform modernist infrastructure: the creation of homogeneous categories and an ideal of work as stable, predictable, and intrinsically valuable.

Specifically, we examine how a new sanitation guide, developed for use in Kampala, is based on a recognition of the need to work with, rather than control nature. The guide counters modern assumptions by emphasising the need to adjust technological choices to the heterogeneity of site and situation. Yet its representation of the heterogeneity of users is limited. We draw on longstanding arguments that the creation of knowable categories, and the treatment of people as homogeneous within the category, is central to modernity. Applying this understanding into infrastructure studies, we argue that an imaginary of the sameness of users – or of user-types – is fundamental to modernist infrastructure. Colonial states, for example, typically divided residents into racial categories and then defined infrastructural needs accordingly (Appelblad Fredby and Nilsson, 2013). While such racialised practices no longer explicitly exist, the basic framework here has not been overturned: across the Global South, modern infrastructure continues to be prevalent in areas of cities built for white colonists and often absent elsewhere.

More broadly, across the North and South, homes are regularly built to house nuclear families (on homes in the US, see Norman, 2011; in South Africa, Lemanski, 2017). The associated infrastructure is built for 'normal' use, including regular flows of water and electricity based on 'normal' consumption. Social assistance also relies on such normalisations: in South Africa, for example, the volume of free water provided to households was initially based on usage by a family of four (Smith, 2004). This volume is the same regardless of whether there is a large family, extended family, or additional households renting space on a plot (see also Muller, 2008). And yet, as we well know and is particularly true in Global Southern cities, different people use different amounts of water, water use changes across seasons, and households size varies. The number of people living on a plot may change by the day and across the seasons. Across the North and South there are challenges to the norm of the nuclear family as well as the universalisation of appropriate infrastructure use. Such debates might be best exemplified in debates over basic income and basic services (e.g., Standing, 2019). Yet despite widespread realisation of the empirical reality of such heterogeneity, a modernist imaginary of a healthy nuclear family continues to dominate political practices; this imaginary is built on and reinforced by both a false set of assumptions and normative judgements about what appropriate urban behaviour entails (see Lawhon et al., 2020).

In our examination of urban waste, we draw on less well-established but equally significant analyses of modernist views of work. Scholars of infrastructure have increasingly called attention to the role of people in making infrastructure work, including both domestic (often female) and waged labour (Anand, 2017; Fredericks, 2018; Gidwani, 2015; Kaika, 2004; Simone, 2004). We believe it is crucial to situate ongoing explorations into infrastructural labour within wider critiques of modernity, including questioning what types of work we value and why (Lawhon et al., 2018b;

Monteith et al., 2021). We build on growing calls to move the left away from seeing the modern (full-time, set hours, set pay) worker as the pinnacle of liberation and to valorise care, autonomy, serendipity, and non-work identities (Kaika, 2004; Scott, 2014). This matters for our analysis of infrastructure because non-modern infrastructure is often underpinned and enabled by non-modern labour patterns, including less clearly defined rules and responsibilities and a need for intimate, location-specific knowledge. In what follows, we focus on the ways in which the modernist notion that work ought to be stable and predictable contrasts with descriptions by waste pickers that valorise autonomy, flexibility, and serendipity.

Beyond the modernist search for the perfect toilet in Kampala

Researchers have usefully traced the emergence of modern sanitation, demonstrating how toilets and sewers came to dominate our imagination of safe and dignified sanitation (see Nilsson, 2006, in Kampala; Gandy, 1999, in Paris). In Kampala, sanitation service provisioning is shaped by colonial history as well as the socio-economic status of urban residents. Only about one in ten households has a connection to the national sewer line and the remainder use onsite options (KCCA, 2016; Government of Uganda, 2015). Households connected to the sewer are located in the parts of the city formerly occupied by colonial administrators and their Asian counterparts. Thus, the spatial extent of the network is limited and is primarily accessible to high and middle-income earners who now reside in these places (Appelblad Fredby and Nilsson, 2013).

State policies generated since independence have emphasised the expansion of the sewer network, yet there have been recent changes that legitimise and seek to govern alternatives (Nakyagaba et al., 2021; Lawhon et al., forthcoming). Examining this process is both about understanding changing imaginaries of infrastructure and, more broadly, aligning urban political ecological scholarship more closely in line with policies (Tzaninis et al., 2021). Sanitation planning documents, for example, envision 100 per cent coverage of the sewerage network, although there is no timeframe assigned to this goal (see Lawhon et al., forthcoming). Yet the extension of sewerage infrastructure to areas not covered during the colonial area has been extremely difficult. Flush toilets can be found across the city, but these are connected to septic tanks rather than offsite conveyance. Such toilet configurations are found in high- and middle-class homesteads as well as some government properties such as schools, hospitals, and barracks. Most urban residents use onsite toilets such as pit latrines, many of which fall short of public health guidelines (KCCA, 2016). Faecal sludge builds up in the pit under a latrine; this sludge is intended to be emptied by a cesspool emptier that takes it to a state managed treatment plant, although for various reasons many go unemptied (Nakyagaba et al., 2021). With the expansion of urban boundaries and continued population growth, city and municipal authorities are even more challenged (Lwasa and Owens, 2018).

Until recently, the predominant approach of the city, as has been observed more widely in southern contexts, has been to ignore and at times penalise residents for using such infrastructure without providing affordable alternatives. Yet city officials increasingly accept that onsite technologies cannot be done away with soon. In this context, as Nakyagaba et al. (2021) and Sseviiri et al. (2022) argue in more depth elsewhere, the state is shifting away from a legal and technical framework that promotes the modernist infrastructure ideal and towards working with and facilitating improved, heterogeneous infrastructure. And yet, as we demonstrate below, letting go of the modernist imaginary underpinning infrastructure remains difficult (see also Lawhon et al., forthcoming).

In what follows, we examine a recent handbook that provides a useful lens into the reworking of modernist approaches to infrastructure. Kampala City is governed and managed by Kampala Capital City Authority (KCCA) on behalf of the central government. One of its roles is to coordinate and harmonise sanitation services in the city with urban development planning. This role has sparked controversy around the type of technologies that are acceptable, informed by pre-existing ideas of what ought to be and what actually is (Lwasa and Owens, 2018; Nakyagaba et al., 2021). Kampala has an undulating landscape, and in some places, the lowlands have a high water table. In a modernist vision, piped networks would cut through the hills, reworking nature to enable uniform, sewer-connected flush toilets across the city. Yet, the KCCA handbook recognises both that sewers are unlikely to be built and that the existing sanitation situation needs to be improved.

The minimum standards handbook developed by KCCA is intended to guide households and developers through various options for improved onsite sanitation, including septic tanks, bio-fill toilets, pit latrines, and Urine Diversion Toilets. It is written to enable users to work with, rather than attempt to control, this diversity of sites (physical context) and situations (proximity to modernist infrastructure) across Kampala. The decision-making process is usefully summarised in a flow chart, asking whether a site is near to water and sewerage networks, and the height of the water table and ground conditions. We suggest this is an important shift away from modern uniformity and towards a recognition that different technologies are better suited to particular locations. Further, onsite sanitation does not seek to control its environment in the same way that modernist sewers must. Onsite systems, especially pit latrines, require engineers, masons, and developers to work with and adjust to the biophysical surroundings as they construct these technologies to minimise pollution. This includes thinking through the appropriate depth and materials for the containment chamber.

The manual also provides environmental and technical aspects to be aware of while constructing sanitation facilities. These include measurements for superstructures as 1m by 1.5m; the materials with which the superstructures and containment chambers should be made from brick, cement, and sand in specific ratios; the depth of the faecal containment chamber vis-à-vis the water table in a particular location. The standards also grant enforcement rights to the authority against anyone acting contrary to these.

In sum, we suggest this manual is evidence of KCCA accepting technologies that are underpinned by a principle of working with rather than control of nature. Technological choices must be adapted to the site and situation; in the world we have, there is no one magic toilet design that works across Kampala.[3] And yet, in developing this manual, the state has not rejected modernity in total: there is still logic and reason, prediction and patterns, experts and users. What is different here is reworking two of the core components of modernist infrastructure. First is the idea that engineers and planners can and should rework the built environment in order to create a uniform infrastructure.

There is also a second, less attended-to way in which onsite sanitation infrastructure challenges the modern infrastructure ideal: it reworks the assumption that waste should flow out of the city. This is a partial reworking at present, for while pipes are rejected, much of the onsite technology still relies on the movement of waste materials out of the city through pit emptying, and a whole appendix explains the importance of accessibility to septic trucks. Technologies that maintain the flow of waste materials out of the city, then, retain part of the modernist vision in which infrastructure takes the waste away.

And yet, there is a type of sanitation included in the manual which is not premised on this: bio-latrines. Here 'nature' and 'the city' are more intimately connected as there is no outside or periphery where the faecal sludge is sent. This waste is even turned to benefit: some bio-latrines produce biogas, and many put the processed waste into gardens and green spaces. The creation of these more circular, small-scale patterns reworks our common ideas of urban flows. It also requires attentiveness and more space than is possible in all parts of Kampala. Yet for those who choose this approach, it creates an awareness and attunement with possibilities and opportunities absent from other technological configurations.

Finally, we observe that the heterogeneity recognised in the KCCA manual is primarily physical and technological. Importantly, the authors recognise users as part of the configuration and have special observations and accommodations for people with disabilities. Further, the framing of the section meant to guide the selection of technology for households notes the importance of 'socio-cultural [factors] including acceptability, perception, and usability' as well as 'socio-economic' factors, including cost and number of users. And yet, when presented with the decision-tree described above that is meant to help handbook users select a technology, this complexity is lost. No guidance is provided to help determine which technology might better accord with household budgets or which accord with faecal-phobic cultures, with small children, elderly or unwell residents. Nor do they help us understand which are more able to withstand changing patterns of use that arise in households that frequently change size. (Worms, for example, require a reasonably set amount of food and cannot accommodate sudden increases in faecal sludge or long periods of low input.)

In sum, the basic premise of the KCCA manual works against modernist assumptions of a uniform and teleological notion of progress, controlling nature and providing uniform infrastructure. Specifically, the handbook is designed to enable users to choose the sanitation technology that works best for their particular site and situation. Most of the technological options continue to rely on the modernist assumption that waste should move and be processed at the urban periphery, but some rewrite modernist ideas of infrastructural flows. Finally, despite much here that reworks modernist assumptions and an explicit recognition of cultural and socio-economic factors, households and their residents are largely treated in a modernist way as a homogeneous group with known, stable, and definable needs.

Serendipity and autonomy as anti-modern values in waste work

In this section, we continue to inquire into how modernist imaginaries shape infrastructure and examine different visions from African cities through a focus on labour. We locate ongoing debates over infrastructural labour, and particularly waste labour, within wider discourses of modernity. Waste picking is, we suggest, non-modern work: it is characterised by flexibility, self-determination, non-hierarchical relationships and negotiated permissions (Makina, 2020). Yet waste picking is increasingly threatened by state efforts to formalise the waste sector (Samson, 2020). Formalisation efforts often draw on modernist assumptions that good work is regular and predictable, with set hours, wages, responsibilities, and hierarchies. We suggest that much of the ongoing conflicts over waste work in Global Southern contexts are founded on different notions of what good work entails (more generally, see Barchiesi 2011; Weeks, 2011). More specifically, modernist approaches to formalise infrastructural labour often eliminate what attracts many waste workers to the profession in the first place.

Waste workers regularly experience stigma for their association with waste (Fredericks, 2018; Peres, 2016; Dias and Samson, 2016); for those working in the informal sector, this is compounded by negative judgements about informality. Three longstanding perspectives of the informal sector all consider it to be something temporary, to be fixed and improved upon. These include: the dualist approach, which considers informal workers as those who could not find employment in the formal sector; the structuralist perspective, which ranks informal work as lower in status due to lack of benefits and poor compensation when compared with formal employment; and the legalist view that considers informal work as a product of inefficient government regulation (Coletto and Bisschop, 2017). Additionally, the informal sector is sometimes associated with criminal activities (Potts, 2008). Those working in the informal sector are thus often seen as criminal, lazy, and lacking discipline, and to be workers without better options.

In these various frames, the formal economy, or at least, more formal, regulated and predictable work, is positioned as the preferable way in which to earn a livelihood. This intersects with the perception that waste picking is considered backward and archaic, in contrast to a modern waste management system which is one that should utilise machines that are capital-intensive and new technologies (Dias and Samson, 2016; Dias, 2016; Scheinberg and Anschutz, 2006). Further, in many cities, waste pickers are often framed as a problem because they do not conform to the ideals of a modern waste management sector (Coletto and Bisschop, 2017). Formal waste management systems do hire waste pickers (Marello and Helwage, 2018), but in other instances, either fail to include them (Mbiba, 2014), or include them at unfavourable terms so they exit the process (Sekhwela and Samson, 2020; Samson, 2020).

Questions have risen about how not to displace waste pickers while improving waste work and waste infrastructure. However, there is no clarity on the manner with which to do so given multiple usages and application of the terms 'inclusion', 'formalisation', and 'integration' in the waste management sector, and the fact that these terms are used interchangeably (Velis et al., 2012, see Scheinberg, 2012, for definitions of these terms).

In South Africa, the formation of cooperatives has been the main mode in which to formalise waste pickers, albeit with dismal results: 91.8 per cent of these cooperatives were unsuccessful, raising questions about the ability of formalisation to bring about secure employment (Godfrey et al., 2017). In reference to integration and in accordance with our data examined below, Samson (2020) asserts that independence is important to waste pickers (see also Schenck et al., 2016). We agree that this point needs greater exploration particularly in contexts where worker autonomy is overlooked in favour of dominant narratives about the desirability of modern (stable, predictable, hierarchical) work.

We extend the discussion on what good work entails through our analysis of participant observation and interviews with 23 waste pickers conducted by Anesu in 2018 in Tshwane (formerly Pretoria), South Africa. Cautious of celebrating what is, no doubt, a difficult means of accessing a livelihood, we do believe that it is imperative to articulate and give weight to what waste pickers value about their work. Specifically, many explained that this work can be more remunerative (see also Coletto and Bisschop, 2017; Scheinberg and Anschutz, 2006; Medina, 2010) and even preferred over formal employment because of autonomy, flexibility, and serendipity. This contrasts with the dominant characterisations of waste picking as precarious due to exploitation by buyers and middlemen, and the inability to control prices in addition to occupational hazards (Marello and Helwege, 2018; Schenck et al., 2019). Our point here not to oppose these alternative views – we agree that there is precarity – nor universalise our findings to all waste pickers. Instead, we seek to add to and emphasise the non-modern values asserted by these workers.

In conversations with waste pickers, some described that they were offered a job and turned it down in favour of waste picking. They were not, thus, unable to find modern work options, but found particular aspects of waste picking compelling. One respondent recalled an offer to work as a formal recycler for a fixed wage, recounting how this was not a good deal because if he worked hard, he could make double what was on offer. He also noted the importance of his own experiential knowledge in evaluating what a fair wage would be: because he knew the resale value of the recyclable materials, he was able to judge that someone else would be making money off his labour.

Waste pickers emphasised their autonomy to make their own decisions, including over when, where and how much they worked; they did not have a boss or respond to a set hierarchy (see also Coletto and Bisschop, 2017). Participants described working extra when they wanted (either to account for a thin day or to cover extra costs) and that they could take as much time off as they needed. Further, they could change working locations if a new opportunity in a different city or neighbourhood opened, but also retain the possibility of returning to their current work. For instance, some waste pickers would visit friends for long periods of time and work in those neighbourhoods, then return and pick up their old routes and routines. (As we detail more extensively elsewhere, many waste pickers work according to a code of conduct that enables regular access to particular bins. These are sometimes contested, but enable some stability and reduce the potential for conflict over access. See Makina and Lawhon, forthcoming).

Such patterns bear striking resemblance to those described at earlier points in African history. Colonial and capitalist powers routinely complained about worker mobility, while many African workers moved for a variety of reasons including that repetitive labour is dull. They also complained that African workers would work less when they had accumulated sufficient income. Both presented problems for accumulation, and the state and capital often worked together to suppress this activity and instead create reliable modern workers (Cooper, 1996). This modernist view on good workers was largely adopted, rather than contested, by postcolonial states (Barchiesi, 2011; Lawhon et al., 2018b).

Even within the wider category of waste picking, there are many options and decisions made on a continuous basis. Some waste pickers chose to pick only high value recyclables such as copper and aluminium cans, while others salvaged the waste stream for items to sell, including mobile phones, laptops, clothing, and children's toys. Some picked all recyclable and sellable materials as a strategy to maximise their earnings. While there were broad patterns here, these were not static and could be adjusted. In 'lean times', such as over the Christmas holidays, when many people leave Tshwane, participants reported they might draw from a wider array of materials.

Some respondents described the uncertainty and the occasional serendipitous find to be part of the allure of the work. For instance, waste pickers were excited upon finding a high value item such as a laptop, as it could be sold or gifted to family. One waste picker had sent laptops to his children, proudly claiming he 'wanted them to be in the technological era'. Yet another mentioned 'you can find nice things in the bins' then proceeded to show a set of earphones he found that day as evidence. A few weeks later, he found some name-brand T-shirts but the luckiest find was a pair of new name-brand sneakers still in the box. Sometimes waste pickers were pleasantly surprised to find items they needed. One participant described finding a discarded mattress which he immediately took because he had been wanting one.

Our point here in sharing these stories of discovery is, again, is not to laud precarity. Relying on chance certainly does have its risks and respondents noted that it can sometimes be difficult to make set plans. We emphasise from our findings that some described their earnings as sufficient, and found some joy from the possibility of finding valuable, sellable items. These unexpected bonuses boosted earnings and created emotionally important stories of success to be shared with other waste pickers as well as friends and family.

Our discussion here should also not be read as lauding the status quo: much as in our analysis of sanitation, we intend to raise questions about what new forms of work might be possible and preferable as we imagine infrastructural possibilities. We are not interested in a world comprised by low-incomes and high-risks, but in thinking through how we might rework our ideas of what a good job is, what work is necessary, and how we organise and attribute responsibility for the work of infrastructure. While it is beyond our task to elaborate here, we believe that there are possibilities for redistributing our global wealth in ways that ensure security and increase autonomy; a basic income grant, as advocated for by many in South Africa (Standing and Samson, 2003), would enable waste pickers to retain their autonomy and flexibility and likely increase their bargaining power (Wright, 2004; see also Lawhon and McCreary, forthcoming). Recognising diverse ways of valuing work underpins this wider project.

Conclusion

This chapter starts from the premise that the idea of modernity has failed, yet continues to retain powerful influence. The modernist conceit that underpins the modern infrastructure ideal is compelling, hard to let go of because it is so desirable, so comfortable, so convenient for users. Our concern is that the modern infrastructure ideal is based on a fundamentally inaccurate belief in our ability to know and control the world as well as a false belief that people are homogeneous and want stable, predictable, dependent lives.

To call the modern infrastructure ideal into question is, importantly, not to give up on the goal of safe and dignified services and livelihoods. It is to open conceptual and political spaces for thinking about other modes of infrastructural provisioning. We point towards ways that the state in Kampala supports technological diversity and waste pickers in Tshwane valorise their autonomous and serendipitous work as examples that are not underpinned by modern ideals. Crucially, they are not fully developed alternatives, but are useful starting points for spurring scholarly analysis of practices and imaginaries that do not accord with the modern imaginary.

We use these cases to begin thinking about what a 'modest' imaginary might entail (see Lawhon et al. 2021, forthcoming). In a world underpinned by a modest imaginary, technology will surely be more heterogeneous, more attuned to and in relation with its immediate surroundings. Providers of infrastructure will need to grapple with social heterogeneity, including varying needs, wants, practices, and values. The work that makes the infrastructure go may not be stable, predictable, centrally organised waged labour. A modest politics might mean we need other ways to ensure autonomy and security for all those who engage with infrastructure.

While we have focused on examples from two African cities, we are clear that there are emergent and longstanding practices that do not accord with the modern infrastructure ideal in many different places across the Global

North and South. Some have existed long before the idea of modernity, others have been developed in response to the social and ecological shortcomings of modern practices. In this time of crisis, they provide empirical cases and conceptual provocations for thinking differently. We thus see such urban political ecologies not as fully developed alternatives but as inspiration for rethinking and developing new imaginaries that better accord with the messy, uncertain and dynamic world we have.

Acknowledgements

Funding was received from Riksbankens Jubileumsfond for the project 'Examining nature-society relations through urban infrastructure' (P19-0286:1) and the Economic and Social Research Council–Department for International Development joint fund for poverty alleviation research for the project 'Turning Livelihoods to Rubbish? Assessing the Impacts of Formalization and Technologization of Waste Management on the Urban Poor' (ES/M009408/1).

Notes

1 Critical urbanists have called for more research into non-modern infrastructures but this work is typically analytical rather than normative. Literature on alternative/appropriate technology, in contrast, is primarily normative but not critical (see Lawhon et al., 2018a, 2020).
2 Some versions of socio-ecological theory, such as some versions of resilience, translate a new ontology of uncertainty into programmatic action. Although widely critiqued by critical scholars, there are components of resilience thinking that resonate with our wider project (Grove, 2018; see Lawhon et al., 2018a).
3 This is quite a contrast from design approaches that often seek 'the' best sanitation technology, see Kass (2013) and Njeru (2014).

References

Appelblad Fredby, J. and D. Nilsson. 2013. From 'all for some' to 'some for all'? A historical geography of pro-poor water provision in Kampala. *Journal of Eastern African Studies* 7(1): 40–57.
Anand, N. 2017. *Hydraulic city: Water and the infrastructures of citizenship in Mumbai*. Durham: Duke University Press.
Arboleda, M. 2016. In the nature of the non-city: Expanded infrastructural networks and the political ecology of planetary urbanisation. *Antipode* 48(2): 233–51.

Barchiesi, F. 2011. *Precarious liberation: Workers, the state, and contested social citizenship in postapartheid South Africa*. Albany, NY: Suny Press.
Bond, P. 1998. Privatisation, participation and protest in the restructuring of municipal services. *Urban Forum* 9(1): 37–75.
Bresnihan, P. 2017. Thinkery on water, anti-privatization struggles and the commons. *Undisciplined* Environments. https://undisciplinedenvironments.org/2017/06/09/thinkery-on-water-anti-privatization-struggles-and-the-commons/, accessed 12 August 2022.
Budds, J. 2004. Power, nature and neoliberalism: The political ecology of water in Chile. *Singapore Journal of Tropical Geography* 25(3): 322–42.
Cooper, F. 1996. *Decolonization and African society: The labor question in French and British Africa*. Cambridge: Cambridge University Press.
Coletto, D. and L. Bisschop. 2017. Waste pickers in the informal economy of the Global South: Included or excluded? *International Journal of Sociology and Social Policy* 37(5–6): 280–94.
Dias, S.M. 2016. Waste pickers and cities. *Environment and Urbanization* 28(2): 375–90.
Dias, S. and M. Samson. 2016. *Informal economy monitoring study sector report: Wastepickers*. Cambridge, MA: WIEGO. www.wiego.org/sites/default/files/publications/files/Dias-Samson-IEMS-Waste-Picker-Sector-Report.pdf, accessed 12 August 2022.
Escobar, A. 2006. Difference and conflict in the struggle over natural resources: a political ecology framework. *Development* 49(3): 6–13.
Fredericks, R. 2018. *Garbage citizenship: Vital infrastructures of labor in Dakar, Senegal*. Durham: Duke University Press.
Gandy, M. 1999. The Paris sewers and the rationalization of urban space. *Transactions of the Institute of British Geographers* 24(1): 23–44.
Gandy, M. 2005. Cyborg urbanization: Complexity and monstrosity in the contemporary city. *International Journal of Urban and Regional Research* 29(1): 26–49.
Gidwani, V. 2015. The work of waste: Inside India's infra-economy. *Transactions of the Institute of British Geographers* 40(4): 575–95.
Godfrey, L., A. Muswema, W. Strydom, T. Mamafa, and M. Mapako. 2017. Co-operatives as a development mechanism to support job creation and sustainable waste management in South Africa. *Sustainability Science* 12(5): 799–812.
Government of Uganda. 2015. *Second National Development Plan 2015/16 vision: A transformed Ugandan society from a peasant to a modern and prosperous country within 30 years*. Kampala: Government of Uganda.
Graham, S. and S. Marvin. 2001. *Splintering urbanism: Networked infrastructures, technological mobilities and the urban condition*. London: Routledge.
Grove, K. 2018. *Resilience*. London: Routledge.
Gunn, S. and A. Owens. 2006. Nature, technology and the modern city: An introduction. *Cultural Geographies* 13(4): 491–6.
Huber, M.T. and T.M. Currie. 2007. The urbanization of an idea: Imagining nature through urban growth boundary policy in Portland, Oregon. *Urban Geography* 28(8): 705–31.
K'Akumu, O.A. 2007. The political ecology of water commercialisation in Kenya. *International Journal of Environment and Sustainable Development* 6(3): 290–309.

Kaika, M. 2004. Interrogating the geographies of the familiar: Domesticating nature and constructing the autonomy of the modern home. *International Journal of Urban and Regional Research* 28(2): 265–86.

Kaika, M. 2006. Dams as symbols of modernization: The urbanization of nature between geographical imagination and materiality. *Annals of the Association of American Geographers* 96(2): 276–301.

Kaika, M. and E. Swyngedouw. 2000. Fetishizing the modern city: the phantasmagoria of urban technological networks. *International Journal of Urban and Regional Research* 24(1): 120–38.

KCCA. 2016. *Kampala fecal sludge management (FSM) project: Improving onsite sanitation in Kampala City, Uganda.* Project launch, press release.

Kass, J. 2013. Bill Gates can't build a toilet. *New York Times*, 19 November. www.nytimes.com/2013/11/19/opinion/bill-gates-cant-build-a-toilet.html?_r=0, accessed 12 August 2022.

Keil, R. 2007. Sustaining modernity, modernizing nature. In R. Krueger and D. Gibbs (eds.), *The sustainable development paradox: Urban political ecology in the US and Europe.* New York: Guilford Press, pp. 41–65.

Latour, B. 2012 [1991]. *We have never been modern.* Cambridge, MA: Harvard University Press.

Lawhon, M. and T. McCreary. Forthcoming. Making UBI Radical: On the potential for a universal basic income to underwrite transformative and anti-kyriarchal change. *Economy and Society.*

Lawhon, M., D. Nilsson, J. Silver, H. Ernstson, and S. Lwasa. 2018a. Thinking through heterogeneous infrastructure configurations. *Urban Studies* 55(4): 720–32.

Lawhon, M., N. Millington, and K. Stokes. 2018b. A labour question for the 21st century: Perpetuating the work ethic in the absence of jobs in South Africa's waste sector. *Journal of Southern African Studies* 44(6): 1115–31.

Lawhon, M. with L. Le Roux, A. Makina, and Y. Truelove. 2020. *Making urban theory: Learning and unlearning through southern cities.* London: Routledge.

Lawhon, M., M. Henderson, and T. McCreary. 2021. Viewpoint: Neither more nor less, but enough: towards a modest political ecology of the future. *Political Geography* 76.

Lawhon, M., G.N. Nakyagaba, and T. Karzopouglou (forthcoming). Towards a modest infrastructural imaginary? Sanitation in Kampala beyond the modern infrastructure ideal. *Urban Studies.*

Lemanski, C. 2017. Citizens in the middle class: The interstitial policy spaces of South Africa's housing gap. *Geoforum* 79: 101–10.

Loftus, A.J. and D.A. McDonald. 2001. Of liquid dreams: A political ecology of water privatization in Buenos Aires. *Environment and Urbanization* 13(2): 179–99.

Makina, A. 2020. Logics used to justify urban appropriations: An examination of waste picking in Tshwane. Doctoral dissertation, University of Oklahoma.

Makina, A. and M. Lawhon. Forthcoming. MPermission to appropriate: Waste pickers' 'guidelines' for contesting and consolidating claims to waste on the streets of South Africa *Geoforum.*

Mbiba, B. 2014. Urban solid waste characteristics and household appetite for separation at source in Eastern and Southern Africa. *Habitat International* 43: 152–62.

McDonald, D.A. and G. Ruiters (eds.). 2012. *Alternatives to privatization: Public options for essential services in the Global South.* Durham: Routledge.

Medina, M. 2010. Solid wastes, poverty and the environment in developing country cities: Challenges and opportunities (No. 2010/23). WIDER Working

Paper. www.econstor.eu/bitstream/10419/54107/1/63649439X.pdf, accessed 12 August 2022.
Millington, N., K. Stokes, and M. Lawhon. 2022. Whose value lies in the urban mine? Reconfiguring permissions, work and the benefits of waste in South Africa. *Annals of the American Association of Geographers* 112(7): 1942–57.
Miraftab, F. 2004. Neoliberalism and casualization of public sector services: The case of waste collection services in Cape Town, South Africa. *International Journal of Urban and Regional Research* 28(4): 874–92.
Monteith, W., D.-O. Vicol, and P. Williams (eds.). 2021. *Beyond the wage: Ordinary work in diverse economies.* Bristol: Bristol University Press.
Muller, M. 2008. Free basic water: A sustainable instrument for a sustainable future in South Africa. *Environment and Urbanization* 20(1): 67–87.
Nakyagaba, G.N., M. Lawhon, S. Lwasa, J. Silver and F.R. Tumwine. 2021. The politics of new sanitation technologies in Kampala: Legitimacy, access and benefits of the gulper. *Singapore Journal of Tropical Geography* 42: 415–30.
Neimark, B. et al. 2019. Speaking power to 'post-truth': Critical political ecology and the new authoritarianism. *Annals of the American Association of Geographers* 109(2): 613–23.
Njeru, J.N. 2014. Rethinking public toilet technologies in Nairobi: The case of Ikotoilet facilities. *Journal of Water, Sanitation and Hygiene for Development* 4(2): 324–8.
Nilsson, D. 2006. A heritage of unsustainability? Reviewing the origin of the large-scale water and sanitation system in Kampala, Uganda. *Environment and Urbanization* 18(2): 369–85.
Norman, J.R. 2011. Housing for families but not for people: Federal policy and normative family ideals in midcentury California. *Sociological Focus* 44(3): 210–30.
Peres, T.S. 2016. Stigma management in waste management: An investigation into the interactions of 'waste pickers' on the streets of Cape Town and the consequences for agency. PhD thesis, University of Cape Town.
Potts, D. 2008. The urban informal sector in sub-Saharan Africa: From bad to good (and back again?). *Development Southern Africa* 25(2): 151–67.
Robbins, P. 2020. Is less more … or is more less? Scaling the political ecologies of the future. *Political Geography* 76: 102018.
Robins, S. 2014. The 2011 toilet wars in South Africa: Justice and transition between the exceptional and the everyday after apartheid. *Development and Change* 45(3): 479–501.
Rodríguez, I. and M.L. Inturias. 2018. Conflict transformation in Indigenous peoples' territories: Doing environmental justice with a 'decolonial turn'. *Development Studies Research* 5(1): 90–105.
Samson, M. 2020. Whose frontier is it anyway? Reclaimer 'Integration' and the battle over Johannesburg's waste-based commodity frontier. *Capitalism Nature Socialism* 31(4): 60–75.
Scott, J.C. 2014. *Two cheers for anarchism: Six easy pieces on autonomy, dignity, and meaningful work and play.* Princeton, NJ: Princeton University Press.
Scheinberg, A. 2012. *Informal sector integration and high performance recycling: Evidence from 20 cities.* WIEGO Working Paper (Urban Policies) No 23. www.wiego.org/sites/default/files/publications/files/Scheinberg_WIEGO_WP23.pdf, accessed 12 August 2022.
Scheinberg, A. and J. Anschutz. 2006. Slim pickin's: Supporting waste pickers in the ecological modernization of urban waste management systems. *International*

Journal of Technology Management & Sustainable Development 5(3): 257–70.

Schenck, R., D. Blaauw, and K. Viljoen. 2016. Enabling factors for the existence of waste pickers: A systematic review. *Social Work* 52(1): 35–53.

Schenck, C.J., P.F. Blaauw, E.C. Swart, J.M. Viljoen, and N. Mudavanhu. 2019. The management of South Africa's landfills and waste pickers on them: Impacting lives and livelihoods. *Development Southern Africa* 36(1): 80–98.

Sekhwela, M.M. and M. Samson. 2020. Contested understandings of reclaimer integration: Insights from a failed Johannesburg pilot project. *Urban Forum* 31(1): 21–39.

Simone, A. 2004. People as infrastructure: Intersecting fragments in Johannesburg. *Public Culture* 16(3): 407–29.

Smith, L. 2004. The murky waters of the second wave of neoliberalism: Corporatization as a service delivery model in Cape Town. *Geoforum* 35(3): 375–93.

Sseviiri, H., S. Lwasa, M. Lawhon, H. Ernstson, and R. Twinomuhangi. Forthcoming. Claiming value in a heterogeneous solid waste configuration in Kampala. *Urban Geography*.

Standing, G. 2019. Why 'Universal Basic Services' is no alternative to Basic Income. *Open Democracy*. www.opendemocracy.net/en/oureconomy/why-universal-basic-services-is-no-alternative-to-basic-income/, accessed 12 August 2022.

Standing, G. and M. Samson (eds.). 2003. *A basic income grant for South Africa*. Cape Town: Juta and Company Ltd.

Star, S.L. 1999. The ethnography of infrastructure. *American Behavioral Scientist* 43(3): 377–91.

Tzaninis, Y., T. Mandler, M. Kaika, and R. Keil. 2021. Moving urban political ecology beyond the 'urbanization of nature'. *Progress in Human Geography* 45(2): 229–52.

Velis, C.A., D.C. Wilson, O. Rocca, S.R. Smith, A. Mavropoulos, and C.R. Cheeseman. 2012. An analytical framework and tool ('InteRa') for integrating the informal recycling sector in waste and resource management systems in developing countries. *Waste Management & Research* 30(9): 43–66.

Weeks, K. 2011. *The problem with work*. Durham: Duke University Press.

Wright, E.O. 2004. Basic income, stakeholder grants, and class analysis. *Politics & Society* 32(1): 79–87.

Zimmer, A., N. Cornea, and R. Véron. 2017. Of parks and politics: The production of socio-nature in a Gujarati town. *Local Environment* 22(1): 49–66.

Part III

More-than-human urban political ecologies and relational geographies

11

Extending the boundaries of 'urban society': The urban political ecologies and pathologies of Ebola virus disease in West Africa

Roger Keil, S. Harris Ali, and Stefan Treffers

If urban political ecology (UPE) is, at its core, about urban life, infectious disease, its origin, trajectory, and the response to it must be among its prime occupations.[1] After all, cities and infectious disease have a joint history which is shaped and characterised by the relationships between human and non-human nature in and around urban settlement. Zoonoses – the leap of diseases from animal to human reservoirs – the spread of disease vectors such as mosquitoes and ticks in the outskirts of growing cities, and the mobility of bodies through an increasingly urbanised space are aspects of those relationships. Those are not separate from other physical and social articulations of what is commonly referred to as 'city' and 'nature'; disease spread is related to metabolic exchange which is the signature concept of UPE. Both urbanisation and the production of nature have changed in recent decades as we have seen more extended forms of urbanisation around the world (Connolly et al., 2020; Tzaninis et al., 2021). Accordingly, this chapter will examine the histories and geographies of the relationships of cities and infectious disease as a problem of the political ecology of extended urbanisation in a moment of intensified climate emergency.

As the world continues to flirt with unprecedented climate change and species extinction, it appears humans are claiming ever-more space and putting more and exceedingly damaging pressure on natural systems; yet at the same time, massive urbanisation also remakes those natural conditions, some would even speak of influence on evolutionary change (popular discussions in this context include those on the Anthropocene and on 'human-induced rapid evolutionary change'; see Quammen, 2018). More than 3 billion people are projected to be added to the 7 billion that already inhabit the planet before the world population is projected to plateau. It is likely that most of these new earthlings will live in some form of extended, suburban environment. This settlement pattern cuts into existing agricultural land and drives urbanisation into feral and previously uninhabited regions of the world. This involves the loss of prime forest areas which has been connected to the spread of disease (Olivero et al., 2017; Pontes, 2020). The consequences of this massive expansion in human settlement add up to a redefinition of what urban life, or life generally, will mean for humans on the suburban planet. These consequences test the conditions of our collective existence in ways we have not seen since the emergence of the 'bacteriological city' (Gandy, 2006) a century ago, and they challenge the socio-technological networks we have introduced to live in what Lefebvre (2003) calls 'urban society'.

While the hygienic city of the twentieth century in many parts of the world created infrastructures and public health institutions that contributed to the containment of outbreaks which had plagued urban life in previous centuries, recent decades have seen a (re)emergence of infectious disease in cities. This emergent phenomenon coincides with what has been referred to as planetary urbanisation/suburbanisation and the formation of 'urban society' or 'the prodigious extension of the urban to the entire planet' (Lefebvre, 2003: 169). While noting the possible 'rupture' caused by this development for 'industry and finance', Lefebvre is explicit about the fact that industrial society 'simply ravages nature and everything associated with "naturalism"'. Lefebvre (2016: 149) is concerned about how 'Mastery over nature, associated with technology and the growth of productive forces, and subject solely to the demands of profit (surplus value), culminates in the destruction of nature', but he also holds out the possibility that urban society brings forth new forms of 'nature' and new modes of management of scarcities related to that emergent nature (2003: 25–7).

Somewhere in there, urban society also needs to find new ways to live up to the challenges of human physical nature, including the management of health and disease (left, as we know, to the methods and devices of the industrial city in the past). One obvious point of entry into this discussion is the recognition of public health as part of the development of 'social needs' which Lefebvre says '*defines socialism*' (2016: 131, emphasis in original). Lefebvre explicitly exposes the fallacy of equating the city with disease – although he carefully explicates Engels's early writings on the deprivations of the working-class quarters (Lefebvre, 2016, 1: 3–18). He critiques the tendency in some of the twentieth century's revolutionary efforts to assume that 'the large city is nothing but vice, pollution, and disease (mental, moral, social)' (2003: 92). Instead, he proposes a dialectical model that notoriously argues that the urban revolution is predicated on the end of the city and its replacement by urban society (2003). Taking up Lefebvre's dialectical method that builds on the contradiction of general urbanisation and the end of the city, this chapter looks at the ways in which a 'spatialized political ecology' (Connolly et al., 2020) can help understand the challenges a generalised urban will encounter and how it can contribute to mitigating the impact of disease outbreaks that appear to be endemic to emerging urban society.

In developing our conceptual argument, we bring together two areas of thought that have different origins and histories but are compatible in our current context. One area is Sub/urban Political Pathologies, i.e., the interrelationship of peripheral urbanisation with the spread of (re-)emerging infectious disease and with new and persistent chronic health conditions (Connolly et al., 2020); and the other area is Sub/urban Political Ecologies, in other words, the political ecologies of extended urbanisation (Tzaninis et al., 2021). Through these lenses, we subject the political *pathologies* and the political *ecologies* of the urban periphery to similar analytical principles: humans are embedded in ecologies of more-than-human environments that are structured by human action while being both enabled and constrained through the conditions of what we refer colloquially as nature.

Urban political pathology (UPP) is here understood as the intersection of urbanisation and the governance of health. This is based on David Fidler's use of the term during the SARS crisis when he noted that political pathology 'contains a message that responses to pathogenic microbes are deeply political' (2004: 18). Fidler's notion of political pathology entails an attempt to 'analyze the scientific, medical, and public health challenges [a given infectious disease] creates through a political lens' (2004: 8). The relationships of urbanisation and health/disease have long been the subject of scholarly study (Rossi-Espagnet, 1983). It has been known that patterns of urbanisation can increase the statistical odds that microbes are being spread and have played a key role in the tripling of the total number of disease outbreaks per decade since the 1980s (Keil and Ali, 2007: 848). The 'promiscuity' of urban interaction is seen as key to the spread of infectious disease (Wald, 2008: 14) and the proliferation of urban settlement initiates a new research agenda:

> there is something peculiar about urban environments and their impact on human health and this problem is potentially global in scale. This observation presents a problem worthy of more detailed exploration: seen from a theoretical angle, the ways in which urban complexity can be distinguished from other kinds of complexity are still far from clear. What exactly constitutes 'the urban' within the complex assemblages of disease interactions?
>
> (Wolf, 2016: 959)

The most significant global disease outbreaks in recent years have originated in China and Africa, which are also among the most rapidly urbanising countries and where the urban periphery in particular has been a focus of attention (Ali et al., 2016). But under current conditions of mobility and connectivity, those infections are not contained at the point of origin. Diseases that used to be exclusively isolated and rural phenomena, like the Ebola outbreaks of the past, are now becoming urbanised. The most recent outbreaks of this haemorrhagic fever have typically occurred in the sprawling towns and cities of West and equatorial Africa. And as COVID-19 showed in utmost clarity, the transmission from an urban centre to the entire world can now occur in days and weeks, rather than months and years. The political governance systems in place have not proven to be calibrated to these changes as they continue to be tethered to the 'Westphalian' state system.

The political aspect of UPP does not just mean hierarchical or networked institution-building. Urban society develops in a dialectic of exposure and containment that needs political contestation, negotiation, and decision-making. Politics is therefore critical in any discussion of disease governance and political pathology in urban society. As research on SARS, widely considered the first pathogen of the global era, has shown, past hierarchical and hermetic, nation-state-based regulation needed to be complemented by institutions and actors at the international, sub-national, sub/urban, and community level, especially through civil society-based advocacy and monitoring systems (Ali and Keil, 2008: 50). Consequently, asking how and why suburban or peri-urban areas are conducive to disease outbreaks is an important question to explore (Connolly et al., 2020). During the COVID-19 pandemic, the regulation of social, spatial, and institutional peripheries was thrown into the spotlight in many geographical regions (Biglieri et al., 2020). Comparative political pathologies render important insights on the vulnerability of particular groups in different spatial and socio-economic settings (Kapiriri and Ross, 2020).

Urban political ecology (UPE) looks at the urbanisation of nature and investigates urban metabolisms through a material and materialist lens that recognises both physical processes of exchange and societal mediation of such processes. During the current period of urbanisation much attention will be on urban peripheries. We can therefore speak of a *sub*urban political ecology, which brings into relief the vast swathes of residential territories where people make their home around the globe but also the 'non-places' where people work, travel, and dispose of their leftovers, like airports, oil fields, and garbage dumps. Instead of seeing these spaces as a mere appendage to the central city, we propose to look at the metabolism of the urban region from the outside inwards (Tzaninis et al., 2021).

Urbanisation is now the conditioning process through which political ecologies and political pathologies gain shape. It is an engulfing process that is not restricted to specific confined places but creates an overreaching way of life that is resourced by planetary streams of goods and services and is vulnerable to often unexpected shocks (health emergencies, disasters, economic crises) that can originate anywhere in the system but have consequences beyond that point of origin. Martin Murray has called the 'distended urban form ... the template for global urbanism' (2017: 46). To Murray and other urban theorists, the bloated, unbounded form of urbanisation finds its equivalence in the solution of political governance and rational planning. The result is 'a seemingly random aggregation and spatially discontinuous collection of fragments always in motion' (2017: 31). Yet, there are differences across the globe that are etched into narratives of progress, stasis, and decay. The creative city discourse that has characterised the urbanism of the West for much of this century was counterposed to the 'deadening homogeneity – characterized by slums and informality – [in the so-called] prototypical Third World City' (Murray, 2017: 31). Both extremes and stereotypes have subsided as the creative city has been largely illusionary and the city of the Global South has become characterised less by homogeneity than by splintered enclave urbanism.

The distended urbanisation that is now common in the world poses fundamental questions to political ecology and political pathology alike. Thomas Bollyky (2018) has pointed to the 'paradox of progress', meaning that 'the world is getting better in worrisome ways', in a spiral through which metabolic processes like sanitation, and the establishment of healthier environments are intertwined in rapid urbanisation. Today, the fastest and most extensive forms of urban growth, uneven and convulsive as they are, occur in what Bollyky calls 'poor world cities' like Dhaka, New Delhi, Jakarta, Lagos, or Kinshasa. Those cities, with their dramatic socio-economic disparities and socio-ecological deficiencies (no clean water, no sewage disposal, no networked infrastructure generally), one might assume, are also the most vulnerable to emerging infectious disease.

COVID-19, like pandemics before it, exposed the inequalities in and of cities in much the same way as past environmental emergencies (floods, earthquakes, bushfires) highlighted the vulnerabilities of some populations that tend to be subject to economic and social marginalisation even in the best of times (Kapiriri and Ross, 2020). In many cities of the Global North tuberculosis had long made a reappearance among poor and vulnerable populations; in the Global South, where urbanisation has been concentrated over the past decades, many vector-borne infections continue to affect newly urbanised populations, especially in informal settlements. The SARS outbreak of 2003 highlighted the ways in which a global network of cities exacerbated the exposure of the urban world to infectious disease (Ali and Keil, 2008); and the West African Ebola pandemic of 2014/15 revealed the relationships of rapid urbanisation and disease spread (Ali et al., 2022).

In the suburbs of North America, tick-borne disease spreads at the edges of sprawl (Kaup, 2018) and Zika hit the poverty populations in Brazil's cities hard in 2015 (Chang et al., 2016; Imperato, 2016; Lowe et al., 2018). The COVID-19 pandemic has led to a reassessment of (urban) development policy and practice in light of the challenges highlighted by this and other pandemics (Leach et al., 2021). But the results of these outbreaks are not predetermined and their lessons for future pandemic preparedness efforts need to be carefully assessed.

The COVID-19 pandemic led to containment measures that involved an unprecedented quarantine of entire urban regions and highlighted the connectivities of economies and populations in a world of extended urbanisation (Keil et al., 2020). The pandemic has additionally called into question the traditional divisions between the urbanism of networked infrastructures, welfare state institutions, and rational city planning on one side and that of infrastructure deficits, failing institutions, and informality on the other (Bhan et al., 2020). The virus ravaged the depleted institutions of long-term care in the Global North (Biglieri, et al., 2020) while it was held in check by the culture of community-based health care in the Global South (Ali et al., 2022); while access to clean water and spaces that allowed social distancing were assumed as given in the rich urban centres of the Global South such certainties did not readily exist in the informal settlements of the Global South or in austerity-racked metropoles of the Global North (e.g., water crisis in Detroit). Concepts like culture and trust seemed to be as important to survival during the pandemic as access to beds and respirators (Napier and Fischer, 2020).

The breadth and variety of the intersections of political ecologies and political pathologies in the current urbanisation process suggests the importance of close analysis of particular outbreaks and health emergencies to increase our understanding of the interrelationships of the societal relationships with nature and disease in a world of extended urbanisation.

Ebola virus disease in an urbanising West Africa

In the remainder of this chapter we discuss the political ecologies and the political pathologies of urbanisation in West Africa – Guinea, Liberia, and Sierra Leone to be specific – where an outbreak of Ebola virus disease (EVD) affected more than 30,000 in 2014/15, 10,000 of whom died. The disease, which had never before existed in this part of Africa, emerged in the urbanising hinterlands and at a crossroads of mobilities in the rural southwest of Guinea, where trading and travel routes connect to Sierra Leone and Liberia. Paul Richards (2016: 21–2) notes that at the time '[i]nsufficient attention was paid to the intensive cross-border networking that catapulted the disease in the direction of adjacent, crowded, capital cities on the coast'. There were concerns that an 'epidemic in city environments, with crowded slums, was uncharted terrain, and a degree of panic ensued' (Richards, 2016: 22). Still, while 'Freetown and its peri-urban fringe' (Richards, 2016: 24) and the large Monrovia informal settlement of West Point with its 70,000 inhabitants became hotspots of the outbreak, they also became centres of political and community intervention that helped stem the outbreak eventually. In fact, Richards (2016: 40) reports that '[r]esponding was in some ways easier in urban environments since so much in Ebola prevention hinges on logistics' and '[u]rban community structures proved to be not noticeably less effective than their rural counterparts in supporting activities requiring citizen support, such as case-finding and quarantine'.

Though the epidemic was eventually contained, the outbreak revealed deeply entrenched weaknesses in the early response by government officials and the international community. The narratives that dominated early understandings of the disease and informed policy in the region tended to focus on West Africans' cultural practices, extensive social networks, and non-compliance with public health directives. However, the reality was being dictated by a much more complex socio-political landscape; one shaped by a nexus of imperial and colonial rule, civil war, political strife and corruption, and exploitative economic arrangements. For decades, these factors have shaped the region's socio-economic developmental trajectories and have helped define patterns of mobility and settlement. Today, Guinea, Liberia, and Sierra Leone rank among the poorest countries in the world with rising levels of rural impoverishment and rapid population growth heavily concentrated in urban informal settlements that are highly susceptible to disease spread (Howard, 2017; Wilkinson, 2020a, 2020b). It is unsurprising that decades of political strife and plundering of the region's natural resources by multinational corporations and local ruling elites have led to the severe underdevelopment of social, physical, and health infrastructures, the fragility of which became exposed once the pandemic hit. These arrangements also contributed to widespread distrust of government and even seemingly benign foreign NGOs that further exacerbated challenges in effectively responding to the outbreak.

Regional political ecologies and extended urbanisation

It is now well established that the spread of EVD in West Africa followed a regional trajectory, moving from the remote, forested hinterlands of the border region to the heavily interconnected capital cities of Monrovia, Freetown, and Conakry. According to Howard (2017), Guinea, Liberia, and

Sierra Leone have historically been, and still are today, integrated by complex social, economic, and cultural networks. The three countries 'constitute a single region with complementary ecologies, which has been integrated from the nineteenth century onwards by socio-cultural commonalities, flows of people and ideas, and commercial and socials exchanges' (Abdullah and Rashid, 2017: 4). Though the movement of people and goods grew out of earlier pre-colonial routes of commerce (Howard, 2017), patterns of mobility and settlement have been augmented in significant ways as a result of the region's colonial history and present-day socio-political arrangements.

The Ebola outbreak in West Africa is often considered exceptional for the simple reason that EVD had never before entered the fully urbanised context of Africa's major cities. Shortly after the first case was identified, EVD spread rapidly to several villages in Guinea before making its way to the densely populated capital cities of Conakry and Monrovia. As Green (forthcoming) and others have argued, we should not presume the urbanisation of Ebola lay in an inherent ability for the virus to mutate, but rather in the ways human networks created amplified pathways for its spread and how these networks were mediated by social, economic, and political factors. Centralisation of economic and political activity in the capital cities also accelerated Ebola's spread from villages and smaller towns to the cities, as many migrated to cities in search of employment (Azétsop et al., 2020: 170). Also, movement from the rural areas to urban informal settlements was not exclusively unidirectional as there was periodic back-and-forth travel between these locations, which contributed to the rapid spread of the epidemic not only in Liberia but in West Africa more generally (see Richards et al., 2015).

The introduction of EVD in the rapidly growing and overcrowded informal settlements provided a concentrated mass of host populations and breeding ground for the virus. Here, underdeveloped, fragmented, or otherwise inaccessible health systems left many ill-prepared to deal with an outbreak of the magnitude of the one that ravaged West Africa. West Africa's capital cities of Freetown, Conakry, and Monrovia have more than quadrupled in size since the 1960s (Howard, 2017), with much of this growth concentrated in informal settlements. Today, nearly three quarters of Sierra Leone's urban population lives in slum conditions, with 68 informal settlements in Freetown alone (Conteh et al., 2020; Sanderson, 2020). It is here where viral transmission exploded due to high population densities as well as poor access to water and sanitation, and health care (see Wilkinson, 2020a, 2020b). Indeed, informal settlements typically have ten times the density of adjacent areas in the same city with overcrowding common in single dwellings, making physical distancing and quarantine challenging (Muggah and Florida, 2020). While urban infrastructures 'act as conduits, circuits and sites for processes of socio-natural transformation' (Silver, 2016: 986), their disruptions can create major barriers for containing spread. The fragmented and splintered nature of infrastructural development meant that few inhabitants in West Africa's informal settlements had access to clean water, with others forced to rely on polluted sources for drinking and sanitation. This is particularly problematic for populations suffering from food insecurity, as nutritional deficiencies can heighten susceptibility to infection.

Yet, the swiftness with which Ebola spread through informal settlements is not merely a result of their physical forms, nominal densities, or availability of infrastructures, but of a complex web of historical, economic, political, and spatial relationships. In particular, the extraction-based political economy, a prominent feature of racial capitalist economic relations across the continent (Rodney, 1972), had important implications for the spatialised aspect of the EVD spread. In Liberia, for example, the concentration of employment opportunities in the capital city of Monrovia served as a magnet for impoverished rural inhabitants who settled primarily in overcrowded informal settlements. This was closely related to the fact that Americo-Liberian elites who largely located in Monrovia, tended to neglect the needs of those in the rural/peripheral areas while benefiting from their labour and catering to the needs of foreign investors. Those in rural areas never had any real representation and were not even considered as counties until 1964 (Howard, 2017). This led to certain level of distrust and tension between the urban elite and the rural dwellers that was further accentuated by civil wars that led to massive displacements. Escaping the violence, many fled to informal settlements situated on the periphery of the more developed urban cores. As Howard (2017) notes, during this era cities grew massively while social resources shrunk, making urban populations especially vulnerable to contagious disease. The rapid spread of Ebola through deeply impoverished urban informal settlements led Liberia to have the highest caseloads of the three affected Mano River Union Countries.

Deforestation, extractive industry, and the contested zoonotic origins of the West African Ebola outbreak

Despite countless investigations of exactly how the Ebola virus came to spread so rapidly across the region, the origins of the outbreak and the particulars of the index case of the disease remain unclear. According to the commonly accepted narrative adopted, for example, by the World Health Organization (WHO), the outbreak is presumed to have originated in the remote forest region of Guinea where a young boy in the village of Méliandou was believed to be infected while playing near a roosting place for free-tail bats

(WHO, 2020; see also Wallace and Wallace, 2016). It is thought that the virus spread from there through extensively connected and intensively used travel routes that connected small and large urban areas in the West African countries that were hit by EVD. The assumed trajectory of the virus is closely related to the idea that urban landscapes are embedded within a 'series of interconnected heterogeneous (human and non-human) and dynamic but contested and contestable processes of continuous quantitative and qualitative transformations that re-arranges humans and non-humans in new and often unexpected ways' (Swyngedouw, 2006: 106). Here, socio-spatial and socio-natural processes are grounded in metabolic exchanges and circulation of various physical, chemical, and biological components that can be disrupted, augmented, or transformed to form new urban 'natures'. In the case of emerging diseases, urbanisation as a process of socio-ecological change produces numerous pathways for new human–non-human interactions and relationships that may enable microbes to exploit new ecological niches. This is particularly true of extended forms of urbanisation such as those that produce spaces of resource extraction, known to routinely breach and disrupt ecosystems on the urban fringe (Arboleda, 2015). It is, however, not sufficient to speak about environmental impact or ecological disturbances by merely referencing the various mining areas, logging camps, or monoculture plantations that dot the extended urban landscape. Rather we must consider the wider operational landscapes that result from and facilitate urban agglomeration (Brenner, 2014). These include roads, highways, power lines, satellite towns, and other infrastructures that connect spaces of extraction to the wider global urban fabric and fundamentally alter nature in an effort to produce 'frictionless', homogenised spaces for the circulation of raw materials. It is here where the possibilities of zoonoses might be amplified due to encroachment by humans of nature, displacement of wildlife, destruction of natural habitats and biodiversity, and disruption of natural buffering systems that reduce the chances of 'spillover' events – that is, the transmission of a pathogen from wildlife reservoirs to humans.

However, some suggest that zoonosis might only explain the index case rather than the entirety of the pandemic, the severity of which might be better explained by human-to-human transmission (Richards et al., 2015). Other scholars question the link of deforestation and disease outbreak as 'people and bats have long co-habited in this ancient, anthropogenic forest landscape with its mosaic of forest, bush, and savannah, shaped by settlement and farming, war and trade, and everyday social and ecological life' and such a theory might lay 'the blame for the epidemic at the feet of the rural people now suffering from it' (Wilkinson and Leach, 2015: 145).

Several African scholars too have argued that despite hundreds of publications on the subject, there is still 'no clear scientific evidence or indisputable explanation of how EBOV [Ebola virus] moved from wild animals to humans in the Mano River Union sub-region' (Abdullah and Rashid, 2017: 3). In a critical analysis of the zoonotic narrative, Bah (2017) argued that the scientific team credited with authenticating the bush meat thesis did so on the basis of circumstantial evidence, having found no conclusive proof of the virus in the surrounding animal population in the Southern Guinean region. Others suggest a need to consider alternative hypotheses, including examining a broader spectrum of ecological, social, and politico-economic factors (Howard, 2017; Leendertz, 2016). Despite contestation over its origins, what we might be more certain about is that beyond the index case, the rapid spread of the disease was amplified by a number of political, social, and spatial relations. Indeed, as Bausch and Schwarz (2014: 3) argue: 'Biological and ecological factors may drive emergence of the virus from the forest, but clearly the sociopolitical landscape dictates where it goes from there.'

Conclusion

This chapter argued that during our current period of urbanisation, the intensified activities occurring at the urban peripheries must be given greater attention. As accelerating climate crises and emerging infectious diseases pose catastrophic risks to human and non-human life, we must be cognisant that these phenomena are intricately connected to one another through unprecedented urban transformations, including the extended urban fabric of dense forested regions and hinterlands of emerging cities. New urban-industrial agricultural and mining frontiers as well as new centres of agglomerations characterised by urban informality constitute some of the emerging nodes in this polycentric urban system. Applying an urban political ecology perspective helps underscore that as capitalist relations of production are extended into the furthest reaches of the urban landscape and test new ecological limits, they inevitably transform socio-cultural and material flows in ways that increase possibilities for emergence and spread of infectious disease. Whether it is through the pushing of urban boundaries into previously undisturbed ecological niches, the disruption of natural ecosystem homeostasis that keeps pathogens in check, or the expanding networks and geographies of mobility that accelerate the spread of infectious disease, an urban political ecology lens helps us understand the various urban metabolisms that link together country and city. Moreover, emerging infectious disease and its intimate connections with ecological disruptions and climate change is as much political as it is ecological. Indeed, one cannot fully reconcile the severity of the West African Ebola outbreak, its weak public health response, and its unevenly distributed impacts without explicating the (post)colonial nature of urbanisation and the racial capitalist system that underpins it.

If, finally, Lefebvre was concerned with 'the prodigious extension of the urban to the entire planet' (2003: 169), Ebola and other deadly infectious diseases at the frontier of this 'prodigious extension' should warn us of the potential perils of ignoring ecological degradation. As we emerge from the COVID-19 pandemic, 'urban society' must confront not only the threat of irreversible climate change, but also global, existential risks posed by yet-to-be discovered deadly pathogens.

Note

1 This is an abridged version of an argument we are making at greater length in Treffers et al. (2021).

References

Abdullah, I. and I. Rashid. 2017. Introduction: Understanding West Africa's Ebola epidemic. In I. Abdullah and I. Rashid (eds.), *Understanding West Africa's Ebola epidemic: Towards a political economy*. London: Zed Books, pp. 1–13.

Ali, H. and Keil, R. 2008. *Networked disease: Emerging infections in the global city*. Oxford: Wiley-Blackwell.

Ali, S.H., B. Dumbuya, M. Hynie, P. Idahosa, R. Keil, and P. Perkins. 2016. The social and political dimensions of the Ebola response: Global inequality, climate change, and infectious disease. In W.L. Filho, U.M. Azeiteiro, and F. Alves (eds.), *Climate change and health: Improving resilience and reducing risks*. Cham: Springer International Publishing, pp. 151–69.

Ali, S.H., M. Fallah, J. McCarthy, R. Keil, and C. Connolly. 2022. Mobilizing the urban social infrastructure of informal settlements in infectious disease response: The case of Ebola virus disease and COVID-19 in West Africa. *Landscape and Urban Planning* 217: 1–13.

Arboleda, M. 2015. Spaces of extraction, metropolitan explosions: Planetary urbanization and the commodity boom in Latin America. *International Journal of Urban and Regional Research* 40(1): 96–112.

Azétsop, J., L. Lado, and A. Fosso. 2020. Ebola crisis in West Africa as the embodiment of the world: Arguing for a non-conventional epistemology of disease aetiology. *African Sociological Review* 24(1): 4–33.

Bah, C. 2017. Eurocentric epistemology: Questioning the narrative on the epidemic's origin. In I. Abdullah and I. Rashid (eds.), *Understanding West Africa's Ebola epidemic: Towards a political economy*. London: Zed Books, pp. 47–66.

Bausch, D. and L. Schwarz. 2014. Outbreak of Ebola virus disease in Guinea: Where ecology meets economy. *PLoS Neglected Tropical Diseases* 8(7): e3056. DOI: 10.1371/journal.pntd.0003056.

Bhan, G., T. Caldeira, K. Gillespie, and A. Simone. 2020. The pandemic, southern urbanisms and collective life. *Environment and Planning D: Society and Space*. www.societyandspace.org/articles/the-pandemic-southern-urbanisms-and-collective-life, accessed 12 August 2022.

Biglieri, S., L. De Vidovich, and R. Keil. 2020. City as the core of contagion? Repositioning COVID-19 at the social and spatial periphery of urban society. *Cities & Health*. DOI: 10.1080/23748834.2020.1788320.

Bollyky, T. 2018. *Plagues and the paradox of progress: Why the world is getting healthier in worrisome ways*. Cambridge, MA: MIT Press.

Brenner, N. 2014. Urban theory without an outside. In N. Brenner (ed.), *Implosions/explosions: Towards a study of planetary urbanization*. Berlin: Jovis, pp. 14–31.

Chang, C., K. Ortiz, A. Ansari, and M. Gershwin. 2016. The Zika outbreak of the 21st century. *Journal of Autoimmunity* 68: 1–13. DOI: 10.1016/j.jaut.2016.02.006.

Connolly, C., R. Keil, and H. Ali. 2020. Extended urbanisation and the spatialities of infectious disease: Demographic change, infrastructure, and governance. *Urban Studies* 58(2): 245–63.

Conteh, A., M. Sirah Kamara, and S. Saidu. 2020. COVID-19 response and protracted exclusion of informal residents: Why should it matter to city authorities in Freetown, Sierra Leone? *Arise*, 22 July. www.ariseconsortium.org/covid-19-response-and-protracted-exclusion-of-informal-residents-why-should-it-matter-to-city-authorities-in-freetown-sierra-leone/, accessed 12 August 2022.

Dias, S. and M. Samson. 2016. *Informal economy monitoring study sector report: Waste pickers*. Manchester: WIEGO. Available at: www.wiego.org/sites/wiego.org/files/publications/files/Dias-Samson-IEMS-Waste-Picker-Sector-Report.pdf, accessed 12 August 2022.

Fidler, D. 2004. *SARS, governance and the globalization of disease*. New York: Palgrave Macmillan.

Gandy, M. 2006. The bacteriological city and its discontents. *Historical Geography* 34: 14–25.

Green, M. Forthcoming. *What places Ebola in the realm of the 'global'? A view from history*. Working Paper.

Howard, A. 2017. Ebola and regional history: Connections and common experiences. In I. Abdullah and I. Rashid (eds.), *Understanding West Africa's Ebola epidemic: Towards a political economy*. London: Zed Books, pp. 19–46.

Imperato, P. 2016. The convergence of a virus, mosquitoes, and human travel in globalizing the Zika epidemic. *Journal of Community Health* 41(3): 674–9. DOI: 10.1007/s10900-016-0177-7. PMID: 26969497.

Kapiriri, L. and A. Ross. 2020. The politics of disease epidemics: A comparative analysis of the SARS, Zika, and Ebola outbreaks. *Global Social Welfare* 7(1): 33–45. DOI: 10.1007/s40609-018-0123-y.

Kaup, B. 2018. The making of Lyme Disease: A political ecology of ticks and tick-borne illness in Virginia. *Environmental Sociology* 4(3): 381–91.

Keil, R. and S.H. Ali. 2007. Governing the sick city: Urban governance in the age of emerging infectious disease. *Antipode* 39(5): 846–73.

Keil, R., C. Connolly, and S.H. Ali. 2020. Outbreaks like coronavirus start in and spread from the edges of cities. *The Conversation*, February 17. https://theconversation.com/outbreaks-like-coronavirus-start-in-and-spread-from-the-edges-of-cities-130666, accessed 12 August 2022.

Leach, M., H. MacGregor, I. Scoones, and A. Wilkinson. 2021. Post-pandemic transformations: How and why COVID-19 requires us to rethink development. *World Development* 138(7): 105233. DOI: 10.1016/j.worlddev.2020.105233.

Leendertz, S. 2016. Testing new hypotheses regarding Ebolavirus reservoirs. *Viruses* 8(2): 30.

Lefebvre, H. 2003. *The urban revolution*. Minneapolis, MN: University of Minnesota Press.

Lefebvre, H. 2016. *Marxist thought and the city*. Minneapolis, MN: University of Minnesota Press.

Lowe, R., C. Barcellos, P. Brasil, O.G. Cruz, N.A. Honório, H. Kuper, and M.S. Carvalho. 2018. The Zika virus epidemic in Brazil: From discovery to future implications. *International Journal of Environmental Research and Public Health* 15(1): 96. DOI: 10.3390/ijerph15010096.

Lwasa, S. and K. Owens. 2018. Kampala: Rebuilding public sector legitimacy with a new approach to sanitation services. World Resources Institute. https://policycommons.net/artifacts/1360135/kampala/1973416/, accessed 12 August 2022.

Muggah, R. and R. Florida. 2020. Megacity slums are incubators of disease – but coronavirus response isn't helping the billion people who live in them. *The Conversation*, May 14. https://theconversation.com/megacity-slums-are-incubators-of-disease-but-coronavirusresponse-isnt-helping-the-billion-people-who-live-in-them-138092?utm_source=twitter&utm_medium=bylinetwitterbutton, accessed 12 August 2022.

Murray, M. 2017. *The urbanism of exception*. Cambridge: Cambridge University Press.

Napier D. and E. Fischer. 2020. The culture of health and sickness. *Le Monde Diplomatique*, July. https://mondediplo.com/2020/07/04uganda, accessed 12 August 2022.

Olivero, J. et al. 2017. Recent loss of closed forests is associated with Ebola virus disease outbreaks. *Scientific Reports* 7. www.nature.com/articles/s41598-017-14727-9, accessed 12 August 2022.

Pontes, N. 2020. How deforestation can lead to more infectious diseases. *Deutsche Welle*, 29 April. www.dw.com/en/how-deforestation-can-lead-to-more-infectious-diseases/a-53282244, accessed 12 August 2022.

Quammen, D. 2018. The urban jungle. *The New York Review*, 8 November. www.nybooks.com/articles/2018/11/08/concrete-urban-jungle-evolution/, accessed 12 August 2022.

Richards, P. 2016. *Ebola: How a people's science helped end an epidemic*. London: Zed Books.

Richards, P., J. Amara, M.C. Ferme, P. Kamara, E. Mokuwa, A.I. Sheriff, R. Suluku, and M. Voors. 2015. Social pathways for Ebola virus disease in rural Sierra Leone, and some implications for containment. *PLoS Neglected Tropical Diseases* 9(4): 1–15.

Rodney, W. 1972. *How Europe underdeveloped Africa*. London: Bogle-L'Ouverture Publications.

Rossi-Espagnet, A. 1983. Primary health care in the context of rapid urbanization. *Community Development Journal* 18(2): 104–19.

Sanderson, D. 2020. Coronavirus an existential threat to africa and her crowded slums. *The Conversation*, 9 April. https://theconversation.com/coronavirus-an-existential-threat-to-africa-and-her-crowded-slums-135829?utm_source=twitter&utm_medium=bylinetwitterbutton, accessed 12 August 2022.

Silver, J. 2016. Disrupted infrastructures: An urban political ecology of interrupted electricity in Accra. *International Journal of Urban and Regional Research* 39(5): 984–1003.
Swyngedouw, E. 1996. The city as a hybrid: On nature, society and cyborg urbanisation. *Capitalism Nature Socialism* 7(25): 65–80.
Swyngedouw, E. 2006. Circulations and metabolisms: (Hybrid) natures and (cyborg) cities. *Science and Culture* 15(2): 105–21.
Treffers, S., S.H. Ali, R. Keil, and M. Fallah. 2021. Extending the boundaries of 'urban society': The urban political ecologies and pathologies of Ebola virus Disease in West Africa. *Environment and Planning E: Nature and Space*. https://doi.org/10.1177/25148486211054932
Tzaninis, Y., T. Mandler, M. Kaika, and R. Keil. 2021. Moving urban political ecology beyond the 'urbanization of nature'. *Progress in Human Geography* 45(2): 229–52.
Wald, P. 2008. *Contagious: Cultures, carriers, and the outbreak narrative*. Durham: Duke University Press.
Wallace, R. and R. Wallace. 2016. Ebola's ecologies. *New Left Review* 102. https://newleftreview.org/issues/II102/articles/rob-wallace-rodrick-wallace-ebola-s-ecologies, accessed 12 August 2022.
Wilkinson, A. and M. Leach. 2015. Briefing: Ebola – myths, realities, and structural violence. *African Affairs* 114: 136–48.
Wilkinson, A. 2020a. What is the impact of COVID-19 in informal settlements? *LSE Blog*, March 13. https://blogs.lse.ac.uk/africaatlse/2020/03/13/what-is-the-impact-of-covid-19-coronavirus-informal-settlements-africa/, accessed 12 August 2022.
Wilkinson, A. 2020b. Local response in health emergencies: Key considerations for addressing the COVID-19 pandemic in informal urban settlements. *Environment and Urbanization* 32(2): 503–22. DOI: 10.1177%2F0956247820922843.
WHO. 2020. Ground zero in Guinea: The Ebola outbreak smoulders – undetected – for more than 3 months. *World Health Organization*. www.who.int/csr/disease/ebola/ebola-6-months/guinea/en/, accessed 12 August 2022.
Wolf, M. 2016. Rethinking urban epidemiology: Natures, networks and materialities. *International Journal of Urban and Regional Research* 40(5): 958–82. DOI: 10.1111/1468-2427.12381.
Worster, D. 1977. *Nature's economy: The roots of ecology*. San Francisco: Sierra Club Books.

12

In formation: Urban political ecology for a world of flows

Kian Goh

Interconnected urban sites[1]

In October 2012, Hurricane Sandy hit the New York City region. The storm reinforced ongoing initiatives and precipitated new efforts to protect the city from climate change-exacerbated storms and sea level rise. Among these was Rebuild by Design. Launched by the Presidential Hurricane Sandy Rebuilding Task Force in June 2013, the competition was charged with finding 'innovative, implementable proposals that promote resilience in the Sandy-affected region' (Rebuild by Design, 2013). Ten teams produced design proposals for sites in New York, New Jersey, and Connecticut. They envisioned, among them, the 'BIG U', protective landscapes and buildings along lower Manhattan (by the BIG team) and 'living breakwaters' of oysters and shellfish along the eastern shore of Staten Island (by the SCAPE team).

In January 2013, massive floods hit Jakarta, Indonesia, considered among the most vulnerable cities to climate change. This followed severe inundations in 1996, 2002, and 2007. The floods bolstered initiatives to address the city's failing infrastructure, including projects to dredge and widen waterways and evict residents of informal *kampung* settlements along them. In April 2014, on a Jakarta visit, then-Dutch infrastructure and environment minister Melanie Schultz announced the National Capital Integrated Coastal Development (NCICD) masterplan. Known as the Giant Sea Wall, it proposes a new city for 1.5 million people on reclaimed land in the Jakarta Bay. Shaped like the Garuda, the mythical bird that is Indonesia's national symbol, the plan promises to solve flooding, function as a freshwater reservoir, and provide a modern waterfront and central business district.

Cursory studies of Rebuild by Design and the Giant Sea Wall reveal extensive Dutch involvement. Rebuild by Design principal Henk Ovink was formerly the Netherlands director general of spatial planning and water affairs. Participating teams prominently featured Dutch designers and engineers.[2] The cause of the 2007 Jakarta floods, attributed to severe land subsidence, was determined in part by Dutch research institute Deltares. The NCICD masterplan, funded by the Dutch government, is authored primarily by Dutch engineering, design, and development firms.[3] The triangulation was completed when, in September 2014, the Netherlands Water Partnership organised a delegation from Indonesia to visit New York and New Orleans to learn about adaptation projects (Connecting Delta Cities, 2014).

How might we understand the relationships between actors, institutions, and physical places of the Netherlands, renowned for spatial planning and water management, and sites of environmental challenges and adaptation initiatives in New York and Jakarta? Urban researchers have long emphasised interconnectivities of capital and information across geographic scales (Friedmann, 1986; Sassen, 1991) and the material and social conditions of networked societies (Castells, 1996). Environmental researchers recognise emerging cross-scalar institutions of global climate governance (Bulkeley et al., 2014). And yet, much discourse around urban climate change adaptation, developed on the bases of case studies, comparisons, and surveys, still approaches the city as a distinct, analytically bounded entity.

Among the primary contributions of urban political ecology (UPE) scholarship includes the conceptualisation of cities as socio-natural, that is, an outcome of contested metabolic processes (Swyngedouw, 1996; Heynen et al., 2006; Heynen, 2014; see also Keil, 2003, 2005), and a challenge to analytical views of cities as distinct and bounded (Angelo and Wachsmuth, 2015). In various ways, UPE scholarship has pushed urban researchers to look deeper and more historically into and more expansively about interconnected urban processes, including the literal cores and pipes of cities and their far-flung extensions (see Gandy, 2002; Kaika, 2005). This chapter builds on my research on the 'relational geographies' of global and urban interconnectivities in the context of climate change and globalised urban development, tuned to the conceptual precepts of UPE. How do the emerging geographies of global and urban climate change responses inform and revise our understanding of urban socio-ecological change?

Exploring the spatial interconnections, international geopolitics, and their remaking in the context of climate change, I explain how a look at different set of sites and flows reframes and revises the notion of the socio-natural city. In particular: urban sociological change as not only historical and regional – expanding beyond the city per se – or even global, but more interconnected and distributed in relational ways across space and over time. The findings here also elaborate on more recent UPE debates on the understanding of scale and scope of political ecologies (see Tzaninis et al., Introduction in this volume; Gandy, 2021), more embodied (Heynen, 2014) and situated, heterogenous urban socio-natural processes (Lawhon et al.,

2014), as well as pointed questions about the concept of ecology in urban theory (Gandy, 2021).

In this chapter, I trace the development of emerging urban environmental plans, and propose the concept of a 'network formation' to understand relationships that bridge geographic scales and institutional levels. I argue that these emerging networks form in response to shifting political-economic and environmental conditions to mobilise ideas and influence across sites and boundaries. They build on economic relationships, including promises of economic growth, situational relationships, defined by historical bases of knowledge and power, and specific interface conditions, including narratives of culture and environmental urgency.

Urban adaptation to climate change

Climate change threats to urban centres include disrupted livelihoods in coastal areas from storm surges and sea level rise; the breakdown of infrastructure networks and critical services due to extreme weather events; health impacts in periods of extreme heat; and food insecurity linked to warming, drought, flooding, and uncertain precipitation (IPCC, 2014). Adaptation to climate change has been emphasised by the increase of climate-related disasters, inadequate action on mitigation, and the inclusion of the 'loss and damage agenda' in multilateral negotiations and courts (Khan and Roberts, 2013).

Research on urban adaptation, developed based on case studies of city vulnerabilities and responses (see Alam and Rabbani, 2007; Awuor et al., 2008; Dodman et al., 2010; Moser et al., 2010; Porio, 2011), is expanding, with varied, contested trajectories (Meerow and Mitchell, 2017; Shi and Moser, 2021). Scholars have conducted surveys of plans (Carmin et al., 2012a; Castán Broto and Bulkeley, 2013; Hughes, 2015). They have explored policy strategies and motivations (Carmin et al., 2012b), capacities of governance (Birkmann et al., 2010), policy guidelines and assessments (ACCCRN, 2013; Rosenzweig et al., 2011), and adaptation frameworks (Da Silva et al., 2012; Tyler and Moench, 2012). They assert the disparate vulnerabilities faced by poor residents (Dodman and Satterthwaite, 2008; Huq et al., 2007), the role of civil society (Chu et al., 2016), and issues of injustice in adaptation planning (Anguelovski et al., 2016; Shi et al., 2016).

Much of this research approaches the city as an analytically bounded territory, with complex yet cohesive governance structures and relationships of power. Social, spatial, and economic inequality feature heavily. But interconnections across space and processes of globalisation, urbanisation, and geopolitics are neglected.

This bounded emphasis is inadequate. Climate change causes and impacts traverse the global to the local, involving an array of governance entities. Nation-states engage in multilateral negotiations through the United Nations Framework Convention on Climate Change (UNFCCC), receiving input from a global scientific body, the Intergovernmental Panel on Climate Change (IPCC). Local governments respond to state regulations and learn and share through transnational municipal networks such as C40 Cities. Development agencies, lending institutions, and philanthropic and environmental organisations participate at each of these scales and levels, in a system of 'multilevel governance' (Bulkeley and Betsill, 2005, 2013).

Furthermore, we see the 'metropolitanisation' of climate change, where cities are viewed as a large part of the problem and a necessary part of the solution (Reid and Satterthwaite, 2007; Rosenzweig et al., 2010). Coalitions of economic and ecological interests in cities position themselves as the obvious actors and places to address climate threats. They propose interventions to secure and protect resource flows and economic zones, often resulting in infrastructural unevenness, deepening inequities, and 'ecological enclaves' (Hodson and Marvin, 2010). This heightens the ideological and material stakes of the city in climate change responses, making it critical to understand the broader relationships behind them.

Researchers of 'relational geographies' – cities as 'spatial formations' understood in relation to each other – respond to the problem of dynamic, interconnected sites, tracing urban space as flows and relationships beyond territory (Amin, 2004; also, Jacobs, 2012; Massey, 2011; Roy, 2009). Roy and Ong (2011: 3) point to the urban as a field of experimentation – a 'nexus of situated and transnational ideas, institutions, actors, and practices' – and to 'inter-referencing' – cities borrowing from and measuring by other cities. Peck (2011) asserts that policymaking processes are increasingly mobile – crossing horizontally across geographic scales, and vertically between institutional levels – and accelerating – shortening development cycles – a 'relational interpenetration of policy-making sites and activities'. And scholars stress the fragmentation of authority and shifts in responsibility to local governments and non-state entities, with subnational governments, NGOs, and firms experimenting with transnational environmental governance (Bulkeley et al., 2014).

These theories illuminate emerging global-urban processes and provide some conceptual specificity. But, besides the work on fragmentation, they have not engaged with the problems of climate change. Why, how, and under what conditions do these interconnections among sites and cities form?

Thinking relationally, Jacobs (2012) asserts, necessitates going beyond discerning simple presence (of policies and actors). Jacobs underscores the differences between topographical understandings of interconnectivities – the networked city, municipalities linked by institutions – and topological ones – city 'as mobility', crumbling aspects of physicality, territoriality, and distance. My analysis proceeds between these distinctions. It attends to interactions between urban processes that happen beyond and despite the territorial and political delineations of the city, but then reflect back on them. The 'city' as a construct remains, inasmuch as processes smaller and larger than the territorial unit are informed by its politics and its position as an object of imaging and contestation.

In tracing how and why networks form, I focus on relationships between biophysical environmental change and the institutional shifts motivated by political-economic change. In effect, I investigate multiple adaptations: on one level, the (institutional and physical) modifications directly in response to climate change, and, on another, the adaptations to reconfigured global and urban spaces of possibility. In particular, for the latter, I explore the emerging governance arrangements across scales – motivated both by global political-economic trajectories and environmental change – and changing ideologies and capacities of spatial interventions in cities.

In the following sections, I describe the formation of multiscalar, multilevel connectivities. I trace the inwards and outwards forces changing urban and environmental planning in the Netherlands. I then illustrate their links to initiatives in New York and Jakarta, two cities made exemplary by the strength of their interconnections within global networks, and the ways in which they reveal the globalising and relocalising efforts. I explain the motivations behind such mobilising, the conditions of their emergence, and their implications.

Multiscalar, multilevel interconnections

Nation-state to the world

The Netherlands has embarked on a concerted effort to promote its urban water expertise. The reasons for this are rooted in political-economic and ecological conditions at home and globally.

Almost a third of the country, reclaimed from peat bogs and shallow seas, is under sea level, with another third requiring protections from river flooding. Historically, it accomplished this reorganisation of land and water through the 'polder' system, a collective social, environmental, and spatial framework through which farmers contribute towards the drainage and maintenance of land. The first 'water boards' were formed in 1250, with increasingly extensive and centralised flood protection since. The 1953 North Sea Flood prompted the formation of the Delta Commission and the planning of the Delta Works – dikes, dams, and barriers to protect the most populated areas from a 10,000-year storm – culminating in the Maeslant storm barrier on the Nieuwe Waterweg, near Rotterdam, in 1997.

Planning for water management has been controlled by the national government in conjunction with regional water boards (Kuks, 2009). It has focused, historically, on hard infrastructure and hydrological engineering – 'dredge, drain, reclaim' (Stive and Vrijling, 2010). But economic restructuring and climate change have shifted this. First, economic liberalisation has led to the decentralisation of decision-making and more local, market-driven approaches to planning and development (Gerrits et al., 2012; Marshall, 2014). Restructuring coupled with the post-2008 recession has motivated agencies and firms to find different ways to fund projects.

Second, climate change poses new threats, including rising seas, warmer temperatures, increasing precipitation, and uncertainty in a system dependent on balance and predictability. A new Delta Commission (2008) proposed increasing protections of diked areas by a factor of ten, and also recommended more flexible responses. Approaches like 'Room for the River' – reconstructing selected dikes to allow occasional, localised flooding (Rijke et al., 2012) – and the 'sand engine' – using the power of wind and waves to help distribute sand – combine engineering with natural dynamics. Proponents call this 'building with nature' – still technocratic, yet ecological (De Vriend and Van Koningsveld, 2012).

On one level, many environmental projects are now conceived on a local scale. On another level, there is an outward shift toward international relationships. Rotterdam is a prime example of this dual outlook. It launched Rotterdam Climate Proof in 2008 – tasked with ensuring climate change resilience by 2025 – and promotes itself as a model for adaptation. The Rotterdam programme adheres to the Dutch emphasis on spatial planning. But it is strongly economic in strategy, emphasising liveability, attraction, and image (Rotterdam, 2013).

Rotterdam Climate Proof builds on the second International Architecture Biennale Rotterdam (IABR) in 2005, titled 'The Flood,' and the city's second Water Plan, with its vision of a 'water city' linking spatial development with water management (Rotterdam et al., 2007). These events reframed water from a problem to an opportunity.[4] Officials tout pilot projects such as garages with stormwater storage, floating pavilions, and 'water squares' – recreational spaces that protect against flooding from cloudbursts. They talk of 'serendipity' and 'coincidences' in explaining Rotterdam's visibility, but also of urging the Mayor to take on a larger role in national climate initiatives and writing their own narrative around the city's propensity for adaptability and change.[5]

City to globe

If urban spatial visions animate the emerging expertise of the Netherlands, they circulate globally through multiscalar, multilevel, and historically defined frameworks. Several entities play key roles in linking municipal programmes like Rotterdam's with international relationships. One is Connecting Delta Cities (CDC), a network of 13 cities (including Rotterdam, New York, and Jakarta), part of C40 Cities. Coordinated by a secretariat in the Rotterdam climate programme, it convenes member cities and serves as a depository of knowledge and best practices. CDC increases its reach by linking with larger international conferences, including the C40 summits.[6] Another is Deltares, formed in 2008 through a merger of public and private hydraulic and geotechnical entities. Deltares maintains its independent status while partly funded by the Netherlands Ministries of Economic Affairs, Agriculture and Innovation, and Foreign Affairs (Deltares, 2012). Its primary purpose is to produce knowledge for the Dutch government and private sector,[7] creating symbiotic relationships between businesses and policies. It has been involved in developments in Dubai and Singapore, and in the Dutch Dialogues planning sessions in New Orleans after Hurricane Katrina. A third is the Netherlands Water Partnership (NWP), consisting of 200 businesses, government agencies, and NGOs. NWP helps the Dutch water sector gain international impact by providing 'network, knowledge, visibility and influence' (NWP, n.d.). It enables consortia of members to enter 'markets in clusters, offering expertise as a one-stop-shop', and partners with Dutch agencies on national policy initiatives.

These entities, alongside the national and municipal programmes, provide capacities for city modelling, scientific research, and marketing. While Dutch planning is generally seen as centralised, these initiatives show a more reflexive, multiscalar operation. Shifting conditions are embraced as opportunities to rework Dutch socio-spatial relationships, and to retune planning and knowledge institutions to an increasingly climate-aware and alarmed global audience. The adaptations are in the systems of planning as well as the objects of planning. Flood protection that has largely focused on regional infrastructure, such as the Delta Works, now includes coordinated urban projects. In this shift, social and spatial adaptation is not just in response to climate change, it is towards new modes of urban environmental project making. Cities are not just protected by the dikes. They are a feature of the protection.

Nation-states to the cities

On a national level, the Netherlands has affirmed memorandums of understanding (MOUs) with both the United States and Indonesia. In March 2013, the Netherlands Ministry of Infrastructure and the Environment (IenM) and the US Department of Housing and Urban Development (HUD) agreed to a MOU for cooperation in sustainable urban development and water management, signed by Dutch Minister Schultz and then-HUD Secretary Shaun

Donovan in Washington, DC (US HUD and Netherlands IenM, 2013). Minister Schultz's April 2014 visit to Jakarta to announce the NCICD masterplan was also to reaffirm a 2012 MOU between the Netherlands and Indonesia on water and environment (Indonesia, Ministry of Public Works, 2014). A multitude of MOUs have been brokered between national and subnational governments and Dutch entities towards cooperation on sustainable urban development and water management.[8]

Dutch involvement in New York and Jakarta long predates these initiatives. Both cities served formative periods as Dutch colonial settlements – New York as Nieuw Amsterdam in 1624, Jakarta as Batavia in 1619. Jakarta continues to bear the physical, social, and institutional marks of three centuries of colonisation. In New York, colonial traces are more ceremonial. In these diverse contexts, present-day Dutch initiatives land with varying ease.

In both cities, a specific environment event marked a shift in longer relationships. In New York, post-Hurricane Sandy efforts including the Presidential Hurricane Sandy Rebuilding Task Force and the state-led NYS 2100 Commission (HSRTF, 2013; NYS 2100, 2013) followed ongoing initiatives such as PlaNYC (the sustainability plan) and the New York City Climate Change Adaptation Task Force (NYC, 2007, 2011; NPCC, 2010, 2015), as well as the *Rising Currents* exhibition at the Museum of Modern Art in 2010, exploring design responses to sea level rise. Launched by the presidential task force and overseen by HUD, Rebuild by Design's organisational entity and competition phase were privately funded, primarily by the Rockefeller Foundation. The implementation phase is backed by $930 million in federal Community Development Block Grants – Disaster Recovery (CDBG-DR). This operationally links an international, climate change-focused design competition with federal funding.[9]

This arrangement empowered HUD officials to play a greater role in urban resilience conversations at local and international levels, while the promise of federal funds motivated local government cooperation and enthusiasm.[10] It also enabled a fluency and flexibility not always found in federal programmes. The Rockefeller Foundation had already conducted workshops and published papers on urban resilience and funded the Asian Cities Climate Change Resilience Network (ACCCRN) since 2008. Pre-existing relationships between the philanthropic organisation and HUD's leadership enabled rapid response in the wake of the storm.[11]

The fluency of globally circulating ideas then encounters the relative obduracy of local politics and fragmented governance. Rebuild by Design aspired to be regional and multilevel in scope, providing the planning and protection evident in the Dutch examples. But CDBG funds are targeted for particular localities, implemented by local and state authorities. There was cooperation but not formal implementation mechanisms between Rebuild by Design and these localities. Furthermore, Hurricane Sandy had exposed the region's disparate vulnerability. Systemic inequities of poverty, joblessness, and access to housing and services predated the storm and were accentuated in its wake – what researchers have called a 'tale of two Sandys' (SRL, 2013). Rebuild by Design's participatory process assuaged some local community concerns. But, in some ways, it postponed the discontent. Notably, in late 2014, community organisers in the Lower East Side in Manhattan questioned the prioritising of specific areas in the implementation plan.[12] In mid-2017, four years since its start, the winning projects were variously making their way through local public comment and tendering processes.

Dutch involvement in Jakarta environmental planning experienced a turning point after the 2007 floods. A flood hazard mapping study by Deltares concluded that severe land subsidence – at rates up to 12cm per year – was exacerbating flooding (Brinkman and Hartman, 2009; Abidin et al., 2011). These findings led to the Jakarta Coastal Defence Strategy (JCDS), conducted jointly by the Dutch and Indonesians (Indonesia, Ministry of Public Works, 2011). It detailed hydrological conditions, social and economic ties, infrastructural capacities, and governance roles, and outlined strategies for floodwalls in the Jakarta Bay.

The JCDS findings became the basis of the NCICD masterplan (Indonesia MENKO, 2014). Often billed as a climate change and sea level rise plan, the Giant Sea Wall is more a 'sinking city' plan (Goh, 2019), the 'wings' of the seawall creating massive retention ponds designed to enable the drainage of rivers and canals and counter the effects of subsidence. This strategy is somewhat reflective of the Netherlands, where much of the population lives below sea level, protected by dikes, canals, and pumps. But while planners there have been advocating for smaller scale and ecologically attuned projects, the Giant Sea Wall harks back to classic, 'hard' models of Dutch planning.

Broadly, the NCICD takes technical lessons from the JCDS, and creates an urban development plan – in which the infrastructural 'wall' is privately funded by leasable reclaimed land. The masterplan has provoked pitched debate about large-scale development, environmental protection, and social inequality. Environmentalists express concern about its impact on ecological systems and fisheries. Activists question the masterplan's claim of knowing what the real problem is and presupposing a solution that, once again, downplays or neglects the concerns of poor urban residents for their livelihoods and community networks.[13]

Global-urban network

We see a multiscalar, multilevel network – through which capital, knowledge, and influence flow. In contrast to a static view defined by stable

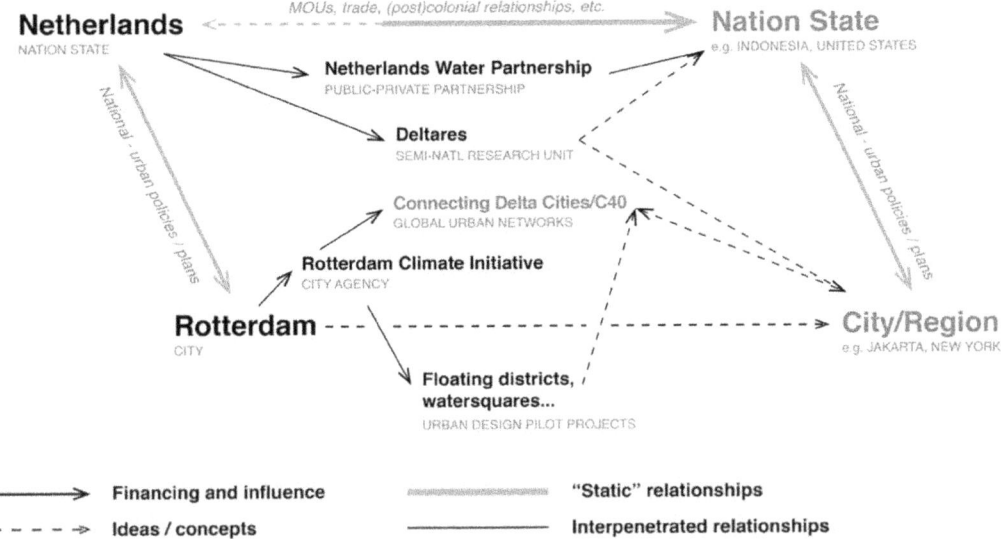

Figure 12.1 Diagram of global-urban networks.

external state relationships and internal national policies, and bounded, cohesive cities, a relational view reveals connections and interpenetrations across scales and levels (Figure 12.1). This network is driven and defined by interrelated factors: economic relationships, historically defined situational relationships, and a set of interface conditions.

Economic relationships

Economic development, primarily privatised urban development, underpins Dutch involvement and investment in Jakarta and New York. The Netherlands' 'top sectors', national priority sectors, include water, creative industries, technology, and logistics (Netherlands EZK, 2016). Planning for water is a key export for which the Dutch hold undeniable pedigree. Economic conditions at home have motivated the emphasis on global relationships. Climate change has only made more urgent the need for solutions. Water is a way for the Dutch to brand themselves to the world – at once economic development and foreign policy.

For Indonesia, Dutch officials are eager to see a relationship characterised by postcolonial influence and development aid transition into something more reciprocal in economic exchange – if not necessarily more equal in political power. The opportunities transcend Indonesian borders. A high-profile development in Jakarta constitutes a scaffold onto which Dutch firms can establish themselves in expanding regional markets. According to a NWP official, the Giant Sea Wall serves as a showcase for the Dutch water sector to establish their expertise and be seen as a trustworthy partner especially for private investors and development officials in other Asian cities.[14]

For Rebuild by Design in New York, the federal funds for winning proposals – a fraction of the projected costs – are meant to spur private investment. Participation in the initiative reinforces Dutch influence and expertise. This could enable the consolidation of work in the region and country by transnational engineering and project management firms such as Arcadis (involved in three of ten finalist teams). But it also broaches new roles for small firms such as De Urbanisten, designer of the Rotterdam water squares. Its participation in Rebuild by Design has opened new opportunities across the Atlantic.[15] This success, in turn, positions its designs, prominently featured in Rotterdam's climate programme and Dutch water sector marketing, within a global discourse on Dutch creative industries and environmental planning.

Situational relationships

These economic relationships highlight associated situational ones, involving historically determined and evolving geopolitical power relationships. Minister Schultz, unveiling the NCICD masterplan in Jakarta, said, 'We Dutch feel very much at home here. We feel *senang* [at ease]' (Netherlands, 2014), a remarkable statement in a former colony. The Giant Sea Wall, in many ways, conforms to traditional notions of international development, involving top-down planning, Western expertise, and a technocratic approach. Relating economic development and private investment with imminent catastrophe, it is a kind of environment-induced disaster capitalism – perhaps a projective 'shock doctrine', what Klein (2007) has called efforts to secure private profits around disasters and wars. In Indonesia, where Deltares's office is embedded in the public works ministry, these processes are empowered by persistent postcolonial ties.

And yet, the NWP official describes the struggle of proving that they are the trusted long-term partners when Korean and Japanese companies are promising solutions for less money. The NCICD may be a 'showcase', but its implementation has continually been in flux and doubt. In late 2015, a trilateral letter of intent was signed by Indonesia, South Korea, and the Netherlands to study joint implementation of the NCICD. In mid-2016, progress had slowed due to uncertainty around governance support in Indonesia.[16] In 2017, a Deltares representative stated that the plan would no longer involve the ambitious Garuda landform, possibly relying on existing, tendered reclamation projects[17] – a decision later echoed by a government official.[18] While postcolonial influence continues to define the terms of environmental vulnerabilities and urban governance, it is not a sufficient determinant of success.

In the US, such explicit appeals are tempered by a sense of mutuality – perhaps a more certain feeling of being 'at ease'. US HUD Secretary Shaun Donovan met Henk Ovink while touring the Netherlands to observe water infrastructure after Hurricane Sandy. Ovink suggested to Donovan that he help with the presidential task force effort.[19] Ovink credits his background in spatial planning and policy, experience in public and private sectors, academic ties, and skills in building coalitions and alliances as key factors in making him the 'ideal partner' for the US.[20]

The extensive involvement of Dutch firms in New York preceded Hurricane Sandy. However, the accelerated activity after Sandy illustrates the manoeuvrings of large firms like Arcadis in a scenario of environmental risk. At a conference in 2014, an Arcadis planner recounted how the firm was central to the climate change work precipitated by Sandy. The panel moderator, a New York-based climate change scientist, corrected him, calling it a 'mischaracterisation' to suggest that little was happening in the city before the storm.[21]

Ovink, now essentially an ambassador with dual roles – for Rebuild by Design and the Dutch water sector – sees it diplomatically. For him, the competition created a process through which US-based engineers and designers could learn about comprehensive planning and water management, and those from the Netherlands could understand regionalism, fragmented governance, and community engagement differently.[22]

In Indonesia, long-time Dutch governmental and institutional relationships guide a process of problem-framing and solution-making. In the US, transnational corporate and diplomatic activities are institutionally boosted after a disaster.

Interface conditions

Economic and situational relationships are reinforced by interface conditions – specific characteristics or the dynamic between the sites or actors – including cultural narratives and invocations of urgency.

The origin story of Dutch water expertise is rehearsed on multiple levels. In Rotterdam, officials talk of writing their own narrative. In public speeches worldwide, Henk Ovink recounts the development of the Netherlands' culture of living with water, promoting its relevance for other places confronting risk (although its 800 years of societal learning is not on offer). These narratives are effective. An evaluation of the first phase of Rebuild by Design found that: first, HUD Secretary Donovan's leadership and the commitment of federal funds were critical motivators, and second, so was

Ovink's 'charisma and vision' (Urban Institute, 2014). Sustaining partnerships is seen as critical in New York as it is in Jakarta.

While the overall image of globalising Dutch water is one of coherence and organisation, friction appears around specific initiatives. Critics of the Giant Sea Wall in Jakarta express fears of a 'black lagoon' – sewage-laden canals draining into the proposed catchment ponds. A Dutch hydrologist acknowledges these concerns and opines that closing off the wall might be considered a last resort. He did not foreclose alternatives, such as Room for the River-like approaches, but asserted that the problems and potential solutions should be understood as distinctly Indonesian.[23] This sentiment is prevalent among Dutch individuals, who are mindful of past criticisms.[24] But the most ambitious version of the NCICD was carried to its launch, despite the concerns, propelled by promises of modernisation, invocations of urgency by Dutch research reports and public statements about the sinking city, and the acquiescence of local officials. A Jakarta city official expressed doubt that they could find another option to solve the flooding.[25]

Climate change researchers have pointed to 'adaptation regimes' (Paprocki, 2018) and 'resilience machines' (Davoudi et al., 2019). The 'machine-like', systemic characteristics are ascribed to differential power relationships, appeals of threats and uncertain futures, and dominant modes of development. These factors are apparent in Jakarta: there is evident threat, and a draw towards modernisation and infrastructural fixes; there are few alternatives to consider, and Dutch influence and long-term power relationships and urban development dynamics are hard to shake. In New York, processes are less informed by historical power relationships, and more by an aligned vision of new urban futures promoted alike by government agencies, transnational corporations, and global philanthropies. Systemic, structural factors hold firm, propelled by economic-ecological shifts on a global scale. But they are enabled by situational and specific, conditional relationships.

Network formation

The global-urban network reveals relationalities that are cross-site and multiscalar. On one level, the motivations behind the initiatives in New York and Jakarta cannot be fully understood without relational tracings to sociospatial changes in the Netherlands. On another level, the Dutch engagements in New York and Jakarta are illuminated by relational distinction from the other; generalised forces inflected to meld to historically defined socio-spatial conditions. Seeing each site from the others shows how shifting,

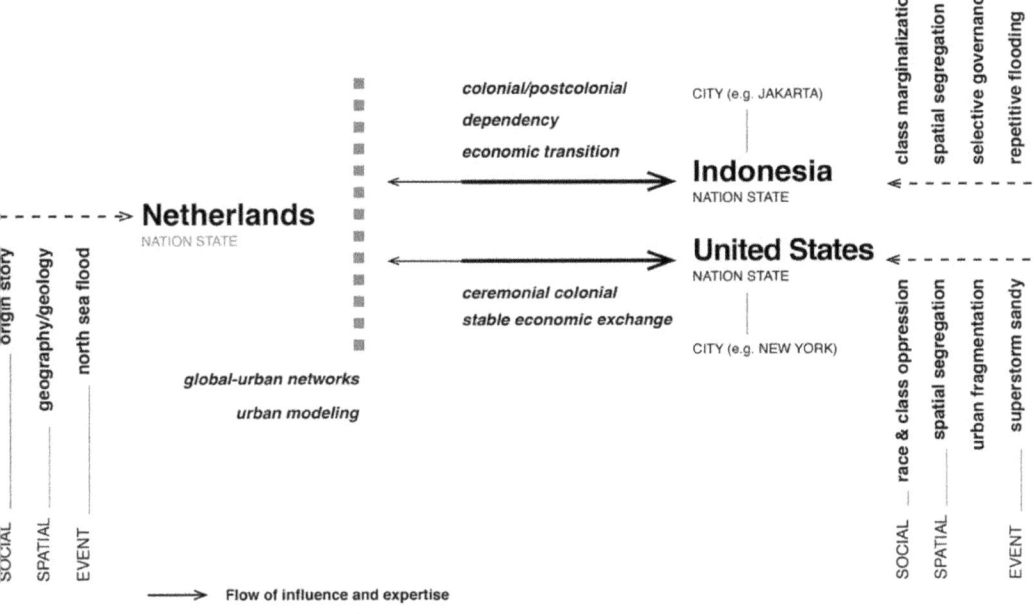

Figure 12.2 Diagram of conceptual interfaces, relationships, and formations.

distinct political economic conditions guide the terms of engagement and the trajectory of the relationships.

New York, Jakarta, and Rotterdam comprise a sample of dynamic global phenomena – a *network formation*. This concept offers a way to see and understand the terms of such interconnected processes, and to categorise a set of relationships – not to denote a concrete and unique, or exclusive, network. Nations like the Netherlands and cities such as Rotterdam – with a convincing origin story, expertise pedigree, and internal and external motivators – cities like Jakarta – in rapidly growing economies facing environmental and social challenges – and cities like New York – already a central node in global economic flows, contemplating new urban futures – represent a distinct and exemplary formation (Figure 12.2). Rotterdam, here, functions as a *reflexive* site – the site itself, and the relationship between it and other sites, sharpening the analysis of each of the strategies, and the comprehension of the whole.

This view illustrates the ways in which national and corporate strategies might be operationalised through cities. The Netherlands priority sectors are foregrounded by urban projects, municipal planning, and a web of institutions – including Connecting Delta Cities, a transnational municipal network, and Deltares, a research institute given the latitude to function as a global consultant, with public ties and private opportunities. These networks and entities, conceptually, pull the global and urban together. Besides creating symbiotic links across scales, they enable local, physical interventions such as the water square in Rotterdam to play an outsize role in international discourse, and in national and corporate strategic market making.

Recognition of the broader network is critical in light of prevalent assertions about the 'obvious' importance of cities, and other invocations of the 'Urban Age' (Burdett and Sudjic, 2007), that veil a large part of the motivations behind cities' environmental project-making. These findings reaffirm yet complicate assertions about the 'metropolitanisation' of climate change. We should not too quickly accept the discourse of cities as sole or primary actors, even if we agree with the precept of strategic security and economic interests as their key drivers. We should be attendant to the operations of cities as part of broader agendas, and the extent to which city-centric emphases are driven by self-reinforcing urban development visions.

Circulating ideas reflect concrete spaces. In the context of climate change and crises, the networks mobilise and transform ideas about the spaces of society and water, bringing the biophysical workings of infrastructure and hydrology into the realm of interconnected global economic flows. It is a sort of socio-hydrological addendum to Castells's 'space of flows' – ideas and images about actual/material flows of water join the organisational processes of capital, information, and technology.

Seeing the network in formation also broaches specific possibilities for understanding alternative ideas and visions. These findings raise a critical line of questions. Globally circulating ideas are not so free-flowing on the ground and tend to be deformed and refracted in response to local political-economic and spatial conditions. In each site, historical trajectories and geographic conditions have shaped social and environmental marginalisation and contesting visions of urban futures. Protests arising from this contestation have often taken form against perceivable unequal distribution of resources or direct threats of displacement and dispossession. Have urban spatial protest movements reorganised themselves in response to global-urban networks? And if so, how have the concerns around locally and materially specific inequities been transposed to larger geographic scales and higher governance levels of planning?

Conclusion

I have traced the development of a kind of global-urban environmental project-making. In terms of understanding places, it is neither comparative nor singular. Each site helps to reveal the others. Tracing the formation of global-urban networks transcends bounded, city-centric emphases in urban climate change research. It explains the spatial and temporal interconnections within and across sites, and the ways in which urban spatial interventions operate within broader political economies and ecologies.

These findings reframe and elaborate on debates in urban political ecology in a number of ways. In a world of climate-changed flows, processes of urban socio-natural change are further mediated and reconstituted through global-urban formations involving intertwined global political-economic and biophysical-environmental change, and historically determined and situated relationships and interface conditions. The findings here highlight the transhistorical and relational constitution of urban socio-ecologies – how power relationships manifest across space and over time. They show how situated, positional, and indeed embodied struggles are interwoven with generalised political economic and environmental processes. And they suggest how both the knowledge systems of and realities of biophysical, ecological limits in a world facing a climate emergency are invoked and wielded as part of contested urban socio-ecological struggles.

The formations explored here, and permutations thereof, are emerging as the crucial framework through which environmental projects are conceived and justified. I have illustrated an approach to understanding the social, spatial, and event-driven factors behind the claims on expertise and the formation of risk, and as well how different historical relationships and interfaces impact such factors. As researchers continue studying how cities respond to changing environmental and geopolitical conditions, we will need to define further new conceptual categories for the interfaces, the relationships, and the types of risk and expertise formation within networks such as this one.

Notes

1 This is part of a larger study of the urban spatial politics of climate change adaptation, involving field visits, participant observation, approximately 45 interviews with officials, consultants, and organisers in Southeast Asia, US, and Netherlands, and review of 35 documents, between 2013 and 2019 (Goh, 2021). This chapter revises and elaborates Goh (2020).
2 Six of ten finalists were selected to receive implementation funds (a seventh was added later). Five of seven funded proposals have Dutch involvement. On the BIG team's proposal for Manhattan, One Architecture (design) and Arcadis (engineering/project management); Interboro team's proposal for Nassau County South Shore, Bosch Slabbers (landscape/urban design), Deltares (research), H+N+S (landscape architecture), Palmbout (urban design), and TU Delft; MIT CAU+ZUS+URBANISTEN team's proposal for Meadowlands, NJ, ZUS and De Urbanisten (design), Deltares, and 75B (graphics); OMA team's

proposal for Hoboken, NJ, OMA (architecture) and Royal Haskoning DHV (engineering/project management); WB unabridged w/ Yale ARCADIS team's proposal for Bridgeport, CT, Arcadis. (No explicit Dutch firm involvement on PennDesign/OLIN and SCAPE teams.) Among the other three finalist teams were West 8 and Arcadis on the WXY/WEST 8 team. (Data from Rebuild By Design and firm material, May 2015.)

3 Including, on the masterplan team: Witteveen+Bos (engineering/consulting), Grontmij (engineering, now Sweco), Kuiper Compagnons (urban/landscape design), Ecorys (economic/social research), Triple-A, Deltares; in the programme management unit: Royal Haskoning (engineering/management), Rebel Group (economic advising), UNESCO-IHE (water education).
4 Manager of Rotterdam Climate Proof, interview by the author, Rotterdam, 1 October 2014.
5 Advisor, Water Department of Rotterdam, interview by the author, Rotterdam, 1 October 2014.
6 Advisor, Rotterdam Climate Proof, email correspondence with the author, 19 August 2015.
7 Representative, Deltares, interview by the author, Jakarta, 11 July 2014.
8 The Netherlands has signed MOUs with Mexico, Egypt, Bangladesh, Colombia, Indonesia, and the US on water management and climate change adaptation. There are numerous subnational MOUs between Dutch entities and municipalities and agencies in countries such as Singapore, Vietnam, South Africa, and India (see www.netherlandswaterpartnership.com and www.dutchwatersector.com, accessed 12 August 2022).
9 The format has inspired numerous initiatives including the Changing Course competition in New Orleans; the National Disaster Resilience Competition; and the Global Resilience Partnership.
10 Official, HUD, interview by the author, Washington, DC, 16 June 2014.
11 Senior representative, Rockefeller Foundation, interview by the author, New York, 16 June 2014.
12 Activist, LES Ready!, interview by the author, New York, 18 December 2014.
13 Housing activist and urban researcher, interview by the author, Jakarta, 10 July 2014.
14 Representative, Netherlands Water Partnership, interview by the author, The Hague, 30 September 2014.
15 Director, De Urbanisten, interview by the author, Rotterdam, 30 June 2014.
16 Representative, Netherlands Water Partnership, interview by the author, The Hague, 14 July 2016.
17 Presentation at Tarumanagara University, Jakarta, 22 May 2017, reiterated in email correspondence, 18 July 2017.
18 See Anya and Wijaya (2017).
19 See Shorto (2014).
20 Teleconference interview by the author, 24 November 2014.
21 Session titled 'Managing urban water under changing climate conditions', at the Deltas in Times of Climate Change II conference, Rotterdam, 26 September 2014.

22 Interview by the author, 24 November 2014.
23 Representative, Deltares, interview by the author, Jakarta, 11 July 2014.
24 Also conveyed by a landscape architect involved with the project, interview by the author, Rotterdam, 1 October 2014.
25 Official, Jakarta Climate Change Task Force, interview by the author, Jakarta, 16 July 2014.

References

Abidin, H.Z., H. Andreas, I. Gumilar, Y. Fukuda, Y.E. Pohan, and T. Deguchi. 2011. Land subsidence of Jakarta (Indonesia) and its relation with urban development. *Natural Hazards* 59(3): 1753–71.
ACCCRN (Asian Cities Climate Change Resilience Network). 2013. ACCCRN city projects. Bangkok, Thailand: Rockefeller Foundation, Asia Office. http://hatyaicityclimate.org/upload/forum/ACCCRNCitiesProjectCatalogueHatyai.pdf, accessed 12 August 2022.
Alam, M. and M.D.G. Rabbani. 2007. Vulnerabilities and responses to climate change for Dhaka. *Environment and Urbanization* 19(1): 81–97.
Amin, A. 2004. Regions unbound: Towards a new politics of place. *Geografiska Annaler: Series B, Human Geography* 86(1): 33–44.
Angelo, H. and D. Wachsmuth. 2015. Urbanizing urban political ecology: A critique of methodological cityism. *International Journal of Urban and Regional Research* 39(1): 16–27.
Anguelovski, I., L. Shi, E. Chu, D. Gallagher, K. Goh, Z. Lamb, K. Reeve, and H. Teicher. 2016. Equity impacts of urban land use planning for climate adaptation: Critical perspectives from the Global North and South. *Journal of Planning Education and Research* 36(3): 333–48.
Anya, A. and C.A. Wijaya. 2017. Govt cancels great Garuda seawall. *The Jakarta Post*, 11 December.
Awuor, C.B., V.A. Orindi, and A.O. Adwera. 2008. Climate change and coastal cities: The case of Mombasa, Kenya. *Environment and Urbanization* 20(1): 231–42.
Birkmann, J., M. Garschagen, F. Kraas, and N. Quang. 2010. Adaptive urban governance: New challenges for the second generation of urban adaptation strategies to climate change. *Sustainability Science* 5(2): 185–206.
Brinkman, J.J. and M. Hartman. 2009. Jakarta flood hazard mapping framework. http://edepot.wur.nl/140833, accessed 12 August 2022.
Bulkeley, H. and M. Betsill. 2005. Rethinking sustainable cities: Multilevel governance and the 'urban' politics of climate change. *Environmental Politics* 14(1): 42–63.
Bulkeley, H. and M. Betsill. 2013. Revisiting the urban politics of climate change. *Environmental Politics* 22(1): 136–54.
Bulkeley, H., L.B. Andonova, M.M. Betsill, D. Compagnon, T. Hale, M.J. Hoffman, P. Newell, M. Paterson, C. Roger, and S.D. Vandeveer. 2014. *Transnational climate change governance*. New York: Cambridge University Press.
Burdett, R. and D. Sudjic (eds.). 2007. *The endless city: The Urban Age Project by the London School of Economics and Deutsche Bank's Alfred Herrhausen Society*. London: Phaidon.

Carmin, J., N. Nadkarni, and C. Rhie. 2012a. *Progress and challenges in urban climate adaptation planning: Results of a global survey.* Cambridge, MA: MIT Press.

Carmin, J., I. Anguelovski, and D. Roberts. 2012b. Urban climate adaptation in the Global South planning in an emerging policy domain. *Journal of Planning Education and Research* 32(1): 18–32.

Castán Broto, V. and H. Bulkeley. 2013. A survey of urban climate change experiments in 100 cities. *Global Environmental Change* 23(1): 92–102.

Castells, M. 1996. *The rise of the network society.* Cambridge, MA: Blackwell Publishers.

Chu, E., I. Anguelovski, and J. Carmin. 2016. Inclusive approaches to urban climate adaptation planning and implementation in the Global South. *Climate Policy* 16(3): 372–92.

Connecting Delta Cities. 2014. Indonesian officials meet experts on US East Coast. *Connecting Delta Cities*, 2 September. www.deltacities.com/newsletter/indonesian-officials-meet-experts-on-us-east-coast?news_id=65, accessed 12 August 2022.

Da Silva, J., S. Kernaghan, and A. Luque. 2012. A systems approach to meeting the challenges of urban climate change. *International Journal of Urban Sustainable Development* 4(2): 125–45.

Davoudi, S., J. Lawrence, and J. Bohland. 2019. Anatomy of the resilience machine. In J. Bohland, S. Davoudi, and J. Lawrence (eds.), *The resilience machine*. Abingdon, Oxon; New York: Routledge pp. 12–28.

De Vriend, H. and M. Van Koningsveld. 2012. *Building with nature: Thinking, acting and interacting differently.* Dordrecht: Ecoshape, Building with Nature.

Delta Commission. 2008. *Working together with water: A living land builds for its future – findings of the Deltacommissie 2008, summary and conclusions.* The Hague: Delta Commission. www.deltacommissie.com/doc/deltareport_full.pdf, accessed 12 August 2022.

Deltares. 2012. *Deltares 2.0: Strategic plan 2012–2015.* Delft, Netherlands: Deltares. www.deltares.nl/app/uploads/2015/02/Deltares-Strategic-Plan-Def-ENG.pdf, accessed 12 August 2022.

Dodman, D. and D. Satterthwaite. 2008. Institutional capacity, climate change adaptation and the urban poor. *IDS Bulletin* 39(4): 67–74.

Dodman, D., D. Mitlin, and J.R. Co. 2010. Victims to victors, disasters to opportunities: Community-driven responses to climate change in the Philippines. *International Development Planning Review* 32(1): 1–26.

Friedmann, J. 1986. The world city hypothesis. *Development and Change* 17(1): 69–83.

Gandy, M. 2002. *Concrete and clay: Reworking nature in New York City.* Cambridge, MA: MIT Press.

Gandy, M. 2021. Urban political ecology: A critical reconfiguration. *Progress in Human Geography.* https://doi.org/10.1177/03091325211040553

Gerrits, L., W. Rauws, and G. de Roo. 2012. Dutch spatial planning policies in transition. *Planning Theory & Practice* 13(2): 336–41.

Goh, K. 2019. Urban waterscapes: The hydro-politics of flooding in a sinking city. *International Journal of Urban and Regional Research* 43(2): 250–72.

Goh, K. 2020. Flows in formation: The global-urban networks of climate change adaptation. *Urban Studies* 57(11): 2222–40.

Goh, K. 2021. *Form and flow: The spatial politics of urban resilience and climate justice.* Cambridge, MA: MIT Press.

Heynen, N. 2014. Urban political ecology I: The urban century. *Progress in Human Geography* 38(4): 598–604.
Heynen, N., M. Kaika, and E. Swyngedouw. 2006. Urban political ecology: Politicizing the production of urban natures. In N. Heynen, M. Kaika, and E. Swyngedouw (eds.), *In the nature of cities: Urban political ecology and the politics of urban metabolism*. London and New York: Routledge, pp. 609–19.
Hodson, M. and S. Marvin. 2010. *World cities and climate change: Producing urban ecological security*. Maidenhead and New York: Open University Press.
HSRTF (Hurricane Sandy Rebuilding Task Force). 2013. Hurricane Sandy rebuilding strategy: Stronger communities, a resilient region. http://portal.hud.gov/hudportal/documents/huddoc?id=HSRebuildingStrategy.pdf, accessed 12 August 2022.
Hughes, S. 2015. A meta-analysis of urban climate change adaptation planning in the US. *Urban Climate* 14: 17–29.
Huq, S., S. Kovats, H. Reid, and D. Satterthwaite. 2007. Editorial: Reducing risks to cities from disasters and climate change. *Environment and Urbanization* 19(1): 3–15.
Indonesia MENKO (Coordinating Ministry for Economic Affairs). 2014. National Capital Integrated Coastal Development Master Plan. http://ncicd.com/wp-content/uploads/2014/10/MP-final-NCICD-LR.pdf, accessed 12 August 2022.
Indonesia, Ministry of Public Works. 2011. Jakarta Coastal Defence Strategy (JCDS). Jakarta, Indonesia: Indonesia, Ministry of Public Works.
Indonesia, Ministry of Public Works. 2014. Kerjasama Indonesia Dan Belanda Bidang Air Dan Lingkungan. PU-Net, 1 April. www.pu.go.id/berita/view/10158/kerjasama-indonesia-dan-belanda-bidang-air-dan-lingkungan, accessed 12 August 2022.
IPCC. 2014. *Climate change 2014: Synthesis report. Contribution of Working Groups I, II and III to the Fifth Assessment Report of the Intergovernmental Panel on Climate Change*. Core writing team, R.K. Pachauri and L.A. Meyer (eds.). Geneva, Switzerland: IPCC. www.ipcc.ch/report/ar5/syr/, accessed 12 August 2022.
Jacobs, J.M. 2012. Urban geographies I: Still thinking cities relationally. *Progress in Human Geography* 36(3): 412–22.
Kaika, M. 2005. *City of flows: Modernity, nature, and the city*. New York: Routledge.
Keil, R. 2003. Progress report – urban political ecology. *Urban Geography* 24(8): 723–38.
Keil, R. 2005. Progress report – urban political ecology. *Urban Geography* 26(7): 640–51.
Khan, M.R. and J.T. Roberts. 2013. Adaptation and international climate policy. *Wiley Interdisciplinary Reviews: Climate Change* 4(3): 171–89.
Klein, N. 2007. *The shock doctrine: The rise of disaster capitalism*. Toronto: Alfred A. Knopf Canada.
Kuks, S.M.M. 2009. Institutional evolution of the Dutch Water Board model. In S. Reinhard and H. Folmer (eds.), *Water policy in the Netherlands: Integrated management in a densely populated delta*. Washington, DC: Resources for the Future, pp. 155–70.
Lawhon, M., H. Ernstson, and J. Silver. 2014. Provincializing urban political ecology: Towards a situated UPE through African urbanism. *Antipode* 46(2): 497–516.
Marshall, T. 2014. Infrastructure futures and spatial planning: Lessons from France, the Netherlands, Spain and the UK. *Progress in Planning* 89: 1–38.
Massey, D. 2011. A counterhegemonic relationality of place. In E. McCann and K. Ward (eds.), *Mobile urbanism: Cities and policymaking in the global age*. Minneapolis, MN: University of Minnesota Press, pp. 1–14.

Meerow, S. and C.L. Mitchell. 2017. Weathering the storm: The politics of urban climate change adaptation planning. *Environment and Planning A* 49(11): 2619–27.

Moser, C., S. Georgieva, A. Norton, and A. Stein. 2010. Pro-poor adaptation to climate change in urban centers: Case studies of vulnerability and resilience in Kenya and Nicaragua. Washington, DC: World Bank.

Netherlands, Government of. 2014. Speech by Melanie Schultz, at the Round Table on Coastal Development, Borobodur Hotel, Jakarta, Toespraak, Rijksoverheid. Government of the Netherlands, 2 April. www.rijksoverheid.nl/documenten-en-publicaties/toespraken/2014/04/02/speech-for-melanie-schultz-at-the-round-table-on-coastal-development-borobodur-hotel-jakarta.html, accessed 12 August 2022.

Netherlands EZK (Ministry of Economic Affairs and Climate Policy). 2016. Top sectors in the Netherlands. Ministerie van Economische Zaken en Klimaat. www.topsectoren.nl/publicaties/brochures/2016/03/16/hoe-en-waarom-topsector-engels, accessed 12 August 2022.

NPCC (New York City Panel on Climate Change). 2010. Climate change adaptation in New York City: Building a risk management response. *Annals of the New York Academy of Sciences* 1196(1): 1–354.

NPCC (New York City Panel on Climate Change). 2015. Building the knowledge base for climate resiliency: New York City Panel on Climate Change 2015 report. *Annals of the New York Academy of Sciences* 1336 (1): 1–150.

NWP (Netherlands Water Partnership). n.d. Wat is NWP. NWP: Meer impact in het Buitenland. www.nwp.nl/over-nwp/wat-is-nwp, accessed 12 August 2022.

NYC (New York, City of). 2007. PlaNYC: A greener, greater New York. New York, NY: Office of the Mayor. www.nyc.gov/html/planyc/downloads/pdf/publications/full_report_2007.pdf, accessed 12 August 2022.

NYC (New York, City of). 2011. PlaNYC: A greener, greater New York – update April 2011. New York, NY: Office of the Mayor. www.nyc.gov/html/planyc2030/html/theplan/the-plan.shtml, accessed 12 August 2022.

NYS 2100 Commission. 2013. Recommendations to improve the strength and resilience of the Empire State's infrastructure. www.governor.ny.gov/sites/governor.ny.gov/files/archive/assets/documents/NYS2100.pdf, accessed 12 August 2022.

Paprocki, K. 2018. Threatening dystopias: Development and adaptation regimes in Bangladesh. *Annals of the American Association of Geographers* 108(4): 955–73.

Peck, J. 2011. Geographies of policy: From transfer-diffusion to mobility-mutation. *Progress in Human Geography* 35(6): 773–97.

Porio, E. 2011. Vulnerability, adaptation, and resilience to floods and climate change-related risks among marginal, riverine communities in metro Manila. *Asian Journal of Social Science* 39(4): 425–45.

Rebuild by Design. 2013. *Promoting resilience post-Sandy through innovative planning and design*. Rebuild by Design. http://portal.hud.gov/hudportal/documents/huddoc?id=REBUILDBYDESIGNBrief.pdf, accessed 12 August 2022.

Reid, H. and D. Satterthwaite. 2007. Climate change and cities: Why urban agendas are central to adaptation and mitigation. Sustainable Development Opinion, December. http://pubs.iied.org/pdfs/17025IIED.pdf, accessed 12 August 2022.

Rijke, J., S. van Herk, C. Zevenbergen, and R. Ashley. 2012. Room for the river: Delivering integrated river basin management in the Netherlands. *International Journal of River Basin Management* 10(4): 369–82.

Rotterdam, City of. 2013. Rotterdam Climate Change Adaptation Strategy. Rotterdam: Rotterdam Climate Initiative. www.urbanisten.nl/wp/wp-content/uploads/UB_RAS_EN_lr.pdf, accessed 12 August 2022.

Rotterdam, City of, Schieland and Krimpenerwaard Water Control Board, Hollandse Delta Water Authority, and Delfland Water Control Board. 2007. Rotterdam Waterplan 2: Working on Water for an Attractive City. Rotterdam. www.rotterdamclimateinitiative.nl/documents/Documenten/WATERPLAN_engels.pdf, accessed 12 August 2022.

Rosenzweig, C., W. Solecki, S.A. Hammer, and S. Mehrotra. 2010. Cities lead the way in climate-change action. *Nature* 467 (7318): 909–11.

Rosenzweig, C., W.D. Solecki, S.A. Hammer, and S. Mehrotra (eds.). 2011. *Climate change and cities: First assessment report of the Urban Climate Change Research Network*. Cambridge and New York: Cambridge University Press.

Roy, A. 2009. The 21st-Century metropolis: New geographies of theory. *Regional Studies* 43(6): 819–30.

Roy, A. and A. Ong (eds.). 2011. *Worlding cities: Asian experiments and the art of being global*. Chichester: Wiley-Blackwell.

Sassen, S. 1991. *The global city: New York, London, Tokyo*. Princeton, NJ: Princeton University Press.

Shi, L. and S. Moser. 2021. Transformative climate adaptation in the United States: Trends and prospects. *Science* 372(6549): 1–9.

Shi, L. et al. 2016. Roadmap towards justice in urban climate adaptation research. *Nature Climate Change* 6: 131–7.

Shorto, R. 2014. How to think like the Dutch in a post-Sandy world. *New York Times*, 9 April.

SRL (Superstorm Research Lab). 2013. A tale of two Sandys. http://superstormresearchlab.org/white-paper/, accessed 12 August 2022.

Stive, M. and H. Vrijling. 2010. Draining, dredging, reclaiming: The technology of making a dry, safe, and sustainable delta landscape. In H. Meyer, I. Bobbink, and S. Nijhuis (eds.), *Delta urbanism: The Netherlands*. Chicago, IL: American Planning Association, pp. 20–43.

Swyngedouw, E. 1996. The city as a hybrid: On nature, society and cyborg urbanization. *Capitalism Nature Socialism* 7(2): 65–80.

Tyler, S. and M. Moench. 2012. A framework for urban climate resilience. *Climate and Development* 4(4): 311–26.

Tzaninis, Y., T. Mandler, M. Kaika, and R. Keil. 2021. Moving urban political ecology beyond the 'urbanization of nature'. *Progress in Human Geography* 45(2): 229–52.

Urban Institute. 2014. Evaluation: Rebuild by design phase I. New York: Rockefeller Foundation. www.urban.org/sites/default/files/alfresco/publication-pdfs/413256-Evaluation-Rebuild-by-Design-Phase-I.PDF, accessed 12 August 2022.

US HUD and Netherlands IenM (United States, Department of Housing and Urban Development and Netherlands, Ministry of Infrastructure and the Environment). 2013. *Memorandum of understanding between the Department of Housing and Urban Development of the United States of America and the Ministry of Infrastructure and the Environment of the Kingdom of the Netherlands in the fields of sustainable urban development, water management, and integrated planning and cross sector collaboration*. Washington, DC. http://portal.hud.gov/hudportal/documents/huddoc?id=OPA3-4-13DOC.PDF, accessed 12 August 2022.

13

Insurgent earth: Territorialist political ecology in/for the new climate regime

Camilla Perrone

Introduction: Opening urban political ecology to the terrestrial

Over the past two decades, the debate about the planet's future has revolved around the climate crisis and colonised the political discourse on the link between urban and ecological questions. Moreover, it produced metanarratives of the global urban condition and a varied debate on urban sustainability that oscillated between divergent positions on the role of cities, both as places where environmental crises are severely experienced and as socio-technical systems capable of elaborating innovative responses to such crises. In certain cases, this *problematique* of sustainability is critically related to neoliberalism, uneven territorial development, neoliberalisation, and fights for environmental and spatial justice (Rees and Wackernagel, 1996; Atkinson, 2009; for critical review on this framework, see Brenner and Schmid, 2015; for a deeper focus on the contemporary policy discourse see Angelo and Wachsmuth, 2020; Keil, 2020a).

This chapter contributes to this discourse by interpreting the intertwining between two components of the climate crisis – the political-ecological and the social – from an urban political ecology (UPE) perspective addressed in the 1990s and recently reframed within the discourse of extended urbanisation (Keil, 2018a; Brenner and Schmid, 2015), postcolonial, feminist, and Global South scholarship, comparative and southern urbanism (Lawhon et al., 2014; Simone, 2019; Robinson, 2014, 2022), and the understanding of human and more-than-human actors in the production of space (Connolly, 2019).[1]

The political-ecological component of the climate crisis is understood as the reduction of the planet's habitability resulting from a continuous dialectic capital–nature relationship. It is mirrored in what Eric Swyngedouw (1996), the pioneer of the UPE discourse, defines as a metabolic (circulatory) process of commodity consumption and circulation, but also as a dialectic between this process and the biosphere that generates at the same time capital accumulation and everyday (human) life.

The social component of the climate crisis is related to an increase in gaps and inequalities in access to rights and goods, and the migration crisis.

The UPE perspective recombines these two components of the climate crisis with the view that the fundamental streams of contemporary literature are defined as Capitalocenic.[2] Such a vision moves beyond the dualist framing of nature *and* society, or 'capitalism *plus* nature' (recently defined also as green arithmetic), which consider capital as separate from nature and attribute it to an algorithmic sum of the two climate crises. This moves through the core concept of circular urban metabolism. In certain radical environmental studies, the authors argued for a relational view of humanity-in-nature and nature-in-humanity, as in the case of Harvey (1974). However, UPE explicitly analyses this discourse. Such a view enables rethinking capitalism as the web of life, 'as a way of organising nature as multispecies, situated, capitalist world-ecology' (Moore, 2016: 5). Accordingly, climate change is not the result of human activity in the abstract but the most apparent consequence of centuries of domination by capital.

In this chapter, climate crisis is addressed as a problem in political ecology. Moreover, it is proposed from a territorialist perspective. This perspective develops around the political concept of territory, understood as a metabolic process that reassociates spatial and physical processes with the forms of social, cultural, and political mediation that determine them in the cycles of territorialisation, deterritorialisation, and reterritorialisation (Raffestin, 1980; Magnaghi, 2010, 2020; Schmid, 2015; Elden, 2013). The final effort is to address territorialist political ecology (TPE). This is also a key to understanding the planetary socio-spatial-ecological transformations that characterise the contemporary extended urbanisation processes and include, produce, and reproduce inequalities and marginalisation at the global periphery, conflicts between human and non-human actors, the spread of new viruses and pathologies, processes of modernisation and rebirth of places, and so forth (Keil, 2018a; Brenner and Schmid, 2015; Connolly, 2019; Ranganathan, 2022).

This effort to open a new discourse that associates the territorialist perspective with political ecology follows some recent developments and redirection of urban political ecology (UPE) (Tzaninis et al., 2021; Keil 2020a, 2020b; Connolly et al., 2020).

The UPE discourse 'is rooted in the Marxist production-focused framework' (Keil, 2020b: 1127) and, as already pointed out, developed around the concept of urban circular metabolism addressed by Erik Swyngedouw (1996) in his seminal contribution on the 'city as a hybrid' with reference to the process of commodity consumption and circulation, capital accumulation, and social reproduction, which was further addressed in a co-authored contribution with Maria Kaika and Nick Heynen, *In the nature of cities*' (Heynen et al., 2006).

The core idea and motivation of UPE thinking is that these processes of circular metabolism include dialectics between the destruction of nature through capitalist urbanisation and the simultaneous creation of a second nature (or the urbanised nature as defined by Henri Lefebvre, 1991), which boosts a new capital-driven metabolism. In these flows, interruptions and rifts between the processes of the self-sustaining biosphere and environmental destruction occur and generate the critical contradictions and limits of the Capitalocene (Keil, 2020a; Gandy, 2018).[3]

In particular, UPE relates to 'the examination of continuous socio-ecological transformations as a dialectic between inside and outside, urban core and periphery, local and global' (Tzaninis et al., 2021: 232), apparently offering a theoretical and political apparatus for understanding the contemporary extended urbanisation processes and the climate crisis. Nevertheless, a strand of literature has recently enriched this field.

In a paper published in *Progress in Human Geography*, Yannis Tzaninis, Tait Mandler, Maria Kaika, and Roger Keil (2021) systematically reorganised the variegated contributions and critiques of UPE and addressed four larger streams in UPE as the development of the fundamental research agenda. I refer to the two that are most closely related and inspirational to the TPE discourse. The first is a call for a situated UPE inspired by feminist scholars and discourse on the Global South. It relates to the 'new geographies of theorising' (Roy, 2009, 2016; Robinson, 2014, 2022) and a politicised understanding of situated and contested practices of place and environmental production (Keil, 2020a; Lawhon et al., 2014; Heynen, 2016, 2018). This UPE stream is inspirational, as TPE thinking aims to navigate the rifting among multiple scales that encompass opposite poles: a situated understanding of the local environment and the knowledge–power relations that shape such an environment, and the global understanding of the twenty-first-century urbanisation processes that consider theories and practices of decolonisation (Heynen, 2016, 2018). Moreover, and accordingly, this UPE stream allows trespassing of the UPE postcolonial viewpoints into TPE (Heynen, 2016, 2018),[4] which turns into a framework to change the understanding and analysis of different trajectories of socio-spatial, political, and ecological territorialisation processes that do not conform to the hitherto dominant Western models of development.

The second inspirational strand of the UPE discourse concerns rethinking the role of human and more-than-human actors in the production of space (soil, water, air, concrete, bacteria) by showing 'not only how cities are produced through socio-natural metabolic flows originating "elsewhere" but also that cities and their specific sociopolitical contexts and spatial configurations have strong implications for how these various non-human natures are urbanised' (Connolly, 2019: 64, quoted in Keil, 2020a: 2361).

TPE extends the focus beyond the city and concentrates on territories understood as socio-political contexts whose spatial configurations reflect and affect the way various non-human natures are produced and reproduced in territorialisation, deterritorialisation, and re-territorialisation processes.

Recently, Roger Keil (2020b) further elaborated on the UPE discourse and reformulated the question in terms of 'spatialized political ecology'.[5]

This last epistemological opening of the debate on political ecology, which looks at the spatial ecologies of planetary urbanisation, results in a twofold contribution: on the one hand, it helps understand the rift between ecology and economics that characterises the 'capitalocenic climate change' (Keil, 2020b: 11; Perulli, 2020, 2021); on the other, it paves the way to a renewed focus on the territory as a situated synthesis of the political and the social. Both aspects contribute coherently to the perspective of TPE thinking.

Overall, the territorialist political ecology addressed in this chapter borrows nuances from each of these UPE developments, draws inspiration from the first attempt made by M'Gonigle (1999), and strives for a further nuanced UPE in and for the new climate regime.

This effort relies on a philosophical-political analysis of the context of the ongoing climate crisis addressed by Bruno Latour. It is inspired by Latour's ontological perspective of *Terrestrial* argued in the book *Où atterrir? Comment s'orienter en politique* (2017), to mark a crucial distinction between the poles, the Globe and the Terrestrial:

> The Globe grasps all things from far away, as if they were external to the social world and completely indifferent to human concerns. The Terrestrial grasps the same structures from up close, as internal to the collectivities, and sensitive to human actions, to which they react swiftly. Two very different versions of the way for these very scientists to have their feet on the ground, as it were.
> (Latour, 2017: 66–7)

Latour's discourse on the climate regime introduces the Terrestrial perspective to raise the question of the political centrality of the earth (2015, 2017) as an actor (who reacts and rebels) of the complex interweaving between the social and ecological dimensions defined by the Anthropocene (Crutzen and Stoermer, 2000; Crutzen, 2002; Moore; 2016).[6]

The background idea is that the earth is no longer a scenario of human action. Still, the earth takes part in this scenario of human action as an agent/actor of a new political interplay between the geosphere, socio-sphere, and biosphere. The earth is the protagonist of resistance initiatives (and in the power of transformation) that oppose the existing situation. To some extent, the earth claims the right of co-citizenship as an alternative to rebellion to the actor–network assemblages that seek to metabolise land and labour to produce commodities and feed the metabolism of uneven development conditioned by certain interests, groups, and logics. In so doing, the earth echoes the biological, existential, and political meaning of the term insurgent described by James Holston (1999), Leonie Sandercock (1998), and John Friedmann (2000). Insurgent Earth is the idiom that best summarises the situation with which to renegotiate the political and ecological conditions of the earth's habitability.

Accordingly, this contribution proposes a theoretical frame to explore the possibilities of renegotiation and chart the course for politics of uncertainty and preparedness for the new climate regime that imposes a 'contract' (a symbolic space context of confrontation and politicised conflict) between human, non-human and more-than-human.

The reasoning develops along three consequential discourses about the earth in the attempt to introduce a tentative argument around the transition from the terrestrial to the territorialist perspective – in particular, 'the rebellion of the earth between climate crisis and pandemic', and 'the contract with the earth and the perspective of the earth, the return of the earth' – and ends with the perspective of a territorialist political ecology for/in the new climate regime as a way to continue the debate.

In this contribution, the oft-referenced concept of earth is enriched by the Latourian definition of Gaia (Latour, 2015) and Michel Serres's (1992) meaning attributed to it (see below). The earth is then dressed as a political concept and represents the interdependency and the co-agency between capital, nature and society well described by the concept of Capitalocene: a 'world-ecology of power, capital and nature' (Moore, 2016: 4).

The rebellion of the earth: Climate crisis and pandemics

The scientific debate in recent months has highlighted how the pandemic is one of the possible implications, although certainly not the only one, of the progressive destruction and erosion of ecosystems that disrupts the planet and challenges territories (Balducci et al., 2020). In general, epidemics are an expression of environmental stress and a modification of the balance between humans and their living environment, to which the earth reacts.

Understanding the similarities, differences, and broader relationships between pandemics and climate risk is a critical first step in deriving practical implications that inform our actions (Pinner et al., 2020). There is no direct or substantial evidence that climate change affects the spread of COVID-19, but we do know that it alters the way we relate to other species, which is important for our health and the risk of infections.

Pandemic and climate emergencies represent physical and material traumas, which then translate into a series of socio-economic impacts. In this sense, the effects of COVID-19 can be interpreted as a taste of what a full-fledged climate crisis could entail in terms of exogenous shocks, which simultaneously involve the relationships between supply and demand for services, disruption of supply chains, procurement of goods and resources, and global mechanisms of transmission and amplification. The relationship between climatic and environmental issues and the spread of the 'transspecies' pandemic is, in essence, configured as a real vicious circle (Bernstein, 2021). Above all, there are many relationships and similarities between climate change (which undermines the health of the earth) and pandemics (which directly impact health and relationships between people), and the second finding that we are deeply unprepared is a lesson of no small importance.

Pandemics and climate risk are systemic, as their direct manifestations and ripple effects spread rapidly in an interconnected world. For example, the reduction in oil demand in the wake of the initial outbreak of coronavirus triggered a price war, which further exacerbated the decline in the stock market, with significant impacts on economies and production processes.

Pandemics and climate risk are both non-stationary and characterised by unpredictable ways of manifesting themselves. The processes underlying them are also non-linear, as their socio-economic impact grows disproportionately and even catastrophically once certain thresholds are exceeded (such as the hospital's ability to treat pandemic patients or the onset of cataclysms). Both are risk multipliers, as they highlight and exacerbate previously untested vulnerabilities inherent in financial and health systems, and the real economy. Both are regressive, as they disproportionately affect the world's most vulnerable population (Pinner et al., 2020).

Instead, the climate crisis and pandemics profoundly differ in the effects they generate and, above all, in the speed at which these effects become visible.

The COVID-19 pandemic and its action as a magnifying glass of problems and risks that have already emerged for some time (Marchigiani et al., 2020) lead one to reflect on the need to undertake long-term pathways (projects, actions, and policies). This is to come to terms with what Bruno Latour (2017) defines as the 'rebellion' of the earth against the processes of occupation, exploitation, and urbanisation of the planet that triggered the great climate crisis. Such processes are associated with the logic of capital under which land and labour have been reworked through an intensification of land use and extended urbanisation, which in turn has led to a biophysical agency here denoted 'the earth'.

As anticipated in the introduction, the earth rises (insurges), claiming its own actorship, which is a type of non-human citizenship that imposes a different relationship between ecology and society (Holston, 1999; Sandercock, 1998; Friedmann, 2000).

These long-term pathways call for a different epistemological frame to grasp the relationships between the earth and the complex system of ecological-political-economic actions and relations included in certain conceptions of the Anthropocene. However, this is a highly controversial concept. In the mainstream discourse, on a geological and cultural level, it defines the era we are living in; that is, a period in the history of the planet in which human activity represents one of the most relevant factors for environmental transformations (Crutzen and Stoermer, 2000; Crutzen, 2002). A more critical approach reflects the complex intertwining of capital, society, and nature.

According to critics, including Donna Haraway (2016) and Jason Moore (2016), the term is anything but happy for two basic reasons. From a theoretical point of view, it only underlines anthropocentrism typical of the human perspective on the world and is unable to decentralise to obtain a clearer vision. From a political point of view, it places abstract anthropos at the centre of the scene and veils the responsibilities of capitalist development, the real engine of the ongoing environmental catastrophe. This second meaning draws Moore to rephrase the term 'Capitalocene'.

According to this meaning of Anthropocene and Latour's perspective, earth becomes part of a multiagent relationship between humans and non-humans. This relationship has visible implications and operational dimensions within a territory. Caring by communities that inhabit and produce it represents the only possibility of habitability of the planet (Magnaghi, 2020; Latour, 2017). The concept of territory is complex and varies in the literature. I refer to Christian Schmid's genealogy of the concept (inspired by Stuart Elden's book titled *The birth of territory*, 2013) to briefly introduce it to define a territorial approach to urbanisation processes.

Schmid has identified two interpretative fields. The first, particularly prevalent in political science and in the Anglo-Saxon cultural context, is linked to the concept of state sovereignty and power, and is indifferent to the materiality of the territory; the second, which established itself mainly in the field of geographical and architectural disciplines, developed in French, Italian, and Spanish cultural contexts, focuses precisely on the materiality of the territory. Schmid included in this field the following meanings: first, the definition of territory as a complex product (including political, ethical, and aesthetic dimensions) by the architect Saverio Muratori (1967); second, the interpretation of territory as a socially produced space proposed by the geographer Claude Raffestin (1980) as a synthesis of the intertwining between Lefebvre's theory of space and Foucault's conception of power; third, the conceptualisation of the territory as a palimpsest by André Corboz (1983);

and finally, the territorialist approach of Alberto Magnaghi (2015) (inspired by Raffestin in the 1990s) which interprets the territory as a neo-ecosystem that reunites the natural milieu, the built environment, and human beings.

This section considers the second field of interpretation as a reference. In particular, it considers the recent developments in Magnaghi's concept of territory. The concept of territory dissolves into that of territorial heritage by means of

> the *mediance* of a local society that recognises it, takes care of it [treats it] to produce lasting wealth, transforming it into a resource according to the principles of resilience, within the limits of reproduction (or growth) of its existence value.
> (Magnaghi, 2020: 126; see also Raffestin, 1980; Berque, 2000).

Magnaghi's perspective is proposed later as a long-run operational dimension (compared to the ontological political-philosophical one of the terrestrial) to face both the ecological-climatic crisis and territorial uneven developments as two sides of an argument, preparing for the conditions of radical uncertainty exasperated precisely by the climate crisis.

This perspective considers the active role/agency of earth and the consequent need to stipulate a contract with it.

The contract with the earth: The end of the 'game for two' and the horizon of the terrestrial

Michel Serres in *Le contrat naturel* (1992) shows how the earth forcefully enters the great tale of the *Fight with Cudgels / Duelo a garrotazos* (a picture painted by Francisco de Goya between 1820 and 1821). With the description of the painting, the author illustrates the complex system of relationships between the human (the two duellists) and non-human (the earth) by recognising the role of the third actor while arguing about the need for a contract with the earth.

Serres points out how Goya, in portraying the Hegelian clash between servant and master, immerses the duellists in quicksand (neither of them, of course, will be saved from the density of the silt), contextualising the fight in one place, and making evident the presence of a third agent, the earth.

> [The] two-player game that thrills crowds and that pits only humans, the Master and the Servant, the left against the right, the Republicans against the Democrats, one ideology against any other, the green against the blue [...], it partially vanishes when this third intervenes. And what third! The world itself. Here, quicksand, tomorrow, and the climate. Water, air, fire, earth, flora and fauna, all living species, this archaic and new, inert, and living country, which

I will later call Biogea. End of two-player games: start of a three-way game. Here is the contemporary global state.

(1992: 42–3)

Paba, who re-proposes this story to argue about the earth's rebellion, further underlines: 'Shaken by the movements of the conflict between humans and the conflict between nature and humanity, the Earth shakes in turn and shakes the widespread traces of human settlement' (Paba, 2019: 107). In this discourse, humans are an embodiment (or actor–network) of historically and ecologically configured social interests such as transnational companies, colonial powers, and states. Earth becomes part of the contract for life on earth itself: a 'natural contract', which is different from adopting policies of respect, protection, and conservation of nature.

The question is much more demanding: nature is entrusted with a direct agency (an actorship) consolidated by signing a contract, which requires a certain degree of freedom and autonomy of the contracting parties (with rights), and establishes the impossibility of actions and unilateral decisions. Serres also gives us the keys for an epistemological repositioning of the relationship with nature, confirmed, for example, by the centrality of the theme of water in the crisis of environmental and human systems, and by the complex interweaving of economic, ecological and social, political, legal, identitarian factors around the management of water resources in all its manifestations (Paba, 2019). Moreover, this approach is in line with some seminal, innovative, and still-original experiences in the field of (bio)regional planning (Magnaghi, 2020; Fanfani and Mataran, 2020a, 2020b).

The challenge, therefore, becomes, in Latour's words, that of finding a new geopolitical horizon, the terrestrial, understood as a new delimitation of conflicts or a credible political alternative beyond the logic of dualism: the right and the left; the utopias without 'topos' (without land and without soil) of the local, of the global; the social and the ecological.

On the one hand, the earth inherits materiality, heterogeneity, thickness, and dust from the ground; on the other hand, it articulates this inheritance with the planetary dimension of movement, overcoming scales, boundaries, and borders. Becoming radically terrestrial finally means opening to all other terrestrials, the earthbound, in a conversation extended to all forms of existence, even fragile and precarious ones, which manage, even indirectly, to speak and act – in some way (Paba, 2019). The terrestrial takes part in human action, constituting itself as a third between the two attractors that have generated the crises: the local and the global.

In Latour's view, earth's centrality, its ability to act autonomously, is the subject of bio-political argumentation. The lives of humans on earth are affected by three dynamics of upheaval, intertwined with each other: (1) climate change and the advent of a Nouveau Régime Climatique (climate is understood in the broad sense of the relations between human beings and the material conditions of their lives); (2) deregulation (and the advent of globalisation); and (3) the dizzying explosion of inequalities and amplification of human and non-human migrations (Latour, 2017: 1–2; Paba, 2019). Latour states, 'we are in a condition of migration of ourselves from ourselves, of a crisis of belonging to the globe, to the world, to the provinces, to particular plots of ground, to the world market, to lands or to traditions' (2017: 16). The return of the earth and the opening to the earth mark the fundamental passage we are experiencing: 'there is nothing more innovative, nothing more present, subtle, technical, and artificial (in the positive sense of the word), nothing less rustic and rural, nothing more creative, nothing more contemporary than to negotiate landing on some ground' (2017: 53). This statement paves the way for an awareness of the new role that humanity is called to play. It has become part of either the construction or the destruction of the globe. Globalisation perpetrated through plans for the modernisation of rich countries – responding alternatively to free-market logics and colonial models – is now going through a profound crisis. Countries that have forcefully imposed it on those that must manage the consequences of this model and generate large migrations are experiencing the same problems as the latter:

> If Terrestrial is no longer the framework for human action, it is because it participates in that action [...]. Space has become an agitated history, in which we are participants, among others, reacting to other reactions. It seems that we are landing in the thick of geohistory.
> (Latour, 2017: 41–2)

The earth reacts to human actions and humans (actor networks of historically and ecologically configured social interests) are no longer the only actors.

In the current era of the Anthropocene/Capitalocene, we are witnessing an upheaval involving the Earth System where the action of human beings is no longer distinguishable from the framework that takes part in the action (Hamilton et al., 2015; Lenton, 2016).

The return of the earth: From the terrestrial to the territory

In the years of the 'great acceleration' (Steffen et al., 2015; Polanyi, 1957 [1944]) or the exponential growth of the influence of human activity on the planet, progressive or reactionary politics continue to be defined only based on the vector of modernisation. On the one hand, social movements have not embraced ecological challenges; on the other hand, ecology has not been able to grasp alternative energies. Social and ecological conflicts have been kept distinct as if there were pure and simple human beings and non-human objects. However, these two issues are inseparable. In Latour's view, the error depends on the role that both have given nature (Latour, 2017) as a subject outside society deprived of the power to act. In this sense, he claims for a politicised return of the earth in the political-ecological discourse in the new climate regime (not to be confused with the back-to-the-land movement promoted in France during the Second World War).

By moving attention from nature to the terrestrial, Latour suggests that there has been repositioning of politics that contributed to maintaining social and ecological (based on nature) struggles disconnected since the emergence of the climate threat. Latour, therefore, suggests a shift from an analysis in terms of production systems (rooted in a division between human actors and their resources, namely nature) to one in terms of engendering systems that involve and bring into confrontation actors (agents, animate beings) with distinct abilities and capacities to react, and where the role attributed to humans is dispersed. The basic principle is dependence on the other. The interest of a generative system is to engender terrestrials (not just humans); it is not focused on producing goods for humans based on resources. Therefore, it assigns different functions to politics and reflects the very nature of the Anthropocene: 'the earth system reacts henceforth to your action in such a way that you no longer have a stable and indifferent framework in which to lodge your desires for modernisation' (Latour, 2017: 84).

The concept of generating systems helps to introduce the operational dimension of the earth. It is the territory understood as a human environment where a new climatic civilisation can be tested and the conditions for the habitability of the earth can be reconstructed in a game of situated interdependencies between the parts in a political, ecological, and social context.

> A territory therefore not intended only as an artificial product of man's domination over nature, but above all, having to deal with it, created by producing living neo-ecosystems: a third outcome of the co-evolution processes between human settlement and the environment that have occurred over the long period of history: that is, processes of construction (by trial and error) of wise rules of relationship with which each civilisation has interpreted the 'taking care' of the other (in this case nature), contravening in part to the biblical dictate of subjugation.
>
> (Magnaghi, 2020: 20, my translation)

Downstream of a long process of exploitation and deterritorialisation coinciding with the civilisation of machines and Western modernity, the co-evolutionary synergistic relationships between human settlements (organised on biological and cultural bases and times) and environmental (organised on geological and biological bases and times) have stopped. In this context, Magnaghi's vision proposes a return to the territory to face the return of the Earth according to a holistic approach, *not compensatory or mitigative* (which proved weak in the hands of politics), *non-oppositional or radical* (too sectorial and unsuccessful in proposing experiments), *nor suited to the renaturation of the earth* (counter-intuitive concerning the state of an anthropised earth crust) (Magnaghi, 2020: 15). The hypothesis is that: 'An effective turnaround, able to strategically address the environmental crisis, is possible only by reconstructing the relationship between inhabitants and inhabited territory in its complexity, calling into question all the elements of the production of space' (2020: 15). The proposal is for an eco-territorialist future based on the care of the territory to prevent crises and diseases, and to operate an ecological conversion.

The crucial and perhaps less explicit question of such an interpretation of territory lies in the concept of territoriality. In Raffestin's interpretation, it represents the set of relationships that society and, therefore, the individuals who are part of it have with exteriority (territory) and otherness (other actors/subjects). This relationship is addressed to obtain autonomy, possibly considering the system resources. Territoriality plays the role of cultural, symbolic, cognitive, and practical *médiance* between the materiality of places and social action in territorial conservation/transformation processes and is therefore politicised and contextual.

Moreover, territoriality is situated in everyday practices, local knowledge, bottom-up theoretical understandings, and variegated forms of power in human-environment interactions that might entail new grounds for radical change. As such, territoriality is also described and can be inscribed in the postcolonial UPE tradition that addresses a situated UPE (as a field characterised by critical analysis of power). This UPE offers critical lenses to evaluate situated questions of inequality, justice, and poverty, and encourages the production of more just urban environments as radical incrementalism toward recursive empowerment and systemic change: 'radical incrementalism is thus a situated, unfolding process which differs over time and across space' (Lawhon et al., 2014: 511) and replaces the systemic change towards structural change and revolution (as is understood in the traditional UPE).

Michael M'Gonigle (1999), in his paper on 'Ecological economics and political ecology: Towards a necessary synthesis', made a similar conceptual move relating this political dimension of territoriality back to a perspective of political ecology, that he defined as territorialist, concerning a new conception of territorial and institutional 'space'.

> Territorialist political ecology points to the reverse of the critical importance of protecting and rebuilding territorial forces as the essential foundation of social and ecological sustainability. Indeed, at the heart of this analysis is the dialectical struggle between a hierarchical centre that draws its wealth from afar and from below, and a territorial community that sustains itself locally and from within.
>
> (M'Gonigle, 1999: 18)

M'Gonigle's territorialist perspective enables the conceptual connection between Earth (as an agent), territory (as a synthesis of co-evolutionary processes and assemblages of relations represented by territoriality), and the terrestrial as the biopolitical horizon of the new climate regime. It introduces a specific ecological policy dimension around the territory concept, highlighting the possible move toward a political ecology for the territory (definable as territorialist) in a new civilisation and climate regime.

Conclusion: The tentative perspective for a territorialist political ecology

Political ecology is a highly dynamic field of research in geographical development studies. Since Blaikie and Brookfield (1987; Blaikie, 1999) laid the foundations for this approach and formulated its first definition, it has evolved in many different directions (Zimmer, 2010).

In the past 30 years, a tendency has developed, especially within Anglo-American geography, to translate questions of political ecology into theoretical contexts; thus, urban political ecology has been formed, which today is nuanced into various streams and discourses surveyed in a few recent fundamental contributions (Tzaninis et al., 2021; Keil, 2020b; Connolly, 2019; Swyngedouw and Ernstson, 2018). As stated by Keil (2020a), if one were to give a start date to the debate associated with urban political ecology (UPE), this coincides with Erik Swyngedouw's (1996) article on the city as a hybrid.

UPE examines the urbanisation of nature as a dialectic process. Rather than simply the manifestation of nature in the city (Connolly, 2019; Keil, 2018a); it explores the material and infrastructural connections forming the 'socio-spatial continuum' between the city and the countryside (Kaika, 2005). The notion of metabolism is indeed key to UPE's definition of the city and by-passes the idea of the border between the city and nature, counterposing the idea of interconnection between the two realms (Heynen et al., 2006). Accordingly, the city is conceived as 'a sub-system located within a larger socio-spatial system, for example, an urban region, which are linked through various socio-natural metabolisms' (Keil and Macdonald, 2016: 1518). More specifically,

> particular place-based metabolic relationships are embedded and constituted by external scalar and topological relationships that define metabolism in a particular region [...]. However, those metabolisms have to be stabilised and reproduced through local action under regional regulation.
>
> (Keil, 2018a: 152–3)

The terrestrial geopolitical perspective is proposed here as an epistemological and political key. Pursuing this suggestion, the text proposes an association between potentially converging perspectives, such as that between terrestrial and territory (through its political ownership or territoriality), which opens up new possible discourses on political ecology from a territorialist perspective (TPE) as a key to rethinking the relationships and policies between institutions and territories in the new climate regime. The terrestrial is an attractor that opposes the local and the global (and other binary contrasts perpetuated by modernism, such as ecological/social), decreeing the end of what Michel Serres has defined as the game of two, thus changing the political delimitation of conflicts. This terrestrial geopolitical perspective is proposed here as an epistemological and political key. Pursuing this suggestion, this text proposes an association between potentially converging perspectives, such as that between terrestrial and territory (through its political ownership or territoriality), which opens up new possible discourses on political ecology from a territorialist perspective (TPE) as a key to rethinking the relationships and policies between institutions and territories in/for the new climate regime.

Notes

1 There are numerous strands of literature on this topic. Here I mention the ones that originated the debate. For an extended compendium of the new directions and challenges in UPE, see Tzaninis et al. (2021). For more details on the fundamental UPE research agenda, see Swyngedouw (1996); Keil and Graham (1998); Keil (2003); Swyngedouw and Kaika (2014); Keil and Macdonald (2016); Heynen (2014, 2016, 2018); Heynen et al. (2006); Zimmer (2010).

2 For a deeper exploration of the UPE discourse, see the survey on UPE by Nik Heynen in the series of reports for *Progress in Human Geography* (2014, 2016, 2018) where the author suggests a reframing of the UPE discourse to push forward the field beyond its Marxist (and urbanist) comfort zone and engage with the abolitionist, feminist, and queer traditions and ecologies.

3 The Capitalocene is taken as a way of understanding capitalism as a connective geographical and patterned historical system of power, capital, and nature (Moore, 2016; Haraway, 2016).

4 For an integrative account of the postcolonial UPE tradition see the contributions in this volume by Lawhon et al. (Chapter 10), Kimari (Chapter 8), Velicu (Chapter 16), and Gururani (Chapter 9).

5 In the paper, Keil carries the debate forward and encompasses three areas of discussion: urban political ecology as it has been understood and debated since the 1990s, therefore concentrated on urbanisation processes read in terms of socio-natural relationships; the landscape of political ecology as it has been

made operational in the research through a series of human-non-human constellations between city and countryside (Connolly, 2019); finally, a suburban political ecology, which speaks specifically of the dimension of extended urbanisation (Keil and Macdonald, 2016).

6 For a review of the Anthropocene concept under an UPE perspective see Keil (2020a): 2359–60 and the quoted authors: Swyngedouw and Ernstson (2018); Ruddick (2015); Gandy (2018). For a deeper understanding of the concept with reference to the concept of capital, see Moore (2016).

References

Angelo, H. and D. Wachsmuth. 2020. Why does everyone think cities can save the planet? *Urban Studies* 57(11): 2201–21. DOI: 10.1177/0042098020919081.

Atkinson, A. 2009. Cities after oil – one more time. *City* 13(4): 493–8.

Balducci, S., D. Chiffi, and F. Curci. 2020. *Risk and resilience: Socio-Spatial and Environmental Challenges.* Berlin: Springer, Politecnico di Milano.

Bernstein, A. 2021. Coronavirus, climate change, and the environment. A Conversation on COVID-19 with Dr. Aaron Bernstein, Director of Harvard Chan C-CHANGE. C-Change Center for Climate, Health, and the Global Environment. www.hsph.harvard.edu/c-change/subtopics/coronavirus-and-climate-change/, accessed 12 August 2022.

Berque, A. 2000. *Médiance, de milieux en paysages.* Paris: Belin.

Blaikie, P. 1999. A review of political ecology. *Zeitschrift fur Wirtschaftsgeographie* 43(1): 131–47.

Blaikie, P. and H. Brookfield. 1987. *Land degregation and society.* London: Methuen.

Brenner, N. and C. Schmid. 2015. Towards a new epistemology of the urban? *City* 19(2–3): 151–82. DOI: 10.1080/13604813.2015.1014712.

Connolly, C. 2019. Urban political ecology beyond methodological cityism. *International Journal of Urban and Regional Research* 43(1): 63–75. https://doi.org/10.1111/1468-2427.12710

Connolly, C., R. Keil, and S. Harris Ali. 2020. Extended urbanisation and the spatialities of infectious disease: Demographic change, infrastructure and governance. *Urban Studies.* DOI: 10.1177/0042098020910873.

Corboz, A. 1983. *Ordine sparso. Saggi sull'arte, il metodo, la città e il territorio.* Edited by P. Viganò. Milan: Franco Angeli.

Crutzen, P.J. 2002. Geology of mankind. *Nature* 415(51): 211–15.

Crutzen, P.J. and E.F. Stoermer. 2000. The Anthropocene. *Global Change Newsletter* 41: 17–18.

Elden, S. 2013. *The birth of territory.* Chicago: University of Chicago Press.

Fanfani, D. and A. Mataran. 2020a. *Bioregional planning and design. Volume I. Perspectives on a transitional century.* Switzerland: Springer Nature.

Fanfani, D. and A. Mataran. 2020b. *Bioregional planning and design. Volume II. Issues and practices for a bioregional regeneration.* Switzerland: Springer Nature.

Friedmann, J. 2000. The good city: In defense of utopian thinking. *International Journal of Urban and Regional Research* 2: 460–72.

Gandy, M. 2018. Cities in deep time: Bio-diversity, metabolic rift, and the urban question. *City* 22(1): 96–105.

Hamilton, C., C. Bonneuil, and F. Gemenne. 2015. The Anthropocene and the global environmental crisis: Rethinking modernity in a new epoch. *Routledge Environmental Humanities Series*.
Haraway, D. 2016. *Staying with the troubles: Making kin in the Chthulucene*. Durham: Duke University.
Harvey, D. 1974. Population, resources and the ideology of science. *Economic Geography* 50: 256–77.
Heynen, N. 2014. Urban political ecology I: The urban century. *Progress in Human Geography* 38(4): 598–604. https://doi.org/10.1177/0309132513500443
Heynen, N. 2016. Urban political ecology II: The abolitionist century. *Progress in Human Geography* 40(6): 839–45. https://doi.org/10.1177/0309132515617394
Heynen, N. 2018. Urban political ecology III: The feminist and queer century. *Progress in Human Geography* 42(3): 446–52. https://doi.org/10.1177/03091 32517693336
Heynen, N., M. Kaika, and E. Swyngedouw (eds.). 2006. *In the nature of cities: Urban political ecology and the politics of urban metabolism*. London and New York: Routledge.
Holston, J. 1999. Spaces of insurgent citizenship. In J. Holston (ed.), *Cities and citizenship*. Durham and London: Dike University Press.
Keil, R. 2003. Urban political ecology. *Urban Geography* 24(11): 723–38.
Keil, R. 2018a. *Suburban planet: Making the world urban from the outside*. Cambridge: Polity.
Keil, R. 2018b. Extended urbanization, 'disjunct fragments' and global suburbanisms. *Environment and Planning D: Society and Space* 36(3): 494–511.
Keil, R. 2020a. An urban political ecology for a world of cities. *Urban Studies* 57(11): 2357–70.
Keil, R. 2020b. The spatialized political ecology of the city: Situated peripheries and the capitalocenic limits of urban affairs. *Journal of Urban Affairs* 42(8): 1125–40. DOI: 10.1080/07352166.2020.1785305.
Keil, R. and J. Graham. 1998. Reasserting nature: Constructing urban environments after Fordism. In B. Braun and N. Castree (eds.), *Remaking reality: Nature at the millennium*. London: Routledge, pp. 100–25.
Keil, R. and S. Macdonald. 2016. Rethinking urban political ecology from the outside in: Greenbelts and boundaries in the post-suburban city. *Local Environment* 21(12): 1516–33. https://doi.org/10.1080/13549839.2016.1145642
Latour, B. 2015. *Face à Gaïa. Huit conférences sur le nouveau régime climatique*. Paris: La Découverte.
Latour, B. 2017. *Où atterrir? Comment s'orienter en politique*. Paris: La Découverte.
Lawhon, M., H. Ernstson, and J. Silver. 2014. Provincializing urban political ecology: Towards a situated UPE through African urbanism. *Antipode* 46(2): 497–516.
Lefebvre, H. 1991. *The production of space*. Oxford: Blackwell.
Lenton, T. 2016. *Earth system science: A very short introduction*. Oxford: Oxford University Press.
M'Gonigle, R.M. 1999. Ecological economics and political ecology: Towards a necessary synthesis. *Ecological Economics* 28: 11–26.
Magnaghi, A. 2010. *Il Progetto locale. Verso una coscienza di luogo*. Torino: Bollati Boringhieri.
Magnaghi, A. 2015. *The urban village: A charter for democracy and sustainable development in the city*. London: Zed Books.

Magnaghi, A. 2020. *Il principio territoriale*. Torino: Bollati Boringhieri.
Marchigiani, E., C. Perrone, and G. Esposito. 2020. Oltre il Covid, politiche ecologiche territoriali per aree interne e dintorni. Uno sguardo in-between su territori marginali e fragili, verso nuovi progetti di coesione, *Working papers. Rivista online di Urban@it* 1: 1–9.
Moore, J. 2016. *Anthropocene or Capitalocene? Nature, history, and the crisis of capitalism*. Oakland, CA: PM Press.
Muratori, S. 1967. *Urbanistica, Civiltà e Territorio*. Rome: Centro Studi di Roma Urbanistica.
Paba, G. 2019. La ribellione della terra e il terrestre come orizzonte. In C. Perrone and G. Paba (eds.), *Confini, Movimenti, Luoghi: Politiche e progetti per città e territori in transizione*. Rome: Donzelli, pp. 105–15.
Perulli, P. 2020. *Il debito sovrano. La fase estrema del capitalismo*. Milan: La nave di Teseo.
Perulli, P. 2021. *Nel 2050. Passaggio al Nuovo Mondo*. Bologna: Il Mulino.
Polanyi, K. 1957 [1944]. *The great transformation*. Boston, MA: Beacon Press.
Pinner, D., M. Rogers, and H. Samandar. 2020. Addressing climate change in a post-pandemic world. *Quarterly* 1–3.
Raffestin, C. 1980. *Pour une géographie du pouvoir*. Paris: Librairies Techniques.
Ranganathan, M. 2022. Towards a political ecology of caste and the city. *Journal of Urban Technology* 29(1): 135–43. https://doi.org/10.1080/10630732.2021.2007203
Rees, W. and M. Wackernagel. 1996. Urban ecological footprints: Why cities cannot be sustainable – and why they are a key to sustainability. *Environmental Impact Assessment Revie* 16: 223–48.
Robinson, J. 2014. New geographies of theorizing the urban: Putting comparison to work for global urban studies. In S. Parnell and S. Oldfield (eds.), *The Routledge handbook on cities of the Global South*. New York: Routledge, pp. 57–70.
Robinson, J. 2022. *Comparative urbanism: Tactics for global urban studies*. London: Wiley.
Roy, A. 2009. The 21st century metropolis: New geographies of theory. *Regional Studies* 43(6): 819–30.
Roy, A. 2016. Who's afraid of postcolonial theory? *International Journal Of Urban And Regional Research* 40(1): 200–9.
Ruddick, S. 2015. Situating the Antropocene: Planetary urbanization and the anthropological machine. *Urban Geography* 36(8): 1113–30.
Sandercock, L. 1998. *Toward cosmopolis: Planning for multicultural cities*. Chichester and New York: John Wiley & Sons.
Schmid, C. 2015. Specificity and urbanization: A theoretical outlook. In R. Diener et al. (eds.), *The inevitable specificity of cities*. Zürich: Lars Müller, pp. 287–307.
Serres, M. 1992. *Le contrat naturel*. Paris: Flammarion.
Simone, A. 2019. Maximum exposure: Making sense in the background of extensive urbanization. *Environment and Planning D: Society and Space* 37(6): 990–1006. https://doi.org/10.1177/0263775819856351
Steffen, W., W. Briadgate, L. Deutsch, O. Gaffney, and C. Ludwig. 2015. The trajectory of the Anthropocene: The great acceleration. *The Anthropocene Review*, 1–18.
Swyngedouw, E. 1996. The city as a hybrid: On nature, society and cyborg urbanization. *Capitalism Nature Socialism* 7(2): 65–80. https://doi.org/10.1080/10455759609358679

Swyngedouw, E. 2006a. Circulations and metabolisms: (Hybrid) natures and (cyborg) cities. *Science and Culture* 15(2): 105–21.
Swyngedouw, E. 2006b. Metabolic urbanization: The making of cyborg cities. In N. Heynen, M. Kaika, and E. Swyngedouw (eds.), *In the nature of cities: Urban political ecology and the politics of urban metabolism*. London: Routledge, pp. 21–40.
Swyngedouw, E. and H. Ernstson. 2018. Interrupting the Anthropo-obScene: Immuno-biopolitics and depoliticizing ontologies in the Anthropocene. *Theory, Culture & Society* 35(6): 3–30.
Swyngedouw, E. and M. Kaika. 2014. L'ecologia politica urbana. Grans promeses, aturades ... i nous inicis? [Urban political ecology: Great promises, deadlock ... and new beginnings?], *Documents d'Anàlisi Geogràfica* 60(3): 459–81.
Tzaninis, Y., T. Mandler, M. Kaika, and R. Keil. 2021. Moving urban political ecology beyond the 'urbanization of nature'. *Progress in Human Geography* 45(2): 229–52.
Zimmer, A. 2010. Urban political ecology: Theoretical concepts, challenges, and suggested future directions, *Erdkunde*, 64(4): 343–54.

Part IV

Addressing disjunctions between policy, politics, and academic debate

14

Populist political ecologies? Urban political ecology, authoritarian populism, and the suburbs

Alex Loftus and Joris Gort

> We submit that this analysis of authoritarian populism requires urbanizing. The exercise of rule – and hegemony – is a space-forming practice. That is to say, it intervenes in dynamics of uneven development with territorial state strategies (that organise social relations hierarchically) and symbolic claims to particular spatial forms.
>
> (Kipfer and Saberi, 2014: 130)

Introduction

For the past few years, the question of how right-wing nationalist leaders have achieved electoral success through appeals to 'the people' has dominated political discussions well beyond the left, generating a raft of studies addressing authoritarian populisms and echoing an earlier wave of work focused on the Global South (see Laclau, 1977). More recently, political ecologists have also begun to grapple with authoritarian populism, as seen in special issues of both the *Journal of Peasant Studies* (*JPS*) and the *Annals of the American Association of Geographers*. To date, *urban* political ecology appears to have been less interested in authoritarian populism: political ecological studies concerned with the phenomenon have instead tended to focus on extractivist landscapes, on pipeline politics and – in the case of the *JPS* special issues – on agrarian transformations. While such an intellectual division of labour is understandable, there is a risk that right-wing populism will be presented as a rural phenomenon, thereby replicating the kind of spatially fetishistic analyses critiqued by Kipfer and Dikeç (2019) among others. In this chapter, we offer one small attempt to redress this balance. We do so through bringing together disparate literatures on authoritarian populism, on global suburbanisms, and on urban political ecology.

Given the profoundly uneven political economic conditions out of which authoritarian populisms have emerged, and the invocation of a fetishised metropole to be pitted against its supposed antipode, we argue that it is crucially important to foreground the kind of process-based understanding developed within urban political ecology. Such an approach is exemplified within works that seek to go beyond the urbanisation of nature thesis (Tzaninis et al., 2021) and we will therefore draw on such work to better understand how authoritarian populisms are woven through and out of particular – albeit relationally produced – material conditions. The conditions in which right-wing populisms have flourished consist of *lived* processes. These lived processes shaped by changing political ecologies, from the experience of racialised environmental injustices to the loss of jobs in a resource sector. Lives lived in the latter days of neoliberalism have been profoundly altered by the vicissitudes of a changing global political economy, one reliant on the continued exploitation of the Global South, and one that has served to reconfigure spatialities from the suburbs to the desakota landscapes of Southeast Asia. If we are to begin to find a way out of the mess we're in – a mess a long time in the making – then reckoning with the lived environments in which the majority of the world live is a necessity: urban political ecology provides one valuable resource in such a struggle.

We begin by reviewing literatures on authoritarian populism and the environment, before turning to a more detailed analysis of writings on authoritarian populism. In seeking to develop an urban political ecological approach, we then review what is specific about that approach as well as more recent attempts to move 'beyond the urbanisation of nature thesis'. The latter becomes more important as the suburbs acquire a particular status within authoritarian populist interpretations, being viewed by some as the crucible for social conservatism. In a final section, we therefore seek to establish key principles upon which we can build an urban political ecology of authoritarian populism.

Authoritarian populism and the environment

From the outset, political ecology provides a particularly strong set of resources for analysing the apparent support for 'authoritarian populisms'[1] given its attention to lived material conditions and its circumspection towards the knowledges articulated within hegemonic forms of governance (Loftus, 2019). While consistently challenging the ways in which those on the political right have sought to mobilise 'the people vs. the power bloc', political ecologists are acutely aware of the potential antagonisms within popular movements of varying persuasions. In challenging dominant readings of environmental politics – one might think of the normative framework of sustainable development or the technocratic prescription of ecological modernisation – political ecologists have prioritised subaltern perspectives, contextualising them within the lived environments out of which they emerge. Rather than romanticising the voice of an imagined 'people' – in opposition to that of imagined environmental technocrats – political ecology is well-positioned to tease out the relationship between knowledge claims around the environment, how these are woven through and out of different contexts, and how they come to be politicised. Through excavating the sedimented knowledges – or 'conceptions of the world' (see Wainwright, 2010) – that connect specific social groups to the environments of which they are a part, political ecology places particular emphasis on the situatedness of knowledge claims. It can thereby become a tool through which to dissect authoritarian populisms and it can also potentially serve as a weapon through which to challenge xenophobic and totalitarian appropriations of 'the people'.

Particularly notable contributions on authoritarian populisms and the environment appear in the aforementioned special issues. McCarthy (2019), writing the introduction to the *Annals* special issue, is prompted by questions around the relationship between neoliberalism and authoritarianism, by questions around the descent of right populisms into regimes that resemble fascism, as well as by more hopeful interrogations of the possibilities for 'progressive populisms'. McCarthy (2019: 302) contends that while literatures on populism have burgeoned in recent years, surprisingly few authors (at least prior to the vast special issue McCarthy's paper introduces) have sought to tease out 'the myriad connections between authoritarianism, populism, and environmental politics and governance'. For McCarthy, these connections range from attacks on scientific knowledge, particularly around climate change; the articulation of 'nativist' conceptions of the people, woven through visions of the environment; the development of extractivist politics and resource nationalisms; attacks on environmental regulations; and the exploitation of tensions between the rural and the urban.

Within the same special issue, Kojola (2019) focuses on identities emerging out of livelihoods associated with mining, analysing associated nostalgic connections with resource extractivism. 'Extractive populism' therefore helps to explain the shifting voting patterns within former Democratic Party strongholds in northern Minnesota, where right-wing extractivism gave voice to local sentiments of marginalisation. With the exploitation of tensions between the rural and the urban, and with the claim that cities are dominated by liberal metropolitan elites, it becomes clear how geographical context is critical for the conditions that authoritarian populism exploits.

The relationship between extractivist politics and resource nationalisms are therefore explored in several other pieces. Thus, Kenney-Lazar (2019) analyses what he refers to as neoliberal authoritarianism and its relation to resource extraction in Laos. Unpicking the distinctive articulation of neoliberalism and state authoritarianism in Laos, he sees the potential for forms of resistance to emerge among the Laos peasantry. As Graybill (2019) argues, to some extent echoing Kojola, resource extraction engenders distinct forms of 'emotional environments'. Through a study of energy extraction in Russia, she therefore analyses the ways in which extractivism is lived and experienced in contradictory ways. Lyall and Valdivia (2019) turn their attention to how the Correa administration in Ecuador attempted to cultivate forms of popular legitimacy by speculating on global oil markets and channelling subsequent rents into spectacular projects. In so doing, their analysis echoes other recent political ecological engagements with 'post-neoliberal' Ecuador such as Purcell and Martinez (2018) and J. Wilson (2017). Nevertheless, for R. Wilson (2019) political ecology's focus on neoliberal and post-neoliberal environmental governance has led to a neglect of authoritarian regimes' longstanding relationship with an environmental politics. Whether or not these historical relations have been neglected (and whether political ecologists have been busily distracted by neoliberalisms) is something of a moot point, even if the attention to historical political ecologies is well taken.

Several others have developed nuanced historical analyses of the relationship between political ecological concerns and changing forms of authoritarian governance, focusing, for example, on the relations between infrastructure and the terrain of ideology. Thus, Kaika's (2004) work moves between a focus on ambitious dam-building projects and the intimacies of the home. For Kaika, water helps to establish a city of flows, tracing out the infrastructure networks through which resources circulate, bringing to the fore different connections. More recently, Mullenite (2019) teases out the relationship between infrastructure and authoritarian forms of governance, emphasising how flood infrastructure comes to be enrolled in both colonial and postcolonial governments in Guyana. In some respects, these concerns also echo the work of Swyngedouw (2014), who charts the ways in which fascist rule in Spain came to be consolidated through a massive programme of hydraulic engineering. Water and power therefore develop in a mutually symbiotic manner.

Several studies have focused in greater depth on how the environment is woven into the specific mix of white supremacy and economic nationalism that characterises the Trump era. Thus, Melissa Wright (2019) focuses on Trump's wall, while Pulido et al. (2019) note how 'spectacular racism' has allowed the rolling back of environmental regulations to go relatively unnoticed. Drawing on the Black Radical Tradition, Pulido et al. set out to understand the specific relationships between environmental politics and white nationalism in Trump's government. And Sparke and Bessner (2019) seek to interpret what they define as the Trumpist behemoth – a particular fusion of neoliberalism and nationalism. They go on to explore this behemoth in relation to the politics and practices of resilience, and through engaging with Wainwright and Mann's (2018) work on *Climate leviathan*.

A further set of papers draws together insights around the politics of knowledge and environmental governance to better make sense, not only of knowledge production under authoritarian forms of governance, but also of how political ecology, environmental studies, and geography more broadly might respond to the specific challenges of authoritarian populism. Exploring these connections in greater depth, Neimark et al. (2019) consider the appropriate response for political ecology, a sub-discipline that has often been critical of dominant conceptualisations of the environment: their proposal is to continue 'to speak power to post-truth', thereby shoring up political ecology's critique of dominant frameworks while also distinguishing it from post-truth discourses. In slight contrast, for Bosworth (2019), the counter-expertise that developed through contestation of the Keystone XL and Dakota Access pipelines suggests opportunities for new coalitions to develop that permit 'a science for political ends'. These discussions of how environmental knowledges intersect with authoritarian populisms have been supplemented by more detailed analyses of how they are woven through distinct environmental contexts.

While the *Annals* collection brings together geographical engagements around authoritarian populism and the environment, paired special issues of the *Journal of Peasant Studies* have deepened work loosely associated with agrarian studies. The breadth and depth of these studies is impressive, and they make the case clearly for why the environment matters in struggles over – and in the consolidation of – authoritarian populisms. As we argue in a subsequent section, it is all the more surprising that scholars interested in urban environments have neglected such questions. First, however, it is crucial to better conceptualise the shifts in governance captured under such a broad-brush term as authoritarian populism.

Authoritarian populism as process and relation

The need to carefully dissect 'populisms' only seems to have become more important over the past few years. With the disastrous handling of the COVID-19 pandemic by right-wing nationalists, from Trump to Bolsonaro, and from Johnson to Modi, the question of how so many around the world find themselves at the whim of such necropolitical administrations has, unsurprisingly, become one of the defining questions of the current moment (Mbembe, 2008). For Hart (2020) such a question is slightly misplaced. Asking how 'we' find ourselves in this mess, points to a chauvinism for – and a methodological nationalism when it comes to studying – the liberal democracies of the Global North. In the US, the portrayal of Trump as an aberration only serves to occlude much longer and more deeply rooted processes. Indeed, the surprise among the liberal left at how democracies in the Global North 'find' themselves in such a situation points to ignorance of the institutional racism, the white nationalism, and the settler colonial relations shaping lives within those same places. The conditions for 'a demagogic figure like Trump' have been present in the US for several decades at least, and the question for Hart should instead be 'Why did it take so long?' Her detailed dissection of the globally interconnected historical geographies that have enabled right-wing nationalism to flourish point to the influence of imperialism, of white nationalism, and of the Dollar-Wall Street regime. Such influences helped to generate the conditions for a particular fusion of neoliberalism – apparently in its death throes only a few years earlier – and authoritarian populism.

Political ecologists have much to gain from such an analysis. For while studies of authoritarian populism and the environment have done an excellent job of highlighting the relation between the two, they have often done much less to explore what the blanket term 'populism' refers to. Without further excavating the many different political forms collapsed under the term, there is a risk that critiques become part of the problem that Hart identified – a dismissal of right-wing populisms in the Global North as an aberration, antithetical to what are assumed to be the flagbearers for liberal democracy. Furthermore, there is a risk that populism is framed as what Hart refers to as a ' "manipulated mindless masses" model' (2013: 306).

As in other works, one of Hart's crucial reference points is Laclau's (1977) 'Towards a theory of populism' in *Politics and ideology in Marxist theory*, a study that Hart carefully distinguishes from Laclau's (2005) more recent writings on populism, writings that too often slip into the 'manipulated mindless masses' model. Combining an Althusserian language with a Gramscian sensibility, Laclau (1977) argues against the dominant interpretations of populism in the 1970s. Each one of these interpretations, he argues, places too much emphasis on the content, as opposed to the form, of populism. Through focusing on form, Laclau becomes interested in how particular social groups articulate complex political and ideological relations with respect to dominant ideologies. Prior 'conceptions of the world' come to be integrated within specific articulations of the people vs. the power bloc. In a move that becomes crucial to Hart's reading of shifting political moments in the US, in South Africa, and in India, Laclau distinguishes between the *parliamentary right*, which seeks to neutralise antagonisms emerging from popular mobilisations, and the attempt by the *populist right* to further develop those same antagonisms, while keeping them within certain limits. These two positions characterised the very different strategies of Thabo Mbeki and Jacob Zuma in South Africa, with the latter's unseating of Mbeki at the ANC conference in Polokwane in 2007 representing a populist shift within the party. This shift also captures a broader trend towards increasingly generalisable calls to 'the people', a shift noticeable within the British Conservative Party around Brexit, as David Cameron's leadership gave way to Theresa May and then Boris Johnson.

Thus, following a more empirically grounded study of the development of populisms in Latin America – and specifically the case of Peronism in Argentina – Laclau (1977: 197) briefly lays out some of his hopes for a socialist strategy: 'Socialist hegemony does not mean the pure and simple destruction of the previous society, but the absorption of its elements into a new articulation.' In a markedly Gramscian move, Laclau thereby avoids a simple counterposing of populism and socialism, recognising, as Kipfer (2016: 316, emphasis added) has subsequently argued, that 'any radical politics that aspires to become majoritarian *cannot do without* appeals to "the people"'. Kipfer (ibid.) goes on to write that '[s]ocialist politics can only become hegemonic by linking particular dominated and exploited groups – workers, the unemployed, peasants, and others – to whole social formations'. Laclau's attempt to define populism not by content but by form, in short, serves to shift our attention away from the specific ideologies of ostensibly populist movements and more towards the articulation of those ideologies with material and political processes and movements. Although bound up in the languages of structuralism, Laclau (1977) points to a far more relational take on populism, and one that has proven highly productive when put to work within Hart's (2018, 2020) distinctive form of relational comparison.

If Hart's attention has turned in recent years to questions of Trump-Bannonism, this distinctive US phenomenon is always read through its extended geographical relations. Deeply resistant to forms of methodological nationalism, Hart demonstrates how changing international divisions of labour, and consumer spending patterns in the US, connect workers and the US domestic sphere to the fate of other producers and their forms of social reproduction. Such analysis builds on Hart's (2002) earlier work on relational comparison in South Africa, in which the divergent trajectories of two neighbouring small towns are analysed through their different relationship to racialised dispossession. Racialised dispossession in apartheid South Africa, in turn, articulates with the investment strategies of Taiwanese industrialists in the country, investments that were made possible through the industrialists' own changing relations with land and mainland China. Intuitively, one might assume a relation between the emergence of right wing or authoritarian populisms in the US, in India, and in South Africa. However, rather than simply capturing this as an 'age of anger' or ressentiment (Mishra, 2017), Hart teases out the material relations that come to be articulated within populist projects of quite different types. If Mishra points to some of the colonial ideologies pervading populist rage, Hart forces us to recognise how these imperial relations are material and ongoing, bound up in forms of (re)production and distinct spatio-temporalities. Often in conversation with Hart, Stefan Kipfer (2016) along with other authors (Kipfer and Saberi, 2015; Kipfer and Dikeç, 2019) has further troubled recent conceptions of populism. Rather than simplistically positing a left populism as the antidote to right-wing populism (as is advocated in different ways in the work of Mouffe (2019) and Fraser (2017)), Kipfer (2016) identifies 'two basic conditions for a popular democratic politics': working and organising with an understanding of the people that is opposed to those xenophobic and exclusionary forms of 'the people' mobilised by the political right; and recognising 'the differentiated and uneven relations among dominant groups'. Thus, while recognising that any radical politics must work with and mobilise from a popular political base if it is to be successful, Kipfer carefully points to the ways in which fetishised abstractions must be challenged in order not to reproduce the violent exclusions of the right. Elsewhere, Kipfer with Dikeç (2019: 35) is similarly dismissive of more sympathetic critiques of 'liberal disdain' for populism, as seen in the work of Thomas Frank. While Frank recognises that populist leaders such as Trump were in some instances able to tap into genuine material concerns, the former simultaneously fetishises the 'small-town agony, job loss, and poverty [to be found] "somewhere in the Midwest"' (Kipfer and Dikeç, 2019: 36). Such spatial fetishisms overlook the cross-class support that Trump was able to mobilise, and, perversely, mirror the homogenising vision of 'the people' mobilised by authoritarian populists. Perhaps the key point to emerge from Kipfer's various studies concerns the risks of universalising from a false abstraction of 'the people' and from peripherality more broadly, as we expand on below.

Crucially, various authors have argued such imperial relations have materialised alongside contemporary white nationalist practices. Inwood (2019), for instance, has forcefully argued that Trump's rise signified the mobilisation of whiteness as a populist means to establish a counter-revolutionary politics, a strategy employed intermittently in the history of the US racial state. Racial superiority is thereby constructed through legal discourse, as Wright (2021) demonstrates in relation to a prevailing conservative constitutional narrative, and as Inwood (2015) shows through the 'Southern Strategy'. Following Bonds and Inwood (2016), racist calls to 'the people' reveal the relations of white supremacy as a set of materially grounded practices. In this way, white supremacy is an important frame through which to analyse taken-for-granted conceptions of racial privilege that produce populist support (Pulido, 2015).

As we have alluded to, these more relational takes on authoritarian populism can be contrasted with several other important interpretations of populism in recent years. Brown's (2019) important analysis of 'antidemocratic politics in the West', for example, seeks to interpret the transformation of ostensibly liberal (at least neoliberal) regimes into authoritarian, xenophobic, and exclusionary political projects. In its most obvious manifestation – and taking up much of the concrete analysis within the book – Brown seeks to understand Donald Trump's rise to power in the US. For Brown, the 'composite left account' of the rise of the authoritarian right is inadequate. While not denying the broader context of de-industrialisation, rising joblessness in the former industrial heartlands, growing cultural and religious divides, and flames being fanned by the 2008 economic crisis, Brown calls for an analysis that pays far greater attention to the fundamental principles on which neoliberalism was built. At the heart of neoliberal thought, Brown finds, is a deep hostility to key democratic principles as well as a mistrust for the social. In championing the individual as opposed to society and democracy, neoliberalism sowed the seeds for a Frankensteinian monster that was, on the surface at least, its other. While there is much to be gained from Brown's brilliant rereading of key texts within neoliberalism, there are difficulties in directly transposing these texts to lived realities. In short, reading Hayek feels like the wrong starting point for seeking to understand popular anger in this age of multiple crises.

Brown's work has some similarities to Melinda Cooper's (2017) argument that social policies developed under neoliberalism have focused on the family in a manner that explicitly (even if apparently paradoxically) sought to foster a moral conservatism. In short, moral conservatism's focus on 'family values' finds its roots in the social policies of neoliberalism. While Cooper's book is also focused on reading key Chicago School thinkers such as Gary Becker, her analysis feels more rooted in material concerns such as how a struggling family can access the resources needed to get by in the current moment. It thereby moves closer to the kind of analysis we propose in this chapter.

Before briefly concluding this section, it is worth considering one final contribution. In many respects a more generalist analysis, Nancy Fraser (2017) has developed a related account of how progressive neoliberalism enabled the rise of Donald Trump. The latter's simultaneous crushing of reactionary neoliberalism permitted an authoritarian populist response. Exploring the possibility for a progressive (or 'counterhegemonic') alternative, Fraser proposes a form of progressive populism, something that was briefly embodied in the campaigns of Bernie Sanders and Jeremy Corbyn, as well as in more successful municipal projects such as *Barcelona En Comu*. As Ekers et al. (2020) argue, this simple typology occludes many of the complex relations embodied and expressed within very different 'populist' projects. Furthermore, they ignore the imperial dimension, remaining tightly focused on discrete national projects. Hart (2020), in comparison, develops a nuanced philosophy of praxis that is rooted in the material shifts taking place in a range of relationally produced contexts, while always situating these within a broader global political economy. We find this a useful starting point for considering urban political ecology more broadly.

Urban political ecology against peripheral reification

As we have argued, drawing on Laclau (1977) to define populism by form instead of content shifts attention away from the specific ideologies of ostensibly populist movements and more towards the articulation of those ideologies with material and political processes and movements. Since its inception, urban political ecology has, similarly, proposed a relational and process-based understanding of the city: in short, the field is interested in what Laclau argues gives populism its meaning. Like Harvey's (1996) admonition of urban theorists for focusing on the city and not the process of urbanisation, urban political ecology is interested in the urbanisation of nature, recognising the form in which it presents itself as an outcome of those processes. Urban political ecology is therefore well-placed to cut through the fetishisms through which town is opposed to country, metropolitan to provincial, rust belt to Silicon Valley. Nevertheless, while challenging such spatial or environmental fetishisms, the best research has been acutely aware of how lived experience articulates with ideology and discourse. Because the forms of authoritarian populism are sedimented within the material and political processes of peripheries, the interactions between right-wing nationalisms and their ex-centric political ecologies warrant much closer attention. Focusing on the centrality of the margins, urban political ecology has recently sought to apply such epistemologies to explicitly ex-centric perspectives. Crucial to such perspectives, and to much of this edited collection, is the call by Tzaninis et al. (2021) to 'move urban political ecology beyond the "urbanization of nature thesis"'. By addressing the reification of spatial relations, this view attempts to negate conventional boundaries between the urban and the rural, instead seeking to understand how particular peripheries are *produced* (Ekers et al., 2012) and, in turn, how they *produce* various acts of dissensus (Kaika, 2017).

Situating political ecology within these dynamics appears more vital than ever. Thus, Tzaninis et al. (2021) suggest that moving urban political ecology into more-than-urban sites, such as agricultural landscapes or suburbs, can challenge mainstream perceptions of urban and rural spaces by focusing on the ideological relations shaping and being shaped by peripheral urbanisation. Therefore, in thinking 'from the outside in', Tzaninis and colleagues assert that this expansion can address the need to remain true to the focus on material cultural ecologies central to political ecology while also expanding the field's analytical focus to extended urbanisation.

Recent work heralding a more-than-urban political ecological epistemology has produced a rich body of work on relational suburbanism that highlights precisely how suburbanisation is more diverse and complex than simply 'suburbia' (see Keil and Macdonald, 2016; Angelo, 2017): the processes and relations producing the 'thing' we call suburbia should be the focus of research. Such peripheral urbanisation is shaped not only through symbolic representation but also by situated political, economic, and ecological practices. Focusing on the confluence of these processes becomes even more important when one considers the exploitation and representation of a suburban-metropolitan divide by right populists who reify landscapes of uneven development in their attempts to consolidate a power base through spatial division. Within these representations, processes of uneven development that have shaped the de-industrialising northeast of England, the rust belt of the US, or the 905 area code of Toronto are transformed into discrete spatial containers of cultural difference. The supposed winning electoral combination for the twenty-first century – 'go left on the economy and right on cultural matters' – is one that is assumed to win in these suburbs. The liberal left, according to such a narrative, will find itself increasingly confined to barricaded metropolitan centres.

That right-wing nationalists and cultural conservatives have been able to exploit already constituted representations of spatial separation is evident in the apparent support for right populism in the 'suburbs'. An analysis of these tensions, however, relies on a nuanced historical approach, one that recognises the broader territorialisation of politics as well as how such territorialisation remains situated in distinctly uneven geographical developments. As was clear in the reactionary politics of Rob Ford in Toronto between 2010 and 2014, the bungalow-esque sprawl of Toronto's post-war built outskirts became a battleground for an antagonistic spatial politics. Kipfer and Saberi (2014: 129), therefore, argue: 'Toronto's Ford-ism can be understood as a deeply racialized form of authoritarian populism, an attempt to re-order relations of force in the current conjuncture by articulating fragments of support from a contradictory array of social forces.' However, as the authors further demonstrate, the territorial juxtaposition called for by mayor Ford was only made possible by the dynamic deindustrialisation of the suburbs while simultaneously perpetuating the stigmatisation of working-class suburbanites.

Moreover, in France, an apparent rejection of egalitarian values is often expressed through the reification of difference between the *banlieues*, inner cities, and 'peripheral' France. Guilluy (2014), as critiqued by Kipfer and Dikeç (2019), argues that peripheral France is characterised by 'cultural insecurity' brought on by a reliance on the neighbourhood scale and one that is ultimately resigned to further political marginalisation. Moreover, Guilluy's selective interpretation of census data and electoral maps to support such a claim has contributed to a homogenised picture of the French 'hinterlands' – a picture that ignores spatial difference within these reified forms. Visual fixation on electoral maps, in which support for right-wing nationalists appears homogenous in certain regions (just as with 'the Red Wall' in the north of England) juxtaposes peripheral with centre spaces, thereby fuelling stigmatisation of migrants, a practice exploited with some precision by the *Front National* (Kipfer and Dikeç, 2019). Dikeç (2017) therefore argues that such spatial claim making is central to the representational denouncement of 'illegality' and disorder at the hand of disparate French media and politicians focusing on the spatial other, the *banlieues*. Yet, the mobilisation of negative sentiments against spatial categories such as the *banlieues* or Toronto's suburbs are not only materialised through repressive measures. Instead, Dikeç (2012) contends, antagonistic framings of space instil a 'securitarian ideology' that works on the conditions of possibility *within* such spaces and *with* its populations, even if these facets are themselves a consequence of such perverse imaginaries. Crucially, we are attuned to the fact that peripheral marginalisation is explicitly mobilised by right-wing populists which is then corroborated by scholars reproducing such territorial schisms, *even when* voting patterns do not strictly follow the metropole-periphery rationale reproduced within their studies.

A forceful mobilisation by urban political ecologists of extended urbanisation resides within the ability to recognise how reified conceptions of urbanisation are part of a relational urban fabric. The urban can, as Kipfer (2009) argues, be an epistemology mediating between different scales, elucidating the situated effects of spatial reification within the urbanisation process. Such a relational urban epistemology allows us to situate peripheral caricatures within respective historical development, in turn providing a lens through which to grasp the ideological playpen of, in this case, authoritarian populism. A more-than-urban political ecology of authoritarian populism builds on recent concerns in geography and rural studies while taking seriously the importance of the environment in right-wing ideological developments by analysing the spatial categories developed by right-wing populist assertions. We find the potential for a situated critique to be especially pertinent given contemporary conditions. As such, in this final section we affirm what an urban political ecological critique of authoritarian populism might look like.

Situating authoritarian populism through urban political ecology

If Kipfer and Saberi (2014: 130) make a brilliant case for why 'authoritarian populism requires urbanizing', we have argued that any such analysis should be complemented by insights from urban political ecology. We follow closely in the steps of the former here: their analysis of how the Ford administration prospered in Toronto through racial and homophobic stigmatisation includes a nuanced take on struggles over transit in which an environmental politics is woven through the supposed battle lines between the car-owning suburbs and the public transit riding/cycling downtown. The complexities of such a politics are, of course, also woven through the emergence of the *Gilets Jaunes* in France, as well as through the differing reactions to congestion charging and Low Traffic Neighbourhoods in London.

Challenging the simplistic claims of authoritarian populist movements through urban political ecological critique involves building on relational ways of thinking: we need to recognise the connections between – and the legacies of – neoliberal practices and authoritarian social imaginaries to build alternative futures. If urban political ecology is to assert such a *scholarship of presence*, as Kaika (2019) argues, and if it might do so through a critique of authoritarian populisms, we suggest it might build on the following principles.

Through developing a process-based perspective, such an approach would challenge the reification of the suburb versus the centre.

As we have argued throughout this chapter, our critique of authoritarian populism rests on a process-based perspective that challenges the reifications of the periphery versus the centre. A focus on more-than-urban political ecologies of populist conditions allows for an interrogation of the metabolisms of peripheral relations (Keil and Macdonald, 2016; Angelo, 2017). Rejecting normalised urban oppositions simultaneously allows one to recognise how categories such as the 'urban' or 'rural' are mobilised as forceful spatial categories. Attention to the legal production of spatial difference should also remain aware of its anti-racist power. Cowen and Lewis's (2016) intervention highlights that the contradictions of capitalism increasingly present themselves as spatial anti-Black strategies. Thus, undertaking the kind of cartographic practices that the Black Lives Matter movement exhibits can connect struggles of oppressed peoples against spatial repression and dispossession. And, as Wilson (2021) reaffirms in the case of Chicago's suburbs, such acts of resistance also occur on a mundane level demonstrating the potential within such peripheral spaces.

We therefore believe that a more-than-urban political ecology cements political ecology's heterodox tradition in a way that is attuned to the diverse practices of spatial reification.

While focusing on the relational production of difference, an urban political ecological critique would also draw attention to the geographically specific practices – from car ownership to transit use and lawns – through which everyday life is lived in relationally produced centre-suburbs.

As Sultana (2020) recently reaffirmed, it is vital to analyse the crises of capitalism as they materialise through different forms of marginal contestation. In processes of peripheral urbanisation, such contestation often resides alongside geographically specific practices that are mediated through specific infrastructures from transit to green space. We are deeply resistant to forms of left critique rooted in reified notions of the 'rural' or 'suburban' given how these reproduce the same colonial territorial hierarchies of authoritarian populisms. Recent work using Ekers and Prudham's (2017) 'socioecological fix' has further exemplified how spatial sentiments are woven through authoritarian populist discourses. In different contexts, for example, the (de)concentration of corporate power and profits in struggling ex-coal mining communities is increasingly fuelling right wing movements, as evident in the Appalachian mountains (Harris and McCarthy, 2020) and eastern Germany (Brock et al., 2021). The production of peripheral difference should thus remain attentive to the specific – often infrastructural – relations fostering and facilitating authoritarian populist coalitions.

Such an approach might build upon a philosophy of praxis that captures the movement from situated (relationally understood) practices to conceptions of the world. These conceptions of the world are always articulated with and through sedimented worldviews.

We follow Keil (2019: 173) in arguing that peripheral spaces often 'share to some extent a moment of political disempowerment' that can challenge the elision of specific ideologies (liberal metropolitans vs. provincial populists) with spatially reified regions. Moving away from spatial reification rooted in ostensibly urban lifeworlds thus challenges the political imaginaries fixed in the urban verticality of capitalism (Bordiga, 2016). In turn, drawing on Gramscian interpretations of 'the terrain of ideology' permits a deep engagement with the nuanced histories of (anti-) authoritarian populism in places less obvious to the naked eye (Ekers and Prudham, 2018: 28; see also Wainwright, 2010). Where ex-centric theorisation attunes scholars to the extended capitalisation of space, mobilisation through such epistemologies of relational comparison can point to the shared socialisation of peripheral reification. Or, put differently, as authoritarian populism often resides in the manipulation of peripheral spaces, particularly at the margins, it is crucial to situate such practices within their respective socioecological lifeworlds. Through the evaluation of such imaginaries we must realise, as Wainwright (2010) stresses, that the transformation of (authoritarian populist) conceptions of the world requires conscious labour. The articulation of sedimented worldviews thus further dissects non-dialectical understandings of urban–rural and authoritarian–neoliberal juxtapositions.

Such an approach would learn from – and seek to build upon – an immanent critique of the everyday (sub)urban, thereby formulating both a challenge to right wing populisms and a democratic socio-ecological politics.

As we have sought to emphasise throughout this chapter, any left challenge to authoritarian populism will not go very far if it does not also aspire to being majoritarian. Both political ecology and its urban articulation have developed through an engagement with knowledges and practices 'from below'. Urban political ecology is concerned with environments *as they are lived* rather than Romantic conceptions of a pristine wilderness devoid of human interactions. Necessarily, urban political ecology articulates a popular conception of the environment, a conception that builds on the lived experience of urban populations, always relationally understood. Rather than developing a critique that is removed from such ironments, urban political ecology develops an immanent critique that is rooted within them: it thereby points to a popular political ecology that might challenge authoritarian populisms in their various forms.

Note

1 Although recognising the ambiguities around the term, we will use authoritarian populism as something of a placeholder, given its prevalence within the literatures. Broadly, we follow Stuart Hall's (1985: 118) understanding of *authoritarian populism* as a form of hegemonic politics that incorporates *some* strategic elements of popular opinion into its own hegemonic project and thus represents seemingly contradictory conjunctures with 'a movement towards a dominative and "authoritarian" form of democratic class politics'.

References

Angelo, H. 2017. From the city lens toward urbanisation as a way of seeing: Country/city binaries on an urbanising planet. *Urban Studies* 54(1): 158–78. https://doi.org/10.1177/0042098016629312

Bonds, A. and J. Inwood. 2016. Beyond white privilege: Geographies of white supremacy and settler colonialism. *Progress in Human Geography* 40(6): 715–33. https://doi.org/10.1177/0309132515613166

Bordiga, A. 2016. Space verses cement. In *Espèce Humaine et Croûte Terrestre*. Paris: Payot.

Bosworth, K. 2019. The people know best: Situating the counterexpertise of populist pipeline opposition movements. *Annals of the American Association of Geographers* 109(2): 581–92. https://doi.org/10.1080/24694452.2018.1494538

Brock, A., B.K. Sovacool, and A. Hook. 2021. Volatile photovoltaics: Green industrialization, sacrifice zones, and the political ecology of solar energy in Germany. *Annals of the American Association of Geographers*, 1–23. https://doi.org/10.1080/24694452.2020.1856638

Brown, W. 2019. *In the ruins of neoliberalism: The rise of antidemocratic politics in the West*. New York: Columbia University Press.

Cooper, M. 2017. *Family values: Between neoliberalism and the new social conservatism*. New York: Zone Books.

Cowen, D. and N. Lewis. 2016. Anti-Blackness and urban geopolitical economy. *Society and Space*. www.societyandspace.org/articles/anti-blackness-and-urban-geopolitical-economy, accessed 12 August 2022.

Dikeç, M. 2012. Immigrants, banlieues, and dangerous things: Ideology as an aesthetic affair. *Antipode* 45(1): 23–42. https://doi.org/10.1111/j.1467-8330.2012.00999.x

Dikeç, M. 2017. Disruptive politics. *Urban Studies* 54(1): 49–54. https://doi.org/10.1177/0042098016671476

Ekers, M. and S. Prudham. 2017. The metabolism of socioecological fixes: Capital switching, spatial fixes, and the production of nature. *Annals of the American Association of Geographers* 107(6): 1370–88. https://doi.org/10.1080/24694452.2017.1309962

Ekers, M. and S. Prudham. 2018. The socioecological fix: Fixed capital, metabolism, and hegemony. *Annals of the American Association of Geographers* 108(1): 17–34. https://doi.org/10.1080/24694452.2017.1309963

Ekers, M., P. Hamel, and R. Keil. 2012. Governing suburbia: Modalities and mechanisms of suburban governance. *Regional Studies* 46(3): 405–22. https://doi.org/10.1080/00343404.2012.658036

Ekers, M., S. Kipfer, and A. Loftus. 2020. On articulation, translation, and populism: Gillian Hart's postcolonial Marxism. *Annals of the American Association of Geographers* 110(5): 1577–93. https://doi.org/10.1080/24694452.2020.1715198

Fraser, N. 2017. From progressive neoliberalism to Trump – and beyond. *American Affairs* 1(4): 46–64.

Graybill, J.K. 2019. Emotional Environments of Energy Extraction in Russia. *Annals of the American Association of Geographers* 109(2): 382–94. https://doi.org/10.1080/24694452.2018.1537843

Guilluy, C. 2014. *La France Périphérique: Comment on a Sacrifié Les Classes Populaires*. Paris: Champs actuel.

Hall, S. 1985. Authoritarian populism: A reply. *New Left Review* 1(151): 115–21.

Harris, D.M. and J. McCarthy. 2020. Revisiting power and powerlessness: Speculating on West Virginia's energy future and the externalities of the socioecological fix. *Environment and Planning E: Nature and Space*. https://doi.org/10.1177/2514848620935751

Hart, G. 2002. *Disabling globalization: Places of power in post-Apartheid South Africa*. Berkeley: University of California Press.

Hart, G. 2013. *Rethinking the South African crisis: Nationalism, populism, hegemony*. Scottsville, South Africa: University of KwaZulu-Natal Press.

Hart, G. 2018. Relational comparison revisited: Marxist postcolonial geographies in practice. *Progress in Human Geography* 42(3): 371–94. https://doi.org/10.1177/0309132516681388

Hart, G. 2020. Why did it take so long? Trump-Bannonism in a global conjunctural frame. *Geografiska Annaler: Series B, Human Geography* 102(3): 239–66. https://doi.org/10.1080/04353684.2020.1780791

Harvey, D. 1996. *Justice, nature, and the geography of difference.* Cambridge, MA: Blackwell Publishers.

Inwood, J. 2015. Neoliberal racism: the 'Southern Strategy' and the expanding geographies of white supremacy. *Social & Cultural Geography* 16(4): 407–23. https://doi.org/10.1080/14649365.2014.994670

Inwood, J. 2019. White supremacy, white counter-revolutionary politics, and the rise of Donald Trump. *Environment and Planning C: Politics and Space*, 37(4): 579–96. https://doi.org/10.1177/2399654418789949

Kaika, M. 2004. Interrogating the geographies of the familiar: Domesticating nature and constructing the autonomy of the modern home. *International Journal of Urban and Regional Research* 28(2): 265–86. https://doi.org/10.1111/j.0309-1317.2004.00519.x

Kaika, M. 2017. 'Don't call me resilient again!' The New Urban Agenda as immunology or what happens when communities refuse to be vaccinated with 'smart cities' and indicators. *Environment and Urbanization* 29(1): 89–102. https://doi.org/10.1177/0956247816684763

Kaika, M. 2019. Reclaiming a scholarship of presence: Building alternative socio-environmental imaginaries. In H. Ernstson and E. Swyngedouw (eds.), *Urban political ecology in the Anthropo-obscene: Interruptions and possibilities.* London: Routledge, pp. 239–52.

Keil, R. 2019. Paved paradise: The suburb as chief artefact of the Anthropocene and terrain of new political performativities. In H. Ernstson and E. Swyngedouw (eds.), *Urban political ecology in the Anthropo-obscene: Political interruptions and possibilities.* London: Routledge, pp. 165–83.

Keil, R. and S. Macdonald. 2016. Rethinking urban political ecology from the outside in: Greenbelts and boundaries in the post-suburban city. *Local Environment* 21(12): 1516–33. https://doi.org/10.1080/13549839.2016.1145642

Kenney-Lazar, M. 2019. Neoliberalizing authoritarian environmental governance in (post)socialist Laos. *Annals of the American Association of Geographers* 109(2): 338–48. https://doi.org/10.1080/24694452.2018.1537842

Kipfer, S. 2009. Why the urban question still matters. In R. Keil and R. Mahon (eds.), *Towards a political economy of scale.* Vancouver: UBC Press, pp. 67–83.

Kipfer, S. 2016. Populism. In K. Fritsch, C. O'Connor, and A.K. Thompson (eds.), *Keywords for radicals: The contested vocabulary of late-capitalist struggle* (Oakland, CA: AK Press), pp. 311–19.

Kipfer, S. and M. Dikeç. 2019. Peripheries against peripheries? Against spatial reification. In K.M. Güney, R. Keil, and M. Üçoğlu (eds.), *(Re)building the global periphery, one large scale housing project at a time.* Toronto: University of Toronto Press, pp. 142–64.

Kipfer, S. and P. Saberi. 2014. From 'revolution' to farce? Hard-right populism in the making of Toronto. *Studies in Political Economy* 93(1): 127–52. https://doi.org/10.1080/19187033.2014.11674967

Kipfer, S. and P. Saberi. 2015. The times and spaces of right populism: From Paris to Toronto. *Socialist Register* 52. https://socialistregister.com/index.php/srv/article/view/25603, accessed 12 August 2022.

Kojola, E. 2019. Bringing back the mines and a way of life: Populism and the politics of extraction. *Annals of the American Association of Geographers* 109(2): 371–81. https://doi.org/10.1080/24694452.2018.1506695

Laclau, E. 1977. Towards a theory of populism. In *Politics and ideology in Marxist theory: Capitalism, fascism, populism*. London: Verso, pp. 143–98.

Laclau, E. 2005. *On populist reason*. London: Verso.

Loftus, A. 2019. Political ecology III: Who are 'the people'? *Progress in Human Geography* 44(5): 981–90. https://doi.org/10.1177/0309132519884632

Lyall, A. and G. Valdivia. 2019. The speculative petro-state: Volatile oil prices and resource populism in Ecuador. *Annals of the American Association of Geographers* 109(2): 349–60. https://doi.org/10.1080/24694452.2018.1531690

McCarthy, J. 2019. Authoritarianism, populism, and the environment: Comparative experiences, insights, and perspectives. *Annals of the American Association of Geographers* 109(2): 301–13. https://doi.org/10.1080/24694452.2018.1554393

Mbembe, A. 2008. Necropolitics. In S. Morton and S. Bygrave (eds.), *Foucault in the age of terror*. London: Palgrave Macmillan, pp. 152–82.

Mishra, P. 2017. *Age of anger: A history of the present*. London: Allen Lane.

Mouffe, C. 2019. *For a left populism*. London: Verso.

Mullenite, J. 2019. Infrastructure and authoritarianism in the land of waters: A genealogy of flood control in Guyana. *Annals of the American Association of Geographers* 109(2): 502–10. https://doi.org/10.1080/24694452.2018.1490635

Neimark, B. et al. 2019. Speaking power to 'post-truth': Critical political ecology and the new authoritarianism. *Annals of the American Association of Geographers* 109(2): 613–23. https://doi.org/10.1080/24694452.2018.1547567

Pulido, L. 2015. Geographies of white supremacy and ethnicity 1: White supremacy vs. white privilege in environmental racism research. *Progress in Human Geography* 39(6): 809–17: https://doi.org/10.1177/0309132514563008

Pulido, L., T. Bruno, C. Faiver-Serna, and C. Galentine. 2019. Environmental deregulation, spectacular racism, and white nationalism in the Trump era. *Annals of the American Association of Geographers* 109(2): 520–32. https://doi.org/10.1080/24694452.2018.1549473

Purcell, T.F. and E. Martinez. 2018. Post-neoliberal energy modernity and the political economy of the landlord state in Ecuador. *Energy Research & Social Science, Energy Infrastructure and the Fate of the Nation* 41: 12–21. https://doi.org/10.1016/j.erss.2018.04.003

Sparke, M. and D. Bessner. 2019. Reaction, resilience, and the Trumpist behemoth: Environmental risk management from 'hoax' to technique of domination. *Annals of the American Association of Geographers* 109(2): 533–44. https://doi.org/10.1080/24694452.2018.1549469

Sultana, F. 2020. Political ecology 1: From margins to center. *Progress in Human Geography* 45(1): 156–65. https://doi.org/10.1177/0309132520936751

Swyngedouw, E. 2014. 'Not a drop of water …': State, modernity and the production of nature in Spain, 1898–2010. *Environment and History* 20(1): 67–92. https://doi.org/10.3197/096734014X13851121443445

Tzaninis, Y., T. Mandler, M. Kaika, and R. Keil. 2021. Moving urban political ecology beyond the 'urbanization of nature'. *Progress in Human Geography* 45(2): 229–52.

Wainwright, J. 2010. On Gramsci's 'conceptions of the world'. *Transactions of the Institute of British Geographers* 35(4): 507–21. https://doi.org/10.1111/j.1475-5661.2010.00397.x

Wainwright, J. and G. Mann. 2018. *Climate leviathan: A political theory of our planetary future*. London and New York: Verso.

Wilson, D. 2021. People as infrastructure politics in Global North cities: Chicago's South Side. *Environment and Planning C: Politics and Space*. https://doi.org/10.1177/23996544211004165

Wilson, J. 2017. Perplexing entanglements with a post-neoliberal state. *Journal of Latin American Geography* 16: 177–84. https://doi.org/10.1353/lag.2017.0014

Wilson, R. 2019. Authoritarian environmental governance: Insights from the past century. *Annals of the American Association of Geographers* 109(2): 314–23. https://doi.org/10.1080/24694452.2018.1538767

Wright, M.W. 2019. Border thinking, borderland diversity, and Trump's wall. *Annals of the American Association of Geographers* 109(2): 511–19. https://doi.org/10.1080/24694452.2018.1542290

Wright, R. 2021. Whiteness, nationalism, and the US constitution: Constructing the white nation through legal discourse. *Annals of the American Association of Geographers*. https://doi.org/10.1080/24694452.2020.186578

15

Greenwashing and greywashing: New ideologies of nature in urban sustainability policy

David Wachsmuth and Hillary Angelo

Green and grey sustainable cities

In the face of intensifying global environmental crisis, where do the world's hopeful eyes turn? To the city. 'The environmental challenge we face,' writes David Owen (2004: 112), 'at the current stage of our assault on the world's non-renewable resources, is not how to make our teeming cities more like the pristine countryside. The true challenge is how to make other settled places more like Manhattan.' According to economist Nicholas Stern (2015), cities 'afford multiple opportunities to dramatically reduce carbon emissions while sustaining prosperous standards of living'. One think tank recently declared that 'climate-smart' cities could save the world $17 trillion (Global Commission on Economy and Climate, 2015). And urban leadership pundit Benjamin Barber (2013: 131) made the case as follows: 'Cities cannot wait for states to come to terms with climate change ... Political leadership by mayors and city councils ... and voluntary intercity cooperation ... are key in confronting both the urban consequences of climate change and the underlying causes.'

What does the city as a solution to the world's environmental problems look like? It is not simply a return of nature to the city, but rather a distinctive pairing of 'grey' high-tech environmental strategies with traditionally 'green' interventions such as parks and gardens. New master-planned eco-city projects – of the sort which may soon comprise half of new urban developments in China (Shepard, 2015) – promise sustainability through high technology, thanks to cutting-edge solar power, public transportation, thermal insulation, water filtration, and waste management systems. But optimistic renderings of these spaces inevitably surround shiny new skyscrapers with lakes, trees, and lush parks and plantings, and festoon residential buildings with verdant rooftops or hanging gardens. Planners in North America and Western Europe draw on the same tropes even when not planning new developments from scratch. Urban sustainability plans promote energy efficiency with LEED-certified buildings and smart infrastructure while promising new street trees, expanded park space, and support for urban agriculture and community gardening.

This pairing of high-tech 'grey' with natural 'green' aesthetics is urban sustainability in its paradigmatic contemporary form. And though it appears self-evident, this representational configuration is a thing to be explained. Why do attempts to address climate change and related sustainability challenges take the form of green and grey? Why are high-tech mitigation and adaptation efforts so often dressed up in green? This chapter offers a framework for interpreting contemporary urban sustainability thought and practice, based on a distinction between *green urban nature* and *grey urban nature*. Green urban nature is the return of nature to the city in its most verdant form, while grey urban nature is the concept of social, technological urban space as already inherently sustainable.

This chapter operates in the zone where urban political ecology (Angelo and Wachsmuth, 2015; Gandy, 2003; Heynen et al., 2006; Keil, 2003; Swyngedouw, 1996) overlaps with the urban political economy of climate change (Bulkeley et al., 2015; Cohen, 2017; Rice, 2014), in order to disentangle the power-laden forms of contemporary urban sustainability practices. Here, we add a representational dimension to this analysis by unpacking the distinct aesthetic representations – green and grey – that urban nature takes in responses to the climate crisis. To do so, we develop Henri Lefebvre's ideas of the realistic and transparent illusions as the constitutive ideologies of the production of space to argue that urban sustainability planning today is constituted by twin ideologies of green and grey urban nature, and thereby to make a distinction between the 'greenwashing' and 'greywashing' of climate change.

Urban sustainability thinking's common sense

Contemporary urban sustainability thinking contains a number of diverse and often contradictory elements. But current plans to reorient cities to either mitigate or adapt to global environmental crises generally emphasise some combination of the following key features, which together form a kind of emerging elite 'common sense' (Gramsci, 1971).

Density: Even as suburban modes of urban growth have continued to expand and intensify across the globe in the past 20 years (Keil, 2017), this period has also seen the emergence of something close to a policy consensus around the idea that urban density has environmental value (Jenks et al.,

1996), particularly with respect to the necessity of reducing greenhouse gas emissions. As Glaeser (2009) argues: 'Thoreau was wrong. Living in the country is not the right way to care for the Earth. The best thing that we can do for the planet is build more skyscrapers.'

Smart technology: The 'smart city' is an increasingly diffuse label for a variety of urban development, governance, and branding policies being pursued by governments, corporations, and civil society organisations around the world (Hollands, 2008; Söderström, 2014; Vanolo, 2014). In its early incarnations the smart city was strongly technological but only weakly sustainable. Efficiency, rapidity and ubiquity were its keywords, and the internationally recognisable smart-city projects such as Songdo, South Korea were marketed in these terms. But over the past ten years, smart-city policies have increasingly been pitched on the basis of their environmental potential – a fact which urban research has begun to document (Herrschel, 2013; Neirotti et al., 2014; Viitanen and Kingston, 2014). Today, smart cities such as Songdo and Masdar are upheld as new paragons of urban sustainability.

Resilience: In the face of growing environmental threats, particularly linked to global climate change, urban policymakers have begun to understand sustainability in part as the need to proactively restructure cities' physical and social landscapes to protect them against these threats. This has been accompanied by the arrival of 'resilience' as a new urban policy buzzword (Ahern, 2011), which is arguably beginning to supplant 'sustainability' itself as the master concept for urban environmental thinking (Wilkinson, 2012).

Liveability: Parks and green spaces have been important elements of humane urban development since the nineteenth century, and environmental justice advocates have long argued for more equitable access to these amenities. But today, entrepreneurial urban governance routinely leverages these amenities as a development strategy via 'liveability' – a kind of tangible expression of sustainability at the local scale (Ruth and Franklin, 2014). Urban climate adaptation plans include policy items such as bike lanes, walkability, farmers' markets, and other green infrastructure. And the rising property values and 'green gentrification' more recently associated with proximity to environmental amenities underscore their perceived centrality to contemporary sustainable urban life (Anguelovski and Connolly, 2022; Gould and Lewis, 2016; Johnson Gaither, 2019).

In any combination of these features, today sustainability planning is most often a market-oriented and pro-growth concept (Greenberg, 2015). This is doubly true of *urban* sustainability, since it is precisely the productive power of cities which is supposed to meet global environmental challenges. But even as market- and growth-oriented sustainability planning has become dominant, counter-proposals led by community groups, non-profits, and social movements draw on similar discourses of sustainability as they aim to de-commodify urban environments and offer alternative visions of sustainable urban life (Agyeman, 2005; Greenberg, 2014; Heynen et al., 2006).

Scholars have likewise begun to critique mainstream urban sustainability thinking and policy along several lines. First, researchers have repeatedly identified the underlying conceptual muddiness of urban sustainability policy, from Campbell's (1996: 296) early characterisation of its 'vague idealism' to Gunder's (2006) depiction of sustainability as urban planning's key empty signifier. Similar lines of critique have been developed with respect to 'resilience', the increasingly influential social-ecological policy discourse that conceives urban sustainability goals mostly in terms of risk management, adaptability, and disaster recovery (Evans, 2011; McPhearson, 2014; Meerow and Newell, 2016; Wilkinson, 2012). Human geographers and planners have argued that, for all its new discursive trappings, resilience thinking is in many respects an intensification of existing, politically conservative strands of sustainability discourse (Fainstein, 2015; MacKinnon and Derickson, 2013; White and O'Hare, 2014).

Second, scholars have documented the equity deficits of actually existing urban sustainability planning. The negative impacts of sustainability planning tend to fall disproportionately on the poor and marginalised, while benefits accrue to the wealthy and powerful (Anguelovski et al., 2016; Caprotti, 2014). Following While et al.'s (2004) notion of the 'greening of the growth machine', researchers have explored how urban development actors mobilise the environment as a means of capital accumulation (Evans and Karvonen, 2014; Jonas and While, 2007). Similarly, the growing literature on 'green gentrification' illustrates how environmental amenities meant to 'improve' neighbourhoods can be channelled into regressive neighbourhood change projects (Checker, 2011; Gould and Lewis, 2016).

A final emerging line of critique of contemporary urban sustainability discourse concerns its spatial limits and city-centrism (Angelo and Wachsmuth, 2015). Prior to the 1990s, cities were almost always subject to environmental thought and political action with respect to limiting their negative impacts on the surrounding countryside, where nature and the environment were understood to 'really' be located. Today, sustainability analysis and policy tends to focus on individual cities and city-regions to the exclusion of their wider contexts (Miller and Mössner, 2020). Theoretically, this narrowness forecloses more holistic conceptions of urban nature and sustainability which seek to transcend city boundaries – for example, through the implosion-explosion dialectic of planetary urbanisation (Angelo and Wachsmuth, 2020; Brenner and Schmid, 2015) – and also corresponds to a reductive understanding of the urban as 'the city' (Angelo, 2017; Millington, 2016; Wachsmuth, 2014). Practically, city-centric urban environmental interventions can undermine the very sustainability goals they are driving. When planned and evaluated within narrow spatial parameters, the sustainabilities they achieve within these boundaries are frequently predicated on unsustainabilities elsewhere (Ala-Mantilla et al., 2014; Miller and Mössner, 2020; Wachsmuth et al., 2016).

Green urban nature and grey urban nature

To these important critical appraisals we add a new one: the aesthetic dimensions of contemporary urban sustainability thinking, and the common-sense ideology of nature that underlies them. For all of its diversity, we argue that urban sustainability policy is consistently characterised by two distinct strategies for achieving the sustainable city, corresponding to two very different aesthetic representations of urban nature.

We call these representations *green urban nature* and *grey urban nature*. Green urban nature is the return of nature to the city in its most verdant form. It is signified by street trees and urban gardens, local food and farmers' markets, vertical farming, and greened post-industrial landscapes. In policy it is mobilised in a range of different urban sustainability strategies which leverage self-evidently natural nature, from green walls, bioswales, and urban agriculture up to large-scale landscaping initiatives such as soft coastlines and new parks. Grey urban nature, by contrast, is the concept of social, technological urban space as already inherently sustainable. It is signified by dense urban cores, high-speed public transit, and energy-efficient buildings. In policy terms we see it deployed in strategies which leverage that inherent sustainability of urban space through density and efficiency, ranging from transit and walkability promotion schemes to new smart city construction. We argue that these two sets of phenomenal forms offer two distinct concepts of urban sustainability with corresponding associative pairs: simple/complex; surface/depth; everyday/expert.

We describe these two concepts of urban nature as ideologies: partial representations of reality tied to hegemonic social practices and power relations. Following Henri Lefebvre (1982 [1966], 1991 [1974]), we particularly emphasise the dual *representational* and *historical* character of ideology. First, ideologies are representations in the sense that they express intuitions and common sense about social reality, given that society is too complex and multifaceted to be apprehended directly (Goonewardena, 2005; Wachsmuth, 2014). If common sense emphasises some aspects of this complexity more than others, it does so in a context of unequal power relations – reproducing those relations, contesting them, or some mixture of the two. And so the concept of ideology can be an important lens for identifying and challenging injustices and inequalities – denaturalising social relations to reveal that things could be otherwise.

Second, ideologies are always tied to particular historical and geographical circumstances. While some power-laden social representations (e.g., of class relations or individual liberty) correspond to durable features of capitalist society and have therefore been present throughout its modern history, ideologies can also be embedded in more specific historical-geographical contexts. The neoliberal resurgence of faith in the market to solve social problems is just one of a number of possible examples of historically specific ideologies that are widespread, familiar, and influential.

Green urban nature and grey urban nature are ideologies in this dual representational and historical sense. They express contrasting common senses about urban environments, and the way they do so reflects contemporary power relations – about whose lifestyles and bodies count as environmental concerns and what kinds of environmental interventions they merit. While we propose a categorical distinction that might look 'just' aesthetic, we do so because the differences in aesthetics structure and reflect the strategies, priorities, and assumptions that follow. In other words, the aesthetic differences are important because they do ideological work.

We further argue that the ideological work of green and grey is interconnected: the two are materially and aesthetically opposed but imaginatively mutually supportive. To interpret their relationship we draw on Lefebvre's exploration of the ideologies of modern social space. Lefebvre (1991 [1974]) posits that a new form of social space emerged in the West in the early twentieth century, displacing a tradition stretching back through the Renaissance to Ancient Greece. This new homogenised, fragmented, hierarchised 'abstract space' is the characteristic space of capitalist modernity, but, according to Lefebvre (1991 [1974]: 27), its status as a social product is concealed by 'a double illusion, each side of which refers back to the other, reinforces the other, and hides behind the other'. He terms these double illusions the 'illusion of transparency' and the 'realistic illusion'.

The illusion of transparency is the illusion of transcendentalism and idealism, which sees reality as encrypted but thought as pure and unimpeded: 'Here space appears as luminous, as intelligible, as giving action free rein' (1991 [1974]: 27). The illusion of transparency privileges the ability of thought, language, and design to transform society, by suggesting that social and mental space exist in a direct correspondence with each other. It is therefore a technocratic imaginary which informs planning and representations of space. To a planner or a designer, reality is a complicated ('encrypted') system, but thought can decrypt it, in order to intervene in it and solve its problems.

The realistic illusion – 'the illusion of substantiality, naturalness and spatial opacity' (1991 [1974]: 30) – is the view of space which takes objects at face value, and hence suggests that social space is directly derived from physical space. It is the illusion of natural simplicity, and Lefebvre equates it with a naturalistic materialism, according to which the symbolic meaning of objects lies within the objects themselves. So in contrast to the illusion of transparency, where language and thought are imbued with interpretive and social power, according to the realistic illusion they simply convey reality itself. If the illusion of transparency is a technocratic ideology, the realistic illusion is the ideology of spatial practice and everyday life. It corresponds to the affective dimensions of social space – to the phenomenological experiences through which the reality of 'things' is confirmed.

These two illusions, for all that Lefebvre presents them as opposites, are not in competition with each other. Instead, they are mutually sustaining, masking each other's gaps, and shoring up each other's weaknesses. The 'mental space' of the illusion of transparency and the 'physical space' of the realistic illusion together draw our attention away from the social production of space Lefebvre is seeking to uncover. And, since the social production of space is a historical process, an implication of this analysis is that different socio-historical contexts will host different concrete configurations of the transparent and realistic illusions – masking social complexity through an apparent opposition of the physical and the mental, the evident and the obscure in each case. It is in precisely these terms that we understand green urban nature and grey urban nature. Green and grey are the twin ideological representations of contemporary urban sustainability, that oppose each other and prop each other up. The realistic illusion of green urban nature – the appearance of simplicity, or the materialist distortion of the socio-natural – is the older and the more familiar of the two. But green urban nature now travels hand-in-hand with the newer transparent illusion of grey urban nature – an idealist distortion of the socio-natural through the appearance of complexity.

The realistic illusion of green urban nature

According to the realistic illusion of green urban nature, *if it looks green it is green*. The self-evidently natural is assumed to in fact be natural, and moreover to be sustainable. The conceptual breakthrough of green urban nature is that society and nature are linked in material terms, and that cities can be made more sustainable by bringing nature into them. The realistic illusion thus intertwines two related premises. The first is that nature is a real material thing to be discovered outside the city and imported into it – as Lefebvre (1991 [1974]: 30) describes it, a 'hard dense reality delivered direct from mother nature'. Once it arrives in the city, green urban nature is characteristically low-tech, small-scale, and harmonious, which places it in contrast with the rest of the city.

The straightforward appearance of nature offered by green walls, bioswales, urban agriculture, and the like causes us to overlook the technology and planning required to implement them, as the 'rational is thus naturalized' (Lefebvre, 1991 [1974]: 30). Even where green urban nature interventions in fact rest on complex and large-scale engineering feats, they are represented as simple and direct. This ideology made it possible for New Yorkers to accept Olmsted and Vaux's Central Park as an escape from the city in the nineteenth century (Rosenzweig and Blackmar, 1992), and led the designers of New York City's High Line to plant wildflowers as replacements for the 'real' wild growth that had accumulated on the rail line during the decades it was not in use – in spite of the long history and present diversity of meanings, both positive and negative, of nature (Fitzsimmons, 1989; Nash, 2014; Selin, 2013).

The second premise of the realistic illusion of green urban nature is that nature is per se sustainable, and that the things that look like nature must be more sustainable than the things that do not. Green urban nature has the appearance of unspoiled 'first nature': plants and vegetation are obviously sustainable because they are synonymous with first nature itself. It is for this reason, we argue, that urban sustainability plans are literally green – that their imagery emphasises trees, parks, and waterways. And even planning that relies predominantly on technological means of achieving sustainability tends to include straightforwardly green components to make the case for its ecological benefits. Green walls, gardens and eco-roofs may not be central to the actual ecological impact of these projects (more likely determined by water and energy use, waste disposal systems, etc.), but they tend to feature heavily in promotional materials. The aesthetics of green urban nature are used to communicate sustainability to lay audiences.

The underlying conceptual foundation of green urban nature – that nature is 'real' in a non-social or even pre-social sense, and thereby exists as a resource to improve the urban social – has been critiqued from both cultural (Williams, 1973) and political-economic (Smith, 2010 [1984]) perspectives. It was also the target of much of the first generation of urban political ecology scholarship (Heynen et al., 2006; Swyngedouw, 1996), which introduced the concept of 'socio-nature' to dissolve society–nature binaries in urban contexts. Nevertheless, as this discussion of the realistic illusion illustrates, extra-social representations of urban nature persist. The realistic illusion of green urban nature is an ideology of spatial practice; whether or not planners truly believe greener things are actually more sustainable, they are reproducing this ideology when they cover their energy-efficient smart buildings in decorative plants.

The transparent illusion of grey urban nature

According to the transparent illusion of grey urban nature, sustainability is a thing lurking beneath the surface of the city, to be uncovered through science, technology, and expertise. The conceptual breakthrough of grey urban nature is that the environment is not separable from the social production of urban space, but exists to be revealed, shaped, or enhanced within cities as they actually are. While a version of this analysis was a foundational insight for urban political ecologists and critical geographers (Braun and Castree, 2005; Heynen et al., 2006; Swyngedouw, 1996) who made their critique of green urban nature in order to render grey urban nature visible, it has more recently found public champions among economistic urban environmentalists such as Glaeser (2011), who have made the case that, in sustainability terms, 'grey' is really greener than 'green'.

The ideology of grey urban nature rests on two premises. The first is that reality is complex and requires decoding to be properly understood, but that *knowledge* is transparent and able to accomplish this decoding. According to the illusion of transparency, planners and engineers are the experts with the knowledge and skills required to uncover the city's environmental content. In this sense, even though it is primarily concerned with the management of natural resources (above all energy, water, and carbon dioxide), grey urban nature rejects the romanticism of the realistic illusion's green 'first nature' (Marx and Engels, 1970 [1846]; Schmidt, 2014 [1962]). Instead, it emphasises a technologically mediated 'second nature'. If the realistic illusion of green urban nature is the ideology of spatial practice and everyday life, we might understand the transparent illusion as the technocratic imagination at work in planning and representations of space.

The second premise of grey urban nature is that sustainability is not a property of nature per se, but rather a characteristic which can be discovered or engineered in complex social systems. The current emphasis in sustainability-oriented urban planning on transit development and densification reflects this principle. And the rhetorical thrust of many of the most influential grey urban nature arguments (including Owen's [2009] *Green metropolis* and Glaeser's [2011] *Triumph of the city*) has been a wilful counter-intuitiveness – a celebration of the triumph of scientific and evidence-based reasoning in establishing the importance of grey urban density over merely aesthetic appeals to green nature. These arguments treat sustainability problems as complicated ones to which we must apply sophisticated technology and expertise. The transparent illusion of grey urban nature claims to have pierced the surface of complex urban reality and found the sustainability underneath. Grey urban nature aesthetics correspondingly look like electric car chargers, high-tech smart-city infrastructure, and green building design.

The transparent illusion implies a certain idealistic or even utopian belief in the promise of 'smart' technology to solve sustainability problems by out-thinking and out-planning bad outcomes and continuing to support economic growth. And indeed, the critique of grey urban nature has come most forcefully from sceptical appraisals of the smart city. As scholars such as Greenfield (2013), Hollands (2008), and Söderström et al. (2014) have demonstrated, smart city proponents' claims to a comprehensive technocratic rationality have always been highly overstated. The knowledges underlying the smart city in general, and 'grey' smart city sustainability strategies in particular, are always fragmented, partial, and distorted. They model resource flows with sophistication but struggle to incorporate the cultural or political flows which may prove more consequential for how resources get deployed and appropriated. Grey urban nature is an ideological representation of sustainability that communicates it through the promise of high-tech engineering.

In sum, the imagery, discourse, and designs of contemporary urban sustainability planning are characterised by these two distinct ideologies. The realistic and transparent illusions of urban nature oppose each other and prop each other up to create the image of a sustainable city. Even the most technology-centric smart city plan is likely to deploy green imagery to emphasise its sustainability objectives, and images of urban agriculture likewise often emphasise its embeddedness within the grey city.

Grey substrate, green surface: Abu Dhabi's Masdar City

We now explore the interrelation of green and grey representations of urban nature through the case of Masdar City in the United Arab Emirates (UAE) – one of the world's most infamous urban sustainability schemes, and perhaps the place which most efficiently embodies the urban dialectic of climate crisis. Initiated in 2006 by the Abu Dhabi government, Masdar City was an environmental, high-tech smart city, created with the dual ambitions of being the world's first zero-carbon city and a means of reorienting the national economy away from fossil fuels. Though the project has so far failed to reach its ambitious environmental goals (Goldenberg, 2016), Masdar City arguably remains the world's leader in the emerging policy terrain of 'sustainable smart cities'. Although Masdar is an archetypally grey sustainability project, leveraging smart-city technology towards environmental ends, it relies heavily on the aesthetics of green urban nature to make this environmentalism legible. In this configuration of 'grey substrate, green surface', a veneer of green urban nature helps communicate the ecological content of grey sustainability interventions, and the affective dimensions of the latter and the techno-rational dimensions of the former mutually support each other.

Masdar City is substantively a grey urban nature project. Its major infrastructural systems all use renewable and alternative energy technologies, including energy (solar), transit (electric) and water and waste treatment systems. The orientation and surfaces of the buildings, and the narrow, pedestrian-friendly streets were designed to counter energy-intensive forms of contemporary urbanism, creating cooler interiors and exteriors to reduce dependence on cars and air conditioning. And the city itself has been leveraged for larger state development goals. From the beginning, the project was meant to help transform Abu Dhabi's economy for a post-oil future by providing a new national template for sustainable economic growth. And so, in addition to using solar and renewables in the city's design, Abu Dhabi planned for the city to house a 'community of academics, researchers, start-up companies and financiers – all focused on developing renewable energy and sustainability technologies' (Nader, 2009: 3952).

Yet Masdar City's attempts to achieve sustainability through grey forms of design, building materials, and transportation and energy systems have, since the project's inception, been promoted through signifiers of green urban nature. In renderings, promotional photographs, and the city's master plan, residential areas, schools, and the visitor centre are surrounded by plants, trees, and green lawns. Photographs of many of the development's office and research buildings are foregrounded with foliage, signalling the LEED certifications of the buildings and the alternative energy research occurring inside (Masdar, 2015). The city's plans also include 'biodiversity protection areas' and green corridors that are to provide habitat for native species and serve as recreational areas (Masdar, 2015: 56). In each of these designs and representations the green veneer of palm trees and gently waving grasses 'remind' us in everyday, phenomenal terms that Masdar City is designed to promote more sustainable ways of living and working.

The plans use these signifiers of apparently straightforward reality (green urban nature) to communicate a complex reality (grey urban nature) in intuitive terms. The green veneer is the realistic illusion; the grey substance the illusion of transparency. While the project's sustainability goals will really be achieved (to the extent they are achieved at all) through often-invisible, highly engineered materials and systems, Masdar City's superficial greenness represents the city as sustainable.

This pairing of green surface and grey substrate is also readily apparent in the way third parties have interpreted and digested Masdar City's sustainability plans. On the green side, an article in the UAE's leading English-language newspaper called 'Sowing the seeds of gardening-based change at Masdar City' quotes Masdar City's project directors describing the intention of the city's landscaping to 'imbue a new mindset that promotes the concept of living in harmony with our culture and environment' (Hunt, 2015). The designers are working with local nurseries to supply Masdar City with native plants large enough to create a 'landscape regime' that promotes the 'experience of engaging with nature'. On the grey side, a story in *Renewable Energy Focus* prepared on Masdar City for the 2010 World Future Energy Summit describes Masdar City's sustainability entirely in terms of a 'brave new world' of futuristic, high-tech research, that requires solar investments, innovations in electricity and engineering technology, wind power, and biotech (Hopwood, 2010). For this professional audience, the environment to be saved and promoted is a complex, technological system in which industry leaders '[forge] our energy future by developing a renewable fuel supply [and] developing and commercializing … low-carbon energy sources' (Hopwood, 2010: 23). The green urban nature perspective offers sustainability on the surface of reality, while the grey urban nature perspective looks for it underneath.

Conclusions: The ideological work of urban sustainability

'Sustainability' is frequently criticised for being an amorphous concept or an empty signifier (Brown, 2016). In spite of the truth in this, we have argued that in the domain of urban policy sustainability is nevertheless consistently characterised by two distinct ideas: green urban nature and grey urban nature. These are pervasive but unacknowledged common-sensical frames for understanding what counts as sustainable and what should be prioritised in urban-environmental policy. The purpose of this chapter has been to offer a framework for decoding contemporary urban sustainability thinking in these terms.

We have applied this framework to the case of Masdar City, where 'uncovering' the urban environmental symbolism at work risks falling into a trap of over-credulity, since the entire project is fundamentally a public relations exercise. The UAE is one of the hubs of the fossil fuel industry, which is central to the production of global climate crisis. And while Masdar City no doubt embodies some degree of good-faith effort to invest in renewable energy research which could see the UAE transition to a post-fossil fuel economy, it arguably has more in common with longstanding fossil fuel industry attempts at greenwashing their ongoing unsustainable investments (Scanlan, 2017). Yet the specific form this greenwashing has taken is nevertheless instructive, since it is through the combination of 'green surface and grey substrate' that Masdar City can most convincingly communicate its narrative of eco-modernisation (Cugurullo, 2016) in response to climate crisis. In other words, there is both 'greenwashing' and 'greywashing' at work here: the greywashing of a fossil fuel economy in a smart city sustainability initiative, and the greenwashing of that initiative in green garb.

Abu Dhabi's Masdar City shows an important concrete configuration of green and grey urban natures (what we call grey substrate, green surface) in the context of spectacular (and speculative) urban development. And, while the Masdar City case is valuable simply because it is so spectacular, and thus puts the dynamics of green and grey on clear display, these dynamics can also be seen at work in a variety of historical and geographic configurations (see Wachsmuth and Angelo, 2018).

For example, while green and grey urban nature are twin representational forms of contemporary urban environmentalism, they have distinct historical trajectories. Green urban nature has been a consistent presence in urban design and thought throughout the past 150 years. Grey urban nature, by contrast, is a relatively recent phenomenon. The case of brownfield redevelopment in Germany's Ruhr Valley in the 1990s illustrates this fact. Until the late twentieth century, in the Ruhr as throughout Europe and North America, grey stood for the destruction of nature: polluting technologies of coal extraction and the steel industry. By the 1990s, IBA Emscher Park, a 200km park and regional redevelopment project which turned industrial brownfields into parks, greenways, and heritage and cultural sites, conceived a second 'industrial-nature' (*Industrienatur*) which it deliberately showcased at ecological and cultural heritage sites and used for ecological restoration (Angelo, 2021). This was a first step toward 'grey' as a representational form coming to connote positive environmental outcomes and toward the idea that sustainability could be engineered through technology.

Vancouver's Greenest City 2020 Action Plan, meanwhile, provides a paradigmatic example of how green and grey represent two distinct planning and policy agendas that are nevertheless logically bundled under the rubric of sustainability. The plan, which was launched in 2011, contains robust density- and technology-focused 'grey' interventions aimed at reducing greenhouse gas emissions alongside robust liveability-focused 'green' interventions aimed at creating a pleasant urban environment. But there is very little substantive connection between the two; they simply rest side by side as the two self-evident pillars of urban sustainability. In our analysis this represents a common post-industrial pattern of urban sustainability thinking and practice. Separate green and grey dimensions can be seen in affluent cities' sustainability plans–such as New York's PlaNYC and OneNYC–as well as climate action plans in California cities of all sizes and political orientations (Angelo et al., 2022).

Fifty years ago, Lefebvre highlighted the irony of placing a high value on symbols of nature in the context of ongoing ecological degradation. He wrote:

Theoretically, nature is shrinking, but the signs of nature and the natural are multiplying, replacing and supplanting real 'nature' ... Undiscoverable, fugitive, ravaged, the residue of urbanization and industrialization, nature can be found everywhere. ... Parks and open spaces, the last word in good intentions and bad urban representation, are simply a poor substitute for nature, the degraded simulacrum of the open space characteristic of encounters, games, parks, gardens and public squares.

(Lefebvre, 2003 [1970]: 27)

Contemporary climate crisis has only made these remarks more apropos. Green urban nature enjoys an ongoing popularity stemming from the perceived social and moral value that is a product of modern associations of aesthetic greenness with 'good' (Angelo, 2021), as well as common-sense notions of green as sustainable. Equity-oriented local climate planning efforts are correspondingly often dominated by green policies (Angelo et al., 2022). As we discussed above, grey urban nature is a historically newer idea, but it too has developed a certain fetish character in the elite circuits of global sustainability policy networks, where the confluence of corporate partnerships and fetishisation of technical expertise drives an emphasis on technological and density-driven approaches to fighting climate change. Global inter-urban sustainability networks such as ICLEI, C40, and 100 Resilient Cities have become a key source of momentum behind the slow spread of what Hughes et al. (2019) call 'data-driven urban climate mitigation' policies.

In the end, there are no necessary differences between green urban nature and grey urban nature with respect to either their environmental content or their objective sustainability outcomes. Both are *socio-natures*: hybrid assemblages of the social and natural (Swyngedouw, 1996). Green strategies are not somehow more natural because they rely on visible deployments of non-human nature, nor are grey strategies somehow more social or more technological. Both rely on complex and cutting-edge metabolisms of nature, capital, society, and technology. In practice, both take concrete form in small- and large-scale, top-down and bottom-up ways; for every community garden there is a massive coastal re-engineering effort, and for every transnational corporate smart city there is a neighbourhood infill scheme. Likewise, the relationship between either of these forms of appearance of sustainability and actual sustainable outcomes is an indeterminate one. Even as the low-carbon benefits of high-tech post-industrial cities have arguably been oversold (Wachsmuth et al., 2016), grey urban nature strategies can be effective at reducing greenhouse gas emissions where they take appropriate account of spatial and temporal scale (Ramesh et al., 2010). Conversely, whereas more trees do not guarantee urban sustainability (Escobedo et al., 2011), retrofitting city streets and buildings with more vegetation really does reduce rainwater runoff and urban heat island effects (Susca et al., 2011).

The indeterminacy of these policies' actual impacts thus leaves open arguably the most important question, which is under what conditions political actors mobilise different ideas of urban nature, and to what ends. In the face of intensifying environmental crisis, how can existing progressive and radical visions of urban sustainability be supported, and how can new visions be developed?

References

Agyeman, J. 2005. *Sustainable communities and the challenge of environmental justice.* New York: NYU Press.
Ahern, J. 2011. From fail-safe to safe-to-fail: Sustainability and resilience in the new urban world. *Landscape and Urban Planning* 100(4): 341–3.
Ala-Mantilla, S., J. Heinonen, and S. Junnila. 2014. Relationship between urbanization, direct and indirect greenhouse gas emissions, and expenditures: A multivariate analysis. *Ecological Economics* 104: 129–39.
Angelo, H. 2017. From the city lens toward urbanisation as a way of seeing: Country/city binaries on an urbanising planet. *Urban Studies* 54(1): 158–78.
Angelo, H. 2021. *How became good: Urbanized nature and the making of cities and citizens.* Chicago: University of Chicago Press.
Angelo, H. and D. Wachsmuth. 2015. Urbanizing urban political ecology: A critique of methodological cityism. *International Journal of Urban and Regional Research* 39(1): 16–27.
Angelo, H. and D. Wachsmuth. 2020. Why does everyone think cities can save the planet? *Urban Studies* 57(11): 2201–21. DOI: 10.1177/0042098020919081.
Angelo, H., K. MacFarlane, A. Millard-Ball, and J. Sirigotis. 2022. Missing the housing for the trees: Equity in urban climate planning. *Journal of Planning Education and Research.* https://doi.org/10.1177/0739456X211072527
Anguelovski, I. and J.J. Connolly (eds.). 2022. *The green city and social injustice: 21 tales from North America and Europe.* New York: Routledge.
Anguelovski, I., L. Shi, E. Chu, D. Gallagher, K. Goh, Z. Lamb, K. Reeve and H. Teicher. 2016. Equity impacts of urban land use planning for climate adaptation: Critical perspectives from the Global North and South. *Journal of Planning Education and Research* 36(3): 333–48.
Barber, B. 2013. *If mayors ruled the world: Dysfunctional nations, rising cities.* New Haven, CT: Yale University Press.
Braun, B. and N. Castree (eds.). 2005. *Remaking reality: Nature at the millennium.* London: Routledge.
Brenner, N. and C. Schmid. 2015. Towards a new epistemology of the urban? *City* 19(2–3): 151–82.
Brown, T. 2016. Sustainability as empty signifier: Its rise, fall, and radical potential. *Antipode* 48(1): 115–33.
Bulkeley, H., V. Castán Broto and G.A.S. Edwards. 2015. *An urban politics of climate change: Experimentation and the governing of socio-technical transitions.* London: Routledge.
Campbell, S. 1996. Green cities, growing cities, just cities? Urban planning and the contradictions of sustainable development. *Journal of the American Planning Association* 62(3): 296–312.

Caprotti, F. 2014. Eco-urbanism and the eco-city, or, denying the right to the city? *Antipode* 46(5): 1285–303.
Checker, M. 2011. Wiped out by the 'greenwave': Environmental gentrification and the paradoxical politics of urban sustainability. *City & Society* 23(2): 210–29.
Cohen, D.A. 2017. The other low-carbon protagonists: Poor people's movements and climate politics in São Paulo. In M. Greenberg and P. Luce (eds.), *The city is the factory*. Ithaca: Cornell University Press.
Cugurullo, F. 2016. Urban eco-modernisation and the policy context of new eco-city projects: Where Masdar City fails and why. *Urban Studies* 53(11): 2417–33.
Escobedo, F.J., T. Kroeger, and J.E. Wagner. 2011. Urban forests and pollution mitigation: Analyzing ecosystem services and disservices. *Environmental Pollution* 159(8–9): 2078–87.
Evans, J.P. 2011. Resilience, ecology and adaptation in the experimental city. *Transactions of the Institute of British Geographers* 36(2): 223–37.
Evans, J. and A. Karvonen. 2014. 'Give me a laboratory and i will lower your carbon footprint!' Urban laboratories and the governance of low-carbon futures. *International Journal of Urban and Regional Research* 38(2): 413–30.
Fainstein, S. 2015. Resilience and justice. *International Journal of Urban and Regional Research* 39(1): 157–67.
Fitzsimmons, M. 1989. The matter of nature. *Antipode* 21(2): 106–20.
Gandy, M. 2003. *Concrete and clay*. Cambridge, MA: MIT Press.
Glaeser, E. 2009. Green cities, brown suburbs. *City Journal*. www.city-journal.org/html/green-cities-brown-suburbs-13143.html, accessed 12 August 2022.
Glaeser, E. 2011. *Triumph of the city: How urban spaces make us human*. London: Pan Macmillan.
Global Commission on Economy and Climate. 2015. *Seizing the global opportunity*. Washington, DC: New Climate Economy.
Goonewardena, K. 2005. The urban sensorium: Space, ideology and the aestheticization of politics. *Antipode* 37(1): 46–71.
Goldenberg, S. 2016. Masdar's zero-carbon dream could become world's first green ghost town. *The Guardian*, 16 February. www.theguardian.com/environment/2016/feb/16/masdars-zero-carbon-dream-could-become-worlds-first-green-ghost-town, accessed 12 August 2022.
Gould, K. and T. Lewis. 2016. *Green gentrification: Urban sustainability and the struggle for environmental justice*. New York: Routledge.
Gramsci, A. 1971. Selections from the prison notebooks. Edited by Q. Hoare and G.N. Smith. London: Lawrence & Wishart.
Greenberg, M. 2014. The disaster inside the disaster: Hurricane Sandy and post-crisis redevelopment. *New Labor Forum* 23(1): 44–52.
Greenberg, M. 2015. The sustainability edge: Competition, crisis, and the rise of green urban branding. In C. Isenhour, G. McDonogh, and M. Checker (eds.), *Sustainability in the global city*. Cambridge: Cambridge University Press, pp. 105–130.
Greenfield, A. 2013. *Against the smart city*. Kindle digital edition.
Gunder, M. 2006. Sustainability: Planning's saving grace or road to perdition? *Journal of Planning Education and Research* 26(2): 208–21.
Herrschel, T. 2013. Competitiveness and sustainability: Can 'smart city regionalism' square the circle? *Urban Studies* 50(11): 2332–48.
Heynen, N., M. Kaika, and E. Swyngedouw (eds.). 2006. *In the nature of cities: Urban political ecology and the politics of urban metabolism*. London: Routledge.
Hollands, R.G. 2008. Will the real smart city please stand up? *City* 12(3): 303–20.

Hopwood, D. 2010. Abu Dhabi's Masdar plan takes shape. *Renewable Energy Focus* 11(1): 18–23.
Hughes, S., L. Tozer, and S. Geist. 2019. The politics of data-driven urban climate mitigation. In O.J. van der Heijden, C. Certomà, and H. Bulkeley (eds.), *Urban climate politics: Agency and empowerment.* Cambridge: Cambridge University Press.
Hunt, M. 2015. Sowing the seeds of gardening-based change at Masdar City. *The National*, 26 January. www.thenational.ae/arts-life/home-garden/sowing-the-seeds-of-gardening-based-change-at-masdar-city, accessed 12 August 2022.
Jenks, M., E. Burton, and K. Williams (eds.). 1996. *The compact city: A sustainable urban form?* London: E. & F.N. Spon.
Johnson Gaither, C. 2019. Socioecological production of parks in Atlanta, Georgia's Proctor Creek watershed: Creating ecosystem services or negative externalities? *Environmental Justice* 12(6): 231–41.
Jonas, A.E. and A. While. 2007. Greening the entrepreneurial city. In R. Krueger and D. Gibbs (eds.), *The sustainable development paradox: Urban political economy in the United States and Europe.* New York: Guilford Press, pp. 123–59.
Keil, R. 2003. Progress report – urban political ecology. *Urban Geography* 24(8): 723–38.
Keil, R. 2017. *Suburban planet: Making the world urban from the outside in.* Hoboken: Wiley.
Lefebvre, H. 1982 [1966]. *The sociology of Marx.* New York: Columbia University Press.
Lefebvre, H. 1991 [1974]. *The production of space.* Oxford: Blackwell.
Lefebvre, H. 2003 [1970]. *The urban revolution.* Minnesota, MN: University of Minnesota Press.
MacKinnon, D. and K.D. Derickson. 2013. From resilience to resourcefulness. *Progress in Human Geography* 37(2): 253–70.
Marx, K. and F. Engels. 1970 [1846]. *The German ideology: Vol. 1.* New York: International Publishers Co.
Masdar. 2017. Sustainability report 2015. www.masdar.ae/assets/downloads/content/669/masdar_sustainability_report_2015.pdf, accessed 12 August 2022.
McPhearson, T. 2014. The rise of resilience: Linking resilience and sustainability in city planning. *The Nature of Cities.* www.thenatureofcities.com/2014/06/08/the-rise-of-resilience-linking-resilience-and-sustainability-in-city-planning/#comment-8683, accessed 12 August 2022.
Meerow, S. and J.P. Newell. 2016. Urban resilience, for whom, what, when, where, and why? *Urban Geography* 40(3): 309–29. DOI: 10.1080/02723638.2016.1206395.
Millington, G. 2016. Urbanization and the city image in Lowry at Tate Britain. *International Journal of Urban and Regional Research* 40(4): 717–35. DOI:10.1111/1468-2427.12375.
Miller, B. and S. Mössner. 2020. Urban sustainability and counter-sustainability: Spatial contradictions and conflicts in policy and governance in the Freiburg and Calgary metropolitan regions. *Urban Studies.* DOI: 10.1177/0042098020919280.
Nader, S. 2009. Paths to a low-carbon economy: The Masdar example. *Energy Procedia* 1(1): 3951–8.
Nash, R. 2014. *Wilderness and the American mind.* New Haven: Yale University Press.
Neirotti, P., A. De Marco, A.C. Cagliano, G. Mangano, and F. Scorrano. 2014. Current trends in smart city initiatives: Some stylised facts. *Cities* 38: 25–36.
Owen, D. 2004. Green Manhattan. *The New Yorker* 80(31): 111–23.

Owen, D. 2009. *Green metropolis.* New York: Riverhead Hardcover.
Ramesh, T., R. Prakash, and K.K. Shukla. 2010. Life cycle energy analysis of buildings: An overview. *Energy and Buildings* 42(10): 1592–600.
Rice, J.L. 2014. An urban political ecology of climate change governance. *Geography Compass* 8(6): 381–94.
Rosenzweig, R. and E. Blackmar. 1992. *The park and the people.* Ithaca: Cornell University Press.
Ruth, M. and R.S. Franklin. 2014. Livability for all? Conceptual limits and practical implications. *Applied Geography* 49: 18–23.
Scanlan, S.J. 2017. Framing fracking: Scale-shifting and greenwashing risk in the oil and gas industry. *Local Environment* 22(11): 1311–37.
Schmidt, A. 2014 [1962]. *The concept of nature in Marx.* New York: Verso Books.
Selin, H. (ed.). 2013. *Nature across cultures: Views of nature and the environment in non-Western cultures.* Berlin: Springer Science & Business Media.
Shepard, W. 2015. Can hundreds of new 'ecocities' solve China's environmental problems? *Citymetric.* www.citymetric.com/skylines/can-hundreds-new-ecocities-solve-chinas-environmental-problems-1306, accessed 12 August 2022.
Smith, N. 2010 [1984]. *Uneven development.* Athens: University of Georgia Press.
Söderström, O., T. Paasche, and F. Klauser. 2014. Smart cities as corporate storytelling. *City* 18(3): 307–20.
Stern, N. 2015. Climate change and cities: A prime source of problems, yet key to a solution. *The Guardian,* 17 November. www.theguardian.com/cities/2015/nov/17/cities-climate-change-problems-solution, accessed 12 August 2022.
Susca, T., S.R. Gaffin, and G.R. Dell'Osso. 2011. Positive effects of vegetation: Urban heat island and green roofs. *Environmental Pollution* 159(8–9): 2119–26.
Swyngedouw, E. 1996. The city as a hybrid. *Capitalism Nature Socialism* 7(2): 65–80.
Vanolo, A. 2014. Smartmentality: The smart city as disciplinary strategy. *Urban Studies* 51(5): 883–98.
Viitanen, J. and R. Kingston. 2014. Smart cities and green growth: Outsourcing democratic and environmental resilience to the global technology sector. *Environment and Planning A* 46(4): 803–19.
Wachsmuth, D. 2014. City as ideology: Reconciling the explosion of the city form with the tenacity of the city concept. *Environment and Planning D: Society and Space* 32(1): 75–90.
Wachsmuth, D. and H. Angelo. 2018. Green and gray: New ideologies of nature in urban sustainability policy. *Annals of the American Association of Geographers* 108(4): 1038–56.
Wachsmuth, D., D.A. Cohen, and H. Angelo. 2016. Expand the frontiers of urban sustainability. *Nature* 536(7617): 391–3.
While, A., A.E.G. Jonas and D. Gibbs. 2004. The environment and the entrepreneurial city: Searching for the urban 'sustainability fix' in Manchester and Leeds. *International Journal of Urban and Regional Research* 28(3): 549–69.
White, I. and P. O'Hare. 2014. From rhetoric to reality: Which resilience, why resilience, and whose resilience in spatial planning? *Environment and Planning C: Government and Policy* 32(5): 934–50.
Wilkinson, C. 2012. Social-ecological resilience: Insights and issues for planning theory. *Planning Theory* 11(2): 148–69.
Williams, R. 1973. *The country and the city.* Oxford: Oxford University Press.

16

The peasant way or the urban way? Why disidentification matters for emancipatory politics

Irina Velicu

Introduction

Is capitalism a factory of urbanites? How do dualist identifications such as peasants vs. urbanites support or impede democratic egalitarian politics? The 'planetary urbanization' thesis adopted by some prominent scholars (Brenner and Schmid, 2015; Brenner and Katsikis, Chapter 5 in this volume; Monte-Mór and Limonad, Chapter 3 in this volume) proposed a new epistemology for understanding global spatial transformations: such unidimensional epistemology risks producing 'a potential pernicious ideological position for a universal "urbanism" that inherently negates – that is it also depoliticises – the range of diversity and difference external to, and/or within, urbanisation' (Grange and Gunder, 2019: 393; Jazeel 2018; Schindler, 2017). Such epistemology erases the messiness of everyday life (Lefebvre, 2014 [1991]), epistemological pluralism (Walker, 2015; Oswin, 2018) and the political agency of an 'outside' to the urban (Grange and Gunder, 2019). In other words,

> it could be argued that UPE's call to overcome the distinction between core and periphery, inside and outside, still privileges (at least discursively) the inside, the core, and the center as the spaces that dictate the logic of the outside.
> (Tzaninis et al., 2021: 232)

Therefore, some scholars argue for maintaining the relational dualism where the rural continues to provide the urban with a 'dissensus' necessary for further political transformation (Davidson and Iveson, 2015). In this chapter I engage with these tensions by focusing on the discursive practices of a global peasant movement that promotes the 'peasant way' as an alternative, i.e., *Via Campesina*. The starting observation is that, in order to have an inside or outside of capitalism, one has to accept unambiguously the trajectory of such a path of development. For this to happen, as Tania Murray Li has argued, the transition narrative should be rejected because there is no one trajectory or end point of development.[1]

The rural may not just be the peripheral that feeds and drives the expansion and development of urbanisation: while it has often been seen as the 'outside' left to 'conquer' in the sense of proletarisation (Bernstein, 2014), it has also been seen as the source of 'resilience' for these populations who, in many cases, have never been fully absorbed into the industrial wage-labour force (Visser et al., 2019) or affected by waves of dispossession without prospects of labour (Li, 2010; 2011). While critical vigilance to the 'urbanization of nature' (Kaika, 2005) is crucial, perhaps in order to allow for ambiguousness to play a role in egalitarian social struggles nowadays we have to allow for political imagination to undo the terms of any consensual politics about dualisms. Whether 'peasants living in flats' (Visser et al., 2019: 501) or urbanites investing in the rural to expand, the political strength of such forms of identifications may rather be limited if emancipation is seen as intersectional alliance-building (Sbicca, 2012). To paraphrase Kaika, there can be no value without value-less, no virtue without vice, no identity without 'anonymous'.[2] My proposal to focus on Rancière's theory of subjectification (and disidentification) as opposed to identity politics or justice as recognition aims at expanding understandings about the role of subject positions in social struggles and movements. Specifically, I am looking at the limits of existing classifications such as 'food sovereignty' or 'peasant rights' and illustrating a repetitive tendency to conflate politics with ontology, which may also be observed in the agro-food and *Via Campesina* movements: using Rancière, I am exploring the possibility to reflect on the political as less about subjects with a series of virtues (such as good ecocitizens) and more about political subjects as events of subjectification, which implies processes of disidentification.

Calling themselves 'peasants' in *Via Campesina* has been in itself a political position-statement and performance (Desmarais et al., 2007; Velicu and Ogrezeanu, 2022). Claiming sovereignty for food, seeds, or land is described as a political democratic project or movement credited with 'cooling the planet' by reversing urban unemployment, migration, or hunger, revaluing the countryside, and building ecosystem resilience (McMichael, 2014; Perfecto et al., 2009). In other words, ruralisation or at least the revaluation of the rural as the 'outside' of the urban of society is credited with the power to counteract the damaging effect of industrialisation and urbanisation. As I will elaborate in the next section, the immense literature on food sovereignty is focused on 'validating' and recognising the value (economic, cultural, or spiritual) of the virtuous subject of 'peasant': no longer seen as historically anachronic, they are seen as a new contemporary foundation of civilisation (Wittman et al., 2010). I propose a zooming-out of this debate to observe that such rhetoric places the debate on peasantry again and again in the same meritocratic logic of policy-police that is to blame for the reproduction of inequalities in the first place. I discuss the limits of this politics of rights as an open question about the subject of rights or what Rancière discussed as the limits of justice as recognition (Honneth and Rancière, 2016). Finally, I discuss how such disidentifications may allow reopening the interpretative practices of new generations.

Discussing peasant ontologies as group identification

> Food sovereignty is more than a right; in order to be able to apply policies that allow autonomy in food production it is necessary to have political conditions that exercise autonomy in all the territorial spaces.
>
> (Nyéléni, 2007: 16)

Agrarian communities (peasant wo(men) are being reclaimed as 'guardians of the commons' (McMichael, 2015) and 'bearers of indigenous knowledge' (Altieri, 2010), and thus, invested with the trust of 'cooling the planet' and preserving the commons heritage of our planet (Borras and Franco, 2010; Edelman et al., 2014; Patel, 2009; Wittman et al., 2010). A main focus of the food sovereignty movement seems to be the organisation of a global 'politics of anti-enclosure' (Watts, 2009: 23; also Holt-Giménez and Shattuck, 2011) for it challenges both the modern liberal state and transnational capital in an attempt to create self-governance or popular self-rule (Desmarais and Wittman, 2014; Trauger, 2014). *Via Campesina* and the broader agro-food movement declare that democratisation of the food-system is their main goal: i.e., disabling the monopoly power of corporate agro-foods, redistributing land and livelihoods, community rights, repeasantisation, and repossession of seeds.

The ethico-political values proposed by the food sovereignty movement to counteract such technocratic discourse may be summarised in a few dualisms which support positioning itself as the 'alternative' to capitalist agriculture: autonomy vs. dependence; diversification vs. standardisation/specialisation; cooperation/reciprocity vs. competition; sufficiency vs. efficiency; sovereignty vs. commodification (Bernstein 2014; McMichael, 2010; Wittman et al., 2010). Scholars argue that peasantness is political because, despite its internal divisions and tensions (class, gender, etc.) there is a persistence to unification and mobilisation against the violence of capital (Desmarais et al., 2007; Edelman et al., 2014).

The claiming of rights as an institutional and political process has also been key in the reflective work of a collective peasant building (Desmarais et al., 2007). The recent UN Declaration of the rights of peasants and other rural workers (2018) made scholars confident of the success of decades of activism for the rights to land and other natural resources such as seeds as emergence of an alternative conception of human rights; less individualistic or liberal, less anthropocentric, non-Western, and more collective, cosmopolitan, and multicultural (Claeys, 2018). This strategy has been similar to claiming the right to autonomy recognised in the International Declaration on the Rights of Indigenous Peoples (Golay and Özden, 2012: 24). The efforts to reclaim such rural rights and institutionalise them have their origins in the agro-food crisis of the 2000s and in a context of increasing assault on rural lives, displacements and de-peasantisation, land and resource enclosures, appropriation of genetic resources (seeds), and increasing criminalisation and marginalisation of peasant agriculture around the world (Holt Giménez and Shattuck, 2011; Trauger, 2014). Scholar-activists who support these movements are worried about the growing class of rural labourers and peasants who are further dispossessed and precarious (Altieri, 2010; Borras and Franco, 2010; Edelman, 2013; Patel, 2009; Wittman et al., 2010).

The radicality of the peasant way lies not only in the processes in addressing human rights critically (pushing for collective rights, seed rights for instance) but also in the fact that their claims do not merely imply inclusion to the supposedly benign liberal community and socio-liberal welfare system of recognitions: instead, they move agrarian politics beyond the typical reformist demands to search for structural 'nurturing' alternatives to imagine and organise planetary food production and agriculture in the context of socio-ecological and health crisis (Claeys, 2018). Overall, these conflicts around food sovereignty are social and cultural as well as 'ontological', offering an alternative to the modernity project itself and thus, they are considered political (Escobar, 2010). Surely as in most movements, the claim is that 'rights are that which we cannot not want' (Spivak, 1999: 172) because they are usually conferred by a state which governs through them. My argument on disidentification as emancipatory makes a contribution rather than a critique to this strategic essentialism and societal political imaginary.

The 'peasant way' has been under critical scrutiny from political economists who pointed to the limits of its discourse: Bernstein (2014: 1044) has even summarised the problem by arguing that 'there are no peasants in the world of contemporary capitalist globalization' because commodification of subsistence makes peasants act as petty producers who cannot feed the world by themselves and who are already involved in a plurality of activities which severely diminish their farm-labour time and production. Critical scholars show that the 'peasant' has been assumed rather than investigated and conceptualised as a differentiated social category: sceptical about such reification in strategic progressive populism, scholars urge for more consideration of essentialising and romanticising tendencies or the recurrent inequalities within communities and among various public and private actors (Bernstein, 2014; Soper, 2020). Many authors have already problematised the sovereignty term that is key for the movements and there is an ongoing debate on who is 'included' into the sovereignty paradigm and what to do with the many non-peasant others or with patriarchy (Agarwal, 2014; Beuchelt and Virchow, 2012; O'Laughlin, 2009; Tola, 2018). Moreover, the state is indeed the elephant in the room of food sovereignty (Bernstein, 2014) since it is also a partner rather than an opposer of 'big agri-business' and global financial capitalism.

It is clear that agro-food movements around the world are still unfolding and whether they actually reach out to the goal of being anti-systemic or not remains to be seen (Borras and Slafer, 2008). Here, I do not discuss the need to sociologically advance the classification of peasants and non-peasants or their differentiations or even strategies for collective struggle. A critical approach to the political of agro-food movements necessarily interrogates its solidarity approaches because of their 'conveniences' to coalition building (Bernstein, 2014). My intention here is to invite an approach to agro-food movements that is concerned with what means to perform the political in the 'peasant way' without appeal to ontoepistemological securities such as the 'peasant' as a class or group identification.

Peasant and others' disidentification

> [A]nything may become political if it gives rise to a meeting of these two logics ... police logic, which is opposed to egalitarian/political logic.
> (Rancière, 1999: 32–3)

In this section I discuss the concept of disidentification with a focus on sovereignty and human rights: how does (de)politicising food sovereignty – for instance, by embracing the strategic identity politics of 'proud peasant' or celebratory essentialism (Soper, 2020) – transform its own practice to recentre the political around ecosystems or commons (Vivero-Pol et al., 2018)? Is it still important to use sovereign arguments as political ways for new societal transformations or transitional processes? These are important political and activist questions in the context of new sovereignist populism. In the second subsection I will focus on how attempting to depoliticise sovereignty further through the promotion and institutionalisation of environmental rights or 'rights of nature' might still be insufficient to avoid the 'political' return as extreme manifestation. As I will discuss conceptually, it is a welcoming gesture for UNDROP to represent constituencies rather than social categories – including peasants as well as Indigenous people, migrants, and workers of the land. However, such a move still requires more policy work to decolonise the institutional practice of human rights. Going back to the initial questions: do we need to make sovereignty (and ontology) again and again the only attribute of the political? Is there any other political logic to 'fundament' changes? As I will emphasise, the proposal for disidentification is not a proposal to embrace the existential void as postfoundational: there is an inescapable 'foundation', which is more than the contemporary human rights, and which Rancière calls the presupposition of equality. It is here that a more serious debate about 'the political' is just starting.

Debating food sovereignty as a meritocratic ontology

Food sovereignty is only possible if it takes place at the same time as political sovereignty of peoples.

(Nyéléni, 2007: 16)

Sovereignty is not some static 'traditional' existing object 'out there' to apply: rather, it is 'a living process' which mirrors the continuous changes in relationship-building (Iles and Montenegro de Wit, 2015: 2). As indicated in the previous section, scholar-activists argue that food sovereignty is also a political reclaiming of peasantness as a proud group identification: the appeal to ontological value within the movement is a foundational approach to collective building. However, both this claim and the call for more sociology of peasant differentiation elude the need peasants themselves often indicate, i.e., the problematisation of peasantness itself (Velicu and Barca, 2020). Peasants often adopt or adapt to new technologies, practices, or other forms of identification that seem to clash with a traditional view of how peasantness is conventionally defined. The 'peasants' as fixed political (ontological) subjects do not exist; instead, they themselves are also an ambivalent product (and producer) of power relations and structures. Peasant resistance itself, as a movement, is also a result of what power structures want to control (a Foucauldian take on power). Differentiating among peasants as (some passive) victims who will soon be extinct versus (some active) rebellious opponents is not going to further the cause of democratic (food) politics. My argument here does not build on the sociological/economics pressure on the movement to further validate itself as 'feasible' or 'valuable'.

Zooming out of this dualism we may observe that such rhetoric places the debate on peasantry again and again in the same meritocratic logic of politics which can be called 'policing' for it empowers a 'sovereign' to create arrangements that produce some kind of 'natural' order as ontological coherence: i.e., that destines specific individuals and groups to occupy positions of rule or of being ruled, assigning them to private and public lives, pinning them down to a certain time and space, to specific 'bodies', specific ways of being, seeing, and saying (Rancière, 2010: 139). Whatever is not conforming to such established order is neither clearly seen nor heard but is rather a 'noise'. In order to avoid being 'noise', the peasant way has often had to make itself visible or intelligible in the language of the economic consensus. If only one more movement proves that its 'people' are worthy of respect and recognition in this established policing order! If only one more movement manages to build enough coalitions and critical mass to validate other ontoepistemological perspectives! If only one more movement organises itself well enough to gain the rights that should belong to them in the first place!

As various critical theorists have noted, the current impasse in political reflection and action politics comes exactly from such conflation of politics with a particular meritocratic ontoepistemological order as another manifestation of what is proper to a 'community' (Swyngedouw, 2009). But policies – or police – try to fit people into managerial boxes, that is their purpose: even the 'right' names may pin people down to a place and work that may prove oppressive. This is the 'scandal of democracy' that Rancière is discussing: while basing its emancipatory potential as creating new openings and possibilities, it also creates consensus as some sort of closure and exclusivist orders (Dikeç, 2013).

The production of such meritocratic order is based on practices of categorisation and classification which produce superior and subaltern identities, a widespread 'method of inequality' both in policymaking and social sciences which is often forgotten in the naturalisation of such identities as 'rightfully' entitled to justice (Rancière, 1991: 62, Velicu, 2020). The production of the 'peasant' category itself (including their erasure in policies) was part of such logic of the political as meritocratic policing. As Tsing's historical approach emphasised, such legibility lenses are rooted in a colonial logic of modernisation, which has maintained the dual economic vision of the 'passive' native (peasant) and the 'entrepreneur' coloniser (Tsing, 2003): while the native never seems to fulfil the modern standards, the process of 'integration' produces the native as a citizen of a never-ending modern transition such as 'from farm to factory' or 'from farm to fork' (Alberdi et al., 2020). While the resources peasants usually administered individually or as commons have continued to be enclosed by capitalism – from land to water or seeds – the peasants themselves have been contrived as anachronistic and irrelevant to the consensual thinking about development and agriculture.

As the literature shows, the *Via Campesina* movement is living and confronting these internal contradictions while wishing to loosen its binaries or rigidities in regard to race, class, gender, and other markers of identity which may reiterate abusive relations of power. In this sense, the work of *Via Campesina* and its members may be seen as a work of reimagination of identification at individual and collective level, as many other socio-environmental movements confronting the contradictions of capitalism. No matter how 'feel-good' the grand theory may seem, the life and prosperity of rural laborers (as of everybody) on this planet is a right not because of their virtues: such an approach continues to reproduce a desire to classify people or natures. This invites for more reflection on the need to *not* base politics on such meritocratic policing of the qualities or attributes of some people versus others.

Assuming peasant and nature's rights will be welcomed by states willing to incorporate them into policies, this new ontological politics alone do not guarantee better politics, let alone egalitarianism. The experiences of countries like Ecuador, Bolivia, Venezuela, Nicaragua, Nepal, Mali, and Senegal – which implemented food sovereignty laws and policies – are discouraging not only because of some deviation from the plans of an initially benevolent government which forgot its promises: expansion of local control did not necessarily improve the autonomy and prosperity of small peasants or Indigenous groups and in exchange consolidated state control of resources (Cockburn, 2014; McKay et al., 2014; Schiavoni, 2012; Wittman, 2015), for it assumed the same colonial approach towards peasants as social categories in need of modernisation and progress. More than an argument about state-corporate corruption, I wish to further discuss the logic of inclusive liberal politics itself: egalitarian emancipatory politics is not about the virtues of some virtuous pregressive groups or classes. I build on the debates on the forms of classification of the subjects of food sovereignty to further discuss it as a potential egalitarian politics that disrupts the policing of populations or the reduction of the 'political' to policymaking and managerial consensual governing (Rancière et al., 2001; Swyngedouw, 2009).

Holder of rights or depoliticised subject?

Let us look at peasant seeds (reproduction and exchange) as a practice that requires more in-depth analysis: a fundamental resource of (re)production, seeds and their privatisation play a pivotal role in all contemporary controversies over technical, social, and environmental conditions of production and consumption. However, peasants/farmers are in a structural dependency to firms like Monsanto or DuPont, 'companies that are working aggressively to separate them from self-provisioning of that most fundamental of means of production, the seed' (Kloppenburg, 2010: 370; see also Corrado, 2010). In trying to reproduce their own vegetable seeds, peasants are now being treated like criminals. Therefore, 'peasant seeds' appears more recently in the literature as the cause of small (family-subsistence) farmers who are losing their ability to make their own agronomic choices (Demeulenaere, 2014; Balázs and Aistara, 2018; Bezner Kerr, 2013).

Kloppenburg (2014) insists on the open source activism as a form of 'stealing back' our seed commons. However, peasant movements and scholar activists are often right to problematise the open source seed-commons project (Demeulenaere, 2014): As Ramona Dominicioiu, member of the Eco Ruralis peasant association in Romania argues, 'it's not just about the seed itself as commons, it's about peasants' work to multiply it' (personal discussion, 2020). Even if one manages to empower peasant-led collective action towards on-farm agrobiodiversity restoration through new innovative collaborations between peasants, scientists and other public actors (Mazé et al., 2021; Demeulenaere et al., 2017), we still need to ask: how to stop the waves of dispossession and depeasantisation that have wiped out rural regions all over the world? Are there any prospects on the labour markets to actually support the re-skilling or professionalisation of ancient seeds conservation and reproduction? How do these processes avoid commodification as professionalisation? Perhaps we could imagine a future of seed diversity without peasants: still, structural questions remain unchallenged, as for instance, what would labour transitions look like if we want such ancient praxis to continue? Are there any programmes of vocational schools that teach people how to reproduce seeds? What about the lives and values of still existing peasants, Indigenous or other people of the land? These issues are much more addressed as part of the *Via Campesina* politics focused on decades of transnational advocacy work to promote and institutionalise the rights to seeds, as we can read now as part of the United Nations Declaration for the Rights of Peasants and Other People Working in Rural Areas (UNDROP, 2018).

The radicality of such rights (over natural resources) is one reason for them being called rights against capitalism and expected to break the logic of commodification that underpins the regime of property rights and to rethink of global governance and trade agreements (Claeys, 2015; Edelman and James, 2011). Leaving aside convincing conceptual or historical arguments about the politics of rights as a 'gigantic operation in the depoliticization of subjects' (Badiou, 2008: 139), my theoretical argument here is still focusing on the initial argument about sovereignty vs. disidentification. As the name itself indicated, UNDROP is a good example of the challenge ahead for 'the political': not only to advocate and defend the rights of peasants or their resources but how to rethink the position or the holder of any such rights whatsoever: here is where our argument about disidentification makes more sense, i.e., the political opening 'hidden' in the diverse 'names' or constituencies listed by UNDROP illustrate the 'anonymous' plea for political equality. Such equality is either for anyone or for nothing.

The shift in 'rights subjectivity' is less likely because of the mainstream focus on individual human rights (Vandenbogaerde, 2017). The recognition of rights for a narrowly defined group of peasants is different than the rights of land and resources. These limitations of a rights-politics are not merely procedural: they illustrate what Rancière calls the 'very impoverished virtue' of the pedagogy of 'raising consciousness', unveiling exploitation and its mystifications (Rancière, 2004b: 121). Rancière's critique is in relation to the privatisation of the sphere of rights itself, or the fact that such rights make more sense when one assumes that citizenship is a strong enough political domain to claim state recognition: but politics only starts at the exact ambivalent and porously violent borders separating one life from another, which are not always formally public. He reminds us the famous testament of the revolutionary woman Olympe de Gouges during the French Revolution: 'If women are entitled to go to the scaffold, they are entitled to go to the assembly.' It is not that rights are for those who are not citizens/for whom there is no law/who cannot even be oppressed because they do not even exist in policy (as the peasants in our case). The normalisation-institutionalisation of the human rights is not political in itself.

> When RIGHTS are of no use, you do the same as charitable persons do with their old clothes. You give them to the poor. [...] the Rights of Man become the rights of those who have no rights, the rights of bare human beings subjected to inhuman repression and inhuman conditions of existence. They become humanitarian rights, the rights of those who cannot enact them, the victims of the absolute denial of right.
> (Rancière, 2004c: 307)

For Rancière (1999: 36–7), to 'speak out' is not 'awareness and expression of a self asserting what belongs to it' but rather, a process of *disidentification*, removal from a 'natural' place which one has been pinned down to. In this sense, a political solidarity and egalitarian politics is created not by identification with a 'victim' or his or her cause but as a result of common disidentification with the dominant terms set for subject positioning. If we are to re-politicise and revalue 'rights', Rancière prefers to discuss the presupposition of equality, and specifically of equality in intelligence which requires staging again and again its case. If a life can be stopped because of a political judgement, it is obviously already equally and dangerously political, it does not need to be included as virtuous or expanded as 'citizenship' or as the 'right to rights'. It presupposes an equality that cannot be erased except, maybe, by a crime or legal illegality. Therefore, politics for Rancière begins with addressing this preliminary problem, which is the demonstration of equality staged by any anonymous life.

A political act is not the constitution of a socio-political order and/or subject positions to secure more, inclusive belonging to the social whole, but rather putting the very terms of belonging in question. A political subject is not some actual possessor of rights or citizenness but a capacity for staging scenes of dissensus, i.e., putting two worlds in one and the same litigious world of relations of inclusion and exclusion. Political subjects are surplus subjects, which is not the same as 'the poor' but refers to those who have no specific qualification for public reasoning or ruling. The counting of community as a sum of its parts (each group or class and their qualifications) is a police form of counting: politics as the count of the uncounted separates the community from its parts-qualifications, it is a process rather than a sphere. Therefore, 'there is no man of the Rights of Man, but there is no need for such a man' (Rancière, 2004c: 305). As we will conclude, this brings us closer to the implications for such disidentification for democratic politics, a dissensual rural politics as emancipatory.

Concluding ideas: Emancipation as disidentifications for dissensus

My point in this chapter is that more emancipatory politics does not have to base its assumptions on alternative ('better') procedures, ontoepistemologies, or theories of a virtuous political subject – eco-citizen (peasant or otherwise): there will always be the 'undeserving' if classification (or policing) is the main approach to the 'political'. Such classifications themselves are part of the modern history of colonialism, racism, and patriarchy. In such logic of emancipation, no matter how open, inclusiveness and access to the 'big pie' is bound to fail (Butler et al., 1997; Velicu and Kaika, 2017). When approaching politics as group (or class) politics of inclusion or recognition of rights, we repeat the production of the subaltern involved in such identification itself, and the normalisation of a subjectivity already produced as devoid of political-ness. A collective – such as the peasant one – can dissent from the consensus, for instance, the consensus that they are economic agents to compete internationally: but this act is political not because it constitutes other stable subjectivities that make people reproduce other similar divisions. All predetermined positions are inherently contingent – dissent politics, like a scandal that democracy should be all about, refuses to stay still (Rancière, 2009). Dissent is not a conflict over solutions to some predefined problem or division: it is the active redefinition of the problem that exists in common through acts or events of re-subjectification. The productive tension of the dissensus is in witnessing the melting into air of the terms of any consensus, predetermination of division as the beginning of the political debate, when some oppose their silencing by this 'police'. The force of a 'demos' is neither a sum of social partners nor a gathering together of differences, but quite the opposite – the power to undo all partnerships, gatherings and ordinations (Rancière, 2010: 37). Democracy, therefore, is not some form of government or a mode of social life but a force that allows disidentification and re-subjectification to occur in multiple ways, to make ways for ongoing demonstrations of equality.

> [D]emocracy is neither compromise between interests nor the formation of a common will. Its kind of dialogue is that of a divided community.
> (Rancière, 1995: 103)

I suggest more focus should be placed on the actual acts through which 'peasants' produce themselves as equally political, refusing to be a unified social category. Given the ultimate contingency or all power roles, positions, or knowledges, political communities should aim at resisting transcendent ontological truths and instead ask themselves about the trajectories of such truth-making and how these became dominant in certain historical times. The only necessary political imagination or capacity is to presuppose that people are equal in intelligence for there is no hierarchies of knowledges or virtues because,

> the foundation of politics is ... the lack of foundation, the sheer contingency of any social order. Politics exists simply because no social order is based on nature, no divine law regulates human society.
> (Rancière, 1999: 16)

To the extent that a community of (peasant) sense exists, it is a rather uncommon situation of diverse 'particularities'. Against founding stories of a 'purity' of any community as well as counteracting the perils of populist extremist politics, we should be sharing rather than reconciling different worlds: building a world in common may simply be about encountering each other intersubjectively and intersectionally, sharing these new spaces of encounter, rather than trying to contain each other. Such 'opening work', which seeks renewal of communities rather than reconciliation of differences, needs to undo any mastery figures or ontological certainties. This implies not only de-subjectifying oneself to live one's own 'otherness' even individually but also the reopening of the interpretive practices of new generations of (peasant) communities. Since any ethico-political model of ontology is marked by 'discontinuities that remain in place in "real life"'(Spivak, 2012: 317), one could only hope at sensing new communities with a 'agonistic respect' (Connolly, 2005), which means to approach the other with the same uncertainly, hesitancy and forbearance as we should approach ourselves (Shapiro, 2021).

Acknowledgements

The author acknowledges support as part of the Programa de Estímulo ao Emprego Científico of Centro de Estudos Sociais, Coimbra, Reference DL 572016/CP1341/ CT0022 and FEDER – European Fund for Regional Development funds through the COMPETE 2020 – Operational Programme for Competitiveness and Internationalisation (POCI), and by Portuguese funds through FCT – Foundation for Science and Technology in the framework of the project 029355. Project *JustFood: From Alternative Food Networks to Socio-Environmental Justice*, Reference: POCI-01-0145-FEDER-029355.

Notes

1 Tania Murray Li, 'There is no one trajectory of development', www.youtube.com/watch?v=iELdzQmMEnw, accessed 12 August 2022.
2 I am referring to '[T]here can be no homelessness without an economic, political, and social process that produces "the home" as a commodity; no refugees without practices of exile from a "country of origin"; no margin without a centre; no periphery without a core' (Kaika, 2005: 273).

References

Agarwal, B. 2014. Food sovereignty, food security and democratic choice: Critical contradictions. *Journal of Peasant Studies* 41(6): 1247–68.

Alberdi, G. et al. 2020. A collective response from food sovereignty scholars on the EU's Farm to Fork Strategy. https://foodgovernance.com/eu-farm-to-fork-strategy-collective-response-from-food-sovereignty-scholars/, accessed 12 August 2022.

Alteri, M.A. 2010. *Agroecology versus ecoagriculture: Balancing food production and biodiversity conservation in the midst of social equality*. Gland, Switzerland: IUCN, World Conservation Union and CEESP.

Badiou, A. 2008. Live Badiou: Interview with Alain Badiou, Paris, December 2007. In O. Feltham (ed.), *Alain Badiou: Live theory*. London: Continuum.

Balás, B. and G. Aistara. 2018. The emergence, dynamics and agency of social innovation in seed exchange networks. *International Journal of Sociology of Agricultue and Food* 24(3).

Bernstein, H. 2014. Food sovereignty via the 'peasant way': A sceptical view. *Journal of Peasant Studies* 41(6): 1031–63.

Beuchelt, T.D. and D. Virchow. 2012. Food sovereignty or the human right to adequate food: Which concept serves better as international development policy for global hunger and poverty reduction? *Agriculture and Human Values* 29(2): 259–73.

Bezner Kerr, R. 2013. Seed struggles and food sovereignty in northern Malawi. *Journal of Peasant Studies* 40(5): 867–97.

Borras, L. and G.A. Slafer. 2010. Agronomy and plant breeding are key to combating food crisis. *Nature* 453(7199): 1177.
Borras, S.M. Jr. and J.C. Franco. 2010. Contemporary discourses and contestations around pro-poor land policies and land governance. *Journal of Agrarian Change* 10(1): 1–32.
Brenner, N. and C. Schmid. 2015. Towards a new epistemology of the urban? *City* 19(2–3): 151–82.
Butler, J., E. Laclau, and R. Laddaga. 1997. The uses of equality. *Diacritics* 27(1): 3–12.
Claeys, P. 2015. Food sovereignty and the recognition of new rights for peasants at the UN: A critical overview of La Via Campesina's rights claims over the last 20 years. *Globalizations* 12(4): 452–65.
Claeys, P. 2018. The rise of new rights for peasants. From reliance on NGO intermediaries to direct representation. *Transnational Legal Theory* 9(3–4): 386–99.
Cockburn, J. 2014. Bolivia's food sovereignty and agrobiodiversity: Undermining the local to strengthen the state? *Theory in Action* 7(4): 67.
Connolly, W.E. 2005. *Pluralism*. Durham, NC: Duke University Press.
Corrado, A. 2010. New peasantries and alternative agro-food networks: The case of Réseau Semences Paysannes. In *From community to consumption: New and classical themes in rural sociological research*. Bingley: Emerald Group Publishing.
Davidson, M. and K. Iveson. 2015. Beyond city limits: A conceptual and political defense of 'the city' as an anchoring concept for critical urban theory. *City* 19(5): 646–64.
Demeulenaere, E. 2014. A political ontology of seeds: The transformative frictions of a farmers' movement in Europe. *Focaal* 2014(69): 45–61.
Demeulenaere, E. et al. 2017. Participatory plant breeding and scale issues: On a collaboration between farmer plant breeders and field geneticists. *Natures Sciences Sociétés* 25(4): 336–46.
Desmarais, A.A. and H. Wittman. 2014. Farmers, foodies and First Nations: Getting to food sovereignty in Canada. *Journal of Peasant Studies* 41(6): 1153–73.
Desmarais, A.A., P. Clayes, and A. Trauger (eds.). 2007. *Public policies for food sovereignty*. New York: Routledge
Dikeç, M. 2013. Beginners and equals: Political subjectivity in Arendt and Rancière. *Transactions of the Institute of British Geographers* 38(1): 78–90.
Edelman, M. 2013. What is a peasant? What are peasantries? A briefing paper on issues of definition. First session of the Intergovernmental Working Group on a United Nations Declaration on the Rights of Peasants and Other People Working in Rural Areas, Geneva, 15–19 July.
Edelman, M. and C. James. 2011. Peasants' rights and the UN system: Quixotic struggle? *Journal of Peasant Studies* 38(1): 81–108.
Edelman, M., T. Weis, A. Baviskar, S.M. Borras Jr., E. Holt-Giménez, D. Kandiyoti, and W. Wolford. 2014. Introduction: Critical perspectives on food sovereignty. *Journal of Peasant Studies* 41(6): 911–31.
Escobar, A. 2010. Latin America at a crossroads: Alternative modernizations, post-liberalism, or post-development? *Cultural Studies* 24(1): 1–65.
Golay, C. and M. Özden. 2012. The right to food. Part of a series of the Human Rights Programme of the Europe–Third World Centre (CETIM) Annex.
Grange, K. and M. Gunder. 2019. The urban domination of the planet: A Rancièrian critique. *Planning Theory* 18(4): 389–409.

Holt-Giménez, E. and A. Shattuck. 2011. Food crises, food regimes and food movements: Rumblings of reform or tides of transformation? *Journal of Peasant Studies* 38(1): 109–144.

Honneth, A. and J. Rancière. 2016. *Recognition or disagreement: A critical encounter on the politics of freedom, equality, and identity*. New York: Columbia University Press.

Iles, A. and M. Montenegro de Wit. 2015. Sovereignty at what scale? An inquiry into multiple dimensions of food sovereignty. *Globalizations* 12(4): 481–97.

Jazeel, T. 2018. Urban theory with an outside. *Environment and Planning D: Society and Space* 36(3): 405–19.

Kaika, M. 2005. *City of flows: Modernity, nature, and the city*. London and New York: Routledge.

Kloppenburg, J. 2010. Impeding dispossession, enabling repossession: Biological open source and the recovery of seed sovereignty. *Journal of Agrarian Change* 10(3): 367–88.

Kloppenburg, J. 2014. Re-purposing the master's tools: The open source seed initiative and the struggle for seed sovereignty. *Journal of Peasant Studies* 41(6): 1225–46.

Lefebvre, H. 2014 [1991]. The production of space. In *The people, place, and space reader*. London and New York: Routledge, pp. 323–7.

Li, T.M. 2010. To make live or let die? Rural dispossession and the protection of surplus populations. *Antipode* 41: 66–93.

Li, T.M. 2011. Centering labor in the land grab debate. *The Journal of Peasant Studies* 38(2): 281–98.

Mazé, A., A. Calabuig Domenech, and I. Goldringer. 2021. Commoning the seeds: Alternative models of collective action and open innovation within French peasant seed groups for recreating local knowledge commons. *Agriculture and Human Values* 38(2): 541–59.

McKay, B., R. Nehring, and M. Walsh-Dilley. 2014. The 'state' of food sovereignty in Latin America: Political projects and alternative pathways in Venezuela, Ecuador and Bolivia. *Journal of Peasant Studies* 41(6): 1175–200.

McMichael, P. 2010. *Contesting development: Critical struggles for social change*. London and New York: Routledge.

McMichael, P. 2014. Rethinking land grab ontology. *Rural Sociology* 79(1): 34–55.

McMichael, P. 2015. A comment on Henry Bernstein's way with peasants, and food sovereignty. *Journal of Peasant Studies* 42(1): 193–204.

Nyéléni. 2007. Declaration of Nyéléni. www.nyeleni.org/spip.php?article290, accessed 12 August 2022.

O'Laughlin, B. 2009. Gender justice, land and the agrarian question in Southern Africa. In A.H. Akram-Lodhi and C. Kay (eds.), *Peasants and globalization: Political economy, rural transformation and the agrarian question*. London: Routledge, pp. 190–213.

Oswin, N. 2018. Planetary urbanization: A view from outside. *Environment and Planning D: Society and Space* 36(3): 540–6.

Patel, R. 2009. Grassroots voices: Food sovereignty. *Journal of Peasant Studies* 36(3): 663–706.

Perfecto, I., J. Vandermeer and A. Wright. 2009. *Nature's matrix: Linking agriculture, conservation and food sovereignty*. London: Earthscan.

Rancière, J. 1991. *The ignorant schoolmaster: Five lessons on intellectual emancipation*. Palo Alto, CA: Stanford University Press.

Rancière, J. 1995. *On the shore of politics*. New York: Verso.
Rancière, J. 1999. *Dis-agreement: Politics and philosophy*. Translated by J. Rose. Minneapolis, MN: University of Minnesota Press.
Rancière, J. 2004a. *Disagreement: Politics and philosophy*. Minneapolis, MN: University of Minnesota Press.
Rancière, J. 2004b. *The philosopher and his poor*. Durham, NC: Duke University Press.
Rancière, J. 2004c. Who is the subject of the rights of man? *The South Atlantic Quarterly* 103(2/3): 297–310.
Rancière, J. 2009. *Hatred of democracy*. New York: Verso.
Rancière, J. 2010. *Dissensus: On politics and aesthetics*. New York: Continuum.
Rancière, J., D. Panagia, and R. Bowlby. 2001. Ten theses on politics. *Theory & Event* 5(3).
Sbicca, J. 2012. Growing food justice by planting an anti-oppression foundation: Opportunities and obstacles for a budding social movement. *Agriculture and Human Values* 29(4): 455–66.
Schiavoni, C.M. 2012. Competing sovereignties, contested processes: Insights from the Venezuelan food sovereignty experiment. *Globalizations* 12(4): 466–80.
Schindler, S. 2017. Towards a paradigm of southern urbanism. *City* 21(1): 47–64.
Shapiro, M.J. 2021. *The phenomenology of religious belief: Media, philosophy, and the Arts*. New York: Bloomsbury Academic.
Spivak, G.C. 1999. *A critique of postcolonial reason: Toward a history of the vanishing present*. Cambridge, MA: Harvard University Press.
Spivak, G.C. 2012. *An aesthetic education in the era of globalization*. Cambridge, MA: Harvard University Press.
Swyngedouw, E. 2009. The zero-ground of politics: Musings on the post-political city. *New Geographies* 1(1): 52–61.
Tola, M. 2018. Between Pachamama and mother earth: Gender, political ontology and the rights of nature in contemporary Bolivia. *Feminist Review* 118(1): 25–40.
Trauger, A. 2014. Toward a political geography of food sovereignty: Transforming territory, exchange and power in the liberal sovereign state. *Journal of Peasant Studies* 41(6): 1131–52.
Tsing, A.L. 2003. Agrarian allegory and global futures. In P. Greenough and A.L. Tsing (eds.), *Nature in the Global South: Environmental projects in South and Southeast Asia*. Durham: Duke University Press, pp. 124–69.
Tzaninis, Y., T. Mandler, M. Kaika, and R. Keil. 2021. Moving urban political ecology beyond the 'urbanization of nature'. *Progress in Human Geography* 45(2): 229–52.
Vandenbogaerde, A. 2017. Localizing the Human Rights Council: A case study of the Declaration on the Rights of Peasants. *Journal of Human Rights* 16(2): 220–41.
Velicu, I. 2020. Prospective environmental injustice: insights from anti-mining struggles in Romania and Bulgaria. *Environmental Politics* 29(3): 414–34.
Velicu, I. and S. Barca. 2020. The Just Transition and its work of inequality. *Sustainability: Science, Practice and Policy* 16(1): 263–73.
Velicu, I. and M. Kaika. 2017. Undoing environmental justice: Re-imagining equality in the Rosia Montana anti-mining movement. *Geoforum* 84: 305–15.
Velicu, I. and A. Ogrezeanu. 2022. Quiet no more: The emergence of food justice and sovereignty in Romania. *Journal of Rural Studies* 89: 122–9.

Visser, O., S. Dorondel, P. Jehlička, and M. Spoor. 2019. Post-socialist smallholders: Silence, resistance and alternatives. *Canadian Journal of Development Studies/Revue Canadienne d'études du développement* 40(4): 499–510.

Vivero-Pol, J.L., T. Ferrando, O. De Schutter, and U. Mattei (eds.). 2018. *Routledge handbook of food as a commons*. Durham: Routledge.

Walker, R. 2015. Building a better theory of the urban: A response to 'Towards a new epistemology of the urban?' *City* 19(2–3): 183–91.

Watts, M. 2017. Crude politics: Life and death on the Nigerian oil fields. *Niger Delta Economies of Violence Working Papers* 25: 1–27.

Wittman, H. 2015. From protest to policy: The challenges of institutionalizing food sovereignty. *Canadian Journal of Development Studies/Revue Canadienne d'études du développement* 2(2): 174–82.

Wittman, H., A.A. Desmarais, and N. Wiebe. 2010. Food sovereignty. In *Reconnecting food, nature and community*. Canada: Fernwood Publishing.

17

Urbanising islands: A critical history of Singapore's offshore islands

Creighton Connolly and Hamzah Muzaini

Introduction

Over the past century, many smaller, offshore islands across the Asia-Pacific region have experienced drastic transformations to their social, physical, and symbolic landscapes. These changes have been brought about by transitions in political regimes and migratory flows, national and regional economic growth, and the shifting positions of these offshore islands within their respective nation-states. As a short film shown at the 2014 exhibition at the National Museum of Singapore entitled *Balik Pulau* (Return to the Islands) put it, 'the story of Singapore's islands is one of growth, in size and economic significance, and loss, in numbers and nature, as habitats and homes give way to the needs of a modern city' (Ho, 2014). Indeed, while Singapore's offshore islands have played salient roles in powering the nation's economy and are deeply connected to the mainland, their visibility and historical significance to most Singaporeans remains negligible.

After Singapore left the new Malaysian nation-state in 1965, it became a city-state without a periphery to service the core. While this was later addressed through the development of regional growth triangles in the 1990s by integrating the city to 'new peripheries' in Johor and Riau to benefit from cheaper land and labour for the nation's growing needs (Sparke et al., 2004); an earlier and still ongoing strategy has been the repurposing of Singapore's offshore islands to serve particular functions, including landfilling, oil refinery, shipping, and tourism. We focus here on this particular strategy by examining the evolution of Singapore's Southern and Western Islands over time from uninhabited or traditional Malay villages to industrialised or urbanised islands serving Singapore's various development objectives. We focus primarily on the period since 1965, after which the most dramatic transformations have taken place.

Conceptually, the chapter adapts insights from urban political ecology (UPE) which emphasise how a focus on the metabolic processes connecting the urban core and surrounding peri-urban spaces can demystify the visual and ideological exclusions of particular places and peoples that have been part and parcel of urbanisation. This builds on earlier work in UPE that examined the fetishisation of urban infrastructural networks such as water, electricity, and gas pipelines that are often hidden from view but yet crucial to the functioning of the city (see Kaika and Swyngedouw, 2000). By examining the way in which Singapore's offshore islands have been simultaneously drawn into and transformed through the city-state's development, this chapter contributes to recent literature conceptualising processes of urban metabolism that extend beyond traditional city boundaries (Arboleda, 2016; Cantor, 2020; Connolly, 2019). Accordingly, we consider our work a contribution to 'an integrated research agenda for a UPE beyond the city', by exploring the more-than-urban geographies bound up with planetary, or extended urbanisation (Tzaninis et al., 2021: 332). Though Singapore is ideologically constructed as an independent island city without a hinterland to draw upon, it is in fact heavily dependent upon its material connections to its offshore islands that are separated from, but still deeply connected to the centre.

The empirical section of the chapter is divided into two primary sections, based on some of the functions that the islands were developed to serve: we focus here on industry (petroleum and petrochemical industries) and waste management. These sectors, particularly petrochemical processing, are concentrated along coastal areas, and were central to Singapore's rapid development in the 1980s and 1990s. As we discuss, the Southern and Western Islands have been constructed as 'spatial envelopes' that can contain brownfield activities such as petrochemical industries or landfills, while allowing the simultaneous construction of a 'modern', clean and green Singapore on the mainland (Kaika, 2005: 61; Lefebvre, 1991: 351). While the islands have suffered significant ecological damage through the land reclamation and industrialisation in the 1970s and 1980s, we also note how Singapore has more recently sought to conserve and restore the remaining ecosystems as it has developed. This has taken place alongside renewed popular interest in the Southern Islands, and subsequent efforts to create more awareness about their cultural and natural heritages. We conclude with reflecting on the hybrid rural/urban nature of Singapore's offshore islands and how they both augment and offset Singapore's increasingly urbanised landscapes.[1]

Urbanisation beyond the city: metabolisation and spatial transformation

Earlier work in urban geography has illustrated how territorial organisation operates as a crucial force of production under capitalist systems. This is achieved through the integration and coordination of metabolic processes, infrastructural configurations, and other externalities that are financed by public and private forms of fixed capital and regulated through domestic institutional frameworks within geographically localised production systems (Swyngedouw, 1992). As Brenner (1998: 462) has elaborated, such forms of territorial (re)organisation often underpin the construction, deconstruction, and reconstruction of geographical landscapes throughout phases of capitalist development within countries and regions. Moore (2014: 12) has thus seen capitalism as a way of organising nature, becoming a metabolic engine that leads to the extension of the urban form beyond the city. As we will demonstrate below, Singapore's Southern and Western Islands have gone through a similar cycle over the past 50 years of Singapore's development.

The spatial transformation that has taken place across Singapore's offshore islands since its independence can therefore be explained by the need to create new infrastructures of territorial organisation for subsequent rounds of expanded accumulation as the country developed. Accordingly, the islands have been redeveloped to serve key sectors of the economy, from manufacturing, to tourism, and foreign investment. In this sense, they can be seen as 'operational landscapes' for industrial production, waste management, geopolitical strategies and spaces of recreation and leisure (Arboleda, 2016: 4). However, this has come at a high cost, as 60 per cent of Singapore's coral reefs have been lost, in addition to much of the natural shoreline and Indigenous populations on the islands (International Year of the Reef, 2009). Additionally, the islands have tended to be rendered invisible in the national psyche over the course of Singapore's rapid urbanisation and development which has led to the further marginalisation of their history and heritages.

As Harvey (1989) argues, the urban scale is the fundamental geographical anchor for each spatial reorganisation, in this case being mainland Singapore. Therefore, the spatial transformation has had significant benefits for Singapore as a whole, but has in the process irreversibly transformed the socio-ecologies of the islands. This is because such processes of capitalist accumulation and spatial reorganisation always occur in political and social contexts shaped powerfully, if not exclusively, by central state power (de Koninck et al., 2017). As Neo (2007) observed, Singapore is the quintessential developmental state, which places a premium on physical and economic development to secure its legitimacy. These unequal centre-periphery relationships thus speak to the *political* element of urban political ecology, drawing attention to the social and political relations that are bound up with the transformation of urban environments. Indeed, the ecologies and the former inhabitants of Singapore's offshore islands have assumed most of the negative effects associated with the significant spatial transformations taking place over the past 50 years.

Early work in UPE has documented the material and infrastructural connections forming the 'socio-spatial continuum' between city and countryside in (and beyond) cities like Athens, New York, London, and Chicago (Cronon, 1991; Kaika, 2005). In order to understand these more-than-urban geographies, UPE research is beginning to adopt an explicit spatialised, or landscaped approach in order to integrate key processes of socio-natural metabolisms, power relations, and discourse bound up with the ordering of urban environments (see Connolly, 2019). The concept of metabolism refers to the process of material exchange and interaction between human beings and nature through which both entities are transformed (Swyngedouw, 2006). This approach has some elements in common with the distinct approach of landscape ecology, which describes how urban, suburban, industrial, and natural settings are transformed through processes of contemporary urbanisation that are becoming 'planetary in scope' (see Arboleda, 2016; Yang and Lay, 2004: 1012).

As Kaika (2005) has documented, the separation of 'good' and 'bad' socio-natures through modernist spatial planning is nothing new, but this process is often fetishised so that the socio-ecological inequalities that are generated in the process are concealed and hidden from public view. However, she notes that these socio-natural processes and materials – though kept apart – are very much dialectically related through a process of interdependence, which is required for the ongoing functioning of the whole. Therefore, Kaika (2005: 62) concludes that there can be 'no margin without a center; no periphery without a core'. For example, the case of Singapore's offshore islands presented below illustrates the choreography of materials, places, and people that have been metabolised, transformed, and displaced in order to facilitate the rapid socio-economic development of the city-state.

Singapore's offshore islands: From rural villages to spaces of industry, tourism, and leisure

Singapore currently has a total of 54 islands – down from 77 after the amalgamation of smaller islands through land reclamation works over the past 50 years. Such processes of land reclamation have been an enduring component of Singapore's urban development ever since its initial 'establishment' by the British in the early nineteenth century. Through a process of 'permanent territorial revolution' – justified by Singapore's chronic 'scarcity of land' needed to generate economic growth and house its growing population – Singapore's surface area has increased by nearly a quarter (or 135km^2) since the mid-1960s through land reclamation (de Koninck et al.,

2017). Singapore and its offshore islands are thus illustrative of the perpetual churning of socio-spatial formations under capitalism and the numerous metabolic flows involved (see Brenner, 2013: 99).

While many of these islands have long and important histories, most do not even exist 'on the margins of [Singaporeans'] mental landscapes' (Ho, 2014). A few of the larger islands were once inhabited by vibrant Malay and *Orang Asli* (Indigenous people) communities, often within *kampong* (villages) along the coasts (Wee and Benjamin, n.d.). However, the 1970s saw a rapid depopulation of these islands. Some moved away from their home islands to work on industrialised islands like Pulau Bukom or mainland Singapore, while others were pressured to leave so as to make way for the repurposing of the islands, especially after Singapore lost its hinterland following its departure from Malaysia in 1965 (Cornelius-Takahama and Loo, 2016).

The dialectical relationship between city and countryside is central to the conceptualisation of cities within urban political ecology. One of the foundational texts in this regard is Bill Cronon's (1991: 384) book, *Nature's metropolis*, which argues that 'urban and rural landscapes ... are not two places but one. They created each other, they transformed each other's environments and economies, and they now depend on each other for survival.' The modern history of Singapore's offshore islands is thus illustrative of the interconnectedness between the urban and the rural highlighted by Cronon (1991), as many of these islands were designated as official rural areas and accordingly came under the control of the Singapore Rural Board (SRB) until this was abolished in 1965 (Cornelius-Takahama and Loo, 2016). For planning purposes, Singapore's offshore islands to the south are divided by the Urban Redevelopment Authority (URA) into two clusters: the Southern Islands group and the Western Islands group. Singapore's Southern Islands group comprises eight islands directly to the south of the mainland and the Western Islands group consists of seven islands situated more to the southwest (see Figure 17.1).

Focusing specifically on the impacts of urbanisation on the formerly rural landscapes of Singapore's southern islands, the next section examines the ways in which they have been transformed in order to service the nation's economic, social, and metabolic needs. As we shall show, the islands can be seen as: 'indicators of contradictory yet interconnected processes of socio-spatial restructuring under conditions of ongoing industrial, labour, politico-regulatory and environmental reorganization' in Singapore (Brenner, 2013: 100).[2] This has involved developing a blueprint, or territorial framework for the production of the islands' future spatial forms and social, ecological, and economic functions.

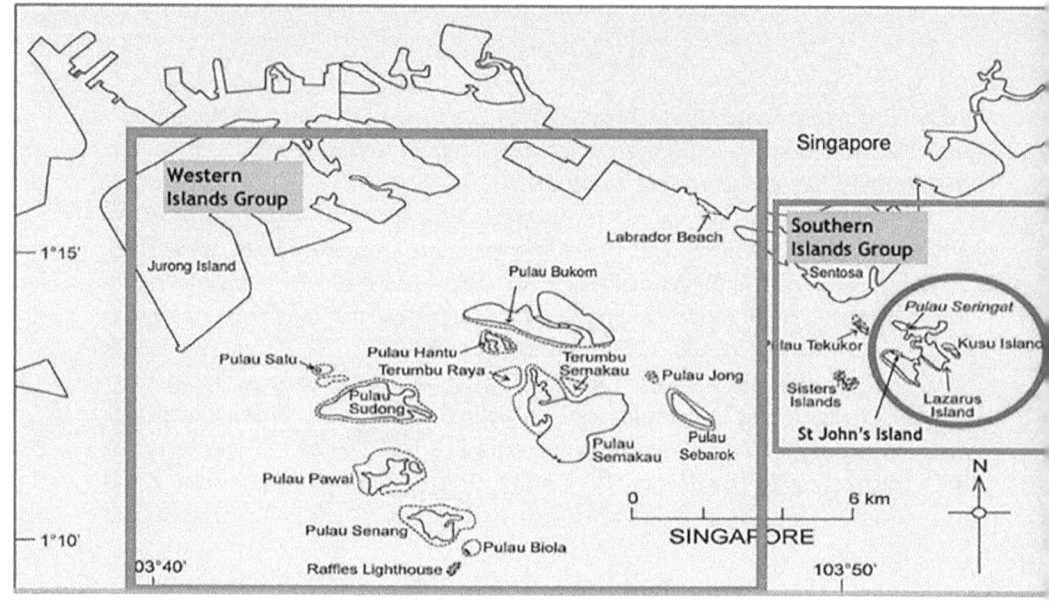

Figure 17.1 Map showing the location of Singapore's Southern and Western Islands, with the Southern Islands of St John's, Lazarus, and Kusu circled as the focus of our field research.

Petroleum and petrochemical industries

The petroleum and petrochemicals industry has been central to Singapore's economic success, as a strategic cluster underpinning the nation's economic development. This is one of the early industries – along with the electronics manufacturing sector – which helped build Singapore's reputation as a value-added economy, rather than as a producer of primary products. However, it was achieved at the expense of the dense mangrove swamps, coral reefs, and Indigenous communities of Singapore's offshore islands, due to the significant amount of land reclamation required to house the industry over the decades. One of the key islands developed for this industry is Pulau Bukom, which is an amalgamation of the former islands Pulau Bukom Besar and Pulau Bukom Kechil.

Pulau Bukom's association with the petroleum industry originated in 1891 for the storage of imported kerosene from Russia by a local merchant Syme & Company (Huff, 1997). The government rejected the company's application to store bulk petroleum on mainland Singapore, which led to the decision to store the kerosene on Bukom due to its proximity to the mainland (Makepeace et al., 1991). Pulau Bukom was greatly expanded through land reclamation in the first half of the twentieth century, which established it as the largest centre for oil storage, blending, packing, and bunkering in Southeast Asia (Huff, 1997; *Straits Times*, 1959). The development of Pulau

Bukom as a site for oil refinery had also displaced its former inhabitants initially to Pulau Sakeng, before the residents were later relocated to the mainland (Wee and Benjamin, n.d.).

Subsequently, neighbouring islands and islets were also reclaimed in order to provide space for the manufacturing of petrochemicals which was seen to be more economically lucrative (Yun and Jin, 2009). Pulau Ular was previously a submerged coral reef with two visible islets that was reclaimed to form part of the petrochemical complex (*Straits Times*, 1974). The island was reclaimed using earth from hills on Pulau Bukom Besar, Club Hill (now Club Street on mainland Singapore) and Pulau Ubin (off the northeastern coast of Singapore), which was a common reclamation strategy in the twentieth century before increased land reclamation required the import of sand from neighbouring countries (Koh and Lin, 2017).[3] This illustrates the way in which redevelopment of individual islands can cause long-term ecological degradation to surrounding islands. It is also representative of the process of creative destruction involving the reorganisation of existing infrastructures and socio-environmental landscapes for the continued accumulation of social and economic capital (see Brenner, 2013: 105).

The connection of previously separate islands has been a common strategy for increasing developable land area of Singapore's offshore islands since the early 2000s. Nearby Jurong Island is also a centre of Singapore's chemical and energy industry, which was targeted as an area for primary investment and growth by the Singapore Government in the 1970s (Lim, 2004). However, as with Pulau Bukom, this economic strategy required more industrial land which was scarce on mainland Singapore, so reclamation of the seafront along offshore islands became the preferred solution (JTC, 1984). Jurong Island was thus formed through successive land reclamation work connecting seven offshore islands, completed in 2009.

As Carpenter and Ng (2013) have argued, the creation of the artificial Jurong Island complex is one of the main reasons for Singapore's emergence as a global leader in the chemical industry. By 2014, the island produced 1.5 million barrels of refined oil, making Singapore one of Asia's top ten exporters of refined oil (Lim, 2004). The petroleum, petrochemical, and specialty chemical industries together form a key pillar of Singapore's economy, which in 2014, accounted for approximately 34 per cent of total manufacturing output worth over S$100 billion (Department of Statistics, 2016). There are also significant financial and commercial networks associated with the industry, as Singapore is now a leading hub in Southeast Asia for petroleum exploration and production (de Koninck et al., 2008). This suggests that Singapore's outlying islands are not only a central part of Singapore's economic core but also that of an export-oriented economy that connects these 'peripheral islands' with other (economic and urban) geographies.[4]

Yet, the development of these islands for the chemical industries also led to the loss of mangrove habitats and resettlement of its former inhabitants, some of whom had settled there as early as 1828 (Savage and Yeoh, 2013: 311). While Singapore's petrochemical industry was initially sited off the coast of the mainland due to potential negative externalities, the second master plan for Jurong Island explicitly ties it into the city-state's larger green vision through the creation of a 'green aesthetic' in the form of tree-lined roads and the restoration of natural ecosystems (Yang and Lay, 2004). This strategy is consistent with other islands like Semakau (discussed in the next section), which combine brownfield sites with ecological conservation measures and recreational amenities. Jurong Island is also being prepared for possible future conversion into a site for the generation of renewable energy, as the petrochemicals industry is recognised to have finite economic viability, particularly in the context of global climate change (Yang and Lay, 2004). The island can therefore be seen as a territorial framework for the production of Singapore's future urban landscapes and economic pathways (see Brenner, 2013: 100).

Waste management

Pulau Semakau is one of Singapore's Western islands, which now contains Singapore's offshore landfill, handling mostly incinerated waste. Incineration reduces the volume of waste by 90 per cent making it an effective waste-management strategy for Singapore due to the shortage of available land within the country. The transformation of Pulau Semakau into a landfill in 1990 (operationalised in 1999) also involved the reclamation of a nearby island, Pulau Seking, which was connected to it. The total reclaimed land consists of 220ha of swamp, foreshore, and seabed around the island, which was initially only 29ha in area (Singapore Parliament, 1975). The total landfill area across the two formerly separate islands now encompasses 350ha, with a capacity of 63 million m^3 of incinerated ash (Chia et al., 1987; Ng, 2012; see Figure 17.2). According to a report in the *Business Times*, this made Semakau Landfill 'probably the largest off-shore dumping ground in South-east Asia' (Lee, 1989: 20), and is in fact the first man-made offshore landfill created mostly out of sea space (Chia, 2019).

Previously, Pulau Seking was home to the last Southern island *kampong* (village) community, the population later supplemented by those from Pulau Bukom as they were displaced from the petrochemical development there. At its height, Pulau Seking had a population of over 300 people, until the islanders were resettled to mainland Singapore to make way for the landfill in the 1990s (Cornelius-Takahama, 2019). Much earlier, there

Figure 17.2 Signboard showing map of Semakau Landfill. Source: Author.

were also about 200 families living on Pulau Semakau although they had already moved to the mainland in 1977 for better employment opportunities (Ng, 2012).

However, in 1989, it was proposed that the site, along with Pulau Semakau, should be used for a landfill due to a lack of space on the mainland. At that time, the waste produced in Singapore totalled 1.9 million tonnes annually and was expected to grow to 2.3 million tonnes a year by the year 2000. It was therefore predicted that both existing landfills on the mainland, in Lim Chu Kang and Tampines at the extreme northwest and northeast respectively, would reach full capacity by the late 1990s, which proved to be accurate (Lee, 1989; Chan, 2016). Other possible sites that were considered on the mainland (such as Punggol, in the Northeast) were needed for new housing estates to accommodate the growing population (Chan, 2016). After Pulau Semakau took over their function, the original landfill sites have become important wetland reserves (Sungei Buloh and Lorong Halus, respectively). Thus, the location of the new landfill offshore, out of sight of most Singaporeans and visitors, can be seen as part of an attempt to build a 'clean and green' Singapore, which of course requires the relocation of brownfield sites into the periphery.

The placement of heavy industry and landfills on the southern islands was a means of – and a basic precondition for – building a 'modern' Singapore through separating 'good' from 'bad' natures (Kaika, 2005: 58). In other words, it is a process of separating the metabolic transformation of nature from that of urbanisation. At the same time, Kaika argues, the domestically metabolised 'bad' nature (e.g., pollution, waste, etc.), become part of the outside, or the antipode to the protected interior of the nation. For instance, Singapore's waste is incinerated at one of four plants on the mainland, and the ashes are then transferred by barge along with non-incinerable waste to Pulau Semakau from Tuas Pier, at the southwestern edge of the mainland. The waste – approximately 2,300 tonnes per day – is transferred at night, keeping it out of sight (Chan, 2016). As such, while modernity in Singapore has been premised upon making 'nature' an intrinsic part of modern life, it has simultaneously positioned many of the Southern Islands as externalised 'others' for the processing of metabolised natures and fuelling economic growth. There are similarities here with 'circular' waste economies elsewhere that have effectively used peripheral and suburban spaces to extend this aspect of the urban landscape's metabolism (see Savini, Chapter 18 in this volume).

Upon construction, it was anticipated that once filled, the reclaimed land on Semakau could be used for more development (Lee, 1989). While this has not yet happened, the original reclaimed area at Semakau was filled by 2016, so the National Environment Agency (NEA) embarked on plans to start work on phase two of the Semakau Landfill in 2013 which would meet Singapore's projected waste disposal needs up to 2035 and beyond (NEA, 2015). A wind turbine and solar panels were installed in 2006 in order to enhance sustainability of the landfill and to reduce greenhouse gas emissions (Tan et al., 2010). The heat released from the incineration is used to power generators and extracted metal is sold for reuse which makes the operation of Semakau financially self-sustaining (Lee, 1989).

However, Chan (2016) has noted that the landfill actually has numerous 'hidden' socio-ecological consequences both within and beyond Singapore, particularly related to the dredging of sand required for the reclamation, which would have had environmental costs for those places and is becoming increasingly unsustainable (Comaroff, 2014). In addition, waste incineration can produce harmful air pollution (particularly dioxins and furans produced from the burning of plastics and other materials) which can be particularly harmful to communities that live in the vicinity of incineration plants. There are also concerns regarding the potential leaching of toxins from the incinerated ash into the ocean, which will require continual monitoring throughout and beyond Semakau's operational lifetime (Chan, 2016). Landfilling of incinerated ash has therefore been increasingly criticised as a viable method of waste disposal due to the possibility of contaminating water supplies and the emission of greenhouse gasses into the atmosphere (Gandy, 1994). This demonstrates the socio-environmental inequalities that are produced through the transformation of the urban landscape to serve the capitalist political economy, even in seemingly 'green' and 'sustainable' ways (Swyngedouw, 2014).

Conclusion

This chapter has sought to complement emerging research explicating the range of spatial processes and more-than-urban geographies bound up with planetary, or extended urbanisation from an urban political ecology perspective. The urbanisation of Singapore's offshore islands helps us to understand how the urban is actually 'distributed, patchy, and not necessarily one coherent space' (Connolly, 2019: 68). In other words, processes of urbanisation impact sites both within and beyond the conventional city as rural places are enrolled as sites of industrial production or sinks for waste (Cantor, 2020: 18; Savini, Chapter 18 in this volume). The case also illustrates the role of the capitalist political economy in generating processes of urban metabolism, and associated socio-spatial transformation.

As we have demonstrated, the Singapore state has mobilised discourses such as 'land scarcity' in justifying the transformation of the offshore islands to facilitate socio-economic development and the displacement of former inhabitants. The transformation of these islands into oil refineries, landfill, and tourism sites has resulted in the loss of many *kampong* landscapes, natural habitats, and the eviction of its former inhabitants. Singapore's offshore islands can therefore be seen as hybrid rural/urban spaces, in that they contain spatial characteristics and features that are typically associated with both urban and rural places. These include a typically rural (sparsely populated) built form with a lack of physical infrastructure and open spaces, no defined core or centre, and a quieter, slower, lived experience; industry, manufacturing and service industries associated with urban places; but also sinks for urban metabolism, such as Singapore's only active landfill, associated with urban peripheries (Cantor, 2020: 5). In this way, the chapter illustrates how taking the rural (or the non-urban) as merely 'the ontological Other of the urban, its radical opposite' is highly problematic (Brenner, 2013: 98).

Notes

1 Methodologically, the chapter is based on a much larger, two-year, interdisciplinary research project investigating the history, heritage, and development of Singapore's Southern Islands (focusing on St John's, Lazarus, and Seringat), spanning 2018–19. This research was based on extensive archival research, interviews with former inhabitants of these islands, surveys with users of the islands, as well as review of existing secondary sources. We conducted several meetings with relevant statutory boards in Singapore, including the Singapore Land Authority (SLA), Sentosa Development Corporation (SDC), and National Heritage Board (NHB). We also made several research trips to the Southern

Islands, at times with representatives from these organisations to share findings and learn more about the Islands' management and future development plans. This chapter in particular draws on insights gleaned from this project, in addition to more specific archival research and review of publicly available reports pertaining to the development of Singapore's offshore islands over the past 50 years.
2 It must be noted that – due to space constraints – the examples we cover here do not include the full range of uses that the islands were developed to serve, but rather a small set of illustrative examples. For other uses, see de Koninck et al. (2017).
3 Another early strategy was the dredging of existing navigation channels within port waters, as some of these were too narrow for the passage of large ships (*Straits Times*, 1975).
4 Thanks to Roger Keil for this point.

References

Arboleda, M. 2016. In the nature of the non-city: Expanded infrastructural networks and the political ecology of planetary urbanization. *Antipode* 48(2): 233–51.
Brenner, N. 1998. Between fixity and motion: Accumulation, territorial organization and the historical geography of spatial scales. *Environment and Planning D: Society and Space* 16(4): 459–81.
Brenner, N. 2013. Theses on urbanization. *Public Culture* 25(1): 85–114.
Cantor, A. 2020. Hydrosocial hinterlands: An urban political ecology of Southern California's hydrosocial territory. *Environment and Planning E: Nature and Space*. DOI: 10.1177/2514848620909384.
Carpenter, K. and W.K. Ng. 2013 Singapore's chemicals industry: Engineering an island. *American Institute of Chemical Engineers*. www.aiche.org/sites/default/files/cep/20130456.pdf, accessed 12 August 2022.
Chan, J.K.H. 2016. The ethics of working with wicked urban waste problems: The case of Singapore's Semakau Landfill. *Landscape and Urban Planning* 154: 123–31.
Chia, J.Y.J. 2019. Pulau Semakau. https://eresources.nlb.gov.sg/infopedia/articles/SIP_1008_2010-03-22.html, accessed 12 August 2022.
Chia, L.S., H. Khan, and L.M. Chou. 1987. *The coastal environmental profile of Singapore*. ICLARM Technical Reports 21. International Center for Living Aquatic Resources, Manila.
Comaroff, J. 2014. Built on sand: Singapore and the new state of risk. *Harvard Design Magazine* 39. www.harvarddesignmagazine.org/issues/39/built-on-sand-singapore-and-the-new-state-of-risk, accessed 12 August 2022.
Connolly, C. 2019. Urban political ecology beyond methodological cityism. *International Journal of Urban and Regional Research* 43(1): 63–85. DOI: 10.1111/1468-2427.12710.
Cornelius-Takahama, V. 2019. Pulau Seking. *Infopedia*. https://eresources.nlb.gov.sg/infopedia/articles/SIP_239_2005-01-19.html, accessed 12 August 2022.
Cornelius-Takahama, V. and J. Loo. 2016. Pulau Bukom. *Infopedia*. https://eresources.nlb.gov.sg/INFOPEDIA/articles/SIP_922_2005-01-19.html, accessed 12 August 2022.

Cronon, W. 1991. *Nature's metropolis: Chicago and the great west*. New York: W.W. Norton.
de Koninck, R., J. Drolet, and M. Girard. 2008. *Singapore: An atlas of perpetual territorial transformation*. Singapore: NUS Press.
de Koninck, R., T.H. Pham, and M. Girard. 2017. *Singapore's permanent territorial revolution: Fifty years in fifty maps*. Singapore: NUS Press.
Department of Statistics. 2016. *Principal statistics of manufacturing by industry cluster*, 4 January. Department of Statistics, Singapore. Available at: www.sings tat.gov.sg/statistics/browse-by-theme/manufacturing, accessed 12 August 2022.
Gandy, M. 1994. *Recycling and the politics of urban waste*. Available at: http://public.ebookcentral.proquest.com/choice/publicfullrecord.aspx?p=1702063, accessed 12 August 2022.
Groen, S. n.d. *Reclaiming the land, protecting the environment: Using EMMP to protect Singapore's natural heritage*. Singapore: DHI Group. www.dhigroup.com/global/references/apac/overview/reclaiming-the-land--protecting-the-envi ronment, accessed 12 August 2022.
Harvey, D. 1989. From managerialism to entrepreneurialism: The transformation in urban governance in late capitalism. *Geografiska Annaler: Series B, Human Geography* 71(1): 3–17.
Ho, A.L. 2014. Singapore's forgotten islands. *The Straits Times*, 3 August.
Huff, W.G. 1997. *The economic growth of Singapore: Trade and development in the twentieth century*. Cambridge: Cambridge University Press.
International Year of the Reef. 2009. *The Singapore blue plan 2009*, 23 May. www.nss.org.sg/old/pdf/blueplan-final.pdf, accessed 12 August 2022.
JTC (Jurong Town Corporation). 1984. *Annual report*. Jurong: Jurong Town Corporation.
Kaika, M. 2005. *City of flows: Modernity, nature, and the city*. New York and London: Routledge.
Kaika, M. and E. Swyngedouw. 2000. Fetishizing the modern city: The phantasmagoria of urban technological networks. *International Journal of Urban and Regional Research* 24(1): 120–38.
Koh, T. and J. Lin. 2017. The land reclamation case: Thoughts and reflections. *Singapore Yearbook of International Law* 10: 1–7.
Lee, H.S. 1989. Big off-shore dumping ground planned. *Business Times*, 11 February.
Lefebvre, H. 1991. *The production of space*. Oxford: Blackwell.
Lim, I. 2004. Jurong Island. https://eresources.nlb.gov.sg/infopedia/articles/SIP_5 05_2004-12-17.html, accessed 12 August 2022.
Makepeace, W., G.E. Brooke, and R.S.J. Braddell (eds.). 1991. *One hundred years of Singapore*. Singapore and New York: Oxford University Press.
Moore, J. 2014. Toward a singular metabolism: Epistemic rifts and environment-making in the capitalist world-ecology. In D. Ibañez and N. Katsikis (eds.), *New Geographies, 6: Grounding Metabolism*. Cambridge, MA: Harvard University Press, pp. 10–19.
NEA (National Environmental Agency). 2015. Phase II Semakau landfill ready to meet Singapore's waste disposal needs to 2035 and beyond. www.nea.gov.sg/media/news/news/index/phase-ii-semakau-landfill-ready-to-meet-singapore-s-waste-disposal-needs-to-2035-and-beyond, accessed 12 August 2022.
Neo, H. 2007. Challenging the developmental state: Nature conservation in Singapore. *Asia Pacific Viewpoint* 48(2): 186–99.
Ng, M.F.C. 2012. *Habitats in harmony: The story of Semakau landfill*. Singapore: National Environment Agency.

Savage, V.R. and B.S.A. Yeoh. 2013. *Singapore street names: A study of toponymics*. Updated and expanded edition. Singapore: Marshall Cavendish Editions.

Singapore Parliament. 1975. Reclamation at Pulau Semakau. Parliamentary Debates, 29 July. https://sprs.parl.gov.sg/search/topic?reportid=034_19750729_S0005_T0 029, accessed 12 August 2022.

Sparke, M., J.D. Sidaway, T. Bunnell, and C. Grundy-Warr. 2004. Triangulating the borderless world: Geographies of power in the Indonesia-Malaysia-Singapore growth triangle. *Transactions of the Institute of British Geographers* 29(4): 485–98.

Straits Times. 1959. $40m Shell refinery for Singapore. The Straits Times, 1 December. Singapore. https://eresources.nlb.gov.sg/newspapers/Digitised/Article/straitstimes19591201-1.2.72, accessed 12 August 2022.

Straits Times. 1974. Chemical complex for Bukom under big expansion plan. *The Straits Times*, 24 October. https://eresources.nlb.gov.sg/newspapers/Digitised/Article/straitstimes19741024-1.2.46.3, accessed 12 August 2022.

Straits Times. 1975. Go-ahead for reclaim land project at Changi. *The Straits Times*, 30 July.

Swyngedouw, E. 1992. Territorial organization and the space/technology nexus. *Transactions of the Institute of British Geographers* 17(4): 417–33.

Swyngedouw, E. 2006. Circulations and metabolisms: (Hybrid) natures and (cyborg) cities. *Science as Culture* 15(2): 105–21.

Swyngedouw, E. 2014. The violence of sustainable urbanity. *Harvard Design Magazine* 37: 24–9.

Tan, H.T., L.M. Chou, D.C.J. Yeo, and P.K.L. Ng. 2010. *The natural heritage of Singapore*. Singapore: Pearson Prentice Hall.

Tzaninis, Y., T. Mandler, M. Kaika, and R. Keil. 2021. Moving urban political ecology beyond the 'urbanization of nature'. *Progress in Human Geography* 45(2): 229–52.

Wee, V. and G. Benjamin. n.d. Pulau Sakeng: The final link to pre-Raffles Singapore. Unpublished manuscript. www.academia.edu/5343730/Vivienne_Wee_and_Geoffrey_Benjamin_Pulau_Seking_the_final_link_to_pre-Raffles_Singapore, accessed 12 August 2022.

Yang, P.P.-J. and O.B. Lay. 2004. Applying ecosystem concepts to the planning of industrial areas: A case study of Singapore's Jurong Island. *Journal of Cleaner Production* 12(8–10): 1011–23.

Yun, H.A. and L.K. Jin. 2009. Evolution of the petrochemical industry in Singapore. *Journal of the Asia Pacific Economy* 14(2): 116–22.

18

The circular economy of cities: The good, the bad, and the ugly

Federico Savini

Urban agglomerations are both engines of the global economy and sources of environmental destruction. Continuing urbanisation means that the overall consumption of materials worldwide will double by 2050. At the same time, urban areas will produce 70 per cent more waste than today (Hoornweg and Bhada-Tata, 2012). The global economy produces nine gigatonnes of waste each year, of which only one third comes from households and another third stems from industrial production. Of the 500kg of (solid) waste that each person produces on average per year, only one third is actually recycled (Tisserant et al., 2017). When non-household waste is added to that calculation, this amount triples. Globally, the urbanised economy extracts 85 gigatonnes of materials each year (excluding water). This means that, on average, every human being requires 11,000kg of materials annually. Each day an urban dweller uses 18kg of sand (United Nations, 2019).

All of this amounts to an unfolding resource and waste crisis. Both geographically and socially, its impact is highly unequal. The materials necessary to sustain urban life will become increasingly scarce. This scarcity will put pressure on all of those zones that supply resources to urban agglomerations. This pressure will exacerbate socio-economic divides and conflicts among areas of concentrated consumption on the one hand and areas of resource extraction and waste disposal on the other. To supply urban life and ensure their prosperity, global cities will depend ever more on the uneven geography of exploitation of both nature and labour.

Against the backdrop of this emergency, the circular economy sketches a vision of hope, even utopia. It suggests the possibility that policymakers can simultaneously reuse available waste, reduce the exploitation of raw materials, shift consumption patterns, and improve economic performance. Because of these combined effects, it is (almost) universally agreed in both policy and research networks that circularity offers a viable paradigm of sustainable development (Gregson and Crang, 2015; Urbinati et al., 2017). Proponents of circularity praise this model's capacity to generate returns from residues of production and consumption processes, while nurturing a business culture and individual lifestyles that are parsimonious with materials (Lacy and Rutqvist, 2016). Critical views, however, warn that circularity will not reduce wasteful consumerism. Instead, it will only precipitate a new circuit of consumption that is premised upon the commodification of waste (Savini, 2019; Valenzuela and Böhm, 2017: 23). Will the circular economy effectively reduce resource depletion while maintaining well-being? Does it diminish wasteful consumerism, the root cause of resource depletion and waste? Or does it instead mark the beginning of a new circuit of capitalist production, which prospers out of the abundance of waste?

Answering these questions means dissecting the emergence and application of the complex narrative of circularity. This chapter reveals the underlying political ecology of waste recovery that has accompanied and fuelled the circularity discourse over the past two decades. It does so by reconsidering how waste flows fit into the processes of urbanisation, moving from a perspective premised on the notion of *abjection* to one based on *valorisation*. Conceived as abjection, the spatiality of waste comes to embody the asymmetric social relations produced by economic accumulation (Baka, 2013; Gandy, 2013). Waste disposal manifests class inequalities: exposure to bacteria, rubbish, and excrement becomes a measure of marginality, exclusion, and exploitation. Aesthetically, the separation between the beauty and cleanliness of production and everyday waste management has been taken as the visible proxy of wasteful consumerism (Lindner and Meissner, 2015). The abjection of waste was a key feature of a paradigm of 'hygiene' that explicitly saw residuals as incompatible with the functioning of cities (Gandy, 2004). When we, however, talk about valorisation, waste becomes a resource in the accumulation process but also a glue around which social and community relations are built (Bulkeley et al., 2007). This shift allows me to address the idiosyncrasies of a circular paradigm of economic growth. While reusing and reducing waste is more crucial than ever in tackling resource depletion, I stress that circular economics also contains the seeds of an economic system that will be even more dependent on waste generation.

Focusing on the Netherlands and in particular the Amsterdam region, the chapter traces the genealogy of circular economy programmes. To this end, I show how waste-processing services have been restructured from around 2005 onward (Savini, 2019). Current realisations of circular economy, I argue, are beginning to lock city-regions into a model of economic development that depends on the perpetual production of waste materials. This waste sector is highly unstable. The notion of circularity, I claim, provides the basis for an emerging wicked cooperation among three distinct submarkets that compete and cooperate with each other: the micro economy of urban waste reuse, the increasingly global waste market, and the incineration sector.

The political ecology of urban waste: From abjection to valorisation

Urban political ecology research has long been concerned with waste. Urban areas crystallise dense flows of materials, whether at the input, throughput, or outputs stages. They metabolise materials such that they become buildings, infrastructures, technologies, energy, and food. The residues left by this metabolisation – reusable or otherwise – are commonly known as 'waste'.

Scholars have generally conceptualised waste as a constructed by-product of capitalist production and socio-environmental exploitation. On this view waste, although a residue of urbanisation, is not found in urban areas (Heynen et al., 2006). Waste's multiple geographies have bifurcated into areas that produce waste and those that process it. The wastelands of urban agglomerations are sites of exploitation necessary for consumerism to prosper and urban wealth to accumulate. Traditionally, then, waste has been seen as *abject* of capitalist accumulation. As the repellent materiality of the unwanted, waste has been identified as an unavoidable 'negative' value: the 'anti-value' of capital (Frow, 2003; Gidwani and Reddy, 2011; Gille, 2010).

Since the Second World War this paradigm has distinguished between what is perceived as properly 'urban' (e.g., places of work and sociality) and all that remains in the background. Areas that could be categorised as neither natural, rural, or suburban were labelled wasteland. This separation was taken as representative of a 'splintered' urban geography of contemporary cities, in which spaces dedicated to waste infrastructures were strictly separated from those allotted to economic growth (Graham and Marvin, 2001).

Both the first and second wave of research in urban political ecology were primarily concerned with waste's economically negative and socially divisive position (Tzaninis et al., 2021). These currents of research were somewhat blind, however, to multiple post-urban geographies of waste flows, for they focused on waste's role in reproducing marginality rather than in producing economic value. The growing interest in narratives of resource efficiency and circular economics indicates a shift in waste's position in contemporary urbanisation. These narratives put waste at the centre of a brand-new paradigm of green urbanisation. Waste's new centrality, particularly in urban spaces, demands that we substitute the concept of *abjection* with that of *valorisation*. Indeed, it is necessary to reposition the role of waste, such that it is seen as central to the analysis of urbanisation processes.

The challenge facing contemporary work on waste in urban political ecology is that of explaining how waste's changing social geography is symptomatic of a different form of capitalist accumulation, which prospers by valorising waste materials. The idea of infinite circularity embodies an emerging paradigm of green urban growth. Although this paradigm imagines the 'end of waste', it does not recognise that waste results from wasteful consumption (Ragossnig and Schneider, 2019). Refusing the negativity imputed to waste in economic processes, it incorporates the materiality of garbage into growth. Circularity envisions a strategy of urban growth that is sustainable in that it constitutes a self-regenerating loop of waste reuse. Through new closed-loop infrastructures and reconfiguration of the way in which urban living relates to waste processing, cities are becoming the testbeds for this valorisation process. As such, circularity also challenges established categorisations of land use, production, and consumption inherited from the linear economy of extraction and disposal. It offers an imaginary of infinite urban growth, in which cities perpetually feed on their own outputs and residuals.

In what follows, I trace the genealogy of this transition between paradigms over the past two decades. Mapping the shifting political ecology of waste valorisation, I show how waste markets and waste processing services have been rapidly repositioned in relation to urban economies. On this basis, I then sketch out the trajectories of waste valorisation in three waste sectors: waste recovery, incineration, and reuse.

Emerging geographies of waste valorisation

At the turn of the century, the European waste market was a patchwork of semi-liberalised sub-national sectors. These were dominated by a diverse landscape of urban waste management companies (OECD, 1999). This market had four peculiarities: a co-dependency between public utilities and private waste services; an institutional upscaling toward homogeneous regulations at the national and European scales; the pursuit of economies of scale; and the suburbanisation of waste infrastructures. Despite increased numbers of private companies in the waste market since the 1970s, the liberalisation of waste came relatively recently in comparison to that of telecommunications, energy, water, and housing (Massarutto, 2007). The reason for this lag was the relatively high risk involved in investing in waste, which meant that private investors remained relatively conservative. The logistics and infrastructures necessary to distribute, store, and process waste materials are expensive, whereas the marginal revenues of processed waste are very low. Moreover, recycled materials were much less valuable than raw materials until around 2010, when the prices of the most critical raw materials – those necessary for building high-tech infrastructures – increased precipitously (European Commission, 2017).

These risks meant that waste processing remained either a tightly regulated public service or resorted to partially illicit means. In collaboration with public actors, joint venture companies or consortia collected, separated, and incinerated household waste. Dense city regions need efficient waste transport systems, involving extensive labour to collect refuse from households. What is more, household waste is of low 'purity', an important factor in increasing yields from recovery. All of this meant that private waste companies generally preferred to invest instead in the industrial waste market, in which waste streams are more homogenous. When raw materials were cheap, converting waste into energy through incineration remained a preferable solution for cities. Accordingly, 300 new incinerators opened worldwide between 2007 and 2013. In Europe specifically, incineration capacity increased by 6 per cent, with Northern and Western EU countries incinerating between 50 and 75 per cent of all their waste. Incineration also discouraged recycling through the so-called 'vacuum cleaner effect' (Wilts and von Gries, 2015).

Unlike financial markets, in which transactions are almost instant, waste processing is at the mercy of long-term shifts in production and consumption. Infrastructural and technological investments in waste processing have extremely long turnover times. For this reason, the waste sector has witnessed a dynamic series of regulatory measures since the late 1990s. Their aim was to consolidate and secure the market and increase recycling at all scales. National governments homogenised waste regulations so as to establish a common waste hierarchy, including at the EU level. They also organised and stimulated the waste market, creating specialised accountancy models and systematically categorising waste into 'mono-streams'. These mono-streams included common recyclates (such as paper, glass, biomass, and metals) and specialised types of waste (such as tyres, mattresses, batteries, chemicals, tapes, and paint). With recognised categories multiplying, the waste market became more fine-grained. This made it possible to valorise different sub-streams.

From the beginning of the twenty-first century, the waste market pursued an economy of scale to reduce the risks of investing in mono-stream processing. Waste companies enlarged their portfolios and specialised in geographically specific services. Financially and spatially, they integrated waste with waster, energy with logistics. As I show below, mergers allowed for synergies among waste streams and other utilities. The waste market simultaneously localised and globalised, with larger corporations and groups managing a constellation of sub-companies, each specialising in a single stream.

EU regulations on landfilling from the mid-1990s bifurcated the geography of waste. At one level, forms of waste that are more difficult (and costly) to process were exported to countries with cheaper manual labour and relaxed environmental regulations (i.e., hazardous) (Gregson and Crang, 2015). At another, more easily treatable (or strictly regulated) waste streams were suburbanised. In the late 1990s specialised waste processing sites began multiplying around urban agglomerations. It was seen as crucial that these be as close as possible to waste sources so as to shorten value chains and reduce logistical costs.

In the first decade of this century, these waste processing sites resembled healthy industrial locations, not marginal areas of social exclusion. Indeed, they were often integrated into the industrial urban fringe. They were transformed from waste*lands* into waste*scapes* (Amenta and van Timmeren, 2018). These locations benefit from close proximity to industrial processing facilities and dense transport networks for exporting materials. On these sites, industrial synergies developed that would become the testbeds of the circular economy (McDonough and Braungart, 2010). Examples of these sites include the clusters of biobased productions in the harbour of Amsterdam, just 4km from the city centre; the petrochemical hubs (i.e., the *ecodistretto*) of Porto Marghera, which extends across the very urbanised Veneto region; energy cluster at the edge of the Rotterdam port, with its large incinerator next to wind turbines; the plastic production industrial cluster in North Rhine-Westphalia.

The suburbanisation of waste offered the geographical conditions under which a new model of regional growth could emerge. Later, when it was combined with concerns about sustainability, it would be labelled the circular economy. As I outline below, this shift is bound up with an ongoing reorganisation of the waste market sector. In rescaling waste streams toward the regional level, this transition has valorised recovered waste materials.

Restructuring waste recovery markets

The growing popularity of the notion of the 'circular economy' in the Netherlands is contiguous with the ongoing expansion and stabilisation of the waste recovery sector. From about 2005, this sector has had to deal with an overabundance of waste processing capacities. The economic downturn of 2008 hit a rapidly expanding market. Volumes of waste, especially from industrial production and household consumables, suddenly decreased. The sector readjusted significantly between 2008 and 2015. A rush of acquisitions and mergers generated multi-utility groups. Waste companies merged into bigger companies. Given their multinational scale, diversified portfolio (encompassing energy, waste, water, logistics, and ecological services at large) and spatial versatility (cross-country and inter-continental), these newly constituted companies had greater capacities for taking on risk.

To grasp this process, it is instructive to look at the legacy of one of the biggest waste companies in the Netherlands in the 2010s: RENEWI-ICOVA (now RENEWI), a listed multinational corporation. Active in nine countries and employing around 8,000 workers, it is the primary private and commercial waste processor in the region of Amsterdam. It recycles 14 million tons of waste annually – and that is only in the Netherlands. Like all waste companies in Holland, RENEWI now presents itself as a forerunner of circularity. This company's development indicates how the waste recovery market has consolidated since about 2010. RENEWI is the result of a 2016 merger between the British utilities group Shanks and van Gasenwinkel, then largest Dutch waste services provider. This was only the latest in a series of mergers and acquisitions. These were initiated to deal with the increased debt of Afvalverwerking Rijnmond (AVR), which was then the largest public waste company and second-largest incinerator in South Holland (processing one-third of the country's waste). Over ten years AVR was bought and sold several times. In 2006, an international private equity investment fund bought it for almost €1.5 billion. One year later AVR merged with van Gasenwinkel, forming the van Gasenwinkel Group, a multi-utility group encompassing water, energy, and waste. In 2013, rising debts forced the group to turn to a Chinese investor, a port services and retail provider named Cheung Kong Infrastructure.

Today RENEWI manages several steps in the waste recovery chain: obtaining waste; transporting it to its own subsidiaries; selling it (when possible) to its own waste processing companies; and finally selling the secondary materials. All of these functions are situated near urban agglomerations to reduce logistical costs. The company owns four mono-stream firms, which process ashes from incineration, electronics, plastic, and glass. It also owns Orgaworld, which produces electricity from biogas and supplies Amsterdam's heating network. The companies are all located in the port of Amsterdam (5km from the city centre), forming an industrial ecosystem of integrated waste and energy services that are oriented toward both local and global markets.

RENEWI's legacy and geographical profile encapsulates broader changes in the Dutch waste sector since the first decade of the twenty-first century, which was then at 'the stage of a fusion wave' (according to the Dutch Financial Daily Newspaper, 2015). Indeed, other Dutch waste companies have followed identical pathways. Remondis, a €7 billion multinational giant, which provides waste and ecological services in 34 countries, purchased Dusseldorp Groep, a Dutch construction waste company. In 2015 SUEZ (the French giant in water, waste, and environmental services) entered the Dutch market, buying 35 per cent of shares in SITA Netherlands. INDAVER, a waste management company active in North Holland, was bought by a consortium of venture capital investors.

The rise (and fall) of the Amsterdam 'circular' incinerator

A closer look at waste-management programs enacted in the Amsterdam city-region affords further insights into the idiosyncrasies of the circular economy, a policy paradigm that makes economic growth dependent on the valorisation of waste. In the first decade of this century, cities across Europe started investing in state-of-the-art new waste-to-energy stations and improving existing ones. They searched for ways of processing the increasing volumes of waste being produced (particularly urban household waste) and supplying urban heat and energy grids, thus reducing consumption of fossil fuels. The large supply of waste, combined with the dearth of processing facilities, led to the increase of tariffs on waste incineration. In turn, this further stimulated long-term investments in waste-to-energy infrastructures. Until recently in Europe, national governments actively minimised taxes on incineration to encourage alternatives to landfilling. Incineration capacity grew everywhere and incineration companies began diversifying their portfolios.

The Amsterdam Waste and Energy Company (AEB) followed this path. The AEB became one of Amsterdam's energy and heat providers in 1999. In that year, it joined the (then-public) energy provider NUON in funding the *Westpoort Warmte* holding, the city's first residual heat provider. This led the AEB to expand its stations, including a new high-efficiency station in Amsterdam Harbour in 2007. These investments deepened the need for a steady and increasing supply of waste to fuel the ovens and meet incineration capacity. In the middle of the first decade of the twenty-first century, the AEB established import routes so as to supply its facilities with waste from abroad. About 20 per cent of its capacity is covered by waste imported from the UK. The AEB also produces about 70 per cent of Amsterdam's supposedly 'sustainable' energy by incinerating organic material (AEB, 2017).

Optimism in the Amsterdam incineration market peaked in 2012. The Amsterdam's former alderman for economic affairs stated that 'our waste-to-energy plant is a money-making machine. So I always say garbage is gold' (*Financial Times*, 2012). This market dynamism was highly fragile, however, and future profits were overestimated. Already in 2013, the AEB's profits were only €7 million, as opposed to the expected €21 million. In 2015, the whole company was valued at half the worth of its total assets (van Zoelen, 2017). Given this uncertainty, Amsterdam's earliest circular economy frameworks (which the municipality approved in 2015 and 2016) aimed to put the AEB at the centre of transitions in both the energy and waste sector. This would make it a player in the city's (circular) economy.

Existing incineration plants provided an infrastructure with which to address national CO_2 reduction requirements and reduce Amsterdam's gas and heat consumption. To establish institutional capacity for this transition, the AEB became a private entity with 100 per cent public shares in 2014. This was supposed to give it a greater flexibility in investing in the growing circular economy; signing contracts with different suppliers; developing substreams of secondary materials; and consolidating the residual heat infrastructure (interview with a project manager at the AEB, November 2019). From 2016, the AEB planned to enlarge *Westpoort Warmte*. Its infrastructure was to expand from covering 140,000 to 350,000 homes by 2050. Further, €35 million were invested in the underground infrastructure servicing Amsterdam's northern and eastern areas.

From 2016, the AEB has also undertaken a series of side projects relating to smart infrastructures and integrated energy services. It invested in a post-collection separation facility for household and commercial waste; initiated programmes for sub-stream specialised recycling; started certifying chemical waste; and planned a biogas station. It also established a carbon-capture utilisation programme to deliver CO_2 produced in incineration to greenhouses in South Holland. This strategy was premised on the idea that the AEB could benefit from its position within an industrial ecosystem. Oriented toward global value chains and located near the city centre, it hoped to become a player in the city-region's circular economy. Transiting toward a circular economy not only impelled the city and AEB toward risky investments but made circular material-reuse programmes dependent on the incinerator's ongoing functioning. By 2019, the AEB's increasing debts had transformed the company 'from a waste dream to a ticking bomb' (Koops and van Zoelen, 2019). The 'bomb' exploded in July 2019, when a technical problem forced four of its six ovens to close for almost five months. Puncturing hopes that the waste market would become increasingly prosperous, this interruption revealed the fragility of the AEB's whole investment strategy from around 2005 onward. The AEB still prioritises incineration today. This highlights the adverse effects of incineration and the toxic nature of its output as discussed also by Connolly and Muzaini (Chapter 17 in this volume).

The new economy of urban waste reuse

Since the mid-2000s, the idea of circularity has provided the basis for an alternative circuit of urban waste valorisation, which both competes with and depends on national and global waste value chains. It turns the city into an 'urban mine' of materials for economic development. The legacy of circular thinking in Amsterdam is rooted in the success of a set of waste reuse and material production initiatives following the global financial crisis. Between 2008 and 2015, the city's handcraft and small manufacturing sector was growing at ten times faster than the national economy (see Municipality of Amsterdam, 2015). At the frontrunner of a new ecological consumerism, this creative economy involved a network of mini start-ups active in DIY production (self-building, repairing, and digitalised manufacturing).

The growth of this sector amid the wider financial downturn motivated a wave of urban experiments geared toward stimulating businesses in sustainability, specifically materials reuse. Politically advertised as the city's new 'resource economy', Amsterdam's first visions of circular economy foregrounded the strategic role of small circular living laboratories, particularly in struggling areas. *Buiksloterham*, *Schoon Schip*, and *de Ceuvel* are all community-initiated projects of off-grid circular buildings in Amsterdam's northern district. Combining principles of sustainable living, DIY, and waste material recovery, they became flagship projects of circular business development. They resulted in the first framework for circular real-estate (Municipality of Amsterdam, 2017) and boosted a local market in materials reuse consultancy. In few years, the firms advising these projects (such as Metabolic and Circle Economy) transformed from start-ups to consultancy companies active all over the country. They fill a gap between circular business models, industrial efficiency, urban policymaking, and popular engagement.

In putting the built environment at the centre of policymaking, these initiatives aim to redirect waste streams away from global circuits of waste processing (involving incineration, landfilling, or backfilling) and toward urban development. In the past ten years, a multitude of start-ups, municipal departments, waste companies, and local associations have begun to invest in the organic waste (particularly local food, beer, and groceries), construction waste, electronics, textiles, and water sectors. These types of waste are both very accessible to urban consumers and directly related to housing and dwelling. Organic and food waste figures an especially dynamic part of the city's eco-consumption strategies. Initiatives trying to urbanise local waste include local compost stations (Warmhotels) that serve groups of at least five households in each city neighbourhood as well as the numerous cafés whose brand is premised on reusing edible food.

As of yet, these initiatives of waste valorisation do not seem to clash with the recovery and incineration sectors. Seemingly, they simply add another circuit of consumption and production. Thanks to partnerships between established waste services and an emerging constellation of urban start-ups, a great deal of R&D has gone into bio-plastics, reused glass, bio-chemicals, 3D printing, smart crushing, and wood architecture. The five years between 2013 and 2018 saw the multiplication of partnerships around notions of urban mining and circular urban development, involving governmental institutions, logistics providers, waste companies, and data companies. A city deal named *Circulaire Stad* is the most representative of these partnerships. Signed in 2017, it consolidated a national coalition of municipal governments, start-ups, logistics firms, and waste corporations around strategies of urban waste recovery.

Today it is impossible to delineate the urban circular economy's exact boundaries in the Amsterdam city-region. It does not correspond to a specific business sector. Instead, it has become an overarching narrative boosting any project that combines the consumption of materials with a narrative of sustainable, green, smart, or social – from the region's smallest social project to the largest waste-recovery stream. The current 'Amsterdam Circular 2020–2025' strategy aims to reduce the city's use of raw materials by 50 per cent by 2030 (Municipality of Amsterdam, 2020). Yet it does so by instituting a policy-to-business synergy across all sectors of innovation in urban material streams, according to a vision of green and sustainable economic growth.

Good, bad, ugly: the ecological politics of circularity

Sergio Leone's movie *The Good, the Bad, and the Ugly* tells the story of three bandits that unwillingly cooperate so as to find buried gold during the American civil war. Each of them has a piece of information about the gold's location. Despite being fully aware that they are silently competing with each other, the bandits work together in pursuit of the treasure.

In responding to the idea of the circular economy, the waste market has come to exhibit this competitive form of cooperation. The circular economy entails three different waste valorisation tactics, which converge in a paradigm of (green) economic growth based on revaluing materials that were hitherto marginal in urban economies. This is achieved by restructuring waste recovery processes, geographies, and finances in urban agglomerations. The city does not so much generate waste as provide a site for waste valorisation. Circularity involves adapting urban and regional infrastructures in the service of waste valorisation.

In this analogy, the good represents the emerging urban economy of waste recovery, including its start-up culture, circular neighbourhoods, climate-neutral estates, and second-hand products. These practices prefigure an alternative lifestyle in which ecologically minded consumers and producers are concerned about the legacy of secondary materials. Advocates present such ventures as stepping stones leading toward the socialisation of waste, with waste becoming the vehicle of ecological economic innovation. That said, these practices are yet to demonstrate their capacity to reduce waste. Instead, they seem to add yet another circuit of consumption.

In Leone's movie, the ugly relates to the most ambiguous character. This reminds us that dealing with unfolding global waste and resource crises is more urgent than ever before. The established waste processing industry boasts about how its infrastructural, geographical, and financial clout can cope with secondary materials of lower marginal value than primary materials. It has become increasingly global and multi-sectoral, incorporating waste, logistic, electricity, and water utilities. On the one hand, the industry portrays itself as essential in the transition towards a circular economy. On the other, it simplifies the notion of circularity, such that it merely entails increasing waste reuse, not reducing waste production.

Finally, the bad in Leone's movie recalls the role of incineration industry in contemporary circular economy discourses. In theory, circular economics posits incineration as the least desirable way of processing waste; as such, it is waste recovery's undesirable competitor. Yet incineration stations (and waste-to-energy facilities more generally) are key to realising circular services. Policymakers see them as crucial sources of energy and heat for the built environment. Incineration therefore follows the good and the ugly in the pursuit of waste valorisation. Urban waste-to-energy plants capitalise on their position as providers for the urban infrastructure, able to combine waste recovery with the imperative to develop forms of 'post-fossil' heating and energy production.

Start-ups of waste reuse, multinationals of waste recovery and the incineration industry each depend on each other in collecting, processing, storing, separating, and distributing waste. Yet they also compete with one another for this valuable material. This competition can be organised and maintained only by avoiding a clear politics of waste reduction and excluding wasteful consumerism and excess from the political arena. Today, the danger of the circular economy lies in its focus on producing a more efficient and capillary system of waste valorisation. We are currently seeing the construction of an unstable economic infrastructure that requires steady flows of waste for its survival.

Things might turn out differently. Cities and urban dwellers are crucial to this economic system's future. In the form of valuable resource, waste is returning to everyday life in cities. Moreover, waste valorisation positions urban consumers and the built environment at the centre of an ecological politics that diverges from the last century's NIMBYism. This politics builds upon an idea that waste is valuable. Asserting that the distribution and ownership of waste is political, it reflects an emerging co-dependency between urbanisation and waste recovery in times of resource scarcity. This incipient politics shows that as political forums, cities have the potential to question the infrastructures and cultural framing of waste production and distribution in deliberate, explicit ways. The urban fringe is key to this politics, for waste valorisation is instantiated in the waste processing industry, which involves warehouses, silos, containers, smart automation, and workers. The circular economy will reshape these areas' future position in waste circulation at the local and global scales.

References

AEB. 2017. *Jaarveslag 2017*. Annual report produced by the AEB, 2017. www.aebamsterdam.nl/media/1777/aeb180709_jvs2017.pdf, accessed 12 August 2022.

Amenta, L. and A. van Timmeren. 2018. Beyond wastescapes: Towards circular landscapes. Addressing the spatial dimension of circularity through the regeneration of wastescapes. *Sustainability* 11(12): 12–15.

Baka, J. 2013. The political construction of wasteland: Governmentality, land acquisition and social inequality in south India. *Development and Change* 44(2): 409–28.

Bulkeley, H., M. Watson, and R. Hudson. 2007. Modes of governing municipal waste. *Environment and Planning A* 39(11): 2733–53.

European Commission. 2017. *Study on the review of the list of Critical Raw Materials Critical Raw Materials Factsheets*. Report no. ET-04-15-307-EN-N. Report produced by the European Commission, Brussels.

Financial Daily Newspaper. 2015. Afvalsector is het toneel van ongekende fusiegolf; Handvol middelgrote bedrijven is bezig aan een opmars.

Financial Times. 2012. Waste opportunity: Creative management of landfill and recycling can transform landscape – and generate income. *Financial Times*, 6 January. www.ft.com/content/8cfd120a-2673-11e1-91cd-00144feabdc0, accessed 12 August 2022.

Frow, J. 2003. Invidious distinction: Waste, difference, and classy stuff. In G. Hawkins and S. Muecke (eds.), *Culture and waste: The creation and destruction of value*. Oxford: Rowman & Littlefield, pp. 25–38.

Gandy, M. 2004. Rethinking urban metabolism: Water, space and the modern city. *City* 8(3): 363–79.

Gandy, M. 2013. Marginalia: Aesthetics, ecology, and urban wastelands. *Annals of the Association of American Geographers* 103(6): 1301–16.

Gidwani, V. and R.N. Reddy. 2011. The afterlives of 'waste': Notes from India for a minor history of capitalist surplus. *Antipode* 43(5): 1625–58.

Gille, Z. 2010. Actor networks, modes of production, and waste regimes: Reassembling the macro-social. *Environment and Planning A* 42(5): 1049–64.

Graham, S. and S. Marvin. 2001. *Splintering urbanism: Networked infrastructures, technological mobilities and the urban condition*. London: Routledge.

Gregson, N. and M. Crang. 2015. From waste to resource: The trade in wastes and global recycling economies. *Annual Review of Environment and Resources* 40: 151–76.

Heynen, N., M. Kaika, and E. Swyngedouw. 2006. *The nature of cities: Urban political ecology and the politics of urban metabolism*. London: Routledge.

Hoornweg, D. and P. Bhada-Tata. 2012. *What a waste: A global review of solid waste management*. Washington: World Bank.

Kaika, M. and E. Swyngedouw. 2000. Fetishizing the modern city: the phantasmagoria of urban technological networks. *International Journal of Urban and Regional Research* 24(1): 120–8.

Koops, R. and B. van Zoelen. 2019. Vuilverbrander AEB: van afvaldroom tot tikkende tijdbom. *Het Parool*, 31 August.

McDonough, W. and M. Braungart. 2010. *Cradle to cradle: Remaking the way we make things*. New York: North Point Press.

Massarutto, A. 2007. Municipal waste management as a local utility: Options for competition in an environmentally-regulated industry. *Utilities Policy* 15(1): 9–19.

Municipality of Amsterdam. 2015. *Amsterdamse Ambachtseconomie 2010–2014*. Amsterdam: Municipality of Amsterdam.

Municipality of Amsterdam. 2017. *Roadmap Circulaire Gronduitgifte*. Amsterdam: Amsterdam City Council.

Municipality of Amsterdam. 2020. *Amsterdam Circulair 2020–2025*. Amsterdam: Amsterdam City Council.

Lacy, P. and J. Rutqvist. 2016. *Waste to wealth: The circular economy advantage*. Cham: Palgrave Macmillan.

Lindner, C. and M. Meissner. 2015. *Global garbage: Urban imaginaries of waste, excess, and abandonment*. London: Routledge.

OECD. 1999. *Competition in Local Services: Solid Waste Management*. Report produced by the Direcotrate for Financial, Fiscal, and Enterprise Affairs and Committee on Competition Law and Policy.

Ragossnig, A.M. and D.R. Schneider. 2019. Circular economy, recycling and end-of-waste. *Waste Management & Research* 37(2): 109–11.

Savini, F. 2019. The economy that runs on waste: accumulation in the circular city. *Journal of Environmental Policy & Planning* 21(6): 675–91.

Tisserant, A., S. Pauliuk, S. Merciai, J. Schmidt, J. Fry, R. Wood, and A. Tukker. 2017. Solid waste and the circular economy: A global analysis of waste treatment and waste footprints. *Journal of Industrial Ecology* 21: 628–40.

Tzaninis, Y., T. Mandler, M. Kaika, and R. Keil. 2021. Moving urban political ecology beyond the 'urbanization of nature'. *Progress in Human Geography* 45(2): 229–52.

United Nations. 2019. *Sand and sustainability: Finding new solutions for environmental governance of global sand resources*. Report produced by the UN Environment Programme. https://wedocs.unep.org/bitstream/handle/20.500.11822/28163/SandSust.pdf?sequence=1&isAllowed=y, accessed 12 August 2022.

Urbinati, A., D. Chiaroni, and V. Chiesa. 2017. Towards a new taxonomy of circular economy business models. *Journal of Cleaner Production* 168: 487–98.

Valenzuela, F. and S. Böhm. 2017. Against wasted politics: A critique of the circular economy. *Ephemera* 17(1): 23–60.

van Zoelen, B. 2017. Niet alles gaat meer deoven in. *Het Parool*, March 29.

Wilts, H. and N. von Gries. 2015. Europe's waste incineration capacities in a circular economy. *Waste and Resource Management* 168: 166–76.

Epilogue: Is an integrated UPE research and policy agenda possible?

Tait Mandler, Roger Keil, Yannis Tzaninis, and Maria Kaika

We set out from three premises. First, that the historical conditions of climate change are intimately linked to the processes and production of new (historically particular) forms of extended urbanisation. Second, that urban political ecology, as a heterodox field, is well suited to examine these linkages. Third, that such a task may nonetheless require a renewed and revitalised integrated UPE research and policy agenda. Importantly, the changing climate(s) that contextualise this book include more than global warming, ravaging wildfires, and an ongoing pandemic; there are geopolitical reorganisations, shifting academic zeitgeists informed by scholarly critical self-reflection, and emerging and reinvigorated insurgent social movements. To no small degree, these conditions have been exacerbated by the coronavirus pandemic which has shone a bright light on the damaged societal relationships with nature in the global urban world. The chapters collected here grapple with these developments as much as with climate change.

Climate change has forced a wider recognition of the argument at the heart of UPE: that nature and society do not occupy ontologically separate domains. In unsettling this modernist binary, as Lawhon et al. write in Chapter 10, 'climate change and the novel coronavirus challenge our collective narratives of progress and technology, have made us question whether we really can know, control, and improve'. There is a certain gratification in seeing greater numbers of activists, policymakers, politicians, non-governmental organisations, and even corporations take up and respond to arguments and ideas that have been central to UPE (as well as much geography, anthropology, and philosophy scholarship). At the same time, this raises a few critical questions for UPE research. Foremost, at least for scholars in any tradition of critical theory, how are these ideas now being taken up and put to work? By whom, for who, and to what ends? As the authors take up in Part IV, as climate change forces a certain confluence of interests there is also a need to address the disjunctions between policy, politics, and academic debate. Relatedly, as climate change implodes/explodes commonplace spatial/scalar categories, how can the realities and everyday lives of those on the peripheries and margins be integrated into (without collapsing/flattening them under) and transform existing policy and research frameworks? As authors take up in Part II, there is a need to attend to situated political ecologies. But if it is no longer (as) necessary to theorise and demonstrate the inseparability of society and nature, where does this take UPE? Gandy (2022), for instance, has recently suggested that UPE is in danger of increasing marginalisation – both within the academy and as a field with the potential to engage with scientists and policymakers. Similarly, as we ask in the introduction, and authors explore in Part I, is it time to move past the urbanisation of nature thesis? Finally, Part III explores how to account for more-than-human assemblages and actors.

This edited volume is in some sense a follow up to Heynen, Kaika, and Swyngedouw's (2006) *In the nature of cities*, which first collected UPE scholarship. In the 16 years that have passed, the field has expanded (empirically and theoretically), engaged with internal and external criticism, etc. Over the same period, however there has also been a disturbing cascade of geopolitical, economic, and ecological catastrophes that together inform our title: *Turning up the heat*. 'Turning up the heat' is a metaphor we use for a condition imposed on the world, while the world remains apathetic at large. The metaphor resonates with the real or fictional narrative of the science experiment about the frog and the pot of water. If the frog is put in water that is already boiling, it will immediately jump out. But if the frog is put in cool water that gets gradually heated, the frog remains in the water until the water boils, and it eventually dies

While 'turning up the heat' works as a metaphor for an apathetic world, it also works as a metaphor for the demand or pressure (especially exerted from below) to act upon what is happening. In either case, a heating planet is an emerging reality to which scholars must respond. Like Ernstson and Swyngedouw's recent edited collection, *Urban political ecology in the Anthropo-obscene*, we also aim to 'push, expand, and hopefully assist in rearranging urban political ecology' (2018: 257).

Our edited book began to take form in early 2019, at a workshop co-organised by York University and the University of Amsterdam, and funded by York University. The editors gathered many of the scholars collected here to discuss the state and future of UPE. In between that workshop and the publication of this volume, a number of authors have published new and exciting work that addresses the themes that organise this book. It feels appropriate to conclude this edited volume by pointing to their recent work, which is already offering pathways for an integrated UPE research agenda woven together of heterodox theories and methodologies. As we state in the Introduction, while maintaining its crucial engagement with new ontologies and epistemologies of the urban and of the environment, an integrated research agenda for UPE that this volume promotes is one that sustains its critical edge while: a) enriching its conceptual and methodological framework; and b) expanding its empirical focus on extended urbanisation beyond Western contexts.

Addressing the concerns raised in Part I, Martín Arboleda's (2020) *Planetary mine* reconfigures the thesis of planetary urbanisation, considering the planetary mine as world-historical spatial form, and emphasises how technologies, practices, and materials from the peripheries are imported into and transform the core. He critically comments that the planetary urbanisation thesis has overlooked the importance of logics and dynamics of resource extraction to processes of capitalist urbanisation. The planetary mine emerges through the new geographies of late industrialisation, which are no longer circumscribed to the traditional core of capitalist development (the West) and through the transformation of labour process by robotics and computerisation (what he calls the fourth machine age). Arboleda argues that modernisation and industrialisation in the Global South since the 1980s has destabilised meta-geographical categories of core/periphery and North/South such that the 'periphery needs to be understood as a ubiquitous socio-spatial condition'. This demands a re-conceptualisation of the scale at which capitalist processes operate. Drawing on standpoint feminism and decolonial theory, he seeks to untangle and theorise global processes through 'their concrete manifestation in the situated, affective fabrics of human and nonhuman existence'. In this way, he highlights how the planetary mine produces conditions for new formations of collective consciousness and agency.

Addressing the concerns raised in Part II, Mary Lawhon's *Making urban theory* articulates the 'southern urban critique' – bringing into question conceptualisations of the urban and geographies of knowledge production (Lawhon, 2020). *Making urban theory* is a personal, theoretical, and empirical reflection on the 'southern urban critique' and the process of, appropriately, making urban theory. She discusses and explores many of the themes that cut across the pages of this volume. Central to her thinking and writing is embracing uneasiness. This includes coming to terms with the instability of our spatial categories, like North/South, urban/rural, centre/periphery. In line with our impetus for a heterodox but integrated UPE, Lawhon also questions the tendency to separate and isolate bodies of thought. Like this volume, Lawhon's book is not a call for a (universal) formula or standardised methodology that might set out to solve this uneasiness. Instead, drawing on postcolonial theory, it is a call for hybridity, juxtaposition, unlearning, and learning anew.

Addressing the concerns raised in Part III, Kian Goh's (2021) *Form and flow* unravels relational geographies of climate change adaptation and emerging insurgent landscapes that criss-cross East/West and North/South. Goh puts the method of juxtaposition to work, exploring relational geographies of Jakarta, Rotterdam, and New York City. Excavating a 'political ecology of design', she examines both plans and counterplans (alternative narratives) that have developed in response to the climate crisis. Goh makes clear that accounting for difference between localities requires attending to particularity as much as cross-scalar generalities – 'the interconnected social, spatial, and environmental conflicts and motivations that now affect cities in every part of the world' (Goh, 2021: 2). Goh places struggle and contestation at the heart of her relational geographies, asking 'In the face of climate change and uneven social and spatial urban development, how are contesting visions of urban futures produced and how do they attain power?' (2021: 3). Climate change disrupts existing understandings and practices of urban planning as well as notions of environmental in/justice.

Finally, Matthew Gandy's (2022) *Natura urbana* develops an interdisciplinary more-than-human (or as he calls it other-than-human) approach to urban ecology through a focus on zones of marginality, such as urban wastelands and cemeteries. These urban fringes are transitory landscapes, neither conventionally urban nor rural, containing intense juxtapositions. He brings together knowledges of urban nature produced by artists, writers, scientists, and even children that may be considered alternative or counterhegemonic. In the obvious presence of species extinction and ecological crisis, Gandy nonetheless offers a rather positive outlook and political perspective as he calls for a perspective that recognises urban natures as a pluriverse of brownfields and rainforests with interlocked political agendas of multispecies urbanism (Gandy, 2022: 241–58).

Addressing the concerns raised in Part IV, Hilary Angelo's (2021) *How green became good* explores green imaginaries that emerge at the intersection of policy, design, and politics. Through a study of Germany's Ruhr Valley, an urban-industrial region, she examines a particular case of urbanisation in the absence of a city. She theorises urban greening as a contemporary global phenomenon. Problematising the distinction between cultural and materialist perspectives, Angelo offers a framework for understanding the socio-ecological imaginaries produced by extended urbanisation.

It is perhaps not unimportant that in all these new publications, edgelands, fringes, far flung locations, in-between landscapes, and colonial interstices are the key focal points of the authors' attention. We note that such an emphasis on the state of the urban world at the margins is emblematic of the kinds of extensive urban political ecologies that, we have argued, need to be the subject of our concern as we leave behind 'central cities' or 'the city' as the only location where urbanisation takes place. We then also enter 'the in-between' as a political space (McFarlane, 2021: 116–21), a space of action from which to regroup as we mobilise (in) urban society against the devastations of climate change. Some of that, as several authors in this book have insisted, will have to involve a different politics, perhaps one of 'fragments' as McFarlane suggests:

> The connective devices between the city of fragments and wholes operate across the liberal city and the 'city in the wild.' The liberal city has a global resonance, even if it is understood in different ways across world-regions. It is the city of rights, state institutions and processes, planning and policy processing, distributions of land, infrastructure and services, and social contracts. It is difficult to imagine addressing fragmented cities without it. At the same time, the liberal city has been complicit in the histories and geographies of fragmentation we find in increasingly unequal cities today.
> (McFarlane, 2021: 223–4)

Yet, the liberal cities rights-based framework of politics is not sufficient as the (majority) 'city in the wild', a 'city of situated everyday negotiating, makeshift political bargaining, forms of protest that might shock and startle, or forms of artistic experimentation and provocation' commands its own attention as a political space as we mobilise the urban political ecologies of global urban society (McFarlane, 2021: 224). And, finally, if we take the city or the urban as a scale at which we need to act in the face of anthropogenic doom and climate emergency, we still need to reconcile the quest for decisive environmental policy and action with the constantly swerving demands of local democracy (Jon, 2021).

The book has made the case for reading UPE as part of a wider project of spatialising political ecologies of the urban in the sense of Lefebvre's urban society.[1] Urbanisation in its now newly concentrated and extended forms, it was argued, is entwined with the affairs of natural landscapes beyond the city. This urban society must be understood as a society of exploding, extended urbanisation. This has consequences on city–nature relationships that are extended as well, and not in a binary fashion. Belting nature against the city means doing the right thing but it does not avoid the hard question of what is inside and outside of the belt and how landscapes on both sides are connected. Mining landscapes are obvious examples to illustrate the conundrums we face on a sub/urban planet. What, finally, do we get ourselves into when we set out to repair the sprawl that everyone thinks kills our planet? This starts from understanding 'Global warming [as] capital's crowning achievement. Global warming is capitalogenic' (Moore, 2016).

Rather than pinning our current environmental predicament on all of humanity, there are reasons to single out the constant search in capitalism for cheap labour and nature as the main driver of the problems the planet faces today. Among the contested and emerging concepts that challenge and complete Moore's *longue durée*, universalist scheme, is the notion of the 'plantation economy' at the basis of racial capitalism (McKittrick, 2013). The related concept of the 'plantationocene' has received considerable debate (Davis et al., 2019). And, just as McKittrick explains that the plantation might have been referred to as a 'town', Simone (2019: 3) extends the urban

> not only in the sense that it covers more ground or becomes an increasingly hegemonic modality of spatial and social production, but that it also incorporates a wide range of logics, social and cultural processes, and vernaculars, thus exposing residents to a larger set factors at work in shaping their own daily experiences. Urbanisation is extensive in that it interrelates all aspects of life that previously could be bounded, separated in space and time.

The resultant urban political ecologies define the reach of classed, gendered, and racialised regimes in and beyond the city, but always on the terrain of the urban fabric.

A growing part of that spatialised capitalist society is characterised by the dominance, in some periods and regions even predominance, of the building and rebuilding of cities and suburbs for the survival of capitalism. Thinking more practically about sustainability strategies, Hillary Angelo and David Wachsmuth (in this book and elsewhere) have examined the ways in which nature and urbanism are currently related. They have thought specifically about the kinds of reformist urbanism (and suburbanism) that are currently presented as the solution to our *rendezvous* with climate change. This includes the 'pairings' of natural (green) and technological (grey) strategies (Wachsmuth and Angelo, 2018: 1039). Seeing the local state as more than physically local is crucial in this context as Andrew Kirby reminds us because 'the striations within society become visible within a city's neighborhoods, and – especially important in this context – it shows why sustainability goals are often subordinated to other concerns, both economic and political' (Kirby, 2019: 12). Despite obvious limitations to these strategies, it is important to recognise efforts towards 'greening the city' and 'greening the suburbs' as real attempts of changing material streams in the city. This begs the question what the consequences of these metabolic shifts (and rifts) may be for urban society and how they relate to issues of justice on a sub/urban planet ravaged by the climate emergency. Beyond the city, restored wetlands and retention ponds are a minimal measure for restitution of natural debts. But they are no match for the injustices of urban societal ownership, use, and abuse.

In addition, and central to any rethinking of the efficacy of practical measures to enhance sustainability in the rapidly urbanising Global South where most urban growth is expected in this century, is the admission that proposed policies, planning directives and technological innovation bear the stamp of

Western origin and are often inappropriate for application outside of Europe and North America (a point clearly made by several chapters in this book). This is made worse by relying almost entirely on concepts and theories that originate in the North (Nagendra et al., 2018) and not recognising established 'modes of Southern urban practice' (Bhan, 2019). Some proposed measures may not have the same urgency in the South, and may have to be evaluated carefully against existing Indigenous and situated practices.

This focus is echoed in work by Pacific northwest based writer-activists Hern, Johal and Sacco, in their timely book *Global warming and the sweetness of life: A tar sands tale* (2018). To them, the complexities of colonial and imperial ecologies revolve around the question of 'who gets to make what decisions for what land?' (Hern et al., 2018: 12). On this land, a spatialised political ecology for an urban society needs to confront the question if and how the 'material lust: the oil and gas, the minerals, the hydroelectric power, the timber, the animals' (Hern et al., 2018: 15) that drive urban life in the current period can be reconciled with what Indigenous scholar Glen Coulthard [2014] calls a 'grounded normativity' (cited in Hern et al., 2018: 14). By this, Coulthard means 'the modalities of Indigenous land-connected practices and longstanding experiential knowledge that inform and structure our ethical engagements with the world and our relationships with human and nonhuman others over time' (cited in Hern et al., 2018: 14). With this, we are moving from a Western-based critique of capitalism to a different kind of ecological analysis that includes a postcolonial critique at its core (Hern et al., 2018: 20). We are, in fact, now returning to the opening call for a making nature part of urban affairs in urban society. In that context, our view of society is profoundly revised. As Jason Moore (2016) reminds us: 'The conflation of human sociality with Society is a conceptual move indebted to a long history of gendered, racialized, and colonial violence.'

Having started from the assumption that we are living in a completely urbanised society, or a suburbanised society, this book ends on this note of programmatic inspiration. If our extended urban or suburban ways of life have become planetary, a spatialised political ecology for the affairs of an urban society under the threat of the capitalogenic climate change must start from where we are: the global urban periphery. Accordingly, our urban affairs need to be adjusted to work on multiple scales, equally global and situated, and always in the presence of the awareness that there is no dividing line between nature and the city (Angelo and Goh, 2020; Kaika, 2005). As we transcend the boundary of urban society and nature, we are also in a better position to chart practical pathways of reconciliation of urban environment and economy (Osgood et al., 2017). In this sense, the book moves the debate on UPE modestly more into the direction of making it relevant for urban and suburban society and for a planet of extended urbanisation.

Politically, we find ourselves 'between catastrophe and revolution' as a collection of essays in honour of our opening author, the late Mike Davis, seems to suggest. However, as Davis suggests, we have no time to give in to catastrophism and must instead fight for 'impossible solutions to the increasingly entangled crisis of urban poverty and climate change' (cited in Monk, 2021: 9). We are held to act, as Ulrich Brand and Markus Wissen note, to replace the 'imperial mode of living' (for which climate change is a modus operandi, not simply a matter of fact) with a 'solidary mode of living – globally and for the long term' (Brand and Wissen, 2021: 202). This kind of thinking raises questions around what is necessary and what is possible in terms of radical reformism faced by capitalogenic climate change. The 'imperial mode of living' which in the Global North is 'imperial inasmuch as it is based on a principally unlimited appropriation to resources, space, territories, labor capacity and sinks elsewhere – secured politically, legally and/or by means of violence' (Brand and Wissen, 2018: 13). Taking their cues from the Latin American discourse on the good life or *buen vivir* (Acosta and Brand, 2018), among others, Brand and Wissen shift the attention from a productivist perspective to a shift in 'the mode of living' as a necessary transition from capitalism.

There are echoes here in the calls – in different camps on the green-left – for all manner of degrowth initiatives, with which we have no space to engage thoroughly here. In this vein, for example, and starting from the actual place where most people live, Australians Samuel Alexander and Brendan Gleeson, make the case for 'degrowth in the suburbs' (2019). Developing a 'radical urban imaginary', they acknowledge the complex, multivalent and situated relationships of urban and ecological processes, noting that 'the primary goal is not to rebuild our cities but instead learn how to reinhabit a built environment that already exists'. Alexander and Gleeson importantly add: 'Unlike the uprisings of the nineteenth century, which tore up slums and tenements of inner cities, this great insurrection must extend to, and in some places, begin from, the suburbs' (2019: 16).

The call for degrowth has in turn invited an emphatic 'critique of commodification' and the propagation of a 'use-value society' (Hermann, 2021). In the 'afterword in times of corona,' of their new book, Brand and Wissen ask:

> What would a left-wing policy of a solidary mode of living look like during Corona virus times, but also as a policy against a possibly solidifying 'Corona capitalism,' in which the tendencies towards inequality, destruction of nature and authoritarianism are continued?
>
> (2021: 217)

They conclude that 'A central task of the left will be the prevention of a renewed policy of austerity' (2021: 219), which falls in line with the insights of an international group of urban scholar-activists who have recently reminded us that 'austerity is a political or ideological choice, not a necessity' but have equally warned that 'moves away from austerity can be partial, selective or illusory, as many leaders of local authorities and public services facing retrenchment will attest' even as it seemed, during COVID-19 that the renewed willingness of governments to spend, could be a blueprint for more decisive action in the fact of burning and flooding urban landscapes around the world (Davies et al., 2022: 156).

If there is a key thing to highlight in the theoretical turn we propose in this book, it is this: The city and its political ecology does not exist in an autonomous and distinct space. Any city-ist approach to the challenges a planetary urban society faces is doomed in a world of extended urbanisation where near-far connectivity in space, and layering across eras of human metabolisms in time determine unprecedented complexities of life.

This conundrum may be most pronounced in attempts to outrun the historical geography of urbanisation by founding new cities to escape the fires, the floods, and the diseases associated with existing urban life. As the Indonesian government pursues its plans to leave behind its sinking capital Jakarta, it seeks to build a new city, on a different island of the archipelago, in an (industrial) forest. The city will be named Nusantara. Sibarani Sofian, a lead architect on the project is quoted as saying:

> The biggest challenge for us is how to put a manufactured city in a natural setting in the most respectful way. Because when we build cities, design cities, we already start to move away so much from the wisdom of the land, the wisdom of nature. You need to really represent how humans relate to nature in this renewed relationship. The city right now we're living in – Jakarta – doesn't have that kind of balance.
>
> (quoted in Irwandi, 2022)

While respectfully acknowledging such good intentions, the authors in this book warn that the kind of balance Jakarta lost may be elusive to Nusantara, if its builders think of it as a place outside of the urban world in which it exists. As the urbanised planets heats, its challenges will need to be met at the scale of its extended urban political ecologies.

Note

1 This section borrows from Keil (2020).

References

Acosta, A. and U. Brand. 2018. *Radikale Alternativen: Warum man den Kapitalismus nur mit vereinten Kräften überwinden kann*. Munich: Oekom Verlag.

Alexander, S. and B. Gleeson. 2019. *Degrowth in the suburbs: a radical urban imaginary*. Singapore: Palgrave Macmillan.

Angelo, H. 2021. *How green became good: Urbanized nature and the making of cities and citizens*. Chicago: University of Chicago Press.

Angelo, H. and K. Goh. 2020. Out in space: Difference and abstraction in planetary urbanization. *International Journal of Urban and Regional Research* 45(4): 732–44. DOI:10.1111/1468-2427.12911.

Angelo, H. and D. Wachsmuth. 2020. Why does everyone think cities can save the planet? *Urban Studies* 57(11): 2201–21. DOI: 10.1177/0042098020919081.

Arboleda, M. 2020. *Planetary mine: Territories of extraction under late capitalism*. London: Verso.

Bhan, G. 2019. Notes on a Southern urban practice. *Environment & Urbanization*. DOI: 10.1177/0956247818815792.

Brand, U. and M. Wissen. 2018. *The limits to capitalist nature: Theorizing and overcoming the imperial mode of living*. London: Rowman and Littlefield.

Brand, U. and M. Wissen. 2021. *The imperial mode of living: Everyday life and the ecological crisis of capitalism*. London: Verso.

Coulthard, G. 2014. *Red skin, white masks: Rejecting the colonial politics of recognition*. Minneapolis: University of Minnesota Press.

Davies, J. et al. 2022. *New developments in urban governance: Rethinking collaboration in the age of austerity*. Bristol: Bristol University Press.

Davis, J., A.A. Moulton, L. Van Sant, and B. Williams. 2019. Anthropocene, Capitalocene, … Plantationocene? A manifesto for ecological justice in an age of global crises. *Geography Compass*. 13: 1–15.

Ernstson, H. and E. Swyngedeouw (eds.). 2018. *Urban political ecology in the Anthropo-obscene: Interruptions and possibilities*. London: Routledge.

Gandy, M. 2022. *Natura urbana*. Cambridge, MA and London: MIT Press.

Goh, K. 2021. *Form and flow: The spatial politics of urban resilience and climate change*. Cambridge, MA and London: MIT Press.

Hermann, C. 2021. *The critique of commodification: Contours of a post-capitalist society*. New York: Oxford University Press.

Hern, M., A. Johal, and J. Sacco. 2018. *Global warming and the sweetness of life: A tar sands tale*. Cambridge, MA: MIT Press.

Heynen, N., M. Kaika, and E. Swyngedouw (eds.). 2006. *In the nature of cities: Urban political ecology and the politics of urban metabolism*. New York: Routledge.

Irwandi, J. (2022) How to move a capital city. *The Globe and Mail*, March 27. www.theglobeandmail.com/world/article-how-to-move-a-capital-city-an-exclusive-look-at-indonesias-plan-to/, accessed 12 August 2022.

Jon, I. 2021. *Cities in the Anthropocene: New ecology and urban politics*. London: Pluto Press.

Keil, R. 2020. The spatialized political ecology of the city: Situated peripheries and the capitalocenic limits of urban affairs. *Journal of Urban Affairs*. DOI: 10.1080/07352166.2020.1785305.

Lawhon, M. 2020. *Making urban theory: Learning and unlearning through southern cities*. London: Routledge.

McFarlane, C. 2021. *Fragments of the city: Making and remaking urban worlds*. Oakland, CA: University of California Press.

McKittrick, K. 2013. Plantation futures. *Small Axe* 42. DOI: 10.1215/07990537-2378892.

Monk, D.B. 2021. Introduction: A dialectic of catastrophe and revolution. In D.B. Monk and M. Sorkin (eds.), *Between catastrophe and revolution: Essays in honor of Mike Davis*. New York and London: O/R Books.

Moore, J.W. (2016) Name the system! Anthropocenes & the Capitalocene alternative, 9 October. https://jasonwmoore.wordpress.com/tag/capitalocene/, accessed 12 August 2022.

Nagendra, H., X. Bai, E.S. Brondizio, and S. Lwasa. 2018. The urban south and the predicament of global sustainability. *Nature Sustainability* 1: 341–49.

Osgood, J.L., S.M. Opp, and M. DeMasters. 2017. Exploring the intersection of local economic development and environmental policy. *Journal of Urban Affairs* 39(2): 260–76. DOI: 10.1111/juaf.12316.

Simone, A. 2019. Maximum exposure: Making sense in the background of extensive urbanization. *Environment and Planning D: Society and Space* 37(6): 990–1006. https://doi.org/10.1177/0263775819856351

Index

Note: Page numbers in *italics* refer to illustrations. Page references with n. refer to the number of a note on that page.

actor/agent, earth as 18, 62, 247–53
   see also more-than-human urban political ecology
Africa
   colonial history 160, 162–7, 192, 198
   disease spread 209–10, 212–18
   extractivism 94, 163, 213
   informal settlements 14, 159–67, 214–15
   labour and modernist values 15, 195–200
   Nairobi 14, 159–67
   racialisation 163–5
   sanitation 15, 190–4, 199–200
   Uganda 15, 190–4, 199–200
   see also South Africa
agrarian urbanism 8, 171, 173, 176–8, 182, 183n.7
agriculture and food
   agri-business 120–1, *120–1*, 305–6
   commodities 99, *117*, 118, *120*
   environmental harm 91–3, 120–2
   food sovereignty 21, 303–10
   global trade 42, 115–18, *116*, *117*, *121*
   hinterlands of hinterlands 116–22, *119*
   solidarity modes 23–4, 85n.8, 85n.9, 85n.10
   waste in circular economies 342–3
Ali, S. Harris ix, 17, 61, 207–21
alternatives *see* capitalism, alternatives; climate crisis, alternatives; modernity, alternatives; utopias
Angelo, Hillary ix, 6, 21, 284–301, 350, 352
Anthropocene
   extended urbanisation 24, 45–7
   territorialist ecology 245–7, 250, 254
   see also Capitalocene; climate crisis; earth; environmental harm
Arboleda, Martín ix, 11, 41, 91–104, 349
Argentina 83n.6, 99, 271
Asia *see* China; India, Gurugram (Gurgaon), water; Japan; Korea, South; Singapore, offshore islands

Atlanta, Georgia 14, 133–7, 140
Australia xvii–xviii, xxv, xxvi, xxxi, 2

Black people *see* racialised peoples; United States, Black people
Bloch, Ernst 67–70, 72, 74–5, 77, 83n.2
Brazil 11, 73, 83n.6, 84n.7, 85n.9, 85n.10
Brenner, Neil ix–x, 11, 105–26, 321
buen vivir (good life) 76–7, 81–2, 83n.5, 85n.9, 354

California xvi–xxvi, 2, 98, 296
Canada 13, 275–7, 296
capitalism
   about 4, 23, 38–9, 43–5, 351–2
   climate crisis as capitalogenic 23–4, 52n.4, 245–7, 250, 351–4
   critiques of 38–41
   expanded reproduction 97–100
   global scale 23–4, 41–2, 46, 64, 349
   imaginaries 39, 44–5, 47–51, 52n.3
   'imperial mode of living' 23–4, 354
   Marx as precursor 37, 39–41
   as metabolic engine 42–3, 321
   neo-colonisation 77–80
   planetary capitalist urbanisation 41–2, 46, 64
   political ecology 47–51
   racial capitalism 3, 4, 130, 133, 137–9, 218, 352
   terminology 38, 43–4, 257n.3
   UPE approaches 3–4, 23–4, 38–42, 46, 64
   waste production 335–6, 343–4
   see also capitalism, alternatives; commodities; extractivism; neoliberalism
capitalism, alternatives
   about 23–4, 67–9, 354–5
   buen vivir (good life) 76–7, 81–2, 83n.5, 85n.9, 354
   cooperatives 135, 196

Index

decolonial turn 74–7, 349
degrowth initiatives 23–4, 40, 189, 354
food sovereignty 21, 303–10
interculturality 69–70, 76–7, 83n.5
interdependency 245, 254–5
progressive transformations 38–9, 47–51
solidarity modes 23–4, 85n.8, 85n.9, 85n.10
utopias 67
see also climate crisis, alternatives; utopias
Capitalocene
  about 45–7, 248, 250, 257n.3
  earth as actor/agent 18, 62, 247–53
  hinterlands 113–15, 118, 120–2
  terminology 248, 250, 257n.3
  see also Anthropocene; capitalism
carbon emissions *see* environmental harm
caste and ethnicity
  intersectionalities 145–6, 148, 150–2, 155
  land politics (India) 171–3, 176–7, 183n.3
  water politics (Nepal) 148–52, 155
  see also racialised peoples
centre/periphery relations
  Global South 170–1, 349
  populism tensions 267–8, 274–9
  UPE approaches 15–16, 22, 170–1, 302–3
China 16, 41, 93–5, 99, 118, 209–10
circular economies
  about 21, 333–6, 343–4
  abjection/valorisation of waste 21, 194, 334–8, 340–4
  Amsterdam 21, 334, 338, 339–43, 348
  critiques of 21, 334, 341, 343–4
  government roles 336–7
  incineration 334, 336–7, 340–2, 344
  local reuse and recycling 334, 336, 337, 341–4
  nature-society binary 189–90
  recovery for markets 334, 336, 337, 338, 342–4
  UPE approaches 18, 21, 334–6, 343–4
  see also economies
cities
  about 64, 105–8, 223–6, 355
  carbon neutral cities 144, 148, 152–5
  city-centric research 6, 8–9, 11–12, 18, 22, 46–7, 105–6, 224–6, 236–7, 287–8
  city/hinterland relations 107–8, 110–16, *112*, 122n.2
  concentrated urbanisation 106
  ecology, as term 57–61
  global-urban networks 144, 225–6, *231*, *235*, 236–7
  global visualisations 108, *109*
  socio-natural vs. bounded 223–6
  urban vs. urbanisation, as terms 105–8
  see also extended urbanisation; global-urban networks; socio-natural processes; urban-natural; urban political ecology (UPE)
climate crisis
  about 1–4, 22–4, 224
  as capitalogenic 23–4, 52n.4, 245–7, 250, 351–4
  cultural politics 48–9, 51
  depoliticisation 19, 49
  disease spread 217–18, 248–51
  dystopias 1–3, 23, 48–9, 52n.3, 81
  earth as actor/agent 18, 62, 247–53
  realities of everyday life 48–51, 224
  regional projections (US) xviii–xix, xxv–xxvi
  as risk multiplier 249
  turning up the heat as a metaphor 23, 348
  see also earth; environmental harm; waste; water
climate crisis, alternatives
  about 18, 22–4, 46–7, 50–1, 64, 105, 156n.1, 224–6
  adaptation, as term 156n.1
  adaptation scholarship 224
  environmental justice 143–6, 152–5
  everyday life 146–7, 154–5
  feminist approaches 14, 144–8, 154–5
  intersectionality 145–6, 152, 155
  knowledge politics 14, 144, 146–8, 152–5
  marginalised people 152–3
  modest vs. modernity 189, 199–200
  politics and policy 18–21, 224
  power relations 145–8
  social inclusion/exclusion 14, 144, 148, 154–5
  subjectivities 145–6, 148
  UPE approaches 5–6, 18, 22–4, 47, 143–4, 223–6, 349–50, 355
  see also capitalism, alternatives; utopias
colonialism
  cities as centres 113–14, 123n.4
  entrepreneur vs. passive peasant 308, 309
  neo-colonialisation 77–80, 113–14
  petro-racial capitalism 137–9
  UPE approaches 131
  see also decolonisation; extractivism; Indigenous peoples; peasants
commodities
  about 91–6, 115–22
  agriculture and food 99, *117*, 118, *120*
  environmental harm 91–4, 116, 120–2
  extractivism 91–100, 349
  global trade 115–18, *116*, *117*, *119*
  hinterland production 110–11, *114*, 114–18, 120–2
  industrial infrastructures 118, *119*
  mining industries 93–9, 100n.2, 349
  waste in circular economies 334–6, 343–4

see also capitalism; extractivism; fossil fuel industry; hinterlands and urbanisation
Connolly, Creighton x, 21, 41, 319–32
COVID-19 see disease spread

Davis, Mike x, xvi–xxix, 11, 161, 354
decolonisation
    about 13, 69–70, 75–80
    decolonial turn 13–14, 349
    of everyday life 74–80
    interculturality 69–70, 76–7, 83n.5
    of knowledge 13–14, 77–80
    of rights 306–7
    of society-nature relations 69–70, 74–5, 77–80
    UPE approaches 13–14, 246, 349
    see also Indigenous peoples; peasants; postcolonialism
democratic processes
    dissent and consensus 312–13
    equality and disidentification 311–13
    grassroots democracy 83n.6, 132–5, 140, 144
    see also environmental justice; politics and policy
disease spread
    about 17, 61, 207–18, 248–51
    climate crisis links 248–51
    COVID-19 17, 23, 61, 64, 209–12, 248–9
    Ebola virus disease 210–18
    extractivism 61, 213, 216–18
    metabolic flows 207, 210–12, 216
    pandemics 248–9
    racialisation and myths of 163–4
    as risk multiplier 249
    SARS (2003) 17, 61, 211
    UPE approaches 17, 61, 207–14, 216–18
    urban political pathologies 209–12
    zoonotic spillover 17, 64, 207, 216–17
dystopias 1–3, 23, 48–9, 76, 81
    see also utopias

earth
    atmosphere 16–17
    earth as actor/agent 18, 62, 247–53
    Earth System 46–7, 253–4
    see also climate crisis; environmental harm; more-than-human urban political ecology; territorialist political ecology (TPE)
Ebola see disease spread
ecological urbanism
    about 56–8, 62–4
    landscape ecology 62–3
    nature as design model 56–7
    systems-based concepts 57, 60–3
    terminology 57–61

    UPE approaches 57, 61–4
ecology, as term 57–61
    see also political ecology; urban political ecology (UPE)
economies
    consumerism 43, 97, 271, 333–6, 342–4
    economic geography 108, *109*, 111–14, *112*, *114*
    extractive economies 92–3, 96–100
    financial system 96–100
    global-urban networks 229–32, *231*, *235*
    as political 40, 355
    solidarity modes 23–4, 85n.8, 85n.9, 85n.10
    see also capitalism; circular economies; commodities; extractivism; hinterlands and urbanisation; neoliberalism
environmental harm
    biodiversity loss 91
    carbon emissions 24n.2, 43, 91–3, 100
    concrete production 16, 41
    extended urbanisation 22–4, 99, 347
    extractivism 91–4, 99–100, 216–18
    in hinterlands 120–2
    invasive species xvi–xxi, xxiv–xxvi, 15–16, 60
    megafires xvi–xxv
    plastics 16, 24n.2, 328, 342
    realities of harm 48–51, 224
    turning up the heat as a metaphor 23, 348
    see also climate crisis; disease spread; extractivism; more-than-human urban political ecology
environmental justice
    informal settlements 159–60
    infrastructure 187, 286
    reparations 133–4, 137–40
    social inclusion/exclusion 133, 144–6
    UPE approaches 61, 133, 138
    see also marginalised peoples; social inclusion/exclusion; water
ethnicity see caste and ethnicity
everyday life
    decolonisation of 74–80
    feminist approaches 146–7, 154–5
    metabolic flows 42
    realities of harm 48–51, 224
    social movements 80–2, 83n.6, 85n.9, 131–5, 140, 305
    territorialist political ecology 251, 255
    UPE approaches 5, 8–9, 12, 22, 42
    utopias grounded in 57–8, 70–6, 79–82, 132
extended urbanisation
    about 6–11, 22–4, 107, 347, 351–2
    agrarian urbanism 171, 173, 176–8, 182, 183n.7

concrete production and use 16, 41
disease spread 207–8, 217–18
diversity in 69
environmental harm 22–4, 99, 347
vs. global/planetary urbanisation 9
hinterlands 107, 113
speculative urbanism 170, 172–3, 175, 177, 180
terminology 7, 9–10, 107–8
UPE approaches 7–11, 16, 69, 99, 107, 349
see also disease spread; extractivism; hinterlands and urbanisation; urban political ecology (UPE)
extractivism
about 11, 41–2, 91–100, 349
capitalist urbanisation 41–2, 99, 349
commodity circuits 92–6, 99–100, 118–19, *119*
disease spread 61, 213, 216–18
environmental harm 91–4, 99–100, 216–18
expanded reproduction 97–100, 349
financial circuits 92–3, 96–100
'hinterlandisation' of the world 113–15, 118, *119*
infrastructure for 95, 118, 216
metabolic flows 92–3, 100, 216
mining industry 93–9, 100n.2, 349
populism and 265, 267–8
productive circuits 92–4, 99–100
terminology 123n.5
transnational circuits 92–3, 99–100, 115–18, *116*
UPE approaches 11, 91–3, 99–100, 349
see also capitalism; commodities; fossil fuel industry

farms and farmers *see* agriculture and food; peasants
feminism
about 14, 144–8, 154–5, 246
knowledge politics 144–8, 153–5
power relations 144–8, 153
social inclusion/exclusion 143–4
subjectivities 145–6
UPE approaches 3, 9–10, 14, 143–4, 154–5, 246, 349
water politics (Nepal) 144, 148–52, 155, 156n.2
ways of knowing 14, 144, 152–3
see also gender/sex; intersectionality
financial system *see* economies
fires, exurban xvi–xxvi, 2
food *see* agriculture and food
fossil fuel industry
climate scepticism 99
financial system 96–9

fossil capitalism 9, 137–9
global trade 41–2, *116*, 116–18
green/greywashing 293–6
Singapore, offshore islands 21, 320, 324–6, 329
UPE approaches 353
see also extractivism
France 85n.8, 276, 277

Gandy, Matthew x, 11, 15, 17, 56–66, 122n.2, 348, 350
gender/sex
LGBTQ 4, 9, 133, 257n.2
patriarchy 79, 146, 312
water politics 148–52, 155
see also feminism; intersectionality
geographies
economic geography 108, *109*, 111–14, *112*, *114*
populism in contexts 265–8, 271–2, 274–9
relational geographies 223, 225, 349–50
territory, terminology 250–2
waterbody mapping 173–6, *175*, 180, 183n.10
water/land blurred boundaries 170, 178–81, 183n.10
see also hinterlands and urbanisation
Germany xxiv–xxv, 60, 278, 296, 350
Gilmore, Ruth Wilson 132–3, 138, 139
Global North
'imperial mode of living' 23–4, 354
North-centric UPE approaches 12
Global South
alternatives to capitalism 76–7
centre/periphery relations 170–1, 349
extractivism 92–3, 349
infrastructure 187, 191, 199–200
solidarity modes 23–4, 85n.8, 85n.9, 85n.10
UPE approaches 3, 12–15, 20, 244, 246, 349
water use 191
global/planetary urbanisation
about 3, 9, 45–7, 105–7
disease spread 208, 217–18
hinterlands 107
planetary urbanisation 9
terminology 9–10, 105–8
visualisation 108, *109*
see also capitalism; disease spread; extended urbanisation; extractivism; hinterlands and urbanisation
global-urban networks
about 17, 64, 222–6, 231, 235, 236–7
C40 Cities 225, 228, *231*, 297
carbon neutral cities 144, 148, 152–5
Connecting Delta Cities 223, 228, *231*, 235
economics 229–32, *231*, 235

formations and relations 225–6, 234–6, *235*
knowledge politics 147–8, 228, 230–1, *231*, 236–7
Netherlands 17, 226–8, *231*, 233–7, *235*, 237n.1, 237n.2, 350
UPE approaches 17, 223–6, 236–7
Goh, Kian x, 17, 222–43, 349–50
Gort, Joris x, 20, 49, 265–83
governance
    about 18–19
    Lefebvre's state 76
    multilevel environmental governance 225–6
    sanitation 192–3
    self-governance by peasants 304–5
    smart technology 286
    UPE approaches 18–19, 209–12
    urban political pathologies 209–12
    wildland gentrification xxi–xxiv, 2
    see also planning; political ecology; politics and policy
Gramsci, Antonio 75, 77, 123n.6, 270–1, 278, 285
green and grey urban nature
    about 21, 284–5, 295–8, 352
    circular economies 342–3
    critiques of 287–8, 293
    density 285–6, 288, 292
    green/greywashing 294–6
    green (natural) strategies 284–5, 288–94, 296–7, 326, 350, 352
    grey (technological) strategies 284–5, 288–94
    Gurgaon, India 180–3
    illusions as realistic and transparent 21, 285, 291, 293–5
    interconnections of green/grey 289–94, 297
    Lefebvre's ideologies of social space 21, 285, 288–91, 296–7
    Masdar City, UAE 293–6
    smart cities 18, 47, 284–6, 288, 293–7
    sustainability and resilience 286–8, 291–8
    terminology 284–5, 288
    UPE approaches 285, 297–8, 350, 352
greenhouse gases *see* environmental harm
Guinea 17, 210, 212–18
Gurgaon *see* India, Gurugram (Gurgaon), water
Gururani, Shubhra x–xi, 7–8, 13, 14–15, 169–85

Harvey, David 41, 98, 99, 245, 274, 321
health *see* disease spread
Heynen, Nik xi, 4–5, 14, 61, 122n.2, 129–42, 257n.2, 348
hinterlands and urbanisation
    about 11, 105–10, 120–2
    city/hinterland relations 107–8, 110–16, *112*, 120–2, 122n.2

commodity production 110–11, *114*, 114–18, 120–2
dispossession 110, 113, 115–16
economic geography 108, *109*, 111–14, *112*, *114*
environmental harm 116, 120–2
extended urbanisation 107, 113
global supply chains 115–18, *116*, *119*
hinterlandisation 113–18, *119*, 121–2
hinterlands, as term 113–15
metabolic flows 110–11, 113–15, 120–2, 256
non-city inputs 110–11, 118, *119*
UPE approaches 11, 105–8, 110–11, 113–14, 122n.2, 123n.3, 123n.6
urban and urbanisation, as terms 9–10, 105–8
von Thünen's model 108, 111, *112*, 116
wildland gentrification xxi–xxiv, 2
see also extractivism
housing
    affordable housing xxii–xxiii, 134–6
    fire ecologies xx–xxvi
    modernist ideal family 191, 192
    UPE approaches 18–19, 137
    wildland gentrification xxi–xxiv, 2
    see also informal settlements
human ecology, as term 57–61
human rights
    civil rights movement (US) 134–5
    Indigenous rights 150, 305
    peasant rights 305–7, 309–13

identity
    colonisation of everyday life 79
    disidentification 303–8, 310–13
    neoliberal subject 44–5
    subjectivity vs. identity 145
    see also intersectionality
India, Gurugram (Gurgaon), water
    about 14–15, 169–71, 176–83
    agrarian urbanism 171, 173, 176–8, 182, 183n.7
    blurred water/land boundaries 170, 178–81, 183n.10
    caste politics 171–3, 176–7, 179–80, 183n.3
    ecological imaginaries 172–3, 180–2, 184n.23
    environmental harm 169–71, *179*, 180–1
    everyday life 169–71, 173–4, 178, 182
    Ghata Lake and Ghata Jheel 169, 171–4, 178–82, *179*
    land politics and urbanisation 169–73, 176–83
    National Capital Region 176–8, 183n.11
    speculative urbanism 170, 172–3, 175, 177, 180

UPE approaches 173, 182–3
waterbodies 14–15, 169–70, 173–6, *175,
179*, 180–3
Indigenous peoples
dispossession (Singapore) 21, 321, 323, 325,
326–7, 329
environmental justice 138, 153
extended urbanisation 13, 85n.9
rights 150, 305
social movements (Brazil) 85n.9
UPE approaches 10, 13–14, 138, 353
ways of knowing 13–14, 153, 353
see also decolonisation; peasants
Indonesia, Jakarta
capital masterplan 222–3, 229–30, 232, 234
global-urban networks 17, 222–4, 228–37,
231, 235, 237n.1, 350
land reclamation 222, 226–7
relocation of city 355
water infrastructure 222–3, 230, 232, 234
informal settlements
depeasantisation 115–16
Ebola virus disease 210–18
'good' and 'bad' human natures 160–7
Mathare, Nairobi 14, 159–67
metabolic flows 160–2
infrastructure
about 12, 186–8
adaptation vs. control of nature 186, 190–1,
193–5, 199–200
categories of users 190–1, 194–5
construction materials 16, 41, *116*, 116–18
environmental harm 16, 24n.2
ethical issues 187–8, 199
extractivist circuits 95–7, 118
global statistics 41
hinterlands 115–16
labour 188, 199–200
modern ideals 15, 186–93, 199–200
nature-society binary 189–90
UPE approaches 12, 15–16, 18, 187–92,
199–200, 200n.1
see also global-urban networks; housing;
waste; water
intersectionality
about 14, 144–6
feminist approaches 14, 144–8, 154–5
multiple subjectivities 145–6
power relations 145–6, 153
social inclusion/exclusion 144, 148
UPE approaches 3, 9–10, 131, 144–6
water politics (Nepal) 144, 148–52,
155, 156n.2
see also caste and ethnicity; gender/sex;
racialised peoples

invasive species xvi–xxi, xxiv–xxvi, 15–16, 60

Jakarta *see* Indonesia, Jakarta
Japan 93, 95, 232

Kaika, Maria xi, 1–34, 61, 72–3, 245–6, 268, 303,
314n.2, 322, 347–57
Kampala, Uganda 15, 190–4, 199–200
Katsikis, Nikos xi, 11, 105–26
Keil, Roger xi, 1–34, 61, 207–21, 246, 247,
257n.5, 347–57
Kenya, Nairobi, Mathare 14, 159–67
Kimari, Wangui xi, 14, 159–68
Kipfer, Stefan 13, 22, 265, 271, 272, 275–7
knowledge
about 13–14, 147–8, 154–5
categories 15–16, 190–1, 194–5, 199–200, 349
decolonisation of 13–14, 77–80
ecology, as term 57–61
feminist approaches 144–8, 153–5
knowledge politics 13–14, 144–8, 152–3, 155
marginalised peoples 152–3
science and modernity 190–1
situated knowledges in UPE 3, 5, 12–15, 20,
22–3, 246
UPE approaches 13–18, 153, 190–1, 269
ways of knowing 14, 144, 147–8
see also geographies; global-urban networks;
more-than-human urban political ecology
Korea, South 93, 95, 232, 286

labour
modernist values 15, 195–200
waste industries 15, 190–2, 195–200, 337
see also peasants
Lacan, Jacques 52n.3
land reclamation 222, 226–7, 320, 322–6, 328
landscape ecology 15–16, 62–3, 322
Latin America
Argentina 83n.6, 99, 271
Brazil 11, 73, 83n.6, 84n.7, 85n.9, 85n.10
buen vivir (good life) 76–7, 81–2, 83n.5,
85n.9, 354
decolonial turn 69
depeasantisation 94
extractivism 93–4, 97, 99, 349
social movements 81–2, 83n.6
Latour, Bruno 181, 247–50, 252–4
Lawhon, Mary xi, 12, 15, 186–204, 347, 349
Lefebvre, Henri
differential spaces 80, 82
ideologies of social space 288–91
nature as real vs. imaginary 285, 290–1, 296–7
planetary capitalist urbanisation 41, 218
planetary crisis 80–3

right to nature 71–2, 82
right to the city 79–80, 82, 132–3
triad dialectics 70–2, 79–80, 82, 86n.11, 246
urban-natural 79–83, 85n.8, 208–9, 351
utopias 67–72, 75–7, 79–83, 85n.8
LGBTQ 4, 9, 133, 257n.2
Liberia 210, 212–18
Limonad, Ester xii, 11, 67–90, 83n.1, 83n.2
Loftus, Alex xii, 9, 20, 49, 265–83
Luke, Nikki xii, 14, 129–42

Makina, Anesu xii, 12, 15, 186–204
Mandler, Tait xii, 1–34, 246, 347–57
marginalised peoples
   exposure to waste disposal 334
   intersectionality 145–6, 155
   sustainability planning 287
   UPE approaches 8–10, 350
   see also social inclusion/exclusion
Marx, Karl, and Marxism
   expanded reproduction 97–100
   industrial capital circuits 92, 95, 96, 97–8
   metabolic rift 42
   racialised difference 137–8
   UPE approaches 37, 39–40, 92, 245
metabolic processes
   about 4, 42–3, 110–11, 256, 322
   capitalism as engine 42–3, 244, 321
   disease spread 207, 210–11, 216
   ecology, as term 60–1
   extractivism 41, 92–3, 100, 349
   flow/fixity dialectics 42–3, 110–11, 244
   hinterland dialectics 110–11
   historical background 60–2
   informal settlements 160–2, 214–15
   non-city inputs 110–11, *119*
   planetary capitalist urbanisation 41–3
   socio-natural flows 244, 256–7, 322
   vs. systems-based concepts 57, 60–3
   territorialist approaches 123n.6, 244–8, 256–7
   urbanisation 110–11
   waste flows 194, 335–6
   see also urban political ecology (UPE)
mining industries see extractivism; fossil fuel industry
modernity
   capitalist modernity 78, 189
   categories 190–1, 194–5, 199–200
   colonial modernity 78–80, 189, 308, 309
   infrastructure ideals 186–91, 199–200
   nature as commodity 73
   nature-society binary 189–90
   progress 190, 195, 211, 347
   terminology 189

modernity, alternatives
   adaptation to nature 190–1, 193–5, 199–200
   anti-modern values 190–2
   decolonisation 75
   labour values 190–2, 195–200
   'modest' imaginary 189, 199–200
   new in-between forms 22, 350–1
   see also capitalism, alternatives; utopias
Monte-Mór, Roberto Luís xii, 11, 67–90
Moore, Jason 46, 123n.5, 250, 321, 352–3
more-than-human urban political ecology
   about 15–18, 23, 37–8, 40
   agency of 40
   atmosphere 16–17
   capitalist entanglements 40, 46–7
   categories 15–16
   contract with the earth 248, 251–3
   earth as actor/agent 18, 62, 247–53
   ecological conflicts 253–4
   ecology, as term 57–61
   metabolic flows 42–3, 256
   subjectivities 145–6
   territorialist political ecology 246, 247–53
   UPE approaches 15–18, 23, 37–8, 40, 246, 350
   zoonotic spillover 17, 64, 207, 216–17
   see also metabolic processes; socio-natural processes; territorialist political ecology (TPE)
Muzaini, Hamzah xiii, 11, 21, 41, 190, 319–32

Nairobi, Mathare 14, 159–67
Nakyagaba, Gloria Nsangi xiii, 12, 15, 186–204
natural resource extraction see extractivism; fossil fuel industry
nature
   concepts 61–2, 72–4
   ecology, as term 16, 57–61
   UPE approaches 40–1, 61–2
   see also more-than-human urban political ecology; socio-natural processes
neoliberalism
   governance 18–19, 43–4, 355
   moral conservatism 273
   nationalism and 268–9
   populism and 266–70, 273
   progressive neoliberalism 45, 273–4
   realities vs. imaginaries 44–5, 52n.3
   UPE approaches 18–19, 43–5, 267–9
   see also capitalism
Nepal 144, 148–52, 155, 156n.2
Netherlands
   Amsterdam 21, 334, 338, 339–43, 348
   circular economy 21, 336, 337–44
   Deltares institute 223, 228, 230, *231*, 232, 235, 237

global-urban networks 17, 226–37, *231*, *235*, 237n.1, 237n.2, 238n.8, 350
post-hurricane networks 17, 222–3, 228–34, *231*, 237n.2, 238n.9
Rotterdam 17, 226–8, *231*, 232–8, *235*, 350
UPE approaches 17, 223–4
water management 226–7, 230
networks *see* global-urban networks
New Orleans 14, 133, 137–40, 223, 228
New York City 17, 222–3, 226, 228–34, *231*, 237n.2, 238n.9, 350
Nightingale, Andrea J. xiii, 14, 143–58
non-human *see* more-than-human urban political ecology

oil and gas *see* fossil fuel industry

pandemics *see* disease spread
peasants
  about 21, 302–4, 312–13
  agrarian urbanism 171, 173, 176–8, 182, 183n.7
  alternative to capitalism 304–5, 308
  disidentification 305–13
  dispossession 21, 94, 99, 110, 115–16, 305, 310
  food sovereignty 21, 303–10
  power relations 307–9
  Rancière on identity 303–4, 306, 308, 311–13
  rights 305–7, 309–12
  Romanian peasants 21, 310
  self-governance 304–5
  sovereignty 303–4, 306–7, 310–13
  subjectification 303, 313
  Via Campesina 302–4, 308–10
Perrone, Camilla xiii–xiv, 17–18, 244–61
planetary urbanisation *see* global/planetary urbanisation
planning
  capital city masterplan 222–3
  density for sustainability 285–6, 288, 292
  design competitions 222–3, 229–30, 232, 233–4, 237n.2, 238n.9
  ecological urbanism 56–8, 62–4
  ecology, as term 60–1
  global-urban networks 222–4, 228–32, *231*, *235*
  grey and green urban nature 284–7, 296–7
  racial inequities 133
  sanitation 192–3
  sustainability planning 286–7, 296–7
  UPE approaches 18, 349–50
  urban ecology 56–7
  see also green and grey urban nature
political ecology
  ecology as always political 40–1

non-urban geographies 265–6, 350–1, 355
terminology 40–1, 61–2
see also extended urbanisation; hinterlands and urbanisation; populism; urban political ecology (UPE)
politics and policy
  about 2–5, 18–21, 40, 133
  carbon neutral cities 144, 148, 152–5
  democratic processes 83n.6, 132–5, 140, 311–13
  depoliticisation of climate issues 19
  ecology as always political 40–1
  knowledge politics 14, 144–8, 155, 267–9
  liberal city of rights 351
  new forms 18–20, 22–4, 350–1
  policy as 'new theory' 133
  political will vs. adaptation 188
  reparations 130–40
  terminology 20, 40–1
  UPE approaches 2–5, 18–21, 40–1, 56, 133
  urban political pathologies 209–12
  water politics (Nepal) 148–52
  see also governance; planning; populism
pollution *see* environmental harm
populism
  about 20, 265–6, 279n.1
  authoritarian populism 20, 265–9, 278–9, 279n.1
  climate crisis imaginaries 48–9, 52n.3
  content vs. form 270–1, 274
  environmental politics 267–70
  extractivism 265, 267–8
  geographical contexts 265–8, 271–2, 274–9
  material conditions 266–7, 271–5, 279
  neoliberalism and 266–70, 273, 277, 279
  progressive populisms 267, 271, 273–4
  racialised forms 268–9, 272–3, 275–6, 277–8
  suburbanisation 266, 274–7
  terminology 270, 279n.1
  Trump's populism 268–74
  UPE approaches 20, 265–9, 274–9
postcolonialism
  centre/periphery relations 170–1
  governance 165–7, 232–3, 268
  territorialist political ecology 246, 255
  UPE approaches 9–10, 246, 349, 353
  see also colonialism; decolonisation; Indigenous peoples
power relations
  alliances of cities 148
  feminist approaches 144–8, 154–5
  intersectionality 145–8, 155
  knowledge politics 144–8, 246
  Lefebvre's ideologies of social space 288–90
  Lefebvre's State 76

neo-colonisation 77–80
patriarchy 79, 146, 312
peasant resistance 307–9
subjectivities 145–6
UPE approaches 37–8, 61
water politics (Nepal) 148–52
see also subjectivities
progress narratives 190, 195, 211, 347
public health *see* disease spread

Quijano, Anibal 69–70, 75, 78–9

racialised peoples
colour-blind urban theory 140
disease spread myths 163–4
dispossession 133
environmental racism 13, 268–9
extractive industries 94
financial discrimination 138
'good' and 'bad' natures 163–4
grassroots movements 132
neo-colonisation 79, 191
populism and racism 268–9, 272–3, 274, 275–6, 277–8
racial capitalism 14, 130, 137–9, 218, 352
reparations for slavery 130–40
right to the city 132–3, 139–40
UPE approaches 14, 130–3, 139–40
utopian social relations 79–80
white supremacy 130–1, 133, 137, 268–9, 272–3, 277–8
see also caste and ethnicity; Indigenous peoples; United States, Black people
Rancière, Jacques 20, 303–4, 306, 308, 311–13
recycling and reuse *see* circular economies
relational geographies *see* geographies
research, UPE *see* urban political ecology (UPE), scholarship
resilience *see* sustainability and resilience
resource extraction *see* extractivism
rights *see* human rights
Rio de Janeiro 83n.6, 85n.10
Romanian peasants 21, 310
rural and urban-natural, terminology 70–1
rural labourers *see* peasants

sanitation *see* waste
SARS (2003) *see* disease spread
Savini, Federico xiv, 11, 21, 41, 333–46
Schmid, Christian 105–6, 250
sciences *see* knowledge
Serres, Michel 248, 251–2, 257
sexuality *see* gender/sex
Sierra Leone 17, 210, 212–18
Simone, AbdouMaliq 10, 352

Singapore, offshore islands
about 21, 319–21, 329
environmental harm 321, 324–6, 328
geography and maps 322–3, 324, 327
green aesthetic 326
historical background 21, 319–20, 322–4
hybrid rural/urban spaces 320, 329
incineration of waste 326–8
Indigenous peoples 21, 321, 323, 325, 326–7, 329
invisibility 321, 323, 327–8
landfills 83n.6, 319–20, 326–9, 327
land reclamation 320, 322–6, 328
metabolic flows 320–3, 327–9
oil industries 21, 320, 324–6, 329
research project 324, 329n.1
shipping 319–20, 330n.3
UPE approaches 21, 319–22, 323, 329
waste management 21, 320, 326–9, 327
slums *see* informal settlements
smart cities 18, 284–6, 288, 293–7
social inclusion/exclusion
about 143–4, 154–5
ecology of exclusion 161, 166–7
environmental justice 143–6, 152–5
knowledge politics 14, 144–8, 152–3, 155
UPE approaches 143–4
see also intersectionality; marginalised peoples
socialism 38, 44, 208, 271
social justice *see* environmental justice; utopias
socio-natural processes
about 10, 143–4, 146, 223–4, 322
vs. binary of nature-society 61, 189–90, 291
cities as socio-natural 223–4
feminist approaches 144–6, 154–5
'good' and 'bad' human natures 160–4, 322
green/gray urban nature 297
interdependency 245, 248, 254–5, 322–3
metabolic flows 4, 216, 223, 245–6, 256–7, 322
subjectivities 145, 149, 154–5
terminology 144, 291, 297
UPE approaches 37–8, 61, 143–4, 154–5, 161, 189–90, 223, 237, 257n.5, 322, 355
see also green and grey urban nature; metabolic processes
solar energy 137–40, 295, 328
South Africa
populism 270–2
waste picking 15, 187, 191–2, 195–200, 200n.4
water consumption 191
South America *see* Latin America
spatialised political ecology 247
see also territorialist political ecology (TPE)

subjectivities
    about 145–6
    colonial subjectivity 79
    ecology of exclusion 161, 166–7
    intersectionality 145–6, 155
    neoliberal subjectivity 45
    social inclusion/exclusion 144–5, 154–5
    water politics (Nepal) 148–52, 155
    see also identity; power relations
suburban, terminology 7
    see also urban and urbanisation, as terms
sustainability and resilience
    critiques of 287–8
    ecological urbanism 56–8, 62–4
    equity deficits 287
    financial support 229
    green/grey urban nature 291–3
    nature as sustainable 46–7, 291
    resilience 20, 46–7, 200n.2, 286–7
    uncertainties 200n.2
    UPE approaches 16, 46–7, 286–8
    waste in circular economies 335–6, 343–4
    see also circular economies; green and grey urban nature
Swyngedouw, Erik 2–4, 11, 19, 37–55, 61, 72–3, 244–5, 256, 268, 348
systems-based concepts 57, 60–3
    see also metabolic processes

technology *see* green and grey urban nature
territorialist political ecology (TPE)
    about 18, 244–8, 254–7
    climate crisis in 251–3
    contract with the earth 248, 251–3
    dialectics in hierarchies 251–2, 255–6
    disease spread 248–51
    earth as actor/agent 18, 62, 247–53
    everyday life 251, 255
    interdependency 245, 254–5
    Latour's perspectives 247–50, 252–4
    metabolic flows 244–8, 256–7
    more-than-human natures 246–7, 251–2
    situated knowledges 246, 254
    terminology 247, 250–2, 254–7
    theory of 245–8, 253–7
    UPE approaches 18, 244–8, 255–7
Toronto, Ontario, populism 275–7
transportation *see* infrastructure
Treffers, Stefan xiv, 17, 207–21
Trump, Donald 268–74
Tsing, Anna 15, 308
turning up the heat, as metaphor 23, 348
Tzaninis, Yannis xiv, 1–34, 69, 190, 246, 274–5, 302, 347–57

Uganda 15, 190–4, 199–200
UN Declaration on the Rights of Peasants (UNDROP) 305–7, 310
United Arab Emirates, Masdar City 293–6
United States
    agriculture 120–1, *120–1*
    authoritarian populism 268–73
    climate crisis projections xviii–xix, xxv–xxvi
    concrete use 16, 41
    environmental politics 268–9
    global-urban networks 17, 223, 228–9, *231*, 233–7, *235*, 237n.1, 237n.2
    hurricanes 137–40, 222–3, 229–30, 233–4
    megafires xvi–xxvi
    Native Americans 13, 134
    Trump's populism 268–74
    wildland gentrification xxi–xxiv, 2
    see also New York City
United States, Black people
    about 14, 129–31, 139–40
    affordable housing 134–6
    anti-Black violence 13, 131, 277–8
    Atlanta 14, 133–7, 140
    community solar 138–40
    grassroots movements 131–5, 140
    land banks 14, 133–7, 139–40
    New Orleans 14, 133, 137–40, 223
    petro-racial capitalism 137–9
    reparations 14, 130–40
    right to the city 132–3, 134, 136, 139–40
    UPE approaches 130–2, 133, 137–40
    utopian dreams 130–1, 140
    white supremacy 129–31, 133, 137, 268–9, 272–3, 277–8
    see also racialised peoples
UPE *see* urban political ecology (UPE)
urban and urbanisation, as terms 9–10, 105–8
    see also cities; global/planetary urbanisation; hinterlands and urbanisation
urban ecology 11, 56–61, 63
    see also ecological urbanism
urban-natural
    about 70–5, 80–3
    alternative to capitalism 72–4, 80
    colonisation of 77–80
    everyday life as basis 72–3
    Lefebvre's approach 70–2, 80–2, 85n.8
    nature concepts 72–4
    terminology 70–2
    utopias 68–70, 80–3, 85n.8
urban political ecology (UPE)
    about 1–11, 22–4, 61–2, 347
    call to action 5–6
    climate crisis 1–6, 245, 347

diversity and multiplicity 4–5, 13–14, 37–8
ecology, as term 57–61
everyday life 5, 8–9, 12, 22, 42
extended urbanisation 3, 5–11
feminism 3, 4, 9, 143–4, 154–5, 246
Global South perspectives 5–6, 12–15, 246
historical background 61–4
Indigenous peoples 4, 10, 13–14, 21
infrastructural turn 12
Lacan's social reality 52n.3
metabolic flows 4–5, 42–3, 210–12
more-than-human ecologies 3–6, 15–18, 23, 37–8, 40
new in-between forms 22, 350–1
politics and policy 4–6, 18–23, 64
postcolonialism 3, 4, 9
racialised people 13–14, 130–3, 139–40
socio-natural processes 2–3, 10
solidarity modes 23–4, 85n.8, 85n.9, 85n.10
terminology 57
turning up the heat, as metaphor 23, 348
see also climate crisis; extended urbanisation; metabolic processes; socio-natural processes
urban political ecology (UPE), scholarship
about 4–6, 13–14, 61–2
centre/periphery relations 15–16, 170–1, 302
city-centrism 6, 8–9, 11–12, 18, 22, 46–7, 110, 224–6, 236–7, 287–8
historical waves and trends 4–5, 6, 56, 61–2, 287–8, 291
recent scholarship 348–55
research agenda 3–7, 13–16, 22–4, 105–6, 246, 257n.1, 348–9
situated knowledges 3, 5, 12–15, 20, 22–3, 246
urban political pathologies (UPP) 209–12
utopias
about 23, 67–75, 80–3, 83n.2
as alternatives to capitalism 23–4, 67–9, 74–7, 354
Black dreams 130–1, 140
Bloch's concrete utopia 67–70, 72, 74–5, 77, 83n.2
buen vivir (good life) 76–7, 81–2, 83n.5, 85n.9, 354
circular economies 333–4
decolonial turn 69–70, 74–5
dystopias 1–3, 23, 48–9, 76, 81
everyday life as basis 57–8, 67, 70–6, 79–82, 132
extended urbanisation 68–9
hope and despair 23–4
interculturality 69–70, 76–7, 83n.5

Lefebvre's approach 67–72, 75–7, 79–82, 85n.8, 132
terrestrial as 252
as unfinished 67, 74–7, 83n.2
urban-natural base 67–77, 79–83
see also capitalism, alternatives; climate crisis, alternatives; modernity, alternatives

Velicu, Irinia xiv, 21, 302–18
viruses *see* disease spread
vulnerable people *see* marginalised peoples

Wachsmuth, David xv, 6, 21, 284–301, 352
Walsh, Catherine 69–70, 76–7, 83n.5
waste
about 335–6, 343–4
abjection/valorisation of waste 21, 334–8, 340–4
adaptation vs. control 193–5
geographies of 337–8
incineration 326–8, 334, 336–7, 340–2, 344
labour 15, 190–2, 195–200, 337
landfills 83n.6, 319–20, 326–9, 327
metabolic flows 194, 335–6, 343–4
nature concepts 73
nature-society binary 190–1
sanitation 15, 190–4, 199–200
statistics 333
UPE approaches 194, 334–6, 343–4
waste picking 15, 187, 191–2, 195–200
see also Singapore, offshore islands
water
blurred water/land boundaries 170, 178–81, 183n.10
climate crisis projections (US) xviii–xix, xxv–xxvi
ecological imaginaries 172–3
floods (India) 14–15, 170, 182
floods (Jakarta) 8, 17, 222–3
hurricanes 137–40, 222–3, 229–30, 232–4
infrastructure design 222–3, 229–30, 232–4, 237n.2, 238n.9
neoliberalisation 43–4
UPE approaches 16
waterbody mapping 173–6, *175*, 180, 183n.10
water politics (Nepal) 144, 148–52, 155, 156n.2
see also India, Gurugram (Gurgaon), water; more-than-human urban political ecology
Williams, Raymond 123n.6, 173

EU authorised representative for GPSR:
Easy Access System Europe, Mustamäe tee 50,
10621 Tallinn, Estonia
gpsr.requests@easproject.com

www.ingramcontent.com/pod-product-compliance
Ingram Content Group UK Ltd.
Pitfield, Milton Keynes, MK11 3LW, UK
UKHW042017140426
5217IPUK00015B/1228